Linux®: Networking for Your Office

Roderick W. Smith

A Division of Macmillan USA
201 West 103rd St., Indianapolis, Indiana, 46290

Linux®: Networking for Your Office
Copyright © 2000 by Sams Publishing

International Standard Book Number: 0-672-31792-3

Library of Congress Catalog Card Number: 99-65181

Printed in the United States of America

First Printing: December 1999

01   00   99   4   3   2   1

Trademarks

Warning and Disclaimer

PUBLISHER
Angela Wethington

ACQUISITIONS EDITOR
Neil Rowe

DEVELOPMENT EDITOR
Tony Amico

MANAGING EDITOR
Lisa Wilson

PROJECT EDITOR
Heather Talbot

COPY EDITOR
Kitty Jarrett

INDEXER
Larry Sweazy

PROOFREADER
Jill Mazurczyk

TECHNICAL EDITOR
Jim Westveer

TEAM COORDINATOR
Karen Opal

MEDIA DEVELOPER
Jason Haines

INTERIOR DESIGNER
Gary Adair

COVER DESIGNER
Alan Clements

COPY WRITER
Eric Borgert

PRODUCTION
Stacey DeRome
Ayanna Lacey
Heather Hiatt Miller

Contents at a Glance

Contents

PART V   REMOTE ACCESS   423

18   USING ssh OR telnet TO LOG ON REMOTELY   425

19   USING VNC OR AN X SERVER TO RUN X WINDOW PROGRAMS REMOTELY   443

About the Author

Roderick W. Smith is an experienced Linux user and system administrator. He's been using and administrating Linux since 1994 when the 1.0.x kernel series was current. Rod has publications in several computer magazines, most notably *Linux Journal*. He maintains several Web pages devoted to Linux, including pages devoted to topics such as fonts and printers under WordPerfect and ApplixWare and creating Red Hat installation CDs. This is Rod's second book, the first being *Special Edition Using Corel WordPerfect 8 for Linux*, published by Que Corporation. He holds a Ph.D. in cognitive psychology from Tufts University and has done postdoctoral research in that field at various institutions. He currently resides in Malden, Massachusetts, just outside Boston.

Dedication

To Donald Becker, Andrew Tridgell, Adrian Sun, and all the many others who have made Linux networking what it is today.

Acknowledgments

I'd like to thank acquisitions editor Neil Rowe, development editor Tony Amico, and project coordinator Karen Opal. These are the people who form the buffer between me and all the myriad details of transforming my words into a book. Without their efforts, this book would not be possible.

Jim Westveer served as technical editor on this book, which means he kept me on the straight-and-narrow path where the truth is concerned. If I nonetheless managed to stray, the fault is, of course, mine alone.

Heartfelt thanks go out to David King, who pointed me towards many useful nuggets of information. Adrian Sun also helped clarify several details of operation of the Netatalk package. Any remaining errors are, of course, my own. I'd also like to thank John Kounios, on whose event-related potential (ERP) laboratory computers I learned much of what I present in this book.

In order to write this book, I used the GIMP image manipulation software by Spencer Kimball and Peter Mattis to capture screenshots in Linux, and Bren Tamilio's ScreenSnatch for Windows screenshots. I used Marko Macek's icewm window manager for controlling onscreen Linux windows (icewm is what you want if you really like the look of the windows in this book). Of course, I used the Linux kernel by Linus Torvalds and others, along with far too many additional programs and utilities to mention by name.

Tell Us What You Think!

As the reader of this book, *you* are our most important critic and commentator. We value your opinion and want to know what we're doing right, what we could do better, what areas you'd like to see us publish in, and any other words of wisdom you're willing to pass our way.

As a publisher for Sams, I welcome your comments. You can fax, email, or write me directly to let me know what you did or didn't like about this book—as well as what we can do to make our books stronger.

Please note that I cannot help you with technical problems related to the topic of this book, and that due to the high volume of mail I receive, I might not be able to reply to every message.

When you write, please be sure to include this book's title and author as well as your name and phone or fax number. I will carefully review your comments and share them with the author and editors who worked on the book.

Fax: 317.581.4770

Email: opsys@mcp.com

Mail: Angela Wethington
            Publisher
            Sams Publishing
            201 West 103rd Street
            Indianapolis, IN 46290 USA

Introduction

In the past few years, an initially little-noticed project has been underway. Started at the University of Helsinki in Finland by Linus Torvalds, the Linux kernel was originally a project to reimplement parts of the UNIX operating system on inexpensive PC hardware. It quickly gathered around it the fruit of years of software development for UNIX, especially what has come to be known as *open-source software*, much of it from Richard Stallman's Free Software Foundation (FSF). The result of this accretion of software, ranging from the Linux kernel itself to the XFree86 windowing system, the Emacs editor, the gcc C language compiler, and others, is frequently referred to as *Linux*, though some prefer the term *GNU/Linux* to spread the credit for the nonkernel utilities, many of which were developed by the FSF's GNU project. By whatever name (I use *Linux* in this book), the result is a very complete UNIX-like operating system that is freely available, stable, and flexible.

One of Linux's greatest strengths has turned out to be its networking capabilities. Thanks to the efforts of individuals like Donald Becker, Linux supports the vast majority of Ethernet networking cards available today. Because most UNIX programs compile and run on Linux with few or no changes, Linux has been blessed by the wide array of networking tools and utilities available for UNIX. As Linux's popularity has grown, it has become the development platform of choice for many networking tool authors. Tools like Samba would probably exist without Linux, but they might not be quite as mature or popular as they are.

This book is designed to help you explore the world of Linux networking. Actually, it might be more accurate to say that this book is designed to help you explore *one continent* in the world of Linux networking. A thorough description of Linux networking is well beyond the scope of a single book. This book focuses upon those networking features of most interest in a small office/home office (SOHO) environment—file sharing, printer sharing, and assorted methods of connecting to the Internet, to name the main topics. Other books in the Sams Linux networking series explore other continents in the world of Linux networking.

Who Should Buy This Book

This book is written with a person possessing moderate to advanced Linux knowledge in mind. I expect the reader has relatively little knowledge of the details of using Samba, Netatalk, IP masquerading, and the other topics covered in this book. You should be familiar with basic Linux operations and principles, such as user accounts, command line shells, and operation of the X Window System. You might or might not be familiar with Linux's model of system administration, such as the locations of configuration files and use of tools such as linuxconf. If you're more of a Linux "newbie," you should still be able to use this book, but you should read it in conjunction with a basic text on Linux operations, such as Pitts & Ball's *Red Hat Linux 6 Unleashed*, from Sams Publishing.

The focus of this book is on using Linux to provide common office services to a small network of computers. The non-server computers could be running Linux, some other UNIX-like OS, Windows, MacOS, or even more exotic operating systems like OS/2 or BeOS. You'll find this book helpful for networks of anywhere from two to dozens of computers. If your network is particularly large or complex, though, you might want to hire a full-time employee to manage it rather than read a book and do it yourself. On the other hand, if you're responsible for one small sub-network—say, your one department of half a dozen computers—this book will help you provide your small corner of the network with the services you need. You will also find this book helpful if you're an experienced network administrator in some other environment, and want to begin integrating Linux servers into your network. Although written primarily with corporate, educational, and other organizations in mind, this book's information applies equally well to an individual running a network at home for personal use.

You'll find a CD-ROM bound into the back of this book that contains a complete version of Red Hat Linux 6.0, along with an assortment of additional Linux and Windows tools that don't normally come with Red Hat. Each distribution of Linux is slightly different in how it handles configuration, and many distributions include GUI configuration tools that differ even more greatly. Red Hat uses linuxconf; SuSE comes with YAST; and Caldera ships with COAS, for instance. (The Mandrake distribution uses linuxconf, but it uses a different method of selecting a specific configuration tool than does Red Hat.) I could have provided instructions for configuring each of these systems, but such detail would have delayed the appearance of this book on store shelves for several months, and possibly made the information obsolete by the time you could read it! I've therefore focused on Red Hat's configuration tools. If you prefer to use another distribution, feel free to do so. You will have to either locate the commonalities between your distribution's configuration tools and Red Hat's linuxconf in order to adapt the instructions I provide, or use the instructions I also provide on text-mode configuration, which varies less from one distribution to another.

One important point to note is that distributions change. You may find yourself using Red Hat 6.1, 6.2, or above; or you might have an older 5.x or still earlier release that you're reluctant to upgrade. The behavior of these systems may not match what I describe in this book. (Indeed, the function of the smbmount command for accessing Windows shared filesystems changed with an update to the Samba package *while I was writing this book!*) So if you're using a more recent, older, or different version of the OS than Red Hat 6.0, don't be surprised if your system doesn't work precisely as I describe in this book. Take a deep breath and delve into the documentation for the relevant package. Using this book's description as a baseline, you should be able to figure out what's changed and how to get the system working as you want it without too much difficulty.

How This Book Is Organized

This book is divided into seven parts ranging from two to five chapters each. Each section covers one set of topics that are closely related to one another. These parts are as follows:

- Part I, "Networking Principles," covers the basics of networking, including both hardware and software. If you're planning a small network and aren't already familiar with networking hardware, you should read this section to learn what hardware is best for your needs. Other chapters in this section introduce concepts that you'll find useful in understanding the rest of the book.

- Part II, "Configuring Linux Networking," covers the basic configuration tasks you'll need to perform other networking operations discussed in the book. These basic tasks include information on Linux configuration, recompiling a kernel, Ethernet networking, and dialup PPP connections to the Internet.

- Part III, "File Sharing," discusses how to use Linux in a file-sharing network. Individual chapters cover basic file sharing principles and each of three major file sharing protocols: NFS, SMB/CIFS, and AppleTalk. The focus in this section is on using Linux as a server, but I also cover using Linux as a client for each of these protocols except AppleTalk, for which Linux support is currently very preliminary and therefore unstable. This section also includes a chapter on backing up your network using Linux as a backup server.

- Part IV, "Printer Sharing," mirrors the organization of Part III, with sections on basic principles and printer sharing details for each of three major printer sharing protocols.

- Part V, "Remote Access," covers using your Linux computer from a distance. You can do so either using text-only tools or using tools that allow you to run X GUI programs from a distant computer. You can use this capability to make a central Linux computer function much like a mainframe of old, handling not just storage but processing; or for occasional remote access to your data and programs when you're at home or travelling.

- Part VI, "Linking Your Intranet to the Internet," discusses two popular and important methods of using a Linux computer as a gateway between an internal network and an external one: IP masquerading and firewalling. The former lets you "hide" an entire network behind one computer so the outside world believes only one computer exists. The latter protects an internal network, but doesn't necessarily mask the presence of those computers from the outside world.

- Part VII, "Final Considerations," covers three important topics that simply didn't fit anywhere else: Hardware considerations when building a new computer; advanced system administration; and security concerns. Each of these topics is touched upon at various other points in the book, but deserves greater attention than was appropriate in chapters about other matters.

If you're new to networking and want to get a good feel for the topic as a whole, you can read this book straight through. If you need information on specific topics, you can read the appropriate chapters, mostly in whatever order you like. Parts III and IV, though, each begin with a chapter that you'll find helpful in understanding the material presented in subsequent chapters in their respective sections. When I think you might want more information on a topic, either as a prerequisite for understanding material or to learn more, I tell you where to look in this book, or in other books or on the Internet.

What's on the CD-ROM?

The CD-ROM that accompanies this book contains a copy of Red Hat Linux 6.0. This copy has had all the patches applied to it that Red Hat has released up to the date on which the CD was mastered, so you don't need to apply these patches yourself. Red Hat will probably have released new updates between the CD mastering date and the time you read this, though, so you should still check Red Hat's Web site and compare the version numbers of updated packages to what you have installed. The text file `updates.txt` on the CD includes information on both where to find updated packages and the updates that have been preapplied to the CD that comes with this book.

The subdirectory `sams-extras` includes most of the programs I discuss in this book that don't come with a standard Red Hat Linux distribution. If you're not using Red Hat Linux, you may want to check your own distribution's CDs for equivalent packages before installing the ones that come with this book's CD, but the packages I've included should be usable with most RPM-based Linux distributions. Some of the included programs do require glibc 2.1, though, and so might not work with older distributions, such as Red Hat 5.x.

Because you may want to read the CD from Windows as well as from Linux, it's been created with both Joliet and Rock Ridge long filenames. You should, therefore, have no trouble getting to the relevant Windows files, or even Linux files if you need to, using Windows or any other OS that understands the Joliet filesystem.

Conventions Used in This Book

This book uses certain conventions to help you get the most from the text.

Text Conventions

Various typefaces in this book identify terms and other special objects. These special typefaces include the following:

Type	Meaning
Italic	New terms or phrases when initially defined.
`Monospaced`	Information presented by the computer, including filenames, command names, and URLs for Web-based information. Examples from configuration files appear as entire lines of monospaced text.
`Boldface Monospaced`	Information that you type into the computer, such as commands entered at a command prompt.
`Italic Monospaced`	Information presented by the computer (or which you type, if the text is also boldfaced) which may vary from what's in the book. Such information could include machine names or IP addresses for computers on your network, arbitrary filenames, and so on.
Capitalization	The capitalization of menu names, dialog box names, dialog box elements, and commands in the text matches the way they appear onscreen. Because Linux is a case-sensitive OS, you must enter commands in the case in which they're presented in this book (generally all lowercase).

Key combinations are represented with a plus sign. For example, if the text calls for you to enter Ctrl+S, you would press the Ctrl key and the S key at the same time.

I represent a series of selections by comma-separated lists of options. For instance, File, Enter means to select the File menu item, followed by the Enter item in the File menu. The `linuxconf` program, as well as a few others, present menus in expanding lists to the left of the window, and I use the same notation to refer to these menus as to the more usual drop-down menus that appear at the tops of windows. I use these same conventions for Linux, Windows, and MacOS.

Special Elements

Throughout this book, you'll find Tips, Notes, Cautions, and sidebars. These elements provide a variety of information, ranging from warnings you shouldn't miss to ancillary information that will enrich your networking experience, but isn't required reading.

TIPS

Tips are designed to point out features, annoyances, and tricks of the trade that you might otherwise miss. Tips generally help you to make better use of Linux networking by providing a quicker or more effective way of doing something than might otherwise be immediately obvious.

NOTES

Notes point out items that you should be aware of, although you can skip these if you're in a hurry. Generally, I've added notes as a way to give you some extra information on a topic without weighing you down.

CAUTIONS

Pay attention to Cautions! These could save you precious hours in lost work. Don't say I didn't warn you.

Sidebars

You can think of sidebars as extended notes—information that's interesting but not vital to understanding the main point of the text. Information in sidebars takes longer to explain than information in notes, though.

Contacting Me

I welcome comments and suggestions concerning this book. You can send me email at smithrod@bellatlantic.net, or visit my Web page at http://members.bellatlantic.net/~smithrod.

Networking Principles

PART
I

IN THIS PART

Networking Hardware

IN THIS CHAPTER

Networks allow computers to communicate with each other. Of course, you're probably not interested in providing a social life for computers *per se*; rather, you're interested in using computer communications to further *your* work with others, or to provide greater efficiency in your own work. You can use computer networks to send and receive email, access files on one computer from another, share a single printer across several computers, and much more. Networks can range in size from a simple two-computer link to the world-spanning Internet. This book focuses on the networking tasks that are of greatest interest to small networks, or to small components of larger networks.

A network requires connections between two or more computers. Generally speaking, these connections are physical, requiring some combination of cables, hubs, switches, network cards, modems, and so on. Wireless networks exist, but even these require networking hardware in the computers. Because networking protocols and software rely upon the underlying hardware, I begin this book with a discussion of common networking hardware, including both the hardware for creating your own local network and what you may need to connect to the Internet as a whole.

Understanding Ethernet

At present, the most common type of networking hardware for small and home offices is *Ethernet*. For this reason, this chapter, and indeed the entire book, focuses upon Ethernet networking. Most of the software and configurations discussed in this book do apply to other types of networking hardware; but if you're using something else, you may need to find documentation on configuring the necessary hardware and drivers elsewhere. The Linux HOWTO collection may contain a document to suit your requirements.

Types of Ethernet

Ethernet comes in several different varieties. The underlying principles are the same for all of these, but these variants differ in terms of speed, cabling, and how computers using these varieties are interconnected. Table 1.1 summarizes the most common forms of Ethernet in SOHO settings.

TABLE **1.1**   Varieties of Ethernet

Name	Top Speed	Cable Format	Maximum Distance
10base-2	10Mbps	Thin coaxial	607 ft.
10base-5	10Mbps	Thick coaxial	1,640 ft.
10base-T	10Mbps	Category 3, 4, or 5 twisted-pair	328 ft.
100base-T	100Mbps	Category 5 twisted-pair	328 ft.

In small networks, 10base-2, 10base-T, and 100base-T are the most common varieties. 10base-2 is most common in older installations. You can easily identify this type of cabling because it resembles the lines used by cable TV, although 10base-2 cable is thinner and the connectors are different. If you're planning a new network, I recommend you use 100base-T, because it's the fastest form of Ethernet in common use. Most 100base-T networking hardware also supports the 10base-T standards. The networking cables for these two types use the same connectors—RJ-45 plugs, similar to telephone plugs but wider, as shown in Figure 1.1.

FIGURE 1.1
Ethernet twisted-pair cabling comes in a variety of colors to help you identify which cables link to which computers.

Aside from the physical cabling and speed, the different varieties of Ethernet vary in how they interconnect computers. The coaxial-based cabling methods allow computers to be connected in a *bus topology*, also sometimes referred to as a *daisy chain*, in which each computer is connected to its neighbor, except for the computers on the ends of the line. A bus topology is depicted in Figure 1.2.

FIGURE 1.2
A bus topology links computers directly to one another in a linear arrangement.

By contrast, the twisted-pair technology requires that a *star topology* be used, as shown in Figure 1.3. In such a network, the computers are not usually connected directly to each other, but to a central device (a *hub* or *switch*) that processes all the network's traffic.

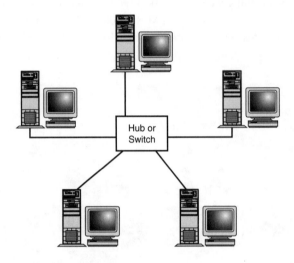

FIGURE **1.3**
A star topology links all computers to a central point.

Alternatives to Ethernet

Ethernet is not the only networking hardware available. Most others are in decline, however, at least for use in small networks. You might find that you need to use one of these network types if you're connecting computers to an existing network. In some cases, though, you might want to set up a small Ethernet network and link it to another network by configuring your Linux computer to use both types, and use it as a router.

Serial and Parallel Ports

You can use the serial or parallel ports found on most PCs to create a simple but low-speed network. In general, you would use the point-to-point protocol (PPP) tools for doing serial-line networking, and the parallel line Internet protocol (PLIP) for parallel port networking. Both of these are Linux kernel protocols, and both require additional configuration. In general, neither of these protocols is very useful for most practical local networks because they're so slow compared to Ethernet. Also, they can be used to connect only two computers. Finally, you lose the use of whichever port is required on both computers. With Ethernet boards selling for $30 and less, the cost of setting up a two-computer network is well under $100.

> **NOTE**
>
> You use a serial port and PPP for connecting to the Internet through a modem, as discussed in Chapter 8, "Using PPP for Dialup Connections." The serial port's speed limitations aren't a major problem in this case because modems can't communicate with each other at a faster rate. You can configure your Linux system to accept dialup connections through a modem, though this topic is beyond the scope of this book.

One exception to the rule of not using serial or parallel connections in a local network is linking palmtop computers or similar specialized devices. With a PPP connection and IP masquerading, you can use your Linux PC's Internet connection to provide Internet access to a palmtop, or you can transfer files between the palmtop and the Linux computer.

Token Ring

Token Ring is a networking technology developed by IBM for small networks. Like Ethernet, Token Ring networks can use a variety of cabling and have two speed options (4Mbps and 16Mbps). As the name implies, Token Ring functions in a ring topology, which is similar to the bus topology of coaxial Ethernet except that the two ends of the bus are joined, creating a circular arrangement. Token Ring's ring is formed inside a hub, however, so the physical arrangement of cables more closely resembles that of 10base-T Ethernet.

The Linux kernel includes support for a number of Token Ring adapters. If you want to connect to a Token Ring network, you should consult the Linux Token Ring mini-HOWTO to learn how to configure the card.

LocalTalk

LocalTalk is the name given to the networking technology Apple built into most of its Macintosh computers until recently. LocalTalk is a slow network technology compared to modern Ethernet varieties. Unless you're trying to connect to an existing LocalTalk network, I don't recommend that you use LocalTalk.

Nonetheless, Linux does include drivers for a small number of AppleTalk cards for PCs. You can also configure Linux to route traffic between an AppleTalk network and another network type, although the details of such a configuration are beyond the scope of this book.

> **NOTE**
>
> The term *LocalTalk* refers to the networking *hardware* used by many Macs, particularly older ones. (Newer Macs include Ethernet hardware, and Apple began dropping LocalTalk support with its 1998 models, such as the popular iMac.) Apple's networking *protocols* are referred to as *AppleTalk*, and AppleTalk can be transmitted over either LocalTalk or Ethernet hardware. Linux can be configured to understand AppleTalk, and to share files and printers with Macs.

Long-Distance Networking

Ethernet and its competitors are primarily *local* network technologies; they're good for linking a single office's computers, but not for connecting two offices across town or across a continent. For these long-distance links, you need to look at other technologies.

ISDN

Integrated Services Digital Networks (ISDN) competes with conventional telephone services. It's a way of transmitting both voice and digital data over the same physical wiring used by the telephone companies for decades.

ISDN is capable of transmitting up to 128Kbps, which at one time was quite speedy compared to conventional modems, but which is now fast but not extraordinarily so. For outside access, cable modems and digital subscriber line (DSL) can now provide much higher speeds, usually at lower cost. If these alternatives are available, there's usually little reason to consider ISDN. For this reason, I don't cover ISDN in this book. Linux does include ISDN support, however. If you want to learn more, check out `http://alumni.caltech.edu/~dank/isdn`.

ATM

Asynchronous Transfer Mode (ATM) networks are relatively new compared to the likes of Ethernet. ATM supports multiple speeds from 25Mbps and up. One of ATM's major strengths is that it permits a combination of voice, video, and data over the same physical wiring, which can be appealing to large businesses. ATM also supports very high speeds, which can be important in applications that require a great deal of bandwidth. For a typical desktop workstation or server, however, ATM hardware is more expensive than Ethernet hardware. For Linux in particular, ATM driver support is not yet integrated into the kernel, although there are projects underway to develop Linux drivers for some ATM boards. If you need to use an ATM board under Linux, check the site `http://lrcww.epfl.ch/linux-atm` for more information.

One final note on ATM is that this technology is closely related to both ISDN and DSL. As discussed later in this chapter, some DSL service providers use an internal card for connecting your computer to the DSL network. These cards are sometimes closely related to ATM cards, and so ATM driver development efforts may be relevant to getting networks such devices working in Linux. This information will mostly interest kernel programmers, however, because as I write this, support for both ATM and internal DSL adapters is rudimentary at best.

Additional Network Types

The number of types of networking hardware is quite large. Linux includes drivers for many of the more obscure network hardware types, but not for all of them. If you have a network built on one of these obscure hardware types, you can check the Linux kernel options to see if there's support for it. If you don't find it, however, don't despair; there may be an add-on module to do what you want that's not yet been integrated into the kernel. Try doing a search on a Web search engine such as Alta Vista (`http://www.altavista.com`), Yahoo! (`http://www.yahoo.com`), or Excite (`http://www.excite.com`); or search the archives of newsgroup postings on Deja News (`http://www.deja.com`).

Dedicated Routers

Larger organizations often use dedicated hardware routers to connect local Ethernet networks to ISPs located miles away. These devices accept Ethernet on one side and output some other protocol on the other. If you're using such a device, you don't need to be concerned about its compatibility with Linux, since dedicated routers aren't OS dependent. In fact, the "modems" used for DSL and cable Internet access (discussed in "DSL and Cable Modems" later in this chapter) are usually routers of this type, albeit scaled down for individual and small-office use.

Network Interface Cards

No matter what type of network you use, you'll need a *network interface card* (*NIC*) to connect your computer to your network. The NIC typically includes one or two connectors for physical network interfacing. (As described earlier, Ethernet has several cabling options, so some NICs include appropriate connectors for more than one such option. Some cards also support more than one interface, each with a unique address, to save slots on computers that need more than one NIC to connect a single computer to two networks.) NICs vary substantially in their features and Linux compatibility, so this section covers these issues.

NOTE

NICs are often referred to as *network cards*, *Ethernet cards* (when they're designed for Ethernet), or other variants.

ISA and PCI Cards

Most modern computers come with both ISA and PCI slots. The ISA slot is an older and slower design, so it's not favored for devices that need high speed access to the rest of the computer, such as video cards and SCSI host adapters. If your network is limited to 10Mbps speeds, an ISA NIC should be adequate, although it may consume more CPU time than would a PCI NIC, especially if the ISA NIC uses an older programmed input/output (PIO) design.

A 100Mbps Ethernet network can exceed the speed capacity of the ISA bus, so 100Mbps ISA NICs are rare. You might want to consider such a card if it is to connect an older computer without PCI slots to a 100Mbps network; but if the computer has any free PCI slots, I recommend the use of PCI NICs whenever possible. Today, most PCI Ethernet cards are 10/100 models, meaning that they can operate at both 10Mbps and 100Mbps. These cards typically auto-detect the network speed and adjust themselves accordingly, so there's little need for explicitly configuring these boards for your network's speed.

> **NOTE**
>
> Many 486 computers and a few older Pentiums used the VESA Local Bus (VLB) or Extended ISA (EISA) instead of PCI. NICs that use these busses exist, but are quite rare today. If you have an older computer with one of these busses, you may want to look for a VLB or EISA NIC.

ISA cards use one of two methods to configure themselves to your computer: jumpers or plug-and-play (PnP) protocols. Jumpers are metal and plastic tabs that slide over metal pins on the board. You place the jumpers over particular pairs of pins to configure features such as the IRQ used by the board. PnP boards are supposed to do away with this by allowing the computer to specify these settings. Unfortunately, PnP often works poorly for ISA devices. Under Linux, PnP devices are configured with the isapnp package. If you have a PnP network card, you can type /sbin/pnpdump > isapnp.conf as the root to create a file called isapnp.conf containing information about your ISA PnP boards. You'll then need to edit this file to specify the IRQ, DMA, and other configuration parameters you want to use. When you're done, place the file in the /etc directory and run /sbin/isapnp -f /etc/isapnp.conf to be sure that the file's syntax is correct and that there are no conflicts with the resources you specified. In theory, you should then be able to use whatever drivers you need for your board. I recommend you reboot to be sure that your Linux system will use these settings when it restarts. (Most modern Linux systems automatically run isapnp when they start, but some may not, in which case you'll need to add an appropriate line to /etc/rc.d/rc.local or some other startup file.)

PCI cards are simpler to configure than ISA cards because they were designed with PnP in mind. Although all PCI cards are PnP devices, they don't require separate configuration tools or explicit instructions on what resources to use; these details should be handled by the BIOS when the system boots. If you suspect you're having problems with a PCI NIC because of resource conflicts, try using your system's BIOS setup features to modify the way it assigns resources to PCI devices. Details vary substantially from one BIOS to another, but there's generally a way to reserve specific resources for non-PCI devices or a selection of algorithms for assigning resources (for instance, assigning IRQs from low to high, from high to low, or in a specified order).

With both PCI and ISA boards, you'll need to configure your Linux drivers appropriately. Before you can do that, however, you'll need to know something about NIC chipsets.

Ethernet Addresses

In order to identify themselves, Ethernet cards have unique six-byte addresses. These addresses are often, but not always, printed on a sticker attached to the card. Even when this is not the case, software can read the Ethernet address of a card. For instance, if you type `/sbin/ifconfig` at a Linux prompt, Linux responds with something like this:

```
eth0      Link encap:Ethernet  HWaddr 00:80:C6:F9:3B:BA
          inet addr:192.168.1.1  Bcast:192.168.1.255  Mask:255.255.255.0
          EtherTalk Phase 2 addr:65280/13
          UP BROADCAST RUNNING MULTICAST  MTU:1500  Metric:1
          RX packets:149265 errors:157 dropped:0 overruns:157 frame:0
          TX packets:186774 errors:3 dropped:0 overruns:3 carrier:0
          collisions:1132
```

The `ifconfig` command provides a great deal of information about the low-level network interfaces, but for the moment, consider only the first line of this output. The six hexadecimal values at the end of this line, labeled `HWaddr`, are the Ethernet address of this NIC.

The NIC's Ethernet address is entirely separate from the numerical Internet address you may have encountered in the past, and which is described in Chapters 2 and 4. (This address is reported on the second line of `ifconfig`'s output, and is labeled `inet addr:192.168.1.1` in the preceding example.) Ethernet boards use their hardware addresses to talk to each other, but not all computers on the Internet are connected via Ethernet, and not all Ethernet networks are connected to the Internet. One of the jobs of the TCP/IP stack, discussed in Chapter 2, is to link these two addresses in a meaningful way.

> **NOTE**
>
> If you need to use DHCP to obtain an Internet address for your computer, you may need to provide the Ethernet address for your network board. Many cable modem and DSL providers use DHCP in this way, as do some businesses on their internal networks. If you're on such a network, therefore, you won't be able to switch network cards on a whim; you'll need to notify your network administrator of the change *before* you do it, or you'll be unable to connect to your network.

Commonly-Used Chipsets

NICs, like most computer boards, use a *chipset* to perform most of their functions. The chipset is a set of chips (or in most cases a single chip) that incorporates the core electronic features needed to implement a function, such as sending and receiving Ethernet frames. It's common practice in the computer industry for board manufacturers to purchase chipsets from any of a number of chipset manufacturers. The board manufacturers then build their products around the chipsets, and sometimes change their chipset supplier. Linux device drivers are written for a specific chipset, not for a specific board. All these facts conspire to produce a potentially confusing situation. For instance, suppose there are three chipset manufacturers, A, B, and C, and three NIC manufacturers, X, Y, and Z. Initially, X and Y might use chipset A, whereas Z uses chipset C. This means that boards X and Y require the same Linux driver—the one for chipset A. Manufacturers Y and Z might both decide to change to chipset B, however, possibly without even changing the names of their products. This means that all samples of NIC X use driver A, but some samples of NIC Y use driver A and some use driver B, while some samples of NIC Z use driver B and some use driver C.

To make life even more difficult, board manufacturers often try to obscure what chipsets they use, which can make selecting a NIC (or other card) for Linux an adventure. You can sometimes get useful information on the chipset a board uses by checking the manufacturer's Web site. Increasingly, these have Linux drivers available for download. You can either use this driver directly or check its comments to see which standard driver it is, and use the latest version of that driver from another source.

Fortunately, a handful of NIC chipsets dominate the PCI NIC marketplace in 1999, and Linux supports all the major players, so you're not likely to go wrong in buying a 10/100 PCI NIC. Common NIC chipsets include

- Intel i82557/i82558—This is the chipset that's used in the Intel EtherExpress Pro 100B boards and in some motherboards with integrated Ethernet.

- 3COM 3c59x and 3c905b series—These chipsets are used in 3COM's EtherLink XL series boards and a few third-party products.

- DEC Tulip 21x4x series—Boards based on these chipsets have been extremely popular, in part because they're less expensive than the Intel and 3COM offerings. Intel bought the rights to this design when DEC folded, however, and genuine DEC/Intel Tulip chipsets have become quite rare.

- Tulip clones—PNIC, Macronix, and others have produced Tulip clone chipsets, which are now found in most of the low-cost PCI NICs on the market.

There are, of course, other chipsets available. This is especially true of ISA products and of 10Mbps boards. Fortunately, most of these NICs are well supported in Linux.

Linux Drivers

Drivers for most NICs come with the Linux kernel itself, and most distributions include support for these NICs "out of the box," so you needn't go looking further. In some cases, however, you'll need to track down a new or updated driver. Many of the Tulip clone chipsets, for instance, work poorly with the version of the Tulip driver included in early 2.2.x kernels (including the kernel that ships with Red Hat 6.0). Two sites that are likely to be useful when trying to track down updated drivers are the NIC manufacturer's Web site and `http://ces-dis.gsfc.nasa.gov/linux/drivers/`. The latter site is maintained by Donald Becker, who wrote many of the Linux Ethernet adapter drivers, and so it contains both the latest stable release and experimental drivers for cutting-edge hardware.

When you download a new driver file, chances are it will be a C source code file (with a .c filename extension). It may come with a text file describing how to integrate it into your kernel. If so, follow those directions. If not, and if the file is an update to an existing file, you can place it in the Linux kernel source tree in place of the old driver (generally in the directory `/usr/src/linux/drivers/net`). You'll then need to recompile your kernel or kernel modules, and probably reboot the computer, as described in Chapter 6.

One question you must answer is whether to compile the driver directly into the kernel or to compile it as a module. If you compile a driver into the kernel, it will always be loaded and present, so there's no chance that the driver will be "lost" on system bootup. Compiling the driver into the kernel proper is also often preferable if you have two NICs that use the same driver. On the other hand, placing the driver in the kernel increases the kernel's size, which may prevent the system from booting in extreme cases. If you compile the driver as a module, Linux will load it only after the kernel itself has booted. You may need to specify what driver is associated with the Ethernet port in `/etc/conf.modules`, which can be a nuisance but can also make it relatively simple to configure a two-NIC system if the boards use different drivers.

Using Hubs and Switches

If you're using a 10base-2 or 10base-5 Ethernet network, you'll link computers together in a bus topology, as described earlier in this chapter. 10base-T and 100base-T networks, however, normally operate in a star topology (depicted in Figure 1.3), using a device called a *hub* or a *switch* at the core of the star. A typical small network hub or switch is a plain box with several RJ-45 connectors and activity LEDs. Because your selection of a hub or switch can have important consequences for your overall networking experience, this section discusses these devices.

> **NOTE**
>
> 10base-2 and 10base-5 are older network technologies. Newer networks generally use 10base-T or 100base-T. I recommend 100base-T for all new installations, because it's the fastest type of Ethernet in common use at the end of 1999.

Why Use a Hub or Switch?

First, if you're using 10base-2 or 10base-5 cabling, you don't need to—and indeed you *can't*—use a hub or switch. As a practical matter, then, you can ignore this question, unless you're considering upgrading your network to 100Mbps speeds, or even to changing to 10base-T.

10base-T and 100base-T cabling is designed for precisely two computers. You therefore can't use it as you do coaxial cable, in which you connect multiple computers to a single run of cable.

If you're using 10base-T or 100base-T networking cards and have only two computers to connect, you have the choice of using a hub, a switch, or a crossover cable. The crossover cable option is the simplest and least expensive in this situation because it's an ordinary Ethernet cable wired so you can directly connect the Ethernet ports on the two computers. For a two-computer network, this is quite adequate, and will save you the expense of a hub or switch. If you later decide to expand your network, you'll have to sacrifice the crossover cable, but nothing else.

If you're using 10base-T or 100base-T and want to connect three or more computers, you have little choice but to use a hub or switch. In theory, you could daisy chain computers by providing all but the endpoint machines with two NICs and configuring all the machines as routers; however, this would be far more effort than it's worth, and would probably cost more than buying a hub.

Why the move from daisy-chainable coaxial cable to the more limited two-connection RJ-45 cable? Why make *you* buy this extra box? In a word, maintenance. A long run of coaxial cable is subject to problems such as breaks. For instance, suppose that an office uses 10base-2 cabling. If one computer's user drops a pen and crawls under the desk to find it, and if that person inadvertently hits the networking cable, pulling it loose from the computer, the network will end up broken into two parts, resulting in mysterious failures that may take some time to track down. If a 10base-T or 100base-T network was in place, by contrast, that same scenario would result in only one person's computer being affected—a problem that's much easier to diagnose.

An additional factor is that stringing cable like Christmas tree lights from one machine to another can result in some convoluted cable paths in some office layouts. While not guaranteed to always be better, a star topology can often produce saner and more flexible cable layouts.

Although I'm discussing Ethernet here, some other network technologies also use hubs, switches, or similar devices. Token Ring, for instance, uses a hub of sorts. The *ring* in a Token Ring network actually exists inside the Token Ring hub. This provides the advantages (and disadvantages) of a star topology to the ring topology used by Token Ring.

The Difference Between Hubs and Switches

Hubs and switches fill very similar roles, but differ in important ways. If you've checked prices in stores, you'll have noted that switches are more expensive than hubs, assuming the same number of connectors. That's because switches are more complex and flexible devices. A hub is a pretty dumb device. When it receives an Ethernet packet from one device, it sends that packet back out to every other device attached to the hub. For instance, suppose you have a network with five computers connected to a single hub. When the computer called polk tries to communicate with the computer pierce, polk's packets do go to pierce, but they also go to the remaining three computers on the network, as shown in Figure 1.4. These computers won't attempt to process these packets because they recognize that the packets are for madison, but this blind relaying of messages to all systems does have negative consequences, as I describe shortly.

A switch, by contrast, is a bit smarter. It keeps within it a list of the Ethernet addresses of the computers it links together. Then, when it sees a packet coming in, it checks its destination address, and if it recognizes that address, the switch sends the packet *only* to that computer (as shown in Figure 1.5).

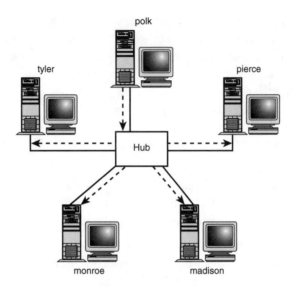

FIGURE 1.4

A hub passes network traffic destined for a single computer (indicated by the dashed lines) to all machines.

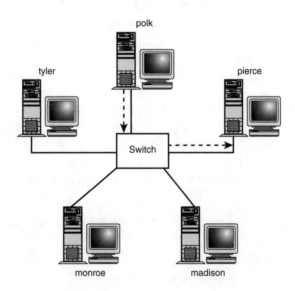

FIGURE 1.5

A switch forwards data only to the intended recipient computer.

1

One consequence of these differences relates to speed. Typically, the speed of a network linked together by a 10/100Mbps hub is limited by its slowest computer. For instance, if four computers in a five-computer network have 10/100Mbps NICs, but the fifth has a 10Mbps NIC, all traffic going over that network will crawl by at 10Mbps. This is true even of traffic between two computers with 10/100Mbps NICs. This fact can be a serious problem if one of the computers has a 100Mbps-only NIC because that computer won't be able to communicate at all with the others.

A switch, by contrast, usually lets two computers communicate at the top speed for communication between them. Thus, two 100Mbps-capable computers can communicate at 100Mbps, even when a 10Mbps-only computer is connected to the same switch.

A related point is that hubs require their connected computers to operate in *half-duplex* mode, meaning that they can send or receive but can't do both at the same time. Switches and crossover cables, by contrast, allow the NICs to operate in *full-duplex* mode, so that transmission and reception can occur simultaneously. Full duplex operation can often speed up network operations substantially.

The line between a hub and a switch is sometimes a blurry one; there are devices that include some features of both products, or which are basically hubs but provide switching features on one or two ports. Such hybrid devices can be a useful compromise to reduce costs while getting the most useful features of a switch, particularly in a network with a mixture of 10Mbps and 100Mbps NICs.

Collisions

Any network architecture has to deal with the fundamental problem of how to cope with the simultaneous need for access by multiple computers. Networks can't handle multiple simultaneous transmissions any better than people can. If three people are sharing a conference call and two try to talk at the same time, the third isn't likely to understand much of what either of the others said—the same is true of computers. How is this fact of networking handled?

In some network architectures, such as Token Ring, it's handled by preventing multiple simultaneous transmissions. In Token Ring, a *token* is "passed" from one computer to another, and each computer is permitted to transmit only when it has received the token. This computer then sends the token on to the next computer, and eventually the token works its way back around the ring.

Ethernet works in a fundamentally different way. In Ethernet, simultaneous transmissions are allowed to happen and are corrected after the fact. A simultaneous transmission is known as a *collision*, and when a collision occurs, neither computer's message is received. Ethernet handles this situation by having each computer delay a random period of time and then try again.

Because the delay period is random, it's unlikely that both computers will try transmitting again at the same time, so both transmissions are likely to work on the second try. (If this second attempt fails, the process repeats itself.)

Collisions are relevant to hubs and switches because hubs do nothing to prevent collisions, whereas switches do. Consider a four-computer network in which the computers maple and oak are exchanging data, while birch and gingko are engaged in their own transfer. With a hub, oak receives data when maple transmits it, but so do birch and gingko. If birch happens to be transmitting data at the same time, a collision occurs, and both maple and birch must retry their transmissions. Because a switch isolates these conversations, though, a collision will not occur in this case, resulting in better network performance. This is true even in a two-computer network because two computers can each attempt to initiate communication at the same time. Crossover cables, like switches, can help prevent collisions, because crossover cables permit full-duplex operation, just as do switches.

The /etc/ifconfig command, mentioned earlier in this chapter, reports the number of collisions detected on one computer. If this number is very high relative to the total number of packets, your network may be overburdened, and you may want to consider replacing hubs with switches, breaking the network into separate segments, or otherwise fixing it. (The ifconfig utility can only report collisions on *one* computer, however, not on the entire network.)

How to Choose a Hub or Switch

Neither hubs nor switches require driver support from the OS; they simply sit on the desk and shuffle Ethernet packets, regardless of the originating and destination operating systems. Hubs and switches are also generally quite capable of interacting well with networking hardware from a variety of manufacturers. You therefore need not purchase a particular brand of hub just because you've got that brand's NICs in your computers. Instead, you should approach the task of picking a hub or switch by asking yourself several questions about your needs and how well the products on the computer store's shelves fill those needs:

- Hub or Switch?—As described earlier, switches are more advanced products than hubs, and switches can improve the performance of your network in several ways. Switches are costlier, though. In general, the extra expense of a switch becomes more worthwhile as you add computers to the network and as those computers generate more traffic. A typical three-computer home network with occasional file sharing isn't likely to benefit much from a switch. An office with two dozen computers with constant sharing of large files, by contrast, likely will benefit from a switch.

- Speed—Although 10/100Mbps NICs aren't much more expensive than 10Mbps NICs, 10/100 hubs and switches are substantially more expensive than their 10Mbps-only counterparts. It may, therefore, be tempting to get a 10Mbps hub if your networking needs are low capacity. This may make sense, even with 10/100 NICs, for modest networks. If and when your needs change or the cost of 10/100 hubs comes down, you can replace the old hub with a new one without opening the computers. Given that the advantage of switches over hubs boils down to speed, I can't see buying a 10Mbps-only switch in most situations, though.

  A related factor for switches is their total internal bandwidth. If a switch is handling two "conversations" between two pairs of computers, and if each of these is transferring data at 100Mbps, the switch itself is processing data at a total of 200Mbps, or perhaps 400Mbps if both connections use full duplex. If you buy a switch, you should check the total capacity of the switch. You'll need higher capacity if your network makes extensive use of peer-to-peer transfers, in which workstations talk to one another, than if it's heavily client/server oriented, in which a large number of clients communicate with a single server.

- Number of Connections—Hubs and routers come in models that support different numbers of connections. You should probably get a hub or switch that has enough connectors for all your existing computers plus at least one or two more. If your network is distributed across a relatively large space, you may want to use two or more hubs or switches, and connect each pair together with a single wire. This may be a particularly useful approach when your computers are clustered together in groups, and each group is separated by some distance. You should be aware of cable length limitations in such situations, however.

- Uplink Connector—Some hubs and switches contain a special connector known as an *uplink connector*. This connector is used to link two hubs or switches together, and is also sometimes used to permit several computers to connect to a single DSL or cable modem. (You can configure a Linux box to do this in a different way using IP masquerading, as described in Chapter 20, "One IP Address, Many Computers: IP Masquerading.") When you link two hubs via their uplink connectors, they effectively become one.

Cabling Choices

If you want to create a 100base-T network, your cabling choices are extremely limited: You must use UTC Category 5 cable with RJ-45 connectors. Such cable is common in computer stores, and can even be obtained from Radio Shack. It does come in a variety of colors and lengths, though. Some Ethernet boards come packaged with a length of appropriate cable, and such bundles are often a bit less expensive than equivalent products purchased separately.

> **TIP**
>
> Take advantage of the varying colors of Ethernet cable. If you can provide each computer that's connected to a hub with a unique color of cable, you'll find it easier to perform maintenance and troubleshooting. The hub's indicator lights can help track down problems with collisions or malfunctioning network cards, and color-coded cables can help you determine which lights refer to which computer. Similarly, different brands of cable often use different types of strain guards and coverings on the RJ-45 clips, and you can use this the same way to aid in diagnostics.

If your network hardware is 10Mbps, you have more substantial choices for cabling. Using 10base-2 coaxial cable may be cheaper for creating or expanding a small network, but you'll need to replace this cabling if you later decide to upgrade the network to 100Mbps. If you decide to use 10base-T, you can use Category 3, 4, or 5 cabling, but given that 100base-T requires Category 5, I recommend using this even for 10base-T networking because the cost difference is minor and upgrades to 100base-T will then be much easier.

When you lay cable for a network, you should follow common-sense safety precautions. Don't leave cable looping about in the open where people might trip over it. Instead, run it behind desks or secure it to baseboards using U-shaped nails or similar cable-stringing products. Particularly in a business environment, you may need to ensure that your cabling meets local fire safety requirements. If you're not familiar with the relevant regulations, you may want to hire a professional who is to purchase and run the cables.

Recently, products have begun to appear that allow you to network computers using unused wires in your home telephone wiring. These products are only capable of slow speeds, however—1Mbps or so. They generally come in kit form and require special Ethernet cards, so be sure to check on Linux compatibility with those cards if you decide to try them. Depending upon your home's wiring, they may conflict with DSL Internet service.

Ethernet Kits

A number of manufacturers sell kits that contain a pair of Ethernet cards, a hub, and two cables. Such kits can sometimes cost a bit less than the equivalent components purchased separately, and so can be a good deal—if you really need those precise components. If you're networking only two computers, for instance, you can make do without the hub by purchasing a crossover cable and using that to directly connect the two computers. You'll get better performance as well because the NICs can use full duplex mode with the crossover cable. You should also be vigilant when it comes to the speed of the components. I've seen kits that include

10/100Mbps NICs but 10Mbps-only hubs, which is hardly a bargain. You should also be sure the cable is UTC Category 5, not a lower grade, and that the cables are of an appropriate length for your needs. Be sure the hub has enough ports for your needs, or that you can expand it with an uplink port to another hub.

If you're networking several computers and determine that a kit is a good starting point, don't feel obliged to purchase the same brand products for additional NICs, cables, or hubs. Doing so may sometimes simplify your life in that you'll need only one type of driver across all your computers, but brand-to-brand incompatibilities in networking hardware are extremely rare.

DSL and Cable Modems

The explosive growth of the Internet in the past decade has been a great boon to large organizations that have been able to afford T1 lines or other high-speed connections to the Internet. Smaller businesses and individuals have had to make do with lesser forms of access, however, and this has become increasingly frustrating as the quantities of data available on the Internet have grown. For instance, in 1994 it was possible to obtain a copy of Slackware Linux (then the rage in the Linux community) in about 20MB of files. With a 14.4Kbps modem, it was possible to download these files in a bit over three hours. Five years later, a Red Hat 6.0 distribution consumes over 500MB—a 25-fold increase from 1994. The fastest modems available, though, are only four times faster, so downloading it all by modem would take over 20 hours! Although this is perhaps not the fairest comparison possible, given that Linux has grown much faster than most software products in that time, it does serve to explain the desire on the part of many for faster Internet access.

High-Speed Access on a Budget

The telecommunications industry is beginning to take note of this demand. In 1999, there are two major approaches to feeding this demand in small business and home Internet access: cable modems and DSL service. Although these technologies are quite different in some ways, they're very similar from the point of view of Linux system configuration. They're also both priced quite low compared to a full T1 connection—usually between $40 and $100 a month for low-level service.

Cable Modems

Cable modems are not actually modems in the conventional sense, as described later in this chapter. Because the cable modem box serves as an interface between the computer and the network much as a conventional modem does, however, the term *cable modem* has come into popular use.

Cable television systems function by transmitting TV-style signals over a coaxial cable. A typical cable TV system has roughly 750MHz of bandwidth, with each TV channel occupying about 6MHz of that, and a certain amount of bandwidth devoted to system control signals, such as those that enable you to order a pay-per-view movie. To support cable modems, one channel (6MHz of bandwidth) is set aside for sending data from the cable company's Internet access line to subscribers (this is referred to as *downstream traffic*). Another channel or some otherwise unused bandwidth is set aside for data going from subscribers to the Internet (called *upstream traffic*). A few cable modem setups don't allocate any upstream traffic, and instead require that you dial up with a conventional telephone line for this function. Such systems are likely to use unusual software and therefore be incompatible with Linux.

One important characteristic of cable modem service is that the amount of bandwidth, and therefore the total amount of data that can flow over the system, is both fixed and shared. The fixed aspect of this arrangement is not unusual, but the shared part is, and this has consequences. Most importantly, your neighbors have access to precisely the same data stream you do; the cable company has no way of directing a specific signal down your cable wire but not your neighbor's. The same is true of cable TV channels. The reason you can order a pay-per-view movie is that these channels are sent out in an encrypted form, and the cable TV set-top boxes contain decryption routines that can be activated remotely after you order the film. Your neighbors receive the same film as you, but unless they order it, the picture will be unviewable. Just as conventional cable TV signals are visible to all individuals on the cable TV system, so too do all the cable modems in an area see all the data going to all the area's cable modems. This fact has two important practical consequences:

- As demand for Internet access via cable modems goes up, speed goes down. This rule applies both on a minute-by-minute, hour-by-hour basis as people surf the Web at particular times, and over days, months, and years as people subscribe to or drop the service. Of course, cable companies can add more equipment to break their territories into smaller regions and improve performance, and they may even be willing to devote more channels to cable modem service, but the bottom line is that the service's speed can vary substantially.

- Network traffic destined for one location is visible at another. In theory, a malicious individual could snoop on the network looking for passwords, credit card numbers, or other information. This doesn't mean you shouldn't use such a system for transferring such data, but it does mean you should be especially aware of security issues. Give your credit card numbers *only* using a browser with security features, for instance, and only to secure Web sites; use `ssh` rather than `telnet` to log in to remote sites (or to your home Linux box from another location); and so on. Fortunately, many cable modem providers encrypt data at the cable modem box, so snooping by your neighbors can be difficult. Not all providers do this, however.

The cable company almost always serves as both the provider of the physical connection to your computer and as the Internet service provider (ISP). You therefore deal with only one company when using a cable modem.

DSL

DSL is a service that's similar in price and performance to cable modems, but it's offered by local telephone companies or other companies that lease the telephone companies' wiring. There are several different varieties of DSL service, each distinguished by a different leading letter, such as ADSL (asymmetric DSL), SDSL (symmetric DSL), and so on. The term *xDSL* is sometimes used to refer to all DSL varieties generically. In most cases, ADSL is the least expensive of these technologies, and it is the one that competes most directly against cable modems. Other DSL varieties (particularly SDSL) are often marketed towards small businesses. You can often subscribe to SDSL for home use or ADSL for business use, however, and you should consult your local DSL providers for information on precisely what services they offer. The Web sites `http://webisplist.InternetList.com/screens/ispsearch/powersearch.asp?From=ADSL` and `http://www.dslreports.com` have information on DSL providers in many parts of the United States.

Like cable "modems," the devices used to connect a computer to a DSL system are sometimes referred to as modems, although this is technically incorrect. DSL systems do resemble cable modems in their operation because both split the bandwidth of the transmission line and use part of it for data and part for other functions. In the case of DSL, a largely inaudible high-frequency portion of the spectrum is used for transmitting data, while the rest of the telephone line is used for conventional voice communication. DSL service can and therefore often does use the same cabling as your phone service. This isn't always the case, though, particularly if a supplier other than your local telephone company provides the network connection.

Unlike cable modems, DSL provides a direct link between your computer and the DSL service's network. Therefore, the bandwidth for which you pay isn't shared as directly (though once at the DSL service, it's combined and there can be bottlenecks here), and your neighbors are less likely to be able to snoop on your network activity. You can also typically subscribe to DSL service at any of a number of different speeds to suit your needs.

Although somecompanies (mostly local telephone companies) provide both the physical wiring and ISP functions, these two aspects of Internet access are more often decoupled with DSL. You can contract with a company like Bell Atlantic, Covad, or Northpoint for the DSL line, and use independent ISPs such as Flashcom, Concentric, or Speakeasy for actual Internet access. Generally speaking, though, one ISP works through only one DSL provider in a given area.

Hardware and Software Requirements

Both cable modems and DSL service generally connect to your computer through a 10base-T Ethernet link. You'll therefore need one Ethernet card in your computer to connect to these services. If you intend to link several computers in this way, you'll need to either subscribe for multiple computers or use your Linux box as a gateway for the others, using IP masquerading, as described in Chapter 20. (There are also third-party products that can perform functions similar to IP masquerading, and sometimes the DSL or cable modem can perform this function.) Connecting multiple computers directly, if your ISP allows this, can be more convenient in some cases, and is more flexible; but it also means you have to be more careful about securing all the systems against intruders, and your ISP may charge more for this service.

Some DSL and cable modem providers include an Ethernet card in their setup charges. You should ask what model card you're getting, and check that it's compatible with Linux before an installer comes to configure your equipment. If your ISP doesn't provide the NIC, or if the ISP provides one that's incompatible with Linux, you'll need to buy your own, preferably before an installer comes to hook everything up. Be sure to tell them you intend to do this because they may need the card's hardware address to configure their system.

A few cable and DSL modems are cards that plug into your computer. At the moment, few or none of these products are compatible with Linux, so you should be sure that you check on this point with your service provider. If the provider uses an all-in-one, Linux-incompatible device, ask if their system is compatible with another device you could get from a third party. If it is, you might be able to get the service working by purchasing this third-party cable or DSL modem.

Most cable and DSL modems are boxes that reside outside the computer, connecting to your computer via an Ethernet cable and to their respective networks with their own cables. In general, cable companies lease the cable modems to their customers, whereas DSL providers sell the DSL modems as part of the installation charge.

Both cable modems and DSL work with standard TCP/IP applications. There's usually very little that's unique to configuring or running these systems as compared to connecting a Linux computer to any other Ethernet network. Many of these systems use DHCP to assign Internet addresses dynamically. This means that your Internet address may not be the same from one day to the next, or even from one hour to the next. This can cause complications if you want to run your own Web server or something similar, but ISPs that use DHCP generally object to such uses anyhow. Other DSL and cable modem providers give you a static Internet address, which you configure in Linux just as if you were connecting to any other Ethernet network.

One trend in the DSL world is to use PPP or similar protocols over the DSL line. The modem itself often handles these functions, so they're transparent to Linux. You should inquire about this, though. If your would-be ISP reports the need for special Windows software, ask more questions to ascertain Linux compatibility. Even if the ISP uses special Windows software, you might be able to get the service working in Linux by purchasing a more expensive modem, which incorporates the necessary protocols.

A Brief Guide to Setting Up Cable Modem or DSL Service

When you call to order cable modem or DSL service, be sure to tell the sales representative that you're running Linux. Some providers balk at this and will refuse to install the service on a computer running anything but Windows or possibly MacOS. Sometimes you can get the service installed by having an "approved" OS running when the installer arrives, and then configure the Linux side yourself. A few ISPs object to your doing this. In general, cable companies are more likely to insist that you run Windows than are DSL ISPs.

The details of what happens when you have these services installed varies widely. It usually involves one or two trips to your home or business by representatives of one or two companies. In the case of DSL service provided by a company other than your local telephone company, for instance, the phone company will usually have to run a wire to your building, and then the DSL provider will install additional hardware, including the DSL "modem" itself.

NOTE

The latest form of DSL service is called G.Lite. This service theoretically eliminates the need for any visit to your home. The provider handles wiring at the phone company's central office and mails you the necessary hardware (or you should be able to buy it at a computer store starting sometime in 2000). You generally have to install *micro-filters* on each phone outlet and then plug the DSL modem in much as you would an analog modem. The trouble is that your inside wiring might not be adequate for this service, in which case you'll need to redo it yourself or have somebody do it for you. If this happens, you won't have saved much time or money compared to conventional DSL service.

In the end, you'll have a new box sitting on your desk. This box will have a standard Ethernet cable to connect to your computer, and another cable to connect to your cable TV system or to your telephone wiring. There may be another box or two involved, sometimes located outside your building.

From a Linux point of view, you configure your system to use either DSL or cable modem service just as if you were configuring any other Ethernet network. In some cases, you'll specify a static Internet address, domain name service (DNS) server, and similar information manually. In other cases, you'll use DHCP to have Linux obtain this information from a server maintained by the ISP. Chapter 7, "Setting Ethernet Options," covers these topics in greater detail. If you want to set up IP masquerading to allow other computers on your home network to use the service, see Chapter 20, but be aware that some ISPs may object to such a configuration.

Telephone Modems

When it comes to linking up with the Internet, not everybody is fortunate enough to have DSL, cable modem, or faster service. For those less fortunate, less needful, or less wealthy, conventional telephone modems provide the usual means for linking to the Internet.

The word *modem* is an acronym for *modulator-demodulator*, referring to the fact that modems modulate digital data into analog form (sound—or, more precisely, the electrical equivalents of sound on telephone wires), and then demodulate these analog signals back into digital form. They are devices for transmitting digital data over the fundamentally analog telephone network, which was designed decades before digital computers became a reality.

What Speed Modem?

Modem speeds have increased dramatically in the past several years. In the mid-1980s, a speed of 300 bps was common; but now, 56,400 bps models are available. Or are they?

The modems you buy in a store that bear the label "56Kbps" can't really achieve that speed, at least in the United States. At best, they can produce 54Kbps, because FCC regulations on signal strength prevent legal use of faster speeds using the v.90 modulation standard. In practice, maximum connect rates are likely to be still lower, on the order of 50Kbps or less.

There's also the fact that v.90 modems produce their high speed in one direction only (downstream—to you). In the opposite direction, the speed is limited to 33,600 bps. This is why it usually takes longer to upload a file than to download one when using such a modem.

All these caveats about v.90 modem speeds should not, however, be taken to mean that you should avoid them. Even a 50% increase in speed over an old 33.6Kbps model can be important and worthwhile. If you're buying a new modem today, there's little reason to buy anything but a v.90 model, at least if the modem is for dialout use. If you want to use the modem to accept calls from others, a 33.6Kbps model will be adequate. This is because the 56Kbps downstream speed can only be attained with a special digital connection to the phone lines on the receiving modem's end. If you buy two v.90 modems and call one from the other, the connect speed will be 33.6Kbps both ways (maximum).

Prior to the acceptance of v.90 as a standard for modem communication, two competing and proprietary protocols were in use, X2 and K56Flex. You're unlikely to find modems that use only these protocols in stores today, but you might find one in the used market. Such models can often be upgraded to use v.90, but a few, particularly from now-defunct manufacturers, may not be upgradeable. Some ISPs may still support one or both of these older protocols, but sooner or later this support is likely to vanish, after which such modems will effectively be 33.6Kbps models.

Telephone modem speeds aren't likely to increase substantially, if at all, in the future. v.90 is more or less at the theoretical limit for data transmission rates over conventional telephone lines when using modem technology. It is possible to coax more speed out of telephone wires, but only by switching to digital technologies such as DSL.

Testing for v.90 Compatibility

Although most phone lines in the United States are capable of handling v.90, not all are. You can test your current phone line by using the line test service operated by 3COM, assuming you have a v.34 (28.8Kbps or better) modem. You'll need to launch a terminal program such as Minicom or Seyon and configure it to use your modem line (generally /dev/ttyS0 or /dev/ttyS1). Type **ATDT1-847-262-6000** to have the modem dial this line test number. (*Note: This is a toll call!*) When you're prompted for your first and last names, enter **line** and **test**, respectively. The system will then diagnose the connection and inform you of the results.

When testing for 56Kbps capability, you should be sure to test from the line you intend to use for the modem connection. It's possible that two phone lines on a street, or even in a building, will have different characteristics, so you shouldn't rely on your neighbor's ability to connect at high speeds; test your own line.

Although generally accurate, the results of the 3COM test aren't perfect. In some cases, you may find that your line tests well for 56Kbps speed, but when you connect an appropriate modem, you only get speeds of around 40Kbps—hardly worth the upgrade from 33.6Kbps. It's conceivable that you could improve matters by removing unneeded telephones from your home wiring or by having the phone company look at your wires, but you may be stuck with it. The v.90 standard pushes the analog telephone system about as far as it can go, and any minor imperfection can cause a substantial drop in performance.

Linux Modem Compatibility

Most modems operate over a conventional serial port (usually /dev/ttyS0 or /dev/ttyS1 in Linux). As such, they don't need special drivers beyond the normal Linux serial drivers. There are some caveats, however, as well as reasons for preferring one type of modem over another.

In addition to their serial port interfaces, modems use command sets to perform actions such as dialing, setting error correction, and so on. The basics of this command set have long been standardized as the *Hayes command set*, named after the modem manufacturer that developed it. The Hayes command set is quite basic, however, and different manufacturers have extended it in various ways. None of these extensions is incompatible with Linux, however. At worst, you'll need to change the modem initialization string you use in your GUI PPP dialer or PPP dial scripts to enable or disable certain features.

External and Internal Modems

You can purchase modems that come as boxes external to the computer and that plug into the computer's external serial port, or as internal cards that plug into an ISA slot (or more recently, a PCI slot). Traditionally, internal modems have contained serial port circuitry, and so appear to Linux as a serial port. The main trick with internal modems of this type is that you may need to configure them as a third serial port (/dev/ttyS2) with its own separate IRQ, or disable one of the serial ports on the motherboard and have the internal modem take its place. Both of these options can be troublesome, and so internal modems tend to be trickier to configure for Linux than external models. External models also have the advantage of indicator lights that can help in diagnosing link problems. On the other hand, external models take up desk space and require a separate power supply. Overall, I tend to favor external models, but this is a matter of personal preference.

A Word About Windows-Only Modems

In the past few years, internal modems have begun to appear that don't use a standard serial interface and offload much of a modem's traditional functionality onto the computer. Such modems often *emulate* the serial port using special Windows drivers. In theory, Linux drivers could be developed for such Windows-only modems, but Linux developers have spurned the challenge for a variety of reasons, including the facts that such modems degrade overall system performance and that modem manufacturers haven't been forthcoming with the specifications needed to develop drivers. Needless to say, you should avoid Windows-only modems for use in Linux.

NOTE

One company, PCtel (http://www.pctel.com), has announced a software-driven modem for Linux similar in concept to Windows-only modems.

Windows-only modems are always internal models, so one way to ensure that you're not getting one is to buy an external model. Manufacturers often include *Win* or *Windows* in the names of such modems, and list Windows as a prerequisite for using the modem. Unfortunately, these characteristics don't indicate that the modem is a Windows-only modem with any certainty because manufacturers also often list Windows as a prerequisite for ordinary modems.

The lesson is that if you want to buy an internal modem, you should buy one from a store with a good return policy. That way, if you install the device in your Linux computer and find that it doesn't work, you can return it and try another. Of course, this is good advice when buying *any* hardware, but it's particularly relevant to internal modems.

Extra Modem Features

Many modems these days sport features in addition to modem functionality. Many of these features can be used in Linux, with greater or lesser degrees of ease.

Fax

One near-universal feature found in modems today is the ability to process faxes. You can configure a modem to both send and receive faxes. You need special fax software to handle both tasks. In Linux, there are several fax programs for sending and receiving faxes, such as `mgetty+sendfax` (which comes with most Linux distributions) or HylaFax.

Modem fax functionality is somewhat standardized. The vast majority of fax machines and fax modems that operate over conventional telephone lines use what is known as Group III fax encoding. This standard is implemented by the fax modem hardware itself, so you needn't be concerned with it from a software point of view. The interface between the fax modem and the software comes into play when considering another fax standard, though, and here there are two major choices: Class 1 and Class 2. Class 1 is an older standard that requires more support from the software for handling page breaks and so on. Class 2 places more of the responsibility of fax formatting in the hands of the fax modem. Unfortunately, Class 2 went for a long time without being ratified by any standards organization, and so many manufacturers shipped slightly incompatible versions of Class 2 fax modems. To help identify models that adhere to the final standard, this standard is referred to as *Class 2.0*, not simply *Class 2*. The common `mgetty+sendfax` program supports Class 2 and Class 2.0 fax modems, but not Class 1 fax modems. Today, most fax modems do support Class 2 or Class 2.0.

Configuring Linux fax software typically involves editing one or more configuration files. Check the documentation that came with your fax software for details. You can configure the software both to send faxes and to receive them. When sending faxes, the fax software generally connects itself to the standard Linux printer queue system to intercept normal printer output. You can configure the software to extract a fax number from the PostScript file that Linux uses as a universal printer document format and send to that number, or to prompt the user with a GUI system for a number, cover page information, and so on. If configured in the first way, you can even send faxes from remote systems using normal Linux printer sharing features, as described in Part IV.

NOTE

When sending faxes, you normally create and "print" a PostScript file. Linux's Ghostscript program then processes the PostScript file into a standard fax file format, which the fax package itself sends to the fax modem. Thus, the information in Chapter 14, "Preparing to Share a Printer," on Ghostscript is relevant to sending faxes.

Voice

An increasingly popular option on modems is voice functionality. This is often used to turn a computer into an answering machine. As with fax functionality, you'll need special Linux software to support this feature. A variant of the `mgetty+sendfax` package, called `vgetty`, is generally used for this purpose. Unlike voicemail packages under Windows or MacOS, `vgetty` presents a crude text-only user interface and is difficult to configure. Configuring `vgetty` is beyond the scope of this book. You can find more information about `vgetty` at `http://www.cis.ohio-state.edu/text/faq/usenet/faxfaq/mgetty+sendfax+vgetty/faq.html`.

Multifunction Units

As the number of SOHO appliances has multiplied, it's become increasingly desirable to combine the functions of two or more devices into one unit to save cost and desk space. Thus, you see combination modem/fax units (with genuine scanners and paper output), printer/scanner/faxes, and so on. In theory, there's nothing preventing such units from working with Linux. You must be cautious about supported protocols, however. For instance, a combination unit might require special software for printing, and be incompatible with Ghostscript, rendering print functions inoperative. Manufacturers of multifunction units seem more reluctant than most others to reveal important specifications, so you'll have to dig deeper to determine whether the functions you want are supported under Linux. If they are, you can save yourself some desk space, and even make such devices' features available to others in your office, just as you would single-function devices, as described in this book.

Summary

This chapter covered the basics of networking hardware. Particularly important for anybody reading this book is the information on NICs and Ethernet. There are many different types of network hardware, but Ethernet is the most popular in small and medium-sized networks today. Ethernet comes in several different varieties, both in terms of speed (10Mbps versus 100Mbps) and cabling (thin coaxial, thick coaxial, and twisted-pair). These different varieties of Ethernet determine the network topologies that are possible, with the most desirable speeds dictating a star topology in which all computers are connected to a central hub or switch.

When it comes to accessing outside networks, most small office and home users will want to use a telephone modem for low-speed access or a cable modem or DSL service for increased speed. Connecting your computer to a cable modem or DSL network is much like connecting to a larger Ethernet network, as described in Chapter 7, "Setting Ethernet Options." Using a telephone modem requires that you configure PPP, which is described in greater detail in Chapter 8, "Using PPP for Dialup Connections."

Table 1.2 summarizes the hardware needed for assorted networking tasks. Note that you might need hardware listed in more than one row of this table, if your system is to function in more than one networking capacity—for instance, as both a node on a local network and as a fax server.

TABLE **1.2**   Hardware Needed for Networking Tasks

Networking Task	10base-T NIC	100base-T NIC	Hub or Switch	UTC Category 5 Cable	Coaxial Cable	DSL or Cable Modem	Second NIC	Analog Modem
Coaxial Ethernet Network	X				X			
10base-T Network	X		X	X				
100base-T Network		X	X	X				
Router Between Two Network Segments		X		X			X	
Router Between Internal Network and Internet Using DSL or Cable Service		X		X		X	X	
Router Between Internal Network and Internet Using Analog Modem		X					X	X
Fax Server		X		X				X

Unless otherwise specified, 100base-T networks are assumed. Hubs and switches are listed once per network; specific functions presuppose the existence of an existing hub or switch, if necessary. This table does not distinguish between 10base-2 and 10base-5 coaxial technologies.

Understanding TCP/IP

IN THIS CHAPTER

Chapter 1 covered network hardware, but hardware is useless without software to use the hardware. This chapter therefore introduces the architecture of networking software under Linux. Networking software uses an assortment of networking *protocols*, which are methods to allow computers to communicate with one another. You can think of a protocol as being something like the rules governing everyday actions, such as ordering a meal at a fast-food restaurant. Components of a "fast food protocol" would include waiting in line, stepping up to the counter, stating what you want to eat, handing over money, receiving change, and receiving your food. Networking protocols are similar to this brief description of buying lunch, but they're much more detailed and precise.

Much of Linux networking—and indeed, much of computer networking in general—is done using the *Transmission Control Protocol* and the *Internet Protocol*, which are known collectively as *TCP/IP*. These two protocols are actually composed of several others, and collectively they allow for computer communications across a room or across the planet. Indeed, there's even been work done on extending TCP/IP to allow for communication across interplanetary distances for NASA space probes! This chapter covers the basics of TCP/IP networking. Although you may be able to get by without reading this chapter, its contents will help you understand the rest of the book. At the end of this chapter, you'll find a brief discussion of protocols that compete with TCP/IP, some of which are important to certain intranetworking tasks to which you may put Linux.

The TCP/IP Stack

TCP/IP, like other networking protocols, can be described in terms of a *protocol stack*. Each layer in this stack performs a different function, and is usually implemented by a unique program. Indeed, different networking applications require an assortment of programs at many different layers of the stack. The end result is that "the" TCP/IP stack used by one program for one connection may be very different than "the" TCP/IP stack used by another program for another connection, even on the same computer. This is similar to the plumbing system used in a town; water can flow through very different pipes to reach two homes, but it's all part of the same network of pipes.

It's important to realize that one computer's TCP/IP stack is useless by itself, however; the whole point of any networking protocol is to exchange data between computers. The TCP/IP stack enables this exchange by "wrapping" the data to be transmitted at each stage for transmission to the destination, or by "unwrapping" data it receives. Each extra layer of wrapping provides information needed by the next layer in the stack to process the data.

Wrapping and Unwrapping Data for Shipment

Let's consider an analogy for a moment. Suppose that you want to send a paper letter to your sister in another city. Once you write your letter, you'll sign it, fold it, and place it in an envelope. You have wrapped data for transmission. You then write an address on the envelope, put a stamp on it, and drop it in a mailbox. The Post Office sorts the letter and places it in a mail bag—another form of wrapping. The bag goes in a truck or some other vehicle (yet another type of wrapping), and the vehicle travels to the destination city. There, the postal workers unload the truck, unpack the bag, and route your letter to an individual mail carrier's vehicle and bag. Finally, with any luck, your sister will receive and read your letter. Your sister can then send a reply by the same means.

TCP/IP works much like the Post Office, wrapping your data on one computer and sending it to another, where it is unwrapped. Instead of wrapping data for physical protection and to group items going to nearby locations, however, TCP/IP wraps data as a means of addressing it and communicating to both intervening and destination TCP/IP stacks how to reassemble the data once it's arrived. This last point is important because, unlike the Post Office, TCP/IP can and does break up a single communication into multiple *packets*, or portions. For instance, if you use a Web browser to download a program file, TCP/IP breaks that file up into small pieces, each of which is wrapped separately and transmitted independently. It's even possible for different pieces of the same file to take entirely different routes from the source to the destination.

For TCP/IP to work as well as it does, it's necessary for each layer of the protocol stack to perform only its own well-defined tasks. Each layer receives a particular type of data from the layer above it when transmitting data, processes it, and sends a transformed data packet to the layer below. On the receiving computer, the corresponding layer of the stack receives the transformed data packet, unwraps it, and sends the unwrapped data up to the next layer, which then sees precisely what its counterpart on the sending computer sent.

Layers of the TCP/IP Stack

So what are these layers of the TCP/IP stack? Figure 2.1 illustrates them. This figure shows the layer twice in order to emphasize the fact that a TCP/IP stack in isolation is a useless thing. Typically, a *client* program on one system initiates a request for data from a *server* program on another computer. Data travels down the stack from the client program, crosses to the recipient computer, and is received by the server program. In many cases, the communication travels both ways, too. For instance, a Web browser sends a request for a Web page, and then receives the text of the page in response. The client may then request further information, such as the image files used on the Web page, and receive them from the server.

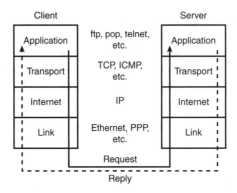

FIGURE 2.1

Each layer of the TCP/IP stack behaves as if it were linked to its twin on the other computer; the intervening layers serve to promote this communication.

NOTE

The terms *client* and *server* are most clearly defined in terms of specific software programs running on computers. The Netscape Navigator Web browser is a client, for instance, whereas the Apache program is a server for Web pages. The terms *client* and *server* are sometimes applied to entire computers, however, as in the statement, "The server is down again today." (Chances are it isn't running Linux!) This simply implies that the primary function of the computer is to run client or server software. You can run both types of programs on a single computer, however, even at the same time. In the case of file and printer sharing, a network in which both client and server software runs on most or all of the computers is typically referred to as a *peer-to-peer* network. In a *client/server* network, by contrast, one or more computers runs primarily server software and other (more numerous) computers run primarily client software. Much of this book is concerned with the configuration of server software under Linux, although I do include information on configuring matching client software, so that your Linux box can participate in both client/server and peer-to-peer interactions.

Application Layer

The topmost layer of the TCP/IP stack is the *application layer*. This layer is comprised of the user applications with which you normally interact on the client end (such as Netscape Navigator, telnet, ftp, and the Windows Network Neighborhood file interface) and the programs that serve requests from these clients on the server end (such as Apache, in.telnetd, in.ftpd, and Samba).

> **NOTE**
>
> In Linux, it's common for a server to take the name of its client counterpart program with *d* appended, and occasionally with *in.* prepended. Thus, in.telnetd serves telnet clients, for example. This isn't necessary, however. The appended *d* refers to the fact that the program runs as a *daemon*—a program that sits in the background doing nothing but waiting for particular events, such as incoming network activity of a particular type.

At any one time, any given computer can have 0, 1, 2, or more programs running in the TCP/IP application layer. For instance, you could be viewing Web pages with Netscape Navigator while simultaneously downloading a file using ftp and accepting a print job from a remote host using Samba. Still more clients and servers could be running but not processing input. Thus, you should not think of the application layer as being a single program or even a fixed set of programs. Instead, it's composed of whatever client and server programs the system happens to be running at any given moment.

In order to communicate with the outside world, a client program running in the application layer makes certain requests of the operating system. Effectively, it creates a message along the lines of *send such-and-such data* and passes it to the OS, along with some way to identify the server. Eventually, the corresponding application layer program on the server system receives that request along with the client's address. The server replies by sending the requested data, or by sending a message stating that the data is not available. (In some cases, the server need not reply, but these situations are the exception rather than the rule. In other cases, the client may send substantial quantities of data to the server, as when a Windows computer stores a file on a Linux computer's hard disk using Windows networking and Samba.) The details of this dialogue are determined by the protocols for the specific service in question, and of course they're usually much more complex than a single request-reply pair, often involving several back-and-forth transfers.

If you've used the Internet much, you're probably used to seeing Internet addresses such as ftp.redhat.com or www.oberlin.edu. These addresses are easy for humans to understand and remember, but they're not ideal for computers. Computers work best with numbers, and at its core, the Internet uses a 32-bit number (called the *IP address*) to address every computer. This number is usually expressed as four decimal digits separated by periods, such as 192.168.1.1. One of the things that the application layer program must do is to *resolve* the human-readable name into its numeric counterpart. It does this by using the *domain name service* (*DNS*), which is a massively distributed database of names located throughout the Internet. Thus, before most application layer programs can do anything at all, they may need to generate network traffic just to look up an address. This is analogous to writing the Post Office in Kalamazoo, Michigan to find the address of an individual who lives in Kalamazoo. Fortunately, TCP/IP networking is normally much faster than delivering paper mail. It's also possible to *cache*, or store locally, frequently-used addresses, thus reducing the need for such traffic.

One of the decisions that the designers of the application layer protocol must make is which TCP/IP transport layer protocol is appropriate for an application. Different transport protocols provide different capabilities, and the application layer program's only means of communication will be through the transport layer protocols.

Transport Layer

Several protocols are available in the transport layer, but three are used most often:

- Transmission Control Protocol (TCP)—This is the protocol that's used for the transmission of large messages, especially when it's most important that the data arrive unscathed. "Large," in this context, means more than a few bytes, and so this is the protocol that's used for the transfer of complete data files. Applications that use TCP include file sharing, remote printing, and Web surfing. TCP supports breaking a transmission down into multiple packets. Because TCP is used by so many important Internet programs, its name is the source of the *TCP* portion of the TCP/IP stack name.

- User Datagram Protocol (UDP)—Systems can send small quantities of data to one another with less-than-perfect reliability using the UDP. UDP messages cannot be broken into multiple packets, which limits the utility of UDP. UDP, however, contains much less overhead than TCP, so it's preferred for certain simple types of transfers. The DNS system for determining a remote system's IP address uses UDP.

- Internet Control Message Protocol (ICMP)—Simpler even than UDP, ICMP is used to send one of a fixed number of simple messages to a recipient machine. If you've used the ping command to determine whether a remote machine and the network between you and it are all working, you've sent ICMP packets because ping simply sends a series of ICMP_ECHO_REQUEST messages and waits for the ICMP_ECHO_REPLY messages in return.

The end user is well-insulated from the details of the transport layer, and even when you're configuring a server for use on an intranet or the Internet, you needn't be very concerned with the details of this layer's operation. If you want to write a new application layer program, though, you'll need to know enough about the transport layer to interface with it. Such details are beyond the scope of this book.

In general, a given application-layer program directly interfaces with only one of the three transport-layer protocols. You can't use ftp to transfer files using ICMP, for instance. Because most application-layer programs use DNS for hostname lookup, however, the UDP protocol will be used indirectly for most network accesses.

Internet Layer

The Internet layer is the only layer that uses only one protocol, the Internet Protocol (from which the *IP* portion of the name *TCP/IP* is derived). The Internet layer's job is to prepare a data packet to leave the computer or to begin decoding a data packet that's been received. The Internet layer doesn't actually receive or transmit packets, though—that's the task of the link layer.

The Internet layer adds data to the start of a data packet received from the transport layer. The data added includes, but is not limited to, the source and destination addresses, the size of the packet, and assorted flags to help systems along the way process the packet. In many ways, this is analogous to writing from and to addresses on an envelope.

In addition to addressing, the Internet layer may sometimes break a data packet into two or more parts. This occurs when two computers with differing capabilities in terms of packet size communicate with each other. If the computer `stark.nephridior.com` is trying to send data to the computer `kent.janet.net`, and if `kent` can receive data in packets only half the size of what `stark`'s Internet layer has prepared, `stark`'s transport layer will compensate by breaking these packets into pieces. Such breakdown and reassembly can also occur because an intervening computer that processes data between `stark` and `kent` can't handle the packet size that `stark` had originally prepared. In any event, this packet breakdown is completely transparent to the layers above the transport layer.

Link Layer

With the link layer, we return to a layer that has multiple options. The options result from the fact that this layer interfaces all the preceding layers to the network hardware, and of course not all computers have the same network hardware. For instance, you might be using an Ethernet card, a Token Ring card, or a PPP dialup connection. None of the software in the preceding layers knows anything about the specific hardware you're using, but those details do need to be handled somewhere, and this is the place.

The link layer takes the packets delivered by the Internet layer and adds appropriate information to make the data transmissible over whatever network hardware exists. The details of what this information is, of course, vary from one type of network interface to another.

One computer can have multiple network interfaces. For instance, you can have a local intranet of half a dozen computers linked via Ethernet, and one of these computers can also have a dialup PPP connection to the Internet. That computer with two interfaces must determine, for each packet its TCP/IP stack generates, to which of the two interfaces it must send the data. It does this by consulting the *routing table*. This is simply a table that lists sets of Internet addresses associated with each interface. For instance, local private Ethernets frequently have IP addresses of the form 192.168.*x.x*. If a computer is connected both to such a network and to the rest of the Internet via a PPP dialup connection, the routing table instructs the link layer to send data destined to 192.168.*x*.*x* addresses to the Ethernet board and everything else over the PPP link.

Note that the sending and receiving computers don't need to use the same type of network hardware. For instance, you can use a PPP dialup connection to communicate with a computer that's linked using Ethernet. In such a situation, however, one or more of the intervening computers must have two interfaces, and the intervening machine must be configured to route the traffic from one interface to another. This *router* strips the link layer's header, places a new header on the packet, and sends it on to the second interface.

One variant on the router model is implemented in IP masquerading. In this case, the intervening computer peels back more layers in the packaging and meddles with the return IP address, thus hiding the originating system's address. The intervening computer then watches for replies to this packet and meddles again to send the packet to the originating system. Does this sound dishonest? In some sense it is, but it's a very useful technique when you have a limited number of IP addresses at your disposal. You can use this technique to link a small home network to the Internet via a dialup PPP connection, for instance. You can then cruise the Web using a Mac with no modem, to name just one possible application.

NOTE

The 32-bit IP address limits the theoretical maximum number of computers on the Internet as a whole to about four billion. In practice, the limit is lower than this for assorted reasons, and we're fast approaching the limit on the number of computers the current IP addressing system can handle. IP masquerading can actually increase the limit because it allows several computers to share a single IP address. IP masquerading is, however, fundamentally a local solution to local IP address limitations.

The Result of Data Wrapping

The end result of the data encapsulation described here is shown in Figure 2.2, which depicts a typical data packet. Figure 2.2 shows an `ftp` packet transmitted over Ethernet, but other protocols and media would result in similar layering.

Upon receipt, each layer of the TCP/IP stack strips away the header (and footer, if applicable) it's assigned and uses the information in that header to pass the data on to the appropriate next layer in the stack. Ultimately, the destination application receives the data at the core of this packet, without the various headers.

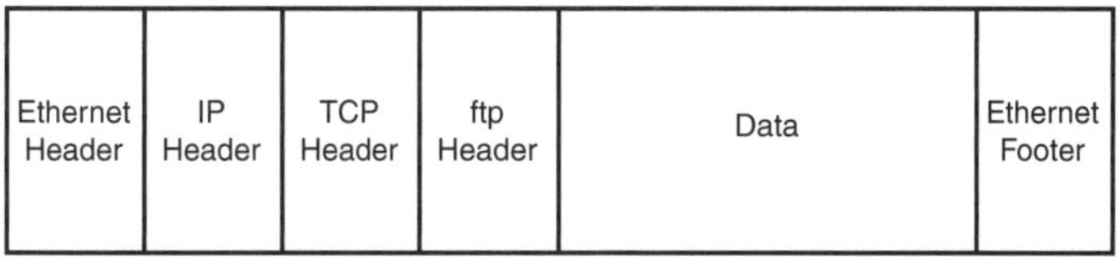

Ethernet Header	IP Header	TCP Header	ftp Header	Data	Ethernet Footer

FIGURE 2.2
Data transmitted over a TCP/IP network is "wrapped" in headers (and sometimes footers) for each layer of the TCP/IP stack.

An Example: Following a Web Page Access

As an example of how all the preceding steps work, let's follow what happens when you access a Web page using a browser such as Netscape Navigator:

1. You type the uniform resource locator (URL) for the Web page into the browser. For instance, you might type `http://www.midwinter.com/lurk/eplist.html` to get a list of episodes from the TV series *Babylon 5*.

2. Netscape calls the Linux library function `gethostbyname`, which links up with DNS. As name resolution could be as simple as looking up an address in a cache or as complex as an entire set of network accesses similar to the one I'm describing, we'll just say it happens and leave it at that. The result is that Netscape now knows the numeric IP address of `www.midwinter.com`, which is 199.165.129.193.

3. Netscape prepares an appropriate hypertext transfer protocol (HTTP) request to ask for the file `/lurk/eplist.html`. Note that although you entered both the address and the file on one line, Netscape has broken these down into two separate parts of the request.

4. Netscape sends the HTTP request to the transport layer, specifying a TCP transmission.

5. TCP adds its own headers onto the request and, if necessary, breaks it down into packets.

6. TCP sends the request to the Internet layer for IP to process. Here, addresses, flags, and more headers are added to the data request.

7. IP passes the request on to the link layer.

8. The link layer determines to which network device the request should go and adds appropriate formatting for that device. Let's suppose for the sake of argument that the request goes out over an Ethernet adapter. Once the Linux Ethernet drivers have transmitted the packet, it's out of the Linux TCP/IP stack.

9. The data packet or packets make their way through some unknown number of intermediate hosts, each of which processes the packet to a greater or lesser extent. Ultimately, it reaches the link layer of `www.midwinter.com`.

10. The link layer of `www.midwinter.com` notices that there's a packet addressed to it coming over its Ethernet wire (or whatever type of networking that system uses). It grabs the packet and begins to decode it; it strips away the Ethernet-specific material, leaving a packet that the Internet layer can handle.

11. When the Internet layer receives the packet, it strips and examines its own layer of material. If it notices that the packet was broken into parts by its counterpart on your system, it will hold onto the first part it receives for a specified period of time, and if more parts arrive, combine them. When this job is done, it passes the packet up to the transport layer, and more specifically, to the TCP handler.

12. TCP, like the Internet layer, checks to see if the packet had been broken up into pieces before transmission, and waits for all pieces to arrive. When they're all present, TCP combines them, checks the destination program (or, more precisely, the destination *port*), and passes the combined data packet on to that program.

13. The recipient program in the application layer is a Web server such as Apache. Apache notes that it has just received a request to send the file `/lurk/eplist.html` to your computer, and it prepares to do so.

14. The process now repeats itself, this time taking the file `/lurk/eplist.html` from `www.midwinter.com` to your computer, and specifically to Netscape.

15. Netscape processes the file. Most Web pages these days contain graphics. These don't come with the original Web page itself. Instead, the Web page includes a reference to another file on the server. Thus, for each graphic image, the entire round-trip sequence repeats. Similar requests go out for embedded sounds, JavaScript, and so on. The need for multiple requests for a single page is why a Web page will sometimes load some graphics but not others; if some sort of blockage occurs on the Internet after your system has received some images but not others, you'll have an incomplete Web page on display.

As you can see, even a fairly simple Internet transfer can take quite a few steps to complete. Similar processes occur for other types of Internet accesses, including printing a file to a remote printer, running an X program on a remote computer, and so on. Some of these processes can involve temporally extended connections (as in running a program remotely). For these, TCP maintains a connection, which basically just means that the client and server programs keep listening for packets from each other, and maintain information in memory such as their respective IP addresses, so they don't need to continue looking up this information.

Alternatives to TCP/IP

Although TCP/IP is a very common set of networking protocols, and the most important one for the Internet as a whole, it's not the only networking stack. Particularly in an office setting, other protocols can be extremely important. Described broadly, these other protocols work much like TCP/IP, though the details do differ.

Linux supports many of these protocols, or provides ways to support them in conjunction with TCP/IP. Because TCP/IP is designed to transmit any type of data, it's possible to *encapsulate* one protocol within another. For instance, you can pass NetBEUI packets within TCP/IP packets. When you do this, you effectively place one network stack on top of another one; the link layer of the first stack serves as the application layer of the second. The resulting data packet is depicted in Figure 2.3. Of course, for this to work you do need support for such encapsulation on both systems.

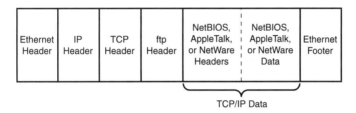

FIGURE 2.3
When TCP/IP is used to transport a secondary networking protocol's packets, the TCP/IP data area carries not only the ordinary data, but also the headers associated with the secondary protocol.

UUCP

UNIX-to-UNIX Copy (UUCP) is a networking protocol that's designed specifically for modem connections. It was in wide use as a means to transfer email and files in the days before the Internet became ubiquitous, but it's not as widely used today. Unlike many other protocols, UUCP can't be used over Ethernet cabling.

As I've already mentioned, TCP/IP can also be used over a modem, via the PPP and SLIP link-layer protocols. Why UUCP, then? For one thing, there's history—UUCP was developed in the 1970s, well before SLIP or PPP. For another thing, UUCP has built-in support for scheduled transfers. For instance, suppose you write several emails on your Linux computer over the course of a day. If you were using PPP, you might connect to your ISP every time you finish an email. With UUCP, the typical procedure would be for your system to keep the emails in a queue and transfer them all at once, without supervision. This can help reduce telephone use and costs if the connections are long distance, particularly because the transfers can be done whenever long-distance rates are lowest.

Of course, you can configure a SLIP or PPP link to work in much the same way, but this isn't typical. UUCP has a long history of being used to transfer data between UNIX systems at scheduled times, and so it's the tool many experienced UNIX administrators choose for such tasks.

Today, when you transfer data using UUCP, chances are the machine with which you exchange information is connected to the Internet via some TCP/IP-based network. Therefore, although the UUCP link doesn't use TCP/IP, sooner or later it will be processed and handled by TCP/IP. You needn't be concerned with the details of this conversion; I mention this fact simply to point out that UUCP networks and the Internet as a whole need not be entirely separate. You can send email via a UUCP link that's destined for any site on the Internet. Similarly, UUCP can be used in conjunction with a local TCP/IP-based network. You could use a UUCP connection as a link between several machines on your local network and the rest of the world.

If your need for Internet access isn't very time-critical (for instance, if you need to occasionally send or receive email and don't particularly care about a few hours' delay in delivery), you might consider using a UUCP link for this access. Most ISPs, however, don't support UUCP, so you'll need to shop and ask about this. Also, be aware that there are different UUCP variants, the most common of which on Linux is called *Taylor UUCP*. You'll need to be sure that your ISP supports this version of UUCP.

For more information is on UUCP, see the UUCP HOWTO, which comes with most Linux distributions, and also on the CD-ROM that accompanies this book, in the doc/HOWTO directory.

IPX

Internet Packet Exchange (IPX) is the networking protocol used by Novell in their NetWare product. Technically, IPX is roughly equivalent to IP in TCP/IP; additional protocols, such as Sequenced Packet Exchange (SPX; equivalent to TCP) round out the Novell network stack. The NetWare Core Protocol (NCP) is NetWare's file sharing mechanism. It is one of the primary tools in the equivalent of the application layer of the Novell networking stack.

If you want your Linux box to interact with Novell NetWare clients or servers, you'll need to include support for at least IPX, and probably SPX and/or NCP, in your kernel. IPX and SPX options are found in the Networking Options portion of your kernel configuration, while NCP is listed under the Network File Systems area. SPX is experimental in the 2.2.x series kernels, and so won't be a visible option unless you elect to include experimental kernel features.

Because Novell's networking system and NetBIOS can be used in most of the same situations, this book doesn't cover IPX and its related technologies. If you want more information on this topic, you can read the IPX HOWTO, which is included with most Linux distributions, and also in the doc/HOWTO directory of this book's CD-ROM.

NetBIOS and NetBEUI

In the 1980s, before the Internet or TCP/IP networking were common in businesses, IBM wanted to sell small intranets to businesses. It chose to design its own networking protocol, which it called the Network Basic Input/Output System (NetBIOS). Microsoft eventually licensed NetBIOS from IBM, and now NetBIOS is the basis of Windows' native file and printer sharing protocols. An extension to NetBIOS is called NetBIOS Extended User Interface (NetBEUI), and serves to encapsulate NetBIOS data on a network.

A NetBIOS network is organized quite differently from a TCP/IP network. Rather than TCP/IP's 32-bit numeric IP addresses, subnets, and DNS system, NetBIOS and NetBEUI organize a network in two ways. First, the network is broken into one or more *workgroups*, each of which is given a unique name. For instance, a college might have workgroups for each department, with appropriate names such as PSYCH, RUSSIAN, and MATH. Within each workgroup, each computer has its own name (perhaps named after the computers' users, such as JAMES and WUNDT). Computers talk to each other using their names, and they know each other's names because they periodically announce them to the entire workgroup.

On the surface, this organization seems similar to the TCP/IP organization, at least from the user's point of view. It's important to recognize, however, that NetBIOS and NetBEUI use the human-readable names to identify computers (not numbers, as in TCP/IP's IP addresses), and there's no provision for an organizational layer above the workgroup.

The NetBIOS and NetBEUI systems don't scale up very well; they generate a lot more traffic than TCP/IP when the network size increases. The naming and limited organizational features of NetBIOS/NetBEUI also limit its expandability. In addition, with the advent of the Internet, Microsoft found it desirable to shift its networking emphasis to TCP/IP. Completely abandoning NetBIOS was undesirable for legacy reasons, however. One approach to this competing set of needs is to transmit NetBIOS over TCP/IP, and Microsoft and IBM have both chosen to support this approach. Linux doesn't support "raw" NetBIOS, but it does support it when it's encapsulated in TCP/IP. This is the basis for Samba, Linux's approach to file sharing with Windows.

2

UNDERSTANDING
TCP/IP

> **NOTE**
>
> The NetBIOS/NetBEUI name for a computer need not bear any resemblance to that computer's Internet identifier. For instance, a computer called frank.nephridior.com on the Internet could be called EAGER on a NetBIOS network. It's generally simpler to use the Internet machine name (frank, in this case) for the computer's NetBIOS name, however.

NetBIOS is used by Windows for Workgroups 3.1, Windows 95, Windows 98, Windows NT, Windows 2000, and OS/2. There are also NetBIOS tools available for DOS. It's therefore quite common in the PC world, though it's increasingly being used as a layer atop TCP/IP.

AppleTalk

Like Novell, IBM, and Microsoft, Apple developed its own networking protocols in the days before the Internet had penetrated most businesses. Apple called these protocols *AppleTalk*, and originally applied the term both to the networking protocols and to the hardware over which they were transmitted. Eventually, however, it became obvious that this dual use of the term *AppleTalk* was confusing, and so Apple began using the term only in reference to the networking protocols. The hardware then became known as *LocalTalk*. Apple included LocalTalk hardware in most of its computers produced until 1998.

Even before 1998, however, Apple also included Ethernet with its computers, and it is possible to use Ethernet as the hardware underlying AppleTalk. Used in this way (which is sometimes referred to as *EtherTalk*), AppleTalk "talks" directly to the Ethernet hardware. Since MacOS 7.5.2, Macs have also been able to transmit AppleTalk using TCP/IP. This ability comes with the Mac Open Transport system extension, and the net result is a substantial increase in the speed of AppleTalk networking. In many ways, these two methods of transmitting AppleTalk are similar to NetBIOS and NetBIOS over TCP/IP, although of course the details differ substantially and the Windows and Mac protocols aren't compatible with one another.

Linux, on the other hand, is compatible with both NetBIOS and AppleTalk (or can be made to be so). To work with AppleTalk in Linux, you'll need to install the Netatalk package, which supports raw AppleTalk. Netatalk has been modified to work with Open Transport-style AppleTalk over TCP/IP, and this modified package is known as Netatalk+asun, after Adrian Sun, the patch's principal creator and Netatalk's current maintainer. These Netatalk packages provide AppleTalk file *server* support in Linux, but not client support. If you want your Linux computer to function as an AppleTalk file sharing client, you'll need to use the afpfs package, which is currently alpha-level and therefore unreliable. Netatalk does include software to allow Linux to share printers that are networked via AppleTalk.

Like NetBIOS/NetBEUI, AppleTalk breaks a network down into groups (called *zones* in AppleTalk) and individual computers. The AppleTalk protocol includes a way to assign each computer a unique identifier automatically, so you needn't be concerned with IP addresses or their equivalent except when using AppleTalk over TCP/IP. A computer's AppleTalk name need bear little resemblance to its Internet name, although as with NetBIOS, you may want to synchronize the two for simplicity's sake.

AppleTalk hasn't caught on much outside of Macintosh networks, so chances are you'll only need to use Netatalk if you want to provide file or print services to one or more Macs. BeOS does use AppleTalk for networked printing, though, so you may want to install Netatalk to share printers with BeOS computers.

Mixing Protocols

In general, it is possible to mix two or more network stacks on a single computer or a single network medium. You can run raw NetBIOS, raw AppleTalk, and TCP/IP on the same Ethernet cable, for instance. Occasionally, however, a Windows computer will get confused if it has too many options available to it. For instance, installing redundant network protocols in Windows can sometimes cause it to fail to see a Linux Samba server. For this reason, it's best to stick to as few protocols as you can on any given network. In particular, you should use NetBIOS over TCP/IP rather than raw NetBIOS. Configuring Linux to understand unused protocols generally won't cause problems, but it will chew up memory you might prefer to devote to other functions.

Of course, there's nothing wrong with using multiple protocols from higher in the TCP/IP stack on one network. For instance, you can run a Web server, an NFS server, a Samba server, and a mail server all on the same network, and even from the same computer. You can also mix in TCP/IP clients on the same computer that runs the servers, and browse the Web with Netscape, print to Windows-hosted printers with Samba, and download files with ftp. The main danger in running so many network programs on one computer is that you may generate so much traffic to and from that computer that it will overwhelm your networking hardware. Lots of network traffic isn't a result of running multiple network stacks *per se*, though, but of transferring a lot of data. If a network is slow when running Netatalk, Samba, and NFS servers, it probably won't help to convert machines from one protocol to another.

If you find your network becoming slow, you should either upgrade to a faster network or use a router to break your network into two or more segments, and isolate these segments as much as possible. If your network is complex and you're not sure where to break it up, you may want to look into using a network diagnostic tool. Linux distributions come with some of these, such as the netstat command, which lists open connections. You can find additional tools, as well, such as netwatch, which provides a real-time display of traffic on a network segment.

Summary

The TCP/IP stack is a way to describe networking functions in Linux or in any other OS that uses TCP/IP for networking. The stack divides networking operations up into four layers, and any networking program operates on one layer in the stack. The programs that you and I as end users and network administrators are most interested in work at the application layer, but the others are just as important.

Although TCP/IP is the dominant networking model in Linux, and is increasingly dominant in most network settings, there are alternatives. Most of these alternatives are more limited or specialized than TCP/IP, but Linux can work with many of them. In addition, it's often possible to encapsulate one of these protocols within TCP/IP to use the alternative protocol more widely or to improve its speed.

Networking Services

IN THIS CHAPTER

This book is mostly about particular types of network services. Just what does this mean, though? As with all things related to computers, network services must be very precisely defined, and the definitions or protocols used vary substantially from one service to another. Examples of services include, but are not limited to

- File transfer
- Remote printing
- Remote login
- Web browsing
- Mail transport
- News transport
- IP routing

These topics are covered in more detail later in the chapter, and throughout the rest of the book. To understand the specifics, though, it's first necessary to know something about the underlying OS mechanisms. Linux handles these mechanisms much as commercial UNIX systems do.

Ports and Sockets

How does a computer tell one TCP/IP connection from another? For instance, suppose you've got a two-computer network, with machines called birch and gingko. Suppose further that a user on birch initiates an FTP connection with gingko to transfer files. With that connection still open, the same or another user starts a Telnet connection to read email. There are now two open connections between birch and gingko, so when gingko receives a TCP/IP packet from birch, gingko can't automatically process it for FTP or Telnet; it has to have some way of knowing to which process to send the packet. To further complicate matters, consider what happens if a *second* FTP session is opened from a user on birch to gingko. Now it's not even enough to know which type of data any given packet contains; it's necessary for both computers to keep both connections separate. This is the problem that the related features of *ports* and *sockets* solve.

Ports

Ports are the most directly related to the solution of this problem. TCP/IP supports the presence of a large number of separate virtual ports, each connected to the same networking interfaces. You can think of a port as being something like separate extension numbers used by a business to route calls to individuals' desks. In the case of extension numbers, several telephones are connected to the same main phone number, and the office phone system directs the call to the correct desk when the caller dials the extension number. Linux (or any OS running server applications) assigns certain server programs to specific ports. When a "call" comes in on a given port, Linux can pass the data on to the program that's assigned to this port.

Common server programs are assigned specific port numbers. For instance, FTP receives the port number 21, and Telnet gets 23. This convention allows you to use these protocols without knowing the port number—the application program you use knows the usual port number assignment, and can add it transparently. In some cases, you can specify a port number explicitly, often by appending it to the machine name after a colon, as in `http://gingko.biloba.com:98`, which attempts to open an HTTP (WWW) connection to `gingko.biloba.com` on port 98, rather than the usual port of 80. (Red Hat's `linuxconf` utility can be configured to allow system configuration via a Web browser using port 98.)

> **NOTE**
>
> The file `/etc/services` contains a list of services that are commonly found on specific ports. An entry in this file does *not* necessarily mean that your Linux computer is configured to accept the connection, though; it just lists the name associated with a port so that assorted utilities can display the name or accept it as input in lieu of a port number.

Similarly, outgoing connections get port numbers on the client system, so that when you open an FTP connection (for example), the client machine makes the connection *from* a specific port. When the client machine makes this connection, it includes its own port number in the initial negotiation of the link, so that the server system can pass back packets with an appropriate port number to ensure that the originating application gets the replies. This fact allows for multiple connections from one machine. If you, on the computer `birch`, open one FTP connection to `gingko` and another to `larch`, the return data from these two machines will come in over two different ports, making it easy for the OS to keep the two properly separated.

How, though, does the *server* keep the data streams separated? If `gingko` receives two FTP connection requests, both directed at port 21, how does it keep the requests straight and know how to direct replies? The server does this by remembering the IP address and port of the originating request. Figure 3.1 illustrates these relationships. Note that `gingko` must maintain a record of which client and client port is needed for each of its FTP server sessions. In practice, `birch` and `larch` also maintain this information, but the use of unique port numbers for outgoing connections does simplify matters somewhat.

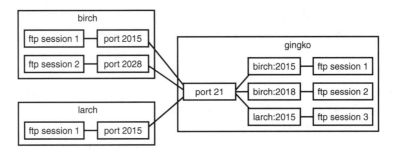

FIGURE 3.1

The use of unique ports on clients and a single port for each service on servers allows multiple connections between an arbitrary number of computers.

This description ignores one important aspect of the situation in practice: the fact that there are separate ports for TCP and UDP packets (p. 44). As described in Chapter 2, TCP is the transport-layer protocol used by many TCP/IP services. UDP is a somewhat simpler transport-layer protocol. Both TCP and UDP require the use of ports. Because the TCP/IP stack can easily distinguish TCP from UDP packets, it uses the same numbers for each type. In many cases, a given number is assigned to an application for both TCP and UDP ports, even if the application only uses one protocol. In other cases, different applications use the same number port, one for TCP and the other for UDP. For instance, port 513 is assigned to the UNIX/Linux login protocol for TCP, but to the whole program for UDP.

Sockets

Internally, the Linux kernel expects certain types of data from different types of connections. This expectation is similar to the different types of protocols used in the transport layer of the TCP/IP stack. Whenever a Linux application establishes a connection with a port, it must register its expectations by specifying the *socket type* for the connection. In some cases, these socket types correspond closely to the TCP/IP TCP and UDP protocols, but there are additional options.

The Client/Server Architecture

Chapter 2, "Understanding TCP/IP," introduced the concepts of the *client* and the *server*. Because these concepts are so important for understanding a typical network, I devote more space to them here.

Broadly speaking, a client initiates a request for services provided by a server. The server then provides those services (or declines to provide them because of resource limitations, authentication failure, or some other reason). Data typically goes both ways during any given exchange between a client and a server, and depending upon the precise nature of the service, more data may go one way than another. A typical exchange with a Web server produces more traffic moving from the server to the client, for instance; but remote printing involves more data going from the client to the server.

One important point to remember when discussing clients and servers is that these terms are most meaningful when applied to individual programs. Although a computer can run nothing but clients or nothing but servers, many computers run a mix of client and server programs. There's more information on this shortly.

Roles of the Client

In general, the client application is an interactive user program, such as Netscape Navigator, ncftp, or the Knews Usenet news reader. Thus, client programs usually initiate data transfers at the request of a human operator. This isn't always the case, though. For instance, it's possible to configure many mail readers to check a remote mail server at regular intervals, and to either download mail automatically or alert the user that there's mail waiting.

Of particular relevance to this book, file sharing systems such as Windows Network Neighborhood contain client elements. When you open a Network Neighborhood window in Windows and use it to open files on a remote Linux machine running Samba, you're using client programs built into Windows and a server running on Linux. It's easy to lose sight of the fact that this is a client/server relationship similar to that of an FTP client and server because the operations are so closely integrated into the client OS, but client/server transfers describe what's happening. In fact, earlier in this chapter I used FTP in a number of examples. Windows file sharing operations could as easily have been used for these examples, although this would have changed some of the details.

Roles of the Server

Servers, in contrast to clients, are generally programs that sit on the server machine and wait for input coming over a particular port. They run with little or no human intervention once configured. This means that server programs must be extremely robust—a server program that crashes can leave the server computer apparently dead to the rest of the world, at least with respect to that one service. (Note that one server program can crash and leave others intact, so a computer might respond to some queries but not others.)

A typical Linux distribution comes set up to provide quite a few standard UNIX-style services. Part of the task of configuring a Linux system involves fine-tuning these configurations—setting up configurations for any services not included by default and disabling unused services. This last aspect is particularly important from a security point of view, as discussed in Chapter 24, "Maintaining a Secure System." Every unnecessary service left running is a potential way for a cracker to gain access to your computer. Of course, most services don't allow meaningful access to your system without authentication such as passwords, so crackers are usually unsuccessful at breaking into systems. If they know of a bug in the server software, though, or if they've obtained a valid username and password through some means, they can gain access to your system via a service, whether or not you or your system's legitimate users actually use that service.

Figuring out which end of a connection is the client and which is the server is generally easy: The program with which you or somebody else interacts most directly on a day-to-day basis is the client. One specific case deserves special mention, however: the X server. Linux's graphical user interface (GUI) environment is the *X Window System*, or *X* for short. One of the great strengths and weaknesses of X is that it's a networkable GUI. That is, you can configure X in such a way that you can use one computer, including running GUI programs, from another physical machine—even one halfway around the planet. (The details of doing this are covered in Chapter 19, "Running X Programs Remotely with VNC or an X Server.") This is great for a networkable, multiuser system such as UNIX or Linux. It does cause some speed degradation compared to a single-user GUI such as that found in Microsoft Windows. The confusing part about this is that the X server runs on the machine that's local to you. For instance, if you're in Tokyo, using the computer `birch.erplab.jp`, and you log on to the Linux computer `eeg.upenn.edu` in Philadelphia, the X server will be running on `birch`, not on `eeg`. The reason for this labeling is that `eeg` (and, indirectly, you) are requesting services located on `birch`— namely, the use of the display, keyboard, and mouse on `birch`. The fact that the server is necessarily in front of you, whereas in most cases it's the client that's nearest you, is irrelevant.

NOTE

X servers can exist as programs that run under any OS. Linux includes an X server, of course, but you can get them for Windows, MacOS, OS/2, and other operating systems. There also exists a class of computers that function as nothing *but* X servers. These machines are called *X terminals*, and they consist of a (typically very large) monitor, keyboard, mouse, and generally a small box containing the CPU, some ROM, some RAM, and an Ethernet connector. X terminals are common in corporate and academic environments in which a large UNIX box is used by many individuals. If you're setting up a Linux computer in such an environment, you may be able to use the X terminals that already exist on this network to access Linux.

When you run X on the computer you're actually using, X still runs using networking protocols; it's just that your X applications connect to the X server that's running locally. This is akin to using ftp to transfer files from one directory to another on a single computer.

The client and server labels are reversed, however (and therefore brought back into line with most peoples' intuitive expectations), when using the Virtual Network Computing (VNC) viewer instead of X's built-in networking capabilities. In this case, the server runs on the system you intend to use, and a client application accesses the server on the system near you. The result from the user's point of view is very similar, however, which is why I cover both X servers and VNC in Chapter 19.

Using One Machine as Both Client and Server

As I mentioned earlier, it's common to run both client and server applications on a single computer. For instance, you might use a Linux computer both as a print server for a network of Mac or Windows boxes and as a desktop system on which you run a Web browser. If this practice is common on many or all of the machines on a given intranet, the network as a whole is often called a *client/server network* (p. 41). It's often convenient to use a client/server architecture on small networks, but as a network grows in size, it becomes more and more tedious to administer and use. For instance, consider a case of two coworkers who want to share files, so that they can easily pass drafts of papers, spreadsheets, and so on, back and forth. Each user can configure his or her computer to admit the other, and it's done. Adding a third computer to this network isn't too difficult; you must simply configure it to read files on the two existing computers, and configure them to read files from the new one. Adding a fourth is just a little bit more difficult than the third, the fifth is just a bit harder than the fourth, and so on. By the time you're up to, say, a hundred computers, the network has become quite tedious to use because users might have to go looking through dozens of machines to find a file. Also, reconfiguring the entire network when one machine is added, removed, or changed can be quite tedious.

For this reason, most administrators favor a client/server architecture for medium-sized and large networks. In such a configuration, one or a small number of computers provide services to many. This centralizes the administration tasks and can make life easier for the users if the file structure on the server is well thought out. Using a Linux server can also help to integrate a multiplatform network. For instance, you can serve the same files to computers running MacOS, DOS, Windows, OS/2, Linux, or any of a number of varieties of UNIX.

Nonetheless, sometimes running both client and server applications on the same machine is desirable, even in a moderate-sized or large network. One method of network backup, for instance, places the backup device on the server, which must then use client software to mount each remote file system for backup. You might also use one system with both client and server software as a "bridge" between two networks. For instance, you could allow Macintosh clients to print to printers connected to Windows machines by using Linux as an intermediary.

3

NETWORKING
SERVICES

There's not much special to consider when running both clients and servers on a single computer. The two types of programs won't normally cause each other trouble. In some cases, such as Samba for Windows network integration, both clients and servers are part of the same package. In other cases, such as afpfs and Netatalk for Macintosh integration, they're separate.

Understanding Linux Daemons

Earlier in this chapter, I've referred to server programs receiving input from client programs on the network. In order for this to happen, either the server program has to be running, or another program has to be running to launch the server when appropriate. Programs that run in the background waiting for input are known as *daemons*, a term derived from the Greek word for *intermediary*. The term *daemon* is nearly synonymous with the term *server* used in the sense of a software program for providing network services, though a server need not always run as a background task, and a few daemons service only local needs. Daemons often have names that end in <u>d</u>, such as smbd or ftpd. (I briefly mentioned daemons in Chapter 2, p. 42.)

Understanding Background Processing

UNIX was designed from the ground up as a multitasking operating system, meaning that it can run multiple programs simultaneously. (Actually, on a single-CPU system, only one program can run at once; but the OS switches execution between programs so rapidly that, from a human timeframe, the programs appear to be running all at once.) As a clone of UNIX, Linux is also a multitasking OS. You're probably used to dealing with several programs, especially in a GUI environment like Microsoft Windows or the X Window System, in which you can click on one program's window to interact with that program, leaving others to do their thing. Figure 3.2 illustrates this with a screen shot of several programs running under X on a Linux system.

Multitasking is not limited to GUI environments, however. In fact, UNIX systems were masters of multitasking before the GUI was invented! As in a GUI environment, when multitasking non-GUI programs, the OS actually switches execution between the programs too quickly for a human to notice. The primary difficulty in multitasking non-GUI programs is with the user interface. Only one program can receive input from the user at any given time—a fact that is also true of GUI programs. Switching between GUI programs, however, is generally simpler than switching between textual programs. Because only one text program can have the user's full attention at any one time, that program is referred to as the *foreground* program, relegating other programs to the *background*.

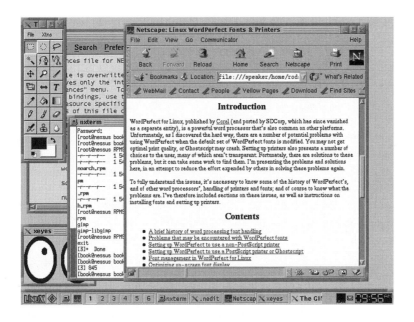

FIGURE 3.2

In a GUI environment, multitasking allows you to see several programs operating at once.

Daemons normally run without direct user intervention. They take all the information they need to run from configuration files or command-line arguments, and if they encounter a problem, they place information of the problem in an error log file. For this reason (and to let you do real work on the computer), daemons run as background processes. The prototypical daemon is started automatically by Linux when the computer starts, runs continuously while the system is up, and is turned off when the system shuts down. When you use your Linux computer, you may not even be aware of the fact that daemons are running in the background.

For the most part, daemons sit idly by; they only need to work when the activity for which they look occurs, such as network access on a particular port. Because of this, daemons consume little CPU time when they're idle (Linux knows not to dish out CPU time where it's not needed). Daemons do occupy some memory, however, even when idle—a fact that's lead to the development of inetd.

inetd: The "Super Server"

Rather than have potentially dozens of daemons sitting around idly waiting for network activity, Linux uses a single daemon that does the watching for many others, and then starts the individual daemons as necessary. The "super server" that does the watching for all of them is known as inetd. When inetd spots network activity that is, say, intended for ftpd, inetd launches `ftpd` with appropriate parameters to let `ftpd` handle that one session and then quit. (Actually, `inetd` often uses yet another intermediary program to launch the daemon that does the real work.)

> **NOTE**
>
> Many Linux distributions ship with versions of daemons intended to be called by `inetd`. These daemons usually have filenames beginning with `in.`, as in `in.ftpd`.

The use of `inetd` allows you to configure which daemons you run by editing a single file—`inetd`'s configuration file, `/etc/inetd.conf`. Each line in `inetd.conf` identifies a single network service to be handled by `inetd`. For instance, here's a line that configures ftp services:

```
ftp    stream   tcp   nowait   root   /usr/sbin/tcpd   /usr/sbin/in.ftpd
```

In the order they appear in the line, the meanings of these fields are

1. Service name (`ftp`)—This is the name of the service. In Linux, services are associated with individual ports in `/etc/services`. Rather than list port numbers in `inetd.conf`, service names appear.
2. Socket type (`stream`)—The type of socket, as discussed earlier in this chapter, is specified here.
3. Protocol (`tcp`)—The protocol is the TCP/IP Internet layer protocol (generally `tcp` or `udp`).
4. Wait/Nowait (`nowait`)—This field specifies how `inetd` handles multiple connection requests.
5. User (`root`)—The username under whose authority the service runs. This is generally `root` or `nobody`, but in some cases you can specify other users to improve system security.
6. Server program (`/usr/sbin/tcpd`)—In many cases, the server program is `/usr/sbin/tcpd`. This program then takes as a parameter the name of the program that *actually* handles the service. If the server program is listed as `internal`, it's a simple service that's handled internally to `inetd`.

> **NOTE**
>
> `tcpd` is part of the *TCP Wrappers* package. This package can help you to secure your system by screening connections and allowing or denying them based on a variety of criteria. I describe this and other packages that achieve similar results in Chapter 24, "Maintaining a Secure System."

7. Server program parameters (`/usr/sbin/in.ftpd`)—If the server program requires parameters, they come last on the line. When the server program is `/usr/sbin/tcpd`, the first parameter is the name of the program that actually processes the service requests.

> **TIP**
>
> One of the first things you should do after you install any Linux system that's connected to the Internet is to disable unused services. You do this by placing a pound sign (#) at the start of the line in `/etc/inetd.conf` that configures the service. By default, most Linux distributions come with many services commented out in this way for security purposes, but you should fine-tune these selections. In fact, you can comment out all the services in `/etc/inetd.conf` except those identified as internal—your computer will still boot and run. The services you're most likely to want include `telnet` (used for remote logins), `ftp` (used for remote file access), and `linuxconf` (on Red Hat and Mandrake systems, this is used for remote system configuration). You might want to use `ssh` instead of `telnet` and `ftp` for greater security, as discussed in Chapter 18, "Logging on Remotely Using `ssh` or `telnet`." I discuss setting up daemons for file and printer sharing in the relevant chapters.

Not all daemons run via `inetd`. Some work better if they're run separately, and come configured to do so. The common `lpd`, for instance, handles print jobs locally, and isn't an `inetd`-launched daemon, though it is a daemon. Even when a daemon can be run via `inetd`, you may want to run it independently because `inetd`'s processing takes a small amount of time. If a daemon responds to a lot of requests, there's little advantage to placing it in `inetd.conf` except for the benefits of being able to "wrap" the daemon using TCP Wrappers, and the extra time to process the daemon's work can be a drawback.

Starting and Stopping Daemons

You may occasionally want to start or stop a daemon without restarting your computer. You might want to do this to change a daemon's configuration, so that it behaves differently, or simply to add or remove a service. Fortunately, this is easy in Linux.

Identifying Running Daemons

If you want to stop or reconfigure a daemon that's already running, the first step is to find that daemon's process identification (PID) number. This information can be most easily obtained by using the ps command in conjunction with grep. For instance, suppose I want to find the PID of the smbd (Samba) program. I could type ps ax ¦ grep smbd - at a Linux command prompt, and the system would reply with something like this:

```
 653 ?         S      0:00 [smbd]
16017 pts/9    S      0:00 grep smbd -
```

The second line is the grep command used to get the output itself, and can be ignored. The first lists the smbd program. At the beginning of that line is the PID—653 in this case. You'll need to use this number to refer to the program when stopping it.

If you don't recall the exact name of the daemon, you can use whatever part of it you do remember, or omit the grep component of the command entirely (that is, just type ps ax). This will increase the number of entries you'll see on your screen, however, making it more difficult to locate the program you want to stop or restart.

In the case of daemons that are invoked by inetd, you may need to modify /etc/inetd.conf and restart inetd instead of directly starting, stopping, or restarting the target daemon. If such a daemon is currently working (say, if smbd had been launched from inetd, and if Windows machines were still accessing Linux shares), it might be necessary to kill that daemon directly, in addition to modifying /etc/inetd.conf. (Stopping a running daemon will, however, disconnect anybody who's currently using it.)

Stopping Daemons

You use the Linux kill command to stop a daemon (or any other program). For instance, to stop the smbd daemon identified earlier, you would type **kill 653**. Sometimes a program won't stop when you kill it this way, but adding a -9 parameter before the PID usually does the trick, as in **kill -9 653**. You should repeat the ps command to be sure that the kill command worked; if it did work, the daemon won't be listed in the output.

If you simply wanted to eliminate a daemon, you can stop here (unless you want to prevent it from starting up when you restart your computer, in which case you'll need to modify /etc/inetd.conf, /etc/rc.d/rc.local, or some other file that launches it automatically). If you want to modify the daemon's actions, you can start it again with modified parameters, or modify its configuration file.

Starting Daemons

You can start a daemon by typing its name at a command prompt. You may need to include a complete path to the executable file, as in /usr/sbin/smbd to start smbd. Like other programs, daemons often take parameters to modify their behavior, and you can include any parameters you need. Most daemons, unlike most user programs, return control of the shell to you as soon as they start, so you don't normally need to include an ampersand (&) at the end of the command line.

If you want to start a daemon that's launched via /etc/inetd.conf, you can do so by adding it to that file and then stopping and restarting inetd.

Once you've restarted a daemon, its PID will be different, so if you want to kill it again, you'll need to use ps again to find the new PID.

Reconfiguring a Running Daemon

Stopping and restarting a daemon can be a nuisance. Fortunately, there's an easier way to reconfigure many daemons if that's what you want to do. Suppose that you find that /etc/inetd.conf is configured to support FTP services, but you don't want these. You can correct the situation by editing /etc/inetd.conf, as described earlier, and then using kill with the -s SIGHUP parameter to tell inetd to restart immediately. For instance, if inetd has a PID of 15953, you could type:

```
kill -s SIGHUP 15953
```

The inetd program then rereads its configuration file and now FTP service won't work. You can add services in this way, as well. What's more, the process keeps the same PID, so if you want to do another reconfiguration, you don't need to use ps to locate a new PID.

The -s SIGHUP parameter doesn't work with all daemons, however, so sometimes you will have to kill a daemon and launch it anew.

A Rundown of Available Services

Linux is an extremely flexible server OS. "Out of the box," it has quite a few services available, either enabled immediately, or disabled but requiring only a small change to /etc/inetd.conf or some other configuration file. Additional services are easy to add by installing an open source server from the Web or a Linux CD.

The following is by no means a complete listing of available Linux services, but the most commonly-used ones are listed. This book doesn't cover all of these services, however, so you may need to look elsewhere for more information on some of these services.

Remote File Access with ftp

The file transfer protocol (FTP) is one of the more popular protocols on the Internet. As its name implies, it's used to transfer files from one computer to another. In its most basic form, FTP provides a text-mode view of files on a remote system (Figure 3.3), but GUI front-ends are available to let you get and put files by clicking a mouse (see Figure 3.4). In addition, Web browsers can use FTP to download files.

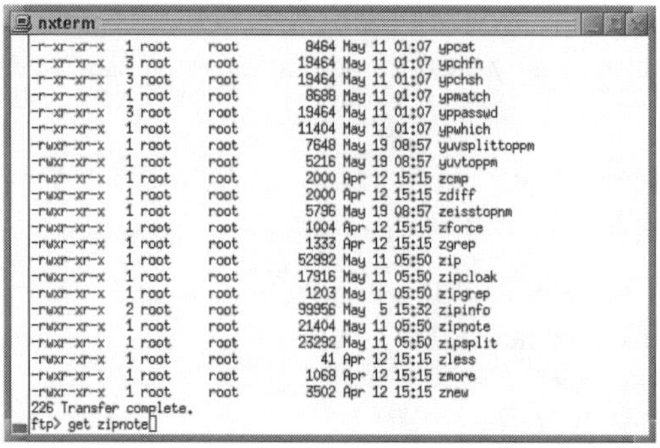

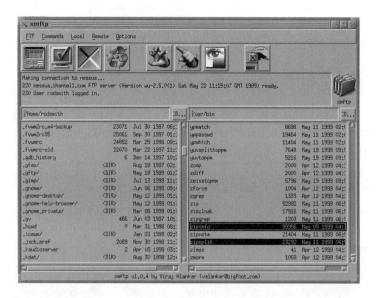

FIGURE 3.3

Although it's shown here in an nxterm *window, basic* ftp *can be used from a textual UNIX or Linux login, or even from MS-DOS.*

FIGURE 3.4

GUI FTP programs let you browse an FTP site's contents and click on files to upload or download them.

No matter what interface is used on the client end, the FTP server configuration is the same, and in Linux this is generally handled by activating the ftp line in /etc/inetd.conf. By default, this requires a username and password. Some FTP sites permit so-called *anonymous* access, in which a username of ***anonymous*** is used in conjunction with any password for read-only access to certain directories. You can configure your Linux system to work in this way, but you'll need to do more work to configure your FTP server. Such a configuration is beyond the scope of this book.

File Sharing with NFS, Samba, and Netatalk

In contrast to FTP, many operating systems include so-called *file sharing* facilities. Functionally, these are quite similar to ftp, but the user interface on the client side is typically much more like that of the host OS's access to local disks. Figure 3.5, for instance, shows how MacOS gives access to both a local hard disk and one shared from a Linux computer via the Netatalk package. In addition to file transfers from one computer to another, file sharing usually allows programs on the client system to directly access files on the server (so you can use an OS/2 word processor to work on files stored on your Linux box, for instance). It's even possible to run programs on the client that are stored on the server, which can greatly reduce the total disk space requirements of an office.

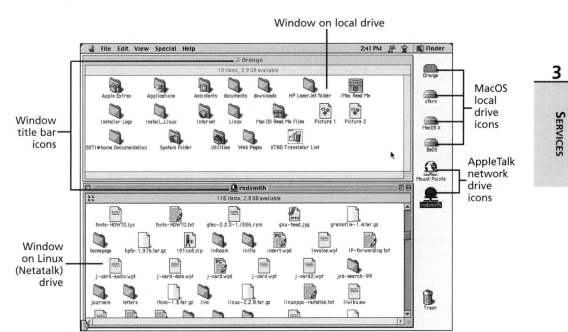

FIGURE 3.5

Shared file systems look and act very much as if they were local. In the case of MacOS, you can tell them apart from local drives by their icons on the desktop and in window title bars.

On Linux, file serving is handled by a variety of daemons, depending upon the client OS. Specifically, the network file system (NFS) is generally used for sharing with other Linux or UNIX computers; Samba is used for sharing with Windows, OS/2, and DOS computers; and Netatalk is used for sharing with MacOS computers. Part III, "File Sharing," discusses these protocols and how to configure them in detail.

In practice, FTP is most often used for file transfers between computers that are geographically remote, whereas file sharing protocols are used for local networks.

Printer Sharing with 1pd, Samba, and Netatalk

The same packages that provide file sharing capabilities often provide *printer sharing* features, as well. In many ways, printer sharing is just like file sharing, except that instead of going to a disk file, the data goes to a printer. On the client OS, a remote printer is generally configured very much like a local one, and the user might not notice much difference in actual use, especially if the printer is physically nearby, as might be the case in a home office setup. Configuring printer sharing in Linux is covered in Part IV, "Printer Sharing."

Serving Up Web Pages

When you use a Web browser to cruise the World Wide Web, you can easily interact with dozens of computers in a minute or two. Each of these computers runs a *Web server* program, such as Apache. If you want to set up a Web server on your Linux computer, you can do so using Apache or any of several other programs. The details of such configuration are, however, beyond the scope of this book.

A few other programs use Web server protocols in their operation, as well. For instance, the linuxconf utility used by the Red Hat and Mandrake Linux distributions has an option to run as a special sort of server to permit remote administration of a Linux computer. This feature can be quite handy, but I advise caution in using it if your computer has a direct connection to the Internet because if an outsider ever gained access to this server, he or she could wreak havoc with your Linux computer. (linuxconf does require an appropriate password, of course, but as with all network services, if it's present, there's a chance that somebody could gain access through a bug or an ill-gotten password.)

Delivering the Mail

Email is one of the oldest and most useful features of the Internet, and there are several protocols, not to mention mail transport agents (MTAs—mail daemons, in effect) devoted to it. Two of the most common email protocols are

- Simple Mail Transport Protocol (SMTP)—This is the protocol most used in UNIX-to-UNIX mail delivery. Many Linux systems (including Red Hat) come configured to use `sendmail` as their MTA, but some use others, such as `exim`. The `qmail` program is a popular replacement MTA.
- Post Office Protocol (POP)—POP is frequently used by end users to download mail from their Internet Service Providers (ISPs), but it's not in common use for other mail delivery tasks. On Linux, you can run assorted POP daemons, but you should only do so if you want to use your Linux box as a mail relay station for clients that expect to use POP. You can also use POP clients on Linux to retrieve mail from your ISP.

CAUTION

SMTP mailers are sometimes abused by so-called *spammers*, who send unsolicited email to large numbers of people. Most Linux distributions therefore configure their SMTP programs to refuse to forward outside mail, although they can still receive outside mail and send local mail to other systems.

You'll generally want some variety of SMTP daemon running on your system, if nothing else just to deliver local mail. (Various Linux programs send email to the root account every now and then to inform you of problems they've encountered, or of routine maintenance they've undertaken automatically.) You might also want the ability to send SMTP mail to remote systems, and perhaps to receive it from the outside. Most Linux distributions configure themselves automatically for such functions when they're installed. If you want to delve deeper into this subject, you should consult your distribution's or SMTP agent's documentation, as this topic is beyond the scope of this book.

Delivering the News

The Network News Transfer Protocol (NNTP) is used for delivering Usenet News (Internet newsgroup) articles. If you've read newsgroups, you've used a client-mode NNTP program—a news reader. The server end of this relationship is known as a news server, and as with most other servers, there are several news servers available for Linux.

Unless you're an ISP, chances are you don't need to maintain a complete set of newsgroups on your Linux server. If you *do*, you'll find that you'll need to devote quite a few gigabytes of disk space to storing just a few days' worth of news. In a SOHO environment, though, there are a couple of more modest uses for a news server:

- Limited news mirror—You can copy the complete contents of a few newsgroups onto your local system from your ISP. This has several advantages over reading the mail directly from your ISP's news server. One is speed: Once the news postings are on your local system, you don't need to connect or suffer through whatever delays are associated with obtaining the news remotely. You can also often download a large number of messages and disconnect more quickly than you could read through the ones you want to read, thus saving online time. These advantages can be multiplied if you have a small local network with several users who want to read a handful of newsgroups. If you want to maintain a mirror of a few global newsgroups, you would normally configure the system to connect to a remote news server and exchange messages once or twice a day.

- Local newsgroups—You can develop and maintain newsgroups that are local to you. For instance, you could have a newsgroup for intra-office communication, in order to make important announcements to your employees. If you're directly connected to the Internet, you can make these newsgroups accessible to your clients or the public at large.

You can combine these two functions in a single news server, maintaining both a mirror of global newsgroups and your own local groups. Hybrids are possible, as well. For instance, it's possible to configure a local news server to accept email from Internet mailing lists. If you subscribe to several mailing lists, this can help you keep track of the goings-on in these lists without overburdening your email box.

As with email delivery, the details of NNTP configuration are beyond the scope of this book. You may find the Linux News HOWTO helpful, though as of this writing, it's not been updated in several years, and so doesn't cover the latest software.

Logging in Remotely

One of the great advantages of Linux (or of any UNIX-style OS) is that you can access the computer remotely, including nearly full functionality. (Only features that require specific local hardware, such as a CD-ROM or VGA graphics without X, are impossible to use from a remote login.) Naturally, Linux runs daemons to help in this remote login process.

Text-Mode Logins

Linux supports several different tools for text-mode logins—logins that provide access only to textual information. One of the most commonly used is the *Telnet* protocol, which is controlled by the `telnet` line in `/etc/inetd.conf`. Telnet clients are available on every platform that supports TCP/IP, which is a great advantage to the `telnet` daemon in Linux because it provides nearly universal access.

Another method of remote login is the *rlogin* protocol. Like Telnet, rlogin lets you log in and use Linux text-mode programs. rlogin is a protocol that's used mostly by UNIX and UNIX-like systems, though; you're not very likely to find an rlogin client on a randomly-selected Windows computer, whereas your chances of finding Telnet on such a machine are quite high.

Both Telnet and rlogin suffer from one potentially serious problem: They send all data, including passwords, in what's known as *cleartext*. Cleartext means that the data isn't encrypted or hidden in any way, so that an Ethernet "sniffer" on an intervening system, or on a network local to either the client or the server machine, can snatch the password or other sensitive data off of the network. This isn't a problem if you're using Telnet to log in to one machine on your private home network from another machine on the same network, but it may be if you're using the protocol in an office environment in which some users should not have access to your data. If you connect to one system from across town or around the world, various intervening systems have access to your data. Worst of all, if you connect to or from a system running a cable modem, it's possible that your neighbors have similar access to your data stream.

Security concerns such as these have prompted the development of new protocols, most prominent of these being the Secure Shell (SSH). The SSH protocol uses cryptographic methods to encrypt data before transmission, so that most prying eyes won't see anything intelligible. After you've set up SSH programs on both systems, its use is quite similar to that of rlogin or Telnet. You can find SSH programs, or SSH plug-ins for existing programs, for most platforms, so it's a good choice for remote logins. If you do use SSH instead of Telnet, you should disable `telnet` in `/etc/inetd.conf` to prevent the possibility that it could be attacked and used by a clever cracker.

3

NETWORKING SERVICES

> **NOTE**
>
> The FTP protocol also uses cleartext passwords and data transmission, and is therefore insecure to network sniffing. You can use the `scp` program, which is part of the `ssh` package, to transfer files between systems using SSH encryption. You can also use `ssh` to process data using other transfer methods, thus encrypting those data streams. Consult the `ssh` documentation for more details.

I cover remote text-mode logins in Chapter 18.

X-Based Logins

If you need to run X-based GUI applications from a remote location, a text-only login won't do you much good. For greater flexibility, you need an X-based login, or at least a way to get X-based programs to use a local display once you've logged in using some other method.

For simplicity's sake, I'll assign labels to the two computers being used for GUI access. The Linux box that has the software you want to use will be `linus`, while the computer to which you have physical access will be `bill`. `Bill` could be another Linux computer, or it could be running Windows, OS/2, MacOS, or some other OS.

Normally, remote X access requires more in the way of software on `bill` than it does on `linus`. As I described earlier in this chapter, an X server actually runs on the computer you're using locally (`bill`), while the X client is the software you're running remotely (on `linus`). You needn't run an X server on `linus`. (In fact, my own home network is configured this way; I've got a Linux computer from which I run many X-based programs, but I run them using X servers on other computers.)

At its crudest, you can run X programs from a remote location by following these steps:

1. Log in to the remote system using `telnet`, `ssh`, or some other means.

2. Set the DISPLAY variable by using a command such as `export DISPLAY=bill:0.0`. Note that the command you type is processed by `linus`, and tells `linus` to send its display to `bill`. If the computers aren't in the same domain, you'll need to specify the complete network address (as in `bill.duck.net`) The numbers *0.0* refer to the display number (0.0 is the default for most X logins at the computer itself, but it may be something else for your particular case).

3. Start the X server on `bill`, if it's not already running.

4. Give authorization to `bill`'s X server to accept the client requests from `linus`. There are a variety of ways to do this. One way is to use the `xhost` command, as in `xhost +linus`. (As with the DISPLAY variable, you may need to give a complete network name, as in `linus.penguin.com`.) You need to issue this command on `bill`. Many X servers intended for Windows or MacOS don't need this authorization.

5. In the `telnet` or other text-mode login window, start whatever X program you want to run. It should appear in an X server window on `bill`.

TIP

If you use a UNIX or Linux `ssh` client program, it automatically handles the authorization details, and it also encrypts all the X data. This fact can make using `ssh` for remote access more convenient—as well as safer—than `telnet`.

To run an X program following these instructions, the only daemon you run on `linus` is used for the text-mode login; you initiate the rest of the configuration on that end manually. `Bill`, however, runs an X server, which includes a daemon looking for X activity.

In addition to the X server option, a program called VNC allows you to run programs remotely using a server program on linus. `Bill` then becomes a client with a relatively simple display program. Note that the roles of the client and server are reversed in this case, and conform to what most people naturally expect.

There are quicker and more secure ways to accomplish this task, as described in detail in Chapter 19, "Running X Programs Remotely with VNC or an X Server."

Connecting to the Wider World

Linux provides several services that are important in connecting a local network to the Internet as a whole. Of particular interest is IP masquerading, in which Linux takes packets from a local network and forwards them over a link to the Internet, hiding the fact that the local network exists, as depicted in Figure 3.6. Linux does this by substituting its own IP address in the outgoing packets and remembering what outgoing ports it uses for traffic originating from a given local machine. Then, when Linux receives a reply addressed to an IP masquerading port, it knows to what local machine to forward that reply. In computers with kernel 2.2.0 and above, you'll need to activate several kernel options and use the `ipchains` utility to configure IP masquerading, as described in Chapter 20, "One IP Address, Many Computers: IP Masquerading."

3

NETWORKING SERVICES

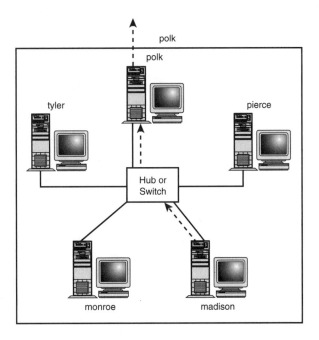

FIGURE 3.6

To the outside world, all data from a local network looks as if it's coming from a single machine when that machine is configured for IP masquerading.

If you use a modem to connect to the outside world, you'll use services related to that connection. Specifically, you'll probably use the point-to-point protocol (PPP) for your connection. Although your machine is technically the client when you dial out with PPP, one of the programs you'll use locally is pppd—the PPP daemon. This is because the task of establishing a PPP connection is so similar at both ends that a single program can do both tasks. Unlike most other services I've discussed in this chapter, PPP is very low-level—it works at the link layer of the TCP/IP stack, as opposed to the application layer where most other daemons work.

Miscellaneous Additional Services

The preceding list, although it covers many of the most-used services, barely scratches the surface of all networking services available in Linux. Just some of the additional ones include

- Font servers—As part of the network-centric nature of X, it's possible to set up one computer to deliver fonts to X servers located on an intranet. In fact, Red Hat 6.0 comes configured with a font server by default, although you can't access it from any system but the one on which it's installed. Font servers can be a great way to quickly update the fonts available on a large number of Linux or UNIX workstations, or on X terminals on a network.

- Dynamic Host Configuration Protocol (DHCP)—It's sometimes desirable to assign IP addresses dynamically—that is, each computer receives its IP address each time it boots. As computers are added to and removed from a network, it's easy to adjust IP address assignments appropriately. This process is handled through the DHCP protocol, which of course Linux can be configured to serve (or to use as a client).

- Time servers—You can obtain the correct time from the Internet from any of a number of time servers. You can also configure your own Linux computer to provide this service to other machines on your network.

- Talk—You can set up systems so that users can "chat" interactively in text on the screen.

- Boot servers—One computer can boot from files stored on another if the system to be booted has a network adapter that supports this ability. This feature is often used by X terminals, which have no hard disks of their own.

- System information—A number of servers, such as fingerd, provide information about a system or its users. This can be handy within a business or university because you can find a person's office phone number or room number by typing a command into the computer. Such information can also be used by remote system crackers, however, and so such servers are often disabled.

Summary

This chapter gives a brief overview of networking services often found on Linux (or other) computers. I reviewed the roles of sockets and ports in helping to direct traffic between computers and the roles of clients and servers in networking. As the use of background processing and daemons are vital to understanding network services, I covered these topics, too. This chapter concluded with a summary of the services you're most likely to want to set up on your system. Many of these services are covered in much greater detail elsewhere in this book.

3

NETWORKING SERVICES

Intranets and the Internet

IN THIS CHAPTER

In the past three chapters, I've tossed about terms like *intranet* and *Internet* on occasion, and I've referred to *your network* and *local networks*. For the most part, the precise meanings of these terms haven't been of critical importance to understanding the main points of those previous discussions, but now it's time to delve into these matters more deeply. Just what distinguishes different types of networks, and how are they related to one another?

This book is about setting up a Linux system at the core of a small network. *Small* is a subjective term in this context, but in my mind it's between two and a few dozen computers. Such a network is frequently referred to as a *local area network (LAN),* as contrasted with a *wide area network (WAN),* which covers more territory, typically both in the number of computers and the distance between them. The terms *intranet* and *local network* are more-or-less synonymous with *LAN.*

One of the key points to understanding networking is that it's possible to link two or more networks in various ways. Such linkages can have the effect of placing every computer on an intranet on the worldwide network of computers called the *Internet*. This chapter in part introduces the concepts you need to understand how this happens.

Network Topologies

Chapter 1, "Networking Hardware," briefly introduces different network *topologies* (p. 10). I return to this topic here because it's important to see how these different topologies differ from one another and—just as important—how they can interact. One key to understanding networking is that it's possible to link different networks, even ones that use radically different topologies and hardware. In order to be useful, of course, linked networks do need to have software protocols (such as TCP/IP) in common. Alternatively, the computer that's used to do the linking may sometimes be able to translate one set of protocols to another, or it can simply function as a server of resources to both networks.

One point to remember throughout this discussion is that these topologies refer to the *logical* structure of the network. It's possible to physically arrange computers in many ways with any of these topologies, but some topologies lend themselves to some physical layouts better than do others.

Some topologies in common use in small networks include

- Bus topology
- Star topology
- Ring topology

The Bus Topology

A *bus topology* involves linking several computers in a row, one to another (sometimes referred to as a *daisy chain*). Figure 4.1 shows such an arrangement, with a simple network of five computers.

FIGURE 4.1

In a bus topology, computers link to a cable, known as the bus, that runs past all the machines.

When dealing with Ethernet (the most common type of networking hardware in small networks), bus topologies are implemented in coaxial cables, which come in thin and thick varieties. Thin Ethernet can run up to 607 feet, and thick Ethernet has a maximum length of 1,640 feet. Both types of Ethernet cable have a maximum speed of 10 Mbps, however, which limits their usefulness in new networks, since 100base-T can achieve 100 Mbps speeds with little additional cost. You'll still find many coaxial Ethernet installations in operation, however, and you may need to link your own network onto such a system. Even if you want to use another topology in your own subnetwork, you can link the two, as described in "Combining Topologies" and "Linking Small and Large Networks," both later in this chapter.

One of the principal advantages of the bus topology, especially as implemented in Ethernet, is that it requires little in the way of networking hardware. You need a network interface card (NIC) in each computer (p. 15), and of course you need cabling, but you don't need any additional centralized hardware, as you do with a star topology (described in the next section). This can make a bus topology easy and inexpensive to set up. If the computers you want to network are all physically located in a row or along multiple walls of a single room, it can also be quite easy to lay the cable for a bus topology.

It can be tricky to expand a bus topology, however, especially if the expansion involves a machine that's physically remote from the rest of the network. Consider the offices in Figure 4.2, for instance. If the computers in Room 1 have all been networked in the neat pattern shown, it might be difficult to add the machines in Room 2. In the case of the offices in Figure 4.2, it would be necessary to do one of two things:

4

INTRANETS AND
THE INTERNET

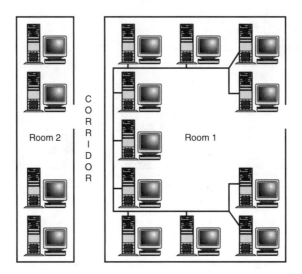

FIGURE 4.2

Room 1's bus topology network is very neat and efficient—until it becomes necessary to add Room 2's computers to the network.

- Run a length of cable from one of the ends of the existing bus in Room 1 over to Room 2 and continue the bus there.

- Splice Room 2's computers into the Room 1 bus near the corridor, using two cable runs through whatever ducts you hope exist between the rooms.

Neither is a particularly elegant solution, and if the bus length limits are exceeded, you might not get either to work, in which case you would have to completely redo the cabling (and possibly the layout of the workstations) so that it is more efficient. Any of these solutions is likely to require at least temporary disruption of network services, as the new network is spliced into the old one.

The Star Topology

The second topology supported by Ethernet is known as the *star*, so called because when diagrammed as in Figure 4.3, it resembles a star, with spokes radiating outward.

In an Ethernet network's star topology (using 10BaseT or 100BaseT cable), the line length limit is 328 feet, which is little more than half of thin coaxial cable's 607-foot limit. This limit effectively applies to each branch of the star, however, so in practice an Ethernet twisted-pair cable network can cover a broader area than can a thin Ethernet coaxial cable network. The same is often true even when comparing twisted-pair to thick Ethernet coaxial cable, though it depends on the precise layout of computers.

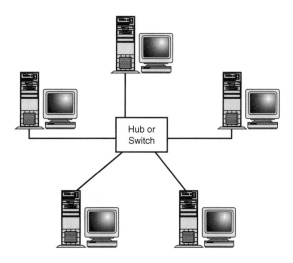

FIGURE 4.3

The star topology uses a central device to manage network traffic.

For instance, consider Figure 4.4. It depicts connections of 14 computers in both bus and star topologies. Depending upon the distance between computers, this arrangement may or may not produce cable length problems for any given form of Ethernet, as detailed in Table 4.1. Twisted-pair cabling is the last to fail, though, supporting a network spread more widely than coaxial Ethernet allows.

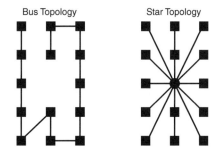

FIGURE 4.4

The computers (squares) are connected to each other or to the hub (the circle) in the most efficient manner possible for each topology.

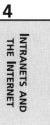

4

INTRANETS AND THE INTERNET

TABLE **4.1**   Cable Lengths from Figure 4.4

Inter-Computer Distance	Bus Topology Total Length	Star Topology Maximum Length	10base-2	10base-5	10base-T and 100base-T
10 ft.	124 ft.	22 ft.	✓	✓	✓
50 ft.	621 ft.	112 ft.	X	✓	✓
135 ft.	1676 ft.	302 ft.	X	X	✓

Furthermore, with Ethernet it's possible to link two hubs or switches, either using a *crossover cable* (p. 20) or *uplink connectors* (p. 24) on the hubs or switches. The result would be two networks like that in Figure 4.3, linked at their central points. If you look again at Figure 4.2, it's not hard to see how the network would be wired initially. Chances are the hub would lie along the wall by the corridor, with cables run along the walls to each of the computers. The expansion into Room 2 could be accomplished either by running multiple lines from that hub into Room 2 or by running a single line and placing a second hub in Room 2 to service Room 2's computers. Either solution could be accomplished without disrupting the existing network, assuming that the main hub or switch had enough room for expansion to begin with.

The Ring Topology

A ring topology is logically similar to a bus topology, except that it's a bus that's linked to its own end, as shown in Figure 4.5. Ethernet doesn't support a ring topology, so you won't encounter one in most small networks. IBM's Token Ring network technology is, as the name implies, based on a ring topology, so you'll encounter the ring topology if you need to set up, maintain, or link to an existing Token Ring network.

Token Ring in particular, however, doesn't *look* like a ring topology—not physically, at any rate. Like 10BaseT and 100BaseT Ethernet, Token Ring uses a hub with cables radiating out from it. This is because Token Ring implements the ring *inside* the hub, thus giving Token Ring many of a star topology's characteristics. In practice, therefore, Token Ring closely resembles twisted-pair Ethernet in its physical cable layout requirements.

Combining Topologies

Today, networks seldom operate in isolation. Networks—of the same or different topologies—can link to other networks in a variety of ways. A comprehensive list of such methods is beyond the scope of this book. I do discuss two important methods (bridges and routers) of linking networks in this section, however, and two more (Internet Protocol [IP] masquerading and firewalls) make appearances toward the end of this chapter, and in detail in Part VI, "Linking Your Intranet to the Internet."

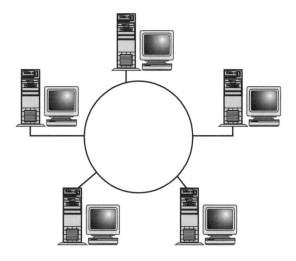

FIGURE 4.5

The ring topology is like a bus topology closed in on itself.

NOTE

Switches and hubs connect individual computers. Routers and bridges, by contrast, connect entire networks, or at least network segments.

Bridges

A network *bridge* is used to combine two similar networks into one logical whole. In a small office environment, bridging is likely to be used to link two otherwise separate Ethernet networks. A bridge can be a specialized hardware device, or it can be a computer that could conceivably function as a node on one or both of the networks it links. Once bridged, the previously separate networks are often referred to as *segments* of a larger network.

> **NOTE**
>
> Many software protocols also break networks up into groups. In the built-in networking in Microsoft Windows, for instance, you can define separate *workgroups*. Details differ from one software product to another, but in general, the software groupings are separate from the hardware segments created by bridging or routing. Hardware segmentation can, however, make it difficult or impossible to create a single group that easily spans the two segments, depending on the protocols used. The segments created by using bridges or routers are distinct from the subnets created by particular uses of IP address assignments, but the two can have similar consequences for software.

A bridge takes the Ethernet traffic from one of its two Ethernet ports and copies it directly to the other port. This makes a bridge a very simple device in principle, much like an Ethernet switch. A bridge typically doesn't care what type of networking protocols it's transferring—TCP/IP, AppleTalk, NetBIOS, or whatever. A bridge can, however, recognize what traffic belongs on each side of the network. The bridge can therefore pass only packets destined for the opposite side, thus reducing overall network traffic. For instance, if Segment A contains a Linux computer that functions as a print server, then when a computer on Segment A submits a print job, Segment B won't see any activity from that job. This characteristic can be particularly handy if you have a network with two easily defined groups, such as Macintosh and Windows computers or workstations that use two different servers.

Bridges can be useful for extending the range of an existing Ethernet network. For instance, if you're using 10Base2 cabling but find you need to expand your network past the 607-foot limit of this technology, you can use a bridge to expand the limit. You can also use a bridge to connect a coaxial Ethernet network to a twisted-pair Ethernet network. Finally, and often most importantly, a bridge's filtering features allow it to reduce overall network traffic and improve performance.

You can configure the Linux kernel to support bridge functions, so that a Linux computer can function as a bridge. (In the Linux 2.2.x kernel series, this support is considered experimental, however, so you should use it with caution.) You can also purchase standalone bridges of various types. Some more complex bridges permit linking networks over some intermediary device, such as linking two Ethernet networks via modem. This practice is known as *tunneling*. Such a use creates what's often referred to as a *virtual network*. A bridge doesn't need an IP address of its own, but if you configure a Linux computer to serve as a bridge, it can have its own IP address, and can participate in normal networking activities.

Routers

A *router* is a more complicated method of linking two networks than a bridge. Whereas a bridge merely copies Ethernet packets from one network to another, a router interprets the IP addressing of the packets and sends them to the appropriate destination. Note that a bridge also checks the destination of packets, but a bridge uses the *Ethernet address* for its filtering, whereas a router uses the *IP address* for this function (you'll learn more on these shortly). Because Ethernet addresses are specific to Ethernet cards, whereas IP addresses are a higher-level construct, a router can link networks that are more dissimilar than can a bridge. For example, you can use a router to link Ethernet and Token Ring networks.

Routers can also serve more complex functions, particularly in an environment in which they're connected to more than two networks. For instance, suppose you've subscribed to both digital subscriber line (DSL) and cable modem service. You could configure a router for your home network to send data to the Internet over either or both of those services. For most sites, it probably won't make much difference which interface you use, but for some it might. If downloads from speedy.cable.com are faster over the cable modem, and if downloads from speedy.dsl.com are faster over the DSL link, then the router can send data over the most efficient link.

Routing can quickly become a very complex topic, but fortunately, most small networks have only modest routing needs. In fact, *all* Linux computers have a routing configuration, but for a typical computer with only a single network connection, it will just route all outgoing traffic over that connection. Such a simple routing configuration is set up more-or-less automatically when you install Linux or configure networking as a whole, as described in Chapters 5, "Basic Linux Configuration," and 7, "Setting Ethernet Options." If you need to set up a more complex router, you should consult the Linux NET-3 HOWTO, which comes with most Linux distributions, and is also on the CD-ROM that accompanies this book in the doc/HOWTO directory.

In general, routing is more complex and more flexible than bridging, but there are exceptions. A bridge, for instance, can easily handle raw AppleTalk and NetBIOS packets. A TCP/IP router, on the other hand, cannot do so because these aren't TCP/IP packets. A router can process these packets when they're encapsulated in TCP/IP, however.

4

INTRANETS AND
THE INTERNET

NOTE

It's possible to link two incompatible network types in a variety of ways. For instance, if you have a Macintosh LocalTalk network and a separate PC Ethernet network, you can set up a Linux box with interfaces to both networks. Using the Samba and Netatalk packages, you can attach to printers and filesystems exported from one network and then re-export them to the other. This adds several layers of overhead, however, so a more efficient configuration in such a situation is to use the Linux computer as a server for the resources needed by both networks.

Hubs and Switches

Hubs and switches serve as the cores of star topologies. In some ways, they resemble routers and, especially, bridges. In particular, a switch is much like a bridge. Like a bridge, a switch examines the Ethernet addresses of the packets it transmits, and sends them on to only the appropriate destination. In fact, if you're using twisted-pair cable and use nothing but switches, you'll probably have no need for a bridge because the switches reduce unnecessary network traffic at least as well as a bridge could. On the other hand, if you have more than a few computers and use hubs, which are less expensive than switches, a well-placed bridge or two can substantially improve network performance.

Switches generally serve as the core of a star topology, whereas bridges generally link two network segments. This distinction is partly a matter of typical use rather than physical differences. In the case of a computer serving as a bridge, it's also a matter of the number of available network interfaces, which is more limited in most computers than in most switches.

Routers are much more complex devices than either switches or hubs, so there really is no comparison between switches or hubs and routers.

A network of a few dozen computers could easily contain all four types of devices—switches to link a cluster of high-performance servers, hubs to link clients or low-bandwidth machines, a bridge to connect all these machines to an older coaxial-based network, and a router to link a Token Ring network. Note that in a case like this, precisely what you define as *the network* is somewhat arbitrary. You could call the Token Ring portion the network, for instance, but for many purposes, the whole grouping could be considered the network.

Some Examples of Combining Networks

Think back to the example presented earlier, in Figure 4.2, concerning the expansion of a bus topology network. You can see where bridges and routers can be quite useful. Instead of attempting to expand the existing bus topology in some awkward way, you could use a bridge to create a link to the new computers, perhaps even using the more modern 100BaseT networking protocols for the recently added computers.

Let's further suppose that you want to link this combined Ethernet network to a nearby workgroup that's been using a Token Ring network for some time. A router is just what you need for that job. Figure 4.6 shows the combination of these three networks. One machine in Room 1 serves as the Ethernet bridge between Rooms 1 and 2, and another machine in Room 1 serves as the router between Room 1's Ethernet and Room 3's Token Ring. This configuration could also be achieved by using standalone bridges and routers.

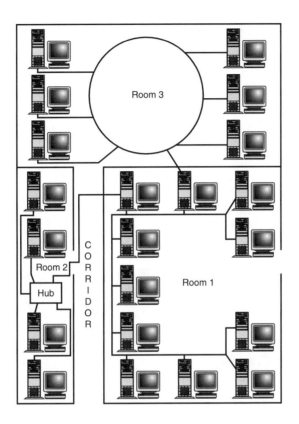

FIGURE 4.6

Although Token Ring uses a physical hub, the Token Ring network is shown here with a ring-like cable arrangement to emphasize its logical ring topology.

As another example of bridges and routers in action, consider *cable and DSL modems*. These devices are actually tunneling bridges or routers, in most cases. They're designed to link your network (possibly consisting of just a single computer) to the cable or DSL provider's network. You might think of this type of modem as a computer peripheral, like a conventional telephone modem. But from a networking point of view, it is a computer with an Ethernet interface, a specialized interface for the cable or DSL connection, and appropriate software to link the two together. In fact, it's often possible to configure these devices to directly service more than one computer. In this case, the modem actually bridges or routes traffic from more than one computer on your local network.

4

INTRANETS AND
THE INTERNET

The Internet Backbones

The discussion so far in this chapter should help you understand how small local networks—like the one you presumably have or want to set up—link together into the Internet as a whole. Let's call the organization that houses the three-room network I've been describing Three Room Company. If Three Room Company wants to link its computers to the nearby Four Room Company, they can do so, and the Four Room Company can link to Guy in a Garage, and so on. This, however, would make for a very haphazard, chaotic, and difficult-to-manage internet.

> **NOTE**
>
> A generic term referring to a network of networks is *internet*; but *the Internet* is the global network with which you're probably already familiar. These terms both contrast with an *intranet*, which as I described at the start of the chapter, is a local network.

In practice, the Internet as a whole follows a hierarchical structure. In order to gain Internet access, chances are that Three Room Company will contract with an Internet service provider (ISP), which is a company that specializes in providing network access. Three Room Company's ISP may contract with a larger ISP, or it may have more direct connections of its own to what's known as an Internet *backbone*. At one time, there was a single Internet backbone, but today there are many. A backbone is a very high-speed network that has *a point of presence (POP)* in several areas, generally large cities. Internet backbones also connect to each other, and so can route traffic from their clients to the clients of other backbones.

> **NOTE**
>
> *POP*, like many computer terms and especially acronyms, has multiple meanings. In addition to *point of presence*, *POP* also means *post office protocol*, which is a networking protocol used to transfer email. In most cases, you can tell which sense is meant if you know both meanings of an acronym, but if you only know a meaning other than the one the author intended, you may get confused! I provide uncommon acronyms' meanings in this book.

Let's examine how this works a bit more closely. Suppose a user at Three Room Company in Boston wants to access a computer at Guy in a Garage in Seattle. Here's what happens:

1. Network traffic traverses Three Room Company's networks until it reaches the machine that serves as the router between Three Room Company and its ISP.

2. The data does a similar traversal of the ISP's network until it reaches the ISP's router to its chosen Internet backbone. (Instead of a backbone, the traffic could travel first to a larger ISP, and perhaps from there to one that's still larger. The number of these steps is generally called the number of *hops* to the backbone.)

3. After the data gets on a backbone, it travels to the nearest connection to the backbone that services Guy in a Garage and jumps to this second backbone. Of course, if both the source and destination computers use the same backbone, this step can be skipped.

4. The destination backbone sends the data to the ISP that services Guy in a Garage (or the ISP closest to the backbone in Guy in a Garage's ISP hierarchy).

5. The ISP delivers the data to the router at Guy in a Garage.

6. Guy in a Garage's router sends the data to its destination computer, possibly via additional routers, bridges, or other distribution means.

Figure 4.7 shows these steps graphically. In reality, each labeled stop on the trip from Three Room Company to Guy in a Garage could represent passage through several computers, however. This is particularly true at the backbone level, and at the ISP level when there are several *tiers* of ISPs between the customer and the backbone.

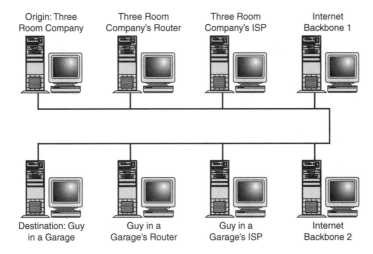

4

INTRANETS AND
THE INTERNET

FIGURE 4.7

Traffic between remote sites typically travels through half a dozen, a dozen, or more intermediate computers.

NOTE

> You can learn something about the path your data takes between you and a remote computer by using the `traceroute` command. Type `/usr/sbin/traceroute` *`remote.`* *`machine.name`* to find the names of intervening computers, along with information on the time it takes data to travel between these computers. These paths can change over time, though, and it's even possible for different parts of a single transmission to take different routes, so don't take `traceroute` output as being absolute.

If all goes well, this process takes no more than the blink of an eye to complete, but of course there can be bottlenecks along the way, such as trouble on the backbone, trouble at any intervening ISP, or trouble on either the source or destination network. Fortunately, TCP/IP was designed to work around such problems. For instance, some ISPs connect to more than one backbone, so if there's a problem on one backbone, traffic can still get through by using another.

This scenario applies even to network traffic that flows from one site to another in a single city. What's more, depending on the ISPs, backbones, and connections between them, network traffic may travel completely outside the locality to reach a local destination. When I lived in Bloomington, Indiana, I spoke to a friend who had high-speed network access. He told me that to connect to the computers at Indiana University just a few blocks away, his network traffic went through Chicago, 200 miles away! Although it sounds preposterous, this sort of situation is common on the Internet. In some ways the situation is analogous to the way overnight shipping companies operate. Rather than ship a package directly from, say, Denver to Phoenix, a package goes through a *hub*, which could be located someplace quite out of the way, such as Cleveland. This arrangement is efficient because it reduces the number of routes the courier must fly. Similarly, seemingly peculiar detours in Internet packet routing can simplify the topology of the Internet as a whole.

Network Addressing

Directing traffic over the Internet is a monumental task. The number of computers on a small office network is so limited that it's usually not a problem that the networking cables often see the traffic for all the computers. If this is a problem, though, using a switch or one or two bridges can reduce the problem to manageable levels.

Imagine, though, if every local network had to wade through the combined traffic of the entire Internet. The resulting speed problems would make people long for the days when carved stone tablets were state-of-the-art telecommunication! Fortunately, a number of technologies described in this and preceding chapters converge to allow network traffic to be addressed and routed efficiently, give or take the occasional 200-mile detour through Chicago.

Numerical Network Addresses

Computers are primarily numerical devices. Even when you write in a word processor, the computer deals in numbers—the computer is simply able to convert the numbers into shapes on the screen that *you* interpret as letters and words. Fundamentally, then, network addressing is a numerical phenomenon. In fact, two different numerical addresses are of vital importance in TCP/IP networking over Ethernet:

- The network hardware address
- The IP address

The first of these is tied to the network hardware no matter what networking protocol is in use—it's the same for TCP/IP, EtherTalk, or any other protocol. The second is associated with TCP/IP, no matter what networking hardware is used—Ethernet, Token Ring, dialup PPP, or anything else.

Network Hardware Addresses

One place to begin a discussion of network addressing is with the addresses built in to network hardware. The details differ from one technology to another, but because most small networks are built on it, I'll describe Ethernet. Each NIC contains a unique 6-byte number. This number is generally expressed as six hexadecimal values separated by colons, as in 00:80:C6:F9:3B:BA. Each manufacturer of Ethernet products has its own unique code, which is part of that address. The manufacturer then assigns additional unique digits to create an Ethernet address that's certain to be different from all other Ethernet addresses (assuming that no mistakes are made). These Ethernet addresses are also sometimes referred to as *MAC (Media Access Control) addresses*.

To transmit data from one computer to another on an Ethernet network, the transmitting computer must know the Ethernet address of the destination. When this information is known, the sending machine can fire Ethernet frames off, and the destination computer can pick them off the wire. All other computers on the local network ignore those frames.

4

INTRANETS AND
THE INTERNET

NOTE

It's possible to program a computer to pay attention to packets addressed to other computers. You can use a *packet sniffer* program to help analyze network traffic flow. Computer crackers also use such programs to obtain passwords and other sensitive data, as discussed in Chapter 24, "Maintaining a Secure System," and elsewhere in this book.

Ethernet transmission is necessarily *local*, though. If you're in Dallas and you want to communicate with a computer in Toronto, knowing the Toronto machine's Ethernet address won't do you much good. You must have a router or some similar intervening system and, most likely, a slew of intermediary computers such as those that make up the Internet's backbone. To get the message through this maze of computers, you need a hardware-independent addressing scheme, and that's the IP address.

IP Addresses

The IP address, as described in Chapter 2, "Understanding TCP/IP," is a 4-byte address that's generally expressed as four decimal digits separated by periods, such as 192.168.1.17. Like Ethernet addresses, with a few exceptions, IP addresses are unique. Unlike Ethernet addresses, IP addresses are not locked into the NIC. Instead, they're assigned, individually or in groups, by assorted organizations.

Traditionally, the Internet Network Information Center, known as InterNIC, has assigned groups of IP addresses to organizations. For instance, if Three Room Company wanted all its computers to have full Internet addresses, it could request a block of these addresses from InterNIC. It's the responsibility of the organization that has registered the addresses to assign them to individual machines. In fact, some companies assign addresses to others. For instance, your ISP assigns you an IP address, either permanently or every time you connect, depending on the technologies involved. In practice, Three Room Company will probably obtain its IP addresses from its ISP, rather than from InterNIC.

IP addresses can be described as belonging to one of several *classes*. The address class defines how many IP addresses belong in that set. Typically, the larger sets go to organizations that need large numbers of computers, such as large multinational firms and large ISPs. Smaller sets of addresses go to smaller organizations, such as Three Room Company and small ISPs. Each IP address is broken down into a network ID and a host ID, and the breakdown depends on the network class:

- Class A—The first bit of a Class A address is always 0, meaning that the first byte is between 1 and 128 (the *0* value has special meaning). The first byte identifies the network, and the remaining 3 bytes identify the computer. For instance, 103.34.23.8 is an address on the 103.0.0.0 Class A network—the trailing *0*s signify the address for a network as a whole. The computer ID is 34.23.8, though this part is seldom used by itself.

- Class B—The first 2 bits of a Class B address are always 1 and 0, meaning that the first byte is between 128 and 191. The address as a whole is split evenly in two, with the first 2 bytes identifying the network and the final 2 bytes identifying the computer. An example of a Class B network address is 143.203.0.0, and a machine on that network might be 143.203.78.9.

- Class C—Class C addresses begin with the bits 1, 1, and 0, so the first byte falls between 192 and 223. They're split, with the first 3 bytes used to identify the network and the final byte to identify the host. For instance, 197.8.33.0 is a Class C network address, while 197.8.33.14 is a computer on that network.

In addition to these standard address classes, there are also Class D addresses (starting with 1, 1, 1, 0), which are used for *multicasts*—Internet traffic destined for multiple hosts; and Class E addresses (starting with 1, 1, 1, 1), which are reserved for future use.

Originally, an organization would register one or more sets of addresses comprising an entire class, but as the number of unclaimed IP addresses shrank, it became necessary to dole them out in a more fine-grained way. It just doesn't do to have, say, two big companies each owning an entire Class A address but collectively using fewer than the 16 million addresses possible with Class A. ISPs, InterNIC, and other organizations have therefore begun to allocate IP addresses by assigning partial classes of addresses.

Not every address in a given network class is usable. Some are "wasted" on various administrative details. One of these details that is particularly important is that any address in which either the host or network address is 0 or filled with 1s (such as 255.x.x.x for a Class C host, or 255.255.x.x for a Class B host) has special meaning. When the host or network bits are 0s, the address represents the network as a whole or the host on the local network, respectively. Addresses in which the bits are all 1s represent broadcasts (for host bits) or network masks (for network bits; network masks are used to help a host identify other computers on its local network).

Several groups of addresses have been set aside for use on private networks. In theory, computers connected only to a private network will never have a need to communicate with the Internet as a whole, and so multiple private networks can each use the same set of private network addresses without conflict. Table 4.2 summarizes the addresses set aside for private networks. Note that there's only one private Class A network address, but there are multiple private Class B and Class C network addresses.

TABLE 4.2   Private Network Addresses

Class	Address Range
Class A	10.0.0.0–10.255.255.255
Class B	172.16.0.0–172.31.255.255
Class C	192.168.0.0–192.168.255.255

The .0 and .255 values are not usable for individual computers, as they have the special meaning described in the text.

To use an IP address, you must configure your computer to use it. In some cases, such as PPP dialup connections or Ethernet connections that use DHCP, your computer obtains its address when it connects to the network. In other cases, you enter the address manually when you configure networking. These options are described in Chapters 7, "Setting Ethernet Options," and 8, "Using PPP for Dialup Connections."

When you communicate with another computer using TCP/IP, you must know the destination computer's IP address. In practice, you generally use a verbal mnemonic, as described later in this chapter, but the TCP/IP stack relies mostly on the numerical IP address.

Linking IP and Ethernet Addresses

You might begin to see a puzzle emerge here. To communicate with another computer on your Ethernet network, you need its IP and Ethernet addresses. Your own computer, if properly configured, knows its IP and Ethernet addresses. If you've entered the remote machine's IP address, you're still missing the remote computer's Ethernet address.

Your computer obtains the final remote address through the use of Address Resolution Protocol (ARP). ARP sends out an Ethernet packet requesting that the computer with the specified IP address reply with its Ethernet address. All the computers on the local network see this packet, and the machine whose IP address matches the query replies, thus providing the sending computer with the information it needs. ARP requests aren't routed, so the Internet as a whole isn't overburdened with ARP requests.

What if you want to send an Ethernet packet to a remote location, though—one that's not on your local Ethernet? You send it to a router. Your computer's routing table should know what the local network's router is, and if no machine on the local network responds to the ARP request, your computer inserts the router's Ethernet address into the Ethernet packet. The router must then continue the routing process by using the IP address in the TCP/IP packet.

> **NOTE**
>
> The router that forwards network traffic off the local Ethernet is often referred to as a *gateway* in network configuration tools. The terms *gateway* and *router* are nearly synonymous, although gateway is sometimes used to refer to a router that routes between two different types of networks (for instance, between Ethernet and Token Ring).
>
> The gateway you set in your computer's basic network configuration, however, is not necessarily the kind that routes between networks of different types; the word is used in a more general sense in this situation.

Each time a router gets hold of a TCP/IP packet, the router consults its *routing table* to determine where to send the packet. For instance, when Three Room Company sends a packet to its ISP, the ISP's router checks its routing table. If the ISP uses only a single Internet backbone, the packet is forwarded to the router in the backbone's local computer. That computer then uses its routing table to determine which backbone hosts the destination computer. The second backbone's computer determines the ISP that hosts the destination site, and the ISP's router locates the router for the destination network. Only at the start and end do the routers need to know anything about specific computers. At the intermediate stages, entire networks are of interest, even though packets go to specific computers on these networks. Enough networks exist to make the tasks of intermediate networks' routers quite complex.

You can examine your Linux computer's routing table by typing `/sbin/route`. This will produce output similar to the following:

```
Kernel IP routing table
Destination     Gateway        Genmask         Flags Metric Ref    Use Iface
192.168.1.1     *              255.255.255.255 UH    0      0        0 eth0
151.209.146.3   *              255.255.255.255 UH    0      0        0 eth1
151.209.146.0   *              255.255.255.0   U     0      0        0 eth1
192.168.1.0     *              255.255.255.0   U     0      0        0 eth0
127.0.0.0       *              255.0.0.0       U     0      0        0 lo
default         polk.threeroomc 0.0.0.0        UG    0      0        0 eth1
```

The table starts with the interface (listed in the final column) used for specific computers, followed by entire networks (machines whose IP addresses end in *.0*), and finally the default route, which is used for any packet for which an ARP request doesn't return an Ethernet address.

Using DNS to Locate IP Addresses

Of course, as a human you probably don't want to be bothered with numeric IP addresses any more than is absolutely necessary. That's why the Domain Name Service (DNS) exists. DNS maps human-intelligible names, such as www.linux.org, onto the matching IP addresses, such as 198.182.196.56. As mentioned in Chapter 2, "Understanding TCP/IP," DNS is effectively a massively distributed database.

DNS works by breaking the Internet as a whole into a number of *zones*, and then further dividing these zones, dividing again, and so on. Each zone contains at least two DNS servers (two for redundancy, in case one becomes unavailable) that know the IP addresses of the DNS servers that manage the first zone's subzones. This structure repeats at every level of the hierarchy until the final DNS server, which provides the target IP address.

In practice, it works like this: When you configure a computer to operate on a network, you give it a list of IP addresses for DNS servers—usually two or three of them. These DNS servers can reside on your own network, but if you're a SOHO user, they'll probably belong to your ISP. When a program needs to look up an IP address from a human-readable address, your system asks one of the DNS servers you specified for the address. This DNS server (I'll call it DNS-1) knows the addresses of the DNS server maintained by the InterNIC (I'll call it DNS-2). This server maintains addresses for the widest-area domains—those for domains such as .com, .edu, and so on. DNS-1 therefore queries DNS-2 about the DNS for the destination domain. When DNS-1 receives the reply, it can query DNS-3 for the next-more-specific DNS, and so on down the chain. Ultimately, DNS-1 gets the IP address for the destination computer, and forwards that address to the program that originated the request.

This might sound like a lot of network traffic just to look up an address, and it is. There are shortcuts, however. Your local DNS can maintain a cache of recently requested domain names, so that it doesn't need to go through the whole process. Large ISPs, for instance, probably get lots of requests for common domains like yahoo.com, and might be able to give the correct IP address without any further action. Your own local computer can do the same thing, resulting in DNS lookup without any network activity. In Linux, you can maintain a completely local list of IP addresses in the file /etc/hosts. If you're maintaining your own local network, you'll probably want to have all your local machines in your /etc/hosts file (particularly if your ISP's DNS doesn't know about them), but you can also add the IP addresses for domains you regularly visit.

Network domain names, like IP addresses, are regulated in a semicentralized way. InterNIC (or, more recently, one of several organizations dedicated to these tasks) lets you choose a domain name and register it. After you register the name, nobody else can use that name for the period of time for which you've registered it. (There are exceptions, particularly in the case of names that match registered trademarks or company names.) You're responsible for naming individual machines, and subdomains if you want them, under your domain name. For instance, if you register the domain name gubron.com, you can assign names to individual computers, such as gingko.gubron.com and larch.gubron.com, as you see fit, without obtaining approval from InterNIC or anybody else for these assignments. One of the responsibilities of owning a domain name, however, is that you must provide at least two DNS servers to inform others of specific machine names. If you're a small company or an individual, you might want to contract with your ISP to provide this service, rather than devote two computers to doing so yourself.

Linking Small and Large Networks

As you are probably aware, there's a great deal of power to be had in linking small networks to larger ones, and particularly in linking small networks to the Internet as a whole. Routers, as just described, are one very common way to do this. There are variants on the router theme, however, that deserve special attention.

Linking to a Large Intranet

If you're maintaining a small network inside a larger organization, you might be able to link to that organization's network to provide more-or-less direct Internet access to all your computers. Because the details of such a link vary substantially from one network to another, I can't provide a simple set of rules for doing this.

In some cases, what you think of as "your" network will end up as just a part of a larger local network, and won't be physically or logically distinct from it. For instance, if you're setting up a laboratory at a research university, chances are your department maintains its own network. You'll be able to plug your computers directly in to this network and let them share services with one another as described in this book. Unless you make special arrangements or provide your own cabling and a router, however, your systems won't be particularly isolated from the rest of the department's network traffic. In many instances this is an effective and easy way to set up your systems.

In other cases, you might need to provide brand-new network cable and link your computers by using a single router. Configuring a generalized router is beyond the scope of this book, but many of the techniques discussed here will help you configure your network.

If you want to connect a number of computers, and your organization can't spare that many IP addresses, you'll want to look into using IP masquerading, described briefly later in this chapter and in more detail in Chapter 20, "One IP Address, Many Computers: IP Masquerading."

In any of these cases, you probably have one or more local networking technicians who can help you plan and implement your network. You *must* consult with these folks if your company has them, even if only to obtain the necessary IP addresses and hardware specifications for connecting to your network.

Linking All Your Computers via an ISP

If you're setting up a network at home or at a small business, chances are you are or will soon contract with an ISP for Internet access. Linking to an ISP can be much like linking to a corporate network. Unlike corporate networks, however, your ISP is probably located physically some distance from you, so you need to use some form of long-distance networking hardware to connect your computers to your ISP. This technology can be as low-end as a modem running

PPP or as high-end as a dedicated high-speed line (which is actually physically quite similar to a telephone line). In deciding on what type of access you want, you need to ask several questions:

- What kind of speed do you need? ISPs offer access speeds ranging from a low of 33.6Kbps dialup modems to ultra-high-speed lines suitable for running the heaviest e-commerce sites. Keep in mind that many services are *asymmetric* in speed, meaning that one direction (typically downstream, to you) is faster than the other. This is great for typical end-user applications, but it's awful if you want to run a heavily visited Web server.

- How much can you afford? As you might imagine, cost goes up hand-in-hand with speed. The relationship isn't perfect, however, and you can sometimes find a bargain price for certain types of service. For instance, in many urban areas the cost of cable modem or low-end DSL service is lower than the cost of a telephone ISP and a dedicated telephone line.

- Do you need uninterrupted service? If you need service that's always up, telephone modems are a poor choice in most cases, although some ISPs offer always-on dialup PPP connections. I consider a cable modem or DSL line a minimum for always-on service.

- How many computers do you want to connect to the Internet with their own IP addresses? A PPP link typically serves only one IP address. Although the technology is capable of serving more, many cable modem and low-end DSL providers also limit you to one IP address. Midrange to high-end DSL service usually gives you the option of running multiple IP addresses, as do dedicated services such as T1 lines.

NOTE

Even if you have several computers on an intranet, you can use them all for many Internet tasks via a single IP address if you configure your Linux box with IP masquerading. IP masquerading does have its limits, but it's a good workaround for many small networks.

- Is your ISP Linux friendly? At the low end, most ISPs don't mind if you run Linux, but they have no expertise with it and are unwilling to provide technical support if you run into problems. A few ISPs are actively hostile toward Linux. When you're looking at the faster and higher-priced connection options, however, UNIX and Linux experience and support are easier to obtain.

> **TIP**
>
> It's easy to greatly miss the mark when it comes to deciding how much Internet access you need. You might think you can get by with an analog dialup modem, only to find it's inadequate. It's just as possible, though, to sign up for a high-end business DSL plan, only to discover you don't use its capacity. It's also quite possible that your needs will change over time. For these reasons, I recommend favoring ISPs that offer several levels of service, such as dialup modems and several types of DSL. If you need to change service in the future, you can then do so relatively painlessly. If you want to maintain a Web page or other corporate Internet presence, you should also seriously consider registering your own domain name with InterNIC. If you then must change ISPs, you can move your domain name with you, and your customers might not even know you made the change.

One important difference between an ISP and a corporate network is that your connection to an ISP usually goes over a single cable, be it a telephone line, a cable TV wire, or what have you. This means that you usually must use some form of router or router-like technology. You can either configure a computer of your own to serve this function, or you can purchase a stand-alone box to do the task. As mentioned earlier, cable and DSL modems are actually routers or bridges, and some of these allow you to connect several computers, either directly or via your own hub or switch. When you use your own computer as a router (or purchase your own stand-alone router), you have more control over what it lets through, which can be a distinct advantage over letting the ISP's hardware do the job. Some poorly configured systems actually link large groups of customers into one virtual network, which can be a serious security problem.

Using IP Masquerading to Use One IP Address

One particularly interesting variant on the router theme is IP masquerading. An ordinary router transfers TCP/IP packets from one computer to another without altering the contents of the message. In particular, an ordinary router doesn't alter the return address embedded in the TCP/IP packet. You can configure a Linux system to substitute its own address in the TCP/IP packet, however, thus fooling the destination system into thinking that the Linux system is the origin of the packet.

IP masquerading is a popular tool among Linux users with small networks because it lets you link that small network to the Internet when you have only one IP address. This is particularly helpful for dialup access via PPP or when you're using a low-end cable modem or DSL system that gives you only one IP address. Another use of IP masquerading is to extend a limited number of IP addresses in a larger networked organization. For instance, if your company has a large number of IP addresses but a growing number of computers, you can extend the life of your large but limited number of IP addresses by using IP masquerading whenever possible. When installing a new cluster of computers, give only one Linux computer a normal IP address, and then network the rest to that one computer, using the private IP addresses in Table 4.2. Note that the machine that does the IP masquerading usually has two IP addresses—one for the internal network and one for the external network. Figure 4.8 illustrates this relationship. Note that, to the outside world, every computer on the network appears to be the masquerading computer.

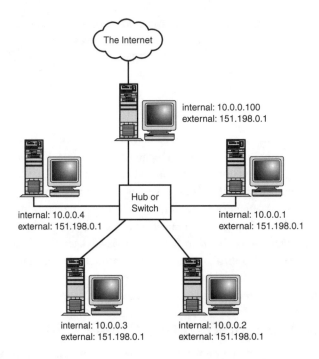

FIGURE 4.8

IP masquerading makes an entire internal network look like a single computer to the outside world.

One of the advantages—and disadvantages—of IP masquerading is that it hides the internal network, including its security vulnerabilities, from the outside world. Because outside sources see only the masquerading router, they won't even realize that the other computers exist. Of course, if the masquerading router itself is cracked, then any resources on the private network will be wide open, so I don't recommend being complacent about internal network security. The advantage of increased security through masquerading can be offset by the fact that this arrangement makes it impossible to run servers on the internal network that are visible to the outside world—at least this is impossible without additional configuration.

> **CAUTION**
>
> It's important that you use private IP addresses for the computers whose identities are to be masqueraded. If you use normal IP addresses, network traffic can be misrouted. For instance, if you use an IP address that happens to be assigned to the Web server at the University of Pangaea, your system will seem to work quite well until one of the users of the masqueraded network tries to access the U of P Web site. At best, the user will get a Web server maintained on the internal masqueraded network. At worst, it simply won't work, making the user think that the U of P Web site is down.

Chapter 20, "One IP Address, Many Computers: IP Masquerading," covers IP masquerading in much greater detail.

Using Firewalls to Protect Your Network

You've probably heard firewalls mentioned with increasing frequency in recent years, but you might not know what a firewall *is*. In fact, not all network professionals agree on this matter—the term is sometimes applied to very specific operations, and other times it's used more globally. In general terms and using broad definitions, a *firewall* is a type of router that's designed to protect a network from outside attack. A firewall scrutinizes network traffic in search of suspicious activity, and can block any packet or connection attempt of which it does not approve. For instance, if a particular remote site is known to be a haven for crackers, you can configure a firewall to block all traffic from that site. If a firewall detects certain types of suspicious activity, such as port scanning (systematically probing a computer for daemons running on particular ports), it can alert you or block the activity. Chapter 21, "Configuring a Firewall," discusses this topic in detail.

Firewalls can be configured to show only a passing interest in the activity of the network, in which case you as a user may not even know it's there. Firewalls can also be configured to be very heavy-handed and block just about anything but approved traffic, in which case the firewall will become the favorite gripe of the office. Linux supports two broad classes of firewall service:

- Packet-filtering firewalls—A packet filter identifies individual TCP/IP packets and passes or rejects them based on criteria such as their origin, destination, and so on. Some people don't consider packet filtering to be firewalling, but in Linux, you implement packet filtering in the kernel by activating a feature called Network Firewalls.

- Proxy server firewalls—A proxy server firewall filters network traffic based on criteria from higher up the TCP/IP chain. At its most restrictive, a proxy firewall can be configured to completely process and then forward to an internal network only a handful of types of data, such as email. Proxy firewalls aren't created by kernel configuration, but by separate software.

For the best security, a firewall machine should serve *only* as a firewall. It should not have user accounts, and it should not offer services of its own outside the firewall functions. When you add services, user accounts, and so on, you degrade the firewall's security substantially.

Summary

Whether they're large or small, networks are defined, in part, by their topologies. Thanks to the popularity of Ethernet, and in particular twisted-pair cabling, star topologies have become quite common in small networks. Any organization with more than a few dozen computers is likely to support multiple networks, however, linked together by routers or bridges, and these networks may come in any of a number of different topologies. The way the networks themselves are linked can create a sort of meta-topology within the organization. The way organizations link their computers to computers worldwide creates the extraordinarily complex web of computers that we refer to as the Internet.

The methods that data packets use to traverse this mass of computers are varied. At each step of its journey, a data packet is partially analyzed and passed on with altered addressing data designed to bring it one step closer to its destination.

If you're an individual or a small business, choosing an ISP and deciding how to link your computers to it can have important consequences on your network connection. Choosing the wrong access method can result in slow network links and frustration, or in money wasted on bandwidth you never use.

Configuring Linux Networking

PART

II

IN THIS PART

Basic Linux Configuration

IN THIS CHAPTER

So far you've learned background information that's vital to setting up networking in Linux. This chapter begins a discussion of more practical issues, including how to install Red Hat Linux 6.0. If you're familiar with Linux installation and the reasons for configuration choices, you can skip much of this chapter. If you're relatively new to Linux or other UNIX-like operating systems, you should read this chapter carefully because it is vital to understanding how Linux operates.

This book comes with a copy of Red Hat Linux 6.0, one of the most popular distributions of Linux. The section on installing Linux contains some very specific information on this particular distribution and version, but many of the general concerns and principles described apply to other distributions, as well. Throughout the rest of the book, I refer to the linuxconf configuration tool Red Hat provides and that is also used by the Mandrake distribution, which is closely related to Red Hat.

Throughout this book I provide information on how to configure a system using textual configuration tools (that is, manually), so you should be able to configure any Linux system using the information in this book. Linux distributions sometimes vary in where configuration files are located and what they're called, but for the most part my descriptions of how to configure a system manually should be helpful whether you're using Red Hat or some other distribution. Some distributions, such as SuSE and Caldera, come with graphical user interface (GUI) configuration tools that are similar to linuxconf in principle, but not in detail. If you're using such a distribution, you might want to investigate these tools.

Installing Linux

If all goes well, installing Linux can take as little as about half an hour. Most people who are not familiar with Linux will take longer to install it, however, and situations such as configuring a computer to dual-boot between Linux and another operating system (OS) can increase the required installation time. If you're diligent about preparing for installation, you might invest an extra half-hour or so at the start. If you're not, you'll save that time, but there's a good chance you'll spend at least as much going back to check on hardware details or repeating an installation.

Red Hat normally releases a new version of Linux every 3–6 months, so there's a good chance that by the time you read this the 6.0 distribution included with this book will be a version or two behind the times. If you want to be absolutely current, you can obtain a new version in several ways:

- Buy an official Red Hat CD from your favorite computer retailer. The list price for Red Hat 6.0 is $79.95, and future versions are likely to be about the same. An official Red Hat package includes technical support, a printed manual, and both demos and fully functional commercial packages not included in the unofficial CDs.

- Buy an unofficial Red Hat CD from a company such as Cheap*Bytes (`http://www.cheapbytes.com`), Linux System Labs (`http://www.lsl.com`), or Linux Central (`http://www.linuxcentral.com`). These CDs typically sell for about $2 plus shipping (which is generally about $5 in the United States).

- Download Red Hat from the Net. You'll need either a fast Internet connection or a great deal of patience to do this (a full download by modem is likely to take a day or more). Red Hat maintains a list of mirror sites that provide Red Hat at `http://www.redhat.com/mirrors.html`. If you want to install Red Hat from a hard disk partition or create your own installation CD-ROM, you should probably check my Web page on the topic at `http://members.bellatlantic.net/~smithrod/rhjol.html`. If you have a direct Internet connection, you can install directly from an FTP site, without storing a copy locally.

The advantage to installing the latest and greatest version of Linux is that you'll be completely up-to-date on performance and security improvements, possibly including new drivers for some of your hardware. The disadvantage is that your experiences may not match what's described in this book as precisely as if you used the version on the book's CD-ROM.

The version of Red Hat 6.0 included on the CD-ROM includes all the updated packages Red Hat has posted to its Web site, up to the day the CD-ROM was mastered. Nonetheless, you might want to check the Red Hat errata page at `http://www.redhat.com/errata/` after installing and check to see if there are any important-sounding bug fixes listed there.

The CD-ROM that accompanies this book includes some extra programs that don't normally come with Red Hat Linux, such as the Netatalk server. You should be able to use these packages even with an updated version of Red Hat or with another distribution.

Partitioning Your Hard Drives

If you want to repartition a system that contains Windows or some other OS, you have two choices:

- Back up all your data, repartition the system, and restore the data. This is effective, but tedious.

- Use a utility such as the freeware First Nondestructive Interactive Partition Splitting Program (FIPS; included on the CD-ROM that accompanies this book) or the commercial Partition Magic from PowerQuest (`http://www.powerquest.com`). Partition Magic is a very handy utility you can use to create and modify Linux partitions in addition to DOS, OS/2, and Windows partitions. It comes with both DOS and Windows executables, including a bootable DOS disk image you can copy to floppy from Linux, so it can be used on a Linux-only system. Figure 5.1 shows Partition Magic in operation.

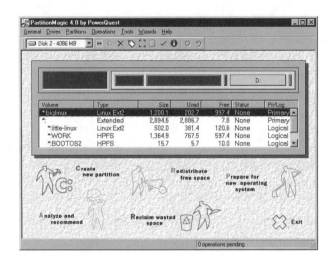

FIGURE 5.1

Partition Magic lets you click on a partition to resize it, move it, or copy it.

CAUTION

Even if you use a utility like FIPS or Partition Magic, it's wise to back up your system before proceeding because dynamic partition modifications are inherently dangerous.

The details of how to use these partition resizing utilities vary substantially, so you should check the documentation of the package you intend to use to learn how to do it.

If you're installing Linux as the only OS on a system, you can use the Linux `fdisk` program during installation to set up the partitions. In fact, you might need to use `fdisk` even if you use a partition resizer. I'll describe this process later, but in case you can set up your partitions before starting the installation, I'll describe Linux's partition requirements here.

A minimal Linux installation typically takes somewhere between 100MB and 500MB, depending on the distribution and what you consider "minimal." To be truly useful, I recommend 1GB or more be devoted to Linux, and if you want to use Linux as a heavy-duty server, you might need quite a few gigabytes of space. Fortunately, the prices of multi-gigabyte hard disks are falling rapidly, so disk space shouldn't be an issue unless you're on a shoestring budget.

For a person who's unfamiliar with Linux, I generally recommend creating only two or three partitions for Linux. One partition, typically 20MB–120MB in size, is the swap partition.

(It's best to err on the side of a large swap partition. Don't make it larger than 128MB, though, since that's all Linux can handle in a single swap partition.) Linux uses the swap partition to supplement the system's RAM. The second partition is the Linux root partition, often referred to by a single slash character (/) because you can access files in this partition by preceding them with that character. If these are your only two partitions, then all your system and user files will reside in the root partition. The optional third partition is the /home partition, in which user files normally reside. Devoting space to a separate /home partition can help when upgrading the system because you can wipe the root partition clean without affecting user files.

NOTE

On rare occasions, a fourth partition is necessary. This is the /boot partition. If your hard disk is large, the computer's BIOS won't be able to access any data past the so-called 1024-cylinder limit on the drive, which generally works out to 8GB, though it's sometimes less. Because the BIOS must read the Linux kernel in order to boot, the kernel must fall below the 1024-cylinder limit.

If you create a single large root partition on a big enough drive, the kernel might not be accessible to the BIOS. The solution is to create a small (5MB–20MB) /boot partition below the 1024-cylinder limit and place the kernel in it. Red Hat Linux places its kernel in the /boot directory during installation, so this works from the start for Red Hat. Some distributions place the kernel in the base of the root directory, so you might need to boot them with a floppy, move the kernel, and reconfigure LILO (as described later in this chapter in "Using LILO to Boot Linux") to get them working in this way.

Maximizing Disk Performance

Try to place the swap partition as close to the center of the drive as you can. Because swap space is used as a supplement to memory, access time to swap space can have a substantial influence on system speed. Putting swap space in the center of the drive minimizes the average seek time, thus improving performance.

If you have two physical disks, you can improve performance by splitting your Linux installation across those two drives. For instance, you can place the /home partition on one disk and the root partition on the other.

If you want the absolute best disk performance possible, you may want to look into Linux's support for redundant array of independent disk (RAID) technology. RAID works best with SCSI disks and improves reliability through redundancy or performance through simultaneous access to both disks.

continues

5

BASIC LINUX CONFIGURATION

> Configuring a RAID setup is beyond the scope of this book, however. You can find more information in the Software RAID Mini-HOWTO, which comes with most distributions and is on the CD-ROM that accompanies this book in the doc/HOWTO/mini directory.

Linux and UNIX professionals often like to create separate partitions for directories such as /var, /opt, /usr/local, and so on. This has certain advantages. For instance, if a filesystem is damaged, the damage is localized to one partition, leaving the others unaffected. Similarly, some actions can fill a partition with gigabytes of gibberish, which can cause serious problems if it prevents files from being created in critical areas. If a user accidentally creates a multi-gigabyte file in the /tmp directory, that need not be immediately disastrous to others working on databases in the /home directory if those directories are each isolated on their own partitions.

Unfortunately, there's no way of advising a new Linux user on the appropriate *sizes* of these partitions. One system might place a lot of files in /var, and another might require a gigabyte of space in /usr/local. Without knowing appropriate values in advance, attempts to partition a system tend to result in extra work when one partition fills up and another is underused. When you're experienced with Linux and know how much space you need in assorted directories, you might want to consider creating multiple partitions. Until then, I advise keeping an installation simple.

Some of the major directory trees that experienced administrators often assign their own partitions installation include the following:

- / (root)—The root partition, off which all others exist. Anything not given its own partition resides in the root partition.
- /usr—Program files reside in the /usr directory tree. Some installations create separate partitions for subpartitions off /usr, such as /usr/local (for locally compiled programs) and /usr/X11R6 (for X programs).
- /opt—The /opt directory contains major program files that aren't part of a Linux distribution. Programs such as WordPerfect and ApplixWare often install themselves in /opt.
- /home—Users' files go in the /home directory.
- /root—Not to be confused with the / directory, /root is the root user's home directory.
- /mnt—When you access a floppy, CD-ROM, or other removable-media device, you normally mount it on a subdirectory under /mnt, or sometimes on /mnt itself. The /mnt directory itself doesn't normally reside on a separate partition, though; each of its subdirectories serves as a mount point.

- /proc—/proc is a special directory and filesystem that contains information about your system.

- /tmp—The /tmp directory stores files that are intended to last for a short period of time.

- /var—The /var directory stores frequently changed spool and log files. A system that serves as a mail or news server is likely to require a large amount of space in /var (either on its own partition or as part of /). The same is true of a system that runs as a print server if it's common for several large print jobs to collect, as might happen near a major deadline in a graphics art department.

- /boot—As mentioned earlier, a /boot partition can be useful if you have a particularly large hard disk, to ensure that the kernel falls below the 1024-cylinder limit.

In addition to these partitions, you might create mount points for any non-Linux operating systems you have on the computer, such as /windows or /c for a Windows C: drive. If your system has a very large number of users creating many large files, you might need more than one physical disk to store all the files, in which case you might create a /home2 mount point and a separate partition on a second disk for some users' home directories.

Modifying an Existing Partition Scheme

If you've previously installed Linux and find that your partitioning scheme is suboptimal, you can recover it in several ways:

- Back up, repartition, and restore—This is a time-tested method that provides maximum flexibility because you can completely redesign the layout of your Linux partitions, without regard to the current layout. It requires that you have adequate backup hardware and software, but you should have such facilities in any event.

- Use Partition Magic to repartition the system dynamically—Although it's written for DOS and Windows, Partition Magic 4.0 can be invaluable if you find that one partition is too large, but an adjoining partition is too small. You can boot a DOS floppy with the DOS version of Partition Magic and use the program to shrink the too-large partition and enlarge the too-small one to fill the space, thus providing a superior partitioning scheme. You can also copy partitions from one hard disk to another. I strongly advise that you back up your system before using Partition Magic, though; it's usually reliable, but the types of operations it performs are inherently dangerous, so any error or problem along the way (such as a power failure) can result in disaster. Also, be sure you get version 4.0 or above, since prior versions didn't support operations on Linux ext2 partitions.

- Add new partitions to an existing setup—If your system has two or more OSs, you might decide to convert space from use in one OS for use in Linux. If the space you want to devote to Linux is contained in a single partition, you can do this by using Linux's fdisk to change the type of the partition, creating a Linux filesystem on the partition with mke2fs, and then mounting the converted partition at an appropriate point in the directory structure. If you want to use the new partition to store existing files, you need to copy them there first, using an intermediary mount point. The tar utility can be very helpful for doing this. For instance, suppose you want to use a new partition to store the contents of the /usr/local directory. You can mount the new directory at some point (let's call it /mnt/temp), change to the /usr/local directory, and then copy the files with the command **tar cplf - . ¦ (cd /mnt/temp; tar xvplf -)**. You then need to delete the existing /usr/local directory tree, edit /etc/fstab to mount the new partition at that location, unmount /mnt/tmp, and type **mount -a** to activate the changes.

TIP

Before deleting the old directory structure, you might want to try mounting the new partition *over* that structure to be sure it works correctly. If you have any problems accessing files or running programs from the new directory tree, you should track down the source of the problem before deleting the original. When you delete the original tree, remember to unmount the new partition first, or you'll just delete the copied files.

- Delete partitions from an existing setup—You might decide that you want to consolidate two or more partitions into one. If one of the partitions is large enough to hold the contents of all the existing ones, you can unmount the to-be-deleted partitions, mount them in a temporary location, and copy their files to the large partition by using a tar command similar to the one just described. You can then remove the references to the small partitions from /etc/fstab, unmount them from their temporary locations, and be done with it. Of course, the old partitions will still exist on your hard disk, but you can change their type to use them in another OS, delete them and combine them together (if they're contiguous) for reuse under Linux, or just ignore them.

Running the Red Hat Installer

Installing Red Hat Linux involves booting a minimal Red Hat installation system, which automatically launches the installer. There are several ways to accomplish this task, but once started, the installation procedure is the same no matter how you launch the installer.

If you've already installed Linux, but want to change your system configuration, you have two basic options:

- You can work from within your existing configuration to add packages, remove them, or change configuration files. If you have a few specific changes you want to implement, this is probably the way to go.

- You can remove the existing installation and begin again. If you want to implement a large number of changes, and especially if you're new to Linux and think you might have misconfigured your first installation in some unknown way, you might want to start from scratch. Unless your partitioning scheme is one of the things you want to change, you can use your existing partitions. Be sure to specify a new installation, not an upgrade, and to tell the installer to format the Linux partitions.

Booting the Installer

If your computer supports booting from a bootable CD-ROM, you can insert the CD-ROM that accompanies this book in your CD-ROM drive and boot directly from it. (You might need to set some BIOS options to boot from a CD-ROM. Check your system's documentation for details on how to do this.)

If your system doesn't support booting from a CD-ROM, you might be able to start the installer by following these directions:

1. Set your system to run in DOS mode. Either boot from a DOS floppy with CD-ROM support or restart Windows in DOS mode.
2. Change to your CD-ROM drive by typing its drive letter and a colon, and then press the Enter key.
3. Type `cd dosutils`, and then press the Enter key.
4. Type `autoboot.bat`, and then press the Enter key. The Red Hat installer should start.

If for some reason you can't follow the preceding instructions, you need to create a Red Hat installation floppy disk. If you have a working DOS or Windows system (it needn't be the one on which you plan to install Linux), you can do so by following these steps:

1. Open a DOS prompt window or boot DOS.
2. Change to your CD-ROM drive by typing its drive letter and a colon, and then press the Enter key.
3. Type

   `cd images`

   and then press the Enter key.
4. Type

   `..\dosutils\rawrite -f boot.img -d a`

5. The program asks you to insert a floppy in the A: drive. Do so. Note that the floppy must have *no* bad sectors, or it won't work correctly. After you insert a floppy, press the Enter key.

6. Your CD-ROM and floppy indicator lights should flicker for a while as the computer makes a copy of the disk image.

NOTE

The CD-ROM that accompanies this book includes a Windows NT version of the RAWRITE utility, in the directory rawriteNT, so you can create a Linux boot floppy from Windows NT or 2000. (The normal RAWRITE doesn't run from Windows NT.)

If you don't have access to a DOS or Windows system, you can create a disk image on a Linux or UNIX system by following these steps:

1. Mount the CD-ROM drive by typing **mount /mnt/cdrom** or something similar (details vary from system to system).

2. Insert a formatted floppy disk in the computer's floppy drive. This floppy must have *no* bad sectors, or it won't work correctly.

3. Type

   `dd if=/mnt/cdrom/images/boot.img of=/dev/fd0`

   to create a Red Hat boot floppy. The path to boot.img might be different if you used a different mount point, and the device file might not be /dev/fd0 on all systems, particularly if you're using a UNIX system that's not Linux. You might need to be root to issue this command.

After you've created a floppy, you can use it to boot the computer into the Red Hat Linux installer. The first screen you'll see is the Red Hat installation boot: prompt, shown in Figure 5.2. You can press the Enter key here to continue the boot process. In rare cases, you might need to track down special parameters to type at this prompt in order to get Linux to recognize your hardware. If, after you press Enter, the system displays some text and hangs, you should consult Red Hat's documentation (in the doc/rhmanual/manual directory on the Red Hat CD-ROM) for help.

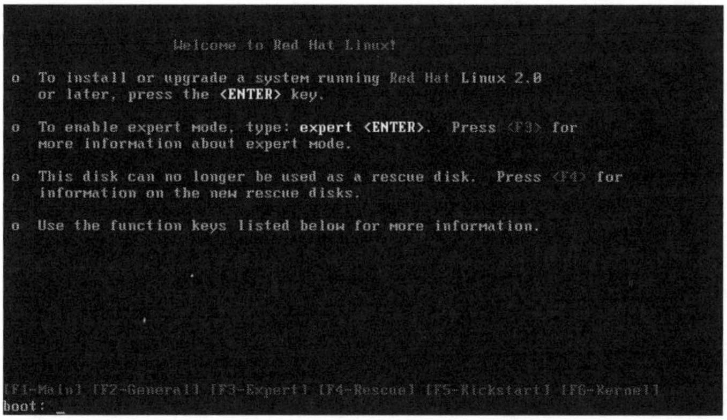

FIGURE 5.2
The Linux boot prompt lets you enter parameters to tell the Linux kernel how to handle unusual hardware configurations.

> **NOTE**
>
> If you want to do a network installation because your target system lacks a CD-ROM or because you want to install a more recent version of Red Hat, you need to create a floppy disk image from the `bootnet.img` file for the version of Red Hat Linux you want to install. You do this much as I've just described. The CD-ROM that accompanies this book includes the Red Hat 6.0 `bootnet.img` file, but if you want to install a more recent version of Red Hat, you need to obtain an appropriate image file for it. You can install Red Hat 6.0 from the CD-ROM that accompanies this book by using a network install with a Linux or Windows computer serving the CD-ROM's files.

Starting the Installation

After you press Enter at the `boot:` prompt, a number of messages appear on the screen. These are status reports from the Linux kernel about your hardware, the drivers being installed, and so on. After these messages are finished, the Red Hat installer welcome screen greets you.

When you press the Enter key at the installer screen, Red Hat prompts you for a number of pieces of information, using prompts similar to those shown in Figure 5.3. At each prompt, you'll see a list of selections. Use the arrow keys to move through the list, and then press Enter when you've reached your selection. You'll be asked about the language, keyboard, and installation source you want to use.

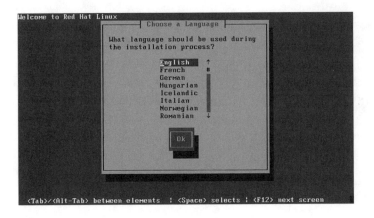

FIGURE 5.3

You navigate installation menus by using the Spacebar and the arrow, Tab, Alt+Tab, and Enter keys.

The installer accesses the CD-ROM, and then asks you more questions, some of which use a multiple-choice format. Use the arrow keys or Tab and Alt+Tab to switch between choices. The installer asks if you want to do a new installation or upgrade an existing one; whether to perform a workstation, server, or custom install; and what type of SCSI host adapter you have. I recommend doing a custom install because this gives you the greatest control over the installation process.

Red Hat gives you a choice of using either of two tools for partitioning your disk: Disk Druid or fdisk. Disk Druid is easier to use, but it has a distressing tendency to produce unusable partitions. I therefore recommend that you use fdisk. When you're in Linux fdisk, you can type single-letter commands and then press the Enter key. The most important command to remember is h, which lists the available commands. I recommend starting with the p command, which displays the existing partition table, as shown in Figure 5.4. You can then use n to create new partitions. By default, Linux's fdisk creates partitions of type 83—Linux native. You should change your swap partition to type 82 with the t command after you create it. When you've created all your partitions to your satisfaction, use the w command to write the partition table and exit. You'll then return to the Partition Disks screen. If you're done, select Done.

> **NOTE**
>
> If you created partitions for Linux with DOS FDISK or most other programs, you can leave them in place, but you *must* change the partition types using the t command in Linux fdisk.

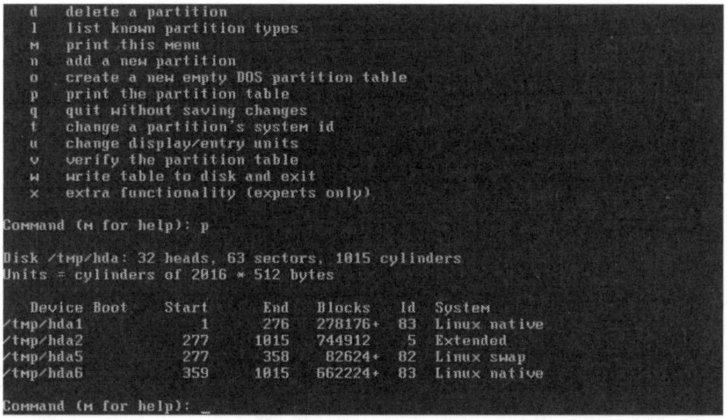

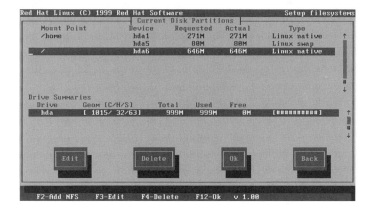

FIGURE 5.4

The Linux fdisk *utility doesn't actually change the disk until you're finished and issue the* w *command.*

You need to tell the installer whereeach partition will reside in the Linux filesystem tree, as shown in Figure 5.5. You *must* specify one partition as the root (/) filesystem. You mount others inside the subdirectory off the root filesystem.

FIGURE 5.5

If you have DOS or Windows partitions, you can include them in your Linux system by giving them mount points just as you do with Linux partitions.

The installer asks you which partitions (both swap space and regular filesystems) you want to format. If you're upgrading an existing system, you should probably not format any partitions. If you're doing a fresh installation, you should format them all unless they've already been formatted.

You've now set up the rough outlines of your Linux system—the partitions and other basic configuration. Now it's time to move on to deciding what specific software you want to install.

Packages to Select and Leave Behind

The Red Hat installer presents a list of OS components you can install, as shown in Figure 5.6. Each component is actually a cluster of several related software packages, some of which are quite large.

FIGURE 5.6

You can select software by positioning the cursor next to the component name and pressing the Spacebar.

Components you're most likely to want for a SOHO Linux server include

- Printer Support—If you want to serve printers or print to local or remote printers, you need this package.

- DOS/Windows Connectivity—Provides tools for working with common DOS and Windows file formats, and for running DOS programs from Linux.

- Networked Workstation—This provides useful network client tools.

- Dialup Workstation—If you connect to your ISP via PPP, select this package.

- NFS Server—If you want to give other Linux or UNIX clients access to your Linux filesystems, select this option.

- SMB (Samba) Connectivity—This is the Samba package, which is necessary for sharing files and printers with Windows clients.

- C Development—Even if you won't be writing new programs yourself, you'll need this to recompile the Linux kernel. Select it.

- Development Libraries—You need these to compile programs, in addition to the C Development packages. Select it.

- Kernel Development—This group includes the Linux kernel source code itself. Select it.

- Extra Documentation—Documentation is always a good idea!

You'll know immediately that you want to leave some packages out. For instance, if you have no intention of playing games, the game packages are obvious. Others might not be so obvious. Chances are you *will* want to install the X Window System packages because these provide a GUI environment. GNOME and KDE are two popular desktop environments for X. They both provide point-and-click file browsers and an assortment of simple applications. They're both big, so if you're short on disk space, you should choose only one of them. There are assorted servers for FTP, DNS, and other protocols that you might or might not want to include.

NOTE

Red Hat uses the Red Hat Package Manager (RPM) system for installing packages. RPM includes information on *dependencies*—packages that are required by other packages. If you select a set of packages that depends on something you've not selected, RPM will force installation of the ones you haven't selected. The installer will tell you about this when it installs the packages, but not when you select them.

Note also that the acronym *RPM* refers to the software for handling packages, the file format for the packages, and the packages themselves.

Don't fret too much over your choices here. Even if you deselect everything, you'll get a working installation, and you can add what you need later. Likewise, if you select too much, you can remove the excess later. If you exceed your disk capacity, you might have more serious problems and need to reinstall from scratch, though. If you're running very short on disk space, try leaving off the X Window System, GNOME, KDE, file managers, and all servers except those you're absolutely positive you must have. You can then see how much disk space you have after you've installed by using the df command, and add packages as appropriate.

After you select the packages you want, choose Ok. The installer informs you that it will place a log of the installation in the file /tmp/install.log. When you dismiss this notification, you'll see a series of messages informing you of the installer's progress at creating filesystems and installing packages, as shown in Figure 5.7.

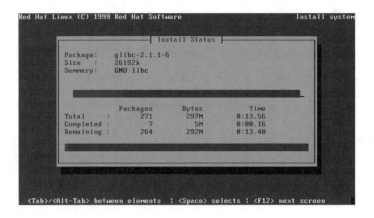

FIGURE 5.7
The installer gives you an estimate of the time to finish the installation, so you know whether to grab a cup of coffee or go out to lunch.

Final Installation Configuration

After the installer has placed files on your hard disk, it goes through a series of tests and configuration routines:

- Mouse Configuration—The installer attempts to identify your mouse, and usually asks for help in identifying the specific model or type.

> **TIP**
>
> If you have a 3-button PS/2 mouse, be sure to hit the down arrow key at this stage. The Red Hat installer defaults to assuming you have a 2-button mouse, but the 3-button option is available on the next line, hidden from view because the 2-button PS/2 mouse option is the last one displayed without scrolling the list.

- Configure Ethernet—I don't present information on Ethernet configuration here because Chapter 7, "Setting Ethernet Options," is devoted to this topic. You can configure your system for Ethernet during installation, but you should check Chapter 7 to find out what the various options mean.
- Configure Timezones—You need to tell Linux in what timezone the computer resides.
- Services—You can tell the system what services (daemons) to start automatically when it boots. You should leave these options at the default values until you're more familiar with Linux. This book tells you how to enable the services that aren't enabled by default.

- Configure Printer—I won't describe printer configuration here, but if you want to do this during installation, you can check Chapter 14, "Preparing to Share a Printer," for details on the information you'll have to enter.

- Root Password—You must type the root password twice to be sure you entered it correctly. When you type the password, you won't see anything happen on the screen. This is normal, and is done for security purposes.

- Authentication Configuration—You have options for how to store passwords: You can use NIS, in which case you must enter an NIS domain and server; you can use shadow passwords; and you can use MD5 passwords. These options are not mutually exclusive. I recommend that you use shadow passwords and MD5 because this results in the most secure passwords. If your network has an NIS server, you can use it; otherwise, you can ignore the NIS option.

- Bootdisk—You can create a boot floppy that will boot your system. I strongly recommend that you do so.

- LILO Installation—The Linux Loader (LILO) is the usual way to boot a Linux system from the hard disk. You have the option of installing it to the Master Boot Record (MBR) of your hard disk or to the first sector of the boot partition. Use the second option if you're currently using another boot loader, such as OS/2's Boot Manager or Partition Magic's Boot Magic. Otherwise, install LILO in the MBR. A second LILO screen lets you enter kernel parameters. If you needed such parameters to get a SCSI adapter or NIC working, you should enter them here, too. Finally, you can enter information in LILO to allow it to boot OSs other than Linux. You need to give each OS a label by selecting it and choosing the Edit option in the Bootable Partitions screen.

- Xconfigurator—The Red Hat installer now configures the X Window System. It asks various questions about your hardware, and then offers to start X. I recommend skipping this step because if the configuration is incorrect, the test might hang your computer.

At this point, the installer has finished, and proceeds to restart the computer.

Testing the Installation

To test the installation, boot into Linux. If you installed LILO, you'll see a LILO `boot:` prompt after the BIOS finishes its tests. You can press Enter at the `boot:` prompt to boot the default OS or type the label for an alternate OS. If after a minute or two you get a prompt that reads `login:`, your installation was at least minimally successful. You can type `root` and enter the password you specified during installation to log in and begin using or further configuring the system.

5

Configuration Files and Tools

After you've done the basic installation on your system, you'll probably need to modify that configuration to suit your exact needs. In some sense, that's the topic of this entire book, although this book covers only a subset of Linux configuration issues. There are commonalities to most Linux configuration procedures, though, and being familiar with them can help you, both in setting up a Linux server and in other Linux configuration tasks.

The /etc Directory and Its Contents

Linux's configuration is done through text files, not binary registry files, as in Windows. Linux stores its configuration files in the /etc directory or subdirectories off /etc. This may sound simple enough, until you take a look at the /etc directory's contents and see the dozens of files there! Here's a rundown of some of the most important files and directories in /etc:

- X11/—This is a subdirectory that contains files for configuring XFree86, the most important of these files being XF86Config.

- atalk/—Netatalk configuration files reside in this directory. It won't exist on a fresh Red Hat install, however.

- conf.modules—You can provide information on how Linux loads and uses device driver modules in this file.

- cron.*/—Several subdirectories beginning with cron are used to configure the Linux cron feature. This feature lets you run programs at specified intervals, and it's used to help clean up system files and temporary directories, among other things.

- fstab—This file controls how Linux mounts its partitions. You'll need to modify it if you add or delete partitions or removable disks, or if you want to modify how an existing partition is handled.

- group—Linux collects users into groups of users, and the group file specifies which users belong to which groups.

- hosts—This file lists the host names and IP addresses of frequently accessed computers.

- hosts.allow—For network services that are controlled by the TCP Wrappers utility, you can specify the computers that are allowed to access the service in the hosts.allow file. Use this if you want to provide a service to only a limited number of computers.

- hosts.deny—If there are computers or domains you want to explicitly forbid from using a service, place them in the hosts.deny file.

- `inetd.conf`—This is the configuration file for the `inetd` daemon. It's a very important file for Linux networking because many distributions (including Red Hat) use `inetd` to launch specific daemons when they're needed and not before.

- `inittab`—The `inittab` file controls many aspects of the boot process, specifying which other files in `/etc` are run and in what order.

- `ld.so.conf`—Linux searches for *libraries* (files with code that's often shared between programs) in certain directories specified in this file.

- `lilo.conf`—The configuration for the LILO utility is stored here. If you change this file, you must reinstall LILO by typing **lilo**.

- `passwd`—Usernames and associated information, sometimes including their passwords, are stored in this file.

- `printcap`—This file defines your printer queues.

- `profile`—Environment variables and startup programs common to all users are stored here.

- `services`—This file lists standard services and their port numbers. Just because a service is listed in this file does *not* mean it's available on your system, though.

- `shadow`—If you enable shadow passwords, users' passwords are stored here rather than in the `passwd` file. The `passwd` file is still used for most user information, though. The idea is that the `shadow` file can have more restrictive permissions than can the `passwd` file, and so an uninvited guest won't be able to obtain users' passwords, even in an encrypted form.

- `smb.conf`—Samba configuration information is stored here.

This is by no means an exhaustive listing of the files in the `/etc` directory, as you know if you've taken a look and compared what you saw to what I've just listed. These are some of the most important files, however, especially for a Linux file and print server.

Using `linuxconf`

If you're new to Linux and UNIX, you might feel intimidated by the need to edit text files to configure your OS. That's one of the reasons Red Hat developed `linuxconf`, a utility to configure a Red Hat Linux system using a textual or graphical user interface rather than a text editor and manuals. You normally have to be root to run `linuxconf`. When you do, the program checks your environment and runs in full GUI mode when you're running in X (see Figure 5.8), or in text-only mode if you're not.

5

BASIC LINUX
CONFIGURATION

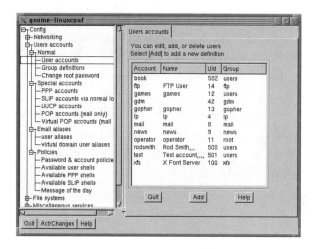

FIGURE 5.8

The linuxconf *utility is expandable, so you can create modules to help configure any aspect of a Linux system.*

NOTE

The window manager I used in preparing this book is called icewm. Red Hat isn't configured to use icewm when it's first installed, so your windows' decorations may be slightly different from what you see in this book's screen shots. The *contents* of the windows you see on your screen should be the same as you see in this book, but the decorations around them may not be.

A potentially useful (and also potentially dangerous) option in linuxconf is to permit access via Web browsers. If you start linuxconf and select Config, Networking, Misc, Linuxconf network access, you can activate network access to linuxconf. You can restrict access to specific hosts, and normal Linux password requirements apply—only people with access to linuxconf from a normal login will be able to access it via the Web, and then they'll need to enter their usernames and passwords. When this is active, you can access linuxconf using a Web browser on any OS by entering the Linux computer's Web address on port 98 (such as http://gingko.biloba.com:98). Figure 5.9 illustrates the result when using Netscape Navigator on a Macintosh to view the same options that are shown in Figure 5.8.

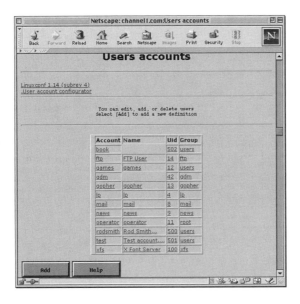

FIGURE 5.9
You can use a Web browser in any OS to control a Red Hat Linux computer via linuxconf.

You might want to take some time to familiarize yourself with linuxconf. I *strongly* suggest that you don't change settings with the utility unless you know what you're doing, however. Although linuxconf makes configuring a Linux computer easier than it is by editing text files, it's still possible to create a configuration in which Linux won't boot by using linuxconf. Although such situations can be corrected, doing so requires more in-depth knowledge than most new Linux users have. You can still investigate linuxconf safely, though; just be sure to click Cancel whenever it's an option, and don't click Accept, particularly if you've made any changes.

Using LILO to Boot Linux

Because booting an OS is such a basic and important task, you should know something about how Linux manages it. The usual way for Linux to boot from a hard disk is to use a program called LILO.

LILO Theory

The PC boot process begins when the system's BIOS checks for hard drives. When it finds a hard drive, the BIOS executes a piece of code that's stored in the MBR. On a typical DOS or Windows PC, this code then executes code stored in the first sector of the boot partition of the hard disk, which in turn loads certain critical OS files, which load more OS files, and so on.

5

BASIC LINUX
CONFIGURATION

The boot process in Linux is both the same and different from the DOS or Windows boot process. Linux uses LILO to direct the boot process in a flexible way. LILO can reside in the MBR, in the first sector of a Linux partition, or on a floppy disk. In any of these cases, it can redirect the boot process to follow any of several paths, according to what you type when LILO executes at boot time. LILO is responsible for placing the boot: prompt on the screen, and in response to this prompt you can press the Enter key to boot the default OS, press the Tab key to see your choices, or type the name of one of your choices to boot it. LILO then redirects the boot process appropriately for whatever OS you've chosen. In the case of Linux, LILO loads the Linux kernel into memory and executes it. The kernel then runs Linux configuration files, which eventually bring up a full-fledged Linux system.

Because LILO can reside in either the MBR or a partition, it can be used as either a primary or a secondary boot loader:

- Primary—When LILO is on the MBR, it controls the boot process and determines what OS will load. This is a useful configuration when Linux is the only OS on the computer, or when you want to use LILO to choose between Linux and one or more other OSs.

- Secondary—If you already use a boot loader such as OS/2's Boot Manager or Partition Magic's Boot Magic, you can place LILO on the Linux partition. In this configuration, you might want to set LILO to boot Linux after a very short delay (a fraction of a second). You can also, however, use LILO to choose which of several kernels you want to boot, or even to boot different versions of Linux or different OSs, for a cascaded boot selection (as in selecting from DOS-like or UNIX-like OSs, and in the latter case choosing Red Hat Linux, Debian GNU/Linux, or FreeBSD).

Microsoft's OSs normally must be installed on primary partitions, but LILO allows Linux to reside entirely on logical partitions. If one of your Linux partitions is a primary partition on the first hard disk, though, you can install LILO on the Linux primary partition. If you then set that partition to be bootable, the normal boot code in the MBR will load LILO. This sort of installation works just like a primary boot loader, although LILO executes from a partition's boot sector, not from the MBR. You might want to use a configuration like this if you prefer not to write data to the MBR unless it's absolutely necessary. Such a setup also allows you to bypass LILO in a multi-OS system, to boot an alternate OS directly.

Configuring LILO with `linuxconf`

You can use `linuxconf` to configure LILO to suit your needs. Under the `linuxconf` Config, boot mode, Lilo menu, you'll find several LILO configuration settings, as shown in Figure 5.10.

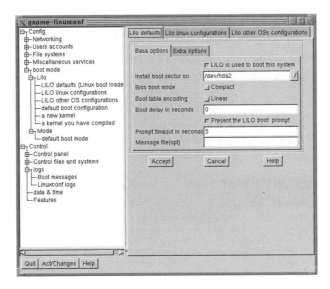

FIGURE 5.10
LILO presents a lot of options across six linuxconf *entries, but you won't use most of these in practice.*

You can configure LILO by using just a few items in the linuxconf setup. Here are some of the highlights:

- LILO defaults, Base options, Install boot sector on—This is where LILO installs itself. To use LILO as a primary boot loader, it needs to be on /dev/hda or /dev/sda. As a secondary loader, it needs to be on your Linux partition (such as /dev/hda2 in Figure 5.10).

- LILO defaults, Base options, Prompt timeout in seconds—This option controls how long the LILO boot: prompt remains on the screen before LILO boots the default option.

- LILO linux configurations—This screen controls the Linux boot configurations. There should be one of these configurations on your installation, created by the Red Hat installer. Click it, and a new tab appears for controlling it. You can create new configurations, say for testing a new kernel.

- LILO linux configurations, Linux boot configuration, Label—The label is what you type to boot this configuration.

- LILO linux configurations, Linux boot configuration, Kernel image file—You must tell LILO where the kernel is located in order to boot Linux.

- LILO linux configurations, Linux boot configuration, root partition—You must tell LILO what partition is the root of your filesystem hierarchy. The kernel looks there for additional configuration files.

5

BASIC LINUX CONFIGURATION

- LILO other OS configurations—You can add non-Linux OSs using this portion of the linuxconf LILO area.

- Default boot configuration—Here you can select any of the Linux or other OS configurations to be the default.

- A new kernel—You can use this item to quickly install a new kernel image in LILO. You must specify the kernel file, give it a label, and so on.

- A new kernel you have compiled—If the utility can spot a freshly compiled kernel, linuxconf can add the new kernel to LILO quite easily when you click this tab.

Configuring LILO with Text Files

If you want to configure LILO the old-fashioned way, you can load the /etc/lilo.conf file into your favorite text editor. Here's a sample lilo.conf file that demonstrates booting from either of two Linux kernels:

```
boot=/dev/hda2
map=/boot/map
install=/boot/boot.b
prompt
timeout=50
image=/boot/zImage-2.2.8
        label=228
        root=/dev/hda8
        read-only
image=/boot/zImage-2.2.9
        label=229
        root=/dev/hda8
        read-only
```

The first line (boot=/dev/hda2) specifies where to place LILO itself. This location is normally /dev/hda or /dev/sda for a primary loader, or a specific partition, such as /dev/hda2, for a secondary loader. The next three lines set standard options, and shouldn't be changed. The timeout line specifies the time the prompt remains on the screen, in tenths of a second. Each of the lines that begins with image specifies a separate Linux boot image, and each image specification includes several subsidiary lines. The image line itself identifies the Linux kernel. The label and root lines specify the boot label and the root filesystem, respectively. The read-only line indicates that the filesystem is to be mounted in read-only mode initially, which is normal; later in the boot process, Linux remounts the filesystem in full read/write mode. Unless otherwise specified, the first system specification in the file becomes the default.

You can learn more about the format of the lilo.conf file by typing **man lilo.conf** at a Linux command prompt.

When you edit your /etc/lilo.conf file, you must be sure to reinstall LILO so that the changes take effect. LILO is really two things: The code that goes in the boot sector and a program for creating that code and putting it there, based on the contents of the /etc/lilo.conf file. The latter task is handled by a program called lilo, located in the /sbin directory, so to install LILO the boot loader, you type **/sbin/lilo**, or just **lilo** if /sbin is on your search path. You'll see messages to the effect that each system specification in the file has been added. If there's an error in the process, you'll see an error message, and *none* of your changes will take effect.

Setting Up User Accounts

Linux is designed as a multiuser operating system. As such, the concept of different accounts for different users is common throughout the OS—from the need to log in, to ownership and permissions on files. Because file and printer sharing operations interact closely with the security needs of Linux, you'll need to be quite familiar with operations relating to account creation and maintenance, file permissions, and so on. This section therefore covers some of this material.

The Importance of User Accounts

The use of separate user accounts provides several key benefits to Linux, just as it does to other UNIX-like operating systems:

- User privacy—On most operating systems designed for desktop use, there's no concept of user accounts, and anybody who sits down to use the system can access all the files on the system. If you want to share such a computer with another person, the only way to ensure that the other user can't read your files is to encrypt them, and that's awkward for you. User accounts let you keep prying eyes away from your data.

- Multiuser access—Several people can use a single Linux computer simultaneously, by using terminals or other networked computers. Keeping separate accounts helps keep the separate actions of these individuals from interfering with one another.

- Access control—User accounts allow a computer to be placed in a public location without fear that it will be used by unauthorized individuals. (This applies both to physical location and to access via a network.) Of course, even a single-user OS such as DOS can be outfitted with a password-protection scheme, but without implementing at least a minimal system of user accounts, there's no way to track just who used the computer when.

- System protection—An OS with differing levels of permissions for different users, such as Linux implements, allows the OS to protect itself from both user error and malicious actions. For instance, it's notoriously easy for a user of most traditional desktop OSs to wipe out the entire OS, just by deleting a critical directory. Although this is possible in

Linux, such actions require root access, which most users don't possess. An ordinary user can generally wipe out his or her own files, but not those of another user of the system and not those belonging to the system as a whole.

This final point is the most relevant to people using Linux as a desktop OS, and is the primary reason that posts to Usenet newsgroups from root accounts are often greeted with scorn, or at least admonitions to create and use an ordinary user account. My own system has an ordinary user account that I use for tasks such as Web browsing, reading email, writing, and so on. Suppose that I accidentally type a command such as

```
rm -r / home/rodsmith/dumbstuff
```

The intent was to delete a specific directory called dumbstuff but, because of a stray space, this command actually tells the system to wipe every file from all mounted filesystems. Linux will not let me do this *if* I'm logged on as an ordinary user. I'll wipe out all my own files if I don't catch the error in time, but I won't damage the system as a whole. If I do everything as root, though, I can wipe out the system. Linux can be cryptic to new users, and it doesn't always warn you that you're doing something dangerous, so you should definitely create and use an ordinary user account, even if you're using Linux as a desktop OS.

> **NOTE**
>
> Although I encourage you to use a user account whenever possible, most of the actions described in this book are system configuration actions, and therefore require that you be root to perform them. You can either log in directly as root or you can use the su command to gain root access. At a command prompt or xterm window, type **su**, and then press the Enter key. Linux prompts for a password. Enter the root password, and anything you type in that xterm or command prompt takes on root authority. If you're running in X, programs that are already running aren't affected by this.

Using `linuxconf`

Creating a user account is quite easy using linuxconf. Choose Config, Users accounts, Normal, User accounts to get the account list window (Figure 5.11). You can click an existing account to alter it or click Add to add a new one. Either way, linuxconf displays the User account creation tab shown in Figure 5.12 (it's called User information if you modify an existing account, though).

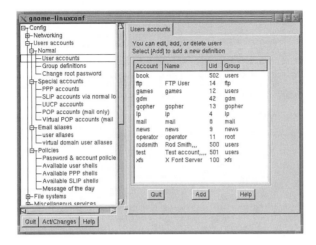

FIGURE 5.11

The User accounts tab shows all the usual user accounts, along with key information about them, such as their primary groups and user IDs.

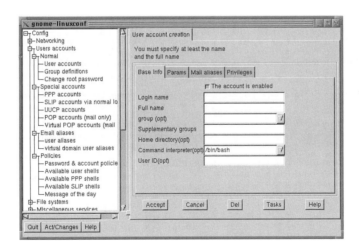

FIGURE 5.12

You can create an account by filling in a few pieces of information and clicking Accept.

The most important information for creating a new account or modifying an existing one is in the Base info subtab. You can enter the user's login name, full name, groups, home directory, shell, and user ID. For most of these fields, if you don't enter any information, linuxconf assigns an appropriate default value. For instance, the default group is a new group with the same name as the login name; and linuxconf assigns the first available user ID.

The additional subtabs on the User account creation tab provide additional options for fine-tuning the features of a user's account:

- Params tab—You can set parameters relating to password expiration here. By default, values of -1 or 99999 appear, indicating that the password won't expire. If you want to force users to change their passwords (which is a good policy in many environments), you can alter these values.

- Mail aliases—You can specify that mail coming into an account should be directed elsewhere, and you can set the name that appears on outgoing mail from an account to be something other than this account.

- Privileges—You can specify that the user be able or unable to perform certain administration-like actions, such as shutting down the computer or viewing system log files.

When you set up a Linux system as a server, and particularly as a file server, you need to consider how you'll implement security. These considerations interact with the options you set for user accounts, as described in "Account Creation Tips," later in this chapter.

When you click Accept to create the account, linuxconf prompts you to enter a password. You have to type it twice to be sure you typed it correctly.

Creating an Account with Text-Mode Tools

If you don't want to or can't use linuxconf, you can use fairly standard textual tools for creating accounts. The principal of these is useradd, generally located in /usr/sbin. To create an account with useradd, you must specify all the parameters on the command line, as in the following:

```
useradd -u 521 -g 100 -d /home/amy -s /bin/bash -p password amy
```

The options you're most likely to use with useradd are

- -u—Indicates the user ID to be assigned.
- -g—Indicates the group ID to be assigned.
- -d—Indicates the home directory.
- -s—Indicates the default shell.
- -p—Indicates the starting password.
- -D—Modifies an existing account rather than creates a new one (this option takes no additional parameters).

The username comes last on the line, without an identifying dashed option.

> **NOTE**
>
> Linux commands are case sensitive. This applies both to the command names them-
> selves and to their parameters. You may have noticed that useradd has both a -d
> option and a -D option, for instance, and specifying one when you meant the other
> can produce unpredictable results.

useradd has additional options. Type **man useradd** to learn more about it.

You can use the userdel command to remove a user account. It's much simpler than the
useradd command; userdel has only a single option, -r, which causes the system to remove
all the files from the user's account.

Account Creation Tips

Linux uses its concept of users for *all* file operations, including operations that originate from
remote computers using a file or printer sharing protocol. You should therefore consider
Linux's security model, and how you intend to work your network into that model.

Each file in Linux has three different sets of permissions, indicated by a string of 10 characters
or a 3- or 4-digit octal number, such as -rw-r--r--, 644, or 0644, respectively. In the 10-
character representation, the first character indicates special files, such as directories (d), and
the remaining 9 are three groups of three characters, which indicate the presence of *read* (r),
write (w), and *execute* (x) permissions for the file's owner, the file's group, and all other users.
The octal representation indicates the same information by encoding the read, write, and execute permissions as bits, resulting in a digit from 0 through 7 for the owner, the group, and all
permissions. Figure 5.13 illustrates this relationship for one triplet. Each file also possesses an
owner and a group, both normally set to the username and primary group of the user who created the file.

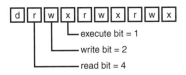

FIGURE 5.13
*Add the values for each bit to obtain the octal permissions value for each triplet—the owner, the group, and all other
users.*

This scheme allows a person creating a file to give tiered access to the file. For instance, the permissions string -rw-r----- (or 640, in octal representation) indicates that the owner can read from and write to the file, users in the file's group can read from but not write to the file, and nobody else can access the file. (One exception to this rule is that the root user has full read/write access to all files.)

Now, suppose you have a small network with three separate Windows computers, each of which has a different user, and a Linux server running Samba. You can use Samba to configure what permissions new files get, but you should consider security and user groups when you create accounts for your three network users. Here are some possible scenarios:

- Use a single username and password on all three Windows machines, with a single Linux account—This option is convenient and easy to configure, but it provides poor security, and there's no easy way to keep users' files separate from each other.

- Use separate accounts with a single group—You can create separate accounts for each user, but place them all in a single group. You can then configure Samba to create files with permissions of -rw-rw-r-- or -rw-r--r-- to provide read/write or read-only access to all users' accounts from other accounts, respectively. You might need to manually change the permissions on the users' home directories when you create them, though, because by default they get permissions of drwx------, which means that only the owner can access them. A setup like this can be good for sharing files among all users of the network.

- Use separate accounts with separate groups—You can create separate accounts for different users, along with two or more groups. For instance, you might place the users kohler and wundt in the group europe but the user james in the group usa. Depending on the group permissions Samba assigns to new files, kohler and wundt will be able to read and perhaps write each other's files, but you can lock out james. Because Linux allows you to assign a user to several groups, you can expand one user's access beyond the usual reach, if you like. For instance, you could turn the tables by adding europe to the list of groups to which james belongs, thus giving james access to kohler's and wundt's files, but restricting them from james' files.

The UNIX-style permissions used by Linux allow for considerable subtlety and flexibility, and you'll need to learn through practice just what this system can accomplish. If you set up one system but decide it's not working, you can change the system. You can alter permissions, ownership, and group status of files by using the chmod, chown, and chgrp commands, respectively. If necessary, you can change a user's primary group affiliation, and associate a user to additional groups by using linuxconf or by editing the /etc/passwd and /etc/group files. You can alter the permissions assigned to files by using the umask command or by altering the configuration for the file sharing server (such as Samba or Netatalk).

Finally, you can create both private and shared directories for file sharing. For instance, you can give each user a default directory (probably the same as the user's Linux home directory) for personal files, along with a separate shared directory for all users, containing shared data files or program files. In this way you can provide relatively free access to some files while maintaining security on other files.

Summary

Before you can configure the networking features you want on a Linux system, you need to have a working basic system. This chapter describes how to accomplish this goal. This book comes with a CD-ROM containing Red Hat Linux 6.0, and the first half of this chapter describes how to install it. The remainder of the chapter describes the most important configuration files and the `linuxconf` utility. You can use `linuxconf` to configure many aspects of a working Linux system by using a GUI environment, or even from a Web browser on a remote computer.

Compiling a Kernel for Networking

IN THIS CHAPTER

Here's a hypothetical but typical Usenet news exchange in certain Linux newsgroups in mid-1999, trimmed somewhat for brevity:

New Linuxer:	I can't get my NIC working in Linux. It's a LinkGear 10/100 PCI model, and I'm using Red Hat 6.0. How do I get this to work? Help!
Experienced Linuxer:	The LinkGear 10/100 uses a clone of the DEC Tulip chipset. This particular clone doesn't work well with the driver that comes with Red Hat 6.0. You'll need to get a new version of the driver and recompile your kernel or your kernel modules.
New Linuxer:	Okay, but how do I recompile the kernel?

This chapter is intended primarily to answer the new Linuxer's second question, but also to provide some insight into why you'd want to do it, even if your system seems to be running fine. I'll begin with the question of what is the benefit to compiling the kernel.

Understanding the Compile Process

If you're not very familiar with computer programming, you might not understand just what good compiling the kernel does. Linux is one of the few operating systems that allows the end user to compile a kernel. This is both a blessing and a curse, as described in this section.

Just What Is Compilation?

Humans understand words. Computers understand numbers. Compiling a computer program is the process of converting the words of a high-level computer language such as C or Pascal into the numbers that computers understand. There are actually several stages to the compilation process, but you don't need to be concerned with most of them specifically. In compiling a Linux kernel, you need to be concerned mostly with the configuration process and with the handful of commands you issue to start everything in motion and to use the end product—a fresh kernel, customized for *your* system.

Advantages and Disadvantages of Compiling Your Own Kernel

There are several very good reasons to compile your own kernel. Not all of them apply to every system, but many of them do, so I recommend that you do compile your own kernel. The reasons for compiling a custom kernel include

- Setting optimizations—You can tell the system to compile the kernel to know what type of CPU you have. This allows the kernel to run more efficiently, thus improving overall system performance. Similarly, you can customize networking and other options to optimize performance in specific areas, such as routing TCP/IP packets.

- Adding features—The precompiled kernels you can download and that come with distributions may or may not support the features you want. This is particularly true of advanced features such as IP masquerading. Also, some exotic drivers haven't made their way into the kernel, but you may want to add them yourself.

- Removing features—Precompiled kernels often includes features you *don't* want or need, such as FPU emulation for 386 CPUs. Removing these features can reduce the size of the kernel, thus saving RAM. For instance, the 2.2.5 kernel that ships with Red Hat 6.0 is 600KB in size, but the 2.2.5 kernel I compiled for my main Linux system immediately after installing Red Hat 6.0 is 500KB in size. As the kernel is stored on disk in a compressed form, this represents a RAM savings of something more than 100KB.

- Updating drivers—The people who write Linux kernel drivers eventually submit their drivers for inclusion in the Linux kernel as a whole, but it can sometimes take a while for updated drivers to make their way into the kernel. This is the situation that prompted the scenario outlined at the start of the chapter; the version of the `tulip.c` driver that works best with the latest clones of the Tulip Ethernet chipset isn't in the standard kernel source for kernel 2.2.5. Replacing one file and recompiling the kernel fixes problems associated with using many recent—and very popular—Ethernet boards.

- Experience—Sooner or later, if you stick with Linux, you *will* find that one of the preceding advantages becomes a necessity. Even if you don't need to compile a kernel now, you should try it and learn how it's done, so that you don't suffer from downtime when you need to compile a new kernel.

There are, of course, disadvantages to compiling your own kernel:

- Uniqueness—Chances are good that not many people will have a kernel compiled with precisely the features you selected, so if that configuration causes unique problems, you might have difficulty diagnosing the trouble.

- User error—If you accidentally leave out an important kernel driver, you might find that some feature doesn't work. You might spend some time trying to diagnose other parts of your system before you find the true cause of the trouble. I once spent an hour diagnosing a printer problem that had been caused by omitting a parallel-port driver in my previous kernel compile, two days before.

- Time—It *does* take time to compile a kernel, and if your system is working fine without taking this time, why bother? There's certainly a lot to be said for this factor, particularly for casual users.

Linux Kernel Versions

The Linux kernel is the core of the operating system. In fact, to be strictly accurate about it, the Linux kernel *is* Linux, and everything else that you probably think of as Linux is *not* part of Linux. The Linux kernel is the part of the operating system (OS) that handles the low-level operations—things like device drivers, memory management, filesystem access, multitasking, and so on. Things like the shell program in which you type commands, the daemons that provide networking services, the XFree86 implementation of the X Window System, and many others are not part of the kernel, and they were all developed independently of the kernel.

> **NOTE**
>
> Many of these non-kernel components were developed under the auspices of the Free Software Foundation, which uses the recursive acronym GNU's Not UNIX (GNU) to refer to its products. For this reason, some people use the term *GNU/Linux* when referring to a complete package of Linux and other components, such as Red Hat. This practice is particularly prevalent in reference to the Debian distribution. I use *Linux* alone in this book because it's shorter, is the more common usage, and is what Red Hat calls its product, which is included on the CD-ROM that accompanies this book.

Linux Kernel History

Each kernel is identified by three numbers, in the form *x.y.z*—for instance, 2.2.5, which is the version that ships with Red Hat Linux 6.0. In Linux, the second number of the triplet (the y in *x.y.z*) bears special interpretation. When y is even, the kernel is considered to be a "release" kernel. Of course, there may be bugs, but there shouldn't be many bugs. Just as important, there won't be major changes in the course of revisions reflected in the z number during a fixed y number's life. When y is odd, on the other hand, the kernel is considered a "development" kernel, meaning that it may have more bugs than a release kernel and, more importantly, developers will be working to produce potentially large changes from one z release to another.

In effect, what all this means is that at any time there are two most-current Linux kernels—a release kernel (in the 2.2 series as I write) and a development kernel (in the 2.3 series as I write). When the kernel developers (prime among them being Linus Torvalds, the kernel's originator) decide they've added enough features to a development kernel, they start concentrating on making it stable, and eventually distribute it under a release number.

NOTE

You might occasionally see references to "Linux 6.0" or some similar high number. Unless you're reading this book several years into the 21st century, such references are incorrect, and ̶ ̶ ̶ ̶ ̶ mangled references to a specific Linux distribution, such as Red Hat L ̶ ̶ ̶ ̶ ̶ ̶ ̶ ̶ ̶ ̶ ̶ ̶ ̶ ̶ ̶ ̶ ̶ ̶ ̶ ams, have their own numbering ̶ nel's—and each other's—number ̶ ̶ ̶ ̶ ̶

All other things bei ̶ ̶ ̶ ̶ ̶ ̶ ̶ ̶ ̶ ̶ ̶ ̶ ̶ ̶ ̶ he latest release series that you can. ̶ ̶ ̶ ̶ ̶ ̶ ̶ ̶ ̶ ̶ ̶ ̶ ̶ ̶ kernel appear on the FTP sites, though— ̶ ̶ ̶ ̶ ̶ ̶ ̶ ̶ ̶ ̶ won't be substantial enough to warrant t ̶ ̶ ̶ ̶ ̶ ̶ ̶ ̶ ̶ ̶ eboot your system. There's always a ch ̶ ̶ ̶ ̶ ̶ ̶

If you want to live ̶ ̶ ̶ ̶ ̶ ̶ ̶ ̶ ̶ ̶ ̶ ̶ ̶ ̶ ̶ ou might want to consider using a de ̶ ̶ ̶ ̶ ̶ ̶ ̶ ̶ ̶ ̶ ̶ ̶ ̶ ady experienced with Linux, though, or i ̶ ̶ ̶ ̶ ̶ ̶ ̶ ̶ ̶ ̶ ̶ orted in a release kernel. Even if you ̶ ̶ ̶ ̶ ̶ ̶ ̶ ̶ ̶ ̶ a release kernel, thus avoiding the possi ̶ ̶ ̶ ̶ ̶ ̶ ̶ ystem.

Obtaining ̶ ̶ ̶

Most Linux FTP ̶ ̶ ̶ ̶ ̶ ̶ ̶ ̶ ̶ ̶ ̶ ̶ ̶ ̶ ̶ kernel in either Red Hat Package Mar ̶ ̶ ̶ ̶ ̶ ̶ ̶ ̶ ̶ ̶ ̶ ̶ ̶ ̶ ends in `.tgz` or `.tar.gz`. I gener ̶ ̶ ̶ ̶ ̶ ̶ ̶ ̶ ̶ ̶ ̶ iles. Pick whichever you like.

If you get a tarb ̶ ̶ ̶ ̶ ̶ ̶ ̶ ̶ ̶ ̶ ̶ ̶ ̶ ̶ ̶ ̶ ̶ ̶ w these steps:

1. Change to ̶ ̶ ̶ ̶

   `cd /usr/ ̶`

2. Create a ̶ re installing kernel 2.2.9, typ ̶

   `mkdir linux-2.2.9`

3. If you already have Linux kernel source, there will probably be a symbolic link from its directory to `linux`. Remove that link by typing

   `rm linux`

4. Create a new symbolic link from the new directory by typing

   `ln -s linux-2.2.9 linux`

5. Extract the new kernel source files. If the tarball is in your home directory, type

   `tar xvzf ~/linux-2.2.9.tar.gz`

   (substituting the appropriate filename for the version you have).

You've now extracted the kernel.

If you get an RPM file, you need to download two files rather than one: `kernel-source` and `kernel-headers` (with appropriate version numbers and `.rpm` extensions). After you've done this, your task is somewhat easier than it is with a tarball; you just need to type

`rpm -Uvh kernel-source-2.2.9-1.i386.rpm kernel-headers-2.2.9-1.i386.rpm`

The filenames may vary from these, even if it's the 2.2.9 kernel source you're installing.

Setting Kernel Compile Options

After you've extracted the kernel source, you should change to the kernel source directory by typing

`cd /usr/src/linux`

You must then specify which of the many drivers and options you want to compile, and how. If you're using X, the easiest way to do this is by typing

`make xconfig`

which produces the Linux kernel configuration window shown in Figure 6.1. If you're not running X, you can type

`make menuconfig`

which produces a textual menu-driven configuration screen that provides the same options as does

`make xconfig`

Alternatively, you can type

`make config`

which causes the configuration scripts to prompt you for each and every option in a rigid sequence. All three of these methods are equivalent from the point of view of the end result: a configuration file that controls what features will be compiled into your kernel.

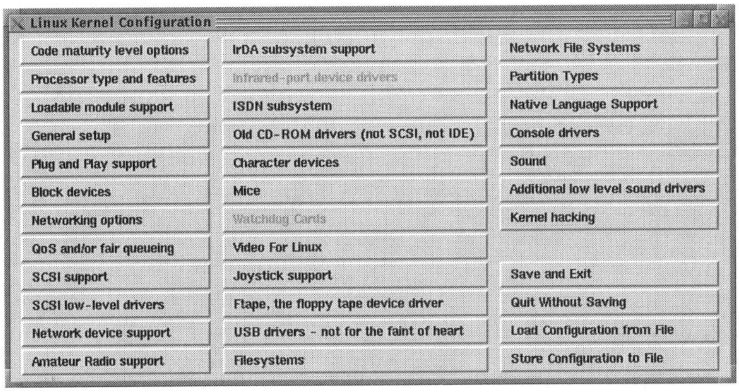

FIGURE **6.1**

Linux kernel configuration options are grouped into several categories, each of which has one button in the Linux Kernel Configuration window.

> **TIP**
>
> If you don't already know what *chipsets* (p. 18) your major devices use, locate this information before proceeding further. This is particularly critical for SCSI host adapters, network interface cards (NICs), and sound cards. You *do not* need information on your video card's chipset for kernel compilation, though. The video display is generally handled by XFree86, not by the kernel. (There is a move to add some video support to the kernel in the Video for Linux configuration area, but you can probably ignore this, especially for a server that's not likely to be used for console games.)

In many cases, specific kernel features have three options, labeled y, m, and n. (See Figure 6.2 for an example of a configuration window.) The first and last of these stand for yes and no, respectively, and refer to compiling the driver or feature directly into the monolithic kernel file. The m option refers to compilation as a module. A *kernel module* is a file that is physically separate from the kernel, but that the kernel can load into memory to supplement its own functions at will. There are two primary advantages to using modules over compiling the driver into the kernel proper. First, kernel modules can be loaded and unloaded as needed, and therefore do not have to occupy RAM when they're not needed. Second, kernel modules permit the creation of relatively compact kernel files with a slew of modules to support a wide variety of hardware. This second advantage is especially important to distribution providers such as Red Hat, but you might want to take advantage of this feature if you have several Linux computers with varying hardware. Rather than include support in the kernel for, say, 3COM, Intel, and D-Link Ethernet boards in three different computers, you can compile a kernel with no specific

Ethernet adapters, along with the three Ethernet drivers as modules. You can then use the same kernel and customize each machine's /etc/conf.modules file to have it use the appropriate module. This keeps the kernel small and avoids the possibility of a driver for nonexistent hardware causing problems with other drivers or with real hardware.

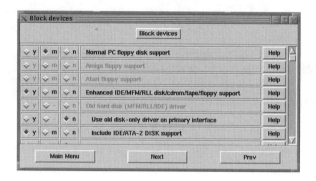

FIGURE 6.2
Configuration options that aren't available are grayed out; those that are available are displayed in black text.

The rest of this section covers some of the most important general and network-specific options in the Linux 2.2-series kernels. I don't cover all of the kernel options, however, because there are so many of them. I recommend that you set aside an hour or so to go through the kernel and click the Help button next to most of the kernel options. In this way you can learn something about these options.

NOTE

Available kernel options change every now and then, mostly during the course of development kernel changes, but also sometimes in release kernel series. If you're compiling a kernel that's newer or older than the 2.2.9 kernel I used as a reference in writing this section, you have to rely on the make xconfig or make menuconfig Help text or on additional sources of documentation. There have been substantial changes to certain options, including parallel port support and the kernel features required to do IP masquerading, from the 2.0-series kernels to the 2.2-series kernels, for instance. You're likely to encounter similar differences if you use a 2.3-series kernel or something newer.

Preliminary Options

The Code maturity level options, Processor type and features, Loadable module support, and General setup buttons on the configuration main menu provide options that are of general interest and that, in some cases, determine what options are available elsewhere in the kernel. These options include

- Prompt for development and/or incomplete code/drivers—Even release-level kernels often contain drivers that are considered experimental. If you select y for this option, you can include these experimental drivers. Some of the networking features described in this book are considered experimental, so I recommend selecting y to this option.

- Processor family—You can select which of several broad classes of x86 CPU you have.

- Math emulation—Linux includes a math coprocessor emulator. You need this emulator only if you have a 386, 486SX, or an early NexGen Nx586 CPU without a matched FPU chip.

- Loadable module support—Select y here, or you won't be able to compile any drivers as modules.

- Kernel module loader—Select y here to allow the kernel to search for and load appropriate modules when it needs them.

- Networking support—Select y here.

- Kernel support for ELF binaries—Executable and Linkable Format (ELF) is the current format for Linux executable files. You *must* have this support, so select y.

- Parallel port support—Set this to m or y if you want to use parallel port devices such as printers or parallel-port Zip drives. When you turn on this option, you'll be able to set the *types* of ports you support, too. On an x86 computer, PC-style hardware is all that's required.

Block Devices

Block devices are those that exchange data in blocks. These are primarily disk drives, but some devices associated with disks (such as SCSI host adapters) have their own configuration screens. Block device options include the following:

- Enhanced IDE/MFM/RLL disk/cdrom/tape/floppy support—If you run the system off EIDE hard disks, select y here. If you have EIDE/ATAPI devices such as CD-ROMs but boot off of a SCSI hard disk, you can compile this as a module instead.

- Include IDE/ATAPI *{device}* support—There are a series of options for specific devices on the menu. Select m or y for any you have. You must select y for hard disks if you boot off an EIDE hard disk.

- Chipset support—A large number of options enable extensions and bug fixes for specific EIDE controllers (many of which are integrated into motherboard chipsets). If you don't know what controller your system uses, it would be wise to select any of these options that includes the word *bugfix* because these options work around bugs in the hardware that can cause data corruption. These bug fixes won't interfere with normal operation if you don't have an afflicted controller.

- Loopback device support—Linux supports mounting a file as if it were a device. This is known as a *loopback device* and is useful for testing CD-ROM images you create with mkisofs, preparing floppies entirely on the hard disk before copying them to floppy, and so on.

> **TIP**
>
> You can use Linux's loopback device support to serve several CD-ROMs simultaneously and to improve CD-ROM access speed if you have sufficient disk space to store multiple CD-ROM images.

- Network block device support—If you select this option, you'll be able to directly mount devices from remote servers. This is different from mounting a filesystem exported via a protocol such as Network File System (NFS); your computer will directly manipulate the external device. This option is useful only if you have two or more Linux or UNIX computers on the network; if you're configuring a single Linux computer as a server for Windows or Macintosh machines, you can select n to this option.

- Multiple devices driver support—This option enables redundant array of independent disks (RAID) support, which can be used for very fast servers with multiple SCSI disks.

- Parallel port IDE device support—Select this option and the appropriate suboptions if you have tapes, CD-ROMs, and so on that interface through the parallel port.

Networking Options

The Networking options group contains some of the most important options for configuring a Linux network server:

- Network firewalls—Select y here if you want your Linux computer to serve as a firewall or an IP masquerading computer, as described in Part VI, "Linking Your Intranet to the Internet." This option enables the kernel to serve as a packet-filtering firewall, which filters network packets based on rudimentary information such as the source address. The more complex proxy firewalls don't need this kernel option.

- TCP/IP networking—Select y for this option.

- IP: advanced router—Select y here if you want to configure your Linux box as a router. You'll then be able to enable a number of more specific routing features. You do not need this option to use IP masquerading, however.

- IP: firewalling—This is a second firewall option. You need to select it, as well as Network firewalls, in order to do IP masquerading.

- IP: always defragment—This option reassembles network packets that have been split during their network travels. You need to select y here to use IP masquerading. In most other cases, you should select n.

- IP: masquerading—Select y if you want to perform IP masquerading, as described in Chapter 20, "One IP Address, Many Computers: IP Masquerading." Several subsequent options allow you to enable support for masquerading specific types of network traffic. Select the ones you think you might need, or all of them if you're not sure which you'll need.

- IP: optimize as router not host—If your system will serve primarily as a router, select y to this option; otherwise, select n.

- AppleTalk DDP—Select y or m if you want your computer to function as an AppleTalk server or client. You also need the Netatalk or afpfs packages, respectively.

- Bridging—Your Linux box can serve as a *bridge* (p. xxx) between two Ethernet segments if you enable this option.

SCSI Support

The SCSI support and SCSI low-level drivers areas list options for SCSI device types (such as disk, tape, and CD-ROM) and specific SCSI host adapters, respectively. If your system boots from a SCSI hard disk, both the SCSI disk support option and the option for your specific model of host adapter must be present in the kernel—that is, compiled with y, not with m. You can compile all other SCSI options as modules if you like.

Network Device Support

The Network device support area includes low-level drivers for most NICs and other network interfaces, such as PPP.

TIP

If your system has two NICs that use the same driver, you might find that it's easier to configure Linux to recognize them both if you compile the Ethernet driver directly into the kernel, not as a module. On the other hand, if you have two NICs that use *different* drivers, you'll probably find that compiling them both as modules gives you greater flexibility.

Network device options include the following:

- Network device support—Select y for this top-level option.
- Ethernet (10 or 100Mbit)—If you're using an Ethernet network, select y. Some drivers appear immediately under this heading, others are grouped in various ways that aren't entirely consistent, so you might have to hunt for your specific driver. Specific option groups include the following:
    - 3COM cards—An entire Ethernet card group is devoted to 3COM cards. Select y here and choose your card if you have a 3COM model.
    - Western Digital/SMC cards—As with 3COM, there's an entire section devoted to Western Digital and SMC boards.
    - Other ISA cards—This area lists an assortment of ISA NICs. If yours is an ISA board, it may be listed in this section. If you have an ISA board but have no clue what it is, try the NE2000/NE1000 driver; many ISA boards are NE2000 compatible, and so work with this driver.
    - EISA, VLB, PCI and on board controllers—An assortment of EISA, VLB, and PCI card chipsets appear here. Some of these are integrated on motherboards, as well.
- PLIP (parallel port) support—If you want to connect two computers via their parallel ports rather than via Ethernet, choose y or m here. You will also have to select Parallel port support in the General setup area.
- PPP (point-to-point) support—Choose y or m here to use PPP to connect to your ISP via a modem.
- SLIP (serial line) support—Choose y or m here to use SLIP to connect to your ISP via a modem. SLIP is largely obsolete. It is used as an intermediary protocol in doing dial-on-demand networking with PPP, however, as described in Chapter 8, "Using PPP for Dialup Connections."
- Token Ring driver support—If you have a Token Ring card, select y for this option and for the appropriate Token Ring board.

Character Devices

Character devices send and receive data one character at a time. This contrasts with block devices such as hard disks, which transfer data in multibyte blocks. Character device options include the following:

- Virtual terminal— Linux maintains several *virtual terminals* to let you switch easily between multiple running programs and even complete X configurations. Select y for this option.

- Standard/generic (dumb) serial support—Select y or m here to use the serial ports on your motherboard, most plug-in one- or two-port serial boards, or an internal modem.

- Parallel printer support—Select y or m if you have a printer connected to the parallel port. You'll also need to select y or m to Parallel port support in the General setup area.

- Mouse Support (not serial mice)—Select y here if you have a bus mouse or a PS/2 mouse.

Mice

If you have a PS/2 mouse or a bus mouse, this area lets you enable drivers for specific types of mouse devices.

Filesystems

One of the great advantages of Linux as a server is that it supports so many other operating systems' filesystems. This isn't very important for a server's hard disks, but it can be for handling removable drives. If your network has mostly Windows computers except for a Linux server, you can read Macintosh 1.44MB floppies and removable disks on the Linux server, for instance. The filesystem options are split across the Filesystems, Network File Systems, Partition Types, and Native Language Support areas. Supported Linux filesystems and filesystem options include

- Quota support—You can limit the amount of disk space each individual user has if you select this option.

- Apple Macintosh filesystem support—This driver supports the Macintosh Hierarchical Filesystem (HFS) format, but not the more recent HFS+. Because HFS+ isn't normally used on floppies or other removable media, this lack isn't normally important.

NOTE

You can read Macintosh 1.44MB floppies on a PC, but not the older 800KB or 400KB floppies. These older floppies use a unique method of low-level encoding, and standard PC hardware can't read that encoding. Apple switched to the same encoding scheme used by PCs with the Macintosh's 1.44MB floppies, but kept HFS rather than the PC's File Allocation Table (FAT) filesystem.

> **CAUTION**
>
> Linux's HFS support is considered experimental in the 2.2 series kernels. This means you may lose data if you try writing files to HFS media. In my experience, the Linux driver is reliable enough for occasional use on removable media, but I recommend keeping backups of all files on such disks. Similar comments apply to other experimental filesystems, though some are more reliable than others.

- DOS FAT fs support—FAT is the name given to both the basic DOS and Windows filesystem and a data structure on that filesystem. FAT comes in 12-, 16-, and 32-bit varieties, the latter having been introduced as FAT-32 late in the Windows 95 lifetime. Linux autodetects which of these varieties is in use, so you needn't concern yourself with that detail.

  Linux includes support for three filesystems based on FAT: MS-DOS, UMSDOS, and VFAT. MS-DOS restricts you to filenames of eight characters with a three-character extension (called *8.3 filenames*); UMSDOS places hidden structures on the disk to create UNIX-style permissions, ownership, and long filenames; and VFAT creates long filenames in the same way Windows does, for easy exchange of documents between Windows and Linux. You can select any or all of these filesystem options.

- ISO 9660 CDROM filesystem support—Select y or m here to read and write CD-ROMs, including CD-ROMs that use the Rock Ridge extensions that are common in the Linux community. If you also select the subsequent Microsoft Joliet CDROM extensions option, you'll be able to read the long filenames on CD-ROMs burned for Windows.

- NTFS filesystem support—You can read and write NTFS partitions using this option, although the write support is quite dangerous, as of kernel 2.2.9. Because Windows NT uses FAT for floppies and other removable media, you probably won't need this option unless your computer dual-boots between Linux and Windows NT.

- OS/2 HPFS filesystem support—As with NTFS, you probably don't need HPFS unless your system dual-boots between Linux and OS/2.

- /proc filesystem support—Select y to this option. It enables a special pseudo-filesystem that gives you and Linux programs easy access to assorted low-level hardware information, such as disk driver options and interrupts used by various devices.

- Second extended fs support—This option enables support for the second extended filesystem, or *ext2fs* as it's more commonly known. This is the standard Linux filesystem, so you *must* select y (not m) to this option to use most Linux systems.

- UFS filesystem support—UFS is the filesystem used by FreeBSD, SunOS, NeXTSTEP, and some other UNIX OSs. Select this option if you want to exchange removable media with these systems. Write support for UFS is experimental, so be cautious about using it.

- NFS filesystem support—NFS is what UNIX systems use for network file sharing. Select y or m here to allow Linux to mount such networked filesystems.

- NFS server support—If you want your Linux box to act as a server of NFS filesystems, you should select y or m to this option.

- SMB filesystem support—Select y or m here if you want your Linux box to be able to mount filesystems exported by Windows or OS/2 computers. You don't need this option to export your Linux filesystems to Windows computers; for that, you need the Samba package (SMB), which is a daemon that runs outside the kernel.

NOTE

Network filesystems such as NFS and SMB describe file transfer across the network, not file structures on a hard disk. A Linux server can serve any disk-based filesystem it supports via either NFS or SMB, and can even re-export a filesystem; for instance, you can mount a filesystem via NFS and then export it via SMB. Similarly, if you mount a remote filesystem, it could originate as ext2fs, FAT, NTFS, or something else.

- Partition Types—PCs use a particular method to break a hard disk into multiple partitions, but other methods are possible, and are in fact used by other computers. You can tell Linux to understand some such systems, which can be handy if you want to swap an entire hard disk from such a computer or if a removable disk has been partitioned on such a computer.

- Native Language Support—VFAT and Joliet support relies on support for assorted codepages and ISO encodings to record non-ASCII characters in filenames. You can add support for such encodings in the Linux kernel or as modules.

Compiling and Installing a Kernel

Now that you've selected the kernel options, the hard part is over—for you. Your computer has yet to do any substantial work, but it will, as soon as you issue the appropriate commands. Then you'll install the new kernel and reboot the computer to use the new kernel.

Compiling the Kernel

There are four steps for compiling the kernel:

1. Type

   `make clean; make dep`

   This step ensures that any old files or configuration features are swept away. Sometimes stray configurations can cause problems, such as not allowing modules to work properly.

2. Type

   `make zImage`

   or

   `make bzImage`

   to compile the kernel proper. These commands mostly do the same things, but they differ in their output formats. The `zImage` file is an older kernel format that's still in common use. `bzImage` is similar to `zImage` but uses a different method for loading the kernel. The advantage of `bzImage` is that this format permits loading of a larger kernel than does `zImage`. Especially since moving to the 2.2-series kernels, kernel images have become so large that it's not uncommon to see LILO refuse to install a kernel that's compiled as a `zImage`.

   After you type the `make` command, you'll see a large number of messages appear onscreen. Depending on your system, these messages scroll by for anywhere from a few minutes to an hour or more. If all finishes well, the last few lines above the command prompt contain information on the root device, boot sector, and system size. If the compiler had problems, you see error messages, but this is quite rare unless you've modified the kernel in some way.

> **TIP**
>
> If you've tried patching a kernel with a newer version of an existing driver or with an entirely new driver, be careful about end-of-line characters. Windows and Linux use different conventions for how to end a line, and if you downloaded source code `.c` or `.h` files on a Windows computer, they may have inappropriate line endings to which the Linux `gcc` compiler objects. You can use many Linux text editors to correct the problem by doing a search and replace on the offending characters, or you can use the `dos2unix` command to do the conversion if this utility is installed on your system.

Compiling a Kernel for Networking

CHAPTER 6

155

6

COMPILING A
KERNEL FOR
NETWORKING

3. Type

```
make modules
```

This command compiles the kernel modules. As with the previous step, you'll see a large number of compiler commands scroll by onscreen. If all finishes without error, you see no error messages in the final few lines.

> **NOTE**
>
> Some programs, including some kernel modules, produce compiler *warnings*, which are not errors. Don't be concerned if you see the word *warning* in the compiler's output.

4. Type

```
make modules_install
```

This command installs the module files where the kernel can find them, in /usr/lib/modules/*x.y.z*, where *x.y.z* is the kernel version (Red Hat kernel source RPMs often have a fourth number, separated from the first three by a dash [-]).

> **CAUTION**
>
> If you're recompiling a kernel of the same version that you already have, I recommend moving the existing kernel modules to a safe location before issuing the `make modules_install` command. For instance, you could type something like
>
> `mv /usr/lib/modules/2.2.9 /usr/lib/modules/2.2.9-working`
>
> That way, if you experience problems, you can use an emergency boot floppy to restore the old kernel modules and reboot with the old kernel.

Preparing to Use the Compiled Kernel

After you've compiled the kernel, you need to tell your system about it so that you can use the new kernel when you reboot. In a Red Hat Linux system, there are two ways you can do this: with linuxconf and manually.

Using `linuxconf`

You type **linuxconf** at a command prompt to start the linuxconf utility. You can then select Config, boot mode, LILO, a kernel you have compiled to get the configuration menu shown in Figure 6.3.

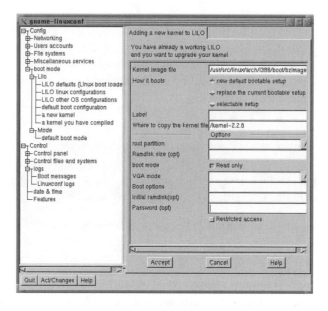

FIGURE 6.3

The linuxconf *utility lets you move a kernel file and configure LILO in a single operation.*

You should change some of the default values chosen by linuxconf:

- How it boots—By default, linuxconf makes the new kernel the new default. You can instead select to replace the current kernel or make the new kernel an additional option in the LILO setup. I recommend the first or last option because replacing the current kernel could result in disaster if the new kernel doesn't work as you expect.

- Label—You must give your kernel image a LILO boot: prompt name, so that you can select it when you reboot.

- Where to copy the kernel file—You should change this field to read /boot, or make it a subdirectory under /boot, unless you have a specific reason to place the kernel somewhere else.

- root partition—Type in the root partition's identifier, such as /dev/hda2, or select it from the pop-up menu of choices.

TIP

If you can't remember the root partition's device name, type **df** / in an xterm window. Linux responds with the name of the root partition's device, along with statistics on that partition, such as free disk space.

- Boot options—If you need to pass any options to the kernel at boot time, enter them here.

After you've entered these changes, click Accept, and linuxconf asks for confirmation that you want to change the boot process. Click Yes to have linuxconf activate these changes. You can now exit from linuxconf and reboot the system, as described shortly.

Manual Preparation

On an x86 system, the fresh kernel file appears in the /usr/src/linux/arch/i386/boot direc-tory, under the filename zImage or bzImage, depending on which variety you compiled. Standard practice is to move or copy the kernel file into the /boot directory. I find it helpful to give the kernel an extended name that includes the kernel version number and possibly some sort of coding to indicate any special features I've compiled into it. For instance, I might issue the command

```
mv /usr/src/linux/arch/i386/boot/zImage /boot/zImage-2.2.9-ntfswrite
```

to move the kernel and identify it as version 2.2.9 with NTFS read/write support.

After you've moved the kernel into its usual location, it's time to configure LILO for the new kernel. You do this by loading /etc/lilo.conf into your favorite editor and creating a new entry. For instance, suppose the existing /etc/lilo.conf file looks like this:

```
boot=/dev/hda2
map=/boot/map
install=/boot/boot.b
prompt
timeout=50
image=/boot/zImage-2.2.8-std
        label=linux
        root=/dev/hda8
        read-only
```

One easy way to create an entry for a new kernel is to copy an existing one. In the preceding sample, the one and only entry is the last four lines (you may have more lines, but probably not fewer, in an entry). Select them and copy them, so that your file looks like this:

```
boot=/dev/hda2
map=/boot/map
install=/boot/boot.b
prompt
timeout=50
image=/boot/zImage-2.2.8-std
        label=linux
        root=/dev/hda8
        read-only
```

```
image=/boot/zImage-2.2.8-std
        label=linux
        root=/dev/hda8
        read-only
```

You can then modify the first copy or the second, depending on which you want to be the default (the first entry becomes the default unless you explicitly specify otherwise). You need to modify two lines: the `image=` line and the `label=` line. Give the complete path to the new kernel for the former, and a complete boot label for the latter. You might end up with something that looks like this:

```
boot=/dev/hda2
map=/boot/map
install=/boot/boot.b
prompt
timeout=50
image=/boot/zImage-2.2.8-std
        label=linux
        root=/dev/hda8
        read-only
image=/boot/bzImage-2.2.9-ntfswrite
        label=ntfs
        root=/dev/hda8
        read-only
```

You should then save the file and exit your editor. Finally, type **LILO** to install the new LILO on your system. You'll see messages something like this:

```
Added linux *
Added ntfs
```

The asterisk (*) at the end of the first line indicates that this is the default LILO boot option.

Rebooting Your System

Before rebooting, ensure that you've done the following:

- Moved the kernel to its new home (`linuxconf` does this automatically, if you used it)

- Run `lilo`, not just edited `/etc/lilo.conf` (again, `linuxconf` does this automatically)

- Typed both **make modules** and **make modules_install**, in addition to **make zImage** or **make bzImage**

> **CAUTION**
>
> If your system is being used by other people, as a server likely is, you should alert them to the fact that you're going to reboot the computer. If you fail to do this, those users could lose work and become understandably annoyed.

When you're sure you've prepared the new kernel and alerted all your users that the system is going down, you can reboot by typing **/sbin/shutdown now -r**. This command shuts down the system and immediately reboots it. There are variants on this command, including versions that halt the system so you can shut it off or that shut it down at some time in the future. Type **man shutdown** to learn more about these variants.

When the system reboots, press the Tab key when the LILO boot: prompt appears. You should see your new kernel in the list. Type its name and then press the Enter key, or just press the Enter key if the new kernel is the default, and it will load. If you made important changes to its drivers or other options, you might want to watch the display for clues that those changes took effect as you intended, but be aware that kernel messages often fly past too quickly to read.

> **TIP**
>
> You can view the kernel messages after you've booted by typing **dmesg**. You may want to combine this with the less page viewer or with a search for a specific key-word, as in
>
> ```
> dmesg | less
> ```
>
> or
>
> ```
> dmesg | grep eth -
> ```
>
> The former lets you read kernel messages one page at a time, and the latter displays any kernel message line that contains the string eth (used to identify Ethernet drivers).

After you boot the new kernel, you should test the system's basic and important functionality. For instance, if you're trying a new Ethernet driver, try using the associated device. Test that you can print, use your modem, read all your filesystems, and so on. When you're satisfied that everything's working as it should, you can go on to other things.

Alternative Methods of Booting

Although LILO is the most common method of booting Linux, it's not the only one. Two other methods are particularly useful:

- Boot floppy—If you copy a Linux kernel directly to a floppy, you can insert the floppy at boot time and, if your computer is configured to check the floppy for a boot sector before it checks the hard disk, you'll boot the Linux kernel. If you want to test your Linux kernel in this way before installing it in LILO, you need a blank floppy disk. If it hasn't been formatted, insert it and type **fdformat /dev/fd0H1440** to do the job. (This command assumes that the disk is a 1.44MB 3.5-inch floppy. You need to use a different device file if it's another type of floppy.) When the floppy formatting is finished, type **dd if=/usr/src/linux/arch/i386/boot/zImage of=/dev/fd0** to copy the kernel file to the floppy. You can then reboot to test the kernel and, if it works to your satisfaction, modify the LILO configuration, or just keep using the boot floppy if you prefer.

- LOADLIN.EXE—The DOS program LOADLIN.EXE, found in the dosutils directory on the CD-ROM accompanying this book, can boot Linux from a DOS boot floppy or partition. You can copy the kernel to a DOS floppy by inserting one in the floppy drive and typing **mcopy /usr/src/linux/arch/i386/boot/zImage a:**, or by mounting the DOS floppy and using Linux's standard file copying tools. You should use similar commands to copy LOADLIN.EXE to the DOS disk. After booting DOS, type **LOADLIN ZIMAGE root=/dev/ hda8 ro** to boot the kernel file ZIMAGE, using /dev/hda8 as the root partition. As with the boot floppy method, you can modify LILO if you're satisfied with the results, or you can continue to use LOADLIN.EXE to boot Linux.

Summary

Compiling a new kernel is a basic skill that every Linux administrator should possess. Compiling a custom kernel lets you optimize the kernel for your hardware and your intended uses of the computer. Most of the work involved in compiling a kernel comes in deciding what options to include in the kernel. This chapter covers the options that are most important in building a kernel for a Linux server, but you should investigate the other options, too.

As you've learned in this chapter, after you've compiled a kernel, you can install it by modifying your LILO configuration, either by using linuxconf or by editing the /etc/lilo.conf file manually. You can then run lilo to configure the system to use the new kernel when you reboot, either by default or by explicitly selecting it at boot time.

Setting Ethernet Options

IN THIS CHAPTER

A networked computer must know five pieces of information about itself and its immediate network environment in order to function properly:

- Its machine name—This is the human-readable name of a computer, such as `gingko.biloba.com` or `www.linux.org`. Although this is the name with which you as a human work, it's actually the *least* important piece of information from the computer's point of view.

- Its Internet Protocol (IP) address—The IP address, as discussed in Chapter 4, "Intranets and the Internet," is critical to network communications on any TCP/IP network.

- Its network interface—Your computer needs to know on which network interface to "talk." This is particularly true of routers, which have multiple interfaces, but it's also true of other computers, as you'll learn in this chapter.

- Its gateway machine—Unless you're running a strictly private network for local services, you need to specify a gateway, which is a machine that serves as a router between your computer and the Internet as a whole.

- Its DNS servers—The Domain Name Service (DNS) runs on a computer and delivers the IP addresses that correspond to machine names for every computer on the Internet, as discussed in Chapter 4. Although you can get by without DNS services for many operations by specifying the IP address directly or by including the machine names you need in your `/etc/hosts` file, it's generally much simpler to tell your computer about some DNS machines.

Traditionally, administrators have supplied these five pieces of information to their computers by entering them into configuration files. This approach is still popular, but many networks now use a service known as *Dynamic Host Configuration Protocol* (DHCP) to do the job. On a network using DHCP, a DHCP server holds the configuration information for all the other computers on the network, and the server dishes this information out when the network's other computers boot. Linux can be configured to use DHCP, as discussed later in this chapter. Linux can also function as a DHCP server, as I briefly discuss in the section "Using DHCP for Dynamic Configuration," later in this chapter.

If you use PPP to link to an ISP, you have to enter some of this configuration information manually, but PPP includes the ability to dynamically configure some parts of your computer's identity. You'll learn about PPP configuration in Chapter 8, "Using PPP for Dialup Connections."

> **NOTE**
>
> You can configure a Linux computer to have two or more identities—two machine names, two IP addresses, and so on. In some cases, you can associate these two identities with two network interfaces, such as two network interface cards (NICs) or a NIC and a Point-to-Point Protocol (PPP) link. If you then configure the computer to transfer IP traffic from one interface to another, the computer has become a router (p. 87) or some similar device. IP masquerading and firewalling are two applications of this basic principle, and both are covered in Part VI, "Linking Your Intranet to the Internet."

Obtaining the Necessary Information

Before you proceed with configuring your system, you must obtain some vital information. If you're configuring a local network, you can generate this information yourself, but if you're connecting to a larger network within your organization, or if you're connecting to an Internet service provider (ISP) via a digital subscribe line (DSL) link or something similar, you need to obtain this information from your network manager or ISP. If you're configuring *both* a local network and a link to the Internet as a whole, you might need to both generate information and obtain it elsewhere.

If you're configuring your system manually (that is, not by using DHCP), you need the following information:

- The machine name (both the host name and the domain name)
- The IP address
- The network mask
- The network's gateway machine
- The network's DNS servers

If you don't know what these terms mean, don't worry; I describe them later in this chapter. For now, just get the information from your network manager or ISP. If you're configuring your own local network, the descriptions provided later will allow you to generate appropriate values or bypass the need for them.

If you're using DHCP, you probably need to give your network manager the Ethernet address (also known as the Media Access Control, or MAC, address) for your Ethernet board. This address is a 6-byte number, often expressed in hexadecimal form with colons between bytes, such as 00:80:C6:F9:3B:BA. It is often printed on a sticker on the board. If you can't find it, you can get it from Linux after you've installed the network device driver. In fact, before you proceed further, you should ensure that you have this driver installed and configured.

Network Driver Configuration

If you compiled your Ethernet drivers into the kernel itself, they are automatically assigned to devices, and you can check these assignments by typing **dmesg ¦ grep eth -**. For instance, here's the result of typing this command on my system:

```
eth0: Lite-On 82c168 PNIC rev 32 at 0xdc00, 00:A0:CC:24:BA:02, IRQ 10.
eth0:  MII transceiver #1 config 3100 status 7829 advertising 01e1.
eth1: Macronix 98715 PMAC rev 32 at 0xda00, 00:80:C6:F9:3B:BA, IRQ 9.
```

These lines indicate that I have a Lite-On 82c168 chipset serving as eth0 and a Macronix 98715 chipset going by the name eth1. These both happen to be Tulip clone chipsets, but that's unimportant; the dmesg command returns this information, allowing me to identify which board is which. I can then use ifconfig to link the appropriate board to the correct IP address.

> **NOTE**
>
> If you have two identical NICs, you might not be able to distinguish them easily from the dmesg output. If that's the case, it's probably easiest to simply guess which is which. If your network doesn't work as you expect, swap the network cables and try again.

If you've compiled the kernel so that your Ethernet drivers are in modules, you need to edit the /etc/conf.modules file to link your boards to the appropriate interfaces. For instance, here's what you might do to link a Tulip board to eth0 and a 3COM EtherLink XL board to eth1:

```
alias eth0 tulip
alias eth1 3c59x
```

When the system boots, it reads /etc/conf.modules and links the named modules to the appropriate interfaces. Use the names of the Linux module files (in /lib/modules/x.y.z/net, where x.y.z is the kernel version) for the drivers at the ends of these lines.

> **TIP**
>
> If you don't know the names of the kernel modules, try running the kernel configuration routine described in Chapter 6, "Compiling a Kernel for Networking." Read the Help screen for the driver of your choice; it should list the module name. If you don't know which of the drivers is appropriate, try examining the board for an indication of the chipset manufacturer. You can also check for recent newsgroup postings concerning your make and model of board on `http://www.deja.com`.

If one or more of your Ethernet cards is an ISA model, you might need to specify the cards' I/O addresses in `/etc/conf.modules`, as well. Here's an example:

```
alias eth0 tulip
alias eth1 ne
options ne io=0x240
```

This example loads a PCI Tulip-based board as `eth0` and an ISA NE2000 clone as `eth1` on I/O port 0x240. Failing to specify the I/O port on ISA boards can be dangerous because probing for ISA Ethernet boards can disrupt other hardware, potentially causing the system to hang.

If you have two or more interfaces that use the same driver and want to use modular drivers, you should list them both in `/etc/conf.modules`. For instance, if you have two Tulip-based boards, you can use the following to configure them:

```
alias eth0 tulip
alias eth1 tulip
```

These lines automatically assign `eth0` and `eth1` to the boards in the order that Linux locates them, much as if the drivers had been compiled into the kernel.

> **TIP**
>
> Configuring Ethernet board drivers is sometimes tricky, particularly if you have two NICs. If you can't get your system to recognize the boards, try recompiling the kernel and placing the NIC drivers in the kernel itself if they were compiled as modules or as modules if they were compiled into the kernel. You can also try splitting the drivers, one in the kernel and one as a module, if you have two boards that use different drivers. NIC initialization can vary depending on the location of the driver, so moving it in or out of the kernel can sometimes clear up problems.

Configuring a System with a Fixed Address

When you configure a Linux computer for networking, one of the things you must do is build a set of links between the assorted names and interfaces of the computer. Ultimately, you want to be able to access your own computer, and other computers, by using a machine name, such as gingko.biloba.com, and have the computer link that name to the appropriate IP address and network interface. This doesn't happen automatically, however; you must create these links by telling the computer which identifiers apply to it. In fact, you must build a sort of trail of crumbs for the computer to follow, leading from the computer name to the IP address to the Ethernet interface.

This section describes how to set up this trail of crumbs, using Linux text-mode configuration files. This method gives you the greatest flexibility, but it's also the hardest way to do it. If you prefer to configure your Red Hat or Mandrake system more quickly, you can do so with the linuxconf utility, as described later in this chapter.

Setting the Machine Name

Many programs and components of Linux expect the computer to have a proper machine name. This is true even when networking doesn't come into play, so you can run into problems if your machine name isn't set properly. For instance, the XEmacs editor expects to be able to find a machine name, and if it can't find one, it will take a long time to start up. Several programs that run during system startup, such as the sendmail mail daemon, also expect to find a proper machine name and pause for a minute or more if they can't find one. If your machine name isn't set properly and you experience this pause, you might think that your system has hung during the boot process.

Parts of the Machine Name

A machine name has two components:

- The *host name*—This is a single word, usually all lowercase, that contains no periods. Examples of host names are gingko in the name gingko.biloba.com and www in www.linux.org.

- The *domain name*—This is the part of the complete network name that comes after the host name, as in biloba.com or linux.org. Some machines may have longer domain names than these. For instance, the computer n400.erplab.pangaea.edu has the host-name n400 and the domain name erplab.pangaea.edu.

> **NOTE**
>
> Valid characters for machine names are letters (a–z), numbers (0–9), and the dash (-).
> Other characters, including the underscore (_) are not valid characters for TCP/IP
> machine names; however, these may be valid in other environments, such as in
> NetBIOS.

It's easy to take the fully qualified domain name (FQDN) that's used to address the computer
from anywhere on the Internet and generate the separate host and domain names. Just split the
name at the first period, and it's done.

The Many References to the Machine Name

If you want to configure your computer manually, you have to edit several files to completely
set the machine name:

- `/etc/HOSTNAME`—This file contains the FQDN, such as `gingko.biloba.com`. Many programs access it to obtain the computer's name, and the initialization scripts in some distributions access this file for the same purpose. In some distributions, such as Debian,
  this file appears in lowercase (`/etc/hostname`) rather than uppercase; but in Red Hat 6.0,
  it's uppercase.

- Initialization files—One or more of the initialization files in the `/etc` directory (perhaps
  in `/etc/rc.d`, if that subdirectory exists on your system) contains a call to the `hostname`
  program. In Red Hat Linux 6.0, this file is `/etc/rc.d/rc.sysinit`, and `rc.sysinit` uses
  a definition in `/etc/sysconfig/network` to set the hostname. If you're using Red Hat
  6.0, you can therefore change the hostname by editing `/etc/sysconfig/network` and
  altering the line that begins `HOSTNAME=`. Other distributions may place the call to
  `hostname` elsewhere, such as in `/etc/rc.inet1`. Some distributions use the contents of
  `/etc/HOSTNAME` to set the machine name in their initialization files (Debian does this, for
  instance).

- `/etc/hosts`—This file sets IP addresses and names for remote computers, in addition to
  the machine name. Because of its multipurpose nature, I describe this file separately.

Note that you can set only a single machine name using the `/etc/HOSTNAME` file and other initialization files. This might seem limiting if your computer resides on two networks, such as
your private internal network and your cable company's cable modem network. This limitation
usually is not a major problem, though, because the host name you set in these files is used primarily to identify your computer to itself and to set identifying information on outgoing communications, such as email headers. Chances are that you want a single hostname on these
communications—those associated with the larger network. You should therefore probably set

this hostname to the name your ISP or network manager gives you. If you don't like this name, you can set the hostname as you like and then edit the configuration files for the individual network clients (such as `sendmail` and your news reader), but this might be more trouble than it's worth.

Despite the fact that you can set only a single hostname in these configuration files, you can have your system respond to more than a single name. You do this by adding configuration files and options, as described in the following sections.

The `/etc/hosts` File

The `/etc/hosts` file contains a list of hosts and their associated IP addresses. At the very least, this file should contain an entry for `localhost`, which is always a valid machine name (but should not be the only name in any networked computer). Each line in `/etc/hosts` contains an IP address followed by an FQDN, optionally followed by additional names for that address. For instance, here's a minimal `/etc/hosts` file:

```
127.0.0.1       localhost
192.168.1.3     gingko.biloba.com gingko
```

If your computer has more than one Ethernet interface, you can give the computer different addresses on the different interfaces. You do this, in part, by specifying the appropriate IP addresses and machine names on separate lines in `/etc/hosts`. If you want to assign multiple names to a single IP address, you can add them all onto the one line. For instance, here's a more complex variant of the previous example:

```
127.0.0.1       localhost
10.0.0.3        polk.biloba.com polk www.biloba.com
192.168.1.3     gingko.biloba.com gingko webserver
```

If two network cards exist in the single computer, one bound to 10.0.0.3 and the other to 192.168.1.3, then that computer understands the names `polk.biloba.com`, `polk`, `www.biloba.com`, `gingko.biloba.com`, `gingko`, and `webserver` all as referring to itself, albeit on two different networks.

The `/etc/hosts` file is intended at least as much for directing traffic *outward* from the computer as for identifying traffic *to* the computer. In fact, adding names to `/etc/hosts` doesn't really do much for specifying your machine's name to other computers. You can, however, add multiple names for *external* machines to `/etc/hosts`. For instance, if the preceding `/etc/hosts` file were on another computer, then that computer could direct traffic to `gingko` under any of its many names.

In general, you should ensure that /etc/hosts contains entries for the following:

- localhost (127.0.0.1)—This is the *loopback interface*, and it's used by a variety of Linux programs when interfacing to the local computer.
- The primary machine name—You should have one entry in /etc/hosts that links the primary machine name (as specified in /etc/HOSTNAME or elsewhere) to its IP address. If the computer isn't on a network, the convention is to use the IP address 192.168.0.1 for this purpose. Because you're presumably configuring a networked system, you should use whatever IP address your machine has.
- Additional machine names—If the computer has multiple interfaces, you can set up two or more lines, one for each NIC, as just described.
- Remote machine names—Enter the names of any computers you like, and their IP addresses. On a small intranet, you might want to enter the names and addresses of all the machines on that intranet. You might then be able to forgo setting up DNS for your network, depending on how you plan to use the computers. You can also enter the IP addresses of machines on the Internet as a whole, if you access them often and want to avoid doing DNS lookups on them. If the IP addresses of such machines change, however, your /etc/hosts file will become inaccurate, so I recommend not adding external computers to /etc/hosts unless you have a compelling reason to do so.

If you're configuring a privatelocal network, you need to choose IP addresses for your computers. You shouldn't do this randomly. A number of IP address ranges have been set aside for precisely this function, and are guaranteed not to match the IP addresses of computers that are publicly accessible on the Internet. These ranges are listed in Table 4.2 (p. 95), but the most common range for small networks is 192.168.0.0 through 192.168.255.255 (the .0 and .255 addresses can't be used, though, because they have special meanings). If you use this range, you should vary only the final number on any given network—for instance, use the computers from 192.168.1.1 through 192.168.1.254.

Activating Interfaces

Specifying names and IP addresses in the configuration files can keep you occupied for a minute or two, but without linking these IP addresses to the computer's network interfaces, not much good will come of it. In Linux, you activate network interfaces with the ifconfig command. This command's basic syntax is as follows:

```
ifconfig interface [options] address
```

The parameters to `ifconfig` are:

- *interface*—The hardware interface. For Ethernet boards, these are `eth`*n*, where *n* is a number from 0 up—for instance, `eth0` for the first NIC, `eth1` for the second NIC, and so on. Token Ring boards use `tr` rather than `eth`, and other networking boards use yet other interface codes.

- *options*—The `ifconfig` command supports a number of options, such as `up` or `down` to enable or disable an interface, respectively (`up` is assumed if it's omitted); `mtu` to set the maximum transfer unit for the interface; and so on. One of the most important options is `netmask` *mask*, which sets the netmask for the IP address, as described shortly. See the `ifconfig` man page for more information on these options.

- *address*—This is the IP address for the computer on this network card.

As an example, consider the following command:

```
ifconfig eth0 192.168.1.3
```

This command tells the system to start using whatever device is driven by `eth0` for the IP address 192.168.1.3. Effectively, `ifconfig` binds an IP address to a NIC—or at least, to a NIC's driver.

One of the items of information you should have received from your network administrator or ISP is a *netmask*. This is a 4-byte number in dotted-quad notation, the same as IP addresses. Some of the numbers of a netmask are 255, though, and the number is not actually an IP address. The netmask indicates what addresses are part of the local network. A 1 bit indicates that the corresponding bit in the destination must be the same as the source if the remote machine is local, whereas a 0 bit indicates that the corresponding bit may be different on a machine on the local network. For instance, if the netmask is 255.255.255.0 and the local computer is 192.168.1.1, then all computers from 192.168.1.1 through 192.168.1.254 are on the local network. All other IP addresses represent nonlocal computers.

Normally, `ifconfig` can deduce the correct netmask based on the class of the network, as described in Chapter 4. Sometimes, though, an organization creates *subnets*, in which a larger network is broken down into smaller networks. When this happens, you must specify the netmask yourself because `ifconfig` has no way to determine how the network has been split.

You can use `ifconfig` without specifying an IP address to see how a network interface is configured. When you do so, you get a list of information, including the NIC's Ethernet address, the computer's IP address on that NIC, the number of transmitted and received packets, and the number of errors.

Linux normally calls the `ifconfig` command, like other network commands, at system startup from a distribution-specific configuration file somewhere in the `/etc` directory structure. If you configure this aspect of networking manually, you might want to place the command in the `/etc/rc.d/rc.local` file or some other file that your distribution runs at startup.

Routing Network Traffic

Activating an interface with `ifconfig` isn't the last of the tasks in setting up a network interface—there's one task left to perform. That task is to set up a *route* for network traffic. When a packet originates from your computer, the computer needs to decide over what network device to send it. Of course, if you've got but a single NIC, that decision is pretty simple—for you or me. A computer needs more specific instructions, though.

Network routing is configured through the `route` command. This command adds to, deletes from, or displays the system's *routing table*—a list of interfaces and associated network addresses, so that the system knows where to send each IP packet it generates or forwards. The `route` command's basic syntax is as follows:

```
route add ¦ del target [gw gateway]
```

The meaning of the parameters is as follows:

- `add ¦ del`—This parameter specifies adding or deleting an entry, respectively. You normally use `add`, but you might use `del` to temporarily remove some set of machines from accessibility.

- *target*—The *target* is the machine or network addressed by the route. If trailing bits in this address are 0, the entry relates to a group of machines—a network. For instance, `192.168.1.0` as a target means that traffic destined for all machines from 192.168.1.1 through 192.168.1.254 is routed through this interface. In addition to using raw numerical IP addresses, you can specify a network by name if it's listed in the `/etc/networks` file, which has a syntax similar to that of `/etc/hosts`, except that `/etc/networks` lists entire networks. One name also carries special meaning: `default`. If you use `default` as the target, the system sends any data that's not matched more specifically through that route. `default` is synonymous with `0.0.0.0`, which matches all networks.

- *gateway*—If you use the `gw` switch, the following parameter is an IP address of a computer that serves as a gateway. A gateway computer accepts traffic destined for more distant networks. Normally, as described in Chapter 4, when a computer sends data over an Ethernet link, the computer attempts to locate the Ethernet address of the destination computer, the assumption being that the destination machine is on the same Ethernet network. Setting a gateway alters that behavior; instead of sending to the final destination, the computer sends to the gateway machine, which serves as a router.

You might have noticed that there's no explicit link between the route command and a particular interface. That's because route can deduce the correct interface based on the target network. For instance, if the target network is 192.168.5.0, then route knows to look for an interface linked to an address that begins 192.168.5, and route attaches the route to that interface.

How does this work in practice? Here's an example of a route command:

```
route add 10.0.0.0
```

This command adds a route to send all data to addresses from 10.0.0.1 through 10.255.255.255, through whatever interface has been assigned an address in that range. Here's another example:

```
route add default gw 10.4.3.100
```

This command sets up the default route to use the machine at 10.4.3.100 as a gateway, so any traffic that's not covered by other entries in the routing table go through this machine.

If you use the route command without any other parameters, Linux displays the current routing table, which can be informative. You might get something that looks like this:

```
192.168.1.1     *             255.255.255.255 UH   0   0   0 eth0
192.168.1.0     *             255.255.255.0   U    0   0   0 eth0
10.0.0.0        *             255.0.0.0       U    0   0   0 eth1
127.0.0.0       *             255.0.0.0       U    0   0   0 lo
default         10.4.3.100    0.0.0.0         UG   0   0   0 eth1
```

This output indicates that the computer is connected to two networks, one of which (192.168.1.0) is presumably a small local network and the other of which (10.0.0.0) is a larger network that contains a gateway machine at 10.4.3.100. All traffic not destined for the 192.168.1.0 network, or for the loopback interface (on 127.0.0.1, though the lo device is configured to take everything on the entire 127.0.0.0 network) goes through the gateway at 10.4.3.100.

As with ifconfig, Linux distributions tend to bury their startup route commands in obscure files in the /etc directory tree, such as /etc/rc.d/init.d/routed. If you want to configure your network manually, you can place an appropriate command in /etc/rc.d/rc.local or some other file that you know runs at system startup.

Preliminary Testing

Now that you've set up the interface, you can test your networking. First, try the loopback interface:

```
ping 127.0.0.1
```

This command should return a series of lines like this:

```
PING 127.0.0.1 (127.0.0.1): 56 data bytes
64 bytes from 127.0.0.1: icmp_seq=0 ttl=255 time=0.2 ms
64 bytes from 127.0.0.1: icmp_seq=1 ttl=255 time=0.1 ms
64 bytes from 127.0.0.1: icmp_seq=2 ttl=255 time=0.1 ms
```

Press Ctrl+C when you've seen enough, and you'll get statistics on the number of packets transmitted and received and the times these transfers took. You should get similar results if you use `localhost` in place of `127.0.0.1` when you issue the `ping` command. If `localhost` doesn't work, then you might have a problem with your `/etc/hosts` file.

Next, you can try the `ping` command on another machine. If you've configured a local network, try `ping`ing another machine from that network. For instance, you might type

ping 192.168.1.2

Of course, the IP address you type depends on how your local network is configured. The results should be similar to the results of `ping`ing your loopback device, though the times might be slightly longer. It shouldn't matter what operating system the target computer is running, as long as its networking features are configured correctly and it has not been configured to ignore ICMP ECHO REQUEST packets. If you've set up `/etc/hosts` correctly, you should be able to use the remote machine's name, such as `polk`, rather than the IP address.

Finally, if you're connected to the Internet through a gateway machine, you should be able to `ping` any computer on the Internet. Until you tell your system what to use for DNS, though, you need to use IP addresses only. As a test, try using the IP address for your ISP's or organization's DNS machine. When you've set up DNS, or if you have some IP addresses and enter them into your `/etc/hosts` file, you can `ping` outside machines by name.

Depending on the resources available on your local network, you can perform additional tests. For instance, if one of your computers runs a Telnet server, you can try using `telnet` on your Linux computer to log on to that machine. Alternatively, if your Linux system runs daemons for some network service, you can test the system by accessing those services from another computer. If you can successfully use `ping` and one or two more sophisticated tools such as `telnet`, `ftp`, or a Web browser, chances are all your networking applications, both clients and servers, will work.

Setting the DNS Server

To access randomly selected computers on the Internet as a whole by name, you need to tell your Linux machine the IP addresses of one or more DNS servers. These servers are normally maintained by your ISP or your organization's networking department, so ask for these computers' addresses. If you're setting up your own private intranet, you might want to run DNS on your Linux computer to provide similar services to machines on that network. This task can be complex, and complete coverage of it is beyond the scope of this book, but later in the section "Setting Up a DNS Server," you'll find a brief outline of how to run a DNS server.

> **NOTE**
>
> If you'll be using your intranet primarily for file and printer sharing using Samba/Windows networking or Netatalk/AppleTalk, running DNS locally might not be important. This is because both NetBIOS and AppleTalk provide their own computer naming conventions, so Internet-style names aren't important to these services.
>
> If you want to access machines on your intranet for TCP/IP services such as Telnet or FTP, though, you have to enter raw IP addresses, run DNS, or maintain /etc/hosts files on all the client computers. If all your intranet's machines are directly connected to the Internet, then your ISP or networking department's DNS machines will handle these services, and you need not concern yourself with it, aside from configuring all of your computers as DNS *clients*.

Specifying DNS Servers Manually

The primary file for configuring TCP/IP name lookups is /etc/resolv.conf. There are three types of commands in this file, in addition to comments, which are indicated by a pound sign (#):

- nameserver—A line that begins with nameserver specifies the IP address of a DNS machine. For instance, a line might read nameserver 192.168.3.100. You can specify several name servers by listing them on multiple lines.

- domain—The domain keyword indicates that the system will attempt to find the named computer in the specified domain. For instance, if the line domain biloba.com appears in /etc/resolv.conf, and if you try to access a service on host gingko, the system looks for gingko in biloba.com—that is, as gingko.biloba.com—in addition to searching for gingko by itself.

- search—The search list is similar in concept to the domain, except that you can specify several domains on a single search line, separated by spaces or tabs.

Here's an example of an /etc/resolv.conf file:

```
# Default domain:
domain threeroomco.com
# Subnetworks to search:
search room1.threeroomco.com room2.threeroomco.com
```

```
# Our nameservers:
nameserver 192.168.3.100
nameserver 192.168.3.101
```

If you were to use this file and try to access services on a computer called `polk`, the system would perform DNS searches on `polk`, `polk.threeroomco.com`, `polk.room1.threeroomco.com`, and `polk.room2.threeroomco.com`. Note that multiple name searches can have some disadvantages. They take time, for one thing, though that's usually not a major problem because the individual transfers are so quick. More importantly, if you specify too many domains in the `search` line, you might get an unintended match to a mistyped name. For instance, if `threeroomco.com` has a machine called `server`, and if `room2.threeroomco.com` has a machine called `serve`, an attempt to access `server` may actually access `serve.room2.threeroomco.com` if you mistype the name. This specific situation calls out for renaming the computers within the organization, but if you start including external domains in your DNS search path, the problem becomes much more serious.

DNS is mainly used for finding the names of remote systems, and particularly those that are on distant networks. Linux includes another mechanism, the `/etc/hosts` file, for finding its own name and the names of local systems. The contents of `/etc/hosts` are described in the section titled "The `/etc/hosts` File." How does Linux know whether to use `/etc/hosts` or DNS, though? The answer lies in the `/etc/host.conf` file, which has several commands:

- `order`—`order` specifies the order in which different name resolution services are tried. You normally want a line reading `order hosts,bind` in your `/etc/host.conf` file. This specifies that the `/etc/hosts` file is tried first, followed by DNS services (BIND is the name of the package that supplies DNS, and it's covered later in this chapter, in the section "Setting Up a DNS Server").

> **NOTE**
>
> A third type of name resolution is known as *Network Information System* (NIS), and Linux can be configured to use it. NIS can provide for unified login information on a network, as well as name resolution services. If your network has an NIS server, you can configure Linux to use it, though this topic is beyond the scope of this book. If your system is configured to use NIS, you can list it on the order line in `/etc/host.conf`.

- `multi`—`multi` indicates whether a host in `/etc/hosts` can have several IP addresses. You normally want this line to read `multi on` to permit such a situation.

- nospoof—*Spoofing* is a technique commonly used by system crackers to make their systems appear to be from somewhere they're not. If you include a line reading `nospoof`, Linux cross-checks the IP address and the FQDN, and rejects suspected spoofed accesses.

- alert—You can specify `alert on` or `alert off` to log spoofing attempts.

- trim—The `trim` line is something like the opposite of a `search` line in the `/etc/resolv.conf` file. If you attempt to access a host on a domain specified in the `trim` line, Linux removes the domain name, leaving only the host name. If your `/etc/hosts` file omits the domain names, this can speed up access slightly. Since `/etc/hosts` allows you to include both FQDNs and shorter "nicknames," the `trim` option isn't much needed in practice.

Between the files `/etc/resolv.conf`, `/etc.host.conf`, and `/etc/hosts`, then, you can control how your system searches for IP addresses when given a domain name.

Setting Up a DNS Server

Configuring your system as a DNS server isn't necessary in most cases. You'll probably only want to do this if you have a private network and want to be able to access hosts on that network by name from any machine on the network. Even in this case, you don't need a DNS server if you're only using Windows networking or AppleTalk because these protocols include their own name resolution.

DNS in Linux is handled by a package called the Berkeley Internet Name Daemon (BIND), which includes a daemon called `named` (pronounced *name-dee*). Thus, the terms *DNS*, *BIND*, and `named` have overlapping meanings, but differing levels of specificity: *DNS* is the most general term, and `named` is the most specific.

If you're running Red Hat Linux 6.0, you need to install the `bind` and `caching-nameserver` packages from your Red Hat CD-ROM. For other distributions, you need to locate the equivalent packages, which might be bundled in a single package or split across more than two. Because configuring DNS can be complex, I'm making the simplifying assumption that you're using the Red Hat 6.0 files, which come configured in a fixed way that makes modification simpler. If you're not using Red Hat, you might need to configure aspects of your system that I don't cover here, or you can use the Red Hat 6.0 `caching-nameserver` package to get the configuration files I use as a starting point.

Red Hat 6.0 uses BIND version 8.2. Older versions of BIND use different configuration file formats entirely, so if you're using an older version of BIND, you either have to upgrade or use different syntax in your configuration file.

After you've installed the DNS packages, you need to edit the following files:

- `/etc/named.conf`—Add an entry to the bottom of this file for your local network. For instance, it might read

```
zone "private" {
        type master;
        file "named.private";
};
```

This entry adds support for the domain `private`, so you can access hosts by names such as `stanislaw.private` and `isaac.private`. While you're editing this file, if you want the name server to respond only to requests on your local network, you can add a line like the following just after the line that reads `options {`:

`listen-on { 192.168.1.1; };`

Be sure to type this correctly, including both semicolons, but substitute the IP address for your Linux computer on the private network. This line causes `named` to respond only to requests received over the physical interface with which the specified IP address is associated, thus improving security.

- `/var/named/named.private`—You need to create this file. It must have the same name you specified in the `file` field in `/etc/named.conf` (Red Hat's distribution of BIND uses the `/var/named` directory as the base for most BIND configuration files). This file should contain entries for each machine on your private network. For instance, here's such a file for a three-computer network:

```
stanislaw IN A 192.168.1.1
isaac IN A 192.168.1.2
mary IN A 192.168.1.3
```

You needn't be too concerned with what the IN A portion of these entries represent; just put the machine name, IN A, and the IP address on a single line.

You can now start the name server by typing **named**, possibly preceded by its complete path, such as **/usr/sbin/named**. You can test it by setting another computer on the network to use the Linux machine as the only name server, then see if you can access computers by name. Be sure to test both those on your local network (listed in `/var/named/named.private`—be sure to specify the complete name, as in `stanislaw.private`, or include an appropriate domain or search path on the remote system) and those on remote networks, assuming that your intranet is connected to the Internet as a whole. By default, Red Hat and many other distributions configure `named` to run automatically on start when you install the appropriate packages. If your system doesn't do so, you can add a call to `named` to a system startup file, such as `/etc/rc.d/rc.local`.

The preceding instructions provide only a *very* brief introduction to the subject of DNS. This description omits configuration of *reverse* DNS lookups, altering default values for DNS cache times, and many other topics. If you need to run your own DNS server for anything but very casual purposes, you should definitely read the documentation files in /usr/doc/bind-8.2 (or possibly a directory with a higher number, if you're running an updated version of the program). You should also be aware of security concerns when running DNS, as when running any service; although DNS isn't designed to give any substantial access to your system, past bugs in DNS have provided system crackers with ways into computers, and this could happen in the future. I therefore advise that you install the latest version of bind that your distribution provides.

Configuring for DSL or Cable Modems

You can connect your Linux computer to the Internet by using a DSL or cable modem. These devices aren't truly modems in the sense that a conventional telephone modem is. These devices come in two basic forms. One is an internal card, which is essentially a NIC. As I write this, no such internal DSL or cable modems are supported in Linux, but that's likely to change in the future. The second form for DSL and cable modems is an external box that connects to your computer through a standard Ethernet line, typically 10BaseT. These devices are essentially *bridges* (p. xxx) or routers (p. xxx)— they're small computers with two network interfaces, and they link your computer or network to your ISP's network, and hence to the Internet.

Given this design, it shouldn't be surprising that there's little or nothing different about configuring a typical DSL or cable modem compared to configuring any other Ethernet connection. Your ISP either provides a static IP address or records the Ethernet address of your NIC in order to provide you with a dynamic IP address via DHCP. You configure your Linux box as appropriate for either of these schemes, as described in this chapter.

A few systems use unusual configurations, such as *one-way* cable modems, which provide only downstream bandwidth, requiring you to dial up with a modem for upstream traffic. Some DSL systems require special client software, but these functions can sometimes be taken over by appropriate DSL modems, and other times the software merely activates features in the modem that you can activate manually or via a script. Check with your ISP to learn what requirements its hardware imposes on your system.

ISPs vary in how friendly they are to Linux. Some are quite happy to let you connect your Linux computer to their network, and even provide you with technical support to help you do so. Others don't really care what OS you use, but don't provide any support for Linux. Still others refuse to provide service if they know you're running Linux. If a potential ISP doesn't forbid Linux, but wants to see a Windows system when the installer comes, you might need to set up a minimal Windows system for the installer's benefit, even if your computer is normally Linux only. When the installer leaves, you can reboot into Linux, configure it for the DSL or cable modem, and when you're satisfied that it's working, wipe out Windows and use that partition for some other purpose, as described in Chapter 5, "Basic Linux Configuration."

If you want your Linux computer to serve as a firewall or IP masquerading server for your private network, you probably want two NICs, and you need to configure them both. It's possible to run into resource limitations in such a situation, and people sometimes find that one NIC works better on the internal network and another works better with the DSL or cable modem, so you might need to experiment with the configuration to get it working to your satisfaction.

Using DHCP for Dynamic Configuration

The preceding discussion should give you a good idea of what's required to configure basic TCP/IP connectivity on a Linux computer, as well as some not-so-basic services—namely BIND. On some networks, including many cable and DSL modem networks, you enter only some of this information yourself. These networks use DHCP to obtain the IP address, netmask, gateway, and DNS server addresses dynamically. Because the IP address can change from hour to hour with such a configuration, some ISPs refer to this as *dynamic IP assignment* or some variant of that term. This contrasts with *static IP assignment*, in which you enter a single IP address as described in "Configuring a System with a Fixed Address," earlier in this chapter.

NOTE

DHCP is backward compatible with a protocol called BOOTP. If your network administrator says to use BOOTP, you can use DHCP and everything should work fine.

Using DHCP as a Client

In order for DHCP to work, you need to have installed the Linux DHCP client package, called dhcpcd in Red Hat Linux. If you're not certain you've installed this package, type

```
rpm -q dhcpcd
```

If the system responds `package dhcpcd is not installed`, then you need to install it from your CD-ROM. If the system responds with a precise package version, then DHCP client support is installed on your system. To configure your system with DHCP on the `eth0` interface, type

```
/sbin/dhcpcd -d -D -H eth0
```

This command tells the system to do maximal configuration through DHCP, including the computer's domain name (the `-D` option) and host name (the `-H` option). You set your own domain and host names by omitting these options from the `dhcpcd` command line and setting them manually, as described in "Setting the Machine Name," earlier in this chapter, or by using the `-h` option to specify a host name manually. You can learn more about `dhcpcd`'s options by typing **man dhcpcd.**

dhcpcd sets the following networking options:

- The machine name—dhcpcd sets this option if configured to do so with the `-H` switch, and if the DHCP server provides this information.
- The network name—dhcpcd sets this option if configured to do so with the `-D` switch, and if the DHCP server provides this information.
- The IP address—This address can change from one session to another, and even midsession if your client and the server need to renegotiate the DHCP "lease."
- The netmask—This is likely the same from one session to another.
- The gateway—This is the computer through which traffic to the Internet as a whole flows.
- The DNS servers—DHCP sets the addresses of remote DNS servers. It does not configure a DNS server on your own computer.
- The Ethernet adapter—DHCP brings up the Ethernet adapter, much as `ifconfig` does.

In other words, DHCP does all the work outlined in the section "Configuring a System with a Fixed Address" *except* for running a DNS server on your system. You shouldn't run a DNS server on a system that obtains its address via DHCP, anyhow, since its IP address isn't guaranteed to remain constant. As a constant IP address is a practical necessity for a DNS server, being a DHCP client and a DNS server are mutually incompatible. (If you also run the DHCP server, you could configure it to provide a fixed address to the DHCP client/DNS server, but in that case you might simply run both servers on one computer.) Running many other types of TCP/IP servers on DHCP-served computers is also suboptimal at best, because remote machines might have trouble locating the server's current IP address if and when it changes.

Configuring a DHCP Server

In most small networks, it's easiest to use static IP address assignment. In some cases, though, you might want your Linux computer to function as a DHCP server. You might do this, for instance, if you maintain a network that's used by a large number of individuals who connect computers to your network sporadically, as in travelling salespeople's notebook computers. You might also want to use DHCP if you have more computers than IP addresses, but most of the computers aren't connected to the network at any given moment. (IP masquerading, as described in Chapter 20, "One IP Address, Many Computers: IP Masquerading," is another tool you might want to use in such situations.)

The Red Hat Linux DHCP server package is called dhcp, and other distributions often use similar names. After you've installed this package, you must set up a configuration file called /etc/dhcpd.conf. Here's an example of a dhcpd.conf file:

```
default-lease-time 6000;
max-lease-time 10000;
option subnet-mask 255.255.255.0;
option broadcast-address 192.168.1.255;
option routers 192.168.1.1;
option domain-name-servers 192.168.1.1;
option domain-name "threeroomco.com";

subnet 192.168.1.0 netmask 255.255.255.0 {
   range 192.168.1.100 192.168.1.150;
}

host polk { hardware ethernet 00:80:C6:F9:3B:BA; }
host tyler { hardware ethernet 00:A0:CC:24:BA:02; }
```

The default-lease-time and max-lease-time lines set the default and maximum times, in seconds, dhcpd is to hold an IP address before attempting to re-negotiate the lease. The subsequent option lines each sets one option, of the form described in the section "Configuring a System with a Fixed Address," earlier in this chapter. The three lines starting with the subnet statement define the network the server is to serve, including the range of IP addresses it's authorized to assign. In this example, dhcpd will assign addresses between 192.168.1.100 and 192.168.1.150. The final two lines identify specific hosts based on their Ethernet hardware addresses, as described in "Network Hardware Addresses," (p. 93). These last two lines are optional; dhcpd can still assign IP addresses (although not consistent hostnames) without them.

After you've created an appropriate configuration file, you can start dhcpd by typing

`/usr/sbin/dhcpd`

or

`/etc/rc.d/init.d/dhcpd start`

Many distributions (including Red Hat 6.0) configure themselves to start dhcpd when you reboot the computer, but for some, you may need to add an appropriate line to /etc/rc.d/rc.local or some other startup file.

This discussion only scratches the surface of DHCP configuration in Linux. For more information, you should consult the dhcpd.conf and dhcpd manpages or the DHCP Mini-HOWTO, available with most Linux distributions and on this book's CD in the doc/HOWTO/mini directory.

Using linuxconf to Configure Networking

The preceding discussions provide the nitty-gritty detail of how Linux goes about configuring itself for networking. This is useful information, particularly if you're trying to debug a network connection that's not working properly. If you just want to quickly configure a machine, however, you might prefer a streamlined configuration approach, particularly if you need to set up static IP addresses. This streamlined approach is provided by the linuxconf utility in Red Hat 6.0. Many other distributions provide similar GUI configuration tools, though the details of their operation do differ.

Setting Basic Host Information

To begin, you should select the Config, Networking, Client tasks, Basic host information option in linuxconf. The first item you can enter here is the host name, and you should enter it. When you click the Adaptor 1 tab, you can enter additional information, as shown in Figure 7.1. If you select DHCP as the Config mode, you only need to enter the Net device and Kernel module; the system obtains the rest of the information from the DHCP server. If you select Manual for the Config mode, you need to enter your machine's full name and IP address, at a minimum, in addition to the Net device and Kernel module.

You should also select Config, Networking, Routing and gateways, Defaults to set the default gateway (again, that's the computer that transfers information from your local network to the Internet at large). You specify this machine by its numerical IP address rather than its machine name.

Name Server Specification

To configure your name server and related options, you should first select Config, Networking, Client tasks, Name server specification (DNS). This produces the display shown in Figure 7.2, in which you can enter the default domain, up to three nameservers, and up to six search domains.

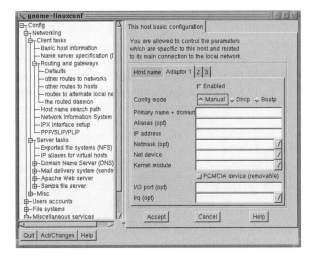

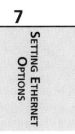

7

SETTING ETHERNET
OPTIONS

FIGURE 7.1

Many network configuration options are combined into a few displays in linuxconf.

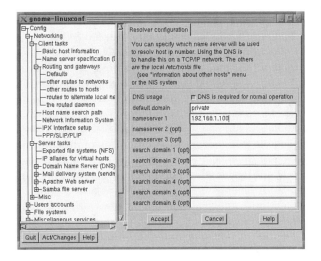

FIGURE 7.2

You can configure DNS-related information with the Resolver configuration tab in linuxconf.

One other name resolution option you should configure is located at Config, Misc, Information about other hosts. This option lets you edit the /etc/hosts file in linuxconf, in order to provide information on local host names without using DNS. As described in "The /etc/hosts File" earlier in this chapter, you should be sure that there's an entry for localhost and for whatever names and addresses by which the computer is known on any networks to which it's attached.

You can modify the contents of /etc/host.conf, in order to tell the system in what order to try different methods of name resolution, by selecting Config, Networking, Host name search path. You can then click a radio button describing in which order to search DNS, the /etc/hosts file, and NIS.

Additional Options

linuxconf provides many additional networking options on its menus. Many of the linuxconf network configuration settings relate to features such as Samba, which are covered later in this book. Some, such as Apache configuration, are beyond the scope of this book.

Even if you use linuxconf, you might want to familiarize yourself with at least the basics of configuring your system via the standard text configuration files. Such familiarity can be useful if you want to do something that's a bit too subtle for linuxconf, or if you need to configure a system on which linuxconf isn't installed or isn't working.

Summary

This chapter covers the basics of Ethernet configuration under Linux. In its most raw form, this configuration involves editing quite a few text files in order to set options and start services. Basically, it's necessary to set the host name, the IP address, the gateway machine's address, and a DNS server's address. Along the way you must enable the Ethernet port itself, including setting Linux's internal routing table.

Fortunately, there are tools to make this task simpler: DHCP and linuxconf (or some other GUI configuration tool). DHCP is a means to offload many of the configuration minutiae to a network server, whereas linuxconf lets you configure networking by using a handful of GUI screens containing relatively obvious fill-in-the-blank spaces for the necessary information.

Using PPP for Dialup Connections

IN THIS CHAPTER

Even if you're setting up a substantial private network, you might need to use a modem to connect to an Internet service provider (ISP). Perhaps your needs for Internet connectivity are modest, or faster forms of access aren't available or are too expensive in your area. Whatever the case, Point-to-Point Protocol (PPP) is the usual means of connecting a single computer to the Internet via a modem.

> **NOTE**
>
> PPP can also be used to connect two computers via a *null modem cable*—a cable that connects one computer's outgoing lines to another's incoming lines and vice versa. This can be a useful technique to connect PPP-enabled devices such as palmtop computers to a Linux computer. If the Linux computer is connected to the Internet, and if it's configured for routing or IP masquerading, you can even give your palmtop full Internet access in this way.

Setting up a PPP link involves many of the same issues discussed in Chapter 7, "Setting Ethernet Options." You must have an IP address for your computer and know the IP address of a router/gateway and DNS servers, for instance. As with Dynamic Host Control Protocol (DHCP; p. 179), PPP can automatically set some, but not all, of these options. Of particular importance, PPP links normally use dynamic IP addresses, meaning that your IP address changes from one connection to the next. This means that PPP isn't normally a suitable protocol if you want to run a server for the outside world on your computer. Of course, you can run servers for an internal network and still connect to the Internet with PPP.

Obtaining a PPP Account

The first step in connecting your computer to the Internet via PPP is to obtain an account with an ISP. You can check your local phone directory under *Internet services* or possibly *computers* for such listings. The Boston phone directory has five pages of listings for ISPs, and other major metropolitan areas are likely to have a similar quantity. If you have Internet access through some other means, you can check `http://thelist.internet.com` or `http://board-watch.internet.com/isp/ac/index.html` for ISP listings; or you can try a Web search engine such as `http://www.yahoo.com`. Most colleges and universities and many companies provide dialup access to their students and employees, so you might be able to use such services if you want to connect your home LAN to your employer's network.

Assuming that you want to use a conventional ISP, you might want to consider several criteria when selecting one:

- Size—ISPs vary in size, ranging from small operations run from an individual's basement to international corporations. You're likely to get the best customer support from a small company—for example, the owner of one small ISP made a house call to help configure a system belonging to a friend of mine! On the other hand, the larger organizations may offer free dialup access from anywhere in the country, and possibly the world, which can be a great boon if you travel or expect to move soon.

- Connection speeds—As of late 1999, the fastest theoretical speed for telephone modems is 56kbps (downstream; it's slower upstream), achieved with the v.90 protocol. The earlier proprietary X2 and K56Flex protocols also achieved this speed, but they're fading fast. I recommend that you only deal with an ISP that supports v.90 (other protocols are a bonus), even if you have a modem that can't make the most of the available speed.

- Additional connection options—An increasing number of ISPs are offering access via dialup modems, Integrated Services Digital Network (ISDN) lines, Digital Subscriber Line (DSL) connections, and sometimes other methods. If you think you may want to upgrade your connection speed in the next few months, try to find an ISP that does or will support the technology you expect to use in the future.

- Number of modems—Some ISPs don't have enough modems to cover the demand for their service. This results in busy signals when you call at popular times of day, such as weekday evenings. ISPs are often reluctant to admit to such problems, of course, but if you can obtain a dialup phone number, you can test availability by making a call or two each day for a week before signing up. You don't even need a modem; just call the number and hang up when you hear the modem tones—or a busy signal.

- Services—Most ISPs offer one or two email accounts, access to a news server, and a certain amount of space for personal Web pages, in addition to raw Internet connectivity for Web browsing, FTP downloads, and so on. ISPs differ in how much of each of these things they offer, though—some give you more email addresses or space for Web pages, for instance, whereas some limit your total monthly online time. Some have special business accounts for large Web pages, even including hosting of a Web site under your own name, such as `www.yourcompany.com`. You'll need to evaluate how well the available services suit your needs—and your budget.

- Linux friendliness—Many smaller ISPs run their systems using Linux or FreeBSD, so it may be surprising that most don't list these operating systems (OSs) as being supported. In most cases, you can still use the ISP's services with Linux; the ISP just won't help you configure your system for PPP. Some ISPs are actively hostile toward Linux, or have systems that require you to perform unusual steps to connect using Linux. I once tried a large ISP but dropped it during the trial period because I couldn't get this ISP's servers and Linux to talk to one another, though I could connect fine from Windows and OS/2.

8

USING PPP FOR
DIALUP
CONNECTIONS

ISPs also differ in how well they handle all the assorted services they provide. Some are rock-solid and seldom experience service outages. Others provide unreliable service—connection difficulties, poor news servers, and so on. Many ISPs offer a free trial period, so if you're dissatisfied with the service in the first month or so, you can change without having expended money on the ISP. You can also consult with your friends, neighbors, and co-workers about the reliability of different ISPs.

CAUTION

Because you reach your ISP via a telephone connection, your phone company might charge you for each telephone call. You should be sure that your chosen ISP has at least one number that's within your local calling area, or be prepared to pay your phone company for your online time. If you have metered phone service, you'll be charged for *all* phone calls, including those to your ISP. Many companies and individuals who make heavy use of Internet access pay for dedicated phone lines for this access, which can easily at least double or triple the monthly costs.

Configuring Your Serial Ports

After you've selected an ISP, it's time to begin configuring Linux to use that ISP. Because PPP works over modems, and hence over serial lines, your Linux configuration task begins with configuring your serial ports.

NOTE

Traditionally, even internal modems have used serial ports. To Linux, these modems are indistinguishable from external modems. Many recent internal modems are Windows-only devices, however, which don't use conventional serial ports. As of this writing, no such devices are usable from Linux. For more information on modems, see Chapter 1, "Networking Hardware."

Setting Kernel Options

For information on how to configure and compile your kernel, see Chapter 6, "Compiling a Kernel for Networking." Red Hat 6.0 comes with the necessary support precompiled for most PPP configurations, but if you want or need to recompile your kernel, you should ensure that the necessary options are included.

There are two kernel options you must enable to use PPP networking via a serial port modem:

- Serial port support—In most cases, this is the Standard/generic (dumb) serial support option under the Character devices configuration menu. This option provides access to the serial ports that are built in to modern motherboards, and to the ports that are used on conventional internal modems. If you're using a multiport serial board, though, you'll need to enable the Non-standard serial port support option and the appropriate specific board's driver in addition to or instead of the standard support.

- PPP support—You activate PPP support by selecting PPP (point-to-point) support from the Network device support configuration menu.

In addition to these two items, you need the usual TCP/IP configuration options. If you plan to use the dial-on-demand feature described later in this chapter, you must also compile in the SLIP (serial line) support option, which in 2.2-series kernels is located just below the PPP option, and the IP: Transparent Proxy Support option under the Networking options heading. Dial-on-demand lets your computer make a PPP connection whenever outgoing network traffic appears. This can be a very useful feature if you want your Linux computer to perform IP masquerading for a local network, as described in Chapter 20, "One IP Address, Many Computers: IP Masquerading."

8

> **TIP**
>
> Because most computers are connected by using PPP only a small portion of the time, you can compile the serial line, PPP, and (if you need it) Serial Line Internet Protocol (SLIP) options as modules. This will save on memory when PPP isn't in use.

You can check that your system includes PPP support in the kernel by typing `/usr/sbin/pppd`. If the system returns a message to the effect that PPP support is not present, then you need to recompile the kernel or ensure that the PPP support module is loaded. If everything is configured properly, the system will return some gibberish, like this:

```
~ÿ}#À!}!}!} }4}"}&} } } } }%}&O*_Í}'}"}(}"v}*~
```

This is the PPP protocol trying to negotiate a link with the screen, which of course fails, so after a minute or two of printing a burst of gibberish every few seconds, pppd gives up and returns control to you.

Checking Your Device File

Linux uses *device files* to connect to hardware devices such as serial ports, parallel ports, hard disks, and so on. These files typically appear in the /dev directory. Serial ports use the /dev/ttySx names, where x is a number 0 or higher. What you know as COM1: under DOS or Windows is /dev/ttyS0 under Linux, and COM2: in DOS is /dev/ttyS1 in Linux. In addition, many systems create a hard or symbolic link between the device that holds your modem and the file /dev/modem. This allows you to use the more mnemonic /dev/modem when configuring PPP networking or other tasks that use the modem. Throughout this chapter, I use /dev/modem as a reference to your modem device.

> **NOTE**
>
> In earlier incarnations of Linux, /dev/cuax was an alternative method of addressing serial ports, and you might run into scripts or documentation that refers to this series of device files. As of kernel 2.2.0, however, /dev/cuax shouldn't be used; though it may still work now, it likely won't for many more kernel revisions.

To check that your serial port devices exist, type the following command at an xterm or command prompt:

```
ls -l /dev/ttyS? /dev/modem
```

You should see output similar to this:

```
crw-------  2 root     tty      4,  65 Jul 28 13:05 /dev/modem
crw-------  1 root     tty      4,  64 Jul 26 22:20 /dev/ttyS0
crw-------  2 root     tty      4,  65 Jul 28 13:05 /dev/ttyS1
crw-------  1 root     tty      4,  66 May  5 1998 /dev/ttyS2
crw-------  1 root     tty      4,  67 May  5 1998 /dev/ttyS3
```

The numbers ranging from 64 through 67 just before the dates are the *device minor* numbers, and they, in conjunction with the *device major* number 4, are a code that tells the kernel what hardware device to use when a program accesses the file. Note that /dev/modem shares the device major and device minor numbers with /dev/ttyS1, because /dev/modem is a hard link to /dev/ttyS1. If you don't have a /dev/modem file but want to create one, you can use a command such as this:

```
ln /dev/ttyS1 /dev/modem
```

You should use the device name that corresponds to the port on which your modem resides. If you don't see any of the serial port devices, first be sure that you typed the filenames correctly, including the case (note that the S in ttyS is uppercase). If you still don't see the appropriate device files, you can run the /dev/MAKEDEV script to create the standard device files. If that doesn't work, you can use the mknod command to create the files individually, as in this example:

```
mknod /dev/ttyS0 c 4 64
```

You need to change the device filename and minor number as appropriate to create your devices.

One final point about the serial port device files is to note their permissions: crw-------, with ownership by root and group tty. The leading c indicates that these are character devices, and the remainder of the string indicates that the owner has full read/write permissions on the device, and other users have no access. Depending on your configuration, you might want to give other users read/write access to the serial devices by using the chmod and chgroup commands. Providing such access could be a potential security problem, though, because users (or crackers who've broken into a user account) can then use the modem devices for just about anything, potentially racking up heavy phone bills or even engaging in illegal activities traceable to your system.

Using a Terminal Program to Test Your Modem

After you've set up your serial ports in what you believe to be the correct way, you should check them by using a simple terminal program. Two common terminal programs for Linux are minicom and seyon. The former is a text-mode program that you can run from a command line or xterm, and the latter is a graphical user interface (GUI) program that requires X. minicom is described in this section, but you can use seyon if you prefer.

To begin the test, type **minicom -s** to enter the minicom configuration utility. You need to select the Serial port setup option from the menu that appears, and then check that the serial device is correct. It defaults to /dev/modem, so you should either have a /dev/modem device or change the setting as appropriate for your system. You might also want to change the port speed by selecting option E, Bps/Par/Bits. For a 56Kbps modem, a speed of 115200bps is appropriate.

After you've configured the program, you can select the Save setup as dfl option, and then the Exit option to run the terminal emulator. minicom displays a few lines of welcoming information, and then initializes the modem with a string like this:

```
AT S7=45 S0=0 L1 V1 X4 &c1 E1 Q0
```

You should also see the modem's response to the line: OK. If you're familiar with modem commands, you might want to change the initialization string, but you shouldn't do that here unless you plan to use minicom extensively; for a PPP connection, you should customize the PPP dial scripts. You can type other AT ("attention") commands at this prompt, including **ATDT** to dial the modem—for instance, ATDT555-1234 dials the phone number 555-1234. You might want to try dialing your ISP or some other number you know will connect to a computer to test basic functionality.

NOTE

If you try to connect to your ISP with a terminal program, chances are you won't get anything intelligible on the screen. You might get a CONNECT message indicating that the modem has connected, and possibly some sort of banner in English, but then you'll probably see gibberish, followed by a NO CARRIER message. This is normal; it indicates that the remote system attempted to use an authentication protocol such as Password Authentication Protocol (PAP) or Challenge Handshake Authentication Protocol (CHAP), but failed, which is understandable because you weren't running your PPP startup scripts.

---

minicom uses command keys prefixed by Ctrl+A, so to control the program, you start by pressing Ctrl+A. If you follow Ctrl+A with Z, minicom displays the menu shown in Figure 8.1. After you've finished your check of basic functionality, you probably want to exit from minicom, which you can do by pressing Ctrl+A, and then either X or Q.

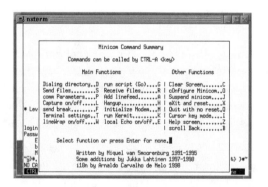

FIGURE 8.1

Whatever you type in minicom *normally goes directly to your modem, but if you first press Ctrl+A,* minicom *interprets the next character as a command.*

If you have problems at this stage, you should resolve them now, or you probably won't have much luck with PPP. Table 8.1 lists some common modem problem symptoms and possible solutions.

TABLE 8.1   Modem Troubleshooting Tips

Symptom	Possible Causes/Solutions
minicom won't run; get a NO GLOBAL CONFIGURATION FILE message	• As root, run minicom -s, enter configuration data, and then save it as dfl.
minicom won't run; get a PERMISSION DENIED message	• Run minicom as root. • Alter permissions on serial port device.
No response from modem	• The modem is not turned on. • The modem is a Windows-only model. • Attempting to use the wrong device file. • Linux serial device driver is not loaded; use **cat** **/proc/interrupts** and check for a serial device interrupt. • Bad modem cable, or cable plugged into wrong port.
Can dial, but get gibberish from ISP	• This is normal when dialing an ISP that expects to make a PPP connection.

PPP Authentication

When you dial an ISP to make a PPP connection, the ISP wants to know who you are for both security and accounting purposes. The process by which you (or your dialing scripts) confirm your identity to your ISP is known as *authentication*, and there are several different methods of authentication in use today:

- Manual login—If you dial your ISP and get a prompt asking for your username and password, it's likely that your ISP supports a manual login procedure. This doesn't mean that a manual login is your *only* option, though. Manual login is distinctly antiquated by today's standards, and few ISPs require manual logins. If yours does, you can create a login script to supply appropriate information at appropriate times, but given the scarcity of systems requiring this procedure, this book doesn't cover creating such a script.

- PAP—PAP is one of the most popular authentication methods in use today. On recent versions of Linux, it requires that you create a special file containing your username and ISP password. The PPP dialing utilities then read this file and send the appropriate password when asked for it.

- CHAP—CHAP works very much like PAP in practice, although it varies in its internal details. As with PAP, you create a special file with your username and password, and the PPP dialer uses that file when the ISP asks who's calling.

In the case of PAP and CHAP, the password files are `/etc/ppp/pap-secrets` and `/etc/ppp/chap-secrets`, respectively. Red Hat Linux includes samples of these files in the ppp package, which you should install if it's not already installed on your system. The Red Hat sample secrets files are very minimal—they contain no entries, just comments. In order to provide the best security, these files should have permissions set to `-rw-------` (600 in octal notation), meaning that only the owner (root) can read or write the file. Each of these files can contain separate authentication for different ISPs or users, one authentication per line. The information on each line is the same for both files:

```
client     server     secret     IP address
```

The meaning of each field is:

> `client`—Your username on the ISP's system.
>
> `server`—The name of your ISP's server. If you don't know the server's name, as you probably don't for most ISPs, you can use an asterisk (*) here.
>
> `secret`—Your password, which is stored in plain text in this file, which is why it's important that this file not be readable by anybody but root.
>
> `IP address`—The IP address you'll be assigned by the remote system. In most cases, you don't know what this will be ahead of time, so you should leave this field blank.

TIP

If you don't know whether your ISP uses PAP or CHAP, you can create one file—say, `pap-secrets`—and create a link for the other file to the one you've created. Your system will then use the same secrets file for both PAP and CHAP.

As an example, here's a `pap-secrets/chap-secrets` file that can be used by three individuals on a single client to connect to three different PPP accounts, which might be on the same or different ISPs:

```
elmo     sesame  elmopw    192.168.1.101
bert     *       bertpw
ernie    *       erniepw
```

In this configuration, `elmo`'s account is the most restrictive because it only allows logging on to the server machine `sesame`, and only accepts the IP address 192.168.1.101. The `bert` and `ernie` accounts are both more flexible; they'll accept any remote server and any IP addresses.

Chances are you only need a single-line `pap-secrets`/`chap-secrets` file, excluding comments (lines that begin with a pound sign [#]). When the system has established a PPP link, any user can use it. So if Bert connects to his ISP, Elmo and Ernie can use that link. If these accounts are on different ISPs, these users may experience difficulties accessing some ISP services, such as email or Usenet news, when the machine is connected to a foreign ISP. This is because many ISPs check the source of incoming requests for services such as these, and refuse such requests if they come from another ISP. Web browsing, Telnet, FTP downloads, and similar functions work fine for all users, though.

Creating PPP Scripts

Red Hat Linux 6.0 includes a few basic PPP support files, including `pppd`, the PPP daemon that's used both for initiating PPP sessions and listening for them if you want your computer to function as a dial-in PPP server. If you want to actually *use* these features, though, you've got to link them together in some way. One way to do this is to write a short script to do the job. In fact, you need *three* scripts: two to initiate the PPP session and one to terminate it. Because you'll be using scripts if you want to configure a dial-on-demand setup, as described in the section "Setting Up Dial-on-Demand for Automatic Connections" later in this chapter, I present more basic scripts here. You might prefer to use a more GUI-oriented approach, and there are several GUI PPP dialers available, so I present instructions on using one in the section "Using a GUI PPP Dialer" later in this chapter.

> **NOTE**
>
> You might need to modify these scripts for your system. At the very least, you need to insert your own username and ISP phone number in the `ppp-on` script. You might also need to change the other scripts to accommodate your hardware or software needs, or the needs of your ISP. Some information on debugging PPP connections appears in the "PPP Problem-Solving" section later in this chapter.

Creating the `ppp-on` Script

First, here's a basic `ppp-on` script. You can type this in, save it in `/usr/local/bin` or some other convenient location, and give it execute permission. There's also a version of this file on the CD-ROM that accompanies this book, in the `sams-extras/ppp` directory. Without further ado, then, here's the script:

```
#!/bin/sh
#
# Script to initiate a ppp connection.
#
# These are the parameters. Change as needed.
TELEPHONE=555-1234        # The telephone number for the connection
ACCOUNT=ernie             # The account name for logon
DIALER_SCRIPT=/etc/ppp/ppp-on-dialer
#
# Export phone number so it's available to ppp-on-dialer script.
export TELEPHONE
#
# Initiate the connection.
#
exec /usr/sbin/pppd debug lock modem crtscts /dev/modem 115200 \
        asyncmap 20A0000 escape FF noipdefault noauth name $ACCOUNT \
        defaultroute connect $DIALER_SCRIPT
```

As you can see, this is a very simple script. A few comments about it are in order:

- You must set the telephone number and account name. pppd then extracts the password from the pap-secrets or chap-secrets file, whichever is appropriate for the authentication system your ISP uses.

- It uses /dev/modem as the modem device. You should either create that device as a link to your real modem device or change the reference in ppp-on.

- It sets the serial port speed to 115200bps. As a practical matter, this is fast enough for most 56Kbps connections (the modem includes built-in compression, but this seldom compresses data by more than a 2:1 ratio, and actual connect rates are usually less than 50Kbps, so 115Kbps is plenty of speed).

- It uses a separate script, /etc/ppp/ppp-on-dialer, as the basis for dialing. I describe this script in the next section.

- The call to /usr/sbin/pppd includes parameters to set assorted options, such as lock and noipdefault. You can read about these options in the pppd man page.

- Some of the options to pppd are *privileged*, meaning that only the root user may use them. This effectively limits the use of this script to root.

Because the /etc/ppp/ppp-on-dialer script does most of the real work, there's not a whole lot to the ppp-on script.

Creating the `ppp-on-dialer` Script

Just as you created the ppp-on script, you must create the ppp-on-dialer script. Either it must go in the /etc/ppp directory or you must modify the reference to this script in the ppp-on script. Here's a sample of ppp-on-dialer (again, you can find this file on the CD-ROM that accompanies this book):

```
#!/bin/sh
#
# This is part 2 of the ppp-on script. It will perform the
# connection protocol for the desired connection.
#
exec /usr/sbin/chat -v                                          \
        TIMEOUT         3                                       \
        ABORT           '\nBUSY\r'                              \
        ABORT           '\nNO ANSWER\r'                         \
        ABORT           '\nRINGING\r\n\r\nRINGING\r'            \
        ' '             'AT'                                    \
        'OK'            'ATZ'                                   \
        TIMEOUT         40                                      \
        'OK'            ATDT$TELEPHONE                          \
        'CONNECT'
```

This script simply runs /usr/sbin/chat, which is a utility to transfer data to the serial port in response to certain strings. Aside from keywords such as TIMEOUT and ABORT, the left column contains *expect* strings, which are what the program expects to see from the modem, and the right column contains *send* strings, which the program sends in response. Some comments on the specifics are in order here:

- The backslash (\) characters at the ends of most lines are line continuation characters; many Linux programs, including shells, recognize these as signaling the extension of one line on the next physical line. They're used here because chat expects its input on a single line, but a multiline format is much easier for humans to understand.

- In response to OK, chat is to send ATZ. This is the modem initialization code, and in this case resets the modem to its defaults. You can change this string to anything else you like—say, to reduce the modem's volume or alter its dial speed. Consult your modem's documentation for details, or copy an initialization string that you like from another program. Different modems use different command codes, though, so don't copy a string from a system that uses a modem that's a different model than yours.

- The TIMEOUT value of 40 should be adequate for most situations, but if your ISP takes a long time to answer the phone, you might need to increase the TIMEOUT value.

8

USING PPP FOR DIALUP CONNECTIONS

Configuring for DNS

Before you can run the ppp-on script to start up your PPP link, there's one more detail to
which you must attend: DNS. As with Ethernet networks, as described in Chapter 7, you must
configure your system to know about your ISP's DNS servers. You do this by editing the file
/etc/resolv.conf. Here's a sample of that file:

```
domain linuxfriend.net
nameserver 10.1.2.3
nameserver 10.1.2.4
```

The domain line lists the domain of which your computer is a part—the fictitious ISP
linuxfriend.net in this case. The nameserver lines each list one name server maintained
by that ISP.

You can configure DNS through linuxconf if you prefer, and you can even set up your own
DNS server using the BIND package. For more information on these topics, see Chapter 7.

Creating the ppp-off Script

Establishing a PPP connection might seem like the important part of the job, but it's not the
only part. When you're done using the Internet for a while, you must disconnect. Of course,
you could hit the power switch if you've got an external modem, but that would leave Linux
thinking it's still connected, which would cause problems the next time you try to connect.
This solution also does no good if your modem is an internal model. For this reason, there's a
third PPP script: ppp-off. Here it is:

```
#!/bin/sh
######################################################################
#
# Determine the device to be terminated.
#
if [ "$1" = "" ]; then
        DEVICE=ppp0
else
        DEVICE=$1
fi


######################################################################
#
# If the ppp0 pid file is present, the program is running. Stop it.
if [ -r /var/run/$DEVICE.pid ]; then
        kill -INT `cat /var/run/$DEVICE.pid`
#
# If the kill did not work, then there is no process running for this
# pid. It may also mean that the lock file will be left. You may wish
```

```
# to delete the lock file at the same time.
        if [ ! "$?" = "0" ]; then
                rm -f /var/run/$DEVICE.pid
                echo "ERROR: Removed stale pid file"
                exit 1
        fi
#
# Success. Let pppd clean up its own junk.
        echo "PPP link to $DEVICE terminated."
        exit 0
fi
#
# The ppp process is not running for ppp0.
echo "ERROR: PPP link is not active on $DEVICE"
exit 1
```

Run ppp-off when you're done with your Internet connection, or if the link drops unexpectedly, as happens often with telephone modem connections.

Testing Your Link

To test your PPP scripts, as root type **ppp-on** (you might need to append the path to the script, as in **/usr/local/bin/ppp-on**). After a brief pause, you should hear your modem dial (unless you turned off the speaker) and negotiate the connection with the remote system. A few seconds after this, you should have Internet access. Try using ping to check basic connectivity, using an IP address to one of your ISP's machines, such as one of the DNS servers. If that works, try using ping to check connectivity using a machine name, such as your ISP's mail or news server. If that works, you shouldn't have problems using ping to check even more remote sites, such as www.linux.org. If you succeed at all these tests, you can try using more advanced features, such as Netscape Navigator or a newsreader.

When you're done, try typing **ppp-off** to close the PPP link. You might hear a click as the modem disconnects, and if you've got an external model, you should see the indicator lights change to indicate a lost carrier.

Using a GUI PPP Dialer

Connecting to your ISP using the script files described so far in this chapter can be quick after you've configured the files, but sometimes you might want more or more easily accessed information, or you might prefer to work within a GUI environment. For this reason, many GUI PPP dialers have become available. In fact, some desktop environments, such as the K Desktop Environment (KDE), now include PPP dialers. Discussing all these dialers would be impractical, so I discuss only one here: X-ISP. This dialer isn't part of the standard Red Hat distribution, but a Red Hat Package Manager (RPM) file for X-ISP is in the sams-extras/ppp directory on the CD-ROM that accompanies this book. Install it as you would any other RPM file, using the `rpm` command-line utility or `gnorpm` GUI tool. If you want to find a more recent version of X-ISP, you can check the X-ISP home page at `http://users.hol.gr/~dbouras/`.

> **NOTE**
>
> The X-ISP package replaces the `/etc/ppp/ip-up` and `/etc/ppp/ip-down` files with enhanced versions of its own. The `rpm` utility alerts you to this fact, and unless you include the `—force` flag, it will not permit the installation of X-ISP. If you remove X-ISP and need the original `ip-up` and `ip-down` files, you can find them saved under the names `ip-up.rpmsave` and `ip-down.rpmsave`, respectively.

By default, X-ISP installs in such a way that only root can use it. If you want other users to be able to dial out, follow these steps:

1. Add the users you want to be able to dial out to the group `uucp`, which should already exist on your system. (These users might need to log out and back on again before these changes will affect them.)

2. Change to the `/usr/sbin` directory and issue the following commands:

```
chown root.uucp chat pppd
chmod 4550 pppd
chmod 550 chat
```

> **NOTE**
>
> The `linuxconf` utility tends to reset the permissions on the `pppd` and `chat` files, so you might need to perform this operation after you use `linuxconf`. If you find that this is a problem, you can create a shell script that sets the files' permissions and ownership, and call that script whenever necessary.

In addition to installing and configuring X-ISP, you need to create an `/etc/ppp/pap-secrets` or `/etc/ppp/chap-secrets` file, as described in the "PPP Authentication" section earlier in this chapter.

After you've done this, you can start X-ISP by typing **xisp** at an xterm window, and Linux starts the program, as shown in Figure 8.2.

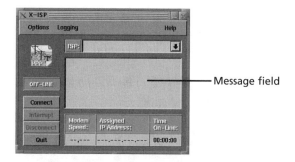

Message field

FIGURE 8.2

X-ISP provides useful information, such as the modem connect speed and IP address, in its dialing window.

You need to enter information on your ISP by selecting items from the Options menu. Start by selecting Options, Account Information, which produces the Account Information dialog box (see Figure 8.3). Click Add in this dialog box to enter the name of your ISP, and thereafter you can enter information such as the telephone numbers (you can enter several, separated by semi-colons, and X-ISP will dial them in sequence until it finds one that's not busy), username, and so on. In most cases, you should enter the username for your ISP account in the User/Name field and select either PAP-Secrets or CHAP-Secrets as the authentication method. If you select None for authentication, you must create select/send pairs for manual login using the Options, Dialing and Login menu item. The PAP option (but not PAP-Secrets) doesn't work with the version of pppd that ships with Red Hat Linux 6.0.

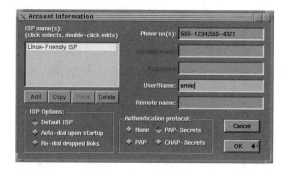

FIGURE 8.3

You can enter your ISP's basic information in the Account Information dialog box.

Chances are you don't need to adjust any of the options available from the Options, Dialing and Login menu item, but you should try Options, Communication Options, which produces the Communication Options dialog box, shown in Figure 8.4. Check that the modem device is one to which your modem is attached, and change the Serial Port Baud Rate setting to 115200. If you like, you can adjust your modem initialization string by changing the contents of the Reset field. If you change the modem device from /dev/modem, X-ISP warns you than you must create a peer information file in the /etc/ppp/peers directory. You can use the /etc/ppp/peers/xisp_modem file as a model—copy it, and then edit it and change references to /dev/modem to the appropriate device.

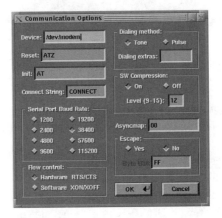

FIGURE 8.4

You can adjust your serial port and modem options in the Communication Options dialog box.

The final configuration you should need to do is in the TCP/IP Options dialog box, shown in Figure 8.5, which you get by selecting Options, TCP/IP Options. You can probably leave the Addressing/Routing settings as they are unless you know you need to change them. Chances are you should select Yes in the DNS support area, and enter the IP addresses for one or two DNS servers provided by your ISP. If you prefer, you can configure DNS as you would for Ethernet devices, as described in Chapter 7, in which case you would select No to DNS support.

After you've entered this information—and created the PAP or CHAP secrets file—you can try dialing your ISP. On the main X-ISP window, click Connect. Your modem should dial, and you should see messages appear in the X-ISP message field relating the status of the connection. When you see an IP address appear, you should be able to use normal Internet tools such as Netscape Navigator, ftp, and so on.

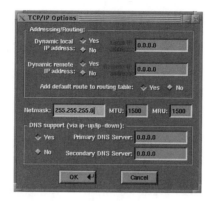

FIGURE 8.5
You can enter your TCP/IP information in the TCP/IP Options dialog box.

Setting Up Dial-on-Demand for Automatic Connections

Using either the PPP connect script or the GUI dialer can be awkward in some situations. For instance, suppose you have an intranet of half a dozen computers in three rooms, plus a Linux server with a modem. Further suppose that you must use a PPP dialup connection through the Linux computer, using IP masquerading, for Internet access for all these computers. Users of any of these computers *could* use one of the techniques in Part V, "Remote Access," to manually connect with the Linux machine and establish a PPP link from there; however, there is an easier way to do this: dial-on-demand.

Dial-on-demand is implemented through the `diald` package. The principle is that your Linux computer establishes a permanent SLIP connection between itself and the `diald` package. When `diald` detects network traffic, it makes a PPP connection between itself and the remote site and serves as an intermediary between your Linux computer's normal network protocols and the PPP-linked computer. In some sense, `diald` acts as if it were a separate router on your network, although it runs entirely within your Linux computer.

Necessary Kernel Options

Aside from the kernel options necessary for PPP networking, `diald` requires the presence of the SLIP (serial line) support option (under the Network device support heading), either as a module or compiled into the kernel.

In addition, `diald` requires that the IP: Transparent Proxy Support option be enabled under the Networking options heading. `diald` uses this kernel feature to do some of the work of juggling IP packets. Note that this option cannot be compiled as a module.

Configuring Dial-on-Demand Services

Assuming that you've compiled an appropriate kernel, you must configure diald to work for you. The first step is to install the package. It's not part of the usual Red Hat Linux 6.0 stable of programs, but you'll find a diald RPM file on the CD-ROM that accompanies this book, in the sams-extras/ppp directory. Install it as you would any RPM, using the rpm utility or a GUI tool such as gnorpm.

> **NOTE**
>
> diald has been changing rapidly recently, in part because of changes in the Linux kernel from 2.0 to 2.2. The version of diald included on the CD-ROM might be out-dated by the time you read this book, so you might want to look for an updated file from the diald home page, at http://diald.unix.ch. If you obtain such a file, how-ever, be aware that it might not contain the same configuration files that come with the RPM on this book's CD-ROM. You might therefore want to install this RPM just to get the configuration files described here, and then upgrade the package.

Before proceeding further, check that you've configured DNS properly, as described earlier in this chapter (p. 198). Without DNS services, you need to specify an IP address, rather than a more reasonable host name, for every outside connection.

After you've installed the diald package, you need to edit two configuration files:

- /etc/diald.conf—Many of the options in this file are identical to those in the standard dialup script ppp-on, and their meanings should be obvious, such as the speed (115200) and device (/dev/modem). Change any of these that you need to change. If you're using either the remote or the local IP address on your local network, you should change the addresses in this file to unused addresses on a private (192.168.x.x) network. What addresses you use is irrelevant, as long as they're unused by any computer. One line you almost certainly have to change is the ISP username, which resides on a line reading pppd-name options ernie in the default file. You must change ernie to your ISP user-name, as recorded in the pap-secrets or chap-secrets file.

- /etc/ppp/diald-dialer—This file is a slight modification of the ppp-on-dialer file presented earlier in this chapter. You should make the same changes to diald-dialer that you made to ppp-on-dialer. In addition, you must change the telephone number to be called (5551234 in the sample file) to one that's appropriate for your ISP.

After you've edited these files, you can test `diald` by starting it. Type **/usr/sbin/diald** to start the daemon. If you don't see any error messages, try a network access, such as `ping` www.linux.org. If `diald` is working correctly, your modem dials after a delay of a second or two, you connect to your ISP, and you start getting back responses from the `ping` command. You can also use a Web browser, an FTP client, or other network applications. If you've configured your machine for IP masquerading, as described in Chapter 20, "One IP Address, Many Computers: IP Masquerading," you should be able to use a computer on your LAN to initiate a PPP dialup connection, just by starting an appropriate Internet application and initiating a network transfer.

If you leave your computer idle for a while, so that it's not transferring new data from the Internet, your modem connection should drop. The precise amount of time before this drop occurs is set in the file `/usr/lib/diald/standard.filter`, and varies depending on the type of the last transfer. For instance, Web transfers keep the link up for 2 minutes, whereas DNS requests without subsequent activity keep the link up for only 30 seconds. You can alter these settings by editing the `standard.filter` file. This file is well commented, so you shouldn't have trouble finding the appropriate section for the type of transfer you want to affect. You specify times in seconds, so a value of 120 indicates a 2-minute delay before terminating the connection.

If you're satisfied that `diald` is working correctly, and if you want it running constantly, you can add a line to `/etc/rc.d/rc.local` or some other initialization script to start it up when the computer boots.

When to Use Dial-on-Demand

Compared to manual PPP dialing, dial-on-demand has unique advantages and disadvantages. Dial-on-demand's strong points include the following:

- It is relatively transparent to users on a small intranet when PPP is the only connection type to the outside world.

- It requires no root access or special groups for dialout access. When the users on an intranet are served through IP masquerading, dial-on-demand doesn't even require that the users have accounts on the dialing Linux box.

- It eliminates the possibility of online charges being driven up by accidentally leaving a link up for extended periods of time.

The weak points of dial-on-demand include the following:

- Delays when initiating a link can cause Internet applications to time out. For instance, if you start a Web access in a Web browser, the browser might report back that the site is unreachable before the PPP link has been established. You can generally just click a retry option or re-enter the address to start again, though.

- Computers often generate seemingly random bursts of Internet activity, which can cause the link to go up unnecessarily. For instance, many mail readers can be configured to check for new mail every few minutes, thus causing a dialout just as often. These occurrences can be difficult to track down, particularly if you're serving an intranet with several computers.

- Links can go down before you'd like them to. This is particularly true when you're reading a lengthy Web page, or if you're composing a long email message or newsgroup posting.

Overall, dial-on-demand can be a very useful tool for certain small networks. I consider it quite worthwhile for a networked home or very small business with two or more computers spread across two or more rooms. Dial-on-demand allows these computers to all be served by a single ISP account, without worry of one user accidentally removing another from the phone line, as could happen if each computer had its own modem.

I find that the drawbacks outweigh the advantages for a single-user network, even one with several computers. I can use a dialup script or X-ISP when I need to initiate a connection, and bring it down manually when I need to bring it down, not when an algorithm computes that I *might* want to do so. For a business of more than half a dozen computers or so, other connection technologies, such as DSL or a T1 line, make more sense than PPP, because they're always up and provide much greater bandwidth. Where available, low-end DSL or cable modem service usually costs about the same as a dialup PPP account and a dedicated phone line combined, but such services are not yet available in all areas.

PPP Problem Solving

No matter what method you choose for making your PPP connections, there's a good chance that you'll run into problems along the way. ISPs vary—often quite substantially—in how they're configured, as do Linux computers. Add in the fact that different models of modems have their own idiosyncrasies, and it's a recipe for trouble, often of a form that's difficult to trace.

General Problem-Solving Advice

No matter what your symptom or where you suspect the problem might lie, there are certain procedures you can follow to help isolate and solve the problem. Here are some places to start:

- Simplify—If you're trying to get dial-on-demand working, drop back to a script-based approach or a GUI dialer. Dial-on-demand involves not just the PPP tools, but `diald`, a SLIP connection, and several extra configuration files. Lots can go wrong there, so if you can get a simpler PPP connection working, it'll help you isolate the problem.

- Try another approach—If you're trying to get a script working, try a GUI dialer, and vice versa. Although these approaches both use pppd, the serial ports, and so on, they tackle the problem of integrating everything quite differently. You might find the alternative approach acceptable, or at least tolerable for getting online and asking further questions. You can also try a different GUI dialer or a different script than the ones presented here.

- Try another account—Problems often occur when you try to connect as an ordinary user but not as root, but sometimes the opposite is true. Some connection tools, such as X-ISP, store configuration files in a user's home account, and if there's a misconfiguration, another user's account might work better. If this approach helps, try to track down the errant configuration files and delete or fix them.

- Try another OS—If possible, boot your computer into Windows, OS/2, or some other OS, and try connecting with it. Whether or not you can connect, you might discover some information that's helpful in diagnosing the problem.

- Check the log files—Many daemons and utilities, including pppd, record important events in a log file, often /var/log/messages. Type `cat /var/log/messages` to see this file. It might be quite large, and the last messages reflect the latest activities.

- Listen to the modem—You can tell a lot by listening to the modem's connect tones, such as whether the connection has completed and at what speed you're connected. (It might take some experience to learn the different sounds, though.) If you normally prefer a silent modem, change your modem initialization string for diagnostic purposes to enable the speaker, and give it a listen.

NOTE

Different modems can make quite different sounds when connecting, even at the same speed. My 3COM Sportster Voice model sounds different from my Apple iMac's built-in modem, even when both connect at v.90 speeds to the same ISP. So if you're trying to diagnose one system's connection problems, don't assume that the connection sounds you hear will be the same as the ones you hear on another computer.

- Study your modem lights—If you have an external modem, its lights can be a treasure trove of information. If your lights blink but the modem doesn't dial, perhaps your dialing or configuration command is incorrect. Perhaps a line quality light is blinking, indicating that the connection is weak.

- Contact your ISP—Especially if you're using a small local ISP that uses Linux or some variety of UNIX in-house, you might be able to get useful tips from the ISP. Some ISPs, even if they don't officially support Linux, have sample configuration files available for download. Sometimes these are quite antiquated, but you won't know until you've checked.

- Check Deja News—The Web site `http://www.deja.com` is a great troubleshooting resource for any computer-related problem. Do a search on keywords that are as specific as you can manage, such as **ppp and linux and pap** if you think you've got a problem with PAP authentication.

- Post a news article—If Deja News turns up nothing promising, try posting your own query. The newsgroup `comp.os.linux.networking` is the most appropriate for Linux PPP questions, but if your problem doesn't appear to be Linux specific, you might want to try `comp.protocols.ppp`. Post as much detail as possible; "PPP doesn't work" won't garner much help, but "PPP fails with a 'PAP authentication failed' message" will do better, and still more specificity will help more.

Of course, these last few options aren't much good without some form of Internet connectivity, and if Linux is your only OS, this can pose a chicken-and-egg problem. Perhaps you can use another computer to check Deja News and even post a query, though; or maybe you can temporarily install Windows to do this.

Modem Connectivity Problems

At the most basic level, you might run into problems getting the modem to connect reliably. You might want to try using `minicom` or `seyon` to establish that your modem works before debugging PPP or your connect scripts—see Table 8.1 earlier in this chapter for information on basic serial port and modem testing.

If you can connect to your ISP with a terminal program, and see either reasonable text or gibberish before the modem hangs up, then you can rule out the possibility of a modem or severe phone line problem. If you don't seem to get this far when attempting a PPP connection to the same phone number, though, it's possible that your modem's initialization string is at fault. Check whatever you're using in your terminal program and implement it in your PPP dial script or GUI dialer.

If when you connect to your ISP with a terminal program you see a login prompt of some sort, it's possible that the ISP requires a manual login rather than authentication through PAP or CHAP. I discuss PAP and CHAP in this chapter because they're used almost universally today, but it's possible that you've located a Coelacanth of an ISP—a variety that lives on in isolated areas, though it's nearly extinct. If so, you'll need to create a more complex `ppp-on-dialer` script or use X-ISP's manual login scripting tools. On the other hand, some ISPs present a manual login prompt but respond to PAP or CHAP queries initiated by the client, so don't assume that you're in this situation just because you see a login prompt.

Occasionally you'll have connectivity problems because of *timeouts*—the time allowed for some action in a script or GUI configuration might not be long enough. This is particularly likely if you're dialing more than seven digits to reach your ISP or if you're using rotary (pulse) dialing rather than tone dialing. If you sometimes connect but sometimes fail just before the connection would normally "take," try increasing the relevant timeout value and see if that helps.

If you hear the modem connect and the carrier immediately drops, it's conceivable that you don't have a connection problem, but an authentication problem. Your system might be connecting, sending login information, and failing the ISP's tests so quickly that you mistake this for a very late modem connection failure.

Authentication Failure

Many PPP connection problems turn out to be problems with authentication. Usually these problems are the result of incorrect configuration—a flawed `pap-secrets` or `chap-secrets` file, say, or incorrect `pppd` options. You should therefore review your configuration for some option you might have overlooked, and double-check that you've typed your username and password correctly in your secrets file. Also, note that in most cases you need an asterisk (*) for the server field of the secrets file, and no entry in the IP addresses field. Your computer refuses a connection if the server field specifies a machine and you don't connect to that computer, or if your ISP tries to assign you an IP address that's not among those listed, if you list any at all.

One of the tricky parts of this process is that what constitutes an "incorrect option to `pppd`" varies from one ISP to another. For instance, most dialup PPP accounts assign an IP address from a pool of addresses, and you're not guaranteed to get the same address on any two connects. Others may give you the same address each time you connect, though, and you might need to specify this address in your GUI dialer or connect scripts. You can type **man pppd** to learn more about the options to `pppd`. If you think you need to change any of them, try editing your `ppp-on` script, the `/etc/diald.conf` file, or the options in the X-ISP configuration dialog boxes.

Postconnection Hangups and Logouts

One unavoidable fact of life with dialup connections using modems is that these links occasionally fail. This is often due to problems with the telephone line—a burst of noise can cause one or both modems to give up and drop the carrier. Of course, Murphy's Law almost guarantees that this happens when you've downloaded 99% of the latest Red Hat Linux release! Other times physical connection problems can cause a modem to *retrain* frequently, meaning that the modem tries to renegotiate its low-level connection to the remote computer. This doesn't cause a carrier drop *per se*, but it does mean that no data gets through during the retrain period. If you have an external modem, you can generally spot a retrain by a blinking light, but with an internal modem, you have no clue when a retrain is in progress. You can often spot connection quality problems after the fact, though, by using a terminal program and issuing an appropriate command. For instance, here's the result of giving the ATI6 command to a 3COM/U.S. Robotics Sportster 56K Voice modem after a successful PPP session:

```
U.S. Robotics 56K Voice EXT Link Diagnostics...

Chars sent            27053     Chars Received        334750
Chars lost                0
Octets sent           16201     Octets Received       188318
Blocks sent            1157     Blocks Received         1858
Blocks resent            15

Retrains Requested        0     Retrains Granted           0
Line Reversals            0     Blers                     24
Link Timeouts             0     Link Naks                  4

Data Compression      V42BIS 2048/32
Equalization          Long
Fallback              Enabled
Protocol              LAPM
Speed                 50666/28800
V.90 Peak Speed       50666
Last Call             00:27:38

Disconnect Reason is DTR dropped
```

Among other things, this report indicates that

- My modem sent 27KB and received 334KB of data.
- 15 of 1,157 blocks were re-sent due to errors.
- There were no retrains during this session.
- The connect speed was 50666bps downstream and 28800bps upstream.

If you experience a large number of calls with dropped connections, low connection speeds, a large number of retrains, or similar problems, you might want to look into several possible solutions:

- Try another access number for your ISP—Sometimes one number works better than another.

- Try another ISP—Sometimes one ISP has poorer lines than another, or hardware that doesn't interface as well with your modem as another's. Free trial periods can be a great way to test this.

- Replace your modem—Modems vary both in overall quality and in how well they cope with specific types of line defects.

- Service the phone line—Problems can sometimes be traced to weak telephone connections. I once had problems with poor connection speeds, retrains, and disconnections after rainfall. Water was seeping into the phone company's equipment outside my apartment and causing static on the lines.

You might also be the victim of an inactivity or usage timer. This comes part and parcel with the dial-on-demand solution, of course, but you can adjust the timing by editing the `/usr/lib/diald/standard.filter` file, as described earlier in the chapter. It's possible to set such timers locally even if you're not using `diald`, however, and you might have inadvertently set such an option, particularly if you used a script or GUI tool you found on the Internet. ISPs sometimes implement similar limits on their end, especially during peak hours.

| NOTE | 8 |

People occasionally post, asking for advice on getting around ISP-imposed inactivity timers. It's a trivial matter to set up a `cron` job that performs some minor Internet traffic at a set interval, but I strongly recommend against such a procedure. Some ISPs consider an attempt to remain connected when you're not using the computer a violation of their fair use policies, and might terminate your account. Even if that doesn't happen, always-on access drives up the cost to ISPs, who must then pass it on to their customers, most of whom don't abuse the system in this way. If you want always-on Internet access, you would be well advised to look into either a dedicated PPP account (one that's sold expressly for this purpose) or an alternative means of access, such as a DSL line, cable modem, or ISDN. DSL and cable connections, in particular, work just like ordinary Ethernet connections from Linux's point of view, and in many metropolitan areas, the price is comparable to that of a dedicated phone line and PPP account, with substantially faster access speeds.

USING PPP FOR
DIALUP
CONNECTIONS

Summary

PPP over telephone lines has been a common method of providing Internet access to individuals and small businesses for several years, and it will likely remain common for several more years. This chapter describes how to set up a PPP link, including the necessary kernel drivers, serial port tests, and PPP configuration itself.

This chapter covers three different ways to start a PPP link: using manually run scripts, the X-ISP GUI dialer, and the `diald` dial-on-demand dialer. Each method has strengths and its weaknesses, so you can pick whichever of these best suits your specific needs.

Setting up a PPP link, using any method, can be a troublesome experience. Problems include difficulties with driver configuration, failures in authentication, and physical defects in the telephone system. Identifying and correcting these problems can be tricky, but this chapter presents some tips to help you in this task.

File Sharing

PART
III

IN THIS PART

Basic Principles of File Sharing

IN THIS CHAPTER

Linux is one of the best operating systems in existence when it comes to file sharing over a network. This is because Linux offers flexibility in two areas: network filesystems and disk-based filesystems. Red Hat Linux supports, out of the box, the Network File System (NFS) protocol for file sharing with UNIX computers; Samba, for file sharing with DOS, Windows, and OS/2 computers; and NetWare Core Protocol (NCP), for file sharing with NetWare computers. With an additional package (included on the CD-ROM that accompanies this book), Red Hat supports AppleTalk, for file sharing with Macintoshes. This range of support, although not unparalleled, makes Linux quite flexible, and you'll be hard-pressed to find an operating system (OS) with more choices.

Similarly, Linux supports a plethora of disk-based filesystems, including its own native ext2fs; various options for the File Allocation Table (FAT) variants used by DOS, Windows, and OS/2; Windows NT's NT File System (NTFS); OS/2's High-Performance File System (HPFS); Macintosh's Hierarchical File System (HFS); the ISO-9660 and Joliet filesystems used on CD-ROMs; UNIX File System (UFS) for various UNIX flavors; and still other more exotic systems. Of course, if you're using a Linux box to serve files stored locally, this unusually wide range of support isn't terribly important. Linux allows you to share *removable* media, though, which could potentially contain any of these filesystems. You can also install a hard disk that had previously been used in another OS and directly share its files, or use this support as a stopgap measure when converting a server from another OS or if you need to dual-boot the machine.

No matter what network or local filesystems you use, though, there are certain concepts with which you must be familiar before you can get the most out of any file-sharing configuration. This is especially true if you're most familiar with Windows or MacOS because Linux's handling of files and filesystems is different from the way these OSs handle them in ways that are both obvious and subtle. Therefore, the goal of this chapter is to introduce important concepts, both of file sharing in general and of Linux's handling of files, particularly as this handling interacts with file sharing with DOS, Windows, OS/2, and Macintosh clients.

Using Mount Points Effectively

In order to understand Linux file-sharing practices, it's important to know something about Linux's partitioning and filesystem philosophy. In general, Linux file sharing is less dependant on partitioning than is file sharing under OSs, such as Windows. Linux also provides ways to access files in an area that's not explicitly exported, which can be both a great convenience and a potential security concern.

NOTE

The word *filesystem* has two meanings in Linux. One is the low-level layout of data on a partition or removable medium. This is the meaning of the word used earlier in this chapter, when referring to ext2, FAT, HFS, and other filesystems supported by Linux. The second meaning of the word, and the one that applies to the previous paragraph, is the high-level logical layout of data on the system—that is, how directories and files are organized in relation to one another. This sense of the word refers to what you would type at a command prompt or in a file open dialog box to access a file. In general, which meaning of the word is relevant should be apparent from context. Where there might be ambiguity, I've tried to clarify it by making the meaning explicit or by using terms such as *partition* or *directory structure* when they're appropriate.

Partitions and Mount Points

Linux, like UNIX, uses a filesystem structure that's substantially different from that of DOS, Windows, OS/2, or MacOS. In all these desktop OSs, you access each partition or removable disk via an identifying label, such as `C:` or `MyFiles:`. Under Linux, there are no drive letters or partition labels. Instead, the first partition, known as the *root partition,* or `/`, serves as a base on which all others stand. Files and directories can exist in the root partition, and you can access them by preceding their names by `/`, as in `/test-file.txt` or `/test-directory/`. You *mount* additional partitions at *mount points*—empty directories—on the root partition. Thereafter, everything under the directory that serves as a mount point resides on the mounted partition. One exception to this rule is that you can mount a partition under a secondary partition, and so on. Figure 9.1 illustrates this relationship. Note that precisely which parts of the filesystem structure exist as separate partitions is arbitrary, and is determined when you install Linux or in subsequent system reconfigurations.

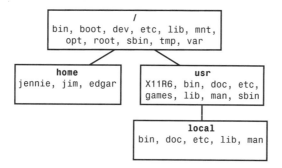

FIGURE 9.1

To the user, it's irrelevant that /home is on a separate partition from /; the partitions are all part of a unified tree.

Exporting Directories

File sharing involves making one or more directories available to users of remote computers. In most cases, you want to export individual users' home directories—the directories storing the users' files in the /home directory tree, such as /home/jennie, /home/jim, and /home/edgar in Figure 9.1. The details of how to do this vary from one protocol to another, but in general you either export the /home directory itself or the individual users' directories.

One important point to note is that in Linux, you export *directories*, not partitions. When you export a directory, you also export all the files and subdirectories available under that directory, whether or not they're on separate partitions. Thus, if you were to export the /usr directory in Figure 9.1, you would also export /usr/local, which resides on a separate partition; but you would *not* automatically export /home or the files and directories that reside physically within the root partition. (There are exceptions to these rules for some file sharing methods, which I discuss in the appropriate chapters.)

> **NOTE**
>
> Linux uses the slash character (/) to separate directory names. DOS, Windows, and OS/2 all use the backslash character (\) for this purpose, and MacOS uses a colon (:), though this fact is generally hidden from Macintosh users. When you export a directory, the client OS's protocols for directory separation take over for access from that client. For instance, suppose you export the /home/jim directory using Samba, and that directory contains a directory called reds and a file in that directory called rose.txt. In Windows, the file might be accessed as E:\reds\rose.txt. It would remain accessible in Linux as /home/jim/reds/rose.txt.

The fact that you export directories means that you need not export entire partitions. For instance, you could export only the /home/jennie directory in Figure 9.1, restricting /home/jim and /home/edgar from network access. If a partition were mounted beneath /home/jennie, then it would be exported along with /home/jennie.

The fact that you can export specific directories gives you precise control over what remote clients can access, with certain caveats with respect to links, as described in the section "What Happens with Links." You might want to give some thought to your desired directory structure when designing your network and your Linux box's filesystem layout. You might want to ask yourself some questions:

- Do users need individualized directory space? If so, they need separate accounts on the Linux server (which is a good idea for security purposes anyway), and you need to export those directories.

- Do users need shared directory space? If users are working together on projects, you might want to give them shared access to one or more directories for this purpose. This could conceivably cause problems if two or more users try to access the same file at the same time, though, so you might want to consider other options, such as storing files in individual users' accounts and letting them copy files to a shared space for transfer purposes.

- Does the server dual-boot? If so, you might want to export the partitions from the non-Linux OS. You can even configure your Linux server to look much the same from the network when running under Linux as when running under its alternate OS.

- Will the server be serving data files only, or program files? If you'll be serving program files, you might want to set aside a separate directory for that purpose. You can even give it permissions so that most network users can't modify the contents of the program files directory. This practice can serve as protection against accidents, malice, and even certain viruses.

In general, maintaining separate user accounts along with one or more directories for shared files is an effective solution in many situations. You can place the shared files directories in the /home directory tree if that's convenient, or you can create a separate directory elsewhere.

One peculiarity of the Linux mount and export systems is that it's possible to export the same files on multiple exports. For instance, suppose you've got a directory called /usr/local/ winfiles/apps. You can export this directory, in which case the files and directories within it will appear on the client in the root directory, such as E:\MegaWord, E:\readme.txt, and so on. You could also export a directory that's higher or lower in this hierarchy, however, such as /usr/local. You'll then have access to the same files as on the previous exports, only with a different root location, as in F:\winfiles\apps\MegaWord and F:\winfiles\apps\readme. txt. Multiple exports like this can be confusing, so I recommend that you avoid them whenever possible.

What Happens with Links

Linux supports *links*, which are pointers from one file to another. When a program tries to open a link, Linux opens the linked-to file, and most programs don't know the difference. Links are similar to Macintosh aliases, Windows shortcuts, and OS/2 shadows, but Linux implements them in a more basic way, particularly compared to OS/2 shadows. In OS/2, shadows exist largely as WorkPlace Shell (WPS) objects, not as fundamental filesystem features, meaning that most programs can't access files through shadows. To a lesser extent, the same is true of shortcuts in Windows. In Linux, any program can access a file through a link. Because file-sharing daemons are Linux programs, links are exported in one way or another, at least potentially. With NFS, links are exported as links, so other Linux or UNIX boxes access them in much the same way as you do locally. With Samba and Netatalk, links are exported as ordinary files, as if they existed twice on the same filesystem.

Types of Links

Linux supports two types of links:

- Hard links—These links are formed by creating two directory entries that point to the same file. It's not really accurate to say that one file is a link to another because both directory entries result in access to the file in the same way. Because hard links are formed by creating multiple directory entries to just one file, they cannot span partition boundaries. You can delete the "original" file and the link to it will remain accessible. You can create a hard link in Linux by typing **ln** *oldfile* *newfile*, where *oldfile* is the existing file and *newfile* is the additional name by which you want to access the file.

- Symbolic links—These links, also sometimes known as *soft links*, are formed by creating a special file that contains the filename of the linked-to file. Thus, there's one definite "original" file and one (or potentially more) link(s) to that file. Symbolic links can span partition boundaries, which makes them popular when linking across directories: You can create a link and be confident that it will continue to work even if you later rearrange your partition structure. If you delete the original file, the link stops working because the file is gone. You can create a symbolic link by typing **ln** **-s** *oldfile* *newfile*—the syntax is the same as for creating a hard link, except that you add a -s parameter just after the ln command name.

Figure 9.2 illustrates the difference between hard and symbolic links.

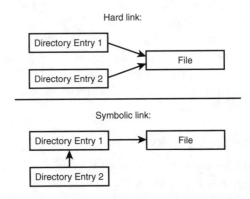

FIGURE 9.2

Because symbolic links point to the original file's directory entry, they take slightly longer to access than do hard links, although this difference is negligible for a single access.

You can generally create links only on ext2fs or other Linux- or UNIX-native filesystems. Because all the mechanisms for soft links reside in the link file itself, though, you can place a soft link on an ext2fs partition to a file that resides on a non-Linux filesystem such as FAT.

Both link types work equally well for files and for directories. When you link to a directory, you can move into the link and access the files within the linked-to directory.

Links Across Exports

Because you can link from just about any point in a Linux directory tree to just about any other point in the tree, you can create a link that leads out of an exported filesystem. For instance, suppose that you export /home/jennie from Figure 9.1. Then, suppose that Jennie logs in to the Linux computer using telnet or some other means and creates a link leading from her home account to the root of the filesystem, /. Jennie now has access to *all* the directories on the computer. This could potentially pose a security problem—but no more of one than exists by giving users login access to a system, assuming that you configure the network so that your users get file-sharing access with their ordinary user permissions. Nonetheless, Samba provides an option to disable the following of symbolic links. If you use this option, your users will get an error if they attempt to follow a symbolic link.

> **TIP**
>
> If you configure permissions properly on your Linux computer, users won't be able to do any damage to the system, even if they create symbolic links into sensitive areas. Most Linux distributions by default have reasonable permissions on most files and directories, so only modest precautions are necessary to maintain this aspect of system security. You should pay close attention to the permissions you give to any sensitive directory structure you create, though, such as directories containing employee performance evaluations or trade secrets.

Symbolic links can be made in either of two forms: relative or absolute. In a *relative* link, the reference to the linked-to file is made relative to the current directory. For instance, if Jennie wants to create a link in her home directory /home/jennie to the file /home/edgar/bone.jpg, Jennie could type **ln -s ../edgar/bone.jpg**, using the .. operator to move back in the directory structure and then forward again, using her home directory as the starting point. An *absolute* reference, on the other hand, uses the root directory as the point of origin, so the equivalent link could be formed by typing **ln -s /home/edgar/string.jpg**. Note that the absolute or relative nature of the link becomes a permanent part of the link; it's not just a matter of how the link is created, but has an impact every time the file is accessed through the link.

Absolute links are useful when the location of the link file itself might change. For instance, if Jennie originally creates the link to string.jpg in her home directory but later decides to move the link to the pictures subdirectory within her home directory, an absolute link can survive that move. A relative link does not survive, though. On the other hand, a relative link can survive a shift of the entire directory structure. For instance, if the system administrator moves both the /home/jennie and /home/edgar directories to a new location (say, /home2, on a new hard disk), then a relative link continues to work whereas an absolute link does not.

Link Quirks

Because Linux links appear as ordinary files or directories when you export a filesystem via Samba or Netatalk, the links present certain quirks:

- If you open a file via a link, make changes, and then save the file, the link is sometimes replaced by a new file, leaving the original unchanged. This happens when the program on the remote system deletes the original and then creates a new file, rather than updating the original file. This situation is quite common with both Macintosh and Windows client computers. Both Microsoft Word and Corel WordPerfect for both Macintosh and Windows exhibit this problem, for instance, although the Macintosh TeachText and Windows WordPad don't.

- If you create a link across partitions, the free space estimate might not be accurate. You might run out of space before the client OS thinks you should, or you might have much more space than the client OS thinks is available. This latter situation can be particularly irksome at times because some programs check available disk space and refuse to let you create a file that they believe can't be created. Although this is normally a sensible precaution on the program's part, when the free space estimate is thrown off by a link across partitions, it can be annoying.

Overall, I recommend avoiding the use of links on exported directories whenever possible.

Client Links

As mentioned earlier, client OSs also support links or link-like structures. You can often create these client OS links on an exported filesystem. In the case of NFS exports to other Linux or UNIX computers, in fact, these links work just like native links—except that references in a link might refer to the host computer. For instance, suppose the user jim creates a link from his home directory /home/jim to files in /opt/wp8/wpgraphics on the client computer. When Jim uses another Linux or UNIX client, or the server itself, and mounts his home directory remotely, chances are he'll find that the link now points to the /usr/wp8/wpgraphics directory on the new computer—if that directory exists at all!

With both Windows and Macintosh clients, links created in the client OS are useful only from that OS. If you're using Linux in a mixed-OS environment, you can't expect a link created in one OS to be usable from another, except in the case of links created using Linux native tools like the ln command. Further, links to files on the server might not always work, particularly in MacOS, which uses file IDs to identify the aliased files. These IDs can change from one mount to another, rendering the alias useless. This fact can also throw off file history features in programs; you might try loading one file, but get an error message or a different file.

Understanding Ownership and Permissions

Linux supports more complex concepts of ownership and permission than do most desktop OSs, such as DOS, Windows, and MacOS. Even when these OSs support such concepts, as does Windows NT, Linux's file permission model usually differs from that of the client OS. This fact can lead to some compromises in how the system maps Linux file permissions onto the client OS.

Ownership and Permission Concepts

In Linux, every file has two ownership characteristics: the *owner* and the *group*. The owner is normally the user who created the file, though ownership can be transferred with the chown command. Every user belongs to one primary group and can belong to several additional groups. For instance, a user might belong to the users group, along with the groups uucp and project10. Ordinarily, this user would create files associated with the group users, and this user would have group access permission to files belonging to the groups uucp and project10.

Each file has separate permissions for the owner, the group, and all other users. Each of these three permissions is broken down into read, write, and execute permissions. Read and write permissions are fairly obvious. Execute permission means that the file can be run as a program. Thus, execute permission is similar to an .EXE extension in DOS or Windows.

> **NOTE**
>
> Execute permission is relevant to running the file as a program *in Linux*. When you export a directory, the client OS makes its own determination of whether the file is executable. In the case of DOS, Windows, OS/2, and MacOS, this determination does *not* depend on Linux execute permissions.

Permissions are normally represented in one of two ways. The first is as a string of 10 characters, the first of which indicates the file type (ordinary file, directory, and so on), the remaining 9 of which represent the permissions in groups of 3 for the owner, the group, and all other users. For instance, here are some sample files:

```
-rwxr-xr-x   1 rodsmith users     10572 Jun 19 12:44 vplay
-rw-rw-r--   1 rodsmith users      2598 Jun 20 13:18 wp-fontinstall.txt
drwxr-x---   2 rodsmith users      2048 Jul  1 11:00 wp-icons
```

The first file, vplay, is a program file—its permission string -rwxr-xr-x indicates that it has execute (x) permission for the owner, the group, and all users. (Dashes indicate no permission, and r, w, and x indicate read, write, or execute permission, respectively.) The second file, wp-fontinstall.txt, is a text file with read and write permission for both the owner and the file's group (users), and read-only access for all others. The third file, wp-icons, is actually a directory (indicated by the d in the first field of the permissions string) with read and write access for the owner, read access for members of the users group, and no access for others. Execute permission carries a special meaning for directories: It means that the directory's contents are accessible. If a directory can be read but not executed, you can find some information about the contents, but you can't access the files in the directory. If the directory can be executed but not read, you can't obtain a directory listing, but you can access the files in the directory if you know their filenames. Thus, directories normally have both read and execute permission. To restrict access to a directory, you need to remove *both* execute and read permissions.

The second way to represent permissions is as a three- or four-digit octal (base 8) number, such as 754 or 0754. Each octal digit is 3 bits in size, and can be expressed as a binary number; for instance, 7 is 111, 5 is 101, and 4 is 100. Link the binary representations together, and you have a permissions string, with 0 equivalent to a dash (-) and 1 equivalent to whatever character is appropriate for the position in question. For instance, 754 is equivalent to -rwxr-xr--. (The leading digit in the 4-digit representation carries special meaning. Aside from d to represent directories, you don't normally need to concern yourself with it, and even the directory coding is handled automatically.)

From within Linux, you can alter ownership and permissions with the chown, chgrp, and chmod commands:

- chown—Changes the ownership of the file, and optionally the group. Type **chown *username.group filename*** to do this. You can omit the period and group name if you want to change only the username.

- chgrp—Changes the group association of the file. This command works much like chown.

- chmod—Changes the permissions for the file. The simplest way to use chmod is with an octal permissions representation, as in chmod 644 *filename.txt* to change *filename.txt* to have permissions 644 (-rw-rw-rw). You can also change individual bits by using the codes u, g, o, and a for the user, group, other users, and all permissions, in conjunction with a plus (+), minus (-), or equal sign (=) and the r, w, or x codes for read, write, and execute permissions. For instance, chmod a+x *progname* gives all users (the owner, group, and all others) execute permissions on the file *progname*. chmod go-rw *filename.txt* removes group and other users' read and write access from *filename.txt*.

The chown, chgrp, and chmod commands all work on both files and directories. There's also a -R or --recursive switch to apply these commands to entire directory trees, as in **chown edgar /home/edgar --recursive**.

Table 9.1 lists a number of common permission codes, their string equivalents, and meanings. Keep in mind that these aren't the only possible permissions; with 9 bits available, there are 512 possible permissions, not counting variants for special files like links and directories.

TABLE 9.1 Sample Permissions and Their Meanings

Octal Code	Permissions	Meaning
644	-rw-r---r--	The owner can read and write the file, everybody else can only read it.
640	-rw-r-----	The owner can read and write the file, members of the file's group can read it, but nobody else can access it.
755	-rwxr-xr-x	The owner can read, write, and execute the file, everybody else can read or execute it.
711	-rwx--x--x	The owner can read, write, and execute the file, everybody else can only execute it.
444	-r---r---r--	Everybody can read the file, nobody can write to or execute it.

Ownership and Permissions on Non-Linux Filesystems

If you're using a Linux server to serve a non-Linux filesystem, and particularly an HFS or FAT filesystem, you'll run into Linux's handling of ownership and permissions on these foreign filesystems. Because Linux relies so heavily on ownership and permissions features, Linux basically *fakes* these features on non-native filesystems. For instance, if you mount a FAT filesystem, Linux assigns some default set of permissions and ownership to the files on that filesystem. You can specify what these are by options to the mount command or by entries in your /etc/fstab file. If you issue a complete mount command, these options appear after the -o parameter, as in **mount /dev/fd0 /mnt/floppy -t vfat -o uid=500**. In the case of the /etc/fstab entries, these options go in the fourth column. In both cases, multiple options can be separated by commas. The options that are most relevant are summarized in Table 9.2.

TABLE 9.2 Mount Options for Non-Linux Filesystems

Option	Filesystems	Meaning
uid=*value*	msdos, vfat, hfs, hpfs, ntfs, iso9660	Sets the owner ID on all files.
gid=*value*	msdos, vfat, hfs, hpfs, ntfs, iso9660	Sets the group ID on all files.
umask=*value*	msdos, vfat, hfs, hpfs, ntfs, iso9660	Sets the permission bits that will be *removed* from a file, in octal notation. For instance, the value 000 results in files with -rwxrwxrwx permissions, and the value 022 results in files with -rwxr-xr-x permissions.
nonumtail	vfat	Normally, the VFAT filesystem creates underlying 8.3 filenames that have *numeric tails* when the filename exceeds the 8.3 limit, as in longfi~1.txt for longfilename.txt. This option eliminates these tails whenever possible, resulting in an 8.3 filename like longfile.txt.
conv=[t]ext¦[b]inary¦[a]uto	msdos, vfat, hfs, hpfs, ntfs, iso9660	UNIX/Linux, DOS/Windows/OS/2, and MacOS each treat line endings differently in text files. This option sets conversion options: text treats all files as text files, binary treats all

Option	Filesystems	Meaning
		files as binary (no conversion), and `auto` attempts to determine which is which through filename extensions or other clues. `binary` is the recommended and default setting.
`case=lower¦asis`	hpfs, hfs	Converts all files to lowercase or leave case as-is. Default is `lower` for `hpfs`, `asis` for `hfs`.
`fork=cap¦double¦netatalk`	hfs	Displays the Macintosh resource fork data in assorted formats. `netatalk` is the preferred format if you're using Netatalk for Macintosh file sharing.
`afpd`	hfs	Makes the handling of the filesystem more compatible with Netatalk.
`creator=xxxx`	hfs	Sets the Macintosh creator code for new files to the four-letter code specified.
`norock`	iso9660	Do not use Rock Ridge extensions, if present.
`nojoliet`	iso9660	Do not use a Joliet filesystem, if present.
`noauto`	All filesystems	Do not mount the filesystem at system startup. Recommended for removable media. Used only in `/etc/fstab`.
`user`	All filesystems	Allow non-root users to mount the filesystem. Used only in `/etc/fstab`.
`loop`	All filesystems	Mount a disk image as if it were a removable disk or partition.

9

BASIC PRINCIPLES OF FILE SHARING

The manpage for the `mount` command lists additional options for these and other filesystems. The filesystems with the newest Linux support (mainly HFS and NTFS) aren't fully described in the `mount` manpage, so you should consult the documentation files in the kernel source tree for further information on these filesystems' mount options.

When you've mounted a filesystem that doesn't support permissions or ownership, you won't be able to change any of these features that the filesystem doesn't support. Most of these filesystems support the write permission bit, but when you change it, you change it for the owner, the group, and all other users (assuming that the umask value doesn't block out write permission to some of these groups). If you need to change the permissions or ownership of files on such a filesystem, you need to unmount it and then mount it again with new options.

Non-Linux clients may support filesystem characteristics that Linux doesn't support. For instance, FAT has a hidden characteristic that, when enabled, hides the file from many commands. Depending on the server and configuration, such characteristics are likely to be lost when a file is copied to a Linux server, but it's sometimes possible to preserve them. In the case of the hidden bit, Samba and Netatalk can be configured to enable this bit for files that begin with periods because a leading period is Linux's indication of hidden files.

Assignment of Ownership and Permissions by Remote Systems

When you export a directory to remote systems, the server must decide how to translate ownership and permissions. For NFS, this information is part of the transfer. The difficulty here is that ownership and permissions are transferred by using numerical codes, not names. Therefore, if you have accounts on two Linux computers, but on one your user ID is 501 and on the other it's 514, you don't have proper permissions to create files on one system from the other. If you alter your permissions to allow such creations, you might not have permission to access the files on the host computer. Fortunately, NFS supports mechanisms to correct for mismatched user IDs on client and server systems. Similar comments apply to group membership and group IDs, although this may not be as critical.

For Samba and Netatalk, the server daemon must decide how to apply ownership and permissions. With these systems, ownership normally goes to the user the daemon believes is using the system; so if the user jennie creates files via Samba, the ownership of those files goes to the user jennie. File access is also restricted in the same way, so jennie cannot access files belonging to jim if the permissions are -rw-------, for instance.

As for permissions, both Samba and Netatalk apply a specific permissions *mask* to files. This mask determines what permissions bits *may* be set, but not necessarily what bits *are* set. These masks are normally set so that files get read, write, and perhaps execute permission for the owner. The permissions for the group and all others may or may not be more restrictive, depending on what you as a system administrator decree. Note that execute permission is largely irrelevant for non-Linux OSs, unless the server maps the execute permission bit onto some other meaning in the client OS. Users can override these settings in two ways:

- Setting a file to be locked or read-only in the client OS. When the user does this, the server daemon removes write permissions from the file for all users, including the file's owner.

- Logging in to the server and altering the permissions with the Linux chmod command. Subsequent accesses from a client system could change the permissions back, though.

The details of how to configure Samba and Netatalk for the permissions strings you want appear in Chapters 11, "Samba: Sharing Files with Windows or OS/2," and 12, "Netatalk: Sharing Files with Macintoshes," respectively. Basically, you need to edit only a line or two in the relevant servers' configuration files.

You should give serious thought to how you want to configure default permissions on your system. If you're configuring a server for a small workgroup in which different users should be able to see each others' files, you might want to put all the users in a single group and give the group read access to new files. I generally do not recommend giving entire groups write access to files, even in a trusted environment; the potential for error is just too high. Read access allows a user to copy the file and modify the copy, which is generally good enough. If the people served by your Linux computer will be working in two or more separate groups, you can create appropriate groups and give read access only within the appropriate group. If an individual needs access to both groups' files, that person can be given membership in both groups. In an environment in which each user works on particularly sensitive files, entirely separate groups for each user or no access to files by group (that is, permissions of -rw-------) may be in order. In a mixed situation, in which users may need access to some, but not all, of another user's files, you or your users can configure subdirectories with customized permissions.

Superuser Access to Files

In most cases, the system administrator (also known as the *superuser* or *root*) has privileged access to all files on a system. The superuser can read, write, delete, copy, or move any file belonging to any user. For this reason, you probably do not want to let the root user access files via a shared filesystem; the danger of tampering is simply too great. The superuser should do administration through a conventional login whenever possible. In Samba and Netatalk, restricting access in this way is easy enough, and in fact the default configurations don't give root access to anybody. With NFS, because usernames transfer with files, it might seem that anybody with root access to one computer could effectively obtain similar access on another. Fortunately, NFS makes an exception for root accounts, and most NFS installations, by default, give root users of foreign systems unusually restrictive access.

9

BASIC PRINCIPLES
OF FILE SHARING

Case-Sensitivity in Linux and Other OSs

In addition to ownership and permissions, Linux treats filename case differently than do most desktop OSs. Once again, this means that file-sharing systems such as Samba and Netatalk must make compromises in handling situations where Linux's and the client OS's case assumptions differ.

There are three types of systems when it comes to handling case in filesystems:

- Case-insensitive—In a case-insensitive filesystem, only one case (uppercase or lowercase) is used. Typically, case-insensitive systems match your filename entries, whether or not they match the case of the file on the disk. Examples of case-insensitive systems include DOS with FAT and the ISO-9660 filesystem used on CD-ROMs.

- Case-retentive—A case-retentive filesystem records the case of filenames, but doesn't care about case when matching files. For instance, a file might appear on disk as `Monthly-Report.wpd`, but you can access it by typing the filename `monthly-report.wpd` or `mOnTHLy-REPort.WpD`. Windows 95 and above with VFAT or NTFS, OS/2 with its HPFS, and MacOS with HFS are all case-retentive systems.

- Case-sensitive—In a case-sensitive filesystem, case is both retained and significant. Thus, to access the file `Monthly-Report.wpd`, you must type precisely that; neither `monthly-report.wpd` nor `mOnTHLy-REPort.WpD` will do. What's more, all three of these filenames could exist in the same directory because their case distinguishes them from one another. UNIX flavors, including Linux, normally sport case-sensitive filesystems such as ext2fs.

Because Linux is a case-sensitive filesystem but the usual clients of Samba and Netatalk are either case-insensitive or case-retentive, the servers normally do extra work to try to match filenames and make the Linux filesystem appear to be case-retentive. Occasionally there are conflicts, though, as when two files in a directory differ only in case. In such situations, you need to log in to Linux and rename one file in order to gain access to both of them. If you don't do that, only one of the files is available to the client.

When Linux accesses media from case-insensitive or case-retentive OSs, Linux normally treats the medium in a case-sensitive way. Exporting such a filesystem then undoes this, returning case-retentive properties to the medium. Details of how this is done differ somewhat from one filesystem to another, though, so check the options in Table 9.2 or in the `mount` manpage for further information.

Serving Removable Media

Although most computers these days have floppy, CD-ROM, and even Zip or LS-120 drives, it's sometimes desirable to let a Linux computer serve removable media. Sometimes this is because the client computer lacks a particular type of drive, as is the case in my home network, where my iMac has no floppy drive, and I share a single Zip drive between all my computers. Other times Linux's great flexibility with filesystems can be a boon. For instance, if you use Windows computers exclusively except for a Linux server, but a client or colleague gives you a Zip disk created on a Macintosh, your Linux box can serve the Zip disk and you can read it on your Windows machines.

Supported Filesystems

The four filesystems you're most likely to encounter in removable media are

* FAT for DOS, Windows, and OS/2 disks—Linux supports FAT using three different filesystem names: `msdos`, `vfat`, and `umsdos`. The `umsdos` filesystem is normally used to install Linux on a FAT partition, so you're not likely to encounter it on a removable-media device. The difference between the `msdos` and `vfat` filesystems is that the former enforces the 8.3 filename length limits of DOS, whereas the latter supports VFAT-style long filenames. Today, you'll probably want to support `vfat` on most or all FAT disks because if you choose `vfat`, you'll still be able to read and write older DOS disks. If you write a file with a long filename to such a disk, though, and then read it on a DOS computer, you'll see a truncated version of the filename. This is no different from writing a disk with Windows 95 or above and then reading it with DOS.

NOTE

Linux normally converts 8.3-style filenames to lowercase when it reads them from FAT floppies. This contrasts with DOS and Windows, which read these filenames entirely in uppercase. (The Windows GUI environment usually converts them to lowercase with a leading uppercase letter, though.) This fact means that your filenames can shift in case if you swap them between Linux and Windows computers via removable disks, but because Windows is a case-retentive OS, this shift normally has few or no practical consequences.

---

* HFS for Macintosh disks—Macintoshes use a filesystem known as HFS, both for removable media such as floppies and Zip disks and often for CD-ROMs. With the 2.2-series kernel, Linux has added support for HFS, so you can read and write these disks. Linux

cannot, however, handle the 400KB and 800KB floppy disk formats from older Macintoshes. This is because PC hardware can't read the low-level formats of these disks. The newer 1.44MB Macintosh floppies are readable by Linux, though.

CAUTION

Linux's support for HFS is good, but still imperfect. Making heavy use of Linux's ability to write HFS may eventually result in a disk with damaged data. I therefore recommend using HFS write capability only when it's absolutely necessary. Most Macintoshes can seamlessly read FAT disks, so you can send data to Macintosh users on FAT disks. If you're writing data to a freshly formatted disk, a failure is less likely, and probably less important, than if you're writing data to a large-capacity removable disk that already contains a great deal of important data.

- ISO-9660 for cross-platform and older CD-ROMs—Naturally, Linux supports the ISO-9660 filesystem for CD-ROMs. You probably only need to share such CD-ROMs if the client computers have no CD-ROM drives, or if you need to access the same CD-ROM simultaneously from several clients. Linux also supports the Rock Ridge extensions to ISO-9660, which are used by Linux and various UNIX flavors to provide long filenames and UNIX/Linux-style permissions and ownership on CD-ROMs. If you have a Rock Ridge CD-ROM and you want to preserve the filenames on a Windows or Macintosh computer, sharing it from Linux is an excellent solution.
- Joliet for recent Windows CD-ROMs—Joliet is the filesystem Microsoft developed to allow Windows 95 and later to read long filenames on CD-ROMs. Joliet normally coexists with ISO-9660, and you can select which you want to read by using the `nojoliet` option, described in Table 9.2 (Linux uses the `iso9660` driver for both ISO-9660 and Joliet CD-ROMs).

In addition to these four major filesystems, you might find media with Linux's ext2fs, the Minix filesystem, OS/2's HPFS, or others. Linux's wide filesystem support lets you serve any of these media to any system on your network.

Mounting a Filesystem

In Linux a removable disk doesn't become available as soon as you insert it into the drive. Instead, you must first *mount* the disk. You do this with the `mount` command, which has the following basic syntax:

```
mount [-t type] [-o options] device-file mount-point
```

There are additional parameters, but you're unlikely to need them in most cases. See the `mount` manpage for details. The parameters listed here have specific meanings:

- `-t` *type*—The filesystem type. The most likely options are `vfat` for FAT with long file-name support; `msdos` for FAT with 8.3 filenames; `hfs` for Macintosh HFS; `iso9660` for ISO-9660 or Joliet; `ext2` for Linux's native ext2fs; and `minix` for the Minix filesystem. The `-t` parameter is largely optional because Linux can usually autodetect the filesystem. You might need to be specific if you want `vfat` or `msdos`, though, and Linux often doesn't detect HFS correctly, so you might need to specify it.

> **TIP**
>
> If you only use `msdos` or `vfat`, not both, then you can omit the filesystem you don't use when you compile your kernel. Autodetection will then detect only the variety you use.

- `-o` *options*—Mount options, as specified in Table 9.2 or the `mount` manpage.
- *device-file*—the device file at which the disk can be found. For instance, the floppy is normally `/dev/fd0`, the CD-ROM is likely to be `/dev/cdrom` but could be `/dev/scd0`, `/dev/hdb`, or something else, and removable-media devices such as Zip or LS-120 disks are likely to be somewhere in the `/dev/sd??` or `/dev/hd??` series.
- *mount-point*—The directory where you want the device to be mounted. This will normally be a subdirectory under `/mnt` for removable media, but you can specify another directory if you prefer.

When you're done accessing a filesystem, you should unmount it with the `umount` command. (That *is* spelled correctly; it's missing the first *n*.) Type **umount** followed by the device or mount point, as in **umount /dev/fd0** or **umount /mnt/cdrom**.

9

BASIC PRINCIPLES OF FILE SHARING

> **CAUTION**
>
> Linux normally locks any removable-media device you access, so you can't eject it before you unmount it. Such locking isn't possible with standard floppy drives, though. Because Linux caches all its filesystems, including floppy disks, it's possible to corrupt data on a floppy disk by ejecting it before you've unmounted it. I suggest always checking to see if a floppy device is mounted by typing **df** at a command prompt before ejecting the disk. The `df` command shows information on all mounted filesystems, so if you see no floppy devices listed, it's safe to eject the floppy.

Many GUI environments provide some means for mounting and unmounting filesystems using a GUI tool rather than a command line. The details differ from one environment to another, though. The text-mode commands offer the advantage of allowing access through a simple `telnet` session to the server computer. Of course, for removable media, you must physically enter the room in which the server exists to insert the medium into the computer, but you can save some time by not having to turn on the monitor of the console if you use `telnet` to log in and mount the device.

Configuring `/etc/fstab` for Removable Media

If you create an entry for a removable disk in `/etc/fstab`, you can use a shortened form of the mount command: `mount mount-point`. If you list the `user` option in `/etc/fstab`, ordinary users can mount the device (normally this is a privilege reserved for the superuser). An `/etc/fstab` entry looks something like this:

```
/dev/scd0    /mnt/cdrom    iso9660    user,noauto    0 0
```

The entries on this line represent the following:

- `/dev/scd0`—The device, in this case the first SCSI CD-ROM.
- `/mnt/cdrom`—The mount point.
- `iso9660`—The filesystem type.

> **TIP**
>
> You can specify a filesystem type of `auto` to have Linux autodetect the filesystem type. This way, you can mount FAT or ext2 media on the same mount point with the same command, for instance. In my experience, this doesn't usually work well with HFS media, though.

- `user,noauto`—Filesystem mount options. In this example, ordinary users can mount the device, and it's not mounted automatically at system startup. It's important that no spaces appear between items, only commas.
- `0 0`—These values represent the dump and filesystem check order. For removable-media devices, these should be `0 0`.

Using the Automounter

There is an alternative to manually mounting and unmounting filesystems: the *automounter*. This is a daemon that watches for attempts to access a specified directory structure. When such an access occurs, the daemon mounts the device associated with that directory, so there's no need to explicitly mount the device. To use the automounter, follow these steps:

1. Check to be sure you have compiled the kernel with Kernel automounter support in the Filesystems area and NFS filesystem support in the Network File Systems area. If you haven't done so, recompile the kernel with these features and restart the system (you might want to put off restarting until you complete the configuration, though).

2. Install the autofs package. This package comes with Red Hat 6.0. If you're using another distribution, you need to locate the equivalent package for your distribution.

3. Edit the /etc/auto.misc file to reflect the devices you want to mount. Here is an example of such a file:

```
floppy          -fstype=auto            :/dev/fd0
zip             -fstype=auto            :/dev/sda4
cdrom           -fstype=iso9660         :/dev/scd0
```

The first column is the mount point, minus a heading, which is set in the /etc/auto.master file, and which defaults to /misc. The second column is a listing of options, as described in Table 9.2, but including the filesystem type (-fstype=). The final column is the device file for the device, preceded by a colon.

4. To start the service, type

```
/usr/sbin/automount /misc file /etc/auto.misc
etc/rc.d/init.d/autofs start
```

If you used the /etc/auto.misc file presented in step 3, and if you have the appropriate devices, you could insert a CD-ROM into the CD-ROM drive, type **ls /misc/cdrom**, and see the contents of the CD-ROM drive. A network access also opens an automounted directory, making the mount process transparent to remote users, with some caveats.

The main drawback to the automounter for use with Windows clients is that the computer can't know when you're done accessing a removable device. You can set a timeout value in the /etc/auto.master file. This value defaults to 60 seconds, which means you can eject a disk 1 minute after the last access to that device. If you find a 1-minute wait too awkward, you can reduce the timeout value, but that can cause problems, too, because the system might end up mounting and unmounting a disk several times in a period of just a few minutes.

Unfortunately, the automounter doesn't do much good for Macintosh clients because Netatalk doesn't export a directory that it doesn't see, and the automounter doesn't create a directory for a device until an attempt has been made to access that directory. This means that you must use conventional mount points and mount commands with Macintosh clients.

You can use both the automounter and conventional mount points, if you like, although you need to use separate mount directories for each. This is because the automounter takes over its mount directory (/misc by default with Red Hat's RPM version of the program), so if you try to use the usual /mnt directory, the mount points in /mnt vanish.

9

BASIC PRINCIPLES OF FILE SHARING

Connecting to Removable Media from a Remote Host

To connect to removable media from a remote computer, you must export a filesystem containing a removable-media mount point. You can either export the mount point itself or you can export a directory in which the mount points reside. Figure 9.3 shows the latter option at work, on a Macintosh client with both a Rock Ridge CD-ROM and a Macintosh floppy disk exported.

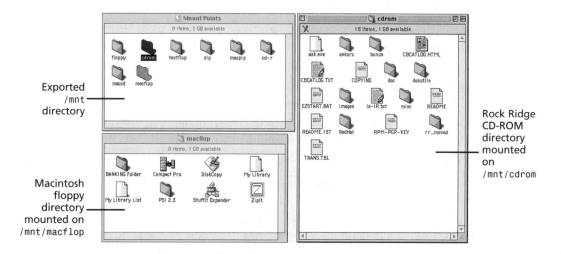

Exported
/mnt
directory

Macintosh
floppy
directory
mounted on
/mnt/macflop

Rock Ridge
CD-ROM
directory
mounted
on
/mnt/cdrom

FIGURE 9.3

Linux handles filesystems well enough that, for example, the Macintosh client can read and write to an HFS floppy, including Macintosh resource forks and other features; and it can read mixed-case filenames from a Rock Ridge CD-ROM.

If you export removable media on a per-device basis, you probably have a large number of possible mount points, which can be tedious to access at times. On the other hand, the root of each device corresponds to the root as it would appear if the disk were used directly. This latter can be a great benefit in some cases because installation programs sometimes expect to find files at particular locations relative to the disk's root.

Exporting the /mnt directory itself, on the other hand, can make life simpler when you want to access a removable device. In this case, you can leave the /mnt directory mounted on a host machine and then have to deal with mounting only the removable media in Linux, not the client machine as well.

If you're using the automounter with a DOS, Windows, or OS/2 client via Samba, you get the best results if you create separate mount points for each device. This is because the automounter doesn't create mount directories until after an attempt is made to access that directory.

If you create an export of the automounter's directory, it will be empty and you won't be able to click on a folder corresponding to the mount point.

Quirks of Serving Removable Media

Removable media sometimes pose unusual challenges to Linux, the client OS, or your users. Some of these quirks are as follows:

- Unmounting—Ordinarily, you can unmount a disk from Linux whenever you've closed all the files on the disk. Sometimes when you access a disk through file-sharing mechanisms, though, a program on the client system keeps a file open long after it needs to, thus preventing you from unmounting the disk. You might need to unmount the shared filesystem from the client system to regain the ability to unmount the removable medium from Linux. Other times you can quit from the errant program or simply wait a minute or two, and you'll be able to unmount the disk.

- Root location—As described previously in this chapter, you can export the mount point, a point above that on the directory tree, or even a directory within the removable media. If the medium contains an installer or some other program, the program might not work properly if it can't find its files where it expects them to be.

- Disk labels—Linux doesn't read or export the labels for removable media. Some installation programs expect media to be labeled in certain ways, and so may not work properly when run from an exported mount. You may be able to customize the Linux export, though, to get around this problem if it's important enough.

- Free space—If you export the /mnt directory, the available disk space measurement is almost certain to be wildly inaccurate.

- Cross-OS quirks—If you're trying to export a disk created on one OS for use with another, you might encounter problems with end-of-line translation in text files, file format incompatibilities, and so on. Many OSs place hidden files on disks, and these typically become visible in the client OS. Linux's handling of Macintosh resource forks is also likely to produce separate visible resource fork files or directories when you view a Macintosh floppy on a non-Macintosh system. If you use the fork=netatalk option, you should usually ignore the .AppleDouble files on Macintosh disks.

Security Considerations

When you set up a Linux server, you should be aware of the security implications of what you do. For every file-sharing daemon you run, you make your computer that much more vulnerable to network attacks—although if you run a network that's isolated from the Internet through a firewall, the risk is greatly reduced.

The Need for Passwords

Both Samba and Netatalk require usernames and passwords for authentication of remote systems. Windows and MacOS both allow users to store their usernames and passwords on disk, so anybody who can access those computers can also access shared files on the Linux computer. This presumably isn't a major problem in a small home network or even in most small businesses, but if it's a concern for you, you might want to look into security products for your client OSs.

NFS doesn't use passwords for security *per se*. Instead, you specify the computers that are allowed to mount NFS shares in the file /etc/exports. Because NFS is largely a UNIX-to-UNIX system, the client machine will have authenticated its users. If the user IDs of users on each machine match, this authentication method means that your Linux computer's files are as secure as the client machine's security allows. As with Samba and Netatalk, this might be a concern in some environments. As a practical matter applied to your local system, you should be sure your /etc/exports file is configured to give access to as few machines as possible, and to give read-only access whenever that's practical.

Cleartext Versus Encrypted Passwords

Network lines aren't always secure. At the very least, all the computers on a local Ethernet network can, if configured to do so, read all the traffic going over that network. In some cases, a "local" network might be less local than you might think. For instance, some cable modem and DSL network providers configure their networks in such a way that many subscribers are on a single local network. If all your computers are directly connected to such a network, then your neighbors may be able to read all your Ethernet traffic.

> **TIP**
>
> You can eliminate the threat of neighbors viewing your network's traffic over cable or DSL systems by configuring a Linux computer as a firewall or an IP masquerading machine and placing all the rest of your computers behind that Linux computer. This practice keeps your local network traffic local. These options are described in more detail in Part VI, "Linking Your Intranet to the Internet."

Some individuals have written programs to watch all Ethernet packets going over a network in search of keywords, such as *username* and *password*. When these keywords appear, the programs record surrounding data, allowing the snoop to extract a password. With the password, the snoop can then break into a computer and, perhaps, wreak havoc.

You can reduce this risk by sending passwords in an encrypted form. One way this can work is as follows: The server, when contacted with a request for an access, sends a randomly selected key value to the client. The client then uses an algorithm to combine this value with the actual password, and sends the result over the network as the password. The server can then decrypt this reply and compare it to the password it has on file. Because the reply can't be decrypted except with information retained by the server (or by using computers far beyond the means of the average cracker), a snoop on the line can't extract a password from such an exchange. If the would-be cracker attempts to gain entrance to the server, he or she is met with a different key value, so the captured reply won't do the cracker any good.

Most versions of Windows 95 sent *cleartext* passwords by default, meaning that they were unencrypted. Later versions of Windows 95 and subsequent versions of Windows all send encrypted passwords by default. You can change these defaults, or you can configure Samba to accept whichever you need. Whether you use cleartext or encrypted passwords has a significant impact on how you maintain your users' passwords on your Linux server, as described in Chapter 11.

AppleTalk also offers multiple levels of password security, but configuring Netatalk in Linux to use encrypted passwords is quite tricky. It's therefore more important with a Macintosh/Netatalk network to ensure that your network is free of snoops, by configuring an entirely private network with a gateway of some sort to the Internet as a whole.

Summary

File sharing is one of the jobs Linux does very well, particularly if your needs are for a single computer to serve files to a variety of different OSs. You can use Linux to serve the same files to DOS, Windows, OS/2, Macintosh, and UNIX clients, or to any OS that uses these OSs' file sharing mechanisms.

Properly configuring a Linux system to do file sharing requires that you understand how Linux handles directories, partitions, and removable media. You must also know something about how Linux and your client OS differ in their handling of filenames and file ownership and permissions. Because Linux provides finer control over ownership and permissions than most client OSs, you can use Linux's permissions features to provide some degree of intranetwork security, keeping users from seeing other users' files. This security is only as good as the security on the client computers, though, so if this matter is important to you, you should look into add-on security products for the client OSs.

NFS: Sharing Files with Other UNIXes

IN THIS CHAPTER

The Network Filesystem (NFS) is the way that UNIX and Linux share files natively. Unlike the Samba and Netatalk file-sharing solutions, NFS was designed for UNIX and supports all the usual UNIX filesystem features, such as case-sensitivity, ownership, and permissions. It's therefore the file sharing solution of choice when both the client and the server are UNIX or Linux computers.

You can use NFS to share files with non-UNIX systems, too, but you almost always need to acquire special software packages for the non-native systems. This solution places the burden of reconciling the differences between Linux/UNIX and foreign file handling in the hands of the foreign system. If you're using a Linux server with several foreign clients, using NFS for the clients can be costly and requires greater configuration, so it's generally preferable to use Samba to serve DOS, Windows, and OS/2 clients (see Chapter 11, "Samba: Sharing Files with Windows or OS/2") and Netatalk to serve Macintosh clients (see Chapter 12, "Netatalk: Sharing Files with Macintoshes").

Kernel Configuration for NFS

As with many networking options, you must configure the kernel properly to use NFS. There are two main NFS configuration options, each of which has one suboption. All of these are in the Network File Systems portion of the kernel configuration:

- NFS filesystem support—You must enable this option if you want your system to function as an NFS *client*. If you only want to *serve* NFS filesystems, you can omit this option. The Root file system on NFS suboption allows you to mount your system's root filesystem via NFS, which is useful for diskless workstations.

- NFS server support—You need this option if you want your system to function as an NFS *server,* using the kernel-level `knfsd` program. The Emulate SUN NFS server suboption makes `knfsd` function like a Sun NFS server in its handling of mount points. Specifically, if you enable this option, partitions that are mounted on an exported filesystem are also exported. If this option is not enabled, you need to explicitly export (and mount on the remote system) each partition separately.

The NFS Daemon

In addition to the `knfsd` program that requires kernel support to function, there's an older NFS server called `nfs-server` that doesn't require kernel support. Red Hat 6.0 ships with `knfsd`, so you probably want to use it and enable appropriate kernel support. `knfsd` is faster than `nfs-server`, but in some cases `nfs-server` is more reliable.

> **NOTE**
>
> The `nfs-server` package doesn't require kernel support, but it's not harmed by the presence of kernel support, either. If you've compiled your kernel with NFS server support, you have the choice of using either package.

If you have problems with `knfsd`, you have two choices:

- Downgrade—You can use Red Hat Linux 6.0 with the old `nfs-server` package that comes with Red Hat Linux 5.2.

- Upgrade—More recent versions of `knfsd` exist than those that shipped with Red Hat 6.0, and these versions appear to be more reliable in many situations.

> **NOTE**
>
> You're more likely to encounter problems with `knfsd` if you've upgraded your system from a Red Hat 5.2 installation than if you've installed Red Hat 6.0 on an empty partition.

The CD-ROM that accompanies this book includes both an older `nfs-server` package and a newer `knfsd` package in the `sams-extras/nfs` directory. If you try the upgrade route, you need to upgrade both the `knfsd` and `knfsd-clients` packages. If you try the downgrade, you need to eliminate these packages (if they're installed) and install the `nfs-server` package. In either case, before you begin you should type

`/etc/rc.d/init.d/nfs stop`

This command shuts down the existing NFS server. After you update your RPMs, you should type the following to start the updated server:

`/etc/rc.d/init.d/nfs start`

Whatever package you elect to install, the NFS daemon sits in the background and waits for a remote system to attempt to connect. When it sees such an attempt, the daemon checks `/etc/exports` to see whether the connecting computer is authorized to mount the requested filesystem. Assuming that the connection is authorized, the daemon provides the remote system with access.

10

NFS: SHARING FILES WITH OTHER UNIXES

As mentioned earlier in the chapter, `knfsd` either exports all of a directory tree, including any filesystems mounted within the tree, or it exports all of the tree *except* for separate partitions or disks mounted in the tree. You choose which behavior you want by setting an appropriate kernel compile option. The former behavior emulates both Sun's NFS server and the older Linux `nfs-server` package. You can exclude a separate partition from an export by using appropriate NFS options, as described in "The `/etc/exports` File."

Setting NFS Options

You can control many aspects of the NFS daemon's operation by setting options in the `/etc/exports` file or by adjusting the options used to start NFS services.

The `/etc/exports` File

The format of the `/etc/exports` file is fairly simple. Here's an example:

```
/home nessus(rw) teela(ro,squash_uids=500-501,503)
/home/edgar nessus(noaccess)
/mnt nessus(rw) teela(rw)
/etc (ro)
```

Each line begins with the name of a directory to be exported and is followed by the names of computers that are allowed to mount this directory. You can specify machine names in the following ways:

- No machine name—If only options in parentheses appear, all comers are welcome to mount that export. This is, of course, a potentially massive security hole unless it's done on a small local network.

- Single machine name—You can give a machine name, either fully qualified or in the local domain.

- NIS netgroups—If your network has a Network Information Service (NIS) server, you can specify a group known to that server by preceding the name by an ampersand (@).

- IP networks—You can specify a network of computers by giving a network address and netmask, as in `192.168.1.0/255.255.255.0`.

- Wildcards—You can use asterisks (*) and question marks (?) as wildcards in the machine name, much as you would in filenames. For instance, `*.pangaea.edu` matches all computers in the `pangaea.edu` domain, except for those with extra dots, such as `n400.erplab.pangaea.edu`.

Each computer name is followed, without a space, by a list of parameters in parentheses. The options allowed for given hosts include

- secure—Requests must originate on a port with a number lower than 1024. This is the default. To turn this option off, use insecure.
- ro—Read-only access to the export. This is the default when using knfsd.
- rw—Read/write access to the export. This is the default when using nfs-server.
- noaccess—Makes all directories below the specified one inaccessible. You must create a separate entry for this option, as in the example on page 245, in which /home/edgar is excluded from the export of /home to the host nessus.
- link_relative—Converts absolute symbolic links to relative symbolic links on export.
- link_absolute—Leaves symbolic link references as they are. This is the default.
- root_squash—Treats accesses from the root user on the remote system as if they came from user nobody, severely limiting write access to the system. This is the default.
- no_root_squash—Turns off root squashing. I don't recommend using this option in most cases.
- all_squash—Treats all access requests as if they came from the user nobody, severely limiting write access to the server.
- squash_uids and squash_gids—Specifies a list of user or group IDs, respectively, to be squashed. The example on page 244 shows this option in use on the first line of the example.
- map_daemon—Remaps user and group IDs, allowing one user to have different user or group IDs on different systems. Requires support from a special daemon on the client system.
- map_static—Maps user and group IDs according to the contents of the specified file-name. This option is covered in greater detail in the "Configuring a User Map File" section later in this chapter.
- map_nis—Maps user and group IDs according to information obtained from an NIS server.

In most cases, you don't need more than a few of these options in a simple network.

Using `nfsd` Options

In addition to the options in `/etc/exports`, you can control certain aspects of the NFS daemon through options specified when you (or your initialization scripts) start the program. In a Red Hat 6.0 system, the NFS daemon is started in the control script `/etc/rc.d/init.d/nfs`. You can edit this script to change the NFS options, which include the following:

- `-f` or `--exports-file`—The name of the exports file. The default is `/etc/exports`.
- `-l` or `--log-transfers`—Logs transfers to the system log. This option can massively increase the size of your system logs on an NFS server, but may be useful if you want to monitor network activity in great detail.
- `-n` or `--allow-non-root`—Allows connections from port numbers higher than 1024. This is similar to the `insecure` option in `/etc/exports`.
- `-p` or `--promiscuous`—The server serves any host on the network.
- `-r` or `--re-export`—Allows the server to export filesystems it's imported from elsewhere.
- `-t` or `--no-spoof-trace`—Turns off logging of attempts to mount an export from an unauthorized source. Normally, `nfsd` logs failed mount attempts so that you can be aware of them.

Check the manpage for `nfsd` for more options, most of which relate to reporting information back on a command-line launch of the program.

The script `/etc/rc.d/init.d/nfs` starts and stops the daemon when the script is run with the `start` and `stop` parameters, respectively. This normally occurs at system startup and shutdown, but if you need to change your NFS configuration, you can shut down `nfsd` and then restart it by executing this script. You can also use the `restart` and `reload` commands to get NFS to restart completely or reload its configuration files, respectively.

Using `linuxconf` to Configure NFS

As with many Red Hat Linux networking features, you can configure NFS by using `linuxconf`. Select Config, Networking, Server tasks, Exported file systems (NFS) to get the main NFS configuration screen, as shown in Figure 10.1. You can add a new entry or edit an existing one from this screen; in either case, you get the One exported file system tab shown in Figure 10.2.

Using `linuxconf` doesn't provide the same range of options available when you configure NFS by editing the configuration files manually, but it can be more convenient.

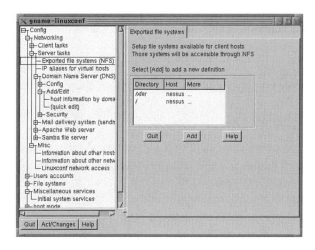

FIGURE 10.1

You can select an existing entry to change its properties or click Add to add a new one.

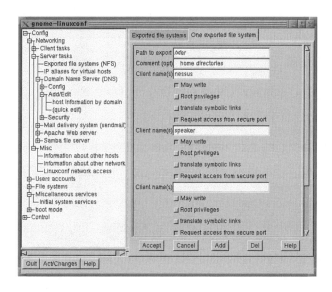

FIGURE 10.2

You can select an export path and then specify a set of clients, each of which can have its unique set of options.

How Permissions Work with NFS

Because NFS is designed for file sharing between multiuser operating systems (OSs), it's necessary for the NFS client and server to communicate user information. They do this by using user and group ID numbers, which can cause some interesting effects.

Remote Users and Local Users

Suppose you've got two Linux computers with accounts on the machines for several users, as outlined in Table 10.1. By default, NFS maps the user IDs in a way that's confusing at best and a security problem at worst. For instance, using Table 10.1's information, the only user who will have proper access to his or her files on both computers is carljones, because his user ID is the same on both computers. If the computer teela exports a filesystem to nessus, then from nessus, jimbrown will have access to bevsmith's files on teela, and bevsmith will have access to susadams' files. If the computer nessus exports filesystems to teela, on the other hand, jimbrown will have access to susadams' nessus files from teela. Similar problems can occur with group IDs.

TABLE 10.1 Hypothetical User and Group IDs on Two Computers

User	*User ID on* nessus	*User ID on* teela
jimbrown	501	504
carljones	502	502
bevsmith	503	501
susadams	504	503

NOTE

The actual usernames are unimportant. For instance, if jimbrown were known as jbrown on one system, the same principles would apply, including the same solutions.

Needless to say, user mapping problems like this are undesirable at best. One way around them is to synchronize the user and group IDs across both machines. This is certainly the simplest solution for a network with a small number of users being configured from scratch on just a few computers; you simply ensure that each user gets the same user and group IDs on all systems. If the machines already have user accounts, though, this solution is more awkward. If you want to try implementing it, you have two choices:

- Use the usermod command to change user IDs. Specifically, use the -u parameter to change the user IDs, as in **usermod -u 512 bevsmith** to change bevsmith's user ID to 512. This command also changes the ownership of files in the user's home directory to match.

- Use linuxconf to do the dirty work. Select Config, Users accounts, Normal, User accounts and click on a user's account name. You can edit the User ID (opt) field to reflect the new ID, as shown in Figure 10.3. When you click Accept, linuxconf informs you that the home directory has an invalid owner. Select the Change ownership recursively option to change the IDs of the user's files.

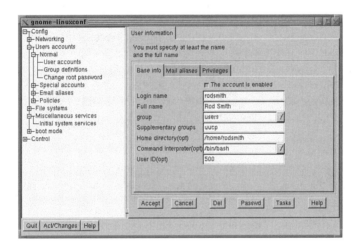

FIGURE 10.3
If you want to change additional aspects of the user's account, you can do so at the same time that you change the ID.

You need to repeat this procedure for every user whose ID needs to be changed. You might need to change some users twice to avoid temporary user ID duplication. If your group IDs need to be changed, you need to apply similar operations to them, using the -g parameter to usermod or the Config, Users accounts, Normal, Group definitions linuxconf screen.

CAUTION

Don't attempt to change any aspect of a user's account, and especially not anything as basic as the user or group ID, when the user is logged in. Be sure all affected users are logged out before attempting this operation.

Configuring a User Map File

A less radical solution, particularly if you have many users or computers, is to set up a *map file* on the server. This file remaps the user and group IDs for NFS access. You specify what map file to use with the `map_static` parameter in the options field within the `/etc/exports` file for each export and remote system. For instance, a line in `/etc/exports` might look like this:

```
/home speaker(rw,map_static=/etc/nfs/speaker.map) \
         nessus(rw,map_static=/etc/nfs/nessus.map)
```

> **TIP**
>
> Because user files normally reside only in the `/home` directory, you probably don't need to create a map file for most other directories you might export, such as `/usr/local`. You might want to use a map file for mount points for removable devices, though, especially if you need write access to the mounted media. You normally use the same map file for different exports to the same host, and different map files for the same or different exports to different hosts.

The sample `/etc/exports` line sets up an export with two different map files, one for the client `speaker` and the other for the client `nessus`. Here's an example of a map file:

```
# Mapping for client nessus:
#    remote      local
# Mapping for client nessus:
uid  0-99        -         # squash these
uid  501         504
uid  502         502
uid  503         501
uid  504         503
gid  0-49        -         # squash these
gid  50-100      700       # map 50-100 to 700-750
```

This map file might be used on Table 10.1's `teela` to correct access for the client `nessus`. Note that there are entries for both user ID (`uid`) and group ID (`gid`) mappings. Pound signs (#) denote comments.

> **CAUTION**
>
> If you create a map file, it's important that you include all your users and groups in it, including users who have the same IDs on both computers. If you omit a user or group, the ID is likely to come through in a mangled form.

Two alternatives to a map file are manifested in the map_nis and map_daemon options to exports in the /etc/exports directory. These options allow an external NIS server or the client computer, respectively, to handle the remapping. These options aren't covered here, because complete configuration is considerably more complex than a server-side map file, which should be adequate for a small network.

The Special Case of root

The superuser normally has extraordinary power on a system, so it's normally unwise to share that power, even with those who are superusers on other systems. For this reason, the root account is handled uniquely by the default NFS setup. File accesses from root (user ID 0) get remapped to a harmless account, such as nobody. If you trust both the superuser of a remote system *and* the security of your network connections, you can use the no_root_squash parameter in /etc/exports to allow the remote system's superuser to have full root access on your system.

> **CAUTION**
>
> Allowing remote NFS root access on any system connected to the Internet is asking for trouble. All a cracker needs to do is *spoof*—pretend to be your trusted computer—to gain full root access, whereupon the normally has cracker could change system files and otherwise wreak havoc. The only situation where I would consider allowing root access via NFS is on a network that's *never* connected to the Internet, and all of whose users I trust.

Mounting Remote NFS Volumes in Linux

If you have a network with two or more Linux computers (or a Linux computer and one or more UNIX machines), exporting NFS filesystems isn't enough; you must know how to mount the filesystems on a remote system.

In order to mount an NFS export, you need kernel support for the NFS filesystem, as described earlier in this chapter. You can think of NFS as being just like a disk-based filesystem in this respect; the difference is that a disk-based filesystem uses a disk device, whereas NFS uses an Ethernet cable. You don't need any other special daemons or utilities to mount an NFS export—just standard tools like mount.

Using **mount** with Remote Systems

Assuming that you don't have an `/etc/fstab` entry for a remote system, you can mount it as root with the usual `mount` command, specifying both the remote host and directory and the local mount point. For instance, here's a sample command:

```
mount teela:/home /mnt/teela/home -t nfs
```

This command is virtually identical to a standard `mount` command of a local filesystem. The main difference is in the device specification, which consists of a computer name, a colon, and a directory specification rather than a standard device file in the `/dev` directory. As with most local filesystems, Linux is smart enough to detect that you're trying to mount an NFS filesystem, so the `-t nfs` portion of the command isn't strictly necessary.

> **TIP**
>
> If the `mount` command fails, try checking the last few entries in the `/var/log/messages` file on both the server and the client machines. There may be clues in those files as to why the mount failed (for example, the client isn't authorized to connect to the server). You get an error message with some information when a mount fails, but `/var/log/messages` often contains more information.

You can specify additional options using the `-o` parameter, as in the following:

```
mount teela:/home /mnt/teela/home -o rsize=8192,wsize=8192
```

Options that you're likely to find most useful include the following:

- `rsize=`*value* and `wsize=`*value*—Specify the size of the transfers for reading and writing, respectively. The default is 1024, which is rather small.
- `hard`—Causes programs to hang if the server becomes inaccessible, but the programs resume operation when the server comes back online. This is the default.
- `soft`—Transfers a timeout when the server becomes inaccessible, potentially causing loss of data but allowing for local interruption of the affected programs.
- `intr`—Allows interrupts to NFS calls, which can be useful for aborting if the server becomes inaccessible, particularly if you also specify the `hard` option.

You can provide many more mount options for NFS filesystems. Check the `nfs` manpage for more details.

Configuring `/etc/fstab` to Allow Users to Mount Remote Volumes

You can add NFS exports to `/etc/fstab` just as if they were normal partitions. This includes the ability to use the `user` option to allow users to mount remote partitions. Here's a sample `/etc/fstab` file illustrating this:

```
/dev/hda10      /                ext2    defaults      1 1
none            /proc            proc    defaults      0 0
speaker:/home   /speaker/home    nfs     defaults      0 0
speaker:/mnt    /speaker/mnt     nfs     noauto,user   0 0
```

In addition to mounting the root and `/proc` partitions, this `/etc/fstab` file gives access to two NFS exports from the computer `speaker`: `/home` and `/mnt`. The system mounts `speaker:/home` at boot time, so it will always be available—assuming that `speaker` is always available! The `noauto` parameter in the fourth column of the `speaker:/mnt` entry prevents the export from being mounted at system boot, and the `user` parameter allows users to mount and unmount the exports by typing **mount /speaker/home** or **mount /speaker/mnt**.

Automounting Remote Volumes

You can add NFS exports to an automount configuration, as discussed in Chapter 9, "Basic Principles of File Sharing." As with adding an NFS export to `/etc/fstab`, you specify `nfs` as the filesystem type and use the NFS *machine:directory* specification as the device in the automounter configuration file. There is one difference, though: When you create the entry for the NFS export, you *omit* the leading colon (`:`) on the device name. Here's a sample `/etc/auto.misc` configuration:

```
floppy          -fstype=auto            :/dev/fd0
cdrom           -fstype=iso9660         :/dev/scd0
teela           -fstype=nfs             teela:/home
```

If the automounter is configured to mount these devices in the `/misc` directory, you could then access `teela`'s `/home` directory by going to `/misc/teela`. The computer automatically unmounts the NFS export after the delay interval specified in the `/etc/auto.master` file unless there's continued access to that directory.

> **NOTE**
>
> The omission of the leading colon when you place an NFS export in an automounter entry isn't really an omission. You may recall from Chapter 9's discussion of the automounter that this feature requires NFS support in the kernel. The automounter uses this support to mount the files, hence the need for a colon in the device names for local mounts—what's really omitted is the machine name for the local device files! When you configure the automounter to handle NFS exports, you have to add the machine name back because the device is no longer on the local computer.

Summary

NFS exports are in many ways the simplest kind of file sharing in Linux. This is partly because the protocol is designed for UNIX-to-UNIX file sharing, and so needn't be concerned with issues of filename or permissions conversion. NFS has mechanisms to deal with differing user and group IDs on the client and server computers, though.

Red Hat Linux ships with a version of the NFS daemon that causes problems on many systems. Other NFS daemons are available, though, and if you have problems with the default daemon, you can try one of the alternatives. In practice, these different alternatives function very much alike, so the configuration information presented here applies to them all, except as noted.

Samba: Sharing Files with DOS, Windows, and OS/2

IN THIS CHAPTER

Given the popularity of Windows as a desktop operating system (OS), chances are good that one of the reasons you're reading this book is to learn how to configure Linux to serve files to Windows computers. You might even have skipped directly to this chapter, bypassing the preceding 10. If so, you would do well to at least skim Chapter 9, "Basic Principles of File Sharing," before embarking on a quest to configure Samba, Linux's server for Windows file and printer sharing. Also, you should be aware that you need Linux's basic networking features running properly before you can configure Samba, so if you're starting from a fresh Linux installation, you may need to go over Chapter 7, "Setting Ethernet Options," and perhaps Chapters 5, "Basic Linux Configuration," and 6, "Compiling a Kernel for Networking," as well. If you want to use your Linux computer to make a printer available to several computers, you should read Chapters 14, "Preparing to Share a Printer," and 16, "Samba: Sharing Printers with DOS, Windows, and OS/2."

Although most people use Samba with Windows clients, OSs besides Windows, including DOS and OS/2, use the same protocols. People even use Samba on occasion to share files from one Linux computer to another, although NFS (Chapter 10, "NFS: Sharing Files with Other UNIXes") is usually better for this purpose. There's even a Macintosh client, known as DAVE (`http://www.thursby.com`), that works with Samba—though the Netatalk package for Linux is usually a better choice for file sharing with Macintoshes. In this chapter, I often refer to "Windows clients," but unless I mention specific Windows characteristics, such as the Select Network Protocol dialog box, these comments generally apply to other client OSs that can communicate with Samba.

NOTE

This chapter doesn't provide information on how to configure Windows or any other OS for networking; I expect that you know how to do that already. Toward the end of the chapter, though, I present a few examples of how to access Samba shares from Windows.

Samba's job is simple in principle, but fairly complex in practice. It must coax Linux into communicating on a Windows network, using Windows native networking protocols. The primary goal is to allow Windows computers to mount Linux directories as if they were exported disks from a Windows computer, and to print to printers controlled by Linux as if they were connected to Windows computers. A secondary goal is to allow the Linux computer to access resources shared by the Windows machines. Samba also supports a number of additional Windows networking tasks, some of which are subsidiary to these primary and secondary goals.

The original Red Hat 6.0 shipped with Samba version 2.0.3, but version 2.0.5a has subsequently been released. Because Red Hat has made a 2.0.5a update available, and because the CD that accompanies this book installs that updated version by default, that's the version described in this chapter. Previous versions of Red Hat shipped with pre-2.0 varieties of Samba, and if you're using an older distribution, you might have such a version. I recommend that you upgrade Samba in this situation.

> **NOTE**
>
> If Samba is not already installed on your computer, install it now. On an RPM-based system, type `rpm -q samba` to see if it's installed.

Samba is a very complex software package, with lots of subtleties. This chapter can get you started using it, but it doesn't cover every aspect of the server. For basic information on the commands and options you don't find here, you can start by reading the manpages for `smb.conf`, `smbd`, or any other relevant tool. You can also check the documentation in the `/usr/doc/samba-2.0.5a` directory, and on the Samba Web site, `http://samba.org`. If you need to delve deeper into Samba, you might want to check out *Sams Teach Yourself Samba in 24 Hours*, which goes into far more detail than one chapter can.

Samba: NetBIOS over TCP/IP for Linux

In the 1980s, IBM developed a networking technology that it called *NetBIOS* (Network Basic Input/Output System) for small networks of PCs. This technology has grown and transformed in various ways over the years, and is now an important component of Windows workgroup networking, and thus for Samba.

Understanding NetBIOS and NetBEUI

If you've configured Windows computers, you've no doubt seen the terms *NetBIOS* and *NetBEUI* in reference to Windows networking protocols, but you may not know what they are. NetBIOS, as mentioned, is the core of the Windows networking protocols. NetBEUI stands for *NetBIOS Extended User Interface*, and is both an extension of NetBIOS and a networking layer upon which NetBIOS rests.

In practice, plain NetBIOS is more important, at least for Samba networking, than is NetBEUI. NetBIOS can run over NetBEUI, but it can also run over the Novell IPX (Internetwork Packet Exchange) protocols or over TCP/IP. In fact, you can see that Microsoft Windows offers IPX, NetBEUI, and TCP/IP as alternative network stacks, as shown in the Select Network Protocol dialog box (see Figure 11.1). In this dialog box, IPX/SPX, NetBEUI, and TCP/IP are all listed as separate items.

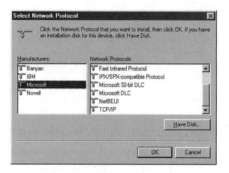

FIGURE 11.1

IPX/SPX, NetBEUI, and TCP/IP are all examples of networking stacks, referred to as network protocols in Windows.

Bridging NetBIOS to TCP/IP

Samba must understand NetBIOS in order to communicate with Windows clients. Samba does not, however, understand NetBEUI. Instead, Samba communicates using NetBIOS as transmitted over TCP/IP. Because Microsoft has been moving toward TCP/IP for years, this approach is quite reasonable in most cases. It does have certain consequences, however:

- Your Windows clients must have TCP/IP networking installed.

- Occasionally, the presence of NetBEUI on client computers interferes with the operation of NetBIOS over TCP/IP. If you're having problems connecting from a client computer, particularly if other clients work, try removing NetBEUI from the problem computer.

- Because TCP/IP routers don't process NetBEUI, NetBEUI can be more secure when linking a small network to the Internet. You might therefore need to exercise greater caution when using NetBIOS over TCP/IP.

This final point deserves a few additional words. If you have a small local network that you want to link to the Internet, Windows-style networking can be a security problem. Depending on how your organization or ISP attaches your network to its wider networks, computers outside your immediate workgroup might be able to see your machines if you enable Windows file sharing over TCP/IP. The best solution is to use a firewall or IP masquerading gateway to connect your network to the Internet. If you use NetBEUI, this problem is also reduced because NetBEUI doesn't get past TCP/IP routers. If you're concerned about these issues, you should consult with your organization's networking personnel or with your ISP to determine how your computers are connected to the Internet.

The SMB Protocols

At the top of the Windows networking protocols, controlling the show as it were, is the *Server Message Block* (SMB) protocol, which has been renamed the *Common Internet File System* (CIFS). In fact, Samba gets its name from the acronym SMB. Figure 11.2 shows the relationship between SMB, NetBIOS, NetBEUI, IPX, and TCP/IP.

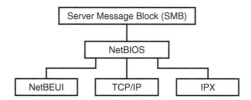

FIGURE 11.2
Samba supports SMB only over TCP/IP, although Windows supports SMB over NetBEUI and IPX, as well.

NetBIOS provides basic functionality—indeed, the *B* in NetBIOS stands for *basic*. SMB provides higher-level tools. This is similar to the relationship between a driver or BIOS for controlling a hard disk and the disk's filesystem. SMB is, much like UNIX's Network Filesystem (NFS), a filesystem for network use. Unlike a hard disk's BIOS, though, in the case of Windows file sharing, there's another level of protocols beneath the NetBIOS—namely TCP/IP, in the case of Samba.

When to Use Samba

NetBIOS and SMB/CIFS were designed with networking for DOS and, later, Windows and OS/2 in mind. These protocols provide support for the specific features that DOS, Windows, and OS/2 programs expect of a filesystem. Other networking protocols, such as NFS, support a different set of features. Therefore, using SMB/CIFS is the best course of action when the client OS is DOS, Windows, or OS/2.

Note, however, that using Samba on Linux means that Samba has to convert the filesystem features supported by SMB into forms that Linux can handle. Basic functionality, such as file reading and writing, isn't a problem; features like the *hidden* attribute, which isn't supported by Linux, can cause difficulties, depending on how Samba is configured. For the most part, Samba has conquered these difficulties, so a Samba server can integrate quite seamlessly into an existing Windows network. In fact, if you're careful to configure the system properly, you could replace a Windows server with a Linux computer running Samba, and your users might not know the difference!

Because SMB doesn't provide for the permissions or ownership information that UNIX computers expect and that NFS provides, it's generally best *not* to use Samba for file sharing between Linux or UNIX computers. You might do so in some limited cases, though, such as when you only need to provide access to users' data files, not program files, or if a user needs quick access to remote files that aren't normally needed from Linux, but are from Windows. As a general rule, I recommend using Samba for file sharing with Linux or UNIX clients only if you have some compelling reason to do so, such as a desire to limit the number of file-sharing protocols your server supports.

Similarly, Macintoshes expect their filesystems to support certain unique features, such as the presence of separate resource and data forks. Samba doesn't support this feature, so SMB/CIFS software for Macintoshes, such as Thursby's DAVE, must emulate it. DAVE also costs money, whereas the Netatalk AppleTalk server package for Linux is free, so there's a financial incentive to not use Samba with Macintoshes. On the other hand, Samba is more polished than Netatalk, so you might find the combination of Samba and DAVE to be better in some situations.

Setting Samba Options

Before you can use Samba to serve files, you must configure the software. As you work with Samba, you'll discover that it offers an extremely broad array of configuration options, giving you much finer control over the behavior of your Linux server than you get with a Windows server. You need to take the time to learn something of what these options do, though.

TIP

When you create your /etc/smb.conf Samba configuration file, you might want to use the testparm utility. This program checks whether the file contains any egregious errors. Try running it on /etc/smb.conf and then on another, unrelated file, such as /etc/fstab. testparm displays many errors for the latter, but should not for the former. The program also dumps a summary of the /etc/smb.conf file's services after doing its test, and this summary can be quite long.

Text Editing and GUI Configuration

You can configure Samba either by editing the /etc/smb.conf file in your favorite text editor or by using the linuxconf utility (assuming that you're using the Red Hat or Mandrake Linux distributions). If you use linuxconf, you need to select the options under the Config, Networking, Samba file server heading. Figure 11.3 shows the Defaults tab from that list, which lets you configure general-purpose settings. The Default setup for user's home option allows you to configure settings for home directory shares, and the Disk shares option lets you select or create a share other than a home directory share.

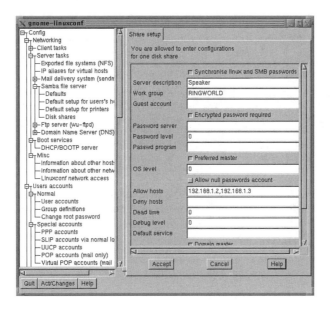

FIGURE 11.3
You don't need to use the Default setup for printers linuxconf item to configure file sharing, but you do need to use the other Samba file server items.

Because the linuxconf options are easy to match with the options for text file configuration, this section focuses on editing the /etc/smb.conf configuration file directly. If you prefer to use linuxconf, just look for appropriately named entries for each of these actions. I recommend that you use linuxconf (or some other administrative tool) to configure Samba initially because using linuxconf reduces the likelihood that you'll produce a corrupt /etc/smb.conf file.

SWATting Samba

You can administer Samba through a Web-based utility known as the *Samba Web Administration Tool* (SWAT). This tool operates much like `linuxconf` in its Web-based mode, but you access it from port 901—for instance, to access SWAT on the computer `n400.erplab.pangaea.edu`, you would enter `http://n400.erplab.pangaea.edu:901` in a browser's address field. To activate SWAT, you must do three things:

- If it's not already present, add a line to `/etc/services` that reads

  ```
  swat      901/tcp
  ```

- If it's not already present, add a line to `/etc/inetd.conf` that reads

  ```
  swat   stream   tcp   nowait.400   root   /usr/sbin/swat   swat
  ```

  If you're not using Red Hat Linux and its default Samba installation, you might need to adjust the path to the `swat` program for your system.

- Restart the `inetd` daemon by using `ps` to find its process ID number and typing **kill -SIGHUP** *pid*, where *pid* is the process ID number.

The SWAT user interface is similar in principle to `linuxconf`'s in Web mode, although the details differ. When you use SWAT, you send your root password in cleartext, so it's generally best to use it only on a local network that you completely control, and only on a server with no direct connections to the Internet at large. SWAT is no more—or less—secure in principle than is `linuxconf` when it's configured for Web access, but because SWAT only controls Samba, I recommend that you use it rather than `linuxconf` if you want to configure *only* Samba through the Web. If you're already running `linuxconf`, SWAT is redundant.

/etc/smb.conf File Structure

The `/etc/smb.conf` file is organized in sections, each of which is identified by a name in square braces, such as `[global]`. Many options apply to multiple sections, but some have meaning only within specific sections. The sections are

- `[global]`—This section controls the most far-ranging aspects of Samba's configuration, such as the NetBIOS name for the computer, what hosts can connect, and so on.

- `[printers]`—You can define default printer operations in this section. Unless you specify otherwise, Linux exports *all* the printers configured on your printer. I discuss configuring Samba for printers in Chapter 16, "Samba: Sharing Printers with DOS, Windows, and OS/2."

- [homes]—If you want users to have access to their home directories, you can create a section to define such access here. When Samba authenticates a user, that user has access to his or her home directory, but not others' home directories, assuming that you've set up Linux's permissions to forbid such access. Using the [homes] section is a great time-saver because you don't need to define each user's home directory separately—one configuration works for all.

- [*sharename*]—Any name other than [global], [printers], or [homes] represents the name of a specific share. You might want to define a directory in which shared program files reside, or where your network's users can place files they need to exchange with each other.

The [global] section is generally the largest because it contains configuration options for many important global parameters. If the defaults are acceptable, though, this section may be fairly small.

Within each section, you set most options by specifying the option name, an equal sign (=), and the value. Both the option name and the value it holds can be multiple words. In some cases, you might want to set some information in the value that you can't know at the time you configure the /etc/smb.conf file, such as the username of the person using the share. For this reason, Samba supports a number of variables in the /etc/smb.conf file, as detailed in Table 11.1. Variables are all preceded by percent signs (%).

TABLE 11.1 smb.conf Variables

Variable	Description
%a	The architecture of the remote machine. May be Samba, WfWg, WinNT, or Win95. Windows 98 shows up as Win95, and Windows 2000 as WinNT.
%d	The process ID of the current server process.
%g	The primary group of username %u.
%G	The primary group of username %u.
%h	The Internet name of the host on which Samba is running.
%H	The home directory for the username %u.
%I	The IP address of the client machine.
%L	The NetBIOS name of the server.
%m	The NetBIOS name of the client.
%M	The TCP/IP name of the client.

continues

TABLE **11.1** Continued

Variable	Description
%N	The name of your NIS home directory server, as specified in the auto.map file. This is the same as %L if Samba hasn't been compiled with automount support.
%p	The path to the service's home directory, as obtained from the auto.map file.
%P	The root directory of the current service.
%R	The protocol selected during the protocol negotiation phase of the connection setup. May be CORE, COREPLUS, LANMAN1, LANMAN2, or NT1.
%S	The name of the current service.
%T	The current date and time.
%u	The username of the current service.
%U	The username the client requested. This may not be identical to %u.
%v	The Samba version number.

Setting Global Parameters

The global parameters control how Samba as a whole behaves—how it announces itself to the network, to what computers it responds, and so on. It's vital that you configure your system's global parameters properly, or you might not even be able to see it in the Windows Network Neighborhood.

Identification Settings

NetBIOS doesn't use TCP/IP machine names to identify computers, even when NetBIOS runs over TCP/IP. Instead, NetBIOS uses its own *machine* and *workgroup* names. In general, you probably want to set your server to use your TCP/IP machine name as the NetBIOS machine name, just to make life less complicated. Your workgroup name might be totally unrelated to any other networking name for your computer. If you're setting up an intranet in a larger organization, though, you might have the luxury of setting the workgroup name to match a portion of your fully qualified domain name (FQDN). For instance, if the network of computers in the domain erplab.pangaea.edu constitutes a single NetBIOS workgroup, you might set the workgroup name to ERPLAB.

> **NOTE**
>
> A NetBIOS workgroup must normally reside on a single Ethernet network, limiting the physical range of the workgroup. You can use a bridge to extend this range, though. Also, with NetBIOS over TCP/IP, you can connect to remote workgroups by specifying an IP address. I've used PPP dialup connections to ISPs to connect to Samba servers that are miles away on networks separate from the ISP's, for instance.

To set the machine name, you use the `netbios name` option, and to set the workgroup name, you use the `workgroup` option. The convention is to specify these values in uppercase. You can also set the `server string` option, which can provide a more descriptive identification of your system. The `netbios name` option defaults to your computer's hostname, and the workgroup name's default varies depending on compile options. You can therefore omit the `netbios name` specification in many instances, but because your workgroup name varies locally, you should be sure to set it.

Here's an example of all three options in use:

```
netbios name = SPEAKER
workgroup = RINGWORLD
server string = Workgroup server computer running Samba %v
```

Note that the `server string` specification includes a variable (`%v`) to announce the Samba version number. In practice, you might not want to give this information out because if there's a security bug in the version you're running, advertising the version number might prove unwise.

Authentication Options

You can configure Samba to use one of four different methods of authentication using the `security` option:

- `share`—Samba requires separate authentication for access to each shared resource. In Windows, *only* a password is required for this type of access, but in Linux, Samba needs a username, too. Some clients send a username, and Samba attempts to use that. In the event that this attempt fails, you can specify a set of users against which to check the password, as in `users = larry, moe, curly`. In general, share-level security is awkward in Linux, so unless you have a compelling reason to use it, I recommend not using it.

- `user`—Samba requires that the client send both a username and a password, and if approved, the user has access to all the shares on the server, within limits imposed by Linux permissions.

- server—Server security works very much like user security, except that Samba offloads the password-checking task to another server computer. This computer can be a Windows NT or Samba machine. If you use this option, you must also specify the password server option, and give the NetBIOS name of the password server as its parameter.

- domain—Domain security works just like server security, but the Samba server then belongs to a Windows NT domain, which is somewhat different from a workgroup, as discussed in "Workgroups, Domains, and Browsing," later in this chapter. If you're connecting a Samba server to a network that uses domains, you should give serious consideration to using this security option.

Windows clients normally send the Windows login name and password, so it's best to ensure that all users have the same usernames (and perhaps passwords) on all systems. If that's not the case, you can use the username map option to specify a file containing a list of Linux and Windows usernames, in the form *linuxname = windowsname*, one entry per line.

Password Encryption

An issue that goes hand-in-hand with the security option is password encryption. Both Samba and Windows support two different encryption options, as discussed in Chapter 9: cleartext and encrypted. Crackers generally find encrypted passwords to be more difficult to break, and so this type of password is preferable from a security standpoint. Two issues complicate the equation, though:

- Some versions of Windows send cleartext and others send encrypted passwords by default. Specifically, early versions of Windows 95 and Windows NT 4.0 prior to Service Pack 3 sent cleartext passwords, whereas subsequent versions of both OSs (including Windows 98 and 2000) send encrypted passwords. You can change the defaults for Windows, but it might be simpler to change what Samba expects.

- The encryption scheme used by Windows is different from that used by Linux. Because both schemes are *nonreversible* (meaning that you can't get the original password from its encrypted version), Samba can't use the normal Linux user authentication methods with encrypted passwords; it has to maintain a separate database of passwords. In Red Hat Linux, this database is stored in /etc/smbpasswd, but it might reside elsewhere in other distributions or if you build Samba from source code yourself. Maintaining two password files can be a nuisance.

You control whether to use encrypted passwords with the encrypt passwords option; set this to yes to use encrypted passwords, or no to use cleartext passwords. If you use encrypted passwords, you also need to create an appropriate /etc/smbpasswd file. Here's a procedure to do so, using the existing /etc/passwd file as a base:

1. Type this command to create an `/etc/smbpasswd` file with entries for each user, but invalid passwords:

   ```
   cat /etc/passwd | mksmbpasswd.sh > /etc/smbpasswd
   ```

2. Edit the resulting `/etc/smbpasswd` file to remove accounts that won't be using Samba services. Such accounts include an assortment of accounts that Linux uses internally, such as `ftp` and `gopher`.

3. For each user, issue the `smbpasswd` command to change the password. (Note that `smbpasswd` is both the name of a command and the name of the Samba password file.) For instance, typing **`smbpasswd larry`** results in a prompt for a new password for the user `larry`.

If you have a large number of users and don't want to call them in to enter their passwords or assign passwords yourself, you can use cleartext passwords initially and migrate to encrypted passwords. Instead of performing step 3, configure Samba to use cleartext passwords and add the option `update encrypted = yes` to the `/etc/smb.conf` file. As users log on and use Samba shares, Samba will run `smbpasswd` itself, using the verified cleartext password to set the encrypted password value. After a while, you can change `/etc/smb.conf` to use `encrypt passwords = yes` and `update encrypted = no`. One caveat is that this procedure assumes that the clients can handle both encrypted and cleartext passwords. Recent versions of Windows insist on using encrypted passwords only, which can make this procedure more difficult.

To change Windows to use cleartext passwords, you need to add an entry to the Windows Registry. If you're using Red Hat 6.0, you can find files to accomplish this task in the `/usr/doc/samba-2.0.5a/docs`; you need the `WinVer_PlainPassword.reg` file, where `WinVer` is your version of Windows. You might find these files in some other directory if you're using a different distribution of Linux. Copy the appropriate file to your Windows computer and double-click on it. Windows should incorporate the change into the Registry, thus enabling cleartext passwords.

Another password-related issue is case. SMB/CIFS servers generally use case-insensitive or all-uppercase passwords, but Linux uses case-sensitive passwords. To cope with this problem, Samba converts passwords to lowercase (because most users have mostly lowercase passwords). If no match is found, Samba can convert individual letters to uppercase to try to find a match. Samba tries all possible permutations of upper- and lowercase letters, using up to the number of uppercase letters specified by the `password level` option. Increasing this level can slow down logins, but may be necessary if your users have uppercase or mixed-case passwords. Similar comments apply to usernames, and there's a `username level` option that works the same way as `password level`.

Limiting Samba Access

If your Linux server is accessible from the Internet, or even from computers in your organization that shouldn't have access to your Samba shares, you might want to limit access on a machine-by-machine basis. You do this with the `hosts allow` and `hosts deny` options. The syntax for these options is very similar, but `hosts allow` lists machines from which access is permitted, whereas `hosts deny` lists computers that should *not* have access. In general, you use `hosts allow` when you want to provide Samba services to only a handful of computers, and you use `hosts deny` when you want to exclude known "troublemakers" or machines that belong to some less-trusted computers, such as public workstations.

You can specify machines for `hosts allow` and `hosts deny` in the following ways:

- As an Internet machine name—This generally means an FQDN, such as `n400.erplab.pangaea.edu`. If your system is on the same network as the target, you might be able to give only the machine name, as in `n400`.
- As an IP address—A full IP address in dotted quad notation, such as `192.168.1.5`.
- As a partial IP address—If you enter fewer than 4 bytes of the IP address and leave a period, Samba interprets this to mean all addresses in the network specified. For instance, `192.168.1.` refers to all computers (up to 254 of them) in the 192.168.1.0 network.
- As an IP address/subnet mask pair—You can specify an IP address and subnet mask to specify a range of computers. For instance, `192.168.1.32/255.255.255.224` refers to hosts ranging from 192.168.1.32 through 192.168.1.63.
- Using `except`—You can exclude a machine or subnetwork from the rule by preceding its name with the keyword `except`. For instance, `192.168.1. except 192.168.1.23` allows or denies all computers in the 192.168.1.*x* network except for 192.168.1.23.

You can mix and match these methods by listing separate addresses or ranges separated by spaces. For instance, here's a sample `hosts allow` line:

```
hosts allow = teela 192.168.1. 192.168.3.2
```

If you have so many hosts that they exceed one line's length, you can place a backslash (\) at the end of one line to continue the list on another. This technique works with other `/etc/smb.conf` options, too.

> **TIP**
>
> You can use the `hosts allow` and `hosts deny` options in individual shares, as well as use them in the `[global]` section of `/etc/smb.conf`.

In general, I recommend using `hosts allow` to explicitly list the authorized hosts by IP address, at least on computers that are connected to the Internet. This practice makes it more difficult for unauthorized individuals to break into your system.

To increase security, Samba normally binds itself to a single interface. If your computer functions as a gateway, firewall, or IP masquerading computer, though, it's possible that you need to specify the NIC it's to use. You do this with the `interfaces` option:

```
interfaces = 192.168.1.1/255.255.255.0
```

You specify the host computer's IP address and netmask on the interface to which you want to bind on the `interfaces` line. The preceding example sets Samba to serve the 192.168.1.0 network on the NIC bound to 192.168.1.1. If you want Samba to serve the networks of two or more NICs, you need to list them all, separated by spaces.

Speed Enhancement Options

Samba generally produces good speed, but in some cases you might need to tweak its settings, or "untweak" some setting that was somehow misconfigured. Unfortunately, details of what works well vary substantially from one network to another because performance-tuning factors interact with issues such as the network hardware type. The following are a few specific suggestions:

- General network performance—If your network is overloaded, Samba doesn't perform well. You might want to check for collisions by typing **/sbin/ifconfig**. If the number of collisions is high compared to the number of packets transmitted (TX) and received (RX), then you might want to look into installing a bridge or replacing a hub with a switch (see Chapter 4, "Intranets and the Internet," and Chapter 1, "Networking Hardware").

- Oplocks—*Opportunistic locks,* or *oplocks,* are a means of controlling multiuser access to files. The `fake oplocks` option can speed up access to read-only media such as CD-ROMs, but is otherwise risky. The `oplocks` option (which is distinct from the `fake oplocks` option) can speed access substantially on all files if set to `yes`, so you should be sure this hasn't been set to `no`.

- Strict sync—The `strict sync` parameter defaults to `no`, and should usually be left that way because it improves performance by not performing a Linux `sync()` operation when the client requests it—which many Windows programs do more frequently than they should. The default setting of `no` increases the risk of lost data should Linux itself crash, though.

In addition to these items, you can use socket options to influence Samba's interface to the TCP/IP stack, thus affecting system performance. The exact effects you see with these options vary from one network to another, though, so I can't offer any specific advice. If you want to experiment, you can create a socket options line in your /etc/smb.conf file and add or delete the following options:

SO_KEEPALIVE

SO_REUSEADDR

SO_BROADCAST

TCP_NODELAY

IPTOS_LOWDELAY

IPTOS_THROUGHPUT

SO_SNDBUF=*integer*

SO_RCVBUF=*integer*

SO_SNDLOWAT=*integer*

SO_RCVLOWAT=*integer*

Configuring a Share

After you've set the configuration options for the Samba server as a whole, it's time to tackle the shares you want to configure. You do this in the section with the name of the share you want to modify, or in the [homes] section to create a share for all users' home accounts. The [homes] section, if present, creates a share that can be accessed either by the name homes or by the username. By default, that share opens onto the user's home directory, and you should *not* specify another directory for this share.

Share Availability Options

Several options affect the availability of a share—either its visibility in a client's browser or the ability of the user to access the share:

- comment—The comment you enter on a share appears when you browse the share in details mode from Windows, as shown in Figure 11.4.
- available—This option defaults to yes. If it is set to no, Samba doesn't let anybody connect to a share. You might use this option to make a share temporarily unavailable while you perform maintenance on a directory.
- guest ok or public—These options are synonymous, and default to no. If they are set to yes, they allow anybody to connect to the share in question, even without a password. Exercise extreme caution in using these options!

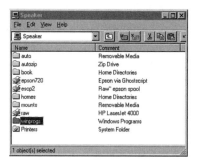

FIGURE 11.4
You use the comment *option to provide a few words of description to each share.*

- browsable or browseable—These options are synonymous, and refer to the visibility of a share in a browser such as the Windows Network Neighborhood. You normally need to set this option to yes, which is the default.

> **NOTE**
>
> A browser for SMB/CIFS is *not* the same as a Web browser, although changes in Windows 98 make the two behave very much alike in that OS.

- path—You specify what directory to share using the path option. In the case of the [homes] section, you don't specify a path; Samba knows to use the user's home directory for this section.
- writable or writeable—These options are synonymous, and refer to the ability to write to a share. The default value is no. After setting a share to writeable = yes and installing program files on it, you might set such a share to writable = no in order to prevent users from accidentally deleting program files. The read only option is an antonym for writable. In many cases you can achieve similar results by using Linux permissions.
- write list—You can specify a group of users who have write access to a share, even when the writable option is set to no. You might be able to achieve similar results by using Linux permissions.

Ownership and Permissions Options

By default, files created by remote users are owned by the user and have file permissions of -rwxr--r-- (0744 in octal notation), or drwxr-xr-x (0755 octal) for directories. You can change these defaults, however:

- `force user`—You can specify a username for files created in a given share. For instance, suppose that you normally use the `larry` login name. You can use `force user` to set the username on files created in a share to `moe`, even though you're accessing the share as `larry`. This feature is particularly helpful for shares that are accessed by multiple users—you can create a special user to own shared files, and use `force user` to let all users access shared files using this special user's permissions. You probably should *not* use the `force user` option on home directories, though because you probably want ownership in home directories to reflect the files' true owners.

- `force group`—This option works very much like the `force user` option, except that you specify a group name, rather than a username.

- `create mask` and `create mode`—These options are synonymous. They set the ownership of files, specified as an octal string. The default setting, `0744`, gives the owner execute permission on files, which is a bit odd when you access the files from Linux itself. I therefore like changing the `create mask` to `0644`. You can set more restrictive modes, such as `0600` or `0640`, to limit read access to the files to the owner and perhaps others in the owner's group, respectively.

- `directory mask` and `directory mode`—These options are synonymous. They set the ownership of directories in the same way that `create mask` sets ownership of files. Because directories in Linux generally have execute permission whenever they have write permission, the default value, `0755`, is reasonable, but you can limit access further by specifying `0750` or `0700`, if you like.

Table 11.2 shows some useful combinations of ownership and masks for various situations.

TABLE 11.2   Some Possible Ownership and Permissions for Samba Shares

Force User	Create Mask	Directory Mask	Description
common[1]	0666	0777	Files shared by many users.
—	0444	0555	A read-only shared directory. This directory could be modified from Linux itself, but not from Windows clients.
—	0440	0550	A read-only shared directory for a group.
—	0644	0755	A home directory account in a low-security environment.
—	0640	0750	A home directory account in an environment requiring groups to collaborate, but little file sharing between groups.
—	0600	0700	A home directory account when no other user should be able to access files.

[1]*User* common *refers to some username set aside to own the shared files for purposes of Linux bookkeeping.*

Of course Table 11.2 only scratches the surface of the possibilities. In a network with many users and groups interacting in complex ways, you might have several different shared directories with differing permissions for assorted groups of users. These options also interact with some of the share availability options discussed earlier in the chapter. In general, actual access is determined by the most restrictive options specified. Fortunately, most small networks can do quite well with just a few simple options.

Filename Case and Mangling Options

Linux is a *case-sensitive* OS (p. 230), whereas Windows is a *case-retentive* OS (p. 230). In addition, Linux supports longer filenames than Windows, and much longer filenames than DOS. Also, DOS is a *case-insensitive* OS (p. 230), which adds yet more complications to the mix.

Samba's default behavior is to take great pains to conform to the client OS's expectations for filename case and length. In some situations, particularly when dealing with DOS clients, Samba must *mangle* a name, or shorten it in such a way that Samba can still match the on-disk filename to the one used by the client. If you've used Windows 95 or later, you're probably familiar with name mangling as performed on FAT/VFAT filesystems because VFAT includes built-in name mangling capabilities. This is demonstrated by a directory listing in a Windows command prompt window, like this:

```
A:\>dir
Volume in drive A is FLOPPY
Directory of A:\
FILE1    TXT            99  10-05-99  2:19p FILE1.TXT
LONGFI~1 TXT            99  10-05-99  2:21p LongFilename.txt
         5 file(s)          198 bytes
```

The file called LongFilename.txt also bears the mangled filename LONGFI~1.TXT, which is used by DOS and older Windows programs that don't understand long filenames. Samba supports a similar feature, even on filesystems that don't include explicit support for name mangling.

NOTE

In Windows, the VFAT and NTFS filesystems provide direct support for name mangling. Even when using VFAT or NTFS, though, Samba's name mangling is self-generated. Therefore, you don't see the same mangled names in a Samba share that you see when accessing the same FAT or NTFS disk directly or from a Windows server. If you dual-boot a server between Linux and Windows, DOS clients therefore see different filenames for non-8.3-compliant names.

Samba options that affect name mangling and case-sensitivity include the following:

- `mangled names`—The default for this option is `yes`. If you set this option to `no`, Samba doesn't perform name mangling; it simply truncates filenames, which can result in two files having the same name. When this happens, you can access only one file.
- `mangle case`—Converts the case of files, normally providing all-uppercase names to the clients. The default is `no`.
- `case sensitive`—If this option is set to `yes`, Samba treats filenames in a case-sensitive manner. The default is `no`, which requires that Samba do more work to match filenames.
- `default case`—This option specifies the default case for new files from case-insensitive clients. The default is `lower`.
- `preserve case`—If this option is set to `yes` (the default), it preserves case from case-retentive OSs, such as Windows and OS/2. If it is set to `no`, filenames are converted to the default case.

The Samba Daemons

Like most networking services, Samba operates by running *daemons* (p. 62). The Samba package contains two daemons:

- `smbd`—The SMB daemon provides the bulk of the services you think of when you think of Windows networking, including the all-important file-exchange services.
- `nmbd`—The name browser daemon is responsible for announcing the presence of your Linux server on the NetBIOS network. If it's not configured properly, you can't access your Linux computer's shares from Windows.

There are two ways to run the Samba daemons: independently and from `inetd`. Each has advantages and disadvantages.

Running Samba Independently

If you type **ps ax ¦ grep mbd -**, you get a report of services running that include the string mbd in their names. This includes both the Samba daemons, and normally not much else. Here's some sample output from my system:

```
8243 ?        S       0:00 smbd -D
8254 ?        S       0:00 nmbd -D
```

> **NOTE**
>
> Don't be concerned if you see several instances of smbd. This occurrence is normal if several clients are connected to Samba shares.

Because both smbd and nmbd appear in this output, it's clear that both daemons are running independently. How do you get to this state, though?

Many Linux distributions, including Red Hat Linux 6.0, start the Samba daemons in the script /etc/rc.d/init.d/smb, which takes the parameters start, stop, restart, and status. So if Samba isn't already running, you can type **/etc/rc.d/init.d/smb start** to start it. The initialization scripts run the smb script at system startup, so after you install Samba and reboot, it should be running.

> **NOTE**
>
> If you've installed Samba and rebooted but it's not running, check for the presence of links called smb in /etc/rc.d/rc3.d and /etc/rc.d/rc5.d to /etc/rc.d/init.d/smb. If there are no such links, create them by typing **ln -s /etc/rc.d/init.d/smb /etc/rc.d/rc3.d**, and **ln -s /etc/rc.d/init.d/ smb /etc/rc.d/rc5.d.**

On some Linux distributions, you might need to start Samba by editing some other initialization script, such as /etc/rc.d/rc.local. You can add lines such as these to whatever startup script is convenient:

```
/usr/sbin/smbd -D
/usr/sbin/nmbd -D
```

You can also enter these lines directly at a command prompt if you want to start Samba manually.

Running Samba independently in this way has the advantage that it can respond quickly to incoming requests. In my experience, this method is also somewhat more reliable than running Samba from inetd. Running Samba independently does, however, consume memory even when Samba isn't serving any clients.

Running Samba from `inetd`

As described in Chapter 3, "Networking Services," `inetd` is a super server that monitors network activity on a large number of ports. When it sees something it's configured to handle, `inetd` starts the appropriate daemon to service that port. In this way, `inetd` can reduce the memory and, to a lesser extent, CPU load on a system that uses a large number of servers. It can also provide some system security benefits, as discussed in Chapter 24, "Maintaining a Secure System."

You can run Samba through `inetd`, and if your computer doesn't serve many Samba requests, you might improve overall system performance, but at the cost of slightly increased response times for starting Samba sessions.

Assuming that you're running Red Hat Linux (or any distribution that starts Samba as Red Hat does), follow these steps to configure Samba to run from `inetd`:

1. Add the following lines to your `/etc/inetd.conf` file:

   ```
   netbios-ssn  stream  tcp  nowait  root  /usr/sbin/smbd smbd
   netbios-ns   dgram   udp  wait    root  /usr/sbin/nmbd nmbd
   ```

2. To stop the current Samba services (if they're running), type

   ```
   /etc/rc.d/init.d/smb stop
   ```

   You should see two lines reporting successful shutdown of Samba's SMB and NMB services.

> **CAUTION**
>
> Stopping Samba disconnects any users who are currently accessing Samba shares. You should notify all your users that you're about to shut down file and printer serving before you stop Samba.

3. Find the process ID of the `inetd` program by typing

   ```
   ps ax ¦ grep inetd -
   ```

4. Use the process ID you found in step 3 to restart `inetd` by typing

   ```
   kill -SIGHUP pid
   ```

   where *pid* is the process ID.

5. Move the `/etc/rc.d/rc.init/smb` file to some other location, to prevent it from running and starting Samba as an always-running service when you reboot.

If you're using a distribution other than Red Hat 6.0, you might need to modify these directions somewhat, by changing the path to the Samba binaries or changing the method used to remove the existing Samba startup code.

Workgroups, Domains, and Browsing

Windows networking is organized around the similar concepts of the *workgroup* and the *domain*. As a practical matter, you're probably familiar with these concepts from browsing through the network with the Windows Network Neighborhood tool, shown in Figure 11.5. You might not know quite what workgroups and domains are, though, or how they differ from one another.

Map Network Drive icon

FIGURE 11.5
Windows lets you browse a network in a hierarchical manner, as if it were a disk drive.

What Are Workgroups and Domains?

Workgroups and domains are extremely similar networking structures in practice. They're both groups of computers that use NetBIOS and SMB to share resources. Both feature machine names for individual computers and a name for the workgroup or domain. Even a small network can contain more than one workgroup or domain, although the network depicted in Figure 11.5 has only one. They differ primarily in how they handle authentication. A domain is more centralized; one computer in a domain serves as the *domain controller*, which is a computer that authenticates users on the domain. In contrast, in a workgroup, each machine is responsible for authenticating its users, and in passing that authentication information on to other machines in the workgroup.

This difference between workgroups and domains has several important implications:

- Each Windows 95 or 98 computer in a workgroup maintains a set of passwords for its users in files with `.pwl` extensions in the `C:\WINDOWS` directory. These passwords are poorly encrypted and are a potential security hole, should an unauthorized individual acquire them. In a domain, there's no need for these distributed password files. (Windows 95 and 98 still store them, though, unless you disable this feature as described shortly.)

- Because passwords are stored on many computers in a workgroup, any attempt to change a user's password requires changing the password on *all* the computers. This is awkward at best. In a domain, because a central computer stores all passwords, changing a user's password is simpler.

- Domain logins allow the domain controller to pass a login script back to the client computer when an individual has logged in to the network. In an environment with multiple more-or-less identical Windows computers and a central file server, this feature allows the server to customize the client for each person, no matter what client the person is using.

Overall, workgroups are generally fine for small networks, and often for somewhat larger networks in which each person uses a single computer. As the number of clients increases, though, the administrative advantages of using a domain system increase.

If you want the security advantages of eliminating the `.pwl` files, you need to disable password caching. You do this with the Windows Registry Editor.

CAUTION

Exercise extreme care when editing the Windows Registry! This file is a database of critical configuration details, and if you change something you shouldn't change, your system can become unstable or even unusable.

To turn off password caching, follow these steps:

1. Start the Registry Editor by opening a Windows command prompt and typing REGEDIT. Windows starts the program, shown in Figure 11.6.

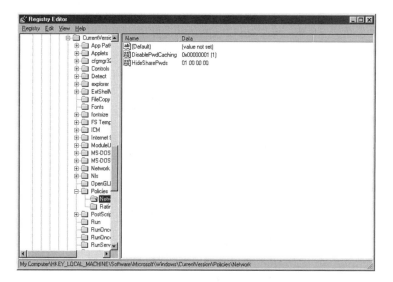

FIGURE 11.6
The Registry Editor allows you to change many of the Windows default settings.

2. *Before proceeding further, select Registry, Export Registry File to save your current Registry!* This way, if you damage your registry, you'll be better able to recover from the damage.

3. In the pane on the left of the window, select HKEY_LOCAL_MACHINE, Software, Microsoft, Windows, CurrentVersion, Policies, Network. Your display should now look something like that shown in Figure 11.6, except that there is no DisablePwdCaching item in the right pane of the window.

4. Select Edit, New, DWORD Value. A new item appears in the right side of the window.

5. While the new item is still selected and editable, type the name **DisablePwdCaching**, and then press the Enter key.

6. Double-click the new DisablePwdCaching item. The Registry Editor displays a dialog box in which you can edit the value. Enter 1 and click OK. Your display should now look like the one in Figure 11.6.

7. Exit the Registry Editor.

8. Type DEL C:\WINDOWS*.PWL at a command prompt to delete the existing .pwl files.

You also need to change Windows to use a domain login, which you can do from the Network tool in the Control Panel. Click Client for Microsoft Network in the Configuration tab, and then click Properties. Select Log on to Windows NT domain in the Client for Microsoft Networks Properties (Figure 11.7), type the name of the domain, and click OK. When you're done, Windows might want to access its installation CD-ROM, and you need to reboot. After you've done this, check to be sure Windows has not created any more .pwl files in the C:\WIN-DOWS directory.

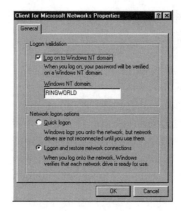

FIGURE 11.7

If you check log on to Windows NT domain, Windows will let the domain controller handle its user authentication, which can greatly improve Windows login security.

Configuring Samba to Appear in Network Neighborhood

If your Linux server is to reside on a workgroup or on a domain that's controlled by another computer, you need to do very little to get the server working. I've already discussed most of the necessary options in earlier sections of this chapter. If you're on a network that has an existing domain controller, though, you should use the domain controller option in /etc/smb.conf to identify that computer to Samba.

If you've configured your Linux computer but can't access it from Windows computers, see Table 11.3 for some tips that might help you fix the problem.

TABLE 11.3   Troubleshooting for Samba Network Access

Symptom	Possible Causes
The Linux computer doesn't appear in Network Neighborhood.	The `workgroup` option is not set correctly in `/etc/smb.conf`.
	The client computer is configured to use NetBIOS over NetBEUI, rather than over TCP/IP.
	If you have set a `hosts allow` or `hosts deny` option, maybe it is not correct. As a test, try removing these options.
The Linux computer appears in Network Neighborhood, but you can't open the computer in the browser—an error message appears.	Samba is not configured for the appropriate password type (cleartext or encrypted). You typed the password incorrectly, either on the client or when setting up the account.
	There is no account for the username you're trying to use. Note that if you're using encrypted passwords, you need an entry in `/etc/smbpasswd`, not just a regular Linux account.
Linux computer appears in Network Neighborhood, but no shares appear on the Linux computer.	You have not created the appropriate shares.
	You have set the `browsable` or `browseable` option to `off`. For good measure, add one of these options to each share and set them to `on`.
Linux computer and shares appear in Network Neighborhood, but you can't access the shares.	You've set the `security` option to `share`. You need to enter a separate password for each share. Check the earlier tips about problems accessing the computer from Network Neighborhood.
	You have restricted access to shares in some way. Samba supports a number of options, many of which are not discussed in this chapter, for locking people out of certain shares.

Becoming the Domain Controller

If you want to configure your Linux computer to be the domain controller, you can do so by following these steps:

1. Be sure the following options are set in the `[global]` section of your `/etc/smb.conf` file:

```
os level = 64
domain master = yes
local master = yes
preferred master = yes
domain logons = yes
```

2. Create a special share for network logons:

```
[netlogon]
    path = /home/netlogon
    writeable = no
    public = no
```

You can choose any directory you like for the `netlogon` share's path; `/home/netlogon` is only one possibility. You do have to create this directory, though.

3. You can create a logon script for clients and place it in the `netlogon` directory. For instance, here's one, called `logon.bat`, that mounts a share at a fixed location:

```
net use m: \\speaker\homes
```

> **NOTE**
>
> Because this script is for use in Windows clients, you need to use Windows end-of-line conventions. The script presented has only one line, so there's no problem with it. If the script had multiple lines, though, you might want to create it using a DOS or Windows text editor, or use a utility such as `unix2dos` on Linux to convert the end-of-line characters appropriately.

4. If you create a script in step 3, you probably want to use it, so add the following line to the `[global]` section of `/etc/smb.conf`:

```
logon script = logon.bat
```

You can create customized scripts for each user. If you do this, you need to use the `%U` variable as part of the script's filename, as in `logon-%U.bat`.

After you've finished making these changes, you need to restart the Samba server. If you've left the Red Hat Linux configuration as it came, you can do this by typing:

```
/etc/rc.d/init.d/smb restart
```

Accessing Shares from Windows

There are several ways to access Samba shares from Windows, some of which are more obvious than others. Some of the most common are described in the following sections.

Browsing a Network from Windows

Browsing the network is one of the most obvious methods of accessing Samba shares. Double-click on the Network Neighborhood icon on your desktop, and you'll get a network browser, as shown in Figure 11.5. You can double-click on a machine in this browser to see its shares, and then double-click on the shares to access the files and directories it contains, much as if it were a local hard disk.

> **NOTE**
>
> With Windows 98, you might only need to single-click to navigate through directories and files.

Accessing a share in this way can be awkward. If you regularly use a particular share, you can create a shortcut directly to it:

1. Open the window that shows the folder icon for the share you want to access regularly.
2. Right-click on this share. You get a pop-up context menu.
3. Select Create Shortcut. Windows displays a dialog box stating that it can't create a shortcut in that location, but that it can place one on the desktop.
4. Click Yes to create the shortcut on the desktop.

Thereafter, when you open the shortcut that's on the desktop, Windows opens the share, without making you go through several layers in the Network Neighborhood browser.

Mounting a Samba Share in Windows

Browsing the network can be convenient, but sometimes you need to assign a drive letter to a share. This is true if you need to access the share by using a DOS program run under Windows, for instance, and even for some Windows programs. There are two ways to assign a drive letter to a share.

The first method is to issue the net use command at a command prompt. For instance, typing **net use m: \\speaker\rodsmith** causes the share \\speaker\rodsmith to be mapped to the drive letter M:.

The second method of assigning a drive letter is to follow these steps:

1. At any open file browser window, make sure the toolbar is visible, and if it's not, select View, Toolbar to show it.

2. Click the Map Network Drive icon in the toolbar (see Figure 11.5). Windows responds by displaying the Map Network Drive dialog box shown in Figure 11.8.

FIGURE 11.8

The Windows Map Network Drive dialog box differs from one version of Windows to another. Shown here is the dialog box in Windows NT 4.0; the comparable dialog box in Windows 98 is simpler.

3. Type the share name in the Path field, as in **speaker****rodsmith**. In Windows NT 4.0, you can instead select the share by using the browser in the lower portion of the dialog box.

4. Select the drive letter you want to assign to the share.

5. Click OK. Windows mounts the share under the letter you specified.

Accessing a Samba Share from a Windows Program

If you're using a Windows program and realize that you need to access a shared directory, you can often do so without mounting the share as a drive letter. A typical file dialog box in a Windows program lets you select Network Neighborhood as one of the options available from the Desktop, as shown in Figure 11.9. You can then browse down from there to your Linux server and open or save files. Alternatively, you can often enter the complete path to the file in the filename field of the dialog box, as in **speaker****rodsmith****a-file.txt**.

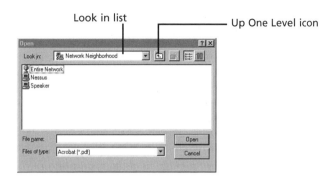

FIGURE 11.9
You can access networked shares by clicking the Up One Level icon several times or by locating Network Neighborhood in the Look in list.

Linux as an SMB Client

File sharing with Windows computers can go both ways—it's possible to access Windows shares from Linux. In fact, there are two principal ways to do this: You can use a quick-and-dirty interface, or you can mount Windows shares as if they were local drives. You can use both methods to access Windows exports from actual Windows computers or from Linux or UNIX computers running Samba. Because Samba emulates Windows networking so well, there are no differences in operation on the Linux client side.

Using `smbclient`

The `smbclient` program provides an FTP-like interface to shared Windows resources. In general, you can start using `smbclient` by typing its name, followed by the resource you intend to use, as in this example:

```
smbclient //nessus/shared
```

> **NOTE**
>
> In Linux, you use slash (/) characters rather than the backslash (\) you use in Windows. Although you *can* use backslash characters in Linux, you need to use twice as many—four in front of the machine name and two between the machine name and the resource.

The program then prompts you for a password, and if you type one that's acceptable to the server, you are greeted by a prompt. You can enter several FTP-like commands, including the following:

- ls or dir—Display a directory listing.
- cd—Change to a new directory on the server.
- lcd—Change to a new directory on the local machine.
- get and mget—Transfer a single or multiple files, respectively, from the server.
- put and mput—Transfer a single or multiple files, respectively, to the server.
- ? or help—Display available commands.
- quit—Exit smbclient.

There are many more smbclient commands, as well as command-line options to alter its behavior. You can check the smbclient manpage for more details.

Mounting Windows Volumes in Linux

Although smbclient can be handy for doing occasional transfers, it's not nearly as flexible as actually mounting a share can be. Therefore, it is fortunate that Linux implements support for SMB/CIFS in the kernel and has utilities that allow you to mount an SMB share much as you would mount a local hard disk or an NFS export.

Compiling Support into the Kernel

The first step you must take if you want to mount Windows or Samba shares is to ensure that you have appropriate support in your kernel. Under the Network File Systems option, you should ensure that you've selected SMB filesystem support, either as a module or compiled into the kernel file. If you plan to mount *only* Windows 95 shares, you should also select the SMB Win95 bug work-around option. If you plan to connect to Windows 98, Windows NT, or a mixture of machines, though, you should *not* select this last option.

Using the smbmount Command

In its simplest form, you can use smbmount as follows:

```
smbmount //nessus/shared -c /mnt/nessus
```

> ### NOTE
>
> The `smbmount` syntax changed between Samba versions 2.0.3 and 2.0.5a. If you're using 2.0.3, you should type
>
> ```
> smbmount //nessus/shared-c 'mount /mnt/nessus'
> ```
>
> to mount a remote Samba share. Also, Red Hat moved the Samba client programs into a separate RPM file with version 2.0.5a, so if you can set up a Samba server, but can't access the client programs, check to see that the `samba-client` package is installed. If it's not, install it (you can find a link to it in the `updates` directory on the CD-ROM that accompanies this book).

After you type this command, `smbmount` asks for a password. (You can instead type a password on the command line, immediately after the share name, but then it is visible for all who walk past to see.) If you type a valid password, you gain access to the remote share.

If you're using pre-2.0.5a versions of `smbmount`, you can provide additional parameters within the single quotes, to modify the permissions and ownership of files in the mounted share:

- `-u`—Specifies the user ID to be used by all files in the share.
- `-g`—Specifies the group ID to be used by all files in the share.
- `-f`—Specifies the permissions, in octal form, to be assigned to files on the share. These permissions can't exceed those given by the server, though—if a file is marked read-only on the server, you can't override that through this option. You can, however, change permissions with the Linux `chmod` command after the share has been mounted.
- `-d`—Specifies the permissions, in octal form, to be assigned to directories on the share.

These options *do not* work with `smbmount` from the 2.0.5a release, unfortunately. This more recent version gives file ownership to the person who mounts the share, and uses permissions of 755 for all files and directories.

As installed on a Red Hat 6.0 system, `smbmount` requires that you be root to operate. If you want to give ordinary Linux users the ability to mount remote shares, you can do so; just type the following commands:

```
chmod a+s /usr/bin/smbmnt
chmod a+s /usr/bin/smbumount
```

Note that in the first line, the filename is `smbmnt`, not `smbmount`—the former is a helper application to the latter. These commands set the `suid` bit on the applications, which means that they run with the authority of the superuser even when an ordinary user runs them.

Your users require ownership of any directory on which they want to mount a share. This shouldn't normally be a problem because a user can create a directory in his or her home directory and mount a share at that location.

As with other mounted filesystems, you must unmount an SMB share when you're done with it. You use the `smbumount` command to do this, as in `smbumount /mnt/nessus`.

Exporting `smbmounted` Shares to Other Machines

It's possible to export to another computer a share that you've `smbmounted`. Ordinarily you wouldn't want to do this using Samba to serve the re-export because a direct connection between the two computers would produce better performance. You might need to do this using NFS or Netatalk, though. For instance, suppose you have a file on a Windows 98 computer that you want to access on a Macintosh. Assuming that you don't have software such as DAVE to allow Macintoshes to participate in Windows networking, but you do have both Samba and Netatalk configured, you could mount the Windows share on a mount point you've configured for export via Netatalk. The Macintosh will then have access to those files. There are some caveats in such an arrangement, however:

- Performance is likely to be poor. This is because you are doing twice as many transfers, which will produce collisions on networks that are prone to them, and put extra strain on the Linux server. If you find yourself needing solutions like this often, you should seriously consider adding disk space to the Linux computer, if necessary, and storing the cross-platform files on it.

- Filename quirks can multiply over such a connection. In the case of a Macintosh/ Windows connection via Linux, you get both Samba's *and* Netatalk's filename quirks. This isn't likely to be a major problem unless you're transferring files that have sensitive or peculiar filenames.

- You get more filesystem clutter. Many OSs create files that are unique to themselves, or Linux servers do so to help in the serving process. This is particularly true of the Netatalk server, which needs to create special directories to hold Macintosh resource forks. If you transfer a file from a Macintosh to a Windows computer via Linux, you are likely to find a directory called `.AppleDouble` on the Windows machine afterward. If the file is a normal data file, such as a Microsoft Word document, you can safely delete the `.AppleDouble` directory. In a few cases, such as font files, the contents of the `.AppleDouble` directory might be more important than what's in the main directory, though.

Overall, re-exporting shares is a trick that can be convenient on occasion, but you shouldn't rely on it too heavily. Instead, it is a good idea to use a Linux computer as a server for cross-platform files. You can export the same directory by using NFS, Samba, and Netatalk, giving every computer on your network access to the same files by using its native file-sharing mechanisms.

Summary

Samba is a versatile program for providing services to DOS, Windows, and OS/2 computers, or for accessing services provided by such machines. You control Samba through its configuration file, `/etc/smb.conf`, which has sections for overall configuration and for each share you export. Because of Samba's flexibility, the configuration file can be tricky for a newcomer, so I recommend that you use `linuxconf` or SWAT to create your initial Samba configuration.

Samba itself is a pair of daemons, which you can run either independently or under the control of the `inetd` super server. Running the daemons independently generally results in better performance, but a server that gets relatively little Samba use might do well with an `inetd`-based configuration.

You can access Samba shares from Windows just as you would shares from a Windows server, and this chapter provides a summary of these access methods. You can also turn this situation around and access Windows shares from Linux, by using the `smbclient` and `smbmount` commands. You can even re-export a Windows share to other clients, turning the Linux computer into a sort of bridge between incompatible hosts.

Netatalk: Sharing Files with Macintoshes

IN THIS CHAPTER

Just as Samba is Linux's means of providing services to Windows computers, Netatalk is Linux's interpreter for the Macintosh world. Netatalk began life at the University of Michigan, but official support from that institution has ended. Fortunately, the slack has been taken up by Adrian Sun, so more recent versions often go by the name *Netatalk+Asun*. I use *Netatalk* as an all-inclusive term throughout the book, but in general, what I describe in this book is Adrian Sun's expanded and improved version of the server.

Red Hat Linux 6.0 doesn't ship with Netatalk as a standard package, but the CD-ROM that accompanies this book includes it in the `sams-extras/netatalk` directory. Before proceeding further, you should install the Netatalk RPM file by using the `rpm` command or a GUI front end to it, such as `gnorpm`.

> **CAUTION**
>
> Netatalk is a tricky package. Many people report problems with one version of the software, but no problems with another. I use the RPM included on this CD-ROM on my own systems that run Red Hat Linux 6.0 and Mandrake Linux 6.0, so I don't expect you'll have problems with the included RPM if you use one of these distributions. If you try downloading a more recent RPM, though, be aware that you might have problems with it. Also, different RPMs might place configuration files in different places or might require you to start Netatalk in a different way than that described here.

Because Netatalk isn't a standard part of Red Hat's distribution of Linux, there are no `linuxconf` configuration modules for it. I therefore describe only how to configure Netatalk by editing its configuration files with a text editor.

AppleTalk: The Macintosh's Basic Networking

Before the Internet became popular, Macintoshes used a proprietary networking technology known as *AppleTalk*. Initially, this term applied to both the networking protocols and the networking hardware, but that became confusing, so Apple decreed that *AppleTalk* would refer to the software and *LocalTalk* would be the new name for the hardware. It's useful to know something about the history of Macintosh networking to understand Netatalk and how it allows Linux to fit into a Macintosh network.

Apple Networking Hardware and Software

All Macintoshes since the Mac Plus have had some sort of networking support built in. In years past, Macintosh owners often used the networking hardware just to connect one or more Macintoshes to the expensive LaserWriter printers that Apple introduced in the 1980s, but more sophisticated uses have long been possible.

AppleTalk

The Macintosh's traditional basic networking software is known as AppleTalk. You can think of AppleTalk as being roughly equivalent to TCP/IP or the DOS/Windows NetBEUI protocol stacks, with file- and printer-sharing protocols thrown in at the top. Most Macintosh users don't like to think about the specific protocols that underlie their networks, but understanding a few of AppleTalk's subprotocols is helpful in configuring Netatalk. These protocols are grouped according to the Netatalk components that implement them:

- Linux kernel—The kernel implements *Datagram Delivery Protocol* (DDP), which is the most basic of the AppleTalk protocols.

- atalkd—The Netatalk component atalkd implements *Routing Table Maintenance Protocol* (RTMP), *Name Binding Protocol* (NBP), *Zone Information Protocol* (ZIP), and *AppleTalk Echo Protocol* (AEP). These protocols, and hence atalkd, serve functions that are roughly analogous to those performed by the Linux routed and ifconfig tools—they control the physical interface and determine how to deliver network traffic.

- afpd—Netatalk's afpd implements *AppleTalk Filing Protocol* (AFP), which provides file-sharing services. AFP is roughly analogous to NFS for UNIX and Linux file sharing or SMB/CIFS for DOS, Windows, and OS/2 file sharing. This chapter deals largely with configuring afpd and the underlying atalkd systems.

- papd—Netatalk's papd implements *Printer Access Protocol* (PAP) for printer sharing. This protocol is discussed in more detail in Chapter 17, "Netatalk: Sharing Printers with Macintoshes."

The original AppleTalk design served Macintoshes well for several years, but it eventually started to show its age, particularly in the face of increasing network hardware speed. Apple therefore overhauled the Macintosh's networking technologies with Open Transport, a set of tools that allow Macintoshes to integrate more easily with more network types. One of the consequences of Open Transport was a means to transmit AppleTalk over TCP/IP. One of the most important of Adrian Sun's improvements to the Netatalk package has been to implement AppleTalk over TCP/IP in Netatalk; prior versions of Netatalk had been limited to "raw" Netatalk, which is much slower than AppleTalk over TCP/IP.

LocalTalk and PhoneNET

The original LocalTalk network hardware used a *bus topology* (p. 81), meaning that Macintoshes linked to each other in a single line. The computer hardware itself resembled a high-speed serial port, and the cables were fairly expensive. LocalTalk's speed was limited to less than 2Mbps—fast at the time of its introduction, but slow compared to coaxial Ethernet speeds of 10Mbps, and downright pokey compared to today's 100BaseT speed of 100Mbps. One other limit was in cable length: Its maximum was 1,000 feet, which places it between the limits of 10Base2 and 10Base5 Ethernet cabling (see Table 1.1, p. 10).

In order to both extend the cable length limits of LocalTalk and reduce cable cost, the company Farallon introduced a product called PhoneNET, which transmitted LocalTalk signals over ordinary telephone wires. PhoneNET had a maximum run length of 3,000 feet, but did not improve LocalTalk's speed. Because PhoneNET uses adapters external to the computer rather than internal hardware, you can use PhoneNET on any computer that supports LocalTalk.

Although quite rare, LocalTalk boards for PCs do exist. If you want your Linux server to handle traffic from an old LocalTalk network, you can try to locate an Apple/Farallon LocalTalk board or a COPS LocalTalk board. Both of these products are supported in the Linux 2.2-series kernel. Their configuration and use are not described in this book, but aside from basic configuration, the same principles described in this chapter should apply to a network using such products.

Ethernet

Because of Ethernet's vastly superior speed of 10Mbps—and now 100Mbps—Apple eventually began producing Macintoshes with Ethernet ports. In fact, recent models such as the iMac no longer support LocalTalk, only Ethernet, and these latest computers support 100BaseT Ethernet.

Fortunately, Ethernet isn't too picky about what types of data it carries, so Apple was able to adapt AppleTalk to Ethernet. The resulting use of Ethernet to carry AppleTalk is sometimes called *EtherTalk*. You can have an Ethernet network that carries nothing but AppleTalk traffic, or one that mixes AppleTalk with TCP/IP. Given the speed benefits of Open Transport, it's best to use Open Transport to encapsulate AppleTalk inside TCP/IP!

Differences Between AppleTalk and TCP/IP

Like NetBIOS/NetBEUI, AppleTalk is designed for *small* computer networks. It's quite effective for up to a few dozen computers on an office intranet, but it doesn't scale well beyond that point. This is partially due to the fact that, like NetBIOS, AppleTalk's naming scheme is essentially two tiered: Each computer has its own name, and computers can be grouped together into collections known as *zones*, which are similar to the *workgroups* or *domains* (p. 277) of Windows networking. There's no way to group AppleTalk zones into larger collections, though.

In contrast, TCP/IP is designed for much larger networks with more levels in the organization. In fact, this is one reason TCP/IP, rather than AppleTalk or NetBIOS, is the basis of the Internet.

AppleTalk uses ID numbers to identify individual computers, but AppleTalk incorporates procedures for the computers on a network to negotiate with each other to determine their ID numbers automatically. Therefore, you need not deal directly with IP addresses or their equivalents in AppleTalk networking—at least until Open Transport and its AppleTalk over TCP/IP enters the equation.

TCP/IP and AppleTalk on the Same Ethernet

Although AppleTalk and TCP/IP are entirely separate protocols, they can coexist on the same Ethernet cable without conflict. This is because Ethernet itself has protocols for data encapsulation, as described in Chapter 2, "Understanding TCP/IP." Any given Ethernet packet is only an Ethernet packet as far as the networking hardware and lowest levels of the drivers are concerned. As the drivers examine the Ethernet packet, though, they quickly discover to which networking stack the data should be sent—TCP/IP or DDP—so the two protocols get sorted out at a very low level of the computer's networking hierarchy.

As mentioned previously in this chapter, AppleTalk can also be transmitted *over* TCP/IP, in which case most of the Ethernet traffic is composed of TCP/IP datagrams. In this case, too, the protocols coexist—only the TCP/IP stack processes much of the data before passing it on to the appropriate portions of the AppleTalk stack.

Compiling AppleTalk Support into Your Kernel

One of the first steps you must take in preparing for AppleTalk networking with Linux is to compile support for AppleTalk's DDP into your kernel. You do this from the Networking options configuration area by selecting AppleTalk DDP, and then recompiling your kernel and rebooting, as described in Chapter 6, "Compiling a Kernel for Networking."

After you've rebooted with the new kernel, you can check to see if the AppleTalk support is actually there by typing:

```
dmesg ¦ grep Apple -
```

If Linux successfully loaded the DDP support, you see a response similar to this:

```
NET4: AppleTalk 0.18 for Linux NET4.0
```

If you don't see such a message, try going over your kernel compile and loading steps again. I find that I often forget to run `lilo` after compiling a new kernel, for instance, which results in the old one loading.

The `atalkd` Daemon

The `atalkd` daemon provides much of the basics of AppleTalk networking, so configuring and running it is the first order of business when you've got a kernel running with DDP support.

`atalkd` Configuration

To configure `atalkd`, you need to edit the `/etc/atalk/atalkd.conf` file. Configuring `atalkd` is unusual because, in many cases, the `atalkd.conf` file can be *completely empty* and the system will still work! Aside from comment lines that start with pound signs (#), `atalkd.conf` contains configuration information on a one-line-per-interface basis. Information on each line may include the following:

- Ethernet device—This is generally `eth0`, although if you have more than one Ethernet board, the device may be `eth1` or above. If you specify any options at all, the Ethernet device must be the first option on the line. If `atalkd.conf` is empty, `atalkd` probes all available interfaces looking for AppleTalk computers.

- `-seed`—If this option is present, you must specify *all* the additional information. Normally you don't have to use the `-seed` option because it's used only if you want your Linux computer to serve as a bridge between two AppleTalk networks and as the provider of configuration rules for one of them.

- `-phase` *number*—This is essentially the revision number of EtherTalk to which Netatalk conforms. The default is 2, but you can set up Phase 1 if you prefer.

- `-net` *netrange*—You can specify a range of numbers within which your computer will attempt to obtain a network address. You specify *netrange* as a pair of numbers separated by a hyphen, as in `4000-4100`. Legal values range from 1 to 65279. Values higher than this are used in automatic configurations.

- `-addr` *address*—You can request a specific address using this parameter. *address* is a two-part number separated by a period (`.`). The first part is a network number (legal values range from 1 to 65279), and the second part is a node number (1 to 255). Examples of valid addresses include `1.1`, `60321.200`, and `5.254`.

> **NOTE**
>
> With Phase 2 EtherTalk, the network and node values of Ethernet addresses can both vary on a single network. For instance, you could have a network with computers taking addresses of `60321.200`, `3243.78`, and `231.231`, and all three computers could talk to one another. If your Macintoshes still use Phase 1 EtherTalk or LocalTalk, you might need to give your Linux server the same network number that's used by the Macintoshes.

- `-zone` *zonename*—Many small AppleTalk networks are zoneless, and Netatalk tries to determine its zone automatically even on zoned networks. You can force Netatalk's hand with this option, though.

Unless you specify `-seed`, all the other items are treated as requests or suggestions, not requirements. For instance, if you specify the address 60321.200, but another computer on the network already has that address, your machine gets another address instead.

As a general rule, I recommend setting a single line in `atalkd.conf` that contains only the name of the interface on which you want to run Netatalk, like this

```
eth0
```

On rare occasions, you might need to specify additional information. On rarer occasions, you should leave out the `eth0` line entirely. Precisely when you need to add information or remove the line entirely appears to be one of those mysteries that will remain unsolved until the end of time, so if you have trouble, you just have to experiment.

> **TIP**
>
> I've seen a few reports of Netatalk servers that stop responding, and cannot be made to work again, although there have been no configuration changes on the Linux server. The solution is to shut down all the computers on the Macintosh network, including the Linux computer, and bring them up again, starting with the seed machine (if there is a dedicated seed machine).

Starting `atalkd` Services

This section describes starting `atalkd` manually, checking each step of the process. This level of control is not needed except for troubleshooting, so you might want to skip ahead to "The `afpd` Daemon," later in this chapter. If you're having problems or if you just want to know more about how Netatalk works, though, read on.

To test basic `atalkd` functionality, you can type `/usr/sbin/atalkd`. After a brief delay, you get back your command prompt. You can check that the daemon is running by typing

```
ps ax ¦ grep atalkd -
```

> **NOTE**
>
> `atalkd` can take close to a minute to start, and conceivably longer on some hardware. Don't get impatient with the daemon and kill it before it's done its thing.

If you see a process other than `grep`, then `atalkd` is running. You can check functionality further by typing

```
cat /proc/net/atalk_iface
```

This command displays information on the devices to which `atalkd` has attached itself. For instance, on my system, this command reports the following:

```
eth0            F500:DA  0000-FFFE  0
lo              0000:00  0000-0000  0
```

This means that `atalkd` is servicing `eth0` by using the address `FF00:DA` (network address 62720, node address 218, expressed in hexadecimal), and is listening on networks 0 through FFFE (65534). The daemon has also attached itself to `lo`, the loopback interface.

A final test of basic `atalkd` functionality is to use the `aecho` command, which is AppleTalk's equivalent of TCP/IP's `ping`—it sends AppleTalk Echo requests to a specified host, waits for the reply, and prints some basic statistics. You can specify either the target computer's AppleTalk name or its address (network and node, separated by a period, as in `41201.173`). Here's the result of giving the command `aecho teela` on my network:

```
14 bytes from 41201.173: aep_seq=0. time=0. ms
14 bytes from 41201.173: aep_seq=1. time=0. ms
14 bytes from 41201.173: aep_seq=2. time=0. ms
14 bytes from 41201.173: aep_seq=3. time=0. ms

----41201.173 AEP Statistics----
4 packets sent, 4 packets received, 0% packet loss
round-trip (ms)  min/avg/max = 0/0/0
```

I terminated this test after four packets by pressing Ctrl+C.

NOTE

You can use either a real Macintosh or another Netatalk-enabled computer as the target of the `aecho` command. You can't use `aecho` on your own computer, though, at this stage of the configuration process.

At this point, I recommend terminating `atalkd` because in the next sections you'll learn how to start it, `afpd`, and `papd` all with a single command.

The `afpd` Daemon

Getting `atalkd` running is good, but essentially useless by itself. To configure Netatalk to do any real work, you must configure and start `afpd`, too.

Configuring `afpd`

You configure `afpd` through four files, all located in the `/etc/atalk` directory:

- `config`—Sets overall configuration options.
- `afpd.conf`—Controls options most relevant to authentication and data transfer. Most of these options can be set in the `config` file.
- `AppleVolumes.default`—Specifies the directories you want to export.
- `AppleVolumes.system`—Specifies the Macintosh creator and type codes used for native Linux files.

Creating a `config` File

The `/etc/atalk/config` file is included with the particular RPM distribution on this book's CD-ROM, and is used by the Netatalk startup scripts. Another distribution of Netatalk might not use this file. It contains important configuration parameters for providing AppleTalk services. You set options in this file by giving an option name, equal sign, and value. Important options you can set in this file include the following:

- `AFPD_MAX_CLIENTS`—This option is the maximum number of client computers the server allows. The default is 5.
- `ATALK_NAME`—This option is the name of your computer on the AppleTalk network. The default setting attempts to base this name on your Internet machine name, and this usually works. In some cases you might need to specify something else, though.
- `AFPD_NOCLR`—You set this parameter equal to `-C` to disable cleartext logins. The version of Netatalk included with this book's CD-ROM doesn't support encrypted logins, so you should leave this line commented out. If you want to enable encrypted logins, you need to obtain the source code to Netatalk and a DES library, and then compile your own custom version of the program.
- `AFPD_NOGUEST`—You set this parameter equal to `-G` to disable guest (no password) logins. The default setting permits guest logins.
- `AFPD_GUEST`—This option specifies the name of the guest user with this parameter. The default is `nobody`, which gives very restrictive permissions to the guest user.
- `PAPD_RUN`—This option specifies `yes` or `no` to have the startup scripts run `papd` for printer services.

- AFPD_RUN—This is another yes/no option, but for file sharing services via afpd.
- ATALK_BGROUND—If this option is set to yes (the usual value), the startup script runs the daemons in the background.

The default config file disables many of these options by commenting them out with pound signs (#). You can enable the option by uncommenting the relevant line.

Creating an afpd.conf File

You specify options to be passed to afpd in the afpd.conf file. In most cases, a completely blank afpd.conf file will do just fine because the config file contains the most interesting afpd options. There are a couple of options you might conceivably want to override here, though:

- -f *defaultvolumes*—You use this option to obtain the list of directories to export from *defaultvolumes*, rather than from AppleVolumes.default.
- -s *systemvolumes*—You use this option to obtain the Macintosh creator and type codes from *systemvolumes* rather than from AppleVolumes.system.

You can also read the afpd manpage for more information on afpd options.

Creating an AppleVolumes.default File

The AppleVolumes.default file contains a list of directories you want to export, one line to a directory. The usual format is to specify the directory name and a Macintosh volume name, as in

```
/usr/local/macprogs "Shared Programs"
```

This line causes the contents of the /usr/local/macprogs directory to appear on a Macintosh as a shared volume called Shared Programs. The default AppleVolumes.default file contains only one single-line (and single-character!) entry: ~. This entry exports the user's home directory under the user's name. For instance, if you log in as stevej, you see a volume called stevej available.

You can specify additional parameters to alter how Netatalk treats various aspects of exported directories. Each parameter begins with the parameter name, followed by an equal sign (=), and then the value you want to give it. These additional parameters are as follows:

- casefold—This parameter takes the values tolower, toupper, xlatelower, and xlateupper. The first two translate the case of filenames in both directions, whereas the second two changes the filename in only one direction, from the server to the client. The xlate options have inconsistent effects on files and directories, though. For instance, suppose you have a file called MixedName on the server, and want to create one called MacName. The tolower option causes the Macintosh to see mixedname and to create macname. The `xlatelower` option, on the other hand, causes the Macintosh to see MIXED-NAME, but to create the file MacName (which it then sees as MACNAME). If these are directories rather than files, `xlatelower` causes the Macintosh to see mixedname. This `xlate` behavior is a bug, and might be fixed in a future version of Netatalk.

- options—You can specify `prodos`, which makes the system compatible with Apple II computers; `noadouble`, which causes the server to create an `.AppleDouble` directory only when it's absolutely necessary; or `crlf`, which automatically translates between Macintosh and UNIX/Linux end-of-line characters in text files. You can specify multiple options by separating them with commas and no spaces.

> **CAUTION**
>
> The `crlf` option might sound tempting, but it can cause problems with some programs, including some versions of Microsoft Word.

- access—This parameter restricts access to the volume to the specified users and groups. You list users by their Linux usernames and groups by their group names preceded by an at sign (@). You separate multiple users by commas and no spaces.

- password—This parameter specifies a separate password for the volume.

Editing the `AppleVolumes.system` File

Macintoshes include certain pieces of information in their filesystems that don't exist in most other computers. Two of the most important of these are the four-character codes for files' creators and types. For data files, the creator code identifies the application that created the file. For instance, MSWD identifies Microsoft Word documents. An application has the creator code APPL. The document type helps applications identify what type of file it is, and for applications, it is the creator code the application applies to its data files. The document type code is often unique to the application, but other times many applications use the same type codes. For instance, JPEG files have the type code JPEG. It's these codes that allow Macintoshes to open an appropriate application when you double-click a document icon.

When you store a file on your Linux server using a Macintosh, Netatalk stores the file creator and type. If you create the file in Linux or some other OS by using a file-sharing protocol such as Samba or NFS, though, the file doesn't have any creator or type codes. Netatalk must therefore fake these codes. It does this by assigning creator and type codes based on the file's filename extension—the part of the filename that follows the final period. This is where the `AppleVolumes.system` file comes into play because it contains a complete listing of these mappings.

The version of Netatalk included on this book's CD-ROM contains a fairly large set of mappings, but you might want to extend or modify it. Each line of this file specifies one file type, and its format is as follows:

```
.ext    TYPE    CRTR    Type_Description    Creator_Description
```

Each of the items on each line has a specific meaning, as follows:

> `.ext`—The filename extension in Linux, such as `.doc` for Microsoft Word files or `.txt` for plain text files.

NOTE

Although Linux itself is case-sensitive in its filename handling, the extensions listed in `AppleVolumes.system` are *not* case-sensitive, so you need only one entry to cover both upper- and lowercase versions of these extensions.

> `TYPE`—The four-character file type code.
> `CRTR`—The four-character file creator code.

NOTE

Although the `.ext` field is not case-sensitive, the `TYPE` and `CRTR` fields are.

Type_Description—A brief description of the file type, such as "Word 6 document" or "Text file."

Creator_Description—The name of the file's creator, such as "Microsoft Word" or "SimpleText."

The last two fields are optional, and in fact are ignored by Netatalk; they exist only for your edification.

CAUTION

A few *TYPE* codes actually have fewer than four characters—or, more precisely, they contain spaces at their ends. All four characters—including any spaces—of such codes need to be enclosed in double quotation marks, or they won't work properly. Unfortunately, the default `AppleVolumes.system` file contains several two- and three-character codes *without* the requisite quotation marks. You might want to browse through the file and correct this matter, especially if you use files of those types. Affected files include Adobe Acrobat Reader (PDF), DL animation, FLI animation, GL animation, Windows icon, LHA archive, M1V MPEG, PackIt archive, VOC sound, Microsoft Excel, zip archive, and zoo archive files. In general, this problem is largely cosmetic because it simply causes the file to display with a generic document icon until it's used by the program; but some programs might refuse to load a file if it doesn't bear the appropriate *TYPE* code.

TIP

You can change the file's creator for easy access in a foreign program. For instance, suppose you want to be able to open zip files created with PKZip on Windows or InfoZip on Linux using StuffIt Deluxe on the Macintosh. You need only change the existing entry

```
.zip ZIP ZIP
```

to

```
.zip "ZIP " SITD
```

When you restart Netatalk, your existing `.zip` files have StuffIt icons and launch StuffIt when double-clicked. Several Macintosh programs find the file type and creator codes of existing files, if you're uncertain of what to use. I use Norton Utilities for this task.

When the Macintosh creates files, it also explicitly stores file type and creator codes, and Netatalk preserves these. You therefore needn't be concerned with these mappings for files that you create on Macintoshes. If you create a file on Linux, open it on a Macintosh, make changes, and then save the file, chances are the Macintosh program will save the file type and creator codes, overriding whatever is specified by AppleVolumes.system.

Starting AppleTalk Filing Protocols

Now that you've created appropriate configuration files, it's time to start your Netatalk server. If you used the RPM file on this book's CD-ROM, you can easily start Netatalk by typing **/etc/rc.d/init.d/atalk start**. (If Netatalk is already running, you should use restart rather than start.) Because atalkd itself takes a minute or so to start up, your server won't immediately appear on the Choosers of your Macintoshes. The atalk startup script forks execution of atalkd, so you don't know when the startup has finished, except by testing it from a Macintosh client computer.

If you can't access the Netatalk server after a minute or two, try checking /var/log/messages. The last few lines of this file should contain messages relating to the startup of atalkd, afpd, and papd, and may contain error messages that can help you track down the cause of the problem.

When you reboot your computer, Netatalk services should start up automatically. Again, though, it might take a minute or so after your system has booted for the exports to become available to Macintoshes on your network. You can use aecho on Linux to test basic AppleTalk connectivity, as described earlier in this chapter.

If you're using a distribution that uses different startup scripts than Red Hat uses, such as Slackware, you will probably have to manually edit your startup scripts to start Netatalk. You can add lines to whatever startup script is convenient, such as the following:

```
/usr/sbin/atalkd
/usr/sbin/papd
/usr/sbin/afpd -n servername
```

You might want to add additional afpd parameters, as described in the afpd manpages and the section earlier in this chapter on the config file (p. 299). Because atalkd can take so long to start up, you might also want to place these lines in a separate script file and fork that file (using an ampersand [&] after the script's name in the main startup file).

Selecting Linux Exports from Macintosh

Now that you have a Netatalk server running on Linux, it's time to test the configuration from a Macintosh. You'll find that, once configured, the Linux server integrates very well into your Macintosh network.

Using the Macintosh's Chooser

MacOS uses the Chooser to mount volumes exported by networked computers, and you use the Chooser to mount your Linux files—at least in versions of MacOS through 8.6.

> **NOTE**
>
> The upcoming MacOS X might abolish the Chooser, so you might need to use some other means of selecting your Linux exports in MacOS X.

To mount a Linux share from a Macintosh, follow these steps:

1. Select Apple, Chooser to open the Chooser, shown in Figure 12.1.

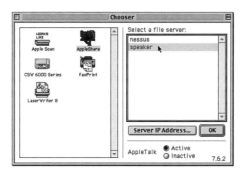

FIGURE 12.1
You use the Chooser to access both shared files and printers (shared or local).

2. Click the AppleShare icon in the left portion of the Chooser. The Macintosh checks the network for AppleTalk servers, and if your Netatalk configuration is correct, you see your Linux computer among them.

> **NOTE**
>
> These instructions presume that you've enabled AppleTalk support in your Macintosh. Examine the AppleTalk radio button near the bottom right of the Chooser. It should be set to Active. If it's set to Inactive, change that setting.

3. Select your Linux server from the list of computers and click OK. MacOS responds by displaying a connection dialog box, as shown in Figure 12.2. If you have enabled guest logins, you can elect to use the guest account, but you won't have access to your home directories. If you want access to your user account files, select Registered User and type your Linux username and password, and then click Connect.

FIGURE 12.2

With the version of Netatalk included with this book's CD-ROM, you are able to send only a cleartext password.

4. The Macintosh now displays the volume selection dialog box, shown in Figure 12.3. Select the volume you want to mount. If you want to mount this volume every time your Macintosh starts, check the box on the right of the list. You can tell the system to save only your username or your username and password. After you select the options you want, click OK, and the Macintosh mounts the volume.

FIGURE 12.3

You can select only one volume at a time in the volume selection dialog box; to open more than one, you need to select the server a second time from the Chooser.

After you mount a volume, a network drive icon appears on the Macintosh desktop. You can double-click that icon to manipulate the files on your Linux server as if they were local to the Macintosh, with some caveats.

Occasionally, there may be a problem with the AppleTalk portion of Netatalk's functioning. In this situation, you don't see your Linux server in the Chooser, but you might still be able to access it by clicking the Server IP Address button. The Macintosh then displays a dialog box asking for an IP address, which you must provide. (Note that this is a numerical IP address, not a TCP/IP machine name.) The login procedure can then proceed normally. The problem with a Linux server not appearing in the Chooser can sometimes be cured by restarting Netatalk, occasionally in conjunction with shutting down and rebooting all the Macintoshes on the network.

Accessing Linux Files

For the most part, your networked Linux filesystem should work as you would expect any other Macintosh drive to behave. There are some caveats and a few bugs, though, particularly as relate to inter-OS interactions:

- As described earlier, Linux uses the contents of the /etc/atalk/AppleVolumes.system file to determine what files map to what application and file type. If the AppleVolumes.system file is misconfigured or if you lack critical applications, you may have difficulty accessing some files.

- Linux supports much longer filenames than does Macintosh—Macintosh is limited to 31 characters, whereas Linux can handle up to 255. If a file has more than 31 characters in its filename, Netatalk ignores it, so you can't access that file on the Macintosh.

- Linux is a *case-sensitive* OS (p. xxx), whereas MacOS is normally *case-retentive* (p. 230). Unless you adjust Netatalk's case-handling features using the casefold option in AppleVolumes.default, Netatalk forces the Macintosh to behave in a case-sensitive way.

- Macintosh aliases to files on Netatalk volumes might not work between sessions. Similarly, the lists of recently accessed files that many programs maintain might not work between sessions.

- Multiuser access to individual files can be tricky. If several users need read-only access to a file, there's normally no problem; however, if two users try to gain write access to the same file, the results can be unpredictable. This is especially true when Macintosh users (using Netatalk) and Windows users (using Samba) try to access the same file, since Netatalk and Samba don't coordinate their file-locking procedures.

- Some Macintosh programs have problems creating large files on large volumes—the Macintosh claims there's not enough free disk space, though there is. The precise limits vary, but the problem normally doesn't appear on files measured in anything less than hundreds of megabytes. This therefore isn't a problem for the average word processing document, but it is when creating a CD-recordable (CD-R) image file or backing up a computer. One workaround to this problem is to create a large empty file in Linux and use the Linux `htools` package to format it as an HFS volume. You can then mount this image file in MacOS by using Apple's free DiskCopy utility and transfer the large files to and from this volume-within-an-export. Although awkward, this workaround is effective if you have sufficient disk space.

When you access a volume by using Netatalk, you do so using the permission of the user whose username and password you enter when you mount the volume. You can use this fact to your advantage as a system administrator by creating appropriate Linux user and group accounts to restrict access to files and directories. For instance, if you create accounts for individuals and place them in two groups, you can restrict all read and write access from members in one group from members of the other by removing world read and execute permissions from the groups' home directories.

Understanding Macintosh Forks

MacOS, unlike Linux and most other OSs, splits files into two parts known as *forks*—the *data fork* and the *resource fork*. The data fork contains the bulk of data for most documents, such as ASCII text, spreadsheet data, and GIF images. The resource fork contains specialized Macintosh information, such as icons, program code, and font definitions. Because Linux doesn't understand forks, Netatalk has to handle this detail. The server performs this feat by creating a special subdirectory, called `.AppleDouble`, in which `afpd` places the resource forks. The files in the `.AppleDouble` directory have the same names as the files in the main directory, but these files contain resource fork information rather than data fork information. (These `.AppleDouble` files actually contain a bit more information, including the file's creator and type IDs.) Because Linux normally hides files that begin with a period, you don't see the `.AppleDouble` directory when you use `ls` or a file browser to see the files.

In addition to `.AppleDouble`, Netatalk creates a directory called `.AppleDesktop`. This file contains information MacOS uses to position icons in windows. The `.AppleDesktop` directory exists only in the root of the exported directory tree, though, whereas Netatalk creates an `.AppleDouble` subdirectory in each directory accessed from the Macintosh.

If you're using a directory strictly for file sharing with Macintoshes, none of this should make much difference to you. You might need to be aware of these facts, and possibly take certain precautions, if you need to access the files from Linux or some other OS (say, via a Samba share):

- You shouldn't delete the `.AppleDouble` directory or any files in it. An exception is if you delete a file in Linux, you can (and should, to reduce wasted disk space) delete its corresponding twin in `.AppleDouble`. If you delete a file from Macintosh, Netatalk removes the file's `.AppleDouble` counterpart automatically. Another exception is if all the files in a directory are of types that are known via the `AppleVolumes.system` file and don't contain any vital resource fork data. Such files include most productivity application data files, raw text files, and cross-platform graphics files.

- If you move or copy a Macintosh file in Linux, you should move or copy the file's `.AppleDouble` counterpart, too. Again, this isn't the case if the file has no vital resource fork data and if its extension appears in `AppleVolumes.system`.

- Some Macintosh files, such as program and font files, have no data in their data forks, but they have substantial resource forks. This means that, in Linux, these files appear to by empty (0 length)—until you examine the files' twins in the `.AppleDouble` directory. Don't make the mistake of assuming that the files in the main directory are superfluous; they are necessary for accessing the resource fork data.

- When you back up your Linux server, you must be sure that you back up the `.AppleDouble` files, too. This happens by default with most backup software.

- If you want to archive a directory of files, say to send them to some other person, you can do so from a Macintosh pretty easily. If you try it from Linux, though, you might get unwanted `.AppleDouble` directories. Many archive programs include an option to exclude certain files, and you can use this option to block the `.AppleDouble` directory.

- Modifying the main (data fork) file from Linux or some OS that shares the same files is normally *not* a problem, as long as you use an appropriate tool for doing so. For instance, you can create a document with Microsoft Word 98 for the Macintosh and modify it with Microsoft Word 97 or 2000 for Windows, and Word 98 on the Macintosh can read the modified file with no problems. The same would be true if you used WordPerfect 8 for Linux to read and modify the file, with the usual caveats about file import/export filters being imperfect.

If you want to burn a CD-ROM from data stored in a Netatalk-served directory, you might need to explicitly exclude the `.AppleDouble` directories. Alternatively, if you want to be able to read the CD-ROM on Macintoshes complete with long filenames and resource fork data, you can use the Linux `mkhybrid` package (which you can find at `http://www.ps.ucl.ac.uk/~jcpearso/mkhybrid.html` and on the CD-ROM that accompanies this book, in the `sams-extras/backup` directory) to create a CD-ROM with both ISO-9660 and Macintosh HFS filesystems. This program also supports Rock Ridge extensions to ISO-9660 and Joliet, so you can create a single CD-ROM with an extremely broad range of OS support. (This book's companion CD-ROM was mastered using `mkhybrid`.) You need to issue the `--netatalk` parameter to `mkhybrid` to get it to recognize the contents of the `.AppleDouble` directory.

Unmounting a Netatalk Volume

You unmount a Netatalk volume in the same way you unmount any other volume in MacOS: by dragging its icon to the trash. The Macintosh then tells Netatalk that the volume is no longer needed, and the connection is closed. If you unmount all volumes from a given server, you might need to reenter your username and password if you try to mount a volume again. Otherwise, the Macintosh remembers your username and password, so you can remount the volume a bit more easily.

Occasionally, a Macintosh program opens a file and doesn't properly close the OS handle on the file. This makes it difficult to unmount the disk *in Linux*. If you're accessing files on a hard disk, such an occurrence isn't normally a problem, but it can be if you're sharing removable media. In such cases, the solution is to either close the program that's holding the file open unnecessarily or to unmount the share in MacOS. Occasionally the latter option may be the only choice. Sometimes you can simply wait a minute or two, and the program belatedly removes its lock on the file, allowing you to unmount the disk from Linux.

Sharing Removable and Networked Media

You can export removable media and those that Linux has mounted from other servers. Figure 12.4 shows a Macintosh that has mounted several filesystems from a Linux Netatalk server:

- A Windows NT C: drive mounted using Samba's smbmount utility
- A Joliet CD-ROM disc read by Linux
- A standard Linux home directory, rodsmith
- A Macintosh HFS Zip disk read by Linux

Whatever the source of the filesystems, the basic principles are the same as far as both Netatalk and MacOS are concerned. Chapter 9, "Basic Principles of File Sharing," discusses different methods of sharing removable media.

A few further comments are in order with respect to sharing Macintosh HFS media, including Macintosh CD-ROMs, Zip disks, and floppies:

- You should use the conv=netatalk and afpd options. The former option sets up Linux's HFS driver to display the resource forks as Netatalk does, and the latter option refines this display to allow better read/write access to the media from Macintoshes.
- Standard PC hardware cannot read the low-level format of 400KB and 800KB floppies, so you can't mount these media in Linux. PC hardware and Linux have no problems with 1.44MB Macintosh floppies, though.

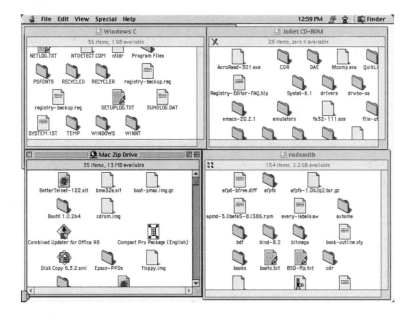

Figure 12.4

Netatalk-exported filesystems give few clues to their origins.

- Macintoshes have traditionally used their own means of supporting long filenames on FAT floppies. These methods are incompatible with VFAT, and therefore with Linux's handling of long filenames. Attempting to share such floppies with Macintoshes therefore loses the Macintosh-created long filenames. Fortunately, recent versions of MacOS use VFAT as DOS does, so this problem should only exist when exchanging FAT floppies with relatively elderly Macintosh systems.

- Linux's HFS support is considered experimental, and may not be 100% reliable. I therefore recommend that you *not* mount large Macintosh removable media with irreplaceable data for read/write access. You're unlikely to run into problems writing a few files to blank media, though, or to small disks.

CAUTION

As of this writing, Linux kernels past 2.2.8 don't work well in conjunction with the export of HFS media via Netatalk. The problem manifests in a hung Macintosh. If you're using a more recent kernel and have this problem, try either the very latest kernel available (which may or may not have fixed the problem) or the 2.2.8 kernel.

12

NETATALK:
SHARING FILES
WITH MACS

If you share disks in a filesystem other than HFS or Linux's native ext2, you might run into that filesystem's peculiarities. For instance, you can't create files with names longer than the DOS 8.3 limit if you use the Linux msdos filesystem. Although this might not sound tragic, it has more serious consequences than you might think—because the .AppleDouble directory's name is longer than the 8.3 limit, Netatalk can't create that directory on msdos floppies, and so file copies won't work. (You get a mysterious message stating that "an error of type -50 occurred.") Much less serious is the fact that, if you use Linux's vfat filesystem, the Macintosh's newfound filename case-sensitivity when using Linux ext2fs partitions is lost.

Security Considerations

Although Netatalk supports encrypted passwords, that support doesn't exist in most binaries because it's implemented through encryption technologies that are restricted for export in some countries, including the United States. Therefore, if you want to use encrypted passwords, you have to either track down a binary that has already linked with those libraries (likely from a non-U.S. site) or compile your own copy of Netatalk. Fortunately, you're not likely to need to use Netatalk over more than your local network, so most sites don't really need encrypted passwords.

Netatalk uses the standard Linux password database, so your Macintosh users need conventional Linux accounts with passwords. If your Macintosh users don't need to log in to the Linux computer normally, you can remove their ability to do so, as described in Chapter 24, "Maintaining a Secure System."

Mounting Macintosh Volumes in Linux

In theory, it's possible to mount volumes exported from Macintosh servers in Linux. To do this, you need to use the Apple File Protocol Filesystem (afpfs). This is a kernel module that's not included in the standard Linux kernel, so you must compile it separately and use it as a kernel module.

Note that I began the preceding paragraph with the words *in theory*. This is because afpfs was never very advanced and is, at the time of this writing, not reliable. In fact, David Foster, the current maintainer of afpfs, states on his Web page (http://www.panix.com/~dfoster/afpfs/) that he doesn't consider afpfs to be usable at the moment. Further, development has stalled, so unless something changes, afpfs may remain unusable for some time.

Nonetheless, if you're interested in this support, you should check the afpfs Web page mentioned in the last paragraph. You might also check the Netatalk HOWTO Web page at http://thehamptons.com/anders/netatalk/, in case somebody else picks up the baton on afpfs.

If you're adventurous enough to try using `afpfs` or—better yet—continuing its development, then by all means download it and try it. I don't provide any instructions here on doing so, though, because I don't recommend it for a production computing environment or for anybody who's not more than qualified to set it up with nothing more than the scant documentation it currently has.

Summary

The Netatalk package does for Macintosh networks what Samba does for Windows networks. Netatalk isn't quite as complete as Samba, though—Netatalk has more quirks, fewer amenities, and currently lacks a Linux client to match its Linux server, for instance. Still, Netatalk gets the job done and is a useful tool on many intranets.

To use Netatalk, you must compile your Linux kernel with AppleTalk DDP support, which provides the low-level protocols similar to the lower layers of the TCP/IP stack. When that's done, you can configure and run the Netatalk daemons, `atalkd` and `afpd`.

In operation, much of the challenge in maintaining a Netatalk server and in allowing it to interoperate smoothly with Linux programs or with Windows files served by Samba is in managing Macintosh resource forks, which Netatalk stores in subdirectories called `.AppleDouble`. You must be careful not to disturb the contents of these directories except when you know that the files contained therein are not vital to the data files as a whole.

Using Linux to Back Up Client Machines

IN THIS CHAPTER

It's 11:00 p.m. and you're working on a report that's due at 9:00 a.m. the next day. You're almost finished, when something goes wrong: The power goes out momentarily, and then comes back, rebooting all your computers. When the systems come back up, they admonish you to shut down properly next time, and then they proceed to check their filesystems. The client machine you were using reports several errors in the directory holding your word processor. When the checks are finished, you try the program anyhow, but it's no good; the word processor crashes on startup. What's worse, you know that these directories hold customizations, templates, and dictionary files, all of which are now suspect at best. Even if you were to reinstall the software, you'd have lost those customizations. What can you do?

If you've been using a Linux file server, and if you've followed the advice in this chapter, you can pull out a backup medium, restore the affected directory tree, and be back in business as quickly as your backup device's speed allows. Linux's file-sharing features make it an excellent choice for duty as a *backup server*—a computer that can back up a potentially large number of networked computers. Maintaining backups of your important data can help reduce downtime due to hardware or software failures, and can rescue you from disaster should irreplaceable data vanish from a hard disk. Do you really want to entrust your business's financial data, or the scientific observations you've collected over the past year to a single hard disk? If not, back it up! Chances are that any person reading this book has a need for backup because the time, effort, and expense of setting up a network suggests an important use for the computers on that network, and hence important data stored on the computers.

Of course, you need backup hardware first. Chapter 22, "Designing a Computer as a Linux Server," includes information on various backup hardware technologies. CD-recordable (CD-R) drives are a good choice for archival storage of up to 650MB of data, or for backing up slow-to-change system configurations if they fit in that space. In general, though, I favor tape drives for routine (daily or weekly) backups. If your network has more than a handful of computers, you should consider a high-end digital audio tape (DAT) or digital linear tape (DLT) drive. These drives can be expensive, but considered on a per-computer basis, the cost can be quite reasonable.

This chapter focuses on open source and freeware backup solutions because they come with Linux or are freely available in other operating systems (OSs). Several commercial backup solutions are also available, such as Enhanced Software Technology's (EST's) Backup and Restore Utility (BRU; http://www.estinc.com) and Knox Software's ARKEIA (http://www.arkeia.com). Some of these include support for both Linux and assorted client OSs, whereas others rely on Linux and the remote system's innate file-sharing mechanisms. Some run entirely on the client OS and rely on Linux's file-sharing or other networking features.

This chapter assumes that you configure file sharing on your network. Depending upon the backup solution you choose, you need to either share your client systems' drives or provide write access to the server's drives. If you haven't already, you should read the appropriate chapters for file sharing for the computers on your network.

Backing Up the Server

This chapter is about backing up a network, but the core of the network is the server. Actually, *the* server might be incorrect wording because a network can have more than one server. In fact, the backup server and the file server could be two entirely separate machines, in which case the file server is a client of the backup server for purposes of backup.

Whatever the arrangements and labels, though, you must not forget to back up the computer that controls the backup hardware. The backup machine's hardware is just as vulnerable to failure as any other hardware on the network, so it must be protected. Because of this, and because backing up clients is often similar to backing up the server, I first present information on server backups to both tape and CD-R.

Backing Up to Tape

Backing up to tape in Linux is quite easy after you've configured your system. The difficulty comes from the need to back up regularly and from disaster recovery procedures. Data recovery is covered later in this chapter, in the section "Restoring Files."

Hardware Preparation

To back up a Linux system to tape, you must have an appropriate tape drive with appropriate support in your kernel. Examples of this support include the following:

- SCSI tape—You need the SCSI support and SCSI tape support options selected, either compiled into the kernel or as modules. These options both appear under the SCSI support section of the kernel configuration menus.

- EIDE tape—Under the Block devices kernel configuration menu, you must select both Enhanced IDE/MFM/RLL disk/cdrom/tape/floppy support and Include IDE/ATAPI TAPE support.

- Floppy-based tape (ftape)—You need to select options under the Ftape, the floppy tape device driver kernel configuration menu. In many cases, enabling Ftape (QIC-80/Travan) support and Ztape, the VFS interface and leaving the other options at their default values is sufficient, but in some cases you might need to tweak additional values. For more information on ftape, see http://www.math1.rwth-aachen.de/~heine/ftape/.

- Parallel port tape—Some parallel port tape drives are supported by ftape, and others are supported by the parallel port AT attachment packet interface (ATAPI) drivers, which you can activate from the Block devices kernel configuration menu. Select Parallel port IDE device support and Parallel port ATAPI tapes. There are also a few unusual devices supported in the Parallel port generic ATAPI devices section, and you might need one of these. In all cases, you also need the Parallel port support item from the General setup configuration menu.

> **NOTE**
>
> Basic tape drive functionality is fairly well standardized, so to use the tools described in this chapter, you don't need specialized drivers for the specific model of tape drive you own, just for the general type of tape drive. Some commercial packages provide special options to use unusual features of specific drives, though, so you might want to check on support for those features before buying hardware or software.

In general, I recommend using SCSI tape backup hardware for large workstations and servers, including network backup servers. SCSI tape drives tend to be the most reliable. EIDE devices are acceptable in some situations, particularly in small and low-performance networks. Floppy- and parallel port–based hardware tends to be slow and unreliable—two characteristics that are anathema to a network backup server.

After compiling a kernel with tape support, you need to reboot and then use an appropriate device file. For SCSI tapes, the most likely devices to use are /dev/st0 and /dev/nst0. For EIDE tape devices, including those interfaced via the parallel port, you generally use /dev/ht0 or /dev/nht0. For ftape devices, you use any of several device files that contain ft in their filenames, such as /dev/nft0 or /dev/zqft0. See http://www.math1.rwth-aachen.de/~heine/ftape/ for details on what these devices do. For all interfaces, the device names that begin with n, such as /dev/nst0, do not rewind the tape after an operation completes. This feature lets you place more than one backup on a tape, if there's room. The devices that don't begin with n automatically rewind the tape after every operation, which is convenient when you want to perform a single backup on a tape.

> **TIP**
>
> You might want to create a link from /dev/tape to the tape device used on your system. Doing so can be particularly convenient if you administer several Linux computers, each of which has a different type of tape drive; you can create one set of backup scripts that access /dev/tape and use the same scripts on all the computers.

Performing a Backup

Because tapes are *sequential-access* devices, in which you must read all the data leading up to the data you want, you can't create a filesystem on a tape and use it as you would a hard disk. Instead, you must use software that's designed to archive data onto tape. One such program is tar—in fact, tar stands for *tape archive*. The tar program is quite complex, and it has lots of options. You can use tar to create archives either on disk files or on a raw device, such as a tape. The general form for using tar is tar [*options*] *filenames*. Some of the most commonly used options include the following:

- -t or --list—Lists the contents of an archive.
- -c or --create—Creates a new archive.
- -x or --extract—Extracts files from an archive.
- -d or --diff—Compares files on disk to those in an archive.
- -f or --file=—Specifies the file or device to use. On some systems, this defaults to /dev/tape, which can be a link to your tape device.
- -v or --verbose—Displays a list of the files as they're being processed.
- -M or --multi-volume—Creates an archive that spans more than one tape.
- -L or --tape-length—Changes tape after writing a specified number of kilobytes.
- -p or --same-permissions—Preserves permission information for all files.
- -l or --one-file-system—Indicates not to process files that are mounted from another partition.
- -z or --gzip—Compresses the archive by using gzip.

> **CAUTION**
>
> One of tar's biggest weaknesses is that gzip compression can cause the loss of all data on the archive. If there's a read error on restoring an archive, gzip won't be able to read *any* data after the point of the error. This is an extremely undesirable characteristic for a backup program. If your tape drive has built-in compression, you should use that rather than the -z option to tar.

When using tar, you can omit the first dash of the options when they're given in single-character form. For example, here's a tar command that backs up the / and /home partitions of a Linux installation to a SCSI tape drive:

```
tar cvlpf /dev/st0 / /home
```

> **TIP**
>
> You should use the -1 option whenever you back up the root (/) filesystem. If you don't use this option, you also back up /proc, which wastes a lot of space on your tape because /proc is a virtual filesystem that contains some very large pseudo-files. What's more, on restoration, you might cause problems when you write to the pseudo-files in /proc, causing system settings to change.

> **NOTE**
>
> Some floppy-based tape devices require that you *format* a tape prior to use. Others, including most SCSI- and EIDE-based drives, have no such requirement, since tapes are sold pre-formatted. The ftape documentation describes how to format a tape.

Although tar is capable of backing up a computer or even an entire network, it has limits, such as the danger involved in creating compressed backups with the program. Therefore, many people prefer to use programs such as cpio and afio, or commercial packages such as BRU. I present backup principles with tar in the rest of this chapter because tar is commonly available and because it's the basis for the smbtar program described later in the chapter. The basic principles are the same for other programs, so if you prefer to use another program, you should have few or no problems adapting the information here to your software of choice.

In addition to separate packages, assorted programs function as GUI front ends to tar or some other tape backup program. Figure 13.1, for instance, shows the KDat program, which comes with the popular KDE GUI environment. KDat serves as a front end to tar, allowing you to create and manipulate backup sets.

> **NOTE**
>
> Although GUI backup software can be convenient and is often less intimidating than command-line utilities, it has two major drawbacks. First, in the case of a complete system recovery, you usually must learn how to use the GUI software's command-line equivalents, and doing so in a disaster-recovery situation is more stressful and difficult than doing so when your system is fully functional. Second, for network backup, you should probably automate the backup process. Although some GUI tools provide schedulers in the GUI environment, one of the best ways to automate backups is to create cron jobs to run the backup from scripts, as described later in this chapter, in the section "Creating cron Jobs to Back Up Regularly." Scripted backups call for command-line tools rather than GUI tools.

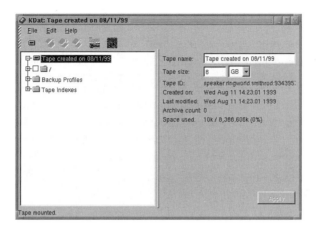

FIGURE **13.1**

KDat uses tar *at its core, but also places its own information on the tape to index the tape's contents.*

Controlling the Tape Device

If all you want to do is create backups on a tape, tar or some other simple backup package, in conjunction with an auto-rewinding tape device, might be sufficient. Chances are good, however, that you need finer control over your tape device. For instance, you might want to do a complete system backup once each week and do incremental backups of only new or changed files once each day. The full backup might consume an entire tape, whereas the incremental backups don't, so to save money, you might want to place all the incremental backups on a single tape. To do so, however, you must skip past the first day's incremental backup, and that's an operation that tar can't do by itself.

To accomplish this goal, you need to use the tape control utility mt. The basic syntax for mt is

```
mt [-f device] operation [count] [arguments]
```

The *device* is the tape device, *operation* is the operation to be performed, *count* is the number of times the operation is to be performed, and *arguments* are any arguments the operation takes. Specific operations include the following:

- fsf—Skips forward *count* files.
- bsf—Skips backward *count* files.
- asf—Positions the tape at the start of file number *count*.
- eod or seod—Positions the tape at the end of existing data.
- retension—Re-tensions the tape. This option is useful for improving tape reliability, especially if a tape hasn't been used in a while.

- erase—Erases the tape.
- status—Displays information about the tape drive.
- load—Loads a tape into the drive. This command isn't needed for all drives.
- offline—Takes the tape drive offline and rewinds the tape.
- compression—Sets the compression option for most tape drives that feature hardware compression. Use a value of 1 to enable compression, or 0 to disable it. Many drives that support hardware compression have jumpers to set the default. The compression option overrides the jumper setting. Some drives, particularly Exabyte units, use specific setdensity settings rather than compression to enable data compression. Consult your drive's documentation or do a Web search to determine what settings you need.

In addition to these operations, mt supports many others, some of which are variants on these that position the tape slightly differently. You might want to experiment with the mt commands, especially as you develop your own backup scripts, to determine precisely what *count* value to give to any given operation to obtain the desired result.

> **NOTE**
>
> To tar and most other tape utilities, a *file* is an entire archive file, not a file on disk. For instance, if you back up the /home directory to tape using tar, that entire backup is one file as far as mt is concerned.

Let's check out an example of using these commands. Suppose that you want to back up two directories, /home/francine and /home/gertrude. You want to keep them on the same tape but in separate tar files. You could do so by issuing the following commands:

```
mt -f /dev/nst0 load
tar cvf /dev/nst0 /home/francine
tar cvf /dev/nst0 /home/gertrude
mt -f /dev/nst0 offline
```

Suppose that the next day, Gertrude comes to you and says that she accidentally deleted the file bug-list.txt from her home directory. You could restore that file by issuing the following commands:

```
cd /
mt -f /dev/nst0 load
mt -f /dev/nst0 fsf 1
tar xvf /dev/nst0 home/gertrude/bug-list.txt
mt -f /dev/nst0 offline
```

The `fsf` command skips past the `/home/francine` backup file, allowing `tar` to access the `/home/gertrude` backup. You could use similar `mt` commands to skip past previous days' backups in an automatic backup script.

> **NOTE**
>
> Tape restores are discussed in more detail later in this chapter, in the section "Restoring Files," so don't pay too much attention to the details ofthe `tar` command in the preceding example.

Backing Up to CD-R or CD-RW

CD-R and CD-RW (CD-rewritable) backups work very differently from tape backups, because the tools are entirely different. You can't write directly to a CD-R drive in the way you can write directly to a tape drive; instead, you must use a CD-R program to do the job. The most common CD-R program for Linux is `cdrecord`, though the older `cdwrite` is still useful in some situations. Various GUI front ends to these programs, such as X-CD-Roast (shown in Figure 13.2, `http://www.fh-muenchen.de/home/ze/rz/services/projects/xcdroast/e_overview.html`) can help you create a CD-ROM, but as with tape backups, they can become awkward when performing scheduled backup operations. This is especially true for CD-R GUIs because these programs aren't designed with backup in mind, but for burning CDs for other purposes.

13

> **NOTE**
>
> CD-R is a write-once technology, whereas CD-RW is a rewritable technology. Both use the same Linux software to create CDs. I use the term *CD-R* to refer to both technologies in this chapter, for brevity's sake.

Because CD-R technology requires a constant and steady stream of data, Linux CD-R software has traditionally required that you first create a single *image file* containing the data to be burned to disc. The `cdrecord` program can then write the data from that single file without having to construct the CD filesystem at the same time it's writing data to the CD. There are efforts under way to develop software that would obviate the need to create an intermediate image file, but what I describe here uses the old style with an intermediate image file.

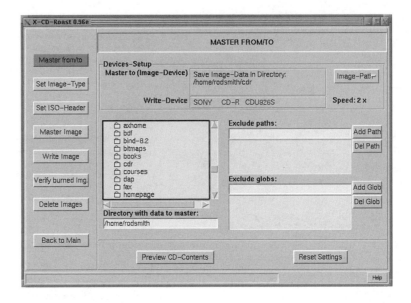

FIGURE 13.2

X-CD-Roast lets you select a directory for backup, then creates an image file and burns a CD from the image file.

You can use `tar` to create your image file. When you need to restore the file, you issue the same commands as if you were restoring from tape, except that you specify the CD-ROM or CD-R drive's device file rather than a tape device file, and the `mt` commands would not work. Such a CD would be unreadable in Windows or most non-Linux/non-UNIX OSs. Alternatively, you can use the `mkisofs` or `mkhybrid` programs to create a standard ISO-9660 image file that can be mounted and read normally. This provides for easier random access to all files on the archive, but you might lose important information. One particularly important problem with creating an ISO-9660 image (even with Rock Ridge extensions) is that all the files on that image are read-only, which can cause serious problems after restoration.

The `mkisofs` package comes with Red Hat Linux, but you need to look elsewhere for the others. `mkhybrid` can be found at `http://www.ps.ucl.ac.uk/~jcpearso/mkhybrid.html`, and provides the ability to create Macintosh HFS CD-ROMs, in addition to the ISO-9660, Rock Ridge, and Joliet supported by `mkisofs`. The `cdrecord` package is available from `http://www.fokus.gmd.de/research/cc/glone/employees/joerg.schilling/private/cdrecord.html`. Both are also on the CD-ROM that accompanies this book, in the `sams-extras/backup` directory.

> **TIP**
>
> If you're using a Linux computer to serve Macintosh files, you can use mkhybrid, in conjunction with its -hfs and —netatalk options, to create a CD-ROM that, when read on a Macintosh, displays the contents of the CD-ROM as they appeared on the Linux server via Netatalk. This can be a very convenient way to distribute Macintosh files from a server. You can also use Apple's Disk Copy utility to accomplish the same goals, but a CD-ROM created with Disk Copy contains *only* HFS structures, so it can't be read on computers that don't understand HFS. If you use mkhybrid, the CD-ROM will also contain ISO-9660 data structures, so you can access the files on PCs or other systems. (Disk Copy is discussed later in this chapter, in the section "Backing Up to Disk.")

As an example, here's how you might back up the /home directory tree to CD-R by using mkisofs and cdrecord:

```
mkisofs -R -J -o outfile.iso /home/
cdrecord -pad dev=6,0 outfile.iso
```

You can eliminate the intermediate file outfile.iso by piping the mkisofs output directly into cdrecord:

```
mkisofs -R -J /home/ ¦ cdrecord -pad dev=6,0 -
```

The problem with this approach is that, because CD recording is very timing-sensitive and because both the CD image creation and burning occur simultaneously, the image creation process is more likely to fail. You're generally safer creating an intermediate file, but if you're short on disk space or have a fast system, you might give the piped solution a try.

The mkisofs command specifies that both Rock Ridge (-R) and Joliet (-J) extensions be used, so you'll be able to read long filenames on the CD in Linux, in other UNIX flavors, and in Windows. The uppercase form of the Rock Ridge switch tells mkisofs to preserve file ownership and permissions, as much as possible. When creating CD-ROMs for distribution, you probably want to use the lowercase form (-r), which changes ownership to root and permissions to -r--r--r-- (with execute bits added when appropriate). This makes the CD readable by all users. For backup, though, preserving the original ownership and permissions is generally more desirable.

To use cdrecord, you must have SCSI generic support selected in the SCSI support section of the kernel configuration. If you're using an EIDE/ATAPI CD-R drive, you should specify SCSI emulation support in the Block devices area; this allows you to access the EIDE/ATAPI CD-R drive as if it were a SCSI device. The dev=6,0 option to cdrecord specifies the device ID— device 6, logical unit (LUN) 0 in this case (most SCSI CD-R drives use a LUN of 0).

After you burn the CD-ROM, you should be able to mount it and access the files. There's no need to keep the `outfile.iso` image file after the CD-ROM has been created. If you prefer to use `tar`, you can substitute an appropriate `tar` command for the `mkisofs` command in this example.

> **NOTE**
>
> Because CD-R media are more reliable than tapes, using `gzip` to compress a `tar` archive is safer with CD-R than with tapes. The potential still exists for compression and a read error to render an archive unreadable, though.

Both `mkisofs` and `cdrecord` support many options that you might need to use. Check their manpages for more details.

In general, I find CD-R media to be too limiting for regular backups of entire systems. They can be useful, however, for backups of clients with small hard disks. The fact that most computers have CD-ROM drives means you can restore data from such backups locally, without involving the server. This can be a great boon in an emergency situation because all you need is an emergency Linux boot floppy to restore the client. Such restores are covered later in this chapter, in the section "Restoring Files."

Server-Initiated Backups

Convincing users to back up their data can be an exercise in frustration. Many individuals are forgetful or find backup procedures to be tedious. Humans also have a common tendency to think that bad things won't happen to them, only to other people, which leads to a minimized sense of risk. As a network administrator, you can't afford to succumb to such attitudes because *when* a computer on your network experiences problems, your users will come to *you* for a solution.

For these reasons, server-initiated backups are often a good idea. All your users need do is leave their computers turned on at some specified time, such as Monday nights, and you configure the Linux server to back up the remote filesystem. Such backups work quite well with NFS and SMB/CIFS networks, but because Linux support for mounting Macintosh file shares is so weak, you can't use this technique with Macintoshes.

13

USING LINUX TO
BACK UP CLIENT
MACHINES

> **NOTE**
>
> Although I've been referring to Linux functioning as a "backup server," when Linux initiates the backup, it is technically the client computer. As far as the remote system is concerned, Linux is just a client system that happens to want to read a lot of files.

Using `tar` to Back Up Mounted Filesystems

Just as `tar` is an effective means of backing up a single computer, it can back up an entire network, or just critical files from the network. In fact, there's not a lot to be said about backing up a networked computer by using `tar`, although if the remote machine is a DOS, Windows, or OS/2 computer, you might want to look into a variant version of `tar` that's included with the Samba package, as described in the next couple sections.

Regular `tar`

One obvious and effective strategy for performing a server-initiated backup is to mount the remote filesystem and use `tar` or some other utility to back up the files. For instance, you could do something like this:

```
mount gingko:/ /mnt/gingko
cd /mnt/gingko
tar cvpf /dev/st0 ./
cd ~
umount /mnt/gingko
```

This sequence backs up the root filesystem on the UNIX or Linux computer called `gingko`. If `gingko`'s NFS daemon exports mounted filesystems, this sequence backs up *all* of `gingko`'s filesystems. Of course, for this procedure to work, `ginkgo` must be configured to export filesystems to the backup server. You can perform a similar backup of Windows filesystems by using `smbmount` rather than `mount`.

> **CAUTION**
>
> Don't attempt to back up a Linux or UNIX system via `smbmount` or `smbtar`. Doing so causes the loss of vital Linux/UNIX filesystem attributes, such as ownership and permissions. You can safely back up a shared FAT partition in this way, though, and this could be convenient if the system dual-boots between Linux and Windows: You can export the same partition under the same name in both OSs, and the backup server need not concern itself with which OS is in use at the time of the backup.

If you prefer to use `cpio`, `afio`, or some other utility, you can do so, in much the way you'd use `tar`, except for whatever changes you need for the alternative utility's syntax.

Samba's `smbtar`

The `smbtar` program is a utility that ties together some of the low-level portions of the Samba client and `tar`. It allows you to back up an SMB/CIFS share without explicitly mounting it in Linux. The format for this command is

```
smbtar options files
```

The available options include the following:

- `-s` *server*—The name of the computer you want to back up. This parameter is required.
- `-u` *user*—The username with which to log on to the remote system. If it is omitted, `smbtar` uses the name of the user who launched the program.
- `-p` *password*—The password for accessing the remote system.
- `-x` *service*—The name of the share you want to back up. The default is `backup`.
- `-X`—An option that `smbtar` uses to exclude any files listed on the command line. Without this parameter, files listed are ones to be *included* in the backup.
- `-d` *directory*—An option to change to the specified directory and back it up, rather than the root of the share. This parameter is optional.
- `-t` *tape*—The name of the tape device or file on the local system to use for backup.
- `-i`—An option to perform an incremental backup—only those files whose archive bits have been set are backed up.
- `-a`—An option that resets the archive bits on files as they're backed up.

> **TIP**
>
> You might want to use the `-a` option on full backups but omit it on incremental backups. That way, you have to do at most two restores in the event of a complete system failure: once for the full backup and once for the most recent incremental backup. If you use the `-a` option on incremental backups, you have to restore all the incremental backups you performed since the last full backup.

- `-r`—An option to restore files, rather than back them up.
- `-v`—An option for verbose mode, which displays filenames as the files are backed up.

As an example, here's a command line that backs up a Windows computer:

```
smbtar -s spruce -u claus -p merry -x cdrive -v -t /dev/nst0
```

This command backs up the computer called `spruce` by using `claus`'s account on that computer, with the password `merry`. All files go to `/dev/nst0`. This command doesn't specify any files to be backed up. In this situation, `smbtar` backs up *all* the files in the specified directory, or in the root directory when you don't give a `-d` parameter, as in the preceding example.

If you want to back up multiple computers, and have adequate storage space on your tape drive, you can issue several `smbtar` commands in sequence to place all the computers' files on one tape—just be sure to use a nonrewinding tape device! On restore, you can use `mt` to space over the intervening backups to get to a particular machine's files.

The tape or file that results from using `smbtar` is an ordinary tar file in all respects. So what do you gain for using `smbtar` rather than mounting a share and using ordinary `tar`? Convenience, mainly; there's no need to explicitly mount and then unmount the remote directory. There's also a security advantage—because the remote filesystem isn't mounted, users who aren't authorized to access that share can't do so through the mount point during the backup procedure. Of course, you could set permissions appropriately in the mount point's directory to restrict unauthorized access, but using `smbtar` ensures that an oversight won't cause problems. Finally, `smbtar` allows you to access the remote filesystem's archive bit, which can be convenient when you perform an incremental backup—rather than keep track of changed files through a file list on the backup server, the target filesystem itself maintains this information.

Creating `cron` Jobs to Back Up Regularly

If you have more than two or three computers to back up, and perhaps even with that few, you might want to create an automated backup schedule. You can configure Linux to do complete backups one night of the week, for instance, and do incremental backups every other night. Backup schedules are covered later in this chapter, in the section "Effective Backup Schedules and Strategies," but for now you should know that you can schedule automatic backups by using Linux's `cron` facility. Linux sports a daemon known as `cron` that can be used to run programs at regularly scheduled times. Linux distributions normally come configured to run `cron` jobs to perform routine maintenance at regular intervals—typically hourly, daily, weekly, and monthly, although not all of these actually do anything. These standard runs occur in the early hours of the morning, typically around 1:00 to 3:00 a.m., so they don't disturb users. They perform tasks such as removing old files from the `/tmp` directory and rotating log files in `/var/log` so that they don't grow to monstrous size. In Red Hat Linux, `cron` job scripts appear in the `/etc/cron.`*`interval`* directories, where *`interval`* is the time period (hourly, daily, and so on). You can easily add backup scripts to this schedule. For instance, to back up your entire network weekly, early Sunday morning, you could add a script to do the job to the `/etc/cron.weekly` directory.

> **CAUTION**
>
> Before you install any scripts or commands for execution by cron, you should be *positive* that the scripts or commands do what you expect them to do. In the case of a script, run it manually, and check how it handles errors. For instance, if a remote machine has been turned off, what does the script do? Does it notify you—say by email—of the error, or does it simply back up an empty directory with no indication that there's a problem? Above all else, you don't want a script that will cause the server's disk to fill, or that will cause CPU use to shoot off the scale to run when you're not around to quickly fix the problem.

Your needs may be more specific than a once-a-week backup, of course. In that case, you need to create a custom cron job. You can do this by typing

crontab -u root -e

The specifics of this example assume that you're running crontab as root and that you want to create a cron job to run as root (you can also create a personal non-root cron job in the same way). The -e parameter to crontab opens an editor in which you can create a crontab file (note the dual use of the word crontab—in reference to both a file and a command). If you prefer, you can create the crontab file in whatever editor you prefer and use the crontab command to install it in the system.

Lines in a crontab file are either environment variable settings or cron commands. Environment variable settings take the form

VARIABLE = value

You might want to set some common variables in this way, such as:

```
SHELL=/bin/bash
PATH=/sbin:/bin:/usr/sbin:/usr/bin
```

cron commands take the form

minute hour day-of-month month day-of-week command

The first five fields specify the time, and the rest of the line is the command to be run. In the case of complex commands, you should probably create a shell script and specify the complete path to the script. The various time fields take values as follows:

   minute—Values 0–59.

   hour—Values 0–23.

   day-of-month—Values 0–31.

month—Values 0–12 or the first three letters of the month's name.

day-of-week—Values 0–7 (0 and 7 both correspond to Sunday) or the first three letters of the day's name.

In all cases, you can specify multiple values in several ways:

- An asterisk (*) signifies all possible values.
- Comma-separated values (as in *0,10,20,30,40,50*) indicate that each specified value matches. This example, if used in the `hour` field, would cause a `cron` job to run once every 10 minutes.
- Values separated by a hyphen (-) signify that the entire range of values matches. For instance, `9-17` in the `hour` field indicates that the job runs between 9:00 a.m. and 5:00 p.m.
- A slash (/) indicates stepped values—a range in which some members are skipped. For instance, `*/10` in the `minute` field would be another way to specify execution every ten minutes, and `9-17/2` in the `hour` field would execute a job every other hour between 9:00 a.m. and 5:00 p.m.

Here's an example of a `crontab` file:

```
SHELL=/bin/bash
MAILTO=rodsmith
#
# run at 2:15am on the first of every month
15 2 1 * *      /root/backup-scripts/monthly-backup
# run at 3:15am on Tuesday mornings (set up MONDAY NIGHT!)
15 3 * * 2      /root/backup-scripts/weekly-backup
# run at 3:15am on mornings following weekdays EXCEPT for Tuesdays
15 3 * * 1,3,4,5 /root/backup-scripts/incremental-backup
```

One potential flaw in the preceding `crontab` file is that the monthly backup can run on days that are also scheduled for weekly or daily backups, depending on the day on which the first of the month falls. This needn't be a problem if the monthly backup is made to a different medium (say, if it's an Internet transfer of files from a regional office to a national office) or if it's a matter of copying files from one directory to another.

To be useful, the preceding `crontab` file must have access to the various backup scripts. Here's a sample backup script, which is also on the CD-ROM that accompanies this book as `sams-extras/backup/backup` (with a few extra comments in the file on the CD-ROM):

```
#!/bin/bash
#
# A *VERY* simple example backup script using smbtar.
total="written"
```

```
# Perform the smbtar operation and dump output in /tmp/bu.log:
smbtar -s machine -u user -p password -x share -t /dev/nst0 -v &> /tmp/bu.log
# Search /tmp/bu.log for the summary string and mail it to root:
grep $total /tmp/bu.log ¦ mail -s "Backup Report" root
# Delete the temporary file. This action is commented out.
# rm /tmp/bu.log
# Unmount the tape device
mt -f /dev/nst0 offline
```

This script backs up the SMB/CIFS share called share on the computer called machine to the /dev/nst0 device. It temporarily stores a list of all backed-up files to /tmp/bu.log and uses grep to search through that file for the summary line that reports the number of bytes written to tape. The script emails that line to the root account (which you should probably configure to forward mail to your ordinary user account). This way, you receive a report concerning the backup activity when you next log on. If the number of bytes backed up is strange, you can check the backup tape itself, or the backup log file if you don't uncomment the line in the script that deletes it.

TIP

You might want to keep the log file available for the expected life of the backup—probably in a directory other than /tmp and under a more descriptive filename than bu.log. Keeping the log file lets you easily locate a filename, so that if a user comes to you with a request to restore a specific file, you can do so easily, even if the user can't recall the precise filename. You can simply search through the file listing for likely files and ask the user to confirm the filename. (In a situation like this, it's best to check that the selected filename doesn't already exist—it wouldn't do to overwrite a newer file because the user misremembered a filename!)

This backup script is intended only as a minimal example. Although you can use it as-is after replacing only specific information on your computer, passwords, and so on, it is limited. It should be easy to modify the script to handle NFS shares, multiple computers, and more complex error reporting. You need to know a bit about Bash shell scripting, though, to do anything more than trivial modifications. Teaching shell scripting is beyond the scope of this book, but you can learn more in *Sams Teach Yourself Shell Programming in 24 Hours*. You could also use a script in any other language you like, such as Perl. *Sams Teach Yourself Perl in 24 Hours* is a useful reference if you want to learn Perl scripting.

Security Considerations

One major concern with server-initiated backups, particularly if those backups use Samba, is that you must store the password in cleartext somewhere on your disk. The password might be in a backup script, a file that's read by the backup script, or even in a crontab file. In any event, you should ensure that the permissions on this file are as tight as possible—probably 0600 with ownership by root, or 0700 if the file is a script. You might even want to create a cron job to check that permission and email you (at a remote computer, if possible) if it changes. Because a backup server that initiates backups in this way stores all your passwords, you should be especially cautious of its own security. Don't make this computer do double duty as a gateway or firewall. If you have the luxury, dedicate a computer to being the backup server, so you can disable all services on that computer. Such a computer's speed is likely to be limited by the tape drive or NIC, so you might be able to "recycle" an older computer as a dedicated backup server.

> **CAUTION**
>
> If you modify the backup shell script on the CD-ROM that accompanies this book, be sure to change its permissions. The CD-ROM–mastering process expands the file's permissions beyond what you want on any file that contains passwords.

> **TIP**
>
> You can create a separate read-only account for backing up SMB/CIFS shares. Windows lets you specify separate passwords for read-only and read/write access to shares. The backup scripts need only read access, so if you use different passwords, you can at least minimize the risk of an intruder doing damage to the Windows systems using the passwords in the backup scripts.

Client-Initiated Backups

Although centrally initiated backups are convenient in many cases, they do have drawbacks. Prime among these is the fact that you can lose certain filesystem attributes, such as the hidden and system bits of Windows files. smbtar is incapable of backing up OS/2 Extended Attributes, and as mentioned previously, Linux-initiated backups of Macintoshes are a practical impossibility at the moment. Therefore, you might want to have your client computers initiate backups. In this scenario, the backup server functions as a shared tape drive, and individual workstations' users must insert a tape and start the backup. In a large network this can produce scheduling difficulties, but it's generally manageable with networks of only a few computers.

Backing Up to Disk

One potential backup procedure is to use Linux's file-sharing capabilities to allow clients to back themselves up to a shared Linux disk. This disk could itself be a removable-media drive, such as a Zip or JAZ drive, in which case somebody must insert a cartridge and remove it when the backup is finished. This method of backup is likely to be expensive because removable-cartridge media tend to cost a lot on a per-megabyte basis. Low-end media such as Zip are also low in capacity, and so are inadequate for doing anything but limited file backups or backups of particularly limited clients.

If the target share is not itself a removable medium, you can back it up to tape from Linux. This two-stage backup procedure might become tedious when it is time to restore, but not so tedious as having no backup at all. As important in many cases, you must have adequate disk space on the Linux server to hold all the files from the client system, at least temporarily.

You can automate some of these procedures. For instance, if you're using backup software on the client that allows it to schedule a backup to a remote share at particular times, you can use the client's scheduling to back up at, say, midnight. You can then use a Linux `cron` job, as described earlier in this chapter, to back up the target directory to tape at 2:00 a.m. and delete the just-backed-up directory tree. Timing is critical in such operations, though, so be sure your clients will be finished with their backups before the Linux `cron` job kicks in.

For a client-initiated backup procedure like this to work, you need appropriate software on the client computers. Software such as NovaStor's (`http://www.novastor.com`) NovaBack or Veritas's (`http://www.veritas.com`) BackupExec should work for Windows clients. For UNIX or Linux, the standard `tar` utility should be adequate. For Macintosh clients, the Retrospect packages from Dantz (`http://www.dantz.com`) work, although they actually use FTP rather than AppleTalk/Netatalk for communication, so you must configure your Linux computer as an FTP server. Alternatively, you can use Apple's free Disk Copy utility, which creates an HFS disk image from your hard disk's files. Disk Copy comes with MacOS, though it's not installed by default. Check the `Utilities Folder` on the installation CD-ROM for MacOS 8.0 or later, or the `Disk Images Folder` for earlier versions of MacOS.

One problem you might encounter when using Disk Copy is that the program sometimes erroneously reports that there's not enough disk space on a Netatalk volume, when in fact there is. This might be fixed in more recent versions of Disk Copy than the one included with MacOS 8.6. You can work around this problem by following these steps:

1. On the Linux server, create an empty file large enough to hold the disk image. You can do this with the Linux dd command, as in **dd if=/dev/zero of=image.img bs=1024 count=1048576**, which creates a 1GB (1,048,576 kilobyte) image.

2. Use the Linux hfsutils package, and in particular the hformat utility, to create a Macintosh filesystem in the image file you've just created, as in **hformat image.img**.

3. From the Macintosh, open the directory in which the image.img file resides. If you've installed Disk Copy on your Macintosh and if your Linux /etc/atalk/AppleVolumes.system file is configured correctly, the image.img file has a Disk Copy icon. You can double-click it to mount the image file. (It might take a while to mount the image file, so be patient.)

> **NOTE**
>
> The default AppleVolumes.system file maps the .img extension onto a Graphics Environment Manager (GEM) bit image file (a rare image file format). You can change the file type and creator codes to dimg and ddsk, respectively, to get the Macintosh to recognize .img files as Disk Copy disk images. Alternatively, you can use some other extension, such as .dsk. You need to restart your Netatalk server to get it to recognize any changes to its configuration files.

4. When you create the image file of the disk you want to back up, specify the empty image file you've just mounted, as shown in Figure 13.3.

FIGURE 13.3

From the Macintosh's Desktop directory, you can double-click the disk image volume (highlighted in this figure) to enter it as you would a hard disk, and then enter a filename to save the backup image.

In this way you create a disk image inside a disk image. If you want to move the Macintosh-created disk image to tape, CD-R, or some other medium, you can do so by mounting the Linux-created disk image with the Linux loopback driver and HFS support, as in

```
mount -t hfs -o loop image.img /mnt/image
```

You can then access the Macintosh-created image inside the /mnt/image directory in order to send it to its ultimate destination medium.

Security Considerations

As with backups initiated by the backup server, those initiated by client computers present security issues. When backing up to disk shares, though, these issues aren't any different from the issues involved in normal file-sharing security, as described in previous chapters. If you write a script on a remote system to initiate a backup, though, you should consider how the script will mount the share. If the script needs to know the share's password, that's a potential security problem. So is leaving a client computer running with a user logged in to obviate the need for a password.

Restoring Files

Backing up is not very difficult. Restoring files to an intact client is also not very difficult. Restoring files to a system that has failed completely, however, can be much more difficult, or at least tedious. I can't begin to cover every option or situation in this chapter, so I present some generalized advice and information that should help you to bring up a working system.

Partial Restores

A *partial restore* is a restoration of some subset of the files that you've backed up. This section covers the subset of partial restores that involve restoring files to a working client. You might want to do a partial restore to a client that's not working—for instance, if Windows 98's C:\WINDOWS directory were damaged. To do that, see the section "Complete Restores and Disaster Recovery" later in this chapter.

Server-Initiated Backups

If you've backed up data by using the Linux box's ability to function as a file-sharing client to grab remote machines' files, you must reverse the steps you took to back up the data. For instance, suppose you used smbtar to back up a remote system with the following command:

```
smbtar -s winbox -x cdrive -u billg -p mypassw -t /dev/nst0
```

Now, suppose you have cause to restore a file or directory, say C:\DOCS\BigFile.doc. You could use the following command to do so:

```
smbtar -s winbox -x cdrive -u billg -p mypassw -t /dev/nst0 -r DOCS/BigFile.doc
```

As you can see, this command is identical to the original backup command, except that it includes the -r switch and the name of the file to be restored. There are some important points to note about this command:

- You must use a read/write account or password to restore files, even if you used a read-only account or password to back up the share. If the client isn't set up for write access via SMB/CIFS, you might need to temporarily modify its settings.

- Linux is case sensitive, so you *must* specify the filename case correctly for this command to work. Note that Linux and Windows handle the case of short filenames differently. Therefore, if the client system dual-boots and you're not sure which OS you used when performing the backup, you might have to check the tape archive itself or try both possibilities (DOCS and docs in the case of the example). Keeping a log of the backed-up files can be extremely useful in this situation.

- Although Windows uses a backslash (\) to separate directories and smbtar displays the same, the files actually appear on the tape with forward slash (/) directory separators. You should use forward slashes to separate the directory names.

- You do *not* specify a leading slash when you list the filenames you want to restore.

- smbtar doesn't take well to filename specifications that contain spaces, so you might need to use smbmount and ordinary tar to restore files with spaces, if you need to list them by name. (The spaces are only a problem in *specifying* the files, so if you have file-names with spaces inside a directory with no spaces in its name, you can restore the entire directory with no problems.)

You can restore multiple files in this way, too—just list the filenames one after another. If you want to restore an entire directory, give the directory's name, and smbtar restores the whole thing.

Because smbtar stores files on tape in an ordinary tar format, you can use tar to restore smbtar-created archives. For instance, here's an alternative means to restore the file C:\DOCS\BigFile.doc:

```
smbmount //winbox/cdrive mypassw /mnt/winbox -U billg
Password: mypassw
cd /mnt/winbox
tar xvf /dev/nst0 ./DOCS/BigFile.doc
cd ~
smbumount /mnt/winbox
```

> **NOTE**
>
> `smbmount` prompts you for the password, which doesn't echo. Because of this prompting, you can't use this procedure in a script that you intend to run from a `cron` job.

A few comments about this procedure are in order:

- The preceding example assumes that you're using the `smbmount` utility from Samba 2.0.5a. If you're using an earlier version of `smbmount`, the syntax is different. See "Mounting Windows Volumes in Linux" (p. 286) for more details.

- `smbtar` places a current directory placeholder (`./`) in front of every filename. You can omit this when restoring files via `smbtar`, but not when restoring files via `tar`. Thus, the third line in this example specifies the filename to be restored as `./DOCS/BigFile.doc` rather than `DOCS/BigFile.doc`.

- If you used `smbmount` and `tar` to back up the remote filesystem, you might need to give the complete path to the to-be-restored files relative to the mount point when you backed up. You probably have to start the restore from the root directory, though, and omit the leading slash. For instance, if you originally backed up using `/mnt/winbox` as the specification of what to back up, you should `cd` to `/` and use `mnt/winbox/DOCS/BigFile.doc` to restore the file. The idea is that `tar`, unless told otherwise with the `-P` parameter at backup, strips the leading `/` from filenames, so if you use it at backup time, you must start the restore from the root directory and omit the `/`, or your filename specifications won't match any in the archive.

- You must be in the mounted remote filesystem to restore files in this way, if you created the archive with `smbtar` or if you used `cd` to move to the remote filesystem and then backed it up by using `./` as the directory specification.

- You can specify filenames that contain spaces, but you should place such filenames in quotation marks. For instance, if `BigFile.doc` had been `Big File.doc`, you would specify the complete filename as `"./DOCS/Big File.doc"`, complete with quotes.

You can restore remote UNIX or Linux files in precisely the same way, except that you use a `mount` command with an NFS filesystem specifier rather than `smbmount` to mount the remote filesystem. You must also ensure that the backup server computer has write access to the mounted UNIX or Linux filesystem. In fact, if you use an emergency Linux boot system for restoration, as described later in this chapter, you can use NFS to restore files you originally backed up with `smbtar` or `tar` with `smbmount`.

Client-Initiated Backups

As with server-initiated backups, you must reverse the steps you took to back up the data when you perform a client-initiated restore. This might involve the following:

- Restoring files from a tape backup and then copying them to the client system with a backup utility or ordinary file sharing.
- Mounting a removable disk and using client-side backup software or file sharing to recover files from the disk.

The details, of course, vary substantially from one implementation to another.

> **TIP**
>
> If you used the image-within-an-image procedure to back up a Macintosh by using Disk Copy, you can restore the image directly from your Linux share. There's no need to create a new disk image and place the backup image in the new disk image. Of course, if you've already got such an image, you can restore the backup file to the empty image if you like.

CD-R Backups

If you use `tar` to create a backup on a CD-R disc, you should follow the same procedures you would for restoring from tape. If you created an ISO-9660, Joliet, or HFS CD-ROM by using `mkisofs` or `mkhybrid`, however, you can restore the files using only the client system—simply insert the CD-R into the client system's CD-ROM drive and read the files from the CD-R disc. You can do the same if you used Apple's Disk Copy utility and burned the resulting image file to CD-R. Of course, you *can* restore files by mounting the CD-R on the Linux computer and sharing it, but unless the client system doesn't have a CD-ROM drive, sharing the mounted CD-R is the more complicated solution.

Complete Restores and Disaster Recovery

Partial restores are fairly easy, but if the client system doesn't boot, you have a much more difficult task ahead of you. This is particularly true of Windows systems because floppy boots don't give you full access to Windows long filenames or (for Windows NT and 2000) NT File System (NTFS).

No matter what approach you take to disaster recovery, you should attempt to test your solution *before* disaster strikes. You can do this either by using your chosen solution to restore a limited number of files or by attempting to restore an entire installation to a spare hard disk or empty disk partition. Doing a complete restore has the advantage that you can check to be sure the system will boot.

Preparation

Before restoring data, you must prepare your hard disk to receive it. This means you must either clean out damaged files or completely repartition and reformat the disk, depending on how badly your system is damaged. I recommend using whatever tools come with your client OS to do this job, or Partition Magic from PowerQuest (http://www.powerquest.com). Although you can use a Linux boot floppy to partition and format a hard disk, Windows some-times has problems with Linux-created FAT filesystems.

You should have, at a minimum, an appropriate set of emergency boot floppies for your OS. Most OSs provide some means of producing these floppies, and you should definitely avail yourself of this capability. In fact, I recommend keeping two or three sets of boot floppies for each computer, since floppies can and do go bad—often at the worst possible time.

Minimal Bootstrap Install

One method of performing an emergency restore is to install on the target computer a minimal working version of the original OS. You can omit all your applications, drivers for all equip-ment except what you need to boot and get on the network, extra utilities, and so on. You need whatever software you used on the client to do the backup, though. In the case of server-initi-ated backups, that's normally just the OS's usual file-sharing mechanisms. You need to config-ure the computer for its file-sharing networking, so that you can mount its shares from Linux. Thereafter, you need only perform a restoration of all the files by using whatever software you used for the backup.

> **TIP**
>
> Microsoft gives you an option concerning the Windows install directory when you install the OS. The default is C:\WINDOWS for Windows 95 and 98, for instance. You should *not* install to the directory in which you originally installed Windows on the computer. That way, when you restore the original Windows directory, it goes in a different location than did the emergency restoration directory, so you don't run into conflicts because of this fact.

Disaster Recovery Disks

Most Windows disk backup programs allow you to create disaster recovery disks. If you used such a program for a client-initiated backup, you might be able to use the emergency disks for a full restore. You must ensure that these disks have full support for whatever networking method you used to access the Linux backup server, or these disks are useless.

Recent versions of MacOS come on bootable CDs; you can insert the CD and hold down the C key as the computer starts to boot from the CD. These CDs include AppleTalk support, so you can use that to restore files from a backup server, provided that you've recovered the files from any secondary storage location you've used.

If you have an Iomega Zip drive, you can use the Norton Zip Rescue software available from Iomega (`http://www.iomega.com`) and bundled with Norton Utilities from Symantec (`http://www.symantec.com`) to boot a Windows 95 or 98 system. You use this utility to create a boot floppy and minimal Windows installation on a Zip disk. You can then use the Zip Rescue disk set to boot your computer and enable file sharing on the drive you want to recover. You can then perform the restore from Linux, if it was a server-initiated backup. If you initiated the backup from Windows, you need a copy of your backup software on the Zip disk. Unfortunately, there is as yet no version of Norton Zip Rescue for Windows NT, and this utility is tightly tied to Iomega's Zip drive, so you can't use it with LS-120 or other removable-media drives.

Linux Disaster Recovery Floppies

You can create a custom set of Linux boot floppies with support for your network card, SCSI adapter (if present), Samba or NFS, and other minimal tools needed to get a system onto the network. You can then use this boot floppy to restore a system, if the backup was initiated from the Linux backup server. This procedure works whether the client is Linux or Windows, though if you're using Windows NT, Linux's preliminary support for NTFS means you might have problems restoring an NTFS system to a fully working state.

Unfortunately, creating the necessary boot floppies for this operation is a challenging task because you need to carefully select the networking software, drivers, and filesystem support you need for your client computers. You might be able to use the Red Hat Linux `bootnet.img` network install floppy image as a starting point if you elect to try this approach. The `bootnet.img` file is a floppy image that contains an image file of its own, `initrd.img`. Although it doesn't bear a `.gz` extension, `initrd.img` is actually gzipped, so you should copy it to the hard disk, rename it `initrd.img.gz`, and use `gunzip` to uncompress it. You can then mount it with the Linux loopback driver (as in `mount -o loop initrd.img /mnt/floppy`) and modify its contents. After you've added the utilities you need and deleted those that you don't need, use `gzip` to compress the `initrd.img` file again, rename it, and copy it back to the floppy.

If you prefer, you can create a fuller-featured Linux system on a Zip disk or other removable media, even including X, GUI text editors, and so on. You must install Linux to the removable media, being careful to select only those packages you need. You can then create a boot floppy with DOS, `LOADLIN.EXE`, and the Linux kernel. Unlike with the Norton Zip Rescue utility for Windows, you can create such emergency Linux disks using LS-120 disks, magneto-optical disks, or other removable-media devices. Although creating an emergency disk setup like this takes some time and planning, it's easier than creating an emergency boot floppy.

> **TIP**
>
> If you have a network with several client systems, investing in a removable-media drive to use as an emergency restore system, either using Norton Zip Rescue or a custom Linux installation, is well worth the small cost. Get a portable unit that interfaces via the parallel port for greatest flexibility, or via a SCSI port if many of your systems have SCSI adapters. If you use static IP addresses on your intranet, you can assign one to the emergency restore system. If your hardware varies, you might need to create more than one emergency disk, particularly if you use Norton Zip Rescue.

Linux Dual Boot

You might want to consider placing a small Linux partition on each client computer. This way, you can boot to Linux to do a complete restore, assuming that the problem is with the client's filesystem and not a completely trashed hard disk. If the hard disk is trashed, you can restore or reinstall Linux first, and use it to recover the primary client system OS.

Disk Partition Image Backups

Several programs exist to make "disk image" backups of hard disk partitions. One such program is Drive Image from PowerQuest (http://www.powerquest.com). Upon restoration, these images recover your filesystem almost precisely as it had been before, even including file fragmentation and perhaps filesystem damage. These last two aspects are undesirable, of course, but the basic concept is quite helpful in disaster recovery situations. You need to run the image-creation program, back up the resulting file, and be prepared to restore it later.

If you can boot Linux on the client OS (through a dual-boot setup or emergency boot disk), you can create a disk image backup quite easily by using the Linux dd utility. For instance, suppose you want to create an image of the partition /dev/hda2. You could type

```
dd if=/dev/hda2 of=disk.img
```

The file disk.img now contains a byte-for-byte copy of the contents of /dev/hda2, whether or not Linux understands that filesystem. You can restore the partition by reversing this process. You can also burn the image file to a CD-ROM or copy it to tape.

One huge advantage of image backups is that they allow you to restore a bootable system with minimal fuss after a major disaster. This is particularly true if the image is small enough to burn to CD-R, so that you can boot Linux and use the CD-ROM device as the input to dd. A major disadvantage to this method of backup is that you might not be able to restore to a partition that's anything but the *exact* size of the original. This is certainly true of Linux's dd approach, though some of the commercial utilities, including Drive Image, are more flexible in this respect. If you use `dd`, don't expect to be able to restore a partition if you need to replace a hard disk; the new drive might have a different geometry that results in slightly different partition sizes.

Postrestore Cleanup

When you restore a DOS, Windows, or OS/2 system, you must often run a special program to ensure that the newly restored partition is bootable. This program is called `SYS.EXE` for DOS and Windows, and should be present on the OS emergency floppy. For OS/2, the program is called `SYSINSTX.EXE`, and is present on the OS/2 installation CD. For DOS or Windows, type `SYS C:` to reconfigure the system to be bootable. The function of OS/2's `SYSINSTX` is similar, except that OS/2 can boot from drives other than `C:`. If you used the minimal bootstrap install method of restoration, you might need to delete the temporary bootstrap installation to be sure you make the restored system the bootable one.

If you're restoring a Linux system, you need to reinstall the Linux Loader (LILO) to restore booting. It's easiest to do this if you have a DOS boot floppy, `LOADLIN.EXE`, and a copy of the Linux kernel with which to boot your system. After the system is booted, type `lilo`, and the system should be back to normal. One further possible complication is that if you changed your partition layout during the restore, you might need to edit `/etc/fstab` to reflect these changes. In fact, your system might not boot until you do so. You should therefore be sure to check `/etc/fstab` against the actual partition layout before shutting down from your emergency Linux boot disk.

Macintoshes are simple to restore compared to most Intel-based OSs; you simply drag the restored files onto the blank hard disk, and the system normally boots correctly. It's possible that you need to set the startup disk from the Startup Disk desk accessory, though, so you might want to check that before rebooting.

Backup Pitfalls

Most operating systems contain some sort of filesystem information that other OSs don't. If you fail to take this fact into consideration when planning your backup strategy, you might find yourself in quite a bind when you lose this information after a restore.

Lost Filesystem Attributes

As mentioned previously, DOS, Windows, and OS/2 all support a few filesystem attributes that Linux doesn't understand, such as the hidden, system, and archive bits. For the most part, these are noncritical, so losing them doesn't cause your system to be unbootable or your programs not to work. You might suddenly see some files that you hadn't seen before a restoration, though. A few boot files need to have their system bits set, but the DOS/Windows `SYS.EXE` utility or the OS/2 `SYSINSTX.EXE` program reinstalls those files over the files that are restored in an emergency restoration.

Losing filesystem attributes isn't a problem if you use a client-initiated backup, which is one of the primary advantages of that method of backup. For this reason, the Macintosh backup methods mentioned in this chapter don't suffer from this problem, although the Macintosh supports similar filesystem attributes.

The Windows Registry

Windows stores many system settings in a file called the *Registry*. This Registry file is open whenever Windows is running, and so it may not be backed up correctly. You can prepare for this potential problem by backing up the Windows Registry file:

1. Start a Windows command prompt.
2. Type REGEDIT.EXE to start the Registry Editor program.
3. Choose Registry, Export Registry File to export the Registry as a text file, as shown in Figure 13.4.

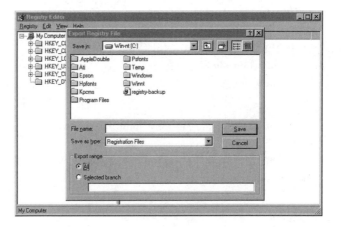

FIGURE 13.4
Exporting the Registry as a text file ensures that it will be available after a restoration.

If you boot your Windows client machine after a restoration and find that it's behaving strangely, try launching the Registry Editor and select Registry, Import Registry File to restore the Registry file you exported before the backup.

If you prefer, you can use any of a number of freeware and shareware Windows utilities designed for backing up the Registry. Many of these perform additional tasks or can maintain several copies of the Registry.

OS/2 Extended Attributes

OS/2 relies heavily upon its Extended Attributes (EAs). These are special pieces of data associated with files, similar to the Macintosh's resource forks, though not as complex. Without EAs, OS/2 won't boot, and many OS/2 programs behave strangely or not at all. Therefore, it's vital that you back up your EAs. The best way to do this is to use an OS/2 backup program to initiate the backup. The second-best way is to use a utility called EABACKUP, which is available from OS/2 FTP sites such as ftp://hobbes.nmsu.edu and ftp://ftp.cdrom.com as EABK203.ZIP, usually in a utilities, disk utilities, or backup directory. EABACKUP stores OS/2 EAs in a file that can be backed up via smbtar or other network utilities. You then run the matching restore utility after a restoration in order to recover the EAs. (You must boot OS/2 with an emergency floppy to run the EA restore utility.)

Macintosh Resource Forks

Because the Macintosh backup strategies discussed here are Macintosh-initiated, you're not likely to run into problems with resource forks when using these methods. If, however, you find that work on afpfs has commenced again and you decide to give it a try for Linux-initiated backups, pay careful attention to the handling of resource forks before using afpfs as a link in your backup chain. Similar comments apply if you decide to try using, say, a Macintosh FTP server or the DAVE SMB/CIFS software to give Linux access to Macintosh files for backup. Because the Macintosh relies on resource forks even more than OS/2 relies on EAs, lost resource forks make your backup useless except for partial restores of certain types of data files.

Effective Backup Schedules and Strategies

The sort of backup schedule you adopt depends largely on the size of your network, the capacity of your backup hardware, your needs, and your tolerance for lost data. In some cases, you might want to do a complete backup of the entire network every night. Other times, you can leave a complete backup as a once-a-month occurrence, or stagger complete backups of client systems across different days. Here are some ideas for backup schedules you might consider:

- Complete backup once per week, incremental backup daily—This is a traditional backup schedule, and ensures that you won't have lost much data if disaster should strike. On a large network, though, you might not be able to fit a complete backup on a single tape.

- Server backup once per week, rotating daily complete backup of clients—If you have, say, eight clients, you can back up two of them each on Monday through Thursday, and back up the server on Friday. If you have enough free space on the tapes, you might also be able to squeeze in incremental daily backups.

- Archival client backup, tape backup of server—If your client machines store relatively little data, you can back them up rarely (once per month or less frequently) to CD-R and use tape for weekly or daily backups of the server. This strategy is effective only if the client systems don't change much, however; if users store data on them, the clients should be backed up more often.

- Mixed archival/tape backup—If you install the client OS on a small partition and place applications and data files on separate partitions, you can back up the OS itself to CD-R on an infrequent basis and back up data and applications to tape daily or weekly.

- Other strategies—The number of possible backup strategies is quite large. Some variant or combination of one of the preceding strategies might serve your particular needs quite well.

In evaluating potential backup strategies, you should ask yourself how inconvenienced you'll be by the schedule itself, by varying levels of recovery, and by lost data. You need to balance each of these factors in deciding what strategy to use. For instance, if your data are vital to your business and can't be done without even for a short time, you should use a backup strategy that guarantees backup of data daily (and perhaps even more often), even if it's inconvenient on a day-to-day basis. If your client systems contain few applications or customizations, you might be able to back them up quite infrequently, particularly if you would be forced to use awkward client-initiated backup procedures.

Remember, too, that you can adopt different schedules for the server and the clients, and even for different clients. A seldom-used public computer with no important files might merit less frequent backups than the fully loaded client systems being used to develop your company's "bread-and-butter" application, for instance.

No matter what schedule you choose, you should consider storing some of your backups off-site. This protects you in the event of burglary, fire, or some other accident that could wipe out your computers *and* any backups you keep. Depending on your needs, simply taking a tape home with you each week (or to work if your network is at home) might be adequate. Those who've watched too many episodes of *The X-Files* might want to send a tape to a safety deposit box in a distant city every now and then.

Summary

Backing up your network is an important task, and one you should not overlook. Linux's file-sharing mechanisms allow you to back up NFS and SMB/CIFS shares quite easily by using the Linux computer to mount the remote shares and copy their contents to tape or some other backup medium. You can also perform client-initiated backups, and indeed this is the most practical way to back up a Macintosh by using Linux.

Restoring a few files from a backup is a fairly simple task, but restoring an entire system (say, because of a crashed hard disk) is not. When restoring an entire system, you must be prepared with emergency boot disks of one form or another and appropriate software to bring the remote system onto the network well enough to reverse the backup procedure. Alternatively, you might be able to restore without the network by using files backed up onto a CD-R or other removable media.

Printer Sharing

PART

IV

IN THIS PART

Preparing to Share a Printer

IN THIS CHAPTER

The "paperless office" was a vision of the 1970s and early 1980s, when personal computers began to enter offices. We could, it was said, exchange documents electronically, without using paper. This vision began to blur and fade by the late 1980s, though, when it became obvious that computers made it easy to produce *more* paper output. Some endeavors certainly use less paper because of computers—I don't need to print the manuscript to this book, for instance. Many other computerized endeavors produce as much or more paper, though, particularly because printers make it so easy to discard an entire page to make a single correction.

With the continued importance of paper output, then, the efficient use of printing hardware has become a priority in offices of all sizes. Some printers are quite inexpensive, but others are not. Even a midrange office laser printer can cost $1,000 or so—more than many computers cost. Thus the popularity and importance of *printer sharing*—making a printer connected to one computer available to others on a network. Rather than place a $1,000 laser printer in each of a dozen offices, a company can place a single printer in a central location, saving $11,000 in initial expenses.

Just as Linux can function as a great integrator across platforms for file sharing, it can integrate access to printers across platforms. Indeed, the UNIX heritage of PostScript printing combined with the universal availability of the Ghostscript PostScript interpreter on Linux makes Linux an ideal platform for sharing even inexpensive printers across client operating systems (OSs). You can even share low-end PC inkjet printers with Macintoshes that work best with PostScript printers, saving on equipment costs.

Before you can do much to configure your system for printer sharing, though, you need to configure *local* printing. When you have your Linux box printing local files, you can configure printer sharing. If you encounter problems at that stage, you know to debug the network aspects, rather than the Linux printer queue itself.

Understanding Linux Printer Queues

Most operating systems more advanced than DOS make use of the concept of a *printer queue*. Linux's printer queues are both similar to and different from printer queues in other OSs. Most importantly, Linux's queues allow you to attach *filters* to queues. These filters process the files you send to a printer in order to convert data to a format that's more amenable to what the printer expects. Filters can be simple or complex, and understanding what they can do is important in configuring and debugging Linux printing.

Printer Queues: Waiting Areas for Printing Files

To print on Linux, you use a special program to transfer a file to be printed to a waiting area called a *queue*. On most Linux systems, the program that performs this duty is known as lpr, and in fact you see references to lpr in various programs' print dialog boxes, such as the xv dialog box shown in Figure 14.1.

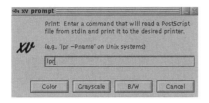

FIGURE 14.1

Graphical user interface (GUI) print dialog boxes sometimes give you hints concerning options you might want to use, like the -Pname *prompt in this dialog box.*

> **NOTE**
>
> Linux's printing model works on *files*, although you might not think in this way, particularly if you're dealing with temporary information. A program either creates a temporary file to be printed and passes this to lpr, or it passes a pseudo-file through *standard output*—data that normally goes to the terminal, but that can be redirected into a program much like a file. This process is mostly transparent to the user, but you should be aware of the emphasis on files to better understand what a printer queue is.

lpr is discussed in more detail later in the chapter (p. 376), but for now I'll just point out one option: -P. You type **-P** followed *immediately* by a printer name (with no space between the two) to print to a printer of that name. For instance, type

```
lpr -Pepson presidents.txt
```

to print the file presidents.txt to the epson printer queue. Traditionally, the default printer queue is called lp, but that might not be true on all systems.

As you might guess from this discussion, Linux supports multiple printer queues, so you can connect several printers to a single computer. These printers can either be directly connected to the Linux computer or they can themselves be network printers shared by other computers or residing independently on the network. Either way, you work with them in Linux in identical ways, and you can export either variety, which can be helpful in some situations, as described later in this chapter.

The lpr program is itself pretty simple; it just copies the file you give it to a waiting area, likely somewhere in the /var/spool/lpd directory tree. By default, Linux configures each printer to have its own subdirectory in that tree. After lpr has copied files to this directory tree, its work is done.

The lpd program then takes a over. lpd is a daemon that watches the queue directories specified in the file /etc/printcap. Normally lpd watches the subdirectories in which lpr stores files for printing. When lpd detects a file in a printer queue directory, the daemon passes the file through filters specified in /etc/printcap and sends the result to the printer's port, also specified in /etc/printcap. Thus a file in Linux is printed.

Queues and Filters

Print filters allow Linux to modify the file before it's printed. Without a filter, lpr places the file in the queue and lpd then sends it, unmodified, to the printer. This is fine if your application produces data in a format that's suitable for your printer, but on modern Linux systems, applications often produce data in formats that the printer doesn't understand, hence the need for a filter. The filter can modify the data before it goes to the printer, thus producing a printout that's what you expect rather than page after page of gibberish.

If you're using a Linux system as a print server for Windows clients, the application that produces the file that lpr delivers to the queue is Samba, and before that the Windows printer driver. In this case, the application *does* (or at least *can*) produce a data file that the printer can understand natively, so no filter is required. Other times, you might want to use a PostScript driver in Windows and send the results through a standard Linux printer queue. Both of these options are discussed in greater detail later in this chapter.

Using Several Queues for One Printer

Linux allows you to configure several queues for a single printer. This capability is useful in several different situations:

- You can temporarily redirect one printer's output to another printer. For instance, suppose your office normally has two printers, called printer1 and printer2, located conveniently for different employees. Now suppose that printer1 breaks. You could temporarily remove the printer1 definition from the Linux print server, of course; but you could also redefine printer1 so that it sends its output to printer2, and tape a piece of paper to the actual hardware that is printer1 to tell users to get their output from printer2.

- You can set up a single printer with two or more different filters. For instance, one filter could print files normally and another could process the output to print two pages to a sheet, reduced in size and turned sideways, to save paper and toner or ink. Alternatively, one queue could pass the print job through without using a filter, and the other could process the job through Ghostscript to interpret the file as PostScript. This latter possibility lets a printer do double duty as both a PostScript printer and whatever type of printer it actually is—a PCL laser printer, a Canon inkjet, or whatever.

- Even when using the same basic filter, you can configure different options for a printer. For instance, you could set one queue to print quickly but at low resolution, as compared to slow but high-resolution printing from another queue.

- You can configure printers with different limits on the size of documents to be printed, differing resolutions, or so on, and make some queues available to some users and other queues available to others. For instance, you might limit students to printing short documents and allow faculty members to print longer ones.

Overall, the ability to define multiple queues for a single physical printer leads to a great deal of flexibility, particularly when combined with access control mechanisms in Samba and Netatalk.

Printer Escape Codes and PDLs

All printers accept input in the form of text or special codes that tell the print mechanism what to display. In the simplest case, the computer sends raw ASCII to the printer, which proceeds to print precisely the characters that the computer sent. In years past, printers did little more than this direct transfer to paper. As hardware improved, however, it became increasingly desirable for printers to do more. For instance, it became possible for the printer hardware to produce italicized text, or to print in condensed or expanded fonts. To support these features, and still more complex features that came along, printer manufacturers developed *escape code sequences* to signal the printer to activate some special feature. These sequences consisted of the escape character (which didn't produce a viewable character in ASCII), followed by some further characters to indicate what feature to activate. One of the most popular such escape code "languages" was developed by Epson for its dot-matrix printers, and was widely copied by other manufacturers. Its derivatives are still in use today in Epson inkjet printers. Another popular language was—and is—Hewlett-Packard's *Printer Control Language* (*PCL*), which Hewlett-Packard used in its LaserJet printer. PCL has evolved through several versions, each new version bringing increased features.

One capability of all but the most primitive printer languages is a capacity to process *bitmaps*—data representing what parts of the page should be black (or some other color), and which should be white. If a computer sends a bitmap to the printer, the printer need not concern itself with fonts, font attributes, lines, or other high-level forms. This characteristic is extremely useful for Linux and Ghostscript, as described later in this chapter.

One of the most sophisticated printer languages of the 1980s was PostScript, which garnered a reputation as an excellent tool for producing high-quality text and graphics. Unlike the escape-code languages of dot-matrix printers, PostScript is a complete programming language, but one geared toward describing the layout of text on a page. It's therefore known as a *page description language* (PDL). A PostScript printer is really a computer, and requires a CPU and memory in order to interpret the PostScript program and produce output. A printer that understands *only* PostScript doesn't know what to do with a raw ASCII file because the printer expects PostScript programs as input. Today, most PostScript printers are dual mode—they understand both PostScript and some other language, such as Hewlett-Packard's PCL, so these printers can process raw ASCII.

Improvements in Hewlett-Packard's PCL have blurred the line between escape-code languages and PDLs. Recent versions of PCL are comparable to PostScript in overall ability and complexity. The evolution of printer driver technology in non-UNIX OSs has also helped to blur the lines for users of those OSs because the printer driver isolates the user from the printer's language.

The Tradition of PostScript in UNIX and Linux

In the worlds of Windows, OS/2, and MacOS, printer hardware and software have evolved along a triple track:

- Applications—Programs have been written to produce output in conformance with the OS's printing *Application Programming Interface* (API)—a set of OS interfaces to help programs print. The printing API allows programs to tell the OS where to place text or graphics, what those elements should look like, and so on. The printing API also allows the OS to tell the applications what the printer's capabilities are, such as its margin limits, whether it can print in color, and so on.

- Drivers—Printer drivers interface to the OS on the other end of the API, as it were. They tell the OS what the printer can do, and they handle the translation from the API's calls to data that the printer can handle. Printer manufacturers normally supply drivers for their printers, although drivers also often come with the OS. If an OS lacks a driver for a printer, that printer is useless in that OS, unless a sufficiently similar model has a driver.

- Printers—The printers themselves take the output from the computer and translate it into words or images on a sheet of paper. As printer technology has evolved over the past few years, the repercussions have worked their way back up the chain, mainly influencing the drivers, but also the applications.

In UNIX, the driver layer of this chain has largely been missing. Instead, applications have been written with the assumption that they would be printing on PostScript printers. This has greatly simplified the design of the UNIX printer queue, but it also results in a certain inflexibility, particularly on low-end systems where it's desirable to use low-cost non-PostScript printers.

This limitation has been met with the print filter concept, in conjunction with *Ghostscript*, a program that can convert PostScript input into output that various low-cost printers can understand. Thus, the combination of a Linux print filter along with Ghostscript takes the place of the printer driver in the printer chain, and PostScript serves as the API. This solution has some subtle consequences compared to a Windows-, OS/2-, or MacOS-style printer driver solution, though:

- The chain moves data in only one direction. In a printer driver configuration, the driver can inform the OS of the printer's capabilities, and the API can then give this information to the application. In Linux, this isn't possible, so applications must make assumptions about the printer's capabilities. In a print-serving environment, it is therefore important to select a printer driver on the client system that's well suited to the capabilities of the printer.

- Applications can produce PostScript that may be more-or-less interpretable by Ghostscript or by a genuine PostScript printer. This is really no different than in Windows, in which an application might have poorly implemented printing API calls. The Linux approach has different consequences, though, because you might be able to adjust the Linux print filter to fix any problems caused by peculiar PostScript output.

- In some sense, there are *two* drivers involved in Linux printing—one in the application (to produce PostScript) and one in Ghostscript (to produce the printer-specific codes). This fact is most important in the handful of applications, such as WordPerfect 8 for Linux, that give you a choice of printer drivers. In a networked environment, one driver exists on the client computer and, if Ghostscript is involved, another is in Ghostscript.

It's important to remember that Linux can, and often does, substantially process data destined for its printers. If you have problems printing from one client system but not another, it might just be that the print filters on Linux can handle the version of the driver you're using on the working client, but not the driver you're using on the problem client. A driver update on the problem client might fix the problem, and so might a change to the Linux printer queue.

Using Ghostscript

Because Ghostscript serves as the driver that produces the output a non-PostScript printer receives, it's important to understand something about Ghostscript. Most Linux distributions, including Red Hat, install Ghostscript as a standard component, and even configure your printer queues to use Ghostscript with the appropriate parameters for many printers. It's still useful to understand what Ghostscript does and where it resides, so that you can update or reconfigure it as the need arises.

Converting PostScript to Other Printer Formats by Using Ghostscript

Recall that a PostScript printer is really a computer, with its own CPU and memory. (The same is true of other printers, but PostScript requires more memory and CPU power than do most other printer languages.) A PostScript printer runs a specialized OS that does one thing: It interprets PostScript programs. In principle, there's no reason you couldn't put the PostScript interpreter on the host computer, thus reducing the memory and CPU needs of the printer. This is precisely what Ghostscript does. Ghostscript is a PostScript interpreter that runs under Linux (or most other OSs). A PostScript interpreter in a printer converts PostScript into a bitmap for display on paper. Ghostscript does the same, but must create a bitmap that's palatable to a particular model of printer—the bitmap must be encoded by using the target printer's language, be that Epson's ESC/P2, HP's PCL, or something more exotic.

To get an idea of what Ghostscript can do, you can use it without directing its output to a printer. Try typing the following at a Linux prompt:

```
gs -sDEVICE=jpeg -dNOPAUSE -dBATCH -r72 -sOutputFile=escher.jpg \
   /usr/share/ghostscript/5.10/examples/escher.ps
```

This command produces a JPEG graphic file, called escher.jpg, from a sample PostScript file called escher.ps. (If you're not using Red Hat Linux 6.0 or if you've upgraded your Ghostscript installation, you might need to change the path to the PostScript file in the command.) What you get when you view escher.jpg in a graphics program such as xv or the GIMP should look something like Figure 14.2, except that you see the image in color if you have a color monitor. Of course, Ghostscript can process PostScript files that produce text as well as graphics, and other sample files in the /usr/share/ghostscript/5.10/examples directory demonstrate this capability.

If you want to know more about what the various Ghostscript options do, try typing `gs – help` to see the help screen. This command is also extremely useful in finding the Ghostscript drivers included in your package—Ghostscript lists the available drivers in one big long list following the text *available devices*.

Fortunately, you don't need to know too much about the Ghostscript command-line options to configure your system to use Ghostscript to drive a printer. Most distributions include configuration programs to help you set up printers, as described later in this chapter, in the section "Configuring a Printer in Linux." You might need to fine-tune your configuration, though, in order to get precisely the printer resolution you want or to print with an alternate driver.

FIGURE 14.2
PostScript is capable of producing complex graphics, in addition to text.

Obtaining and Installing the Latest Ghostscript

The official Web site for Ghostscript is `http://www.cs.wisc.edu/~ghost`, and from there you can obtain the latest Ghostscript source code and binaries. Follow the link labeled Obtaining Aladdin Ghostscript to get the latest version of the program. In most cases, you don't need to do this; the version of Ghostscript that ships with Red Hat Linux 6.0 is quite adequate, although it's not the latest.

Ghostscript Versions

Aladdin is the company that produces Ghostscript. It releases Ghostscript in a version that's free for most uses, but that can't be redistributed in any product that's sold. For that privilege, Aladdin charges money. This restriction prevents Red Hat from distributing Aladdin Ghostscript because Red Hat and others sell Linux CD-ROMs. After a given version has been out for a while, Aladdin changes the license terms to those of the GNU General Public License (GPL), so the program can then be included in Linux distributions. This version of the program is known as GNU Ghostscript. It's identical to Aladdin Ghostscript from some months before. At the time Red Hat Linux 6.0 was released, the latest GNU Ghostscript was version 5.10, and the latest Aladdin Ghostscript was version 5.50.

Although Red Hat or others can't include Aladdin Ghostscript on CD-ROMs without paying licensing fees to Aladdin, it is legal to distribute Aladdin Ghostscript via Web or FTP sites. You can obtain RPMs from the official Ghostscript Web site or from Red Hat's FTP site, `ftp://contrib.redhat.com`.

Ghostscript drivers are compiled directly into the program. Therefore, to add support for new hardware, you must recompile the program. Unfortunately, the default set of drivers doesn't include all available drivers, so for some hardware, you might need to locate an appropriate binary distribution or compile your own version. The Web site `http://www.users.dircon.co.uk/~typhoon/html/ghostscript.html` has a Ghostscript binary distribution with more drivers than most other Ghostscript binary distributions contain.

Ghostscript Files and Configuration

Many of the options you set in a Windows or Macintosh driver, such as the printer's resolution, you set on the Ghostscript command line. In a Linux system, you normally create separate print queues to gain access to different values for these options. For instance, I have four queues for accessing my Epson Stylus Color 400 inkjet printer at differing resolutions.

NOTE

If you configure a queue to pass data directly to the printer, rather than through Ghostscript, you can use a client computer's drivers to set the resolution or other options just as you would if the printer were local to the client computer.

The Ghostscript configuration file that you might want to alter is the `Fontmap` file. On a Red Hat 6.0 installation, this file resides in `/usr/share/ghostscript/5.10`, but if you upgrade your version of Linux, the path to the `Fontmap` file might change. Each line in the `Fontmap` file is one of three things:

- A comment—Comments begin with the percent sign (%) and Ghostscript ignores them.
- A font definition—Font definitions begin with the font name, preceded by a slash (/), and then specify the font filename in parentheses, and end in a semicolon (;). For instance, here's a line to define a font:

```
/NimbusRomNo9L-Regu      (n0210031.pfb) ;
```

> **NOTE**
>
> Ghostscript searches a *font path* to find the font files in font definitions. By default, this path includes the `/usr/share/ghostscript/fonts` directory, and this is where you find the normal Ghostscript fonts. If you want to add fonts that aren't on the font path, I recommend that you use the complete pathname or create a link in the Ghostscript `fonts` directory to the actual file.

- A font alias—Font aliases are much like font definitions, except that they point to an existing font definition rather than to a font file. The result is that the same font can be accessed by using two names: the original and the alias. Here's an example of a font alias:

```
/Times-Roman            /NimbusRomNo9L-Regu ;
```

A PostScript file can specify a font and, if the font name appears in the `Fontmap` file, Ghostscript prints in that font. This emulates the behavior of PostScript printers, which typically ship with several fonts built in to ROM. Ghostscript allows you to easily add to the fonts available to the system, though, merely by editing the `Fontmap` file.

> **TIP**
>
> When using Linux to serve non-PostScript printers, you can serve them as if they were PostScript models. Your client OS needs drivers, though. If you select drivers for a printer that includes several fonts not in Ghostscript's default `Fontmap` file, you get Courier whenever you select the non-included fonts. You can add the fonts by finding the fonts' names in the PostScript file and then adding appropriate entries to `Fontmap`. Check a fonts database such as the one at `http://www.ssifonts.com` to locate fonts that are compatible with the ones you want to use.

Ghostscript can work with Adobe Type 1 fonts in either the .pfa or .pfb formats. The latter is more common on font CD-ROMs. Type 1 fonts also come with additional files with the filename extensions .pfm, .afm, or others. As far as Ghostscript is concerned, you can ignore these files, but you might need them on the client OS or in Linux applications. Ghostscript can also use TrueType fonts (with .ttf extensions), although some characters might print strangely if you use these files. Ghostscript requires fonts in PC (DOS, Windows, OS/2, or UNIX) format. Fonts for Macintoshes come in a special Macintosh format that Ghostscript cannot use directly. This is true even if you're running Linux on a Macintosh. Converter programs are available, however, such as the unpost utility that's part of the freeware t1utils package (included on the CD-ROM that accompanies this book in the sams-extras/printing directory) and the shareware TransType (http://www.fontlab.com/trt_main.htm). If you're using a Linux computer to serve Macintoshes, you can install whatever Macintosh fonts you like on Ghostscript in Linux by first translating them to PC format. Alternatively, you can configure your client OS to download fonts in the PostScript files and Ghostscript can process them on a file-by-file basis. The second is probably the simpler solution in most cases, but it increases the size of the PostScript files, and if you're using a driver that expects a font to be installed in the printer, modifying Ghostscript to meet that expectation is probably the better solution.

> **CAUTION**
>
> United States copyright law as it relates to fonts is peculiar: The fonts themselves—that is, the shapes of the letters—cannot be copyrighted, but the TrueType or Type 1 font files that describe these shapes are considered computer programs, and therefore can be copyrighted. Before installing commercial fonts on your Linux font server or distributing them widely on your network, you should check with the font foundry (the company that sells the fonts) for the terms of use covering the fonts. Laws concerning intellectual property rights and fonts vary substantially from one country to another, so you might need to do further research on your nation's laws on this matter if you aren't in the United States.

Using Ghostscript Versus Printing Directly

A Linux print server can make a printer available to networked computers either in raw form, so that your clients use the driver from the printer manufacturer, or as a Ghostscript-driven printer, so that your clients use a PostScript driver. Each method has advantages and disadvantages. Especially when dealing with Windows clients, you might want to make the same printer available both ways, to give your users a wider range of choices.

Advantages of Using Ghostscript

When you configure a printer to use a queue that incorporates a Ghostscript filter, you use a PostScript driver on the client systems. In general, you use a PostScript driver that comes with the client OS. You probably need to select a specific model of printer when you install a driver in your client OS, but of course you don't see the model you're using on a list, because as far as the OS is concerned, that model is *not* a PostScript printer.

> **TIP**
>
> I've found that drivers for Apple LaserWriter printers tend to work well with Ghostscript when using monochrome printers. When using color printers, drivers for the QMS magicolor printer usually work well. You might want to research the capabilities of the printer whose driver you're using relative to your actual printer. Pay particular attention to resolution. If you use a client-OS driver for a printer with a substantially lower resolution than your printer (or its Ghostscript driver) can produce, you might find that you don't get the maximum benefit of the printer's resolution in all situations.

The strong points of using a client-OS PostScript driver and Ghostscript on Linux include the following:

- Reduced network traffic—When you're printing text, especially to low-end inkjet printers, PostScript tends to produce smaller files, and hence less network traffic. This advantage isn't universal, though; for printing graphics to certain printers, there might be little difference or even more traffic when using PostScript drivers.

- Uniform output across printers—Especially if you use the same PostScript driver for multiple printers, your formatting doesn't change when you change printers. Sometimes changing a printer driver in a client OS also changes your document's fonts, word spacing, and so on. Of course, your documents might still look different when printed on different printers—you don't magically get 600dpi or color printing from a 300dpi laser printer, for instance, and even different color printers can render colors differently.

- Simplified client-driver maintenance—If your network contains several printers, using Ghostscript to turn them all into PostScript printers from the client's point of view can simplify client-side driver maintenance. Rather than deal with drivers for several different printers, you can install and maintain only one driver, connected to several client-OS queues. Even if you select PostScript drivers for several different models of PostScript printers, the client OS might install but a single driver, along with configuration files for each specific model.

- Faster printing—Because of the reduced network load, you might be able to print faster to a Ghostscript-driven printer, especially on congested or slow networks. In some cases, Ghostscript also produces faster output than the host system's driver.

- Ease of Linux setup—Because of the UNIX tradition of using PostScript printers, most Linux distributions assume that you'll want to configure Ghostscript and provide tools to help set up a Ghostscript printer queue. In many cases, it's easier to configure a printer this way than to create a raw queue.

- Easier Macintosh configuration—It's generally much easier to configure a Macintosh to use a PostScript printer than to use a non-PostScript printer served by Linux.

- Printing of PostScript documents—You might occasionally need to print a PostScript document you obtain from another person, a Web site, or what have you. Configuring a remote Ghostscript-driven printer makes this easy from the client OS; you can usually just drag and drop the file onto a printer icon. You might also want PostScript capability to get an idea of how a document will look after it's been printed by a service bureau.

Advantages of Printing Directly

When you configure a raw queue to allow a client system to print using the printer manufacturer's drivers, Linux doesn't process the data, aside from moving it from one port to another (with a brief layover on Linux's hard disk). This approach has its own set of advantages:

- Reduced server CPU and memory loads—Interpreting a PostScript file can require moderate to large amounts of memory and CPU power. If your server is relatively weak in these areas, if it has additional duties, or if you're serving several printers, you might prefer to avoid imposing these loads on the server.

- Easier access to printer features—You can't generally set Ghostscript options such as resolution, paper size, paper trays, or so on from the client system. The solution is to provide multiple printer queues, but this can be awkward, particularly if your printer has several options that you might want to control. Say you have 4 resolutions and 3 paper trays—to provide complete access to these would require 12 printer queues. Using the client OS's drivers to set these features can be much simpler, particularly if your users are already familiar with client-OS driver controls.

- Faster printing—Yes, this *is* (or at least *can be*) an advantage for either type of printing. Client-OS drivers can sometimes produce faster results than can a native Linux driver. In addition, on some systems and with some printers, the parallel port might become a bottleneck when printing bitmaps, which is what Ghostscript does. When printing text to PCL laser printers at faster than six pages per minute, using a raw queue and client PCL driver is probably faster, for instance. You need to try both methods to determine which is faster on your hardware.

- Higher print quality—On some printers, and particularly for low-end color inkjets when printing graphics, you're likely to get better print quality when you use the printer's native drivers on the client OS. This is less likely to be true of laser printers.

- Ability to print—Some low-end printers are designed exclusively for Windows and aren't supported by Ghostscript. Some, but not all, of these printers can work via a raw Linux print queue and native client-OS drivers. I don't recommend purchasing printers like this, but if you already have one, you might be able to get Linux to serve it to other systems.

PostScript Printers

If you use a printer that includes a PostScript interpreter in its firmware, you effectively serve it as a raw printer and use the printer's own drivers on the client OS. Depending on how you configure the printer, Linux might still pass the data through a filter, but if all is configured correctly, the filter doesn't do anything.

> **TIP**
>
> Occasionally a Linux print filter gets confused and tries to convert the PostScript into raw text. You can try another driver on the client OS, reconfigure the client OS driver, or configure a raw queue on the Linux server. One area of recurring trouble along these lines is the Control-D character. Many Windows PostScript printer drivers send Control-D characters, but this practice can confuse Linux filters. Try disabling this feature if it's present in your driver.

Most modern PostScript printers include the ability to process both PostScript and Hewlett-Packard's PCL. You can install both drivers on the client OS and pass them both through a raw Linux print filter, allowing you to print the way that is most convenient or produces the best results for your needs.

Occasionally, particularly with older PostScript printers, the printer may choke on a particular document. This is often due to insufficient memory in the printer to handle a complex image. Occasionally it's because of a buggy PostScript interpreter. You can sometimes work around these problems by using the Ghostscript PostScript drivers (`psmono` and `psgray`). These drivers convert PostScript into PostScript. Odd as this sounds, it can be very useful because the output PostScript is a bitmap, the same as is sent to other printers, but with appropriate PostScript codes enveloping the bitmap. A PostScript printer with insufficient memory to run a complex PostScript program should have no problem with a simple bitmap, so setting up a special queue for this purpose can be helpful. I wouldn't recommend bothering with this unless you have problems with a particular PostScript printer, though.

Adobe is the inventor of the PostScript language, and Adobe originally licensed PostScript to printer manufacturers such as Apple and Hewlett-Packard. Many PostScript printers today, including models from well-respected manufacturers such as Hewlett-Packard, use PostScript clones. These interpreters were not written by Adobe. In fact, some printer manufacturers license their PostScript clone interpreters from Aladdin—they run Ghostscript internally! In general, today's PostScript clones are quite good, and because the clone writers charge less than does Adobe, clones reduce the cost of printers capable of interpreting PostScript. Many clone interpreters have a few subtle incompatibilities with Adobe's PostScript, but there are bugs in specific versions of Adobe-licensed interpreters, too. If you need the utmost in PostScript compatibility, you might want to test a printer before buying it, and check the manufacturer's policy on correcting problems. Some older PostScript clones were not as good as today's. If you have an old printer that uses a clone, and if you have problems, you might want to try Ghostscript's PostScript output on the trouble documents.

CAUTION

A much more serious problem from a Linux perspective is in printers that include "software PostScript." This euphemism refers to a PostScript interpreter hosted on the computer—precisely what Ghostscript is. These PostScript interpreters don't run under Linux, though, so don't pay more for an alleged PostScript printer unless you know that the *printer* hosts the PostScript interpreter. In some cases you can use Ghostscript instead of the manufacturer-supplied interpreter, but you shouldn't count on the manufacturer's computer-hosted interpreter doing any good.

Configuring a Printer in Linux

Printer configuration is an area that varies a lot from one Linux distribution to another. This section describes how to configure a printer in Red Hat Linux 6.0 by using the `printtool` utility. Most distributions include similar GUI configuration tools. In Red Hat and many other distributions, you can configure a printer during system installation. The procedure is much the same as what is described here.

In case you need to fine-tune the configuration, or if you have a distribution without GUI printer configuration tools, I also present some information on the files that are involved in printer configuration, so you can manually tweak the configuration.

Using `printtool` to Set Up a Printer

To start the Red Hat `printtool` utility, type **printtool** at an xterm prompt. Red Hat responds by displaying the `printtool` main window, as shown in Figure 14.3.

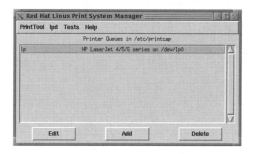

FIGURE 14.3
The Red Hat `printtool` *utility lets you select printers and configure them through options in dialog boxes.*

If you have not configured any printers, the queue list is empty. Figure 14.3 shows one printer already configured. You can edit that configuration by selecting it and clicking Edit, or you can create a new queue by clicking Add. If you edit an existing configuration, you bypass some of the preliminary steps, but the procedure is otherwise similar.

When you click Add, `printtool` displays the Add a Printer Entry dialog box, as shown in Figure 14.4. You select the type of printer you want to configure here. If the Linux computer is functioning as a print server, you have most likely attached one or more printers to the server on parallel or serial ports, so you should select Local Printer. If the printer is accessible via another computer, though, you can select which type of network connection you're using. You might use an option like this if you want to use Linux as a Ghostscript interpreter for a printer shared by another computer or as a gateway for Macintoshes to use printers attached to Windows computers, or vice-versa.

FIGURE 14.4
You should choose Local Printer for printers attached by serial or parallel port, or by universal serial bus (USB) port when Linux's USB support matures.

> **NOTE**
>
> Some printers attach directly to an Ethernet network, and you can purchase small adapters that let you connect parallel-port printers to Ethernet networks without using a computer as a server. If you're using such a printer, you access it as a remote printer. Consult the printer's (or adapter's) documentation to determine whether to select the lpd, SMB, or NetWare queue type. If the printer or adapter uses AppleTalk, "Printing from Linux to Mac Printers," p. xxx, provides instructions on setting up an appropriate Linux queue.

If you choose Local Printer, Linux attempts to locate parallel port hardware to tell you what parallel ports are available. In my experience, Red Hat often gets this wrong, missing ports that do exist, so don't be alarmed if a dialog box lists all the parallel ports as "not detected." You then see the Edit Local Printer Entry dialog box, as shown in Figure 14.5. This is where you enter basic information on what you want to call the printer, to what port the printer is attached, and so on.

FIGURE 14.5
If you set up a networked printer rather than a local one, you have slightly different options in the network equivalents of the Edit Local Printer Entry dialog box.

The name you enter in the Names field is the Linux printer queue name. You can actually enter several names, separated by vertical bars (¦), to make the queue available locally under several names. These names need bear no resemblance to the name under which the printer is available under Samba, Netatalk, or on remote UNIX systems. Likewise, the Spool Directory entry is well hidden from users, even local Linux users. Nonetheless, it's best to name the spool directory after the primary printer name. The Printer Device is the device file for the printer—/dev/lp0 for the first printer port, /dev/ttyS0 for the first serial port, and so on. If you deselect Suppress Headers, Linux prints a header identifying the user who queued the print job, which can be convenient for identifying the owners of print jobs. (Netatalk queues all print jobs under a single username, however, so this option isn't terribly useful on a Macintosh network.)

Finally, you set the model of printer and print options, such as resolution, by clicking the Select button next to the Input Filter field. You get the Configure Filter dialog box, as shown in Figure 14.6. For non-PostScript printers, this dialog box lets you set the Ghostscript options for the printer.

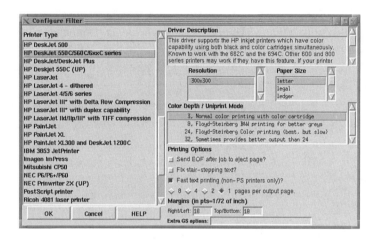

FIGURE 14.6

The Configure Filter dialog box is the core of the printer configuration utility; it lets you select the printer, its resolution, and assorted other options.

TIP

If you want to create a raw queue for printing with the client OSs' native drivers for the printer, *do not* select an input filter. When you leave the Input Filter field blank, Red Hat doesn't set an input filter, so lpd passes the print data to the printer unchanged.

Options you can set in the Configure Filter dialog box include the following:

- Printer Type—If you see your printer model in this list, select it. If not, select something close. Most laser printers today emulate some variety of Hewlett-Packard LaserJet, so select the model of LaserJet that the printer claims to emulate. For inkjet printers, select the model that's closest to the one you use. If you have *any* model of PostScript printer, select PostScript printer. If you're certain you'll never need to print raw text from Linux, or if your PostScript printer can handle raw text, you may leave the Input Filter field of the Edit Local Printer Entry dialog box blank instead of selecting PostScript printer.

- Driver Description—You don't actually set or select anything in this field. Instead, it provides additional information concerning the Printer Type item you've selected.

- Resolution—Many printers provide a choice of resolutions. Select the resolution you want to use.

- Paper Size—Choose the paper size that you normally use in this printer.

- Color Depth/Uniprint Mode—The options in this field vary from one printer to another. They generally relate to paper types, printer-specific options, or dithering options that affect the appearance of printed color. You set the resolution here, rather than in the Resolution field, for some printers.

- Send EOF after job to eject page?—On some printers, you must select this option or else the page isn't printed or isn't ejected from the printer when you print text pages.

- Fix stair-stepping text?—Some printers stair-step their text, as shown in Figure 14.7, when printing ASCII text from Linux. You can select this option to correct the problem.

Type the following:

/usr/bin/yes

to see a string of ys appear

FIGURE 14.7

Stair-stepped text results from a printer expecting DOS-style end-of-line characters and not understanding UNIX/Linux-style end-of-line characters.

- Fast text printing—If you select this option with a non-PostScript printer, Linux sends text files to the printer unfiltered. If you deselect this option, Linux first converts the text to PostScript, which typically results in slower printing.

- Pages per output page—You can reduce the size of each input page to fit several input pages on each physical sheet by using this option.

- Margins—This option adjusts the margins between multiple selected output pages.

- Extra GS options—Any text you enter here gets passed to Ghostscript as an extra option. This could be useful for enabling features that `printtool` doesn't offer.

Testing Your Printer Setup

When you've set all the options you want, click OK in the Configure Filter dialog box, and then in the Edit Local Printer Entry dialog box. You should now see a new entry in the main `printtool` window. You can test the configuration as follows:

1. Choose lpd, Restart lpd to be sure `lpd` is aware of the new printer configuration.

2. Select the printer you want to test.

3. If the printer is local to the Linux server you're configuring, choose Tests, Print ASCII directly to port. You should see a page appear from the printer. If you do not, you might need to select a different port or recompile your kernel with printer support, as described in Chapter 6, "Compiling a Kernel for Networking." (The text you get at this stage may suffer from stair-stepping, as shown in Figure 14.7, but if so, don't be concerned, since this test doesn't apply the filter that corrects for this effect.)

4. Reselect the printer, if necessary, and choose Tests, Print ASCII test page. A text test page should print. If there are problems with it, go back over your printer configuration. One common problem at this point is stair-stepped text, as shown in Figure 14.7, which can be fixed with the appropriate option on the Configure Filter dialog box.

5. Reselect the printer, if necessary, and choose Tests, Print Postscript test page. You should see a PostScript test page print, as shown in Figure 14.8. If the printer is a color model, the output should include color samples. Again, if there's a problem, you should go back to the Configure Filter dialog box and try new options to fix the problem.

It's possible that you won't get satisfactory results at this point, particularly if you have a printer that's poorly supported by Ghostscript. The Red Hat `printtool` utility doesn't know about all the available Ghostscript drivers, particularly drivers in the latest releases of Ghostscript or from nonstandard binaries that include extra or experimental drivers. If you find yourself in this situation, you might need to edit your printer files manually. After you're done, you can restart `printtool` to run the tests again.

Tweaking the Configuration Manually

You're likely to need to edit one of two files when you edit your printer configuration manually: `/etc/printcap` and `/var/spool/lpd/`*queuename*`/postscript.cfg`, where *queuename* is the name of the printer queue you defined in `printtool`. The first of these files is common across Linux distributions, whereas the second is unique to Red Hat and similar distributions. If you're using a radically different distribution, you might need to look elsewhere to configure the printer filter, which is what the `postscript.cfg` file controls. Consult your distribution's documentation for more details.

Printer `printcap` Entries

Here's a sample `/etc/printcap` entry:

```
lp|hp4000:\
        :sd=/var/spool/lpd/lp:\
        :mx#0:\
        :sh:\
        :lp=/dev/lp1:\
        :if=/var/spool/lpd/lp/filter:
```

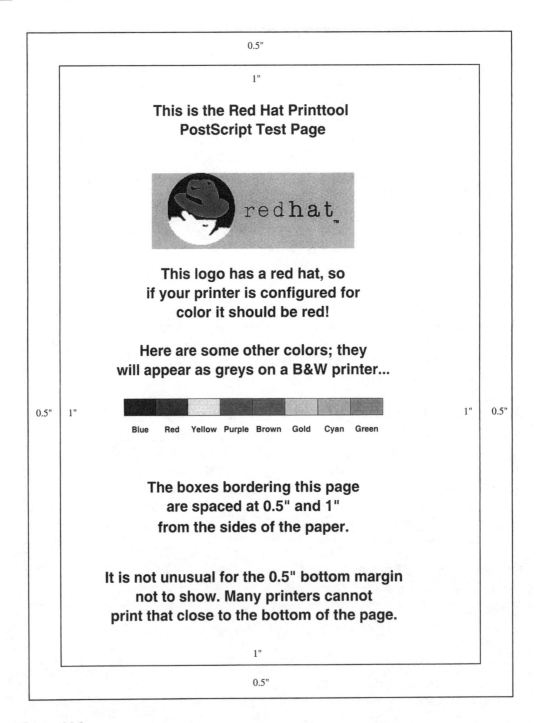

FIGURE 14.8
The Red Hat printtool *PostScript test page helps you evaluate your printer's capabilities under Linux.*

This entry defines a single printer, which is known by two names—lp and hp4000—as defined on the first line of the entry. Entries are separated by colons, with a backslash (\) at the end of most lines. (The backslashes actually signal a *continuation* of a line—each /etc/printcap entry is technically a single line.) Options use an equal sign (=) or pound sign (#) to give values to parameters. Available options include the following:

- sd=—This is the spool directory—where lpr places files and where lpd looks for them.
- mx#—This is the maximum file size. A 0 here indicates no limit. In some environments, you might want to set a limit, to prevent abuse by individuals trying to print ludicrously large files. Be aware, though, that even some very large files can produce relatively few pages of output, particularly for raw printer queues. This is particularly true of color bitmapped graphics, which can easily exceed 1MB per page, even at modest resolutions.
- sf—This option, if present, suppresses the use of form feeds between print jobs. You might want to set it for a raw queue if you otherwise get a blank sheet between print jobs. If you set it when it's not needed, though, you might find that the final page of some jobs doesn't print.
- sh—This option, if present, suppresses the printing of job headers. To get a sheet separating different print jobs, remove this option from /etc/printcap.
- lp=—You set the name of the printer device with this option.
- if=—This option sets the *input filter*, which is what controls the way the queue handles input files. In particular, this filter tries to determine what type of file you're printing, and processes it appropriately. On Red Hat systems, the default filter detects PostScript files (among other file types) and sends them through Ghostscript, when printing to a non-PostScript printer. If you omit this line or leave it blank, the queue becomes a raw queue, suitable for use with client drivers for the specific model of printer.

Most of these options correspond to options you set in printtool. Much of what printtool does is to translate the /etc/printcap entries into easier-to-understand questions, collect your answers to these questions, and translate back to an appropriate /etc/printcap format. In addition, there are several other possible options for /etc/printcap entries. You can type **man printcap** to learn more about them.

Ghostscript Control: The `postscript.cfg` File

Additional printtool options wind up in the /var/spool/lpd/*queuename*/postscript.cfg file, which contains options that are passed to PostScript. This file sets a number of environment variables, which the filter uses when launching Ghostscript. Some of the most important of these variables are as follows:

- GSDEVICE—This is the name of the Ghostscript device, such as `ljet4` for the HP LaserJet 4-, 5-, and 6-series printers. If you're using an unusual or updated Ghostscript binary with drivers that `printtool` doesn't understand, you might need to adjust this line by hand. For instance, I've found that my Epson Stylus Color 400 works better with the older `stcolor` driver than with the newer `uniprint` driver, so I've modified the GSDEVICE line for that printer.

- RESOLUTION—This is the resolution at which you want the printer to print. What you enter here is passed to Ghostscript by using the Ghostscript `-r` parameter. You can enter either a single number, such as `300` or `720`, or a two-number value, such as `300x300` or `720x360`. The former option produces printouts at the same resolution both horizontally and vertically. The latter option is useful when specifying resolutions that are greater in one direction than the other. The `uniprint` driver ignores the RESOLUTION setting, and instead uses the `.upp` file for a specific model of printer to set the resolution.

- COLOR—This field is used to specify a `.upp` file with additional parameters for the `uniprint` driver. This driver is designed to be a universal print driver for inkjet printers, and it uses a separate file—a `.upp` file—to set commands and options for different models. This contrasts with the usual Ghostscript approach of incorporating all printer options into the driver or as command-line parameters.

- EXTRA_GS_OPTIONS—You set any nonstandard Ghostscript options here, between quotation marks. This is the same as the similarly named field in the Configure Filter dialog box. For my Epson Stylus Color 400 using the `stcolor` driver, I must use the `-dSoftweave` parameter to print at resolutions higher than 360dpi, and I can add the `stcolor.ps` parameter to improve the quality of color printing.

It's important to realize that the `postscript.cfg` file is a characteristic of Red Hat and Red Hat–derived distributions (such as Mandrake and LinuxPPC). Other distributions might use entirely different means to control Ghostscript. If you're using such a distribution, check the `if` field in the `/etc/printcap` file for clues about where configuration files go. In the case of Red Hat, `if` points to the `filter` file, which is a script that calls other programs that use the options in `postscript.cfg`.

If you're using a distribution that doesn't come with GUI configuration tools, you can set up the `/etc/printcap` file as described previously in this chapter. If you want to serve a non-PostScript printer as a PostScript model, I recommend that you use a printer "smart filter" package, such as Magic Filter. Your distribution probably comes with such a filter, so check its documentation. When you configure the smart filter according to its documentation, you can create an appropriate `if` line in `/etc/printcap` to use it, and the queue detects whatever file types the smart filter supports. Red Hat Linux's printing system uses its own smart filter, so these extra steps are unnecessary for Red Hat unless you're dissatisfied with the default Red Hat filter.

Managing Printer Queues

Your Linux distribution provides tools to help you control printing. These tools come in the form of several commands you can enter at an xterm or text-mode login. Some of these allow you to do things as an ordinary user; others may require you to be `root`. Most of these commands take at least the `-P` parameter to specify the printer queue on which you want to operate. When you use `-P`, type the name of the printer queue *without an intervening space*; for instance, `lpq -Pcanon` to query the printer queue called `canon`. Without the `-P` parameter, these commands work on the default printer queue, which is generally called `lp`.

You need to have a login account on the Linux computer to use these options; you can't control print jobs remotely in this way, except by using `telnet`, `ssh`, or a similar remote login tool. Samba provides some means for controlling printers remotely using standard Windows printer-control methods, so if you configure Samba correctly, you can perform similar actions from the client computer.

Viewing Print Jobs by Using `lpq`

You use the `lpq` command to determine what print jobs are present in a print queue and whether that queue is printing. Here's some sample output showing a number of files in a printer queue:

```
Rank     Owner      Job   Files                      Total Size
active   rodsmith   152   /tmp/_pp_0000012278_58     10832657 bytes
1st      rodsmith   153   /tmp/_pp_0000012335_59     23967 bytes
2nd      rodsmith   154   /tmp/_pp_0000012365_60     22107 bytes
```

This output shows three print jobs in the queue, all started by the user `rodsmith`. Different programs place files in the print queue in different ways, so the names listed under the `Files` column might take different forms for different programs' print jobs. The first job is the one that's labeled active in the Rank column and has a job ID of 152. When the `lpq` command was issued, that job was being sent to the printer, hence its active status. The second and third jobs have ranks of 1st and 2nd and IDs of 153 and 154, respectively, and are waiting in the queue. The size of the active job is about 1MB, and the next two are each less than 24KB.

When you're doing additional print job management, you need to know the job ID listed under the `Job` column. The job size may or may not be helpful in determining which job is which. If you print two jobs from the same program to the same printer, the document with more pages is likely to be larger, but that might not be the case if the documents use different features (for example, if one is graphics and the other is text).

Removing Print Jobs by Using `lprm`

If you want to stop a print job, either before it begins printing or while it's printing, use the `lprm` command. For instance, you can type

```
lprm -Plexmark 153
```

to remove the second print job identified by the `lpq` command just discussed, assuming that the queue name is `lexmark`. You need to be the owner of that job or `root` to use `lprm` on a print job.

> **TIP**
>
> If you issue an `lprm` command on a printing job, printing might stop in the middle of the page. For inkjet and dot-matrix printers, you might need to eject the half-printed page, and possibly reset your printer, to get it to function correctly. You don't need to eject a page from a laser printer, but a reset might be necessary. Many printers have a button or command available on their front panels to accomplish this task.

Printing a File by Using `lpr`

The `lpr` command prints a file from an xterm or text-mode login. For instance, to print a PostScript file called `file.ps` to a PostScript or Ghostscript-driven printer on the queue `lexmark`, you would type

```
lpr -Plexmark file.ps
```

Red Hat Linux's standard smart filter can handle a number of formats in addition to PostScript and ASCII text, including GIF images, JPEG images, TeX documents, and Hewlett-Packard's PCL printer language. Other smart filter packages support various combinations of file types. For use with a networked printer, only the PCL, PostScript, and ASCII capabilities are likely to be useful. In fact, the filter's detection algorithms don't always work correctly, so you might find it helpful to create a raw queue for PostScript or PCL printers.

Managing the Print System by Using `lpc`

The `lpc` command is the workhorse printer control command for Linux, but you need to be `root` to use many of its features. Also, `lpc` often resides in the `/usr/sbin` directory, which your shell might not search automatically, so you might need to type the complete pathname to use it (that is, type `/usr/sbin/lpc` rather than just `lpc`). I don't give the complete path in the following discussion, however, for brevity's sake.

You use the `lpc` command to enable or disable queues or to rearrange the order of print jobs. You'll probably use it mostly for this last function. Suppose that you want to rearrange the order of the jobs in the queue in the previous example so that job 154 prints before job 153. To do so, you would type

```
lpc topq lexmark 154 153
```

The `topq` parameter tells `lpc` that you want to place the specified print jobs at the top of the queue in the order that you specify. The `lpc` command doesn't interrupt printing on the current job, however, so it remains in place (you can kill it with `lprm` if necessary).

You can also use `lpc` to entirely disable or enable a queue by using the `down` or `up` parameters, as in `lpc down lexmark` or `lpc up lexmark`. Other variants have subtly different effects. You can type **man lpc** at an xterm prompt to read the Linux documentation on `lpc`. You can type the **man** command to find more information about the other print queue management commands, too.

Printer Sharing Security Considerations

As with most networking features, you should be aware of the security implications of running remotely accessible printer queues. The details of these considerations vary substantially from one sharing method to another, but as an overview, you might want to consider the following points:

- An export using UNIX-style `lpd` sharing uses "trusted host" methods similar to those for network filesystem (NFS) file sharing. You should therefore be careful about what hosts have access to your printer.

- Sharing printers via Samba provides the possibility of fine control on a per-user basis with password requirements.

- Printer sharing via Netatalk involves little security. It uses AppleTalk rather than TCP/IP, though, so it's relatively invulnerable to attack via the Internet.

- As with other network services, there's always the risk that a bug in the server could open your system to a cracker, so you should not make services available unnecessarily. This is especially true if your server is visible to the Internet as a whole.

- Assuming that a server bug doesn't lead to bigger problems, leaving a printer share open without adequate security can allow others to print files. A malicious individual might set a printer to churn out a ream of completely black pages late at night. Because ink and toner are far more expensive than paper, this high-density printout could cost substantially more than the $5 or so the paper costs. Turning off printers at night is therefore a sensible precaution, if your office's work habits allow it.

- Because Linux spools print jobs to disk, a vulnerable printer share could also result in depletion of disk space. This is one reason for the presence of the mx# entry in /etc/printcap. It's also one reason experienced administrators often partition a disk—if /var, where print spools are stored, is isolated from user files on /home, system files on /, and program files in /usr and /opt, an intentional or accidental overrun of disk space in /var won't be crippling to the system as a whole.

- Don't forget physical security. If you print sensitive information, be sure not to print it to a publicly accessible printer. Also, many laser printers store their last print jobs for an indefinite period, so you might want to consult your printer's documentation for instructions on how to erase this buffer after sensitive information prints.

Because printing involves the receipt of information by the server, rather than the delivery of information from the server, print services are less likely than file-sharing services to be a source of entry by system crackers. There simply is very little leverage for system entry provided by print services, short of bugs that might provide such access.

One additional point about printers and security: If you suspect that your system's security has been breached by an intruder skillful enough to erase log files, you can reconfigure the system to print all such logs, rather than store them in log files. You might produce quite a few pages of output this way, but a remote intruder can't very well erase a printed document half a world away! You can use the swatch utility, described in "Using swatch to Monitor Log Files," p. 553, to perform such a task.

Summary

Linux makes an excellent print server, particularly in a mixed-OS environment. You can configure a single Linux server to function as a stopping point for several printers to be accessed from UNIX/Linux, DOS/Windows/OS/2, and Macintosh clients. You can serve printers by using either their native printer languages, such as PCL or ESC/P2, or PostScript and translated with Ghostscript (or not translated, if the printer is a PostScript model). For maximum flexibility, you can export a printer both ways, but that might be confusing to users, particularly if you have many printers available.

Configuring a printer in Linux can be quite easy if you're using Red Hat or some other distribution with a good GUI printer configuration utility and if the printer is one listed in the configuration utility's database. If you're not so lucky, you might have to do some research on your printer to find a model with which it's compatible, and possibly find the Ghostscript options to best utilize the printer's features. Alternatively, you might be able to export the printer raw and rely on the client OS's drivers to do the right thing.

Sharing Printers with Other UNIXes

IN THIS CHAPTER

Sharing printers between UNIX or Linux computers is straightforward. In part this is because the UNIX/Linux printing mechanisms were built with networking in mind, so very little needs to be configured. In part this is because both systems are expected to handle printing in the same way, so there's less need to set up special queues or configure extra files, as you might need to do for sharing with Windows or Macintosh clients.

Other OSs can sometimes make use of the UNIX-style printer sharing mechanisms. Chances are you'll have no problems whether you pick UNIX-style or client-style printing mechanisms, but you can ask yourself some questions to help determine which to use:

- Are the clients already configured for UNIX-style printing? If not, it's probably easier to set up client-style printer sharing.
- Are you using Samba or Netatalk to serve files to the client? If so, configuring printer sharing using Samba or Netatalk won't involve much extra work. If you're not already using Samba or Netatalk, using UNIX-style printer sharing will let you avoid installing these packages.
- Are you sharing printers with other UNIX or Linux computers? If not, you can disable Linux's printer sharing mechanisms for increased security.
- Do you want to provide access on a printer-by-printer basis? If so, Samba and Netatalk provide better control over which printers are shared. UNIX-style sharing provides access control by users and groups, though.

Using `lpd` to Share Printers

Prior to this chapter, I've presented `lpd` largely as if it provided services only on and for the computer on which it runs. This isn't necessarily true, however. In fact, `lpd` is a full-fledged network daemon, listening on port 515 for print requests. When `lpd` receives a print job from the network, it places it in the queue for the appropriate printer for processing along with local print jobs. You do need to set a few options to configure `lpd` to work in this way, though, and you should be aware of the methods `lpd` uses to control remote access.

Configuring Linux to Accept Remote Print Jobs

By default, Red Hat Linux comes configured not to accept any remote print jobs, although `lpd` is active for handling local print jobs. This configuration makes sense, of course—Red Hat's designers can't know for what computers you'd want to provide print services, so the only choices for a default configuration are no services, a random selection of supported clients, or *all* computers on the entire Internet as supported clients. If you're not using Red Hat Linux, it's possible that your system is configured for print sharing already, though, if your system's installer asked for relevant information at installation time.

You can configure Linux to accept remote print jobs by editing either of two files: /etc/hosts.lpd or /etc/hosts.equiv. The security implications of these two options are radically different, however, so I suggest you study them carefully.

Editing /etc/hosts.lpd

You can add the names or IP addresses of individual computers to which you want to give print access to the /etc/hosts.lpd file. Simply list the names or addresses one per line, as follows:

```
polk
tyler.threeroomco.com
192.168.2.19
```

This example gives print access to three computers: polk on the host machine's current network, tyler.threeroomco.com, and 192.168.2.19. As you can see, you can list names by the host name only, the fully qualified domain name (FQDN), or the IP address. The FQDN and IP address are the most secure forms.

> **NOTE**
>
> You can use a line containing only + to indicate that *all* computers can print to your printer. I don't recommend doing so, however. Even if your computer isn't currently connected directly to the Internet, if you later change that configuration, it would be easy to forget to change the entry in /etc/hosts.lpd, thus leaving your system open for any prankster who wanted to waste your paper, ink, and toner.

By default, placing a client machine's name or IP address in /etc/hosts.lpd gives the client computer full access to all the printers on the server. This method doesn't give access to any other system resources, though. For instance, /etc/hosts.lpd doesn't give access to NFS exports, as described in Chapter 10, "NFS: Sharing Files with Other UNIXes," p. 241. For that, you must edit the /etc/exports file.

Editing /etc/hosts.equiv

The /etc/hosts.equiv file works much like the /etc/hosts.lpd file—you list client computers that you trust in the file, and those machines are able to print unfettered to your system. The trouble is that /etc/hosts.equiv does much more than give those client machines access to your local printer queue. It also gives users of those machines access to your machine in other ways, such as through the rlogin program, which lets users log in to a remote computer from a trusted host without supplying a password.

For instance, suppose that your computer, `fillmore`, has an `/etc/hosts.equiv` file that lists `polk` and `tyler`. Then, any user with accounts on both `fillmore` and either `polk` or `tyler` can gain access to `fillmore` without supplying a password. This might be convenient in some situations, but it's also a potentially massive security hole. If security on `polk` is weak, for instance, an intruder can then gain access to `fillmore` with ease.

Caution

As with `/etc/hosts.lpd`, a line in `/etc/hosts.equiv` containing only the character + makes *any* host a trusted one. This is a security hole of stellar proportions. I suggest that you check your system to be sure it's *not* configured in this way.

Overall, I recommend not using the `/etc/hosts.equiv` file unless you fully understand the security implications and are willing to accept the risks. For providing printer access alone, `/etc/hosts.lpd` is sufficient.

Tip

To reduce the risks associated with `/etc/hosts.equiv`, you can disable the services that use it—mainly `rlogin` and `rsh`—by commenting out their lines in `/etc/inetd.conf`. I recommend doing this in addition to eliminating `/etc/hosts.equiv`.

Controlling Access to Your Printers

Suppose you want to restrict access to a printer to certain users or groups of users, either locally or on a remote system. Linux's printer queue system provides this functionality through options in the `/etc/printcap` file. Specifically, there are two options of interest:

- `rs`—This option is binary (it's either present or it's not), and controls whether remote users can print to a local queue when those users don't have accounts on the local system. When the `rs` option isn't present, any user can print, as long as the host system is approved in `/etc/hosts.lpd` or `/etc/hosts.equiv`. Thus, the user `sally` on the computer `polk` can print to a queue on `fillmore` even though there's no corresponding account for `sally` on `fillmore`. If you add the `rs` option to `/etc/printcap` on `fillmore`, though, `sally` won't be able to print to any of `fillmore`'s queues. The user `joe`, however, who has accounts on both systems, can print even when `rs` is in place on `fillmore`.

Several versions of Linux's printer queue software have had buggy implementations of the rs feature. In Red Hat 5.2, for instance, the software treated *all* queues as if the rs option were enabled, whether or not it was specified in /etc/printcap.

In Red Hat 6.0, lpd locks out all remote users when rs is set—even users with valid accounts on the server computer. At the time of this writing, Red Hat hasn't issued an official fix for this problem, although it is fixed in the lpr package that Red Hat is distributing with the betas for Red Hat 6.1. That fixed version is included in the sams-extras/printing directory of the CD-ROM that accompanies this book. If you need the rs capability, you should install this updated version of the lpr package.

- rg=—This option specifies a restricted group printer. For instance, if you specify rg=faculty, that printer will be accessible only to the faculty group. You can use this feature to restrict access to some arbitrary group of users. To do so, create a special group for printer access, add all the users you want to have access to that group, and add an appropriate rg= option to your /etc/printcap file.

It's important to realize that these features apply on a printer-by-printer basis. You can provide unfettered access to one printer, but restrict access to another on the same system. The rg= option also applies to users local to the server computer.

As an example of these two access control methods, consider the following sample /etc/printcap entry:

```
bigcolor:\
        :sd=/var/spool/lpd/lp:\
        :mx#0:\
        :sh:\
        :rs:\
        :rg=layout:\
        :lp=/dev/lp0:\
        :if=/var/spool/lpd/lp/filter:
```

This entry restricts access to the printer bigcolor to users who have accounts on the local system and who belong to the group layout.

> **TIP**
>
> The rs option is only useful for restricting printing using native Linux/UNIX printer sharing mechanisms, but the rg= option can be useful with Samba, too. You can restrict printer access just as described here, and as long as your Samba users log on with their own passwords, you can restrict printer access in this way.

Printing to a Remote UNIX Printer from Linux

Because native UNIX/Linux-style printing involves UNIX or Linux clients, it's important to understand the client side of such printer configuration. For the most part, this configuration works much as described in Chapter 14, "Preparing to Share a Printer," p. 351. There are a few unique details, though.

Using printtool to Configure Printing

After you start printtool and click Add to add a printer queue, printtool asks what type of printer you want to add. Select Remote Unix (lpd) Queue and, instead of the Edit Local Printer Entry dialog box, printtool presents the Edit Remote Unix (lpd) Queue Entry dialog box, shown in Figure 15.1.

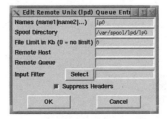

FIGURE 15.1

You must specify a remote host and printer queue when creating a local queue for a remote UNIX or Linux printer.

The Edit Remote Unix (lpd) Queue Entry dialog box works very much like the Edit Local Printer Entry dialog box described in Chapter 14. The only difference is that you must enter the name of the remote computer and the queue name of the destination printer on that computer, rather than the name of the printer device file. Other fields, including the printer name, spool directory, file size limit, and the input filter, work precisely as they do with local printers.

A printer queue can have one name on one computer and another name on another computer. For instance, the printer queue `bigcolor` on the print server `fillmore` might be accessed from the remote computer `polk` as `epson1520`. It's probably best for the sanity of all involved, however, if you attempt to coordinate printer queue names. If name conflict is inevitable (say, because multiple print servers have existing queues with conflicting names), try using a combination of the server and queue names as client computer queue names, as in `fillmore_bigcolor` or `fm_bigcolor`, to identify the `bigcolor` printer on `fillmore`. Alternatively, you might use the printers' locations in a similar way, as in `fl2_bigcolor` for the `bigcolor` printer on Floor 2.

Configuring `/etc/printcap` Manually

An `/etc/printcap` entry for a remote printer queue is much like an entry for a local queue. As with a `printtool`-based configuration, you only need to alter the way the printer device is specified. Instead of an `lp=` option in `/etc/printcap`, you need to specify the `rm=` and `rp=` parameters to specify the remote system's name and the printer queue name on the remote system, respectively. For instance, here's a sample `/etc/printcap` entry for a remote printer queue:

```
bigcolor:\
        :sd=/var/spool/lpd/lp:\
        :mx#0:\
        :sh:\
        :rm=fillmore.threeroomco.com\
        :rp=bigcolor:\
        :if=/var/spool/lpd/lp/filter:
```

This queue directs input to the local `bigcolor` queue to a queue of the same name on the `fillmore.threeroomco.com` print server.

You can, of course, specify any access restrictions you want, remove the `sh` parameter to print a job separator page, and so on. These restrictions apply to jobs generated locally on your computer or accepted from a third computer by your system, but not to jobs sent to the print server directly from another source. Ultimately, it's the job of the print server's administrator to configure that system to print jobs in the desired fashion. If you administer several computers, though, you might want to spread the print queue handling around.

For instance, suppose the computer `polk` is used only by faculty in a college's graphics arts department, all members of whom are authorized to have access to a high-end color printer served by `fillmore`. Suppose further that the computer `tyler` is used by students, some of whom should have access to the color printer, others of whom should not. Most of the individuals who use either `tyler` or `polk` do *not* have accounts on `fillmore`. In this situation, it makes sense to place no access restrictions on the exported color printer queue on `polk`, but to create a color printer group on `tyler` and restrict access to the shared printer on `tyler`. You could then list both `polk` and `tyler` in `fillmore`'s `/etc/hosts.lpd` file and place no restrictions on the printer in `fillmore`'s `/etc/printcap` file. Provided that neither `polk` nor `tyler` exports its printers, you will have restricted access to the printer in a sensible way. Figure 15.2 illustrates this situation.

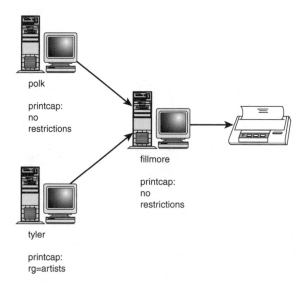

FIGURE 15.2
You can control who has access to a printer from the server or from the server's clients.

Chaining Printer Queues

You can export printer queues that refer to remote printers. You might find this convenient in some cases, but it can lead to access control problems. For instance, suppose you control the computers `polk` and `tyler`, but `fillmore` is out of your control. If `fillmore` is configured as a print server and lists `polk` as an authorized client, but does not list `tyler`, you can, in effect, add `tyler` to `fillmore`'s list by including `tyler` in `polk`'s `/etc/hosts.lpd` file. Figure 15.3 demonstrates this situation.

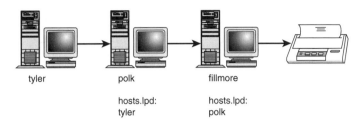

FIGURE 15.3
A print job can hop from one computer to another down a chain, if the computers are configured to allow such actions.

Of course, it's probably more convenient to simply list `tyler` in `fillmore`'s `/etc/hosts.lpd` file. This might not always be possible, though. For instance, you might not have control over `fillmore`, or `tyler` and `fillmore` might not be directly visible to each other (`polk` might serve as an IP masquerading gateway, for instance). You can also link computers in this way across incompatible networks. For instance, if `tyler` is a Macintosh using AppleTalk for printing, `polk` could use Netatalk to convert the AppleTalk print job into a networked `lpd` print job.

> **CAUTION**
>
> Be careful about exporting print jobs that might result in long print chains, particularly when the systems to which you're providing services aren't under your control. Not only are such setups inefficient because of increased network traffic, but they also provide the potential for allowing unauthorized printer access. For instance, if you control `polk` but not `tyler`, but give print access to `tyler`, it's possible that `tyler`'s administrator will misconfigure that system to provide universal access to `tyler`'s printer queue. This could easily overcome printer access controls on `polk` and `fillmore`.

Summary

Exporting Linux printer queues using UNIX/Linux-style printer sharing is reasonably simple, given a working printer configuration. Basically, you need only add the names of client systems to the `/etc/hosts.lpd` file, and you'll be set. You might want to fine-tune your access control, though, by restricting access to those users who have accounts on the server, or by using a group to restrict access further.

Configuring the client system is equally important, and equally easy, if you know how to configure a local printer queue. You need to use only two alternate options in the `/etc/printcap` file to set up a remote printer queue rather than a local one.

Samba: Sharing Printers with DOS, Windows, and OS/2

16

IN THIS CHAPTER

Using a Linux computer running Samba can be an excellent way to share printers on a network of DOS, Windows, or OS/2 computers. As described in Chapter 14, "Preparing to Share a Printer," you can share a printer either "raw," by using Windows drivers for the specific model you're using, or by using Ghostscript to make the printer look like a PostScript printer to Windows. Of course, if the printer has PostScript built in, the two options produce very similar results in practice.

Printer sharing requires that you have Samba installed and running. Basic Samba configuration is covered in Chapter 11, "Samba: Sharing Files with DOS, Windows, and OS/2," particularly in the section titled "Setting Samba Options." This chapter helps you configure your Linux/Samba print server.

Setting Samba Printer Options

Just as with Samba file sharing, you can configure Samba printer shares either using a GUI utility or by directly editing the /etc/smb.conf file. Unfortunately, the version of linuxconf included with Red Hat Linux 6.0 is rather fussy about the form of the printer share information in /etc/smb.conf, and the Samba printer configuration section of linuxconf doesn't work with many configurations. You might therefore need to use the Samba Web Administration Tool (SWAT; see the sidebar on p. 262) for a GUI configuration tool for Samba. Figure 16.1 shows SWAT displaying a Samba printer share configuration.

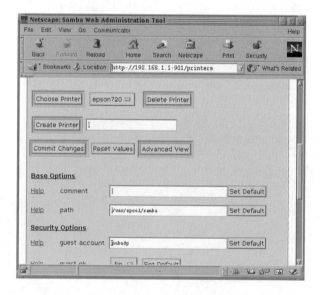

FIGURE 16.1

You can specify an Advanced View or a Basic View in SWAT to provide the desired level of control over your Samba printer configuration.

Because the GUI printer configuration options are so similar to those in the text-mode
/etc/smb.conf file, I focus on the latter. If you're using a GUI configuration tool, you need
only locate appropriately named options in that tool to adapt the information presented in this
chapter.

Sharing Some or All Printers

One of the most important decisions concerning printer sharing is whether you want to share
some or all of your printers. Samba can extract information from the /etc/printcap file to
share all your printers, much as lpd does for UNIX-style printer sharing. Alternatively, you can
create separate share definitions for each printer you want to share.

To create a default share for all printers, create a share named [printers]. Samba reads the
/etc/printcap file and creates a share under the first name of every printer it finds, using the
options set for the [printers] share.

> **NOTE**
>
> You should omit the square braces ([ ]) from the share name when creating a share
> with a GUI tool such as linuxconf or SWAT.

> **NOTE**
>
> If you use SWAT to manage a Samba configuration that includes a [printers] share,
> SWAT displays the names of all the printers that are included from that share. SWAT
> marks these autoloaded printers with asterisks (*). You can't delete them from the
> configuration, but you can edit them. When you do so, SWAT creates a separate
> share for the modified configuration, and this modified configuration overrides that
> of the [printers] share for that one printer.

For instance, here's a sample configuration for a default printer share:

```
[printers]
        path = /var/spool/samba
        print ok = Yes
```

The meanings of the various options are described shortly. Alternatively, suppose the server has three printers defined in /etc/printcap, but you only want to share two of them. You could create entries such as these:

```
[canon]
        path = /var/spool/samba
        print ok = Yes

[lexmark]
        path = /var/spool/samba
        print ok = Yes
```

Collectively, these two entries result in the sharing of the printers canon and lexmark. You can also use the individualized listing to set different options for the different printers. For instance, you can use the hosts allow option (p. 268) to specify which hosts can share a particular printer.

Setting Printer Names

If you elect to use a [printers] share definition, Samba uses the first /etc/printcap name for a printer as that printer's Samba share name. Otherwise, Samba normally uses the name you place in square braces both to search for a matching /etc/printcap entry and as the share name. If you want the Samba export to be available under a name other than the Linux queue name, you can use the printer option to do so, as in the following:

```
[lexmark]
        path = /var/spool/samba
        printer = lp0
        print ok = Yes
```

This share definition makes the Linux lp0 printer available under the name lexmark.

Making Printers Browsable

If you want a printer to appear in the Windows Network Neighborhood, as shown in Figure 16.2, you must ensure that the share is *browsable* (p. 270), just as you do for file shares. There are two ways to accomplish this task:

- Place the load printers = yes option in the [global] section of your /etc/smb.conf file. Actually, yes is the default value for this parameter, so it shouldn't be necessary to specify it if you want all your printers to appear.

- Place the browsable = yes option in the individual share entries. As with load printers, the default value is yes, so you shouldn't need to adjust this parameter in most cases.

SAMBA: SHARING PRINTERS

FIGURE 16.2
Browsable printers show up in Network Neighborhood, so you can easily locate them when setting up drivers or configuring the printer.

In practice, `load printers` isn't of much use because the `browsable` value takes precedence, and it's yes by default.

Even if you set a printer to not be browsable, you can print to it from a client system; the client simply has to know the name of the share. You could use this feature to hide seldom-used variants of printers from a cluttered listing of printers—but if the printer is seldom used, hiding it might be unwise because a user might then have a hard time locating the share.

> **NOTE**
>
> After you configure a queue for a printer on the client system, there's little need to browse the printer share because the client system's queue contains the share name, and the user interacts with the local queue.

Additional Printer Options

Setting a printer name and making the share browsable are only part of the task of sharing a printer. There are many additional options, including the following:

- `print ok` or `printable`—These synonymous options identify the share as a printer share, rather than a file share. One of these parameters is *mandatory* for printer shares. The default value is `no`, so Samba treats a share without this option as a file share.
- `path`—Just as with file shares, Samba needs a location associated with the share. In fact, from the client's point of view, printer sharing is just like file sharing, except that the client uses printer shares almost exclusively for saving the output from printer drivers. The standard Samba installation for Red Hat 6.0 creates an appropriate directory called

`/var/spool/samba` for this function. You can use the same path for multiple printer shares without problems.

CAUTION

Samba stores printed files under the username of the person who's connected via Samba's authentication method. If you're concerned about others being able to read or delete your print jobs, you should be sure to use your own username on client computers, and not print sensitive material if somebody else logged in to the computer and then let you use it. Also, the `/var/spool/samba` directory has its sticky bit set. This means that only the owner of a file can delete the file. (Normally, the ability to delete a file is determined by the ownership and permissions on the directory in which the file resides.) If you change the default Samba path for printer sharing, you should be careful to set the sticky bit on the target directory by using `chmod a+t` on the directory.

- `postscript`—Some Windows PostScript drivers prepend a Control-D character to PostScript files, which often confuses Linux print filters, resulting in the printing of PostScript code, rather than the text or graphics described by the PostScript code. The result can be page after page of PostScript rather than a one- or two-page letter. If you set the `postscript` parameter to `true`, however, Samba prepends a PostScript comment (`%!`) to the file, which corrects the problem. You should use this value for this parameter is `false`.

Samba supports many more printer-related options. You should consult the `smb.conf` manpage or *Sams Teach Yourself Samba in 24 Hours* for more details.

Printing Permissions

You should probably give some thought to the range of users to whom you want to give printer access. Although a printer share might not seem to be as critical to system security as, say, the `root` password, it's possible that a bug in Samba or some combination of printer access and a bug in some other program could give a cracker access to your system. Even aside from issues of access to your system, if anybody can print to your computer, anybody can waste your paper and ink or toner, simply by queuing large print jobs.

Using Passwords to Control Printer Access

The first line of defense against printer intruders is Samba's use of passwords. Chapter 11 provides details on how Samba handles passwords. As a review, recall that the `security` parameter in `/etc/smb.conf` allows you to specify that Samba operate in one of four security modes: `share`, `user`, `server`, or `domain`. In `share` mode, users don't need to give usernames to access the share. Instead, Samba checks the `user` parameter in a share's `/etc/smb.conf` entry to determine which users are authorized to use each share, and Samba tries to match the password that the client gives against each user in turn. Samba requires a new password for each share. In `user` mode, Samba asks for a username and password for each client computer, but doesn't require a separate password for each share. The `server` and `domain` modes work much like the `user` mode, except that in `user` mode the Linux server authenticates the username and password, whereas in `server` and `domain` modes, the Linux server passes that task on to another computer.

In general, `user`, `server`, and `domain` modes best match the Linux security model. If you don't need to restrict access on a printer-by-printer, user-by-user basis, you can provide accounts on the Linux server to users who need access to the server's resources and be done with it. If you don't want a user to have the ability to log on or use file sharing, you can disable these methods of access in various ways, such as by specifying an invalid shell or giving the user's home directory ownership to root and permissions of `000`.

CAUTION

If you don't understand the implications of making changes to login shells and account directory permissions, you should not do these things. Restricting users' access to a system in some ways but not others can be a tricky undertaking. (The basics of this topic are covered in "Disabling Unneeded Passwords," p. 573.) Depending on the system's overall configuration and Samba's specific configuration, you may or may not be able to obtain precisely the results you want by doing creative things to a user's account.

In some cases, you might want to use share-level security. This is most convenient if you need to provide access to some shares to some people and other shares to others. For instance, consider the following printer shares in a `security = share` environment:

```
[canon]
        path = /var/spool/samba
        user = larry, moe, curly
        print ok = Yes
```

```
[hpdj]
        path = /var/spool/samba
        user = lucille, ricky
        print ok = Yes

[lexmark]
        path = /var/spool/samba
        user = larry, lucille
        print ok = Yes
```

In this configuration, only larry, moe, and curly can use the printer canon, whereas only lucille and ricky can use the printer hpdj. The lexmark printer, though, is accessible by two individuals who can access each of the other two printers, namely larry and lucille. As you can see, share-level security is extremely flexible, in terms of its ability to control access to specific printers. On the other hand, it's also quite difficult to maintain because you must frequently add and remove users from multiple shares as the users on the network change. This method of access can also slow down authentication, particularly if shares have many users, because Linux authenticates users in this scheme by checking the provided password against each of the share's authorized users in turn.

An alternative means of applying share-level security would be to create a special Linux account for each share or set of shares, and then distribute the password for this account to everybody who needs to access the shares in question. Of course, this means that a single password will be widely known, so you have to be extra cautious about that account's accessibility in areas other than the sharing for which it's intended. (A cracker who gained knowledge of the password and account name might use it to log in via telnet and attempt further mischief, for instance.) Changing the password could also become a nightmare, as you then need to inform several people of the changed password.

Using Linux /etc/printcap Group Controls

Chapter 15, "Sharing Printers with Other UNIXes," describes a method of printer access control based on Linux group membership. Specifically, you can add a line to the /etc/printcap entry for a printer that is similar to the following:

```
:rg=layout:\
```

This /etc/printcap entry restricts access to the printer to members of the Linux group layout. (You can, of course, use any group you like.) This restriction applies whether the printer queue is exported as a UNIX-style queue or as a Samba queue. You can use it to achieve many aspects of printer access restrictions. For instance, you can create a separate group for each printer, and then add those users who should have access to a printer to each printer's group. When used in conjunction with user, server, or domain security, this method effectively limits access to the printers. In fact, you could implement precisely the same controls in this way for the earlier example's canon, hpdj, and lexmark printers as used by larry, moe, curly, lucille, and ricky.

Using the hosts allow and hosts deny Parameters

You can use the hosts allow and hosts deny parameters in the definition of individual shares to control access to the printer on a client-by-client basis. For instance, suppose your Linux computer hosts three printers that it shares. The printer hp4000 should be accessible to all computers on your intranet, whereas epson1520 should be accessible only to the art department, and okidata should be accessible only to the front office staff. If the art department computers all have addresses in the 192.168.5.*x* range, whereas the front office staff computers are all in the 192.168.7.*x* range, then you could do something like this:

```
[hp4000]
        path = /var/spool/samba
        print ok = Yes

[epson1520]
        path = /var/spool/samba
        hosts allow = 192.168.5.
        print ok = Yes

[okidata]
        path = /var/spool/samba
        hosts allow = 192.168.7.
        print ok = Yes
```

NOTE

This configuration assumes that *all* the computers in the 192.168.5.*x* range belong to the art department and that *all* the computers in the 192.168.7.*x* range are in the front office. If this isn't true, you can use more complex hosts allow statements, such as adding an EXCEPT clause to exclude specific hosts, as in

```
hosts allow = 192.168.7. EXCEPT gingko
```

The details of how to specify computers in hosts allow and hosts deny are described in Chapter 11.

Configuring Windows for Printing

In order to do any good, of course, your Linux print server must have clients. These clients are usually Windows computers, but they can be DOS, OS/2, or even UNIX or Linux computers that themselves run Samba. (The section "Printing from Linux to a Remote SMB/CIFS Printer" later in this chapter provides an overview of how to configure Linux to print to a Windows or Samba server.)

Installing an Appropriate Driver

One of the trickiest aspects of printing to a Samba server is determining what driver to install. Every installation is unique, both in terms of the hardware and the needs of the network's users, so it's impossible to give absolute guidelines on what works all the time. In some cases, you might need to try several configurations before you find one that's to your liking.

Printer Queue Configuration

As described in Chapter 14, you can configure your Linux printer queue in several ways:

- PostScript printer—If you have a printer that supports PostScript in the printer itself, you probably want to configure your Linux printer queue with the standard filters for PostScript printers. You might, however, want to set up a raw queue that feeds its input to the printer without processing, especially if the printer supports both PostScript and some other protocol. This raw queue solution allows you to switch between two drivers on client OSs without trouble.

- Non-PostScript printer via Ghostscript—You can configure a non-PostScript printer, such as one that uses Hewlett-Packard's PCL or Epson's ESC/P2, to behave as if it were a PostScript printer, as far as the client OS is concerned.

- Non-PostScript printer via a raw queue—If you set up a queue that doesn't process its input in any way, you can use the client OS's native drivers for that printer, as supplied by the OS or printer manufacturer.

When you print to a raw queue, whether you use a PostScript or a non-PostScript printer, it's best to use client-OS drivers for the specific printer model you're using. This practice gives you the best access to the printer's specific features, such as built-in fonts, resolution options, sheet feeders, and so on. In many cases, the same is true of PostScript printers when fed through a normal Linux printer queue; but in some cases, Linux's filters misinterpret mode-changing code or Control-D characters and convert the PostScript code to ASCII text, which produces unusable printouts. There are three possible solutions in this situation:

- Select a client driver for a PostScript printer other than the one you're actually using.
- Set the `postscript = true` option in `/etc/smb.conf` for the share in question.

- Set up a raw queue on the Linux server and use it instead of the filtered queue you'd been using.

Not all these options work in all situations. The last, for instance, only works if you're using a PostScript printer or if you switch to the client OS's native drivers for the specific printer you're using.

Selecting a Driver

When you print to a non-PostScript printer by using a client OS PostScript driver with Ghostscript in the Linux filter, you face a dilemma: What specific model of PostScript driver should you select on the client OS? Because the printer you're actually using is *not* a PostScript model, you don't find it listed among the available PostScript printers. Instead, you must select another model of PostScript printer, or a generic PostScript option, if one is available. You should, however, select a PostScript printer with features as closely matched to your actual printer as possible, particularly with respect to resolution, available page sizes, and color support. (You must also select a Ghostscript driver for the Linux server that supports these features, of course.)

In general, I've found that Apple LaserWriter drivers tend to produce good results with Ghostscript-driven black-and-white printers. Older models' drivers, such as the LaserWriter II series, work well with 300dpi inkjet and older laser printers. Drivers for newer models, such as the LaserWriter 630, work well with 600dpi printers.

For color printers, my recommendation is to first try drivers for the QMS magicolor. This is a 600dpi color printer, and drivers for it often work quite well with color inkjet printers driven through Ghostscript under Linux.

If you have printers with unusual capabilities, such as extra-large paper handling, you might need to look further for appropriate drivers. Many such high-end printers have PostScript options, so you can try the manufacturer's Web site to see if there are drivers available for a printer outfitted with such an option.

NOTE

Although the computer-hosted PostScript interpreters sold for some printers aren't useful under Linux, the PostScript drivers the manufacturers make available for printers using the host-based interpreters might be. Conceptually, Ghostscript takes the place of the host-based interpreter, and using the printer from a client would be very much like using the same printer from the same client, with the printer attached to a Windows computer running the manufacturer's interpreter.

Most client OSs come with a selection of PostScript drivers, so you shouldn't have trouble finding a driver for use with a Ghostscript queue. For PostScript printers, you can also check with the printer's manufacturer. You can find other PostScript drivers for some OSs, as well, but you should check licensing terms before using them. For instance, Adobe makes PostScript drivers available, but they're licensed for use only on printers that use genuine Adobe PostScript, so you shouldn't use these drivers with Ghostscript-driven printers or with printers that use PostScript clone interpreters.

Pointing the Driver to the Linux Server

You should follow the directions that come with the driver or OS to install the driver on the client computer. At some point, the OS asks you to locate the printer. For instance, Figure 16.3 shows Windows NT 4.0 Connect to Printer dialog box, prompting for the remote printer's name. Depending on the OS and driver, you might be able to point and click your way to the printer, or you might need to enter a NetBIOS-style identification. In Figure 16.3, for instance, the printer is identified as \\SPEAKER\escp2, because it's the escp2 printer on the server SPEAKER.

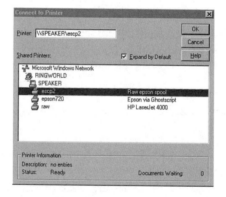

FIGURE 16.3

The Windows NT 4.0 Connect to Printer dialog box shown here lets you select the printer graphically, though not all OSs provide this amenity.

TIP

Some networks develop problems in which servers don't appear in browse lists, but they're still available. You can often access the printers on such computers by entering their names manually, even if you can't locate them by browsing.

When you're done configuring your client's printer queue, you should perform a test printout. Many client OSs prompt you to do just this. Be prepared, though—if something is misconfigured, your printer could begin spewing sheets of paper containing gibberish. You might want to cancel the print job in Linux (by using the `lprm` command, as discussed in Chapter 14). You might also need to cancel the job in the printer itself (most printers have a front-panel control to do this, so consult your manual).

> **TIP**
>
> By removing all but one sheet of paper from the printer, you can ensure that you don't waste a lot of paper in the event of a problem. You might still need to cancel the print job, but in the event of a problem, you at least won't be watching paper come through the printer at top speed while you try to solve the problem!

Printing Files

After you configure a queue, you can print to it just as you would to a local queue. Figure 16.4, for instance, shows a Windows NT 4.0 Print dialog box configured to print a job to an Epson Stylus Color 400 printer connected to the server called `speaker`. You can select other print queues, adjust the printer's properties, and otherwise adjust the print options before starting the print job, just as you would if the printer were local. You can consult the documentation for your OS or printer driver to learn more about the options available to you.

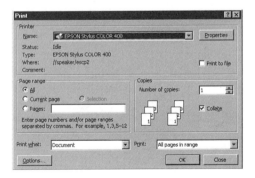

FIGURE 16.4
Print dialog boxes vary substantially from one OS to another, and even from one printer driver to another.

If you regularly print from DOS programs running under Windows, you might want to assign a shared printer to a local printer port, to allow the DOS programs to print. You can do this under Windows 95 or 98 by right-clicking a printer icon and selecting Properties from the resulting pop-up menu. Select the Details tab and click Capture Printer Port, which brings up the Capture Printer Port dialog box (see Figure 16.5). Select the port you want to use for the printer in the Device field, and enter the network path to the port in the Path field. (You might need to enter this path by hand. If you started with the printer to which you want to connect, you can copy the information from the printer's Properties dialog box.) If you want this connection to persist when you reboot the computer, click Reconnect at logon.

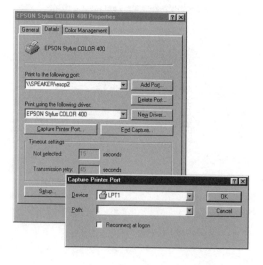

FIGURE 16.5

The Properties dialog box varies from printer to printer, but should always have a Details tab with options that allow you to link a DOS-accessible port to a network printer.

When you're done configuring the port capture, you can print from DOS programs to the captured port. The DOS output isn't processed by the Windows drivers, though. If you've captured a PostScript or Ghostscript-driven Linux share in this way, the DOS program should output PostScript for best results, although some queues might be able to process raw ASCII, too. If you've captured a raw queue, you need drivers in your DOS program for the printer you're using.

Printing from Linux to a Remote SMB/CIFS Printer

In some cases, you might want to print from Linux to a remote printer on a Windows computer or some other system that supports SMB/CIFS. Why would you want to do this? Here are some potential reasons:

- You're using a Linux computer on a peer-to-peer network on which a Windows system has a printer that you want to use.
- You're using a Linux client on a client/server network with a Windows print server.
- You're using a Linux client on a client/server network with a Linux print server that's configured for sharing printers via Samba. The print server's administrator doesn't want to configure UNIX-style printer sharing on that system.
- Your Linux computer serves as a translator between a Macintosh network and a Windows network. You want the Macintoshes to be able to print on Windows printers, so you set up a Linux printer queue that prints to the Windows printers and export that queue to the Macintoshes. (This situation is similar to that depicted in Figure 15.3, in Chapter 15.)

Configuring a Print Queue by Using `printtool`

Red Hat Linux includes direct support for SMB/CIFS print configurations. In the `printtool` utility, if you select SMB/Windows 95/NT Printer at the Add a Printer Entry dialog box, Linux allows you to configure an SMB/CIFS printer by using the Edit SMB/Windows 95/NT Printer Entry dialog box shown in Figure 16.6.

In addition to the information required for local printers, to use an SMB/CIFS queue, you must fill in the following fields:

- Hostname of Printer Server—The NetBIOS name of the server.
- IP number of Server—You can enter the IP address of the server instead of or in addition to the NetBIOS name. Normally you don't need to enter this information.
- Printer Name—The name of the printer on the server. If you're printing to another Samba system, this is the name of the Samba share, which might not be the same as the name in the server's `/etc/printcap` file.

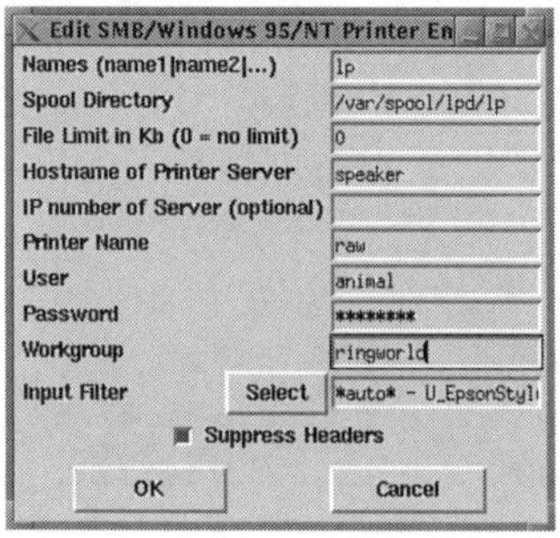

FIGURE 16.6

Configuring an SMB/CIFS printer requires entering more information than does configuring other types of local or networked printers.

- User—All Samba print jobs go through one username. You must enter it here. This is the name of a user on the *server*, not the local machine; the username you enter here need not correspond with a user of the local system.

- Password—You must enter the password for the user authorized to print on the server.

CAUTION

As the `printtool` utility warns you, Linux stores the remote system's username and password unencrypted on the local hard disk when you print via an SMB/CIFS queue. This file is called `.config` and is in the `/var/spool/lpd/`*printername* directory. Unfortunately, this file has permissions `-rw-r--r--`, which means that anybody on the system can read the file. If you restrict the permissions, only root is able to print. This situation therefore represents a potentially major security problem for the print server. You can reduce the severity of the problem by creating a special print-only account on the server. If the server uses share-level security, of course, the username is irrelevant and the password only accesses the printer share, assuming that the server is configured with different passwords for all services.

- Workgroup—The name of the domain or workgroup on which the server resides.

When you finish defining the printer queue, you can print to it much as you would to any Linux printer queue. You can use the `lp` command to print a document, as in `lp fly.ps`; or you can print by using the print commands in the applications you use. There isn't any indication that the printer queue is a Samba queue, just that it exists along with any other local or remote printer queues you might have defined on your system (assuming that the application lists the available queues; not all do).

Configuring a Queue Manually

If you're not using Red Hat Linux, you should consult your distribution's documentation for information on configuring a Samba printer queue. If your documentation lacks this information, follow these steps:

1. Create a printer in whatever way you normally would.
2. Change the `lp=` entry in `/etc/printcap` to point to `/dev/null`.
3. Create a file called `.config` in the spool directory for your printer (`/var/spool/lpd/`*printername*), and type these lines in that file:

```
server=servername
service=printername
password=password
```

   You should replace *servername*, *printername*, and *password* with appropriate strings, of course.

> **NOTE**
>
> The standard `smbprint` script file passes the server's name as the username. This is unimportant if the server is set for share-level security, but if the server is set for user-level security, the server must have an account named after itself with the password specified in the `.config` file. Alternatively, you could alter the `smbprint` script on the Linux client.

4. Change the `if=` line in `/etc/printcap` to point to the `smbprint` script. This script might be in `/usr/bin`, `/usr/local/bin`, or elsewhere, depending on your distribution.
5. Change the `af=` line in `/etc/printcap`, or add one if necessary, to create an accounting file. This can be a file in the spool directory. Its name is unimportant, so long as it doesn't overwrite an existing file. For instance `af=/var/spool/lpd/`*printername*`/afile` should do fine.
6. Restart the printer queue.

The new queue should now work, with one major caveat: Step 4 replaces your filter file, and if you had configured your printer queue to use a smart filter to process PostScript into something that the printer understands, you've now lost that ability. You might therefore want to create a new script that both calls the old print filter *and* calls `smbprint`. You can then enter this new script as the new filter file for the queue. If the server is a Linux computer with its own Ghostscript queues, of course you can print PostScript to the remote system and *the remote system* will do the Ghostscript processing. PostScript processing also happens remotely if the printer is a PostScript model, of course, whether it's hosted on a Linux or a Windows system.

Summary

After you've configured a Linux printer queue and set up Samba for file sharing, sharing the printer with DOS, Windows, and OS/2 machines is a matter of adding an entry for the printer in the /etc/smb.conf file. This entry closely resembles file-sharing entries, and for good reason: Samba printer sharing works very much like file sharing. The client computer opens a share and writes a file to it, whereupon Samba directs that share into a standard Linux printer queue.

The greatest complications in this scenario come from the need to select an appropriate set of printer drivers, both in Linux (for Ghostscript, if you're printing to a non-PostScript printer) and in the client OS (to match both Ghostscript and the printer's capabilities through Ghostscript). Printing by using native client OS drivers and a raw queue can thus be simpler to configure in some cases.

It's also possible to reverse this process and print to a Windows printer from Linux. You should be aware of the security implications of doing so, however, because this configuration requires that the server's password be stored on the client's hard disk in an unencrypted form readable to all users.

Netatalk: Sharing Printers with Macintoshes

IN THIS CHAPTER

Linux's printer-sharing capabilities wouldn't be complete without support for the Macintosh, and Linux doesn't disappoint in this respect. Red Hat 6.0, however, doesn't ship with the necessary software, Netatalk, so it's included on the CD-ROM that accompanies this book in the `sams-extras/netatalk` directory. Netatalk, in conjunction with Apple Datagram Delivery Protocol (DDP; p. 293) support in the Linux kernel, lets Linux participate in Apple's native network "conversations."

This chapter doesn't discuss the basic configuration of Netatalk. For that, you should read Chapter 12, "Netatalk: Sharing Files with Macintoshes," and especially the sections titled "Compiling AppleTalk Support into Your Kernel" and "The `atalkd` Daemon." After you've got basic Netatalk services running, you can read this chapter to learn how to make your printers available to Macintoshes.

Linux can be a great print server for Macintoshes, in part, because Macintoshes work well with networked PostScript printers but not with most inexpensive inkjet printers, whereas with Linux you can convert PostScript into a format that's understandable by inkjets. You do this with the Ghostscript program in Linux, configured to run automatically as part of a print filter. You can therefore set up a Linux computer to serve two or three inexpensive color inkjets to a workgroup of Macintoshes. Even including the cost of the Linux server (which can do more than just serve printers), you may save money compared to buying much more expensive networked PostScript color printers. Macintoshes can also share their own non-PostScript color printers among themselves, but this ties up the server computer, meaning that you either must devote the computer as a server (in which case a Linux computer and PC hardware are less expensive) or the user of the server computer must deal with reduced performance whenever anybody wants to print a job.

An Overview of Macintosh-Style Printer Sharing

Some of the earliest Macintoshes used AppleTalk over LocalTalk networks to print to the earliest LaserWriters (and, soon thereafter, other PostScript printers). In fact, sharing expensive LaserWriter printers was the primary function of most early AppleTalk networks.

Because the early Apple laser printers were PostScript models, Apple's network printing model is heavily PostScript-centric. There are now a wide variety of PostScript printers, however, and so Apple's PostScript drivers make use of a file that describes a PostScript printer's capabilities. This approach allows a single Macintosh printer driver to handle a wide variety of printers with varying capabilities.

Understanding both the protocols and printer description will help you work with Macintosh printing and configure Netatalk to serve Macintoshes, so that information is presented here.

Macintosh Printing Protocols

Macintoshes use the Printer Access Protocol (PAP; p. 293) for printing, so the Netatalk component that handles Macintosh printing requests is called papd. PAP works atop DDP and other Macintosh networking protocols, and doesn't work over TCP/IP. This is unlike UNIX-style lpd printing or Samba's implementation of SMB/CIFS, both of which work through TCP/IP. (Windows computers, though, can implement SMB/CIFS through NetBEUI, which is separate from TCP/IP.) Netatalk—or more precisely, Adrian Sun's updated versions of Netatalk—can share files through AppleTalk over TCP/IP, but it cannot share printers in this way. Netatalk can share printers only over DDP. Although this sounds like a disadvantage, it's not universally so. One of the prime advantages of using DDP as the underlying protocol for Macintosh printer sharing is that DDP isn't transferable over the Internet as a whole—at least not without additional protocols to encapsulate it. This means that a Netatalk printer share isn't susceptible to hacking from an outside source. On the other hand, Netatalk printer shares don't require usernames or passwords, so controlling access to printers locally is difficult. Also, if you print very large files, a TCP/IP-based protocol such as UNIX-style lpd printing might prove faster than PAP sharing.

> **NOTE**
>
> Programs such as lpr and DAVE allow Macintoshes to print using non-Macintosh printer protocols, such as lpd and SMB/CIFS, respectively.

Understanding PPD Files

Depending on who you talk to, *PPD* stands for either *PostScript printer description* or *printer page description*. In the past, PPD files were known as *printer description files* (PDFs), but when Adobe came out with its *portable document format* (PDF; also known as Acrobat) files, using *PDF* to refer to printer description files became too confusing.

Whatever the full name, a PPD file contains information on a printer's exact capabilities, such as its resolution, whether it's a color printer, and what fonts it contains. This information allows the Macintosh printer driver to present reasonable options for the printer, and to produce output that shouldn't overburden the printer—for instance, no 11"×17" page descriptions on a printer only capable of handling 8.5"×11" sheets.

You must specify a PPD file on both the Macintosh and on the Linux Netatalk server. It's best if you use the same file on both sides of the connection. I've encountered situations where mismatched PPD files cause printing to fail. Similarly, picking the wrong PPD file for use on both computers can cause printing to fail.

Where, then, can you find the *right* PPD file? One answer is to check with your printer's manufacturer. If the printer is a PostScript model, or has a PostScript option—even if it's for a host-based PostScript interpreter—the manufacturer should have PPD files for the printer. Another option is to check at `http://www.adobe.com/prodindex/printerdrivers/macppd.html` for PPD files.

> **NOTE**
>
> This is the URL on Adobe's site for *Macintosh* PPDs. This is because Macintosh PPD files include creator and type information and resource fork data that the Macintosh needs to use the files. Netatalk, however, can use the data fork portion of the PPD. It's therefore best to get the PPD files on a Macintosh and extract them using Macintosh utilities. You can then copy the file to Linux by using Netatalk and move it someplace convenient for Netatalk's configuration, as described in "Preparing a PPD File," later in this chapter.

Adobe's Windows PostScript drivers also use PPD files, so you can often find Windows PPD files. I recommend using the Macintosh PPD files throughout the process for consistency's sake, but you might find that using Windows files on Linux and Macintosh files on Macintosh works well in some situations.

What PPD file should you use, though? If you're using a PostScript printer, try to find a PPD file for your model. If you're using a non-PostScript printer driven by Ghostscript, I recommend that you try something simple. Apple LaserWriter PPDs often work well with Ghostscript, and they have the added advantage of coming with MacOS, so you don't have to hunt them down. I've used PPD files intended for the Hewlett Packard DeskJet 1200C and QMS magicolor 2 with color inkjet printers with reasonably good results.

> **NOTE**
>
> Some PPD files have the odd effect of producing pages that print upside-down. (The pages are perfectly readable; they just print bottom first rather than the usual top first.) This peculiarity might be important if you're printing on stationery paper. Upside-down printing can also be a serious problem if you intend to use the Macintosh to "print" to a disk file and produce an Adobe Acrobat PDF file from the PostScript file. If upside-down printing is a problem, you may need to try several PPD files until you find one that produces acceptable results.

Setting Up Remote Access

Configuring Netatalk to export Linux printers involves editing a single file, but you might need to track down other files to get Netatalk itself working, and perhaps debug problems. If all goes well, you might be printing from your networked Macintoshes in no time. If not, you might find yourself delving into the mysteries of PPD files and Ghostscript.

> **TIP**
>
> Be sure that you can print PostScript files from Linux before you begin configuring Netatalk for printing. If you have a Red Hat or Mandrake Linux system, you can use `printtool` to test a print spool's ability to print PostScript files, as described in Chapter 14, "Preparing to Share a Printer." If you're using another Linux distribution, try printing a PostScript test file, such as one in the Ghostscript `examples` directory (`/usr/share/ghostscript/5.10/examples/` on a Red Hat 6.0 system), using the `lpr` command. If you can't print PostScript from the Linux computer itself, it's unlikely that you'll be able to print from a Macintosh.

Preparing a PPD File

As mentioned earlier in the chapter, you must locate a PPD file before you can print from a Macintosh. Because you presumably have a Macintosh that's connected to the same network as your Linux box, you should have no problem extracting the PPD files on the Macintosh from whatever source you locate for them. You can then transfer the files to the Linux computer. Ultimately, you want the PPD file to reside in a convenient directory. I like to use `/etc/atalk/ppds`, but you can select another location if you prefer. Don't copy the file just now, though, because you probably need to convert the file's end-of-line characters first.

If you copy the PPD file without adjusting the end-of-line character, your printer might not work correctly. Fortunately, a pair of simple utilities help make this conversion: `unix2mac` and `mac2unix`. You can install them from the `sams-extras/unix2mac` directory on the CD-ROM that accompanies this book. You can copy these files to a location on your hard disk's path, such as `/usr/local/bin`. If you prefer, you can recompile these utilities from the source code, which is in the `sams-extras/unix2mac/source` directory on the book's CD-ROM.

You call either utility by typing its name, the input filename, and the output filename. For instance, you might use this command:

```
mac2unix "/home/dsmk/SuperPrint 1000 PS" /etc/atalk/ppds/superprint.ppd
```

This converts the Macintosh-style `SuperPrint 1000 PS` PPD file into one that's usable by Netatalk and that's called `superprint.ppd`. This command also places the converted file in the destination directory for the PPD files. You can use `unix2mac` to reverse this process if you have need of reading Linux-style text files on a Macintosh.

If you specify the `options=crlf` parameter to a share in the `AppleVolumes.default` configuration file, Netatalk performs this translation automatically on files it can identify as text files when you copy them from the Macintosh to Linux, using Netatalk. Unfortunately, Netatalk doesn't identify all PPD files as text files, so this feature doesn't always work.

If you don't know which form of end-of-line characters a text file uses, try viewing it in Linux by using `less`. If the file appears properly formatted in reasonable-looking lines, it's got Linux-style end-of-line characters. If, instead, you get a file with the characters `^M` scattered throughout it where you would normally expect line breaks, as in Figure 17.1, the file is in Macintosh format and needs to be converted.

FIGURE 17.1

Linux doesn't cope well with Macintosh-style text files.

NOTE

DOS, Windows, and OS/2 use a third type of end-of-line code. Fortunately, Netatalk can cope with this style of end-of-line code, and it looks like Linux-style coding when you use `less`, so you needn't concern yourself with DOS-style end-of-line codings.

Configuring the `papd.conf` File

Netatalk controls its printing options through the `papd.conf` file, which by default in the package provided on this book's CD-ROM is in the `/etc/atalk` directory. You can edit this file by using your favorite text editor. Because Netatalk isn't part of the standard Red Hat installation, there's no `linuxconf` module to control it; you *must* configure Netatalk and `papd` through the text files.

The `papd.conf` file's format is similar to that of `/etc/printcap`, although `papd.conf` doesn't provide the same options as `/etc/printcap`, nor does it provide direct access to the printer port hardware. Instead, it provides a way to link Linux printer queues, as specified in `/etc/printcap`, to printer share names that a Macintosh can access. Its options include the following:

- `pr=`   The Linux printer queue to be associated with the Macintosh printer name.
- `op=`   The username to be used for print jobs on the server.
- `pd=`   The filename of the PPD file associated with the printer.

For example, here's a `papd.conf` entry for one printer:

```
Epson:\
        :pr=epson720:\
        :op=mac:\
        :pd=/etc/atalk/ppds/epson800.ppd
```

This file sets up a Netatalk printer export that will be visible to Macintoshes as Epson. This export uses the Linux `epson720` printer queue, prints all files under the username `mac`, and uses a PPD file called `/etc/atalk/ppds/epson800.ppd`.

Chances are you need to specify a printer queue that's capable of handling PostScript, because so few non-PostScript printers have Macintosh drivers capable of printing via AppleTalk. Of course, if you've got such a printer, you can try exporting a "raw" queue via Netatalk. Try specifying a completely blank PPD file if you attempt such a configuration.

> **TIP**
>
> You can export a queue that points to a remote UNIX-style or Windows printer, thus providing access to UNIX or Windows printers from the Macintoshes on your network.

The preceding example sets the Netatalk printer user to `mac`. This could be an account for an individual who uses the computer, or it could be an account that's devoted to Netatalk printing. In the latter case, you might want to restrict access to the account by disabling the login password (you can do this by specifying an asterisk [*] in the password field in /etc/passwd or, if you're using shadow passwords, in /etc/shadow). In fact, you can use an existing non-login account, such as nobody.

Because Netatalk requires no authentication for printing, and because it uses only a single username for all printed jobs, accounting of print jobs through Netatalk is effectively impossible. You also cannot restrict access to a printer to certain groups or individuals. In a mixed-operating system (OS) network, however, you can give Macintosh clients access to a different set of printers than you give to Windows or UNIX/Linux clients.

After you've configured your printers, you can type **/etc/rc.d/init.d/atalk restart** to restart Netatalk, forcing it to reread its configuration files.

CAUTION

If you're already sharing files, be sure nobody is using a Netatalk volume before you restart Netatalk. The restart process disconnects all connected Netatalk users, so if people are doing work on shared files, those people might become annoyed at you for disconnecting them and causing them to lose their work!

You might want to check the last few lines of /var/log/messages after you've restarted Netatalk so that you can see its startup messages. You should see something similar to the following, indicating that papd has configured printers for sharing:

```
Aug 21 19:58:42 speaker papd[27276]: register epson360:LaserWriter@*
Aug 21 19:58:48 speaker papd[27276]: register epson:LaserWriter@*
Aug 21 19:58:54 speaker papd[27276]: register epson720:LaserWriter@*
Aug 21 19:59:00 speaker papd[27276]: register hp4000:LaserWriter@*
Aug 21 19:59:00 speaker papd[27276]: child 27301 for "epson" from 41201.173
Aug 21 19:59:01 speaker papd[27301]: lp_print queued
Aug 21 19:59:01 speaker papd[27276]: child 27301 done
```

If you see error messages from papd, or if you don't see the names of printers you thought you'd created, you should go back and check your configuration again. Lack of error messages doesn't necessarily indicate a lack of problems, though. For instance, papd doesn't report an error at this point if a queue name you specified doesn't exist.

> **NOTE**
>
> Netatalk services can take a while to start up. You should therefore wait a minute or so before checking the `/var/log/messages` file or trying to configure a Macintosh printer to use a shared Netatalk printer.

Configuring MacOS for Printing

After you've configured your Linux box to share printers via Netatalk, it's time to head over to a Macintosh and try to print. As far as the Macintosh is concerned, a Netatalk-shared printer looks just like any other networked printer, so if you're already familiar with setting up printers in MacOS, you shouldn't have any problems with this process. If you do have problems, it might be that your Netatalk configuration isn't correct, so you might want to review that side of the setup.

Installing a Driver and PPD File

The first step in setting up a printer is to copy the PPD file. Take the PPD file you obtained from the printer manufacturer, Adobe's Web site, or some other location and drag it into the `System Folder:Extensions:Printer Descriptions` folder on your Macintosh's boot drive. This is where the Macintosh looks for PPD files later in the process.

> **CAUTION**
>
> Be sure to use a *Macintosh* PPD file. The Macintosh doesn't recognize PPD files intended for PCs. If you transfer a PPD file via another system, you might need to deal with MacBinary, BinHex, or some other encoding format. A utility such as StuffIt can be helpful in decoding such formats.

All PostScript and Ghostscript-driven printers use the same driver in MacOS—the LaserWriter 8 driver. (Particularly old versions of MacOS may use older versions of the LaserWriter driver.) This driver is installed by default, so unless you've removed or disabled it, it should be available.

> **NOTE**
>
> These instructions describe setting up a printer in MacOS 8.6, so you may need to adjust them for older or newer versions. In particular, MacOS X will use a radically different design, which is in fact based on UNIX. Chances are that the details of configuring it for printing will differ from what appears here.

You configure the driver as follows:

1. Select Apple, Chooser to bring up the Chooser, shown in Figure 17.2.

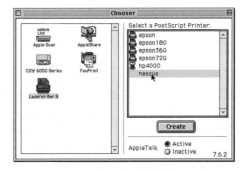

FIGURE 17.2

Apple's Chooser lets you mount networked hard disks or configure printers.

2. Click on the LaserWriter 8 icon. You should see the names of the printers you've defined in your Linux computer's `papd.conf` file appear, along with any printers that are shared by other computers or that exist standalone on the AppleTalk network. Figure 17.2 shows several printers that have already been configured. These existing printers have printer or spool icons next to their names. Figure 17.2 also shows one new one, known as `nessus`.

3. Click the name of the printer you want to define, and then click Create. If you've listed in your Linux `papd.conf` file a PPD file that's also available on the Macintosh, configuration should proceed automatically. You'll see a number of dialog boxes informing you of MacOS's progress in retrieving information about the printer and in setting it up, and then you'll be dropped back to the Chooser. At this point, you should see a new printer icon on your desktop for the new printer, and the Chooser should show an icon next to the printer name.

> **NOTE**
>
> If the Chooser can't find the appropriate PPD file to match the printer name pro-
> vided by Netatalk, the Macintosh will ask you to locate the PPD file manually. If you
> can't find the appropriate PPD file, cancel the operation and try to determine what
> went wrong before proceeding again.

After you've installed a printer, you can change its configuration by using the Chooser. Select
the printer you want to modify and click Setup (the button that's labeled Create in Figure 17.2
changes to Setup after the printer has been created). MacOS presents a dialog box that allows
you to select a new PPD file or go through the automatic setup routine again.

Printing Files

You print files to a Netatalk shared printer just as you do to any other Macintosh printer. In
most applications, the print command is File, Print, or Command+P. This command produces
a dialog box similar to the one shown in Figure 17.3.

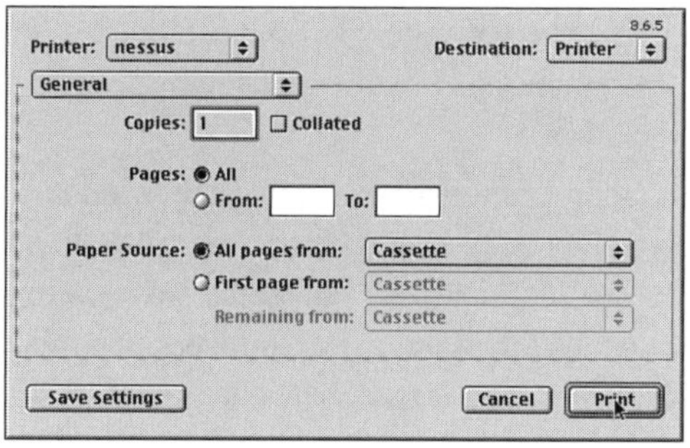

FIGURE 17.3
The Macintosh's print dialog box works the same for Netatalk printers as it does for other PostScript printers.

If you have several printers configured on your Macintosh, you might need to select the appropriate printer from the Printer button at the top left of the dialog box. You can also set the number of copies, page range, and other options. Some of these vary from one printer to another.

I recommend that you print a test document, such as a single page of text, to be sure that printing works correctly on your system. If you have problems, here are some pointers on overcoming some common difficulties:

- Check your Linux printer configuration first! If you had a problem printing in color, try printing in color from Linux to be sure Ghostscript is configured correctly. If fonts look blocky, print a PostScript text file from Linux to be sure the resolution is set correctly in Ghostscript. There's no point in debugging the Macintosh side of the connection if the problem lies in Linux's printer configuration.

- If you get a printout from a Ghostscript-driven printer that lists errors such as invalid-font or nostringval, it's possible that the PPD file on the Linux side is the problem. Check to be sure it uses Linux-style end-of-line characters and that it matches the PPD file you use on the Macintosh. You might also want to try another Linux PPD file.

- If your printer works and produces output that looks accurate but is of poor quality, you might need to select a new PPD file.

- If your printout cuts off the edges of text that's printed with small margins, you might need to try a new PPD file. The PPD file contains information on a printer's margins, and if this information is set incorrectly, the Macintosh might try to print into an area that your printer can't handle. This type of problem is particularly common with the bottom margins of inkjet printers. Alternatively, you can keep track of the margins that the printer requires and not set margins in your applications that would result in printing in unprintable areas of the page.

- If you can't print with landscape orientation, you might need to alter your Ghostscript setup. Specifically, you might need to include the -dFIXEDMEDIA option. You can set this option in the EXTRA_GS_OPTIONS field of your printer's postscript.cfg file, as described in Chapter 14. Unfortunately, this solution doesn't work with all printer drivers. It doesn't work with the stcolor driver, for instance, but it does work with uniprint.

In addition to the options available in the print dialog box, you can set print options *before* printing by selecting File, Page Setup. This option produces the page setup dialog box shown in Figure 17.4, in which you can set an assortment of options. If you're not already familiar with Macintosh PostScript printing features, you might want to explore the available options and see how they interact with your printer as shared from Linux.

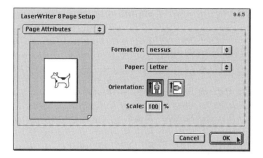

FIGURE 17.4
You can select File, Page Setup before printing to set the options available in this dialog box.

Printing from Linux to Macintosh Printers

The Netatalk package includes three utilities that are useful for printing from a Linux computer to a Macintosh printer. These utilities and their functions are as follows:

- pap—This utility sends a print job to a Macintosh printer. Because Macintosh printers are normally PostScript printers, the input should be PostScript. This program is analogous to lpr for printing to Linux or UNIX printers.

- psf—This program is a filter that's intended to be used in the if= line of a Linux /etc/printcap file to prepare data to be sent to a Macintosh printer.

- papstatus—This program reads the status of a Macintosh printer. It's analogous to the lpq command.

In addition to printing to printers that are shared by Macintoshes, or printers that connect directly to your Ethernet network and use the Macintosh's PAP communications options, you can use these tools to print to printers shared from another Linux or UNIX computer using Netatalk. This feature can be convenient if you're on a Macintosh-dominated network that uses a Linux netatalk printer server if you can't or don't want to configure that printer with native UNIX-style printing.

Using pap Directly

The general syntax for using pap is

```
pap [-c] -p printer_file
```

The parameters to the pap command include:

- -c—Causes pap to lie to the printer, claiming that the Linux box has been waiting for service forever, hence moving your job to the front of the queue. (-c stands for *cut*, as in *cut into line*.) Don't abuse this option, or your co-workers might become annoyed!

- -p *printer*—Tells pap to which printer you want to print.

- *file*—You conclude the command with the name of the file you want to print.

As an example, here's a command to print the file testfile.ps on the printer lw630:

```
pap -p lw630 testfile.ps
```

You can also use pap in place of lpr in many applications. For instance, Figure 17.5 demonstrates using pap to print a graphic directly from xv. Some applications assume that you'll be using lpr, but most let you change the print command in some way. Using pap directly can therefore be quite convenient, especially if you need to print to Macintosh printers only occasionally and from programs that make it easy to use pap rather than lpr. If you administer a Linux computer on a network that contains a frequently changing stable of Macintosh printers, using pap can reduce your administrative duties, too, since you won't need to adjust your /etc/printcap file to make the ever-changing Macintosh printers available to your Linux users.

FIGURE 17.5
Many Linux programs let you select the spooling command at print time, which makes using pap *particularly easy.*

Queuing Jobs by Using psf

The psf program behaves differently depending on the filename with which it's called. This feature can be useful if there are several links to the program, which there are in the /usr/lib/atalk/filters directory. The link you're most likely to need is ifpap, which lets the psf program function as a filter for a Linux /etc/printcap queue definition. An example of such a definition is

```
hp4000:\
        :sd=/var/spool/lpd/hp4000:\
        :mx#0:\
        :sh:\
        :lp=/dev/null:\
        :if=/usr/lib/atalk/filters/ifpap:
```

In order to use this definition, you also need to create a file in the /var/spool/lpd/hp4000 directory called .paprc. This file contains only a single line with the name of the PAP printer to which you want to print, such as hp4000.

After you've created an /etc/printcap entry and .paprc file, you can print to the AppleTalk printer as if it were an ordinary Linux/UNIX printer. Because you're using psf as a filter, though, you are restricted to the types of files that psf recognizes—mainly PostScript and raw ASCII. Some alternate links to psf might be useful in expanding this range, in conjunction with filter entries in /etc/printcap. For instance, you can insert these lines before the if= line to filter TeX DVI and troff files, respectively:

```
:tf=/usr/lib/filters/tfpap:\
:df=/usr/lib/filters/dfpap:\
```

If you want the filter to reverse the page ordering of files, you can call the filter with rev in the name, as in ifpaprev rather than ifpap. This can be useful if your printer outputs jobs face up, because the end result is a printout in forward order—the last page printed is the first one of the job, and it goes on top of the output stack.

If you set up a print queue with psf, you can export that queue again using UNIX-style printer sharing or Samba. This can be useful for making Macintosh printers accessible to Windows or UNIX/Linux clients that do not themselves have Netatalk or similar Macintosh printer-sharing software.

Checking Printers by Using `papstatus`

The papstatus utility gives some minimal information about the status of a printer queue. If you try this command on a Netatalk queue, for instance, you're likely to receive the message *queuename* is ready and printing. If the printer doesn't exist on the AppleTalk network, you get the message NBP lookup failed. You can therefore use this utility to check that a printer's server (or the printer itself, in the case of printers that connect directly to the network) is up and running. As with the pap command, you use the -p parameter to specify the printer's name, as in papstatus -p hp4000.

Summary

Netatalk provides a method of sharing Linux printer queues with Macintoshes or with other OSs that use AppleTalk-style printing. You must explicitly create an export for each queue you want to share, and you must configure each share with an appropriate PPD file on both the server and the client. Because of Linux's ability to print PostScript to non-PostScript printers, using a Linux print server for a Macintosh network can be a very cost-effective means of sharing inexpensive non-PostScript printers with Macintoshes. Similarly, you can share Linux printer queues that themselves print to printers on non-Macintosh networks, such as Windows shared printers.

Netatalk also comes with utilities that let you print from Linux to Macintosh printers. You can use pap as a replacement for the Linux lpr command, or you can create a conventional Linux printer queue and use psf as the queue's filter. Either way, your Linux computer gains access to networked Macintosh printers. When using a conventional Linux queue, you can export these printers, making them available via Samba to Windows computers or via lpd-style sharing to other Linux or UNIX machines.

Remote Access

PART

V

IN THIS PART

Using `ssh` or `telnet` to Log On Remotely

IN THIS CHAPTER

For years UNIX has been a multitasking, multiuser operating system (OS). In the 1970s and 1980s, universities used large UNIX mainframes (often less powerful than today's desktops) to provide dozens or even hundreds of students and faculty members with simultaneous computing resources. Corporations used UNIX mainframes in much the same way, allowing many employees to work at once on a single computer. Of course, these dozens and hundreds of users weren't crowded into a single room staring at a single computer screen; this multiuser aspect of UNIX was implemented with *terminals*—inexpensive hardware consisting of a keyboard, computer monitor, and very little else. Terminals themselves are *dumb*, meaning that they don't contribute to the computational tasks for which computers are useful. Each UNIX mainframe could accommodate hundreds or even thousands of terminals, which could be scattered around a building or campus.

Over the years, as the Internet grew and personal computers came onto the scene, it became possible to use PCs as terminals for UNIX computers, using programs known as *terminal emulators*. It also became possible to access UNIX computers from any networked computer, using a program known as `telnet` or some other program that implemented `telnet`'s protocols.

Security concerns have brought on variants on the `telnet` model. These variants encrypt data—including passwords—so that it can't be easily interpreted if intercepted. One popular encryption system is known as SSH. In its most basic form, the `ssh` client program functions much like `telnet`, but `ssh` is safer to use across any but the smallest and most secure intranets.

Because Linux is modeled after UNIX, Linux can accept remote logins by using `telnet`, `ssh`, and other tools. This capability can be extremely convenient at times—but it also opens your Linux computer to certain risks, as crackers can use these same tools to gain unauthorized entry to your system.

Why Access Programs Remotely?

If you've not used a mainframe computer before, you might not know why you'd want to access a computer remotely. The answer, in brief, is simple: *To use your computer!* With the exception of programs such as graphics utilities or certain games, you can access any non-X program from a remote system, using nothing more than a text-mode terminal program. The tools you can use remotely include text editors, programming languages, email programs, and even text-mode Web browsers. With appropriate software on the system that's local to you, you can even run X programs remotely (as discussed in Chapter 19, "Using VNC or an X Server to Run X Window Programs Remotely").

Computer Access from Your Intranet

If you're reading this book, you presumably have an intranet serving your home or office. In such a situation, you might find that access to your Linux computer from other systems on your intranet is extremely convenient. For instance, you can use this type of access in a number of ways:

- Access from a short distance—If your Linux server is located in one room but you're in another room and have access to another computer on the network, you can use the computer that's local to you to perform work on the Linux computer. This work could be almost anything you would normally do with the Linux computer, but you needn't leave your present location to do it.

- Multiuser access—Two or more people can use the same computer from the same room or different rooms. If your site uses pine on the Linux server for mail reading, several users can read mail simultaneously in this way—while others compile programs, perform statistical tests on data, and write documents. In effect, your Linux computer becomes like the UNIX mainframes of old.

- Access from a specific computer—It's sometimes desirable to access your Linux computer from another machine. For instance, suppose you're using a Mac or Windows word processor to write a document, and you need to include a few lines from a document or program output accessible from Linux. You can open a terminal emulator, log on to the Linux computer, display the text, and then use the client OS's cut-and-paste features to copy the data you want into the word processor document. You might also use this feature to avoid turning on the computer monitor of the Linux machine or to use a better keyboard or monitor, if the Linux computer's hardware is deficient in this respect.

Every network is different, of course, and you might have unique needs. If you ever find yourself thinking, "I wish I could do *x* from this Windows machine," where *x* is some task you normally do with Linux, then a remote login might be just what you need.

Computer Access from Remote Sites

Access from remote sites is extremely appealing in many situations, such as the following:

- Access to work from home—Suppose you're expecting an important email at work at a time when you're home. Remote access to a Linux computer that functions as an email server can allow you to read email from home. Similarly, remote access would be handy if you forget an important file that was on a Linux server and that you intended to work on at home the next day while trapped waiting for the cable installer to come.

- Access to home from work—If you have a small home intranet and an always-on Internet connection, you can gain access to your home system from work. I'm always forgetting to transfer files from one location to another, so such access can be quite useful to me.

- Access when travelling—If you're at a conference or visiting colleagues in another city, you need not be cut off from your usual computing resources. You can use remote access to check email, demonstrate software or data to colleagues, or otherwise use your system from across town or across the globe.

- Access for colleagues—You might occasionally want to give distant colleagues access to your computers, say to help in a collaborative effort. Creating accounts for these people and allowing them to use your system remotely can greatly facilitate your collaboration.

CAUTION

One of the major drawbacks to remote access is that you might tend to drag your work along with you wherever you go. A vacation is no longer a vacation if you spend your time on the beach scrunched over a laptop with a cellular modem link to a national ISP, logged on to your office's computer doing work. It's best to set limits on your use of remote services, and stick to them.

The Terminal Session

When you use your Linux computer remotely, you do so with an old-fashioned hardware terminal or with some variety of terminal program. I therefore refer to a single session of such activity as a *terminal session*. Many of the details of how you operate in a terminal session vary depending on the software you're using (assuming that you're using a computer as a remote access device, and not a dumb terminal). Many other aspects are the same, no matter what access method you choose.

Using Terminal Programs

Terminal programs vary substantially in the complexity of their user interfaces and in the features they support. At the simplest end are programs such as the Linux and UNIX `telnet` command, which open a connection to a remote computer in an existing xterm window or by taking over a text-mode login screen. When a connection is established, you normally don't interact with the local `telnet` program, though you can by typing Ctrl+]. Figure 18.1 shows a `telnet` session from one Linux computer to another, and the built-in `telnet` help describing the commands available after you press Ctrl+].

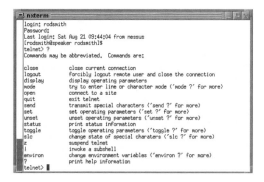

FIGURE 18.1

A telnet *session run in a Linux xterm window uses the fonts and color selection of the host window.*

In Linux, you can use the ssh program to access remote computers much the way you use telnet, but ssh is much more secure because it encrypts data—including your password. ssh is described in more detail later in this chapter, in the section "Using ssh for Security."

OSs other than Linux include telnet programs, although they're sometimes more sophisticated than the basic Linux telnet. Figure 18.2 shows Windows 98's telnet program, which includes a menu bar for access to commands to cut and paste text, select the font, and so on. The Windows telnet program doesn't support Ctrl+] for commands; instead, you use its menu bar commands and dialog boxes to set options via dialog boxes, two of which appear in Figure 18.2.

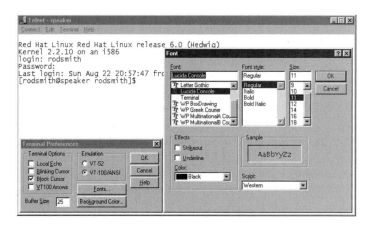

FIGURE 18.2

The Windows telnet *program uses menus and dialog boxes for configuration.*

In addition to standard programs that come with OSs, many third-party programs are available to provide remote access. Many of these programs have a heritage as text-mode dialup terminal programs, which were used to connect with bulletin board systems and mainframes before Point-to-Point Protocol (PPP) connections became common. They've adapted to the times by incorporating the ability to use Telnet, secure shell (SSH), or other protocols instead of, or in addition to, the modem. These programs typically offer many more features than do an OS's standard `telnet` program, such as logging features, the ability to process a wide variety of text control codes (also known as *terminal emulations*), and so on. Figure 18.3 shows one of these programs, Zap-O-Comm (ZOC), connected to a Linux system via the Telnet protocol.

FIGURE 18.3

ZOC and other third-party terminal programs provide expanded features compared to an OS's basic `telnet` *program.*

Table 18.1 lists a number of common terminal programs for several operating systems. You can find these programs by searching on appropriate file archive sites, such as `http://www.cnet.com` or `ftp://ftp.cdrom.com`. Each program supports its own unique set of features, so you might need to try several programs if you're looking for one that meets specific requirements.

TABLE **18.1**   Common Telnet-Capable Terminal Programs

Operating System	*Available Programs*
UNIX/Linux	`telnet`
Microsoft Windows 3.x	Trumptel Telnet, Wintel, Ewan
Microsoft Windows 9x/NT	`telnet`, ZOC, NetTerm, Zmud, WinTel32, Yawtelnet, mTelnet, Teraterm Pro
OS/2	`telnet`, ZOC, mTelnet
Macintosh	NCSA Telnet (largely obsolete), Nifty Telnet, Comet, Better Telnet

Logging In Remotely

Depending on the client software and protocols you use to log in remotely, you'll probably be asked to authenticate yourself at some time—that is, you'll get a prompt for your username and password. Figures 18.2 and 18.3 show typical Linux login prompts when you use the Telnet protocol, for instance. If you use a text-mode login to your Linux computer, these prompts should look familiar because they're the same ones that Linux uses for console access.

Some remote login procedures, such as the `rlogin` program, don't require a username or password; instead, they rely on the concept of the *trusted host*. In this model, the server OS maintains a list of clients that it *trusts* to do an adequate job of authentication. If a client requests a resource, such as printer access or a remote login, the server grants that request on the basis of the client's name alone. The server maintains a list of trusted clients in the file `/etc/hosts.equiv`. Individuals on a Linux server can also maintain their own list of trusted hosts for `rlogin` purposes in the file `~/.rhosts`.

In general, allowing trusted-host access is a risky proposition these days. In part this is because a security breach on a trusted remote system can then translate into a security breach on the server, with very little additional effort on the cracker's part. In part the risk is because crackers can often reconfigure their systems to appear to be another machine, thus gaining access without knowing an individual's password. If you don't need trusted host access, I recommend that you remove the `/etc/hosts.equiv` file and comment out the `login` and `shell` lines in `/etc/inetd.conf`.

> **NOTE**
>
> UNIX-style remote printing also functions on a trusted host model, but you can use a separate file, `/etc/hosts.lpd`, to provide a list of trusted print clients. Because you can separately authenticate print clients in this way, you minimize the risk; short of a bug or some additional misconfiguration, a cracker can't use printer access to do more than waste some of your printing supplies.

Some access methods require that you enter authentication in the client program. For instance, Figure 18.4 shows ZOC's method of initiating an SSH connection. You enter the username and password locally, and ZOC handles the SSH connection and sends that information in an encrypted form.

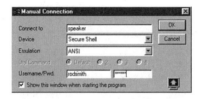

FIGURE 18.4

Depending upon the Device selection, ZOC enables or disables other fields to allow or disallow entry of information such as your username and password.

> **NOTE**
>
> Most programs that ask for passwords either don't echo them or replace the password characters with asterisks or bullets to protect the password from snooping by passersby.

When you use `ssh` from Linux, the program doesn't require a username because `ssh` acquires that information from your local login name; but the program does require a password or passphrase in most configurations. You can configure `ssh` to use a number of authentication methods, though, each of which presents somewhat different password options.

As a security precaution, Red Hat Linux 6.0 comes configured to prevent root logins via Telnet. This configuration makes a cracker's job more difficult. For instance, suppose that a cracker somehow obtains the root password for your computer. To break in using telnet, the cracker would still require an ordinary user's password because telnetd refuses connects for root. (The same isn't true of all other connection methods; for instance, by default sshd allows root logins.) If you want to perform root operations remotely, then, you need to log in as an ordinary user and run su to obtain root privileges.

> **TIP**
>
> If you use SSH for remote logins, I *strongly* encourage you to disallow root logins by SSH. You can do so by editing the /etc/ssh/sshd_config file. Add the line DenyUsers root to that file. (You might want to ensure that DenyUsers isn't already in use. If it is, you can add root to the list of users already denied.)

Capabilities of a Terminal Session

In general, you can do anything from a terminal session that you can do in an xterm or at a text-mode local login. There are some exceptions, though:

- Sound—You can use audio software remotely; however, the sounds play on the speakers directly connected to the Linux computer. This could be disconcerting or annoying to a local user, so you might want to consider whether you really need a login sound if you'll be using the computer remotely with any frequency.

- Video—Most non-X Linux programs use plain text. A few, though, like some games and graphics viewers, use the computer's VGA hardware to display images. You can't use such programs remotely—or, more precisely, you can start them, but you don't see any useful output from them.

- Hardware access—If somebody local to the computer has inserted a floppy, CD-ROM, Zip disk, or similar device in the computer, you can access this device remotely. Unless you possess telekinetic powers, however, you can't insert a disk or tape remotely. If you have the need to access a variety of such devices on a regular basis, a changer may do the trick. *Changers* are variant versions of conventional devices that allow you to access several CDs, tapes, or other media by using one piece of hardware. Alternatively, you could use a large hard disk to store image files of the media in question, and mount them by using Linux's loopback device.

- X Window System—You can't access X-based programs from a terminal program alone. You can, however, run an X server locally to access X programs run on a remote Linux system. This topic is covered in Chapter 19.

You might also encounter problems and limitations depending on the specific program you use remotely. For instance, many Linux programs can use color to improve their displays. Even the lowly ls program can use this feature to display program files in one color, directories in another, and ordinary text files in a third. If your terminal program isn't capable of displaying color, you can't see these colors. Similarly, some programs use more or less sophisticated means of controlling cursor positioning and other text-formatting tasks, and some combinations of server-side application programs and client-side terminal programs don't work very well together.

Linux uses a special environment variable to communicate to programs what terminal type is in use. Normally, Linux queries the terminal program at the time of login to determine how to set this environment variable. Occasionally you might be asked to set it yourself when you log in remotely. To find out what you're using now, type **env ¦ grep TERM** at an xterm, text-mode login, or network login. You should see a response such as TERM=vt220 or TERM=ANSI. Linux uses entries in the /etc/termcap file to determine what features each terminal type supports and how to activate them. Because different terminal programs may implement these features with varying degrees of fidelity, you might find that one terminal program works best when set to one terminal emulation and another works best with another emulation, even though both programs claim to support both emulations. You have to experiment to find what works best for you.

Advantages of `ssh` and `telnet`

As mentioned previously, Linux provides several means of remote login. The two that are discussed in most detail in this chapter are SSH and Telnet. As mentioned earlier, the rlogin program and associated protocol can be convenient in some cases, but they are quite insecure, so I recommend against using them except on small networks that are isolated from the Internet as a whole.

Using `telnet` for Convenience

The Telnet protocol is extremely popular and convenient. Because most modern OSs come with a telnet implementation, you can use it from almost any computer that's connected to the Internet to log on to any computer that has a Telnet daemon running to accept connections. This level of ubiquity is telnet's greatest strength.

If you want to configure your Linux computer to accept Telnet connections, you should check your /etc/inetd.conf file to ensure that it contains a line similar to the following:

```
telnet  stream  tcp    nowait  root    /usr/sbin/tcpd  in.telnetd
```

This line causes inetd (p. xxx) to launch /usr/sbin/tcpd, which in turn calls in.telnetd whenever inetd detects an attempt to access port 23, which is the port assigned to the Telnet protocol. If this line is commented out with a pound sign (#) at the start of the line, Linux doesn't respond to Telnet requests. Red Hat Linux 6.0 ships with the Telnet daemon enabled by default, so unless you've changed /etc/inetd.conf already, you need to change this file only if you want to *disable* incoming Telnet connections.

To start a Telnet connection from a remote system, you should consult the documentation for your terminal program. For Linux, you type **telnet**, followed by the name of the system to which you want to connect, as in the following:

```
telnet gingko.biloba.com
```

You can use a numeric IP address rather than a machine name. You can also add a port address if the server uses a nonstandard port to listen for Telnet connections. Here's an example:

```
telnet gingko.biloba.com 7203
```

This command attempts to connect to a Telnet server that listens on port 7203, rather than the standard port 23.

> **CAUTION**
>
> You might think that by configuring a system to accept Telnet connections on a nonstandard port, you'd improve security. To some extent this might be true, but crackers often use port scanning software that tries to connect to every possible port, and so using a nonstandard port turns back only the most casual of break-in attempts. A better security option is to use SSH for logins, as discussed in the following section.

Using ssh for Security

The principal disadvantage of Telnet is that it's an insecure protocol. When you use Telnet, you transmit all your data—including your username and password—in *cleartext* (p. 72), meaning that the data are easily accessible to any system through which they pass, as well as on any computer connected to, at the least, the local and remote networks. If you use telnet only locally, your passwords and other transactions are vulnerable only to local snooping, but if you use it over the Internet as a whole, you make your passwords available to many others.

Understanding SSH Basics

The SSH protocol is designed to address this concern. If you use SSH instead of Telnet, all the data that passes between two computers is encrypted so that most crackers can't read it. (National security organizations have the means to break some encryption algorithms available to individuals, but even for the likes of the NSA or the CIA, this process takes a while.) Most importantly, SSH encrypts usernames and passwords, so you don't reveal this critical information when you log in. How does this trick work? One computer provides the other with information needed to encode data, but this encoding key is not sufficient to decode the data after it's encoded. To decode the data, a private key is required, and that key is never transmitted.

How do you use SSH? First, you must obtain it. Unfortunately, the ssh package isn't included with Red Hat 6.0, for two reasons:

- U.S. law forbids the export of "munitions" without a proper license. Oddly enough, many encryption algorithms, including those used by SSH, are considered munitions by the U.S. government. Therefore, Red Hat can't place ssh on its CD-ROMs. Similarly, it's illegal to possess encryption technology in some countries, such as France and Russia, without a permit.

> **NOTE**
>
> As this book goes to press, the Clinton administration has announced its intention to change the classification of encryption technology so that it's no longer considered a munition. This change, once enacted, could make encryption programs easier to distribute and therefore more convenient to use.

- Some of the algorithms used by SSH—namely international data encryption algorithm (IDEA) and RSA (named after its inventors, Rivest, Shamir, and Adleman)—are claimed as patented by certain firms in the United States and some other countries. Therefore, in the United States you can only legally use SSH with encryption libraries that have been approved by the owners of these patents. Not all SSH libraries are so approved. These patents will expire in 2000, so this problem will soon go away.

There are two versions of SSH in common use, versions 1.*x* and 2.*x*. Unfortunately, the two are incompatible with each other, but you can configure a 2.*x* SSH server to pass 1.*x* SSH connection requests to a 1.*x* server. Version 1.*x* is the more common variety, particularly in the United States.

Using SSH—The Linux Side

To obtain Linux ssh programs, you need to locate an appropriate distribution site. Because of
U.S. munitions export laws, most such sites are located outside the United States. You can
search for RPMs of ssh software at http://rufus.w3.org/linux/RPM/. You need at least a
basic ssh package. To use a remote SSH program to log on to your Linux computer, you might
also need an ssh-server package. To use ssh locally to log on to a remote SSH-enabled
server, you might need an ssh-clients package. (I say *might* here because different ssh RPMs
can be built in different ways to include different functionality.) In general, the packages
intended for use within the United States have package names that end with *us*, whereas those
intended for international use have package names that end in *i*.

After you've installed ssh and ssh-server, you can start the sshd server by typing
/etc/rc.d/init.d/sshd start. The server also activates itself when you restart your computer.
Alternatively, you can move the /etc/rc.d/init.d/sshd script to another directory and start
sshd via inetd by creating an appropriate entry in /etc/inetd.conf, such as the following:

```
ssh    stream  tcp  nowait  root  /usr/sbin/sshd  -i
```

> **NOTE**
>
> The -i parameter tells sshd that it's running from inetd. The sshd daemon normally
> expects to run continuously, and on a slow machine this might be a practical neces-
> sity because sshd needs to perform some computationally intensive operations at
> startup, which can slow an SSH login attempt if sshd is run from inetd.

18

USING ssh OR
telnet TO LOG
ON REMOTELY

To connect to a remote computer by using ssh, type **ssh** *remotename*, where *remotename* is
the name or IP address of the remote computer. The first time you connect to a host, you might
be told that the host key isn't in the list of known hosts. Respond that you *do* want to continue
connecting. The ssh program asks for your password, but not your username, which it obtains
from your local login name. (If you want to connect remotely as another user, use the -l parameter to specify a remote login name.) When you're connected, you can use an ssh login just
as you would a telnet login, but the computers transparently encrypt all data transmitted, so
it's not easily decoded by snooping parties. In addition, processes started from within an ssh
login are also normally encrypted. For instance, if you start an X program, as described in
Chapter 19, the data transfers associated with that program are encrypted. In fact, SSH can be
used to transfer files, perform backups, and encrypt other network protocols. Type **man ssh** or
check the following URLs for more information:

- http://www.dreamwvr.com/ssh/ssh-faq.html
- http://www.ssh.fi/

Using SSH from Non-Linux OSs

To use SSH to connect to a Linux computer from a non-Linux computer, you need a terminal program that supports SSH on the client OS. This support is becoming increasingly common. Here are a few pointers to available software:

- MindTerm—This is a Java-based SSH client that should run on any platform with adequate Java support. See `http://www.mindbright.se/mindterm` for more information.

- ZOC—This shareware Windows and OS/2 terminal program has SSH support, but in the form of a "non-approved" library, so it might not be legal to use this software in the United States until the relevant software patents expire. The SSH library is therefore a separate download for the program. (You can get as far as the Manual Connection dialog box shown in Figure 18.4 without this library, but not much further.) See `http://www.emtec.com/zoc/` for more information.

- Teraterm Pro—This freeware Windows terminal program (`http://hp.vector.co.jp/authors/VA002416/teraterm.html`) can be used with an SSH module (`http://www.zip.com.au/~roca/ttssh.html`) to provide SSH logins. You must launch the SSH module rather than Teraterm Pro itself to gain access to SSH capabilities.

- F-Secure SSH—This commercial program provides SSH capabilities to Windows, Macintosh, and Linux. See `http://www.datafellows.com/products/cryptography/fsshtt.htm` for more information.

The details of using SSH vary substantially from one program to another, so check your documentation for further information. Some of these programs support both SSH and Telnet protocols (and sometimes others, as well), so you should check to be sure that your program is set to use SSH. If in doubt, consider the method you use to log in. Does it look the same as it does when you use Telnet? If so, it probably *is* Telnet. Some programs can be programmed to automatically log in to remote computers when using Telnet, though, so a lack of a traditional `login:` prompt isn't necessarily evidence that you're using SSH.

Telnet and SSH Security Considerations

Whether you use Telnet or SSH protocols, there are certain security considerations when you access your computer remotely. For that matter, some of these are concerns when you're sitting at your computer's terminal. At the very least, you should be aware of these concerns. You might want to take steps to reduce the severity of the problems that these matters represent by educating your users or by using software to enforce more secure behavior.

Terminals Left Unattended

People often find it inconvenient to log out when they want to run some quick errand, such as collecting a printout or grabbing a snack. Whenever a terminal is left unattended for more than a few seconds, though, there's a chance that somebody could sit down and perform an unfriendly act. In the case of ordinary user accounts, the unwelcome guest isn't likely to be able to do anything that's directly destructive to the system as a whole, but that's not to say damage couldn't be done. For instance, such an individual could send inflammatory email, perhaps to large numbers of external sites. You might want to remind your users that *their* names will be on such emails. Pranks like this have been known to consume system resources for days and effectively block use of the sender's email address forever because of the flurry of angry responses.

Assuming that you're the system administrator, though, the biggest danger from unattended terminals isn't from your users—it's from *you!* When you're performing administrative tasks, you should *never, ever,* even for two seconds, leave your computer unattended. A malicious and knowledgeable passerby could easily wreak serious havoc in just a few seconds, given root access. Skeptical? Consider this command:

```
rm -Rf /
```

This command will wipe out all files on a Linux system, without prompting. I just timed myself; it took me two seconds to type this command. (I did it in a Macintosh word processor, of course—I took *no* chances with this command!)

An intruder after more subtle results would require a bit longer to set up any number of methods of breaking in to the system at a later date, but not by much. For instance, creating a set user ID (SUID; often used to provide a program with root privileges even when run by an ordinary user) version of a shell prompt in some out-of-the-way directory and (if necessary) creating an account with which to access that shell would take perhaps 15 or 20 seconds for a prepared cracker.

So, repeat to yourself, at least 50 times each day:

> ***I will not leave my root login unattended.***

Onlookers Spotting Passwords

Although not as serious a problem as an unattended terminal, the login process itself poses some risks. Specifically, a passerby might be able to decipher a password by watching a person type it in. This is particularly true if the victim is a slow typist, and especially if the victim can't remember the password and so keeps it written down. There are several lines of defense against "shoulder surfing," as this practice is sometimes called:

- Education—Make your users aware of the risk. Ideally, you shouldn't try to lay down strictures against practices like writing down passwords, at least not without explaining their reasons. It's important that your users understand why a practice is risky if they're to be motivated to take preventive actions.

- Adequate password selection—Good passwords are difficult to guess. Shoulder surfing is much less likely to succeed if the user types a password that's odd in some way. For instance, if somebody has the password `doggie`, a shoulder surfer could probably guess the password even if he or she missed a few letters. Change `doggie` to `do3G9giE`, however, and it becomes much more secure, both because of the intervening numbers and because of the mixed case in the alphabetic characters. Better still is `do3GMOp8`, because this password mixes two unrelated words, as well as inserting numbers and mixing letter case. (Of course, these examples will all probably make their way into crackers' databases, so don't use these specific passwords.) Using a single word or minor variant on it as a password is also a poor practice because such passwords are easily guessed by password-cracking programs, as discussed in Chapter 24. On the other hand, you shouldn't make your passwords *too* bizarre, or they'll be hard to remember. Especially if you impose passwords on your users, they're likely to write down passwords that are too complex, which can be a serious security problem.

- Changing passwords—A shoulder surfer might not get a password on the first try. If the surfer gets another chance the next day, though, his or her odds of breaking in go up. If the would-be victim's password has changed in that time, though, the shoulder surfer is again at a disadvantage. Therefore, changing passwords frequently is an important deterrent. When you set up your users' accounts, you can configure them to require a password change at a regular interval. Figure 18.5 shows the relevant screen from `linuxconf`; set the Must change after # days field to some reasonable value, such as 30 for an enforced monthly change (the default value provides an effectively unlimited account duration).

- Physical security—If every computer is in a locked room, and individuals log on only when they are alone in the room, a shoulder surfer has no chance, except perhaps by using a telescope from the building across the street. A locked-room arrangement isn't always practical, but you might be able to take less drastic steps to get the same effect. For instance, in a room with many terminals, as are common on college campuses and corporate "cubicle farms," you can place dividers between the computers so that one person's keyboard isn't visible from another person's chair. A computer that faces a glass wall, so that an individual in the hallway can peer through the glass and watch a keyboard, isn't the most secure arrangement. Frosting the glass could help security in this case.

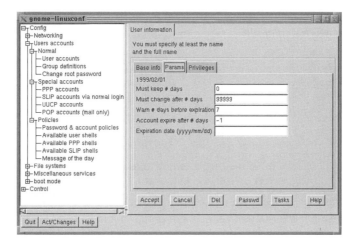

FIGURE 18.5
You can set many aspects of account lifetime and password change requirements when you create an account, or change these details later.

As with unattended computers, you should be especially cautious when entering the root password. A shoulder surfer who's nabbed that password has struck gold, and the unfortunate afflicted system is now completely insecure. Of course, if the system is set up to disallow root logins via Telnet or SSH, the would-be attacker will still need an ordinary user account on the target system—but if he or she was in a position to nab the password from a keyboard, chances are good that this isn't a problem for the attacker.

Password Sniffing

One of the primary reasons for using SSH rather than Telnet to log in remotely is to avoid the possibility of an attacker sniffing a password from the networking hardware, either locally or on intermediate machines. Whereas a shoulder surfer must be physically present and therefore at least potentially detectable, a packet sniffer can be quite invisible, particularly if the sniffer resides on a network between you and the host you intend to use. The primary defense against this possibility is to use a secure login method, such as SSH. One additional precaution is to limit your use of the root account from anything but the console (the keyboard and monitor attached directly to the Linux computer). You should be especially wary of using su to gain root access when you're logged on using telnet, rlogin, or some other insecure method.

One variant of electronic password sniffing is the fake login prompt. This trick is especially common in environments that use dumb terminals. The idea is that a would-be attacker leaves a program running that simulates the login prompt normally seen on the terminal. In fact, the program stores the username and password, fakes a login failure, and quits, dumping the user back to the real login. The unsuspecting user believes that he or she typed an incorrect password and tries again. More sophisticated variants of this scheme can be run on computers that have been partially or completely compromised already, by replacing the actual login programs. One defense against this practice is to advise your users to change their passwords if they ever mistype them at login. Users should also use different passwords on different systems because crackers often use the passwords stolen from one system in an effort to gain entry to another one.

Summary

A Linux computer's capacity to be used from remote locations is one of its greatest strengths. Protocols such as Telnet and SSH are extremely useful in giving your users access to a single Linux computer from across the room or from across the world. Remote access is, however, also a potential entry point for unwanted visitors, so you should be aware of the security implications of running `sshd` or, especially, `telnetd` on your Linux computer. Using SSH rather than Telnet for remote logins and following sensible password procedures can go a long way toward keeping your system from falling into the wrong hands.

Using VNC or an X Server to Run X Window Programs Remotely

IN THIS CHAPTER

Chapter 18, "Using `ssh` or `telnet` to Log On Remotely," describes how to access your Linux computer remotely by using text-based login tools. This ability can be extremely useful in many situations, but it's often not enough. If you need to access graphical user interface (GUI) programs such as the GIMP, WordPerfect, or `xfig`, you need remote access to the X Window System. Fortunately, X was designed with this sort of situation in mind—X is a *networking* GUI environment. Although this design has its downside (it reduces X's speed, for instance), it greatly increases Linux's flexibility.

This chapter covers two methods of remote GUI access. One is to use an X server on the machine that's local to you. This approach places the computational burden of displaying information on the machine you're using. In fact, the computer whose programs you're running need not even be running X itself. This is the traditional X-based remote access method. The second method is to use a program called *Virtual Network Computing (VNC)*. With VNC, the system that hosts the programs you're running has a special X server that displays information remotely. A relatively simple client program runs on the system at which you sit. Each approach has advantages and disadvantages, as you'll learn in this chapter.

Uses for Remote X Access

Remote X access is useful for many of the same reasons that remote text-based access is useful, but with some twists and additions. The following are some examples:

- Access from a distance—Whether you're in the next room or the next state, you might simply need to run a program when you're in one location by using a computer in another.

- Multiuser access—Two or more people can run X-based programs on a single Linux computer.

- Access from a specific computer—You might want to use a certain computer to run software, even when it's in the same room as the Linux computer. For instance, you might have a Macintosh or Windows machine with a large 21-inch monitor, compared to the flickery five-year-old 15-inch monitor on the Linux computer. X-based programs often work best on larger monitors—or more precisely, on monitors with high resolutions. I generally recommend a minimum 1024×768 resolution for X work.

- Access for colleagues—As with text-based logins, you can give colleagues at remote locations access to your computer through X.

- The headless workstation—You can run a Linux computer that doesn't have its own monitor by using X and an X server on a computer that *does* have a monitor. This can be a great way to reduce clutter in a crowded office.

You might have other reasons to use X's networking features. The flexibility of X's design allows you to use remote access in ways that might be important to you but that might not be easy for others (such as X's designers) to predict.

Using an X Server

In X parlance, the *server* handles the display of information for the *client*, which is an application program of some variety. When you aren't sitting at the console, this results in some potentially confusing terminology because the server is the system at which you're sitting, whereas the client is the computer whose resources you want to access. This terminology is exactly backward from what most people expect because the server is usually the distant machine with the resources you want to use. To understand this terminology, though, you should look at it from the point of view of the application program. When you use a word processor on a Macintosh and want to save a file to a distant system, the word processor must access the resources on that distant system. When you use an X-based Linux word processor in a networked environment, though, the word processor must make requests of distant resources merely to display your document—from the *program's* point of view, the display at which you're staring really *is* a server. The same is true when you use a standalone Linux system, except that X runs on the same system as the application program. In this case, you still run an X server program, but it happens to run on the same computer as the applications.

Examples of X Server Software

Many programs exist for handling X displays on various operating systems. The following are some examples:

- XFree86—XFree86 comes with all major Linux distributions, and is capable of handling the display of applications from a distant system. You can therefore use one Linux computer as a remote X display for another Linux computer. XFree86 is also available on assorted non-Linux platforms, including many UNIX flavors and OS/2. You can find out more from the XFree86 Web site, `http://www.xfree86.org`.

- Metro-X—This is a commercial X server for Linux and various UNIX flavors. It replaces the server component of XFree86. In some cases Metro-X may run faster than XFree86 or support hardware that XFree86 doesn't support. In other cases XFree86 is the superior product. For more information, check out `http://www.metrolink.com`.

- Accelerated-X—Accelerated-X is another commercial X server for Linux, FreeBSD, and Solaris. Similar comments apply to Accelerated-X as apply to Metro-X. You can find more information at `http://www.xig.com`.

> **TIP**
>
> In general, the commercial Linux X servers provide support for newer hardware than does XFree86, for a variety of reasons. For older hardware, there's usually less reason to use a commercial server. Each of these three systems, though, has its own strengths, so you might want to check their Web sites just to see what you are—and aren't—missing.

- X servers for UNIX—Most commercial UNIXes come with their own X servers. Such systems should not have difficulty running Linux programs remotely.
- MI/X—This is an inexpensive X server for Windows and MacOS. You can obtain a 15-day sample version of the program to see if it suits your needs. For more information, see http://www.microimages.com/mix for the Windows version, or http://www.microimages.com/freestuf/mix/macindex.htm for the Macintosh version.
- X-Win32—This is another commercial X server for Windows systems. A demo version (with a two-hour time limit per session) is included on the CD-ROM that accompanies this book, in the sams-extras/X directory, or you can obtain a demo version from http://www.starnet.com.
- Exceed—Yet another approach to an X server for Windows is Exceed. You can learn more from http://www.hummingbird.com/products/nc/exceed/index.html, where you can order a demo CD.
- eXodus—This is a commercial X server for the Macintosh. You can obtain more information or download a demo version from http://www.wpine.com.

The details of operation of each of these products differ, though the X servers for UNIX and Linux tend to operate very similarly to one another. On Windows and MacOS, the programs can use one of three methods of operation (most of the programs allow you to select from among at least two of these):

- Rootless with native GUI—The X server can use the native GUI as its window manager. This makes X programs look very much like programs in the host OS, at least at first glance. Figure 19.1 demonstrates this approach, as demonstrated by X-Win32.

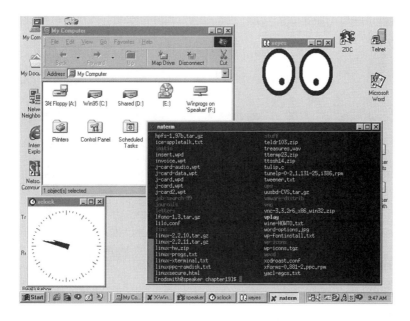

FIGURE 19.1

xeyes, nxterm, *and* xclock *are Linux programs running via X-Win32, whereas the My Computer window is native to Windows 98.*

- Rootless with custom window manager—The X server can place X programs on the host OS's screen, using a UNIX-style window manager (something that resembles mwm or fvwm is common). This makes the Linux programs look distinctive, but they still integrate seamlessly with the native OS's programs. Figure 19.2 demonstrates eXodus using this approach.

- Rooted—The X server can create its own window and then place X programs in that window exclusively. The separate window can then include desktop backgrounds, X icons, and so on. To get a usable amount of space, though, you might need to size the X server's window so large that it obscures native programs you're using. One variant on this theme is to have the X server take over the entire display, eliminating native programs (a special keystroke will often switch between X and native-OS displays). XFree86 running under OS/2 takes this approach. Figure 19.3 demonstrates MI/X running rooted.

19

RUN X WINDOW PROGRAMS REMOTELY

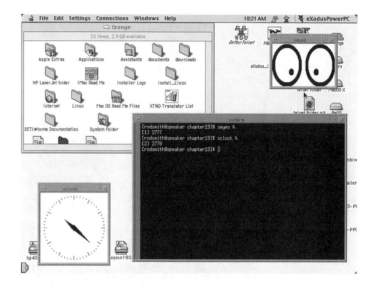

FIGURE 19.2

*When using a custom window manager, the X programs (*xeyes*, *nxterm*, and *xclock*) look quite distinctive, compared to the native Macintosh windows (the Finder window called Orange).*

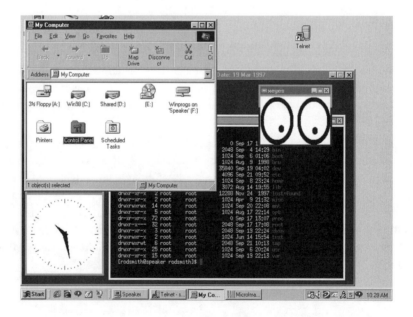

FIGURE 19.3

The MI/X window contains within it the Linux programs running in MI/X's window manager, while Windows programs are entirely separate.

Because most of the commercial X servers have demo versions of some sort, you can try several of them to see which program best suits your needs. X-Win32 is used in the examples throughout the rest of this chapter.

X Terminals

If your *only* reason for having PCs is to use them as X servers for a Linux computer, you might want to consider purchasing X terminals instead. An X terminal is a computer that typically contains no hard disk and very limited RAM and CPU power. It functions exclusively as an X server, so you can think of it as a dumb terminal for X. X terminals often come with large monitors, which means they're often expensive. They are quiet, though, and aside from the monitor size, they are compact. If you have an outdated PC, you can effectively turn it into an X terminal by installing Linux on it and configuring it to function as an X server for another machine. This can be a great way to extend the life of an old PC.

Configuring an X terminal is well beyond the scope of this book. If you want to use one with Linux, I suggest you read the NCD X Terminal Mini-HOWTO, which comes with most Linux distributions. Some of the information in the rest of this chapter applies to X terminals, too, so you can glean some information from this chapter. X terminals generally use the X Display Manager (XDM) logon method described later in the next section.

Logging On

There are two main ways to use an X server: by a textual login start or by an X Display Manager (XDM) login. Each method has advantages and disadvantages.

Textual Login

A textual login is generally the easiest way to begin using an X server. The idea is that you log in to your Linux computer by using `telnet` or a similar program and launch your X-based programs from that `telnet` session. Here's an outline of what to do to use this method:

1. Log in to the Linux computer by using `telnet`, `ssh`, or some other text-mode remote-access program.

2. Set the `DISPLAY` environment variable to point to the computer on which you want to run the X server. If you're using the `bash` shell, you can do this with a command such as

   `export DISPLAY=local.machine.name:0.0`

   You issue this command on the remote machine (that is, through your `telnet` login). `local.machine.name` is the name or IP address of the machine at which you're sitting. The `0.0` part of the `DISPLAY` variable tells the Linux computer *which* display to use on the server. If you're using a Macintosh or Windows computer, `0.0` or `0` is almost always correct. If you're using another Linux computer on which you have several virtual X sessions running, you might need to use a higher value, such as `0.1` or `1`.

> **TIP**
>
> If you use `ssh` to log in to one Linux computer from another, you don't need to explicitly set the `DISPLAY` environment variable. The `ssh` program effectively does this for you. If you use a Macintosh or Windows SSH-enabled program to log in to your Linux computer, though, you may still need to set the `DISPLAY` environment variable, because not all SSH clients on these platforms forward the X protocols. You can look for a configuration option called *forward X protocols* or something similar to enable this feature, if it's present.

3. If you're using a Linux system as the server, you must tell it to provide services to the remote system. There are a number of ways to do this. One is with the `xhost` command, as in

   ```
   xhost +remote.machine.name
   ```

   You must issue this command on the machine at which you're sitting. This command is fairly insecure because it lets any user on the remote computer connect to your X session. You can achieve a similar effect by creating the file `/etc/X0.hosts` and placing the remote machine names in that file. You must create this file on the machine whose X server display you want to use.

> **NOTE**
>
> In general, you don't need to issue the `xhost` command for Macintosh or Windows X servers because these programs accept connections from any computer by default. You can check your server's documentation for details, though.

4. You should now be able to launch programs by using your local display and running them on the host Linux computer. You launch programs by typing their names in your terminal program, as if that terminal program were an `xterm` window.

If you routinely log on from specific computers, you might want to set up an alias in your `.bashrc` (or other shell script initialization) file to set the `DISPLAY` environment variable appropriately for the machines you routinely use. If you do so, you can just type a single word rather than the entire command to set the `DISPLAY` variable. You can create a similar alias for the `xhost` command. Creating an `/etc/X0.hosts` file might also be convenient, but could pose an increased security risk because this file effectively opens *all* X sessions running on the local computer, even when you're not connected to a remote Linux or UNIX system. Overall, an XDM-based login is more secure, and when it's configured, such a login might also be more convenient.

XDM Login

An XDM login allows you to use an X server much as if it were the console. There's no need when you use an XDM login to set the DISPLAY environment variable or to use xhosts. To use an XDM login, follow these steps:

1. If you're using Red Hat 6.0, you first need to enable XDM. By default, Red Hat 6.0 uses an alternative program called GNOME Display Manager (GDM), but GDM doesn't work well with many Macintosh and Windows X servers, so you should disable GDM in favor of XDM. You do this by entering the /etc/X11 directory and changing the file to which prefdm links. To accomplish this task, type

   ```
   rm prefdm; ln -s /usr/X11R6/bin/xdm prefdm
   ```

2. Your system must be running at runlevel 5. If you receive an XDM or GDM login prompt when you start your system, this is already the case. If you receive a text-mode login: prompt at the console, your system is probably set for runlevel 3. You can permanently set the runlevel to 5 by editing the /etc/inittab file. A line early in this file reads id:3:initdefault: if the system is configured for runlevel 3. Change the 3 to a 5 to set the runlevel correctly. If you need to change the runlevel or if you had to reconfigure the system to use XDM rather than GDM, you should change the runlevel manually with the init command, as in init 5 to set runlevel 5. (If you had to change GDM to XDM and had been in runlevel 5, you should first issue an init 3 command.)

3. Configure the X server on the system you intend to use the X Display Manager Control Protocol (XDMCP). Precisely how you do this varies from one server to another. With X-Win32, you select Sessions, New Session from the X-Win32 Utility program and create a session. Be sure to specify XDMCP as the connection method, as shown in Figure 19.4. Depending on your X server and the configuration you choose, selecting the XDMCP option when you later initiate a connection might provide you with a list of computers that offer XDM logins, or may bring you directly to the login screen for the computer you select.

19

RUN X WINDOW
PROGRAMS
REMOTELY

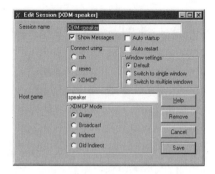

FIGURE 19.4
To use XDM logins, you must configure your X server to request a login from the Linux computer.

4. Launch your X server (if it's not running already) and request an XDMCP login with the Linux computer. In X-Win32, you do this by right-clicking the X-Win32 tab in the Windows toolbar and selecting Sessions, *sessionname* from the pop-up menu, where *sessionname* is the name you gave to your XDMCP configuration. You might see a list of hosts, in which case you should select your Linux box from that list. After you've selected your host, you see a Linux XDM login window, as shown in Figure 19.5.

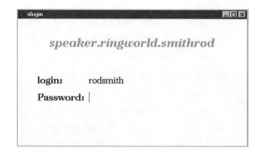

FIGURE 19.5
A Linux XDM login window lets you log in to your Linux account without opening a terminal program.

Ideally, at this point your normal X programs, such as any xterms or other utilities you normally run from .xinitrc, start up. Because many Windows and Macintosh X servers use their own window managers, though, you might find that your programs don't start up correctly. One way to correct this is to switch to a rooted display; this is called *single window* in X-Win32, and you set this from the Options, Window Settings menu in the X-Win32 Utility window. Another is to edit your .xinitrc file to ensure that no window manager is called and that some program, such as an xterm, gets started without exiting; when you exit that program, you are logged off. This second solution can wreak havoc with your console-based logins, though.

Starting X Programs

You can start X programs by typing their names at an xterm prompt or in a terminal program, if the DISPLAY environment variable is set correctly in the terminal program's login shell. You can also use Linux GUI environments, such as GNOME or dfm, to launch programs.

> **TIP**
>
> Many GUI environments, particularly those that include status bars, work best in rooted windows. Many X servers can't display these windowless elements unless they have root windows in which to work.

Performance Considerations

Running X programs via an X server involves certain performance compromises—after all, the GUI information must travel over your networking cable, which is much slower than having that information travel from one program to another in the same computer.

The X server maintains a great deal of information locally. For instance, the X server maintains its own set of fonts, so rather than send textual displays on a pixel-by-pixel basis, the Linux computer can tell the X server to display a particular string of text in a particular font. This fact leads to reasonably good performance when you deal with most textual applications, such as word processors or anything run from within an xterm window.

> **TIP**
>
> You can run an X font server on your Linux computer and add it to the font path of the local server. You can then add any fonts you like to the central font server and use them on any and all X servers on your network. Red Hat Linux comes with a font server called xfs, but it's configured in such a way that remote systems can't access its fonts. You can add another instance of xfs, however, perhaps serving fonts from directories other than the default set, by launching xfs from /etc/rc.d/rc.local or some other convenient startup script. Check the xfs manpage for details.

On the other hand, applications that are heavy on graphics, such as image editors and animation programs, may perform quite slowly, and perhaps even unacceptably slowly on some networks. This poor performance is due to the fact that the entire image data must be transmitted over the network. In some cases you might be able to improve performance by reducing the number of colors used by the X server, thus reducing the network load. Similarly, reducing the size of the displayed image might help.

TIP

Programs and files that produce a dynamic display can chew up network bandwidth. For instance, many Web pages have animated graphics that change in a regular pattern. Although these files need to be transmitted from the hosting Web site to the computer containing the Web browser only once, the animation produces constant local network activity when you view such a page via a networked X server. To improve matters you might be able to disable animations, or all graphics, in your Web browser, or turn off animation options in other programs that use animation.

If you have a substantial need for remote X services but find that your network isn't fast enough, you might want to look into upgrading your network hardware. For instance, if you're using 10BaseT networking connections, upgrading to 100BaseT might improve network X performance substantially. (See Chapter 1, "Networking Hardware," for a discussion of network speed issues.)

Using VNC

In practice, VNC is quite similar to a traditional remote X server configuration, but VNC does its work in a very different way. Rather than run the X server on the machine near you, VNC is an X server that runs on the host computer. On the machine you use, you run a relatively simple VNC client program. The VNC X server sends bitmap images of the screens to be displayed to the VNC client. The bitmap transmission means that VNC typically consumes more network bandwidth than does a traditional remote X server configuration, although this might not always be the case, depending on the applications in use.

VNC has two major advantages over a conventional X setup:

- VNC can be used to control a Windows computer remotely. You can even run a Windows computer from Linux by using VNC. Of course, you can mix VNC and traditional networked X servers on a single network, and even on a single computer, to meet your specific needs.

- VNC is open source software. Most of the Windows and Macintosh X servers are commercial and cost money—often substantial amounts of money, if you want to outfit most computers on your network with the servers. You can obtain VNC from `http://www.uk.research.att.com/vnc/index.html` under the terms of the GNU General Public License (GPL). The software is also included on the CD-ROM that accompanies this book, in the `sams-extras/X` directory.

VNC and traditional remote X servers also differ in a number of ways that have more subtle consequences. For instance, you can use a VNC client on one computer, quit from that session, and then later pick up the same session by using a different computer. Each VNC session can serve only one user. In some sense this is true of other X access methods, too, but for these, Linux automatically starts a new session for each connection request. With VNC, you must explicitly start a new VNC session if you want to run more than one. VNC sessions are also tied to the individuals who start them, so when you log in, you don't need a username, just a session number and a password.

Starting the VNC Server on Linux

To start the VNC server, you should follow these steps:

1. Extract the software—VNC is distributed in a `.tgz` file, which you can extract by using the command

   ```
   tar xvf /mnt/cdrom/sams-extras/X/vnc-3.3.3_x86_linux_2.0.tgz
   ```

   (This assumes that you've mounted your CD at `/mnt/cdrom`.) This command creates a subdirectory called `vnc_x86_linux_2.0` in the current directory, in which VNC resides.

2. Use `cd` to move into the VNC directory, and copy the executables `vncviewer`, `vncserver`, `vncpasswd`, and `Xvnc` to a directory on your path, such as `/usr/local/bin`.

3. Type `vncserver` to start the VNC server on your system. You should type this command as the user who will later log on to the system using a VNC client. In a multiuser environment, you should pay attention to the X desktop identifier returned by the server, such as `gingko.biloba.com:1`. You need the trailing number, especially, to be able to log in to the correct session later.

19

RUN X WINDOW
PROGRAMS
REMOTELY

NOTE

The first time you run the VNC server, it asks you for certain information, especially a password. You can change the password later by using the `vncpasswd` program. The password is stored in an encrypted form in the `~/.vnc` directory.

The vncserver program is actually a Perl script. You can edit this script to change features of the VNC session, such as the virtual screen size and color depth. Check the VNC documentation for details.

VNC includes an option to allow access from any Java-enabled Web browser. This feature might be useful in some situations, but it's not covered here. If you want to use it, read the VNC documentation, which describes how to install the additional files needed to activate this feature in the server.

Using the VNC Client on Windows or Macintosh

When you've run the VNC server on your Linux computer, you can start the VNC client on Windows or MacOS by following these steps:

1. Uncompress the files for the respective OSs by using native utilities. (The CD-ROM that accompanies this book includes the VNC files for both Windows and Macintosh.) In both cases, you should find a folder that contains folders named viewer and either winvnc (for Windows) or server (for Macintosh).

2. Run the viewer as you normally do for your OS, and you get a dialog box asking for the name of the server computer and the display number, as shown in Figure 19.6.

FIGURE 19.6

By default, the VNC viewer's New VNC Connection window includes less information than is shown here, but you can click Show Options to expand the window and see the options in the lower portion of the window.

3. Enter the host name and display number (which the VNC server presented at startup), and VNC prompts you for a password.

4. Enter the password, and you get a VNC screen, as shown in Figure 19.7.

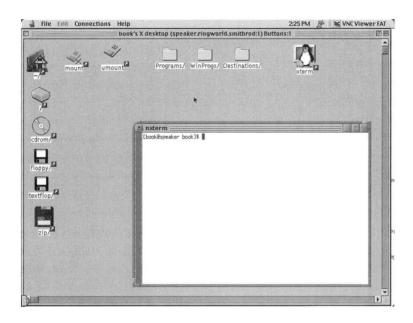

FIGURE 19.7

A VNC window works much like a rooted X server window.

You can use most X-based programs in VNC just as you would in a conventional X server. Because VNC sends whole images, it tends to be slower than using a conventional X server, but it does most things well. One oddity that might take some getting used to is mouse cursor movement. VNC displays two mouse cursors. One is a small dot, which represents the actual location of the mouse. The other is a conventional mouse pointer, which tracks the dot. The conventional mouse pointer might lag behind the dot when you move the mouse quickly or when the network is congested. When you use VNC from MacOS, you must deal with the limiting factor of mouse buttons because Macintoshes usually have only one, but X programs often require three. At present, you toggle which button is sent by using Command+*n*, where *n* is a number key from 1 to 3. Press Command+1 to have a mouse click send a button 1 signal, Command+2 to have a click send a button 2 signal, and Command+3 to set the mouse button to send a button 3 signal.

In my experience, VNC has a few quirks and oddities that aren't shared by the better conventional X servers. For instance, the Nedit text editor doesn't accept keyboard input when run from VNC. Still, VNC is useful, and its bugs might be fixed in the near future, so if you have problems, check for a more recent version at `http://www.uk.research.att.com/vnc/index.html`.

19

RUN X WINDOW
PROGRAMS
REMOTELY

Accessing Windows or MacOS from Linux by Using VNC

You can use VNC in reverse of the usual pattern, to access Windows or Macintosh computers from Linux. This can be useful for much the same reasons remote access to Linux is useful. To do so, follow these steps:

1. If you're using Windows, run the `Setup.exe` program from the `winvnc` subdirectory created when you extracted the VNC files earlier. Follow the directions to install VNC on your system.

2. If you're using MacOS, drag the `vncPatches` file from the `Server:->Extensions` directory and drag the `VNC Controls` file from the `Server:->Control Panels` directory to your `System Folder` directory, and then reboot your computer.

3. Locate the VNC server program for Windows or Macintosh. On Macintosh, this program should be in a subdirectory called `server` in the archive you extracted earlier. (You can move the program elsewhere if you like.) On Windows, the program should be where you specified you wanted VNC to be installed. Run this program.

4. The VNC server should start up and remain tucked out of the way. You can load the program and check options from the OSs' respective task listings. You should definitely check the options and enable a password the first time you run VNC. Without a password, VNC doesn't accept connections.

5. From Linux, type

   ```
   vncviewer remotename:0
   ```

   Make a change to the number, if necessary, and enter your computer name as *remotename*. The program asks for a password.

6. After you enter the password, a VNC window appears on the screen, as shown in Figure 19.8. You can control the Windows or Macintosh system as if you were sitting at its console.

You might want to take note of some characteristics of running the Linux VNC server to control a remote Macintosh or Windows computer:

- The speed isn't as good as when you use a Linux VNC server and Windows or Macintosh VNC client. This is because X's architecture makes it easy for VNC to serve X data, whereas Windows and MacOS aren't designed to allow programs such as VNC to grab their entire screens in this way.

- When using a Macintosh server, you must click the *rightmost* mouse button on the Linux client to make a mouse click.

FIGURE 19.8

At first glance this looks like a Macintosh screen, but notice the Linux icewm window manager border at the top and the icewm toolbar at the bottom, complete with Linux *button.*

- Keyboard mappings might not be perfect. In particular, there are problems with the Macintosh Command key, which doesn't map to anything useful on a Linux keyboard.

- Because Windows and MacOS (through version 9, at any rate) are fundamentally single-user systems, two people cannot use the systems simultaneously—at least not in any useful way. Whatever a user at the console sees is exactly what the remote user sees, too. When one user types something or moves the mouse, that action is reflected on the other's screen. This problem effectively limits the use of the system to one location at a time. The Linux VNC server doesn't suffer from this defect, although each particular run of the server does represent a single instance. For two users to use VNC logins in Linux requires that each user run his or her own instance of the VNC server.

When you're done using VNC, be it the server or the client, you should exit the program. In the case of the Linux VNC server, you might need to locate it with **ps ax ¦ grep vnc** and then issue a kill command against the PID number for the VNC process. (Note that the process is listed under the name Xvnc, not vncserver because the latter is simply a script that calls the former.)

> **CAUTION**
>
> It's easy to forget that the VNC server is running. If you want to run the program at all times, this isn't a problem; but if you only want to run VNC for a while and then close it, you should be careful to shut down the server when you're not using it. As with all servers, VNC could be used by undesirables to gain entry to your system.

X Security Considerations

As with text-mode logins, X-based logins present security concerns, including the same concerns discussed in Chapter 18. In addition, you should be aware of the following:

- XDM and the VNC server both present themselves to the outside world, and so are potential entry portals for crackers. If you don't need these services, you might do well to disable them. You can disable XDM by setting your computer to runlevel 3 rather than runlevel 5, and of course you can disable VNC by not using the server. On the other hand, if you don't have any need for text-based logins, you can use XDM in place of `telnetd`. XDM normally uses encrypted passwords, so it's safer than Telnet-based logins.

- Using `xhost` indiscriminately can be potentially dangerous because `xhost` is, essentially, a form of trusted host security. As described in Chapter 18, crackers can abuse this trust to their advantage in gaining entry to a computer. If you use `xhost`, you can remove a host from the approved list by preceding the hostname with a hyphen (`-`), as in **xhost -gingko.biloba.com**. You can use this feature after you're done using X-based programs to improve security.

- When you use `ssh` to start a UNIX-to-UNIX link, and then launch X-based programs from within that link, the X data gains the benefit of SSH's encryption. This makes `ssh` a good way to start a remote X session if you expect to be dealing with sensitive data, including the use of `su` to gain root privileges on the remote system. You can gain the same benefit when initiating an SSH link from some Macintosh and Windows SSH clients, but not with others.

Overall, providing access to X remotely need not present extraordinary increases in security risks, depending on how it's done. The best method is certainly to use `ssh` to establish the connection because `ssh` then encrypts all data transferred. Even using SSH to establish a connection from a Windows or Macintosh system using an SSH client that doesn't forward X data helps because the initial password is encrypted. Allowing XDM logins presents an additional service on the system, but the exchange of passwords is at least encrypted, which helps with security.

Summary

Linux's remote access facilities are a great boon in any multiuser environment. With X servers on remote systems, a single Linux computer can host multiple users, each running GUI programs such as WordPerfect or the GIMP. Depending on the mix of applications, such a pattern of use may require less in the way of total system resources than would running separate copies of the same programs at independent computers, which can translate into a cost savings. Rather than a dozen midrange computers, one fully decked-out Linux server and a dozen low-end computers can be used.

The assortment of software available for remote X access is impressive. You can use any of several commercial X servers for Windows or Macintosh, or commercial or open source X servers for Linux or various UNIX OSs. If an X server running on each computer isn't appealing, you can use the VNC server running on the central Linux computer, along with VNC viewers, on the bulk of the computers. In a pinch, you can even use VNC to access a Windows or Macintosh computer remotely, although not when somebody else is using that computer at its console.

Linking Your Intranet to the Internet

IN THIS PART

One IP Address, Many Computers: IP Masquerading

IN THIS CHAPTER

The Internet is running out of IP addresses. This may sound odd at first. After all, an IP address is a four-byte (32-bit) number, meaning that there are over four billion possible IP addresses. In truth, the number is smaller than this because certain addresses are reserved or not legal for individual computers. Splitting networks into subnets further reduces the number of available computers. The allocation of IP addresses is also inefficient because ISPs and other organizations often lay claim to more IP addresses than they need at the time they register the addresses in order to have the addresses immediately available when they are needed. Because of these factors, the number of available IP addresses is dwindling fast.

You might not personally feel this squeeze, but maybe you do. This problem manifests itself on a smaller scale in many organizations. You might work for a firm that has assigned your department a handful of IP addresses, but you suddenly find that you need to add more networked computers than you have IP addresses. If you find yourself in this situation, Linux's ability to perform *IP masquerading* can be a great boon. This feature allows a Linux computer to link to two networks in such a way that one network doesn't know the other exists. Typically, the larger network believes that all requests coming from the smaller network originate from the Linux computer that does the masquerading. This fact allows you to hide a potentially very large number of computers behind the Linux box, thus conserving IP addresses.

IP masquerading is particularly helpful for home and small office networks that link to the Internet via a PPP, cable modem, or DSL line. Providers of these services often restrict you to a single IP address. (This is particularly true of PPP links, which support only a single IP address, and many cable and low-end DSL providers that market their services to home users.)

CAUTION

Your ISP might or might not object to your using IP masquerading to connect more than one computer to the Internet. Some ISPs maintain policies that allow them to terminate your service or charge you higher rates if they determine that you're using IP masquerading. You should definitely check with your ISP before engaging in this practice. If you're using IP masquerading on a larger corporate intranet in order to stretch your department's pool of IP addresses, you're less likely to run into such a problem, but you might want to check with whoever manages your organization's network to be sure.

IP masquerading has one additional benefit: It provides many of the characteristics of a fire-wall, protecting the computers on the internal network from outside intruders. Of course, this protection is only as good as the security on the IP masquerading computer; if *its* security is breached, and if you're lax about internal security, an intruder will have free reign over your internal network.

IP Masquerading Versus NAT

If you check non-Linux networking newsgroups, you'll probably run across frequent mention of a technique called *network address translation (NAT)*. NAT and IP masquerading are similar techniques. IP masquerading is more common in the Linux world, whereas NAT is more common in Windows. I therefore describe IP masquerading in this chapter. If you prefer to use NAT, you can do it in Linux. I suggest you check the Web page `http://linas.org/linux/load.html` for more information on NAT for Linux.

The Basic Goal: Linking Networks

Figure 20.1 shows the core of an IP masquerading or NAT configuration. One computer serves as a router between two networks: an internal private network and a larger one (called *the Internet* in Figure 20.1 because the larger network usually *is* the Internet). The larger network doesn't see the smaller network quite as it is, though. Instead, the router performs some sort of translation on packets as they traverse the networks, thus altering the outside's view of the private network. Figure 20.1 depicts a NAT configuration in which two of the internal computers receive the same address as the router itself, as far as the outside world is concerned, whereas two other computers each receive unique addresses unrelated to their internal identities. In an IP masquerading setup, all the computers would appear under the same external IP address.

Characteristics of IP Masquerading

IP masquerading is the simpler of the two techniques. When you configure IP masquerading, all requests coming from the intranet and targeted at the Internet will appear to the Internet server to come from the IP masquerading computer. To the outside world, it looks as if there's one computer, not many. If the internal network generates a lot of Internet traffic, it might appear to be a very busy single computer, but only one nonetheless. Consequences of this approach include

- IP masquerading serves as an effective firewall for the private network. If outsiders can't locate an internal computer, outsiders can't break into the internal computer. (Of course, the masquerading computer must be secure, which is a complex topic itself.)

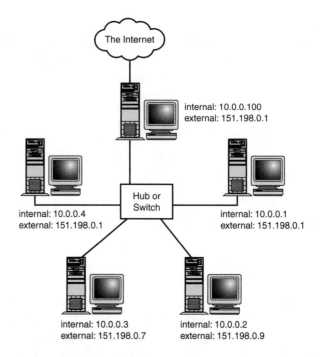

FIGURE 20.1

A computer performing IP masquerading or NAT has the power to hide, re-label, or consolidate machines on its private network, as far as the outside world is concerned.

- It's difficult to run servers for the outside world on computers that reside on the internal network. If an outside client can't see your server machine, that server might as well not exist. There are methods to get around this limitation, but I don't describe them in much detail in this book.

- You can run servers entirely within the internal network. For instance, if you run a Samba server on a computer inside a private masqueraded network, other computers on that private network will have access to the Samba shares. The outside world will know nothing about the Samba server, though.

- Typically, the internal network's computers use IP addresses from the reserved private IP address ranges, such as 10.*x.x.x*. This way, there is no chance that those addresses will accidentally conflict with addresses on the Internet as a whole. The IP masquerading computer must have two IP addresses, one for the private network, and one for the Internet as a whole.

- The IP masquerading software must know something about the protocols used on the internal network to access the Internet. To forward FTP access from an internal FTP client, for instance, the masquerading software must understand something about FTP. Linux IP masquerading does understand many common protocols, including FTP, HTTP (for Web access), SMTP (for outgoing mail), and POP (for incoming mail). Many others exist or are under development, including support for unknown protocols, so long as these protocols don't embed IP addresses in the data stream in unexpected places. Occasionally, though, you may encounter an application that doesn't work from inside an IP masqueraded network.

These characteristics make IP masquerading an excellent choice for many small offices. If you want to provide services internal to your network, have a limited number of public IP addresses, and want to protect your internal network from the Internet as a whole while providing access to the outside for Web browsing and other common activities, setting up a dedicated IP masquerading gateway is just what you need.

Characteristics of NAT

NAT is more flexible than IP masquerading, and in fact many NAT utilities can be configured to do much the same job as IP masquerading. In addition to IP masquerading's features, with NAT you can

- Configure the system to let one or more computers on the internal network be seen from the Internet. You can either show these computers using their real IP addresses or another one. For instance, the internal computer on 10.0.0.2 could appear to the outside world as 151.198.0.9 (as shown in Figure 20.1), although the IP masquerading gateway is 151.198.0.1. This characteristic can be useful when your internal network is subject to frequent reorganization you want to hide from the external world.

- Feed requests from an external source addressed to a single IP address to multiple computers. For instance, suppose you have a very busy Web site and want to devote two computers to serving this site. You can do so with NAT, by configuring the two machines with identical Web pages and telling NAT to split requests for the Web site to those two internal machines. In Figure 20.1, the computers on 10.0.0.1 and 10.0.0.4 could be used in this way.

- Assign multiple external IP addresses to a single internal computer. For instance, one computer can do duty under two names in this way. (In some cases, using aliased DNS entries for a single computer or multiple NICs on one computer can accomplish the same effect.)

20

ONE IP ADDRESS,
MANY
COMPUTERS

NAT can be extremely useful in many cases, but IP masquerading by itself can accomplish a great deal. In particular, IP masquerading is usually adequate if the internal network contains servers for internal services and client computers for Internet access. NAT is best applied when you want to run servers for the Internet at large on your internal network.

> **TIP**
>
> If you want to run one or two Internet servers but use IP masquerading, one alternative to NAT is to place two NICs on the Internet servers. One NIC provides these machines with Internet access; the other with your private network access. This arrangement has the advantage over NAT of reducing the load on the IP masquerading server. This solution does mean, however, that you can't use the IP masquerading machine as a firewall for the Internet servers.

Kernel Options Needed for IP Masquerading

IP masquerading uses both kernel and non-kernel features. You must compile your kernel with a handful of options in order to get the low-level networking support that's required for IP masquerading. In addition, you must use the `ipchains` utility to tell the system *how* to perform the masquerading. I first describe the kernel options required for IP masquerading.

Kernel Version Requirements

IP masquerading can be performed with kernels in the 2.0.*x* or the 2.2.*x* series. The details differ substantially from one kernel version to another, however, including changes in both the kernel options and the supporting utilities. I describe the 2.2.*x* options in this book because Red Hat 6.0 ships with this kernel.

Kernel Modules Needed

To use IP masquerading, your kernel must include support for several options, all in the `Networking options` area of the kernel configuration.

> **NOTE**
>
> Some of the IP masquerading protocols are considered experimental, so you may need to select `Y` for `Prompt for development and/or incomplete code/drivers` in the `Code maturity level options` section of the kernel configuration to see these protocols.

The default Red Hat Linux 6.0 kernel ships with these options enabled, but if you want to recompile your kernel, you should ensure that you select the following options:

- `Network firewalls`—This option lets the Linux kernel filter packets based on low-level information. You need this functionality, so select Y to this option.

- `IP: firewalling`—This option provides kernel services vital to IP masquerading, firewalling, and other features. Select Y to this option.

- `IP: always defragment`—This option causes the Linux box to reassemble fragmented packets before passing them on. IP masquerading may be unreliable without this feature, so select Y.

- `IP: masquerading`—This option builds the kernel-level IP masquerading features, which rely upon the preceding three options. Select Y here.

- Protocol-specific modules—When you select `IP: masquerading`, you'll be able to select several modules that are specific to certain protocols, including `IP: ICMP masquerading` and some experimental support for forwarding protocols not understood by the main IP masquerading support. You may want to select Y for `IP: ICMP masquerading`, in order to let `ping` and other ICMP-based programs work. If you use a networking program that doesn't seem to work with standard IP masquerading, you can try the other options to see if they might help matters.

- `IP: optimize as router not host`—If your system will be used primarily as an IP masquerading router, and not itself as a server or client, you may want to select Y to this option to slightly improve performance. If the system will also function as a server or as a client system, you should probably say N to this option.

- `IP: aliasing support`—Linux supports the use of two IP addresses on a single NIC if you select Y to this option. Doing so allows you to perform IP masquerading using a single NIC. You place the private network on the same physical cabling as the broader network, but using IP addresses that the broader network won't try to use. This approach can be useful if your hardware is limited, but it's less efficient than the traditional two-NIC approach, and may be less secure as well. When you reboot, you can use aliases for the various networks connected to a single device; for instance, `eth0` and `eth0:1` for two networks both connected to the same Ethernet board.

Of course, your kernel also needs support for whatever network interface device you're using, for TCP/IP in general, and so on. You can use IP masquerading to masquerade across network technologies. For instance, if you've got a local Ethernet network and want to masquerade this network over a dialup PPP link, you can do so, but you need both Ethernet and PPP support in your kernel. The same is true if you have a local Token Ring network and want to masquerade this over Ethernet, in which case you need both Token Ring and Ethernet in your kernel. See Chapter 6, "Compiling a Kernel for Networking," for more information on networking kernel options.

20

ONE IP ADDRESS, MANY COMPUTERS

Configuring IP Masquerading

Once you've recompiled your kernel to include IP masquerading support and rebooted, you can configure your system to use this facility. One of the trickier aspects of getting IP masquerading working is properly configuring more than one network interface. Particularly if you're using two interfaces of the same type (such as two Ethernet boards), getting the two to coexist can sometimes pose unusual challenges. The second component of activating IP masquerading is to use the `ipchains` utility to set up the masquerading rules that the kernel will then follow. This aspect of the job is comparatively simple.

Configuring Multiple Network Interfaces

Before reading this section, you should be familiar with the basics of configuring a network interface. If you've not already configured your system to use at least one network, read Chapter 7, "Setting Ethernet Options." If you intend to use IP masquerading in conjunction with a PPP dialup connection, you should also read Chapter 8, "Using PPP for Dialup Connections."

Configuring Two NICs

The simplest way to configure two or more network interfaces is often to use Red Hat's `linuxconf` or whatever configuration tool comes with your distribution. Figure 20.2 shows the `linuxconf` NIC configuration screen (Config, Networking, Client tasks, Basic host information). Note that this configuration screen includes tabs for several network interfaces. Figure 20.2 shows the tab for Adapter 1, but in a multiple-NIC configuration, you can click the 2 tab to set the same options for the second interface, the 3 tab for the third NIC, and so on.

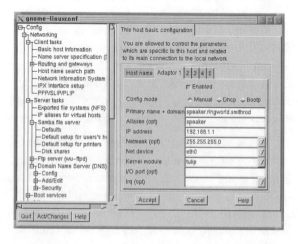

FIGURE 20.2

You can configure each NIC independently using `linuxconf`.

You should be aware of several points when configuring two or more NICs for use on a single system:

- Your computer can have two or more names, one for each network (each name can have several aliases, as well).

- Assuming you're linking a private intranet to the Internet as a whole, one machine name should be the computer's valid Internet name. The other can, and probably should, be a made-up name for a nonexistent top-level domain. Figure 20.2 shows a machine name of `speaker.ringworld.smithrod`, for instance. This naming practice, and giving machines on your private intranet names in the same fictitious domain, will prevent inadvertent name collisions because nobody else will choose the same as you use for one of your systems. Even if such repetition *did* occur, each network will remain invisible to the other because these names won't be propagated through the Internet's DNS system. Thus, creating a fictitious top-level domain serves much the same purpose as does using a reserved private IP address.

- You must specify a different Net device for each interface. On a two-Ethernet-adapter system, these devices will be `eth0` and `eth1`.

- In theory, you can mix-and-match Manual, Dhcp, and Bootp configurations for your NICs. In practice, you may need to use a particular configuration method on one interface or another.

TIP

You can configure either Adapter 1 or Adapter 2 to be the one that's linked to the Internet as a whole. If you have problems getting a configuration working with one assignment, try swapping them. Likewise, you can assign either Ethernet device to either Adapter number tab. Remember to swap the Ethernet cables around, if necessary, to bind the correct set of Linux options to a given physical network cable! Sometimes a specific Ethernet board doesn't work well with one configuration or with a specific physical network, so juggling assignments can occasionally fix problems.

When it comes time to define the default route using the Default gateway option on the Config, Networking, Client tasks, Routing and gateways, Defaults `linuxconf` page (Figure 20.3), you should enter the gateway IP address provided by your ISP or network manager. Linux can normally determine to which interface this gateway is connected. For IP masquerading to work, you'll also want to be sure the Enable routing option is enabled.

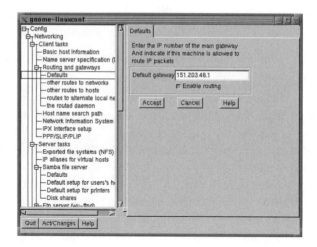

FIGURE 20.3

Specify the gateway provided by your ISP or your organization's networking department.

If you want or need to configure your networking using lines in configuration files like `/etc/rc.d/rc.local`, you need to create one set of configuration commands for each NIC. You configure each one as described in Chapter 7. Remember to set only one default route, though, which should be on the NIC that's connected to the Internet as a whole, leading to the router or gateway address provided by your ISP or network manager.

One of the trickiest aspects of using multiple NICs is in getting Linux to recognize more than one. There are several possible configurations, and depending upon the hardware you use, you may need to try more than one configuration before you find the one that works best for you. Configurations include

- Two NICs using the same driver, driver compiled into the kernel—This configuration sometimes works well automatically, but other times it works only when you include appropriate kernel options in your LILO configuration to tell the kernel to look for two NICs. Specifically, you can add a line like append = "ether=0,0,eth1" to tell Linux to look for a second Ethernet card.

NOTE

The 2.2.x series Linux kernels should be able to detect two PCI Ethernet boards automatically. If you have two ISA boards, you will probably need to use append to tell the kernel to probe for the second board.

- Two NICs using the same driver, driver compiled as a module—If you're using PCI cards, you can usually obtain acceptable results by providing appropriate lines in `/etc/conf.modules` to tell the system you're using two NICs. Specifically, you need one `alias` line per NIC, as in `alias eth0 tulip`, which tells the system to use the `tulip.o` driver module for `eth0`. A second nearly identical line (`alias eth1 tulip`) tells the system to locate the second board. For ISA boards, you may also need to include a line similar to `options ne io=0x280,0x300` to tell the module what system resources to use. (In this example, Linux will look at I/O addresses 0x280 and 0x300 for the boards using the `ne.o` driver.)

- Two NICs using different drivers, drivers compiled into the kernel—As with a single-driver solution, this option often works without intervention, but with ISA hardware, Linux may detect only one board. In this case, you may need to include kernel options in your LILO configuration to force Linux to detect the second NIC. The `append` line mentioned earlier should work in this case.

- Two NICs using different drivers, drivers compiled as modules—This configuration works much like the single-driver/modules configuration, except that the lines in `/etc/conf.modules` each refer to a different driver.

In some cases, you won't have much control over which NIC gets labeled `eth0` and which `eth1`. In particular, when the drivers are in the kernel or when you use two boards that use the same driver, whichever board the kernel finds first will become `eth0`. Therefore, you may need to adjust your configuration to match the way Linux labels your hardware.

If you have problems getting Linux to recognize your multi-NIC setup, you may want to check the Web site `http://cesdis.gsfc.nasa.gov/linux/misc/multicard.html`, which provides additional notes on this topic, including information on cards that sometimes require special treatment in a multi-NIC configuration.

Configuring One NIC and PPP

In some ways, configuring a network to use PPP as an Internet connection method is simpler than using two NICs because there's no need to get two similar NICs working on one system. You should follow these steps to configure a system in this way:

1. Configure your intranet. Follow the directions in Chapter 7 to accomplish this task. *Do not*, however, set a default route for the network; that aspect of the configuration must be done on the PPP side.

2. Configure PPP networking, as described in Chapter 8. If you want to be able to initiate a network connection from your intranet just by starting an Internet client program, you must set up dial-on-demand functionality.

3. Test the intranet connection alone, the PPP connection alone, and both connections when active at the same time. You want to be sure that neither network configuration interferes with the other.

4. Set up IP masquerading using the `ipchains` utility, as described shortly. Once this is done, any machine on your intranet should have Internet access whenever a PPP connection is active on the Linux computer.

Additional Configuration Steps

Depending upon how your system is configured, you may need to perform a few extra steps. In many cases, these aren't necessary. If you have problems getting IP masquerading working, though, you should review this section and try these options:

- Loading modules—If you've configured your kernel to auto-load modules, you don't need to concern yourself with this step. If you haven't, though, you may need to issue a `modprobe` command for each of the masquerading-related kernel modules: `ip_masq_ftp`, `ip_masq_raudio`, `ip_masq_irc`, and others you'll find in the `/lib/modules/`*version*`/ipv4` directory, where *version* is the kernel version number. If you need to issue these commands, you may want to add an entry to `/etc/rc.d/rc.local` or some other startup script to make this step automatic.

- Enable IP forwarding—IP forwarding must be enabled. In Red Hat 6.0, this can be accomplished by checking the Enable routing check box in the Config, Networking, Client tasks, Routing and gateways, Defaults `linuxconf` screen (Figure 20.3). If you're not running Red Hat or you prefer to enable and disable IP masquerading manually, you can perform this step by typing:

```
echo "1" > /proc/sys/net/ipv4/ip_forward
```

This command enables IP forwarding. Using `"0"` rather than `"1"` disables IP forwarding.

The `ipchains` Utility

No matter what type of connection you use for linking to the Internet, you use the `ipchains` utility to tell Linux how to masquerade packets travelling between the networks. The `ipchains` utility allows you to create a very complex set of rules for accepting, denying, forwarding, and modifying IP packets. A basic IP masquerading setup, as I describe here, uses only a fraction of this tool's power. You can read the `ipchains` manpage and HOWTO for more information on this utility. Chapter 21, "Configuring a Firewall," uses `ipchains` in more sophisticated ways than I describe in this chapter.

NOTE

If you're using a system with a pre-2.2 kernel, you need to use the `ipfwadm` utility instead of `ipchains`. The details of what you do with `ipfwadm` differ from what I describe here, but conceptually the two tools do the same thing.

Here is an example of the use of `ipchains` to initiate IP masquerading on an internal network that uses the 192.168.1.*x* range of addresses:

```
ipchains -P forward DENY
ipchains -A forward -j MASQ -s 192.168.1.0/24 -d 0.0.0.0/0
```

If you're impatient, you can try entering these commands on the command line (with appropriate changes to the internal network address, if necessary). If you find that you can then access the Internet from your internal network, you can enter these commands in an appropriate startup file, such as `/etc/rc.d/rc.local`, to have them run when you next reboot your computer.

NOTE

Be sure to enter the `ipchains` commands *after* any commands to start up your network interfaces. If you use a Red Hat system and configured networking with `linuxconf`, anywhere in `/etc/rc.d/rc.local` should do.

The first of the two `ipchains` commands sets the default policy to deny forwarding. Because the next line sets up masqueraded forwarding, denying forwarding may be redundant, but it can help prevent misconfigured systems on your internal network from causing problems.

The second of the two `ipchains` commands sets up forwarding. It's important to realize that `ipchains` allows you to set up a complex set (or *chain*) of rules for forwarding IP packets. Each invocation of `ipchains` modifies or displays the forwarding rules or related data. Some of the options used in the preceding command, or which you might find of use in customizing your setup, include

- `-A` *chain*—Appends a rule to the rule chain. The system maintains four types of chains: the IP input chain, the IP output chain, the IP forwarding chain, and user-defined chains. IP masquerading modifies the IP forwarding chain, hence `-A forward` in the preceding example, to add a rule to the forwarding chain.

- `-j target`—Jumps to a new rule (the *target*). You can specify a user-defined rule as the target, or any of several predefined rules. For IP masquerading, you should use the built-in rule known as `MASQ`, hence `-j MASQ` in the preceding example. The `MASQ` rule does most of the real work in IP masquerading. This rule replaces the originating computer's IP address in the outgoing packets, assigns the outgoing request to a particular port number, and keeps track of that port number so the kernel can reverse the process for replies received from the remote server.

- `-s [!] address[/mask] [!] [port:[port]]`—Specifies the source addresses— that is, the addresses of the machines whose packets are to be masqueraded or otherwise processed. The notation `192.168.1.0/24` indicates that any address matching the first 24 bits of the `192.168.1.0` address will match the rule. You could masquerade the entire 10.0.0.0 network by using `10.0.0.0/8` as the source address. You can give the mask in dotted quad notation, as well—`192.168.1.0/255.255.255.0` is equivalent to `192.168.1.0/24`, for example. You can also include a listing of originating port numbers to forward requests from different originating ports in different ways. An exclamation mark (`!`) preceding either the address or the port inverts the sense of the term, so that you can masquerade everything *but* a certain machine or group of machines, or deny masquerading from certain ports.

- `-d [!] address[/mask] [!] [port:[port]]`—Specifies the destination addresses for the packets to be masqueraded or otherwise processed. The syntax is much the same as for the `-s` parameter. In the example, `0.0.0.0/0` matches all IP addresses, which is generally what you want. You can block specified remote addresses or services by using the exclamation mark (`!`) to invert the meaning of the address or port arguments.

- `-D chain rulenum`—Deletes the specified rule number from the specified chain. The rule number can actually either be a number (such as 1 or 4) or source and destination specifications, as described earlier.

- `-R chain rulenum`—Replaces the specified rule from the specified chain. The `rulenum` is a number, starting with *1* for the first rule in the chain.

- `-F chain`—Flushes (deletes) all rules from the specified chain.

Using these options, you should be able to fine-tune your masquerading setup, using the preceding example as a base. In most cases, you won't need to do much work, as a simple change to the source address and mask should be all that's required. If you need to do more, say to masquerade two internal networks or to block certain addresses, you may need to experiment with the different settings until you attain the results you desire.

Configuring Internal Network Computers

To do any good, you must be able to configure your intranet's computers appropriately. In general, this configuration requires only a few changes to the configuration you use for an unconnected and completely private network:

- It's possible to operate a completely isolated private network using any IP addresses you like. If you do this with IP masquerading active, though, you'll be unable to access sites in the same address range as the IP numbers you've chosen. You should therefore be sure you use internal IP addresses in an approved range of addresses for private networks, as outlined in Table 4.2 (p. 95).

- You should list the IP masquerading Linux computer as the gateway or router. Figure 20.3 shows the Red Hat `linuxconf` window in which you set this option on Red Hat clients, while Figure 20.4 shows the TCP/IP Properties dialog box in which you configure the gateway in Windows 98. Other OSes have similar options.

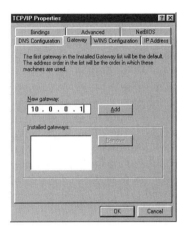

FIGURE 20.4

Type the IP masquerading computer's address and click Add to make it the gateway.

- You must configure the internal network systems to point to one or more appropriate domain name service (DNS) computers, as shown in the MacOS TCP/IP control panel in Figure 20.5. If you're not running DNS on your private network, you can point to an external DNS machine, and IP masquerading will masquerade the DNS requests, as well as the subsequent network connection. If your private network includes a machine running a DNS server, you can specify that server in addition to or instead of external servers.

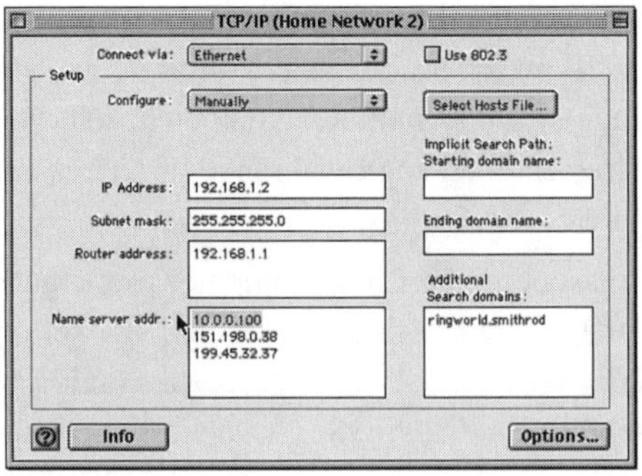

FIGURE 20.5

The Mac's TCP/IP dialog box lets you enter the computer's IP address, the router's address, and the DNS computers all in one dialog box.

NOTE

An isolated private network can usually get by using /etc/hosts files (or their equivalents) on all computers, or even by using raw IP addresses. This is impractical for any serious access to the Internet at large, however, so you'll either need to tell all the intranet's computers about an external DNS machine or run a DNS server locally.

In sum, you configure the computers on your internal network just as if they were directly connected to the Internet, except that you use addresses from the approved list of private IP addresses. You tell your private network computers that the IP masquerading machine is the gateway/router, and you're done.

Testing IP Masquerading

After you configure your Linux computer to perform IP masquerading, you should be able to test it. If the IP masquerading machine uses a connection like PPP that you need to initialize, do so. Then, fire up an FTP client, Web browser, Telnet client, or some other network program on a machine on your private network and try to reach an external site. Here are some tips in case you run into problems:

- Use a Telnet, FTP, or HTTP (Web browser) client—The ping command may or may not work, depending upon your kernel configuration options (you must enable ICMP masquerading to provide support for ping). More exotic protocols may or may not work. It's best to start with something simple.

- Test with raw IP addresses rather than machine names—If you incorrectly specified a DNS address, entering say, www.linux.org won't work, but 198.182.196.56 will. You can use nslookup or a similar utility on a working machine to find some IP addresses. Ultimately, of course, using machine names should work, but as a debugging tool, using IP addresses can be quite helpful.

- Check /var/log/messages for error messages—On the masquerading machine, you may find error messages in /var/log/messages, or possibly in some other log file.

- Check connectivity on the IP masquerading computer itself—If there's something wrong with the IP masquerading computer's Internet connection, this problem will exist for the private network as a whole. Likewise for the connection between the IP masquerading machine and the rest of your intranet.

- Check the status of your IP chains—Type **/sbin/ipchains -L** to check that the masquerading chain is set up correctly. You should see output similar to this:

```
Chain input (policy ACCEPT):
Chain forward (policy DENY):
target     prot opt    source              destination        ports
MASQ       all  ------  192.168.1.0/24      anywhere           n/a
Chain output (policy ACCEPT):
```

The forwarding chain shows a default policy of denying forwarding, but an overriding chain that forwards all protocols originating on the 192.168.1.0 network and destined for any other site on the Internet.

If a basic test with a protocol like FTP or Telnet works, you can try other applications that you might want to use. If a particular protocol doesn't work, go back to your kernel configuration and try adding additional protocols to the IP masquerading options. If that still doesn't work, try a Web search on http://www.deja.com to see if somebody knows of a patch or workaround for the protocol you want to use.

Uses and Abuses of IP Masquerading

IP masquerading is an extremely useful tool, particularly for small and home offices that use dialup PPP, cable modem, or DSL connections to the Internet. IP masquerading does have its limitations, though, both technical and contractual. You should be aware of both the capabilities and limitations of IP masquerading before you begin using it heavily.

IP Masquerading Capabilities and Limits

In many cases, you can configure IP masquerading so that the users on your intranet won't even be aware of masquerading's presence. When IP masquerading supports a client protocol, that support tends to be quite transparent to both the originating machine's client program and to the server on the outside network. Unsupported applications, though, usually don't work at all and won't unless or until a special "helper" module is written for Linux's IP masquerading.

Supported Client Operating Systems

Linux's IP masquerading support is quite agnostic concerning the operating systems (OSs) run on the private network. Reports have appeared of Linux successfully masquerading computers ranging from the common Windows and MacOS machines to quite exotic OSs, such as AmigaDOS, BeOS, and OS/2, as well as any number of UNIX or UNIX-like systems, such as Solaris, AIX, and of course Linux. In short, if the private network machines use TCP/IP, they can be masqueraded.

> **NOTE**
>
> IP masquerading operates on *TCP/IP* data. Linux's IP masquerading *will not* masquerade or otherwise forward Novell's IPX, Apple's AppleTalk, or other non-TCP/IP protocols, except possibly as encapsulated within TCP/IP.

Supported Applications

The more common and simple the protocol, the more likely it is that it's supported by IP masquerading. A *partial* list of supported protocols and applications is

- FTP—The file transfer protocol, as implemented by any application that supports this protocol.
- HTTP—The hypertext transfer protocol, used by Web browsers.
- Telnet—Used by terminal programs for remote logins.
- SMTP—The simple mail transport protocol, used for outgoing and incoming email. (Inside a private network, this will be used only for internal communication and for outgoing mail; internal clients won't be able to accept SMTP connections from the outside.)
- POP—The post office protocol for receiving email from an external server.
- Archie—Used for searching for files.
- NNTP—The network news transfer protocol, used by news readers on all platforms.
- ping—The ping program works by using ICMP packets, and works only if IP masquerading support for ICMP is compiled into the kernel.
- IRC—Internet relay chat is a common real-time "chat" protocol.
- Gopher—Another file search/retrieval protocol.

- Real Audio—Real Networks' audio (and video) transfer protocol works when appropriate support is included in the kernel.

- Miscellaneous A/V protocols—Assorted audio/video transfer programs are supported.

- Assorted games—Games such as Battle.net, Diablo, Quake, and StarCraft work with IP masquerading. Many of these require that the generic `ipportfw` IP masquerading support be compiled into the kernel.

- PC-Anywhere—This program allows remote control of a Windows system. The client program works, but you can't run a server from within a private network for access from the outside.

Unsupported Applications

The list of supported protocols is quite large. By contrast, the list of unsupported protocols is relatively small, although the server side doesn't work well from within a masqueraded network. The list of unsupported tools includes

- Servers—Because IP masquerading reveals only the IP masquerading machine's ports (see Figure 20.6), it's difficult to run a server within the private network. You can run a server on the IP masquerading machine itself, though. More sophisticated configurations permit the running of servers for the outside world within an IP masqueraded network, by forwarding access to specific ports. (One way to do this is to write additional `ipchains` rules. Another is to use the `xinetd` program's `redirect` feature, as described briefly in Chapter 24 [p. 559].) Of course, you *can* run a server within the network if you only want the computers on the private network to have access to the internal server. This feature can be very useful for hiding a file or print server from the outside world.

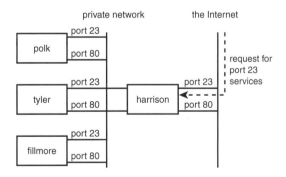

FIGURE 20.6

A request for services comes to the IP masquerading computer, but that request is not passed on to a private network machine without special configuration.

- H.323—This protocol can send outgoing data only, not incoming data. Examples of programs using this protocol include Intel Internet Phone beta 2 and Microsoft Netmeeting.

- Intel Streaming Media Viewer Beta 1—Fails to connect to the server.

- Netscape CoolTalk—Cannot make a connection.

- X—Because the X server runs on the local machine, you can't run X programs on a remote system from a machine in an IP masqueraded network. Because you can't perform a telnet into such a network, you can't run programs located inside the network from the outside. You can get around the first limitation by using SSH to connect to the outside system from a computer on your local network, provided the SSH client forwards X connections. When you do this, the X transmissions go through the existing SSH link, rather than a new link created for the purpose.

- WebPhone—Makes assumptions about IP addresses that aren't valid with IP masquerading.

In some cases, these programs fail because they embed information on IP addresses within the TCP/IP data stream. Unless there's a specific helper module, IP masquerading doesn't know about this information, and so passes it through unchanged. On the other side of the transfer, the software has conflicting information about the IP addresses, and so further transfers fail. Similarly, some protocols may open or close ports in ways that the IP masquerading utility does not expect, resulting in failed data transfers.

NOTE

Because IP masquerading is constantly under development, it's possible that some of these applications may work by the time you read this book. You should see `http://ipmasq.cjb.net/` for the latest official development information. You may also find useful information on `http://www.deja.com` or the newsgroup `comp.os.linux.networking`.

IP Masquerading and Dial-on-Demand

You can use IP masquerading in conjunction with dial-on-demand, as described in Chapter 8. The result is an almost-seamless connection between machines on your intranet and the Internet as a whole. Compared to a true always-on connection, you can expect some quirks:

- Delayed connections—When you initiate a link to a remote site, there will be a delay while the Linux computer dials the modem and makes the connection. This may cause your client program to report a timeout error. Try again (and possibly three or more times, depending upon the timeout value used by the client) to make the connection. Of course, if a PPP link is already up, you won't see this delay.

- Failed connections—If the ISP's line is busy or otherwise down, your connection attempts will fail. If the client system is in a different room from the IP masquerading computer, or if the modem's volume is turned down, you may not realize what's happened because you won't hear the busy signal from the modem.

- Dropped connections—Dial-on-demand automatically drops connections after a period of inactivity. This period varies from one connection type to another, and you may want to adjust the values, as described in Chapter 8, to best match your needs. With some protocols, you may need to exit from the client program and start it up again if dial-on-demand closes the PPP link.

- Speed—PPP links over modems are typically much slower than always-up connections via T1, cable modem, DSL link, or other technologies.

Overall, the combination of dial-on-demand with IP masquerading can be useful for low-cost access for a very small network with modest Internet access needs. A larger network or one with more substantial access needs should look into another access method, either using IP masquerading or several IP addresses for direct connections for all (or at least several) computers.

Bandwidth Limitations

IP masquerading funnels all data for an entire intranet through a single computer. If your network generates a lot of traffic (either incoming or outgoing), you may begin to see the performance limitations of this design. This is particularly true if your link to the outside world is over a low-end connection like a PPP dialup link. Even a DSL or T1 line may be inadequate to the task if your intranet is large enough or if that network generates enough traffic.

For instance, suppose your intranet consists of six computers plus the IP masquerading machine. If the computer `polk` attempts to download the latest Red Hat Linux over a 56kbps PPP dialup, `polk` will demand most of the available bandwidth for several hours—probably over a day, in fact. The user of `polk` may initially see transfer speeds of, say, 50KB/s, which is about as high as can be expected on an average V.90 modem link. Now, suppose that `tyler`'s user tries to download the latest Debian Linux distribution while the Red Hat download is still in progress. The total bandwidth of the modem doesn't change, so `polk` and `tyler` will split that bandwidth, and each will get only 25KB/s. Meanwhile, the other four users will find that their Web browsing and other network accesses are unusually slow.

IP masquerading doesn't magically produce more bandwidth; it's just a way to *share* the bandwidth that's provided to a single computer. You should definitely consider this when planning your network connection.

> **NOTE**
>
> The same comments apply to using any computer as a firewall, router, or bridge of any type. Typically, bandwidth is limited by the slowest networking link in a configuration, be that a 56kbps PPP link, a 640kbps DSL link, a 10Mbps Ethernet link, or something else. This limited bandwidth must be divided among all the computers that use it. If your hardware is particularly high-speed, the bottleneck may become an oversubscribed ISP or even the Internet backbone. At busy times of busy days, this becomes true even of 56kbps dialup lines, as you've probably experienced when browsing the Web at such times.

Being a Good Netizen

IP masquerading's limitations apply not only to the technical side, but also socially. In particular, many ISPs object to the use of IP masquerading. This is because a typical ISP expects users to consume a certain amount of bandwidth and, in the case of dial-up technologies, a certain number of hours of online time. When you subscribe with an ISP for, say, 640kbps DSL service, your ISP expects that you will *not* be using the full 640kbps of bandwidth 24 hours a day, 7 days a week. Instead, the ISP expects that you'll consume brief bursts of 640kbps and average some fraction of that amount. Ten, twenty, or a hundred subscribers together may consume 640kbps of bandwidth for an extended period of time at peak hours. If you use more bandwidth than the ISP expects, that drives up the ISP's costs. Hence, many ISPs impose limits of various sorts on the use of services.

> ### Always-On and On-demand Connections
>
> Some connection technologies, such as DSL and cable modems, are *always-on* technologies, meaning that you're always connected to the Internet, assuming the hardware is always powered up. You might not be using the bandwidth at any given time, however. An ISP providing always-on service expects to provide the basic connectivity 24 hours a day, but does not expect you to transfer data continuously during that period. Other technologies, like PPP, are generally used in an *on-demand* fashion, in which the physical connection is formed and broken as the need for transfers arises. An ISP providing on-demand services may have more subscribers than hardware to connect the subscribers because chances are not everybody using the service will want to use it at once. Even when connected, subscribers probably won't use 100% of their bandwidth.
>
> In an always-on environment, ISPs tend to sell services without temporal usage limits, but sometimes forbid the running of certain servers, or meter the service by the megabyte transferred. On-demand ISPs often limit access by time because the number of connection ports (such as modems) is an important limiting factor to the service. On-demand ISPs also often forbid certain activities, although this is more often to prevent undesirable behavior, such as spamming, than to control costs.

Some common limits on ISP service include

- Total online time—Dial-up ISPs often limit online time to some number of hours per month. If you exceed this limit, the ISP charges by the hour, or perhaps simply raises your monthly charge by a fixed amount.

- Total data transferred—Occasionally an ISP measures the amount of data you transfer, and if you exceed a certain value, raises your rates.

- No servers—ISPs sometimes forbid the use of servers on your system. The idea is that servers, particularly Web and FTP servers, often generate a lot of traffic, hence raising the ISP's costs. Servers may also pose security risks. A misconfigured email server can be used by spammers for email forwarding, for instance, and the ISP might have to deal with at least some of the consequences of your misconfigured server in a case like this.

- No IP masquerading—Because *NAT* is the more common term in Windows, ISPs often specify *NAT* rather than *IP masquerading*, but the idea is the same: ISPs calculate online time based on the assumption of one user. If you link your business's computers via IP masquerading, that action can generate a great deal more traffic and raise the ISP's costs.

So far, I've presented only the ISP's side of the picture. You may view matters differently, and your view may be quite reasonable—for instance, you may be one person who uses IP masquerading at home for convenience and not to transfer more data. Nonetheless, you should be aware of the limits imposed by your ISP's terms of service (TOS). In most cases, you can find an ISP who won't object to your using IP masquerading. In some cases, you may need to pay more money for this privilege. You'll often get more for your money, however. For instance, many DSL ISPs offer two levels of service: one for individual home users, the other for businesses. The business service costs more but provides faster access, guarantees concerning speed or reliability, domain name hosting, or other services you will probably find appealing if you are a business wanting high-speed access for all your computers.

> **CAUTION**
>
> If you decide to violate your ISP's TOS, don't be surprised if your service is unexpectedly disconnected or if you find yourself bumped into a higher rate category. It's a trivial matter for ISPs to probe for servers running on your computer. IP masquerading is more difficult for an ISP to detect, but IP masquerading does leave certain telltales, such as a large number of requests coming out of ports with very high numbers.

One additional aspect of good net behavior is in configuring your IP masquerading computer so that it is secure. Security is mostly a benefit to you, but it can also be a benefit to others. If you deprive a would-be cracker of a platform from which to attack others, you've done those others a service, as well as protected your own system. Throughout this book, I've mentioned security implications of assorted services. On any but the smallest networks, you'll want to dedicate a computer to serve as the IP masquerading machine and disable most or all services on that machine. You can then run your server *within* your private network, where it will be relatively safe from attack. You can learn more about security in Chapter 24, "Maintaining a Secure System," or in the Sams book *Maximum Linux Security*.

CAUTION

Don't assume that your internal network is safe just because you run an IP masquerading computer. If a cracker gains access to the IP masquerading computer, that same cracker can then attack the rest of your network. You should pay particular attention to security in the IP masquerading machine, but you should also take steps to secure your internal machines. Firewall or IP masquerading security will also do you no good if the source of the security breach is *internal*, say from a disgruntled employee.

Summary

IP masquerading is one of the most useful networking tricks Linux can perform. IP masquerading is largely a kernel-level operation, and as such it requires that several kernel options be set correctly. You control this feature with the `ipchains` utility, which you use to set up a *chain* of rules with which the kernel decides how to process a given packet.

IP masquerading is closely related to NAT, which is a somewhat more flexible procedure. Firewalling is another related topic. In fact, IP masquerading is a specialized form of a firewall and, as discussed in the next chapter, you can use many of the same tools to configure a firewall as you do to set up IP masquerading.

Configuring a Firewall

IN THIS CHAPTER

One of the most common computer networking buzzwords these days is *firewall*. Small companies and even individuals post to various newsgroups asking for advice on purchasing a firewall or configuring a computer as one. Employees gripe that their companies' firewalls interfere with their use of the Internet. Companies seek out network administrators with experience configuring custom firewalls.

Ideally, a firewall goes unnoticed by legitimate users of a system while simultaneously blocking access by would-be crackers. Unfortunately, this ideal is difficult to attain. Like many aspects of computer security, it's easy to configure a firewall to be transparent to users but not very secure, or secure but a major nuisance to users. Implementing security *and* ease of use is hard. The goal of this chapter is *not* to present everything you need to know about firewalls; entire books have been written about firewalls, and I can only present some basics in this chapter. After reading this chapter, though, you should know enough to determine what type of firewall you want, the general steps involved in configuring one, and where to go to find the details.

If you haven't already done so, you may want to read Chapters 2, "Understanding TCP/IP," and 3, "Networking Services." Firewall technologies often interact with different layers of the TCP/IP stack, ports, and so on, so it's important that you be familiar with these concepts when you learn about and configure a firewall.

Understanding Firewalls

The first step on the road to firewall installation is to understand what a firewall is, what it can do, and when the use of a firewall may be useful to you. This section covers these issues.

What Is a Firewall?

Most generally, a firewall is a network device that controls the flow of data between two networks. This may sound similar to a *router* (p. 87), but an ordinary router is a fairly passive device; it merely passes packets uncritically from one network to another. A firewall, by contrast, examines the packets to one extent or another and makes a decision about what to do with them.

In this chapter, I discuss two different types of firewalls: *packet filters* and *proxy servers*. These terms aren't used universally; for instance, some people refer to them as *chokes* and *gates*, respectively. Others may consider packet filters in a class by themselves, separate from firewalls. If you do further reading on firewalls, you should be aware of these differences in terminology.

Linux can be configured to serve as a firewall using packet filters, proxies, or a combination of the two techniques. In fact, an old 486 computer can make an excellent firewall for a small network. Alternatively, you may want to purchase a standalone firewall, which could be an ordinary computer configured for this function or a specialized piece of hardware designed expressly as a firewall.

Making Low-Level Decisions: Packet Filters

A packet filter firewall can be fairly unobtrusive. Such a filter makes decisions about what data to pass based on a fairly shallow analysis of the packets it is asked to relay. For instance, a packet filter can examine the source and destination addresses, port numbers, and the type of protocol involved (such as Telnet or HTTP). When you configure a packet filter, you set up a series of rules that define what type of traffic you allow and what to do with traffic that you don't allow (ignore it, send a reject message to the originating host, log the rejection, and so on).

In fact, packet filters are closely related to several other networking technologies. The lines between some of these technologies are rather blurred:

- Routers—A conventional router passes IP packets from one network to another without paying them much attention. Many routers can be configured to perform packet filtering, though, so if you have a dedicated router, you may want to investigate whether it can be configured in this way. If so, you might save yourself some effort in configuring a Linux firewall.

- IP masquerading—Like packet filters, IP masquerading examines packets and makes forwarding decisions based on what it sees. IP masquerading also rewrites the packets' headers, though, to make them appear as if they come from the IP masquerading computer. IP masquerading is an asymmetric technique in the sense that it allows one network to "hide" behind a single computer, but the outside world isn't normally hidden from the private network.

- NAT—Like IP masquerading, network address translation (NAT) allows the router to alter the appearance of an internal network. NAT is somewhat more flexible than IP masquerading in the sense that it can selectively hide computers rather than hiding them all.

In practice, you may want to combine several of these functions. For instance, you could configure a system to use IP masquerading *and* to apply firewall rules to protect the network from outside probes.

To configure Linux for packet filtering, you compile assorted features into the kernel, as described shortly, and use the `ipchains` utility to set up rules for accepting, rejecting, and forwarding packets. This procedure is very similar to that used to configure IP masquerading, in fact, although you might use an entirely different rule set for packet filtering than for IP masquerading.

21

CONFIGURING A
FIREWALL

> **NOTE**
>
> Linux can serve as a packet filter for *TCP/IP packets*. Other Ethernet protocols, such as AppleTalk, go unnoticed by Linux's packet filters. Netatalk can be configured as an AppleTalk router, but it lacks packet filter capabilities. If you want a firewall for non-TCP/IP protocols, you should look into dedicated firewall products, some of which do handle these protocols.

Making High-Level Decisions: Proxies

A *proxy server*, or *proxy* for short, performs higher-level analyses than does a packet filter. Figure 21.1 illustrates the work of a proxy server. Instead of connecting directly to an external computer, an internal computer connects to the proxy server, which then forwards the data. This may sound superficially similar to what a router or packet filter does, but it's much more complex because the proxy server unwraps the data to a greater extent and processes it at the application layer of the TCP/IP stack, as shown in Figure 21.2.

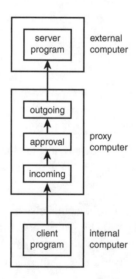

FIGURE 21.1

A proxy server program accepts connections from one network, analyzes the data, and if it approves, makes a new request of the target system, forwarding the response back to the originating computer.

CONFIGURING A
FIREWALL

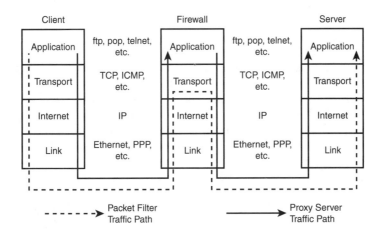

FIGURE 21.2

A proxy server analyzes the data up to the application-layer protocols, whereas a packet filter unwraps a TCP/IP packet only to the Internet or Transport layer.

Many proxy server firewalls require the use of special client or server programs that are aware of the specific proxy server program in use. Other times it may not be possible to make a connection that's anything close to direct. For instance, instead of running a proxy server program *per se* on the firewall, the firewall might be a computer that disallows routing between its networks, but allows at least limited access from each side. A user wishing to do an FTP transfer would therefore log on to the firewall, perform the transfer from the outside, and then move the data to the target system on the protected network.

One point that bears emphasis is that a proxy server disallows direct connections between the internal network and the outside world. Instead, for each protocol to be handled, the proxy server runs a special program that serves as both a client and a server, or requires that the user perform a two-step transfer. This "break" between the inside and outside is reflected in Figure 21.2 by the fact that the proxy server traffic path consists of *two* links, whereas the packet filter traffic path is represented by a single line, albeit one that's partially processed by the firewall's TCP/IP stack.

CAUTION

In general, it's a bad idea to give individual users accounts on a firewall computer because these accounts can serve as points of attack for an outside cracker. It's best to use client software that's proxy-aware and run a real proxy server. If you must use a two-step process for transfers, you may want to create some sort of shared account for each type of transfer. For instance, you could create an account called `ftpaccess` that uses an FTP client as the shell. Users would then be unable to issue ordinary shell commands in this account. Internally, users could retrieve files via a second FTP transfer or by some form of file sharing access—but such a firewall should be configured to respond *only* to the internal network, or they become potential holes in your firewall.

Proxy servers work best when your network requires only limited external access. For instance, your users might not notice a proxy server if their only use of the Internet is email or Usenet news. These protocols can be served directly from the firewall, or forwarded relatively simply from the firewall to internal servers. Such "store and forward" services don't require direct connections between the private network and the outside world; the server running on the firewall accomplishes that task. If you make heavy use of more interactive Internet protocols, such as X servers, Telnet, or FTP, you may find that a proxy server causes more problems than its security improvements justify.

Proxy servers generally don't require special kernel options to operate. They do, however, require careful configuration of available services. There's little point in running a proxy server firewall if you leave lots of servers like Telnet, Samba, or FTP running and accessible to the outside world. You may need to make some such services available only to your internal network. If so, you can use TCP wrappers or `xinetd` to restrict access to these services, as described in Chapter 24, "Maintaining a Secure System." One other important point is that you *must* disable routing of packets from one network to another on a proxy server firewall. If the proxy automatically forwards data between networks, it's not going to be very effective as a firewall.

Standalone Firewalls

Configuring a firewall can be difficult work, and it's easy to misconfigure a firewall so that it provides inadequate protection to your internal network. For that reason, a number of firewall products of various descriptions are available. Some of these are software packages that you run on an appropriate computer. Others are standalone boxes that you insert between your computer and your Internet connection. Prices vary substantially. Some of the choices include

- ISPs—Some ISPs include firewalls on their premises, or in equipment they provide you (such as in a cable or DSL modem). If an ISP's firewall is located between the ISP's network and the Internet, you get some protection from Internet-based attacks, but not from other customers of the same ISP.

- Router hardware—Many routers sold by companies like Cisco and Ascend include firewall features of one sort or another. Check with your router manufacturer for details.

- Linux Router Project—This is a specialized distribution of Linux that's designed to turn a PC into a dedicated router. It includes support for IP masquerading and packet filtering. At the moment, it fits on a single floppy disk. You can find more information at `http://www.linuxrouter.org`.

- FirePlug EDGE—This is an offshoot of the Linux Router Project, and is more specifically tailored to the needs of a firewall. Read more about it at `http://edge.fireplug.net`.

- GNAT Box—Global Technology Associate's (GTA's) GTA Network Address Translation (GNAT) Box is firewall software and an operating system you install on a standard PC to turn it into a dedicated firewall. You can find more information at `http://www.gnat-box.com`.

- WatchGuard Firebox—This is a hardware product that runs Linux internally to provide firewall features. WatchGuard is actively supporting the development of Linux firewall tools. Read more about it at `http://www.watchguard.com`.

- Technologic Interceptor—This is a hardware box that serves as a firewall. Check `http://www.tlogic.com` for more information.

- Galea Avertis—This is another standalone hardware firewall. More information is available at `http://www.galea.com/`.

- Sonic Wall—There are several models in this line of hardware firewalls. You can read more about them at `http://www.sonicwall.com`.

Which of these or the many other firewall products is right for you depends upon your specific needs. You should ask yourself several questions, including

- What is your budget? Some of the available firewall products are quite inexpensive, others aren't. If you have spare hardware gathering dust, a software solution may reduce your costs, particularly if you use Linux for this function (but then only if the labor costs don't offset the savings on software).

- How strong a firewall do you need? The best firewall is an "air gap"—no connection between two networks. This may be impractical, but you might want to consider it for protecting particularly sensitive data. The next step down is a *well-implemented* proxy server with supporting packet filter. A packet filter alone may suffice for some situations.

- How many firewalls? If your network is small, one may suffice. You might want several firewalls, though, to protect separate portions of your organization's network.

One of the most important decisions you'll have to make is whether to use a "canned" firewall product or custom configure a Linux (or some other) system to serve as a firewall. A packaged product is certainly easier to configure, and will probably provide superior protection if you're not already familiar with firewalls. Doing a custom configuration will help you get precisely the protection you need, but will cost more in time, especially if you must first learn the details of firewall configuration.

> **CAUTION**
>
> I cannot do more than provide the briefest overview of firewall principles and Linux firewall tools in this chapter. If you want to learn more, you can begin with the Linux Firewalling and Proxy Server HOWTO, which comes with Red Hat and other Linux distributions. From there, you can read the chapters on firewalls in books such as Sams' *Maximum Linux Security*, or the New Riders title *Linux Firewalls* by Robert Ziegler.

Using Multiple Firewalls in One Network

Many networks can benefit from the presence of two or more firewalls of various types, as illustrated in Figure 21.3. In this configuration, a packet filter blocks the most outrageous connection attempts based on packet analysis. Any traffic coming into the network is then passed directly to the proxy server, which can function as a mail relay, news server, and so on. Outgoing traffic passes through the proxy server, and then through the packet filter. Note that both incoming and outgoing traffic can be blocked at either firewall.

> ### Single- and Multi-Homed Firewalls
>
> In Figure 21.3, both the packet filter and the proxy server are *multi-homed*, meaning that they possess two network interfaces and perform firewall functions to bridge those two interfaces. All other things being equal, a multi-homed firewall is more secure than a single-homed firewall. For instance, in the network depicted in Figure 21.3, if a cracker breaks into the packet filter, the bulk of the internal network is still reachable only through the proxy server. If the proxy server is configured properly, this will present a new set of challenges to the cracker.
>
> It's also possible to tie the packet filter into the main internal network, and use its filtering rules to direct all traffic to the proxy server. In this case, though, if a cracker breaks into the packet filter and gains root access, there's nothing to prevent direct attacks on internal computers, completely bypassing the proxy server.

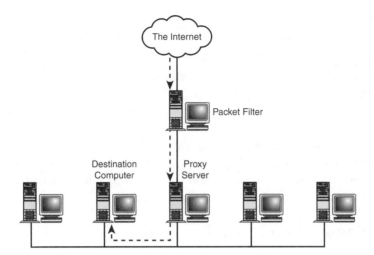

FIGURE 21.3
Each firewall blocks specific types of intrusion attempts.

> **NOTE**
>
> You can configure a single Linux computer to function as *both* a packet filter and a proxy server. This "killing two birds with one stone" approach may be suitable for a small network, but you should be aware that this approach also makes a breach of security on the firewall itself much more serious because the intruder does not need to overcome the second firewall's security.

You can add firewalls in a chain of sorts, each providing additional protection. For instance, you could insert a second packet filter in the chain shown in Figure 21.3 between the proxy server and the internal network, or between that network and a second internal network. Such a multi-layered approach can provide increasing levels of security as you move inward. You can place machines containing insensitive data, such as Web servers, behind no firewall, or perhaps just behind an initial packet filter. To get from there to a payroll computer might require traversing several more firewalls, each configured uniquely. Some such configurations are said to contain *demilitarized zones* (*DMZ*s) near the Internet. A DMZ is a lightly protected area that's used for easy access to the Internet, whereas areas that lie behind additional firewalls may not be very useful for most Internet accesses, though they can gain full access to internal networking services. A DMZ can be particularly useful for running high-visibility servers.

> **TIP**
>
> It's important that each firewall be configured uniquely in a multi-tiered layout. If a cracker can break one firewall, another with similar configuration may pose little challenge.

Another use for multiple firewalls is in segmenting a large internal network. For instance, you might want to isolate the sensitive computers in a research and development laboratory from the accounting computers or from the data entry computers staffed by temporary workers. A large organization might therefore have several firewalls.

When Should You Use a Firewall?

Firewalls are useful security tools, but they aren't panaceas. A poorly configured firewall can actually do more harm than good by lulling you into a false sense of security. This is particularly true if you neglect security on your internal network because you think your network is protected by the firewall. On the other hand, firewalls can provide real protection and convenience. For instance:

- You can block port scans and attempts to use internal services originating from outside your intranet.
- You can deny access to known "troublemaker" sites.
- Firewalls can slow down an attacker. If an attacker takes a month to breach your firewall's security, that's one extra month in which your data are safe. Better yet, the effort involved may deter the intruder from trying.
- If you configure your firewall to log suspicious activity, you may be able to detect a break-in attempt before it succeeds. Monitoring such activity from a single computer is much less time-consuming than monitoring it from an entire network. (See "Using swatch to Monitor Log Files," p. 553, for one approach to system log monitoring.)

Overall, a firewall can be a useful *component* of a security policy for a site. It is only one component, though; you must also tend to the security of the computers on your intranet. You might choose to implement less stringent security on most of the machines on your intranet than you do on your firewall, but you shouldn't ignore security on these machines altogether.

Setting Up a Packet Filter

A packet filter can be fairly unobtrusive to legitimate users, and can provide a great deal of security, particularly if your needs for connectivity with the outside world are limited to a handful of protocols. You can configure a packet filter much as you do IP masquerading, and in fact it's possible to configure a system to do *both* IP masquerading *and* packet filtering. (In this case, though, the packet filtering is likely to be done to protect the IP masquerading router itself, rather than the internal network because IP masquerading by its nature blocks connection attempts from the outside world.)

> **NOTE**
>
> One alternative to using `ipchains` to configure a packet filter firewall is to use `xinetd`, which I describe in Chapter 24. The `xinetd` utility replaces `inetd` and can be configured to ignore requests for a service from one NIC while granting those requests to another. As such, `xinetd` is more flexible than `inetd` but less flexible than `ipchains`. `xinetd`'s advantage is that it's much easier to configure than a packet filter firewall using `ipchains`.

Kernel Options Needed for Packet Filtering

The first step in configuring a packet filter is to set up your kernel to support the necessary options. For the most part, these options are the same as those required for IP masquerading, and they're set in the kernel's `Networking options` configuration area:

- `Network firewalls`—This option is required for packet filtering.
- `IP: advanced router`—For a basic firewall, you can leave this option set to `N`, but if you want to delve into routing esoterica, you may want to set it to `Y` and then set subsequent options to best suit your installation.
- `IP: firewalling`—Again, this is a required option for packet filtering.
- `IP: firewall packet netlink device`—This feature allows you to monitor incoming packets with your own custom software. It's not needed for a basic firewall, but can be extremely useful for more advanced firewalls.
- `IP: transparent proxy support`—This feature allows you to configure a computer as a proxy server in a way that can be relatively transparent to machines on your intranet. It's not required for packet filtering, but you may want to enable it if you want to experiment with more advanced proxy server configurations.

- `IP: optimize as router not host`—If this system will be used primarily as a packet filtering router, and not itself as a server or client, you may want to select Y to this option to slightly improve performance.

You'll also need additional options for your specific type of network and hardware. For instance, you'll need all the usual TCP/IP options and drivers for your network card. See Chapter 6, "Compiling a Kernel for Networking," for more information.

> **NOTE**
>
> I'm assuming that you're using a 2.2.*x*-series kernel. If you're using an older or newer kernel, the options you need may be somewhat different from what I describe here.

Using `ipchains`

Linux uses sets of rules, known as *chains*, to determine the fate of packets coming into the computer. When a packet enters a chain, the rules in the chain determine what happens to the packet. Linux applies each rule to each packet in turn, and each rule can cause certain types of packets to be discarded, modified, or accepted.

Types of Chains

By default, there are three chains on a Linux computer:

- The input chain—This chain processes packets that come into the computer. If you configure an input chain to reject packets from a specific address, your computer will be "blind" to that address, which means that your computer can't be attacked from that address, at least not directly and if the remote site is honest about its address. If an incoming packet is destined for the local computer, it passes from this chain through the local TCP/IP stack.

- The forward chain—If a packet is destined for a computer on one network, but originates on another, it can be routed (or forwarded) through the current computer. The forwarding chain processes such requests. It is here that IP masquerading occurs. You can also implement many firewall rules in the forwarding chain, although the input and output chains can also be used for this purpose.

- The output chain—When a packet leaves the computer, it must traverse the output chain. Like the input chain, the output chain can accept or deny packets. You could implement rules on an output chain to deny access to certain types of services on external computers. For instance, you could block requests to specific Web sites.

You can also create user-defined chains for special purposes. By default, the three standard chains are empty, meaning that they either deny or accept all packets sent through them, depending upon the default configuration (which is normally to accept all packets). Adding rules to the chain can change acceptance to denial or denial to acceptance for particular packet types.

You manipulate the chains' rules with the ipchains utility. Chapter 20 (p. 476) presents the most important options for manipulating chains. The ipchains manpage contains more details.

A Simple Example

Here's an example of a script to set up a *simple* proxy filter firewall. This example script is included on the CD accompanying this book as sams-extras/firewall/firewall.

```sh
#! /bin/sh
# Setup Internal LAN variables here

IntIF="eth0"                # internal network interface
IntHostIP="192.168.1.1"     # internal host IP
IntNETIP="192.168.1.0/24"   # internal LAN IP

# Setup External Internet variables here

ExtIF="eth1"                # external network interface
ExtHostIP="10.0.0.1"        # external host IP
ExtNETIP="10.0.0.0/8"       # external Network IP

IPCHAINS="/sbin/ipchains"

echo -n "*** Flushing all firewall rules and starting clean..."
$IPCHAINS -F input
$IPCHAINS -F output
$IPCHAINS -F forward
echo "done!"

echo -n "*** Setting the default policy to ACCEPT for input, output, and
forward..."
$IPCHAINS -P input ACCEPT
$IPCHAINS -P output ACCEPT
$IPCHAINS -P forward ACCEPT
echo "done!"

echo -n "*** Setting up protection against IP spoofing..."
$IPCHAINS -A input -i $ExtIF -d ! $ExtHostIP -l -j DENY
$IPCHAINS -A input -i $ExtIF -s $IntNETIP -l -j DENY
$IPCHAINS -A input -i $IntIF -s ! $IntNETIP -l -j DENY
echo "done!"
```

```
echo -n "*** Reject connections to ad.doubleclick.net..."
$IPCHAINS -A output -p tcp -d 209.67.38.0/24 80 -j REJECT
$IPCHAINS -A output -p tcp -d 199.95.208.0/24 80 -j REJECT
echo "done!"

echo -n "*** Deny incoming telnet connections..."
$IPCHAINS -A input -i $ExtIF -p tcp -s 0/0 -d $ExtHostIP 23 -j DENY

echo -n "*** allow local connections only, for X Font Server on port 7100..."
$IPCHAINS -A input -i $ExtIF -p tcp -s $ExtHostIP -d $ExtHostIP 7100 -j ACCEPT
$IPCHAINS -A input -i $ExtIF -p udp -s $ExtHostIP -d $ExtHostIP 7100 -j ACCEPT
$IPCHAINS -A input -i $ExtIF -p tcp -s 0/0 -d $ExtHostIP 7100 -l -j DENY
$IPCHAINS -A input -i $ExtIF -p udp -s 0/0 -d $ExtHostIP 7100 -l -j DENY
```

CAUTION

Be sure the permissions on any script that sets firewall options are set appropriately. Specifically, only root should have write access to the script. It's probably best if only root can read or execute the script, too—in other words, set it for 0700 permissions. The CD mastering process sets the permissions more liberally than this, so if you use the firewall script on the CD as a base, be sure to change the permissions.

Here's a brief rundown of what each section accomplishes:

- Variables—The first few lines of the script set variables used internally. These include the IP addresses of both Ethernet interfaces, the Ethernet interface names, and the location of the ipchains utility.

NOTE

The IP addresses used in this script are private network addresses. In reality, the external network address is likely to be a public Internet address, and the internal address will likely be private only if you also enable IP masquerading (which can be done in the same script that configures the rest of the firewall).

- Flushing—The script flushes any existing rules and sets the default policies to ACCEPT, which makes this a fairly lax firewall script.

> **TIP**
>
> You can either set the default policy to ACCEPT and then explicitly deny unwanted connections, or set the default policy to DENY and explicitly accept connections you desire. The latter is generally more secure, but trickier to configure because you must understand the implications of each service you need. You can set the defaults independently for the input, output, and forward chains. For instance, you might set the default for input to DENY and the default for output to ACCEPT.

- Spoofing protection—The script blocks traffic that's destined for the internal network originating from the external network, but that claims to come from the internal network, and vice-versa. When a packet claims to come from the network to which it's going, that's a sure sign that the address has been *spoofed*, or changed in what is likely a break-in attempt.

- Outgoing blocks—The script blocks outgoing traffic to two IP networks on port 80 (used for Web browsing). These addresses are used by `ad.doubleclick.net`, which provides ads for Web pages. Blocking such traffic can speed up Web browsing of some ad-laden pages. (On the other hand, in some cases such a block can also cause a Web page access to hang while the browser waits for images that will never come.) You could use similar blocks to prevent access to X-rated Web sites, software piracy sites, and so on. One drawback of using such blocking for X-rated or piracy sites is that the number of such sites is quite large and is constantly changing, which makes for a great deal of administrative effort.

> **NOTE**
>
> Blocking the *output* chain request for a connection results in no *return* data, hence reducing network bandwidth. You could block return data (on the input chain) instead of or in addition to the output request, but using input blocking exclusively won't result in a reduction in traffic to or from your firewall.

- Service controls—The script blocks telnet service from the external network. It also blocks attempts to access an X font server from the external network, while explicitly allowing such access from the host computer itself.

In most real packet filter scripts, you should include many more service controls than I present in this sample script. Such configurations can become quite complex. If you need fine control over your firewall, you should plan on investing a significant amount of time in setting up and testing your configuration.

In addition to DENY, you can configure your system to REJECT packets. The difference is that DENY makes the packets vanish without a trace, whereas REJECT sends a notice back to the originating machine that the packet was rejected. The latter is the usual behavior when a service isn't running on a Linux computer.

TIP

You can test whether you've successfully blocked a service or port using a Linux or UNIX telnet program. For instance, suppose you're trying to block access to the local SSH server from external sites, but not from internal ones. Log onto an external computer and use telnet to attempt to access the firewall's port 22, which is used for SSH access, as in

telnet gingko.biloba.com 22

If you get a *connection refused* error message or no reply, you've successfully rejected or denied access, respectively. If you get a *connected* message, with or without further prompts, you've connected to the port and need to reexamine your configuration.

In testing your firewall, you may want to set up a test machine as a firewall between your regular network and a small test network of one or two computers. You can then test your firewall and its rules without disrupting the functioning of your main network. When you're satisfied with the results, install your firewall script on the main firewall computer (making any necessary changes to the IP addresses first). You should do this when the main network isn't being used heavily, though, in case there are problems.

Setting Up a Proxy Server

There are several different proxy servers available for Linux. This section provides an overview of using one of them, SOCKS5 (Sockets version 5). Another popular proxy server available for Linux is the Firewall Toolkit (FWTK) from Trusted Information Systems (TIS). You can find out more about TIS and FWTK from http://www.tis.com.

Installing and Configuring SOCKS

You can obtain the SOCKS software from the Web site http://www.socks.nec.com/. The software is available only in source code form, so you need to compile and install it.

Compiling SOCKS

You can compile and install SOCKS by following these directions. If you have problems, consult the SOCKS documentation because it's possible that something about the software's installation has changed since the time of printing.

1. Change to an appropriate directory for building software, such as `/usr/src`.
2. Extract the original source archive, with a command such as

    `tar xvfz ~/socks5-v1.0r10.tar.gz`
3. Change into the newly created SOCKS source directory:

    `cd socks5-v1.0r10/`
4. Type

    `./configure`

    This runs an auto-configuration script to set variables for proper compilation on your system.
5. Type `make` to compile the SOCKS5 package for your system. If your compiler reports any errors, you need to correct these before proceeding.

> **NOTE**
>
> Compiler *errors* and *warnings* are two different things. Don't be concerned if you see compiler warnings, as warnings are minor. Errors prevent a program from compiling properly, though.

6. Type `make install` to install SOCKS5 client and server programs on your system.

If you like, you can clean up by typing `make clean` or by deleting the source code directory.

Configuring the SOCKS Server

You configure the SOCKS server by creating a file called `/etc/socks5.conf`. This file contains rules telling the server how to process access requests. This file contains lines for each of six sections:

*   Ban host—You can forbid connections from specific hosts or groups of hosts by including a line of the form ban *source-host source-port*, as in ban `blue.beard.com 80` or ban `10.323. [100,1000]`. (The latter bans all computers from the 10.323.0.0 network using ports from 100 through 1000.)
*   Authentication—You can configure SOCKS to require that a transfer be authenticated by including a line of the form auth *source-host source-port auth-method*, as in auth `gingko.biloba.com 80 u`. The *auth-method* is generally one of n (no authentication), u (username/password pair), k (Kerberos), or - (any method).

- Interfaces—SOCK5 lets you link certain network interfaces to certain addresses by using a line of the form `interface hostpattern portpattern iface`, where `hostpattern` is the IP address pattern to be bound, `portpattern` is a port or range of ports, and `iface` is the interface. For instance, `interface 192.168.1. - eth0` binds `eth0` to the 192.168.1.0 network. Use of an `interface` line prevents IP spoofing.

- Variables and flags—You can set environment variables by creating a line of the form `set variable value`.

- Proxies—In some cases, you may want to configure two separate networks to accept connections from each other through SOCKS proxies on both ends. You can do this by including a line of the form `proxy-type dest-host dest-port proxy-list` in the `socks5.conf` file. The `proxy-type` is the type of protocol (`socks5`, `socks4`, or `noproxy`), `dest-host` and `dest-port` are the destination address and port number, respectively, and `proxy-list` is a comma-separated list of server daemons.

- Access control—You can permit or deny services by using a line of the form `permit¦deny auth command src-host dest-host src-port dest-port [user-list]`. `auth` is an authentication method, as described earlier. `command` is a comma-separated list of commands that are allowed. The hosts and ports are host and port identifiers, and `user-list` is an optional list of users.

Here's a sample `socks5.conf` file:

```
interface 192.168.1. - eth0
interface -           - eth1
permit - - - - - -
```

The `interface` lines each set up appropriate interfaces—`eth0` is linked to the 192.168.1.0 network, while `eth1` is good for all addresses. The `permit` line is quite permissive and allows any connection by any user. This and the fact that there are no `ban` lines or `auth` lines results in a very permissive proxy server configuration.

One very important aspect of SOCKS configuration is *disabling* normal routing operations. After all, if traffic can get through the router without going through SOCKS, what's the point of running the SOCKS firewall? There are several ways to disable routing:

- Configure a packet filtering firewall in addition to the proxy server firewall. If the packet filter is configured tightly enough, it can let through little or nothing, making SOCKS or some other application-level program the only way to traverse the gap from the intranet to the Internet. The advantage of this approach is that you can open a few services if they're necessary and aren't handled well by SOCKS. For instance, you might want to let a custom server function through the firewall to certain addresses but not others.

- Issue the command:

```
cat "0" /proc/sys/net/ipv4/ip_forward
```

  This will disable forwarding in the kernel.

- Uncheck the Enable routing check button in the `linuxconf` Config, Networking, Client tasks, Routing and gateways, Defaults screen, shown in Figure 21.4. This has the same effect as the preceding command.

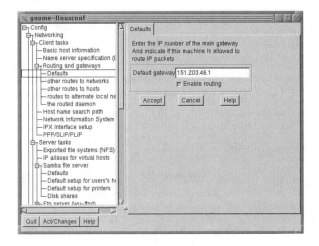

FIGURE 21.4
When you disable routing, Linux refuses to pass a packet from one network to another.

Configuring the SOCKS Clients

On the client side, you must also create a configuration file, called `/etc/libsocks5.conf`. This file contains lines of the form:

```
proxy cmd dest-host dest-port [userlist [proxylist]]
```

The meanings of each of these items is similar to the meanings of equivalent items in the `/etc/socks5.conf` file. For instance, the following line allows any user to connect to the proxy server `gingko.biloba.com`:

```
socks5 - - - - gingko.biloba.com
```

You can create more complex configurations that pass different protocols through different proxy servers, provide services only to certain users, and so on. Once you've created the configuration file, you can use SOCKS-aware client programs.

If you want to use a Linux program for which there is no ready-made "socksified" equivalent, you can recompile the program to use SOCKS. Directions for doing so come with the SOCKS package.

Using SOCKS from Windows

The SOCKS Web site includes a Windows download called SocksCap that allows most Windows TCP/IP applications to work through a SOCKS proxy server. Download the package and install it as per its instructions.

A few programs for Windows and other platforms include support for SOCKS proxies without any additional system patches. This is true of Netscape Navigator, for instance. You can select Edit, Preferences from the Netscape main menu to get the Preferences dialog box shown in Figure 21.5. In this dialog box, select Advanced, Proxies and click Manual proxy configuration to turn on proxy support. You can then click View to configure the SOCKS proxy support using the View Manual Proxy Configuration dialog box shown in Figure 21.6.

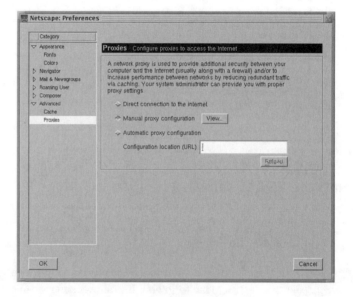

FIGURE 21.5

Proxy support is built into recent versions of Netscape.

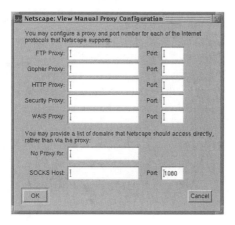

CONFIGURING A
FIREWALL

FIGURE 21.6
Enter the address of the SOCKS proxy server in the SOCKS Host field.

Unfortunately, Netscape's SOCKS support doesn't work well with SOCKS5, although it does work with SOCKS4.

Enabling and Disabling Services

After you've configured your SOCKS server, you can start it by typing **socks5** (you may need to include the path to the binary, which by default is /usr/local/bin). You can stop the service by issuing a `kill` command against it.

After you've got your SOCKS server operating as you like it, you can create an appropriate line in /etc/rc.d/rc.local to start the server when you reboot the system.

Using SOCKS-Aware Applications

After you've created an appropriate /etc/libsocks5.conf file, using SOCKS-aware Linux applications should be transparent. You need only use the SOCKS-aware binary rather than the conventional binary. There are several ways you can accomplish this task:

- Replace the conventional binaries with the SOCKS-aware versions. This isn't recommended because if you ever need the conventional version, it won't be available.

- Install both versions and ensure that the SOCKS-aware binary is in a directory that comes before the conventional binary in the system's PATH environment variable. Linux will then find the SOCKS-aware binary first and use it unless the user specifies the complete pathname to the conventional binary. This approach is often convenient, but can be thrown off if a user alters his or her PATH environment variable, or if a GUI environment calls the original file directly.

- Install the SOCKS-aware binaries under new names, such as s5ftp rather than ftp. Your users can then call the new versions explicitly.

- Rename the original binaries and give the SOCKS-aware versions the original names. For instance, you could rename ftp to ftp-direct and place the SOCKS-aware ftp program on the PATH. The major drawback of this approach on a Red Hat system is that the original binaries come in RPMs, and so when you upgrade the packages, the upgrade will install a new ftp, possibly overwriting the SOCKS-aware ftp or giving the upgraded conventional program precedence because of PATH placement.

If you're using a Windows, MacOS, or other OS's SOCKS-aware program, you should follow the directions for that program or the package you use to enable SOCKS awareness for applications in general.

Firewall Care and Maintenance

After you've set up a firewall, that's not the end of the job. You should regularly perform certain types of maintenance. If you don't, you may miss warning signs of an attack in progress until after your firewall has been breached, or you may leave your system vulnerable to attack by neglecting necessary upgrades.

Monitoring Security Logs

Most firewall tools provide some means of *logging* important information. Linux firewall tools typically log failed access attempts to the /var/log/messages file. For instance, here are two firewall messages:

```
Sep  2 15:43:22 speaker kernel: Packet log: input REJECT eth1 PROTO=17
➡ 192.168.34.98:53 10.17.34.12:137 L=28 S=0x00 I=3955 F=0x0000 T=40
Sep  2 15:45:13 speaker Socks5[14509]: Auth Failed: (192.168.34.98:1029)
```

The first of these entries reflects a packet filter in action—the computer on 192.168.34.98 attempted to access the host computer (10.17.34.12) on port 137, but the packet filter rejected this attempt. Port 137 is the NetBIOS name service, which is handled by nmbd in Linux. In other words, somebody attempted to browse available Samba services on the computer, but the packet filter blocked this attempt.

The second line reflects an attempt, two minutes after the first, to initiate a SOCKS5 proxy connection from the same computer (192.168.34.98), but again, the attempt failed. With two failed attempts to access your system from the same address, you might want to take further action. For instance, you could use nslookup to find out more about the 192.168.34.98 address. (This example is made up, and this address is one of the reserved private addresses, so if you attempt such a lookup, you'll probably find nothing unless your private network happens to use that address.)

Of course, checking through,, which monitors your log files and can take actions such as sending email to an administrative account when it detects something suspicious. I discuss swatch in Chapter 23 (p. 553).

Of course, `/var/log/messages` provides much more than evidence of intrusions. It records use of `su` to gain `root` privileges, successful logins by `ssh` or `telnet`, and other activities that you may find of interest. You can have swatch or some other monitoring utility sift through these logs as well as messages generated by your firewall tools.

You should be aware that crackers often manage to erase evidence of successful intrusions. If a cracker gains `root` access on your system, for instance, the cracker won't have any trouble modifying your `/var/log/messages` file to eliminate evidence of an intrusion. Therefore, although a log file can show evidence of an intrusion attempt, or even of some intrusions, a lack of such evidence doesn't mean that your system has *not* been compromised.

Removing Unneeded Tools

Crackers do break into firewalls. To help slow a cracker down in such an eventuality, you should make your firewall as uninviting a place as possible. Your firewall should be devoid of tools that will help a cracker make further inroads into your system, such as

- Compilers and scripting languages
- Sophisticated editors
- Network access tools that you don't need on the firewall

Of course, if you make the environment, *too* Spartan, you'll have difficulty administering the system yourself. Ideally, though, you won't need to do much with the firewall—just check its logs and perform periodic software updates to keep up with security improvements.

Keeping Up with Security Developments

Crackers often exploit newly discovered bugs in system software in order to gain entry to their target systems. Sometimes these bugs don't create obvious problems or, when exploited, produce logging messages. Your main defense against intrusion through a buggy server is to keep abreast of firewall and security developments. Red Hat maintains a list of errata for programs it distributes at `http://www.redhat.com/corp/support/errata/`. This site includes security-related updates. Chapter 24 discusses this topic further.

NOTE

The Red Hat CD included with this book incorporates all the updated RPMs up to the date the CD was created. Nonetheless, because it takes time to press a CD and distribute it with a book, there may be security updates available by the time you read this, even if you're the first person to buy this ,book.

Summary

A firewall can be a useful component of a security strategy for your network. Firewalls come in two basic types: packet filters and proxy servers. Packet filters operate by examining TCP/IP packets to determine their origin, destination, and type, and block or pass packets based on this information. Proxy filters process TCP/IP traffic much more fully, unpacking it all the way to the application level of the TCP/IP stack. After a proxy server is satisfied that the transfer is legitimate, the server repacks the data and sends it on its way. Because of this, proxy servers provide more sophisticated protection, but at the cost of increased CPU time and, in many cases, reduced convenience for users.

Providing detailed information on how to configure a firewall is beyond the scope of this book; however, this chapter does provide the basics and pointers to additional information. *I strongly urge you to read more on this subject if you want to configure your own firewall "from scratch."* Fortunately, there are several hardware and software firewall packages available, many of which greatly simplify the process of configuring a firewall. As with taking your car to a mechanic rather than fixing it yourself, of course, using a packaged solution such as a "canned" firewall means that you're at the mercy of others' skills. This chapter should at least give you the knowledge you need to understand firewall vendors' claims, and to decide just how much protection you need.

Final Considerations

PART

VII

IN THIS PART

Designing a Computer as a Linux Server

IN THIS CHAPTER

If you intend to build or buy a new computer to use as a Linux server, it's important that you understand something of Linux's hardware requirements, as well as the needs of servers generally. Because the computer industry changes so rapidly, it's impossible to recommend specific brands and models of preassembled computers for use as Linux servers; instead, you must understand something of what Linux needs for each individual component, and then make sure the computer you buy meets those needs.

You can save some time by turning this job over to somebody else. Some companies sell computers with Linux preinstalled, and these systems are almost certain to work well with Linux. If you want to locate a company that builds Linux computers, you might want to check the links available from http://www.linux.org. Even if you purchase this type of machines, you should still read this chapter to determine what hardware is most important for the specific needs of a Linux intranet server, however.

If you have an existing computer you want to adapt to function as a server, similar considerations apply. You might need to replace or upgrade one or more components to get the sort of system you need, and this chapter will help you determine what needs to be done.

CPU Requirements

The *central processing unit* (CPU) is the computational heart of any computer. It's what compares values, does math, and executes instructions in all the software you run. A variety of CPU types are available, and these can have a profound influence on the rest of your computer's design, even including the version of Linux that you run.

CPU Architectures

At the most fundamental level, CPUs use one of several different *architectures*. The CPU's architecture determines what types of program instructions it recognizes. CPUs using different architectures require different software binaries (although the same source code can often be compiled into these different binaries). Fortunately, Linux is available on a wide variety of CPU architectures. Generally speaking, each architecture is proprietary to a specific brand of CPU. For instance, only Motorola or its licensees sell 680x0 and PowerPC CPUs.

Intel designed the CPU used in the earliest IBM PCs, the 8088. Because of the popularity of the PC and its successors, Intel's architecture (known variously as x86, i386, Intel, and so on) has become popular, and in fact Linux was first developed for Intel CPUs. Intel's popularity has spawned *clone* CPUs from companies such as AMD, Cyrix, IBM, NexGen, and IDT. These CPUs reimplement the core functionality of the x86 architecture, and they can be used with the same versions of Linux as can genuine Intel CPUs.

> **NOTE**
>
> IDT's x86 clone CPU is called the WinChip. Despite this name, the CPU runs Linux quite well.

The version of Linux that accompanies this book is compiled for the x86 architecture, and most Linux computers use an x86 or clone processor. Linux has been ported to run on other architectures, however, including 680x0 (used in early Macintoshes, Atari STs, Amigas, and some UNIX workstations), PowerPC (used in later Macintoshes, some IBM systems, and a few others), DEC Alpha (used in some DEC workstations and clones), SPARC (used in SPARC workstations), and others. You can use Linux on any of these architectures, but you might need to look harder to find an appropriate Linux distribution, and chances are you'll pay more for the hardware than you would for an equivalent x86 computer.

On the low end of the scale, there are experimental ports of Linux to outdated and limited CPUs, such as those used in the 3COM PalmPilot organizer. For the most part, such machines aren't suitable for use as servers, although you still might want to use some of the procedures described in this book with them (to transfer files, for instance).

Most of this book's contents apply to any CPU architecture, though because different architectures require different distributions, some details might not apply to any given system. The rest of this chapter, however, focuses on hardware available for x86 systems. In some cases you can use the same hardware on other architectures, and in most cases the same basic principles apply to other architectures, even if the hardware details differ.

Minimal Linux Requirements

Each CPU architecture includes multiple models of CPU within that family, and Linux sometimes has minimal requirements within the family. For instance, on the Intel platform, Linux requires an 80386 or higher CPU; the operating system (OS) does not run on an 80286 or earlier CPU, except in experimental and limited ports similar to the port for the PalmPilot. You don't find new x86 PCs available for sale today that use CPUs so old that Linux won't run on them, but you might find such an antique in your closet or at a garage sale.

The Intel x86 family originally used numeric names to identify each major revision, from the 80286 to the 80386 to the 80486, for instance. This led to the use of the abbreviations 80x86 and x86 to refer to the entire family, and the common omission of the *80* portion to refer to a specific model of CPU, such as 386. Intel's competitors, however, used the same numbers, and Intel found that it couldn't trademark the CPU numbers, so after the 80486, Intel changed to a CPU name: the Pentium. The original Pentium has since spawned the Pentium Pro, the

22

DESIGNING A COMPUTER AS A LINUX SERVER

Pentium II, the Pentium III, the Celeron, and others. Some of these represent substantial improvements over their predecessors, whereas others are intended more to fill specific subniches in the market. Likewise, AMD, Cyrix, and IDT have introduced CPUs to compete against the various Pentium-class and higher CPUs, and these often have names, such as Athlon or M-II. Linux works with all these chips since the 386; you can use an Intel CPU or a competing chip from AMD, Cyrix, or IDT without fear of Linux incompatibility.

Linux relies on the presence of a math coprocessor (also known as a *floating-point unit,* or *FPU*) to perform some functions. Some CPUs, such as the 386 family, the 486SX, and early NexGen Nx586 Pentium clones lacked this FPU. If you want to run Linux on such an old CPU, you can compile the kernel to emulate the FPU functions.

> **NOTE**
>
> NexGen was bought by AMD, and many features of the Nx586 were incorporated into the AMD K6 and later CPUs. The K6 does include an FPU, however.

CPU/Motherboard Compatibility

Each CPU architecture has its own requirements for motherboard hardware. Therefore, if you intend to use, say, an Alpha CPU, you must purchase a matching Alpha motherboard. You cannot use a Pentium motherboard with an Alpha CPU.

In fact, in many architectures the CPU and motherboard must be even more closely matched. In the x86 line, each major CPU revision (386 to 486, for instance) comes with a new method of interfacing the CPU to the motherboard. You therefore can't use an 80386 CPU in an 80486 motherboard. Most Intel clone CPUs since the Pentium (the AMD K5, K6, K6-2, K6-III; the Cyrix 6x86, 6x86MMX, and M-II; and the IDT WinChip) use the same Socket 7 CPU/motherboard interface as the Pentium (shown in Figure 22.1), and so the same motherboard may be usable with old Pentiums, newer Pentiums, or more recent CPUs from the AMD or Cyrix lines. New CPUs in these lines, however, often have unique voltage or other interface electronics requirements, and therefore might not work correctly with older motherboards. If you're building a system yourself, be sure to check with the motherboard and CPU manufacturers to be sure that the models you want to use are compatible with each other.

Intel's Pentium Pro CPU uses a different socket design from the Pentium, and the Pentium II, Celeron, and Pentium III CPUs use a new type of slot, called Slot 1. Intel has also introduced something called Socket 370 as an alternative method of interfacing variants of these CPUs to motherboards. AMD's Athlon (formerly K7) CPU uses its own interface, called Slot A, which looks much like Intel's Slot 1 but is electrically incompatible with Intel products.

FIGURE 22.1
CPUs interface to motherboards by using a socket or slot, such as the Socket 7 interface shown here.

Several companies, such as Evergreen Technologies, sell CPUs that are designed to boost an older system's performance past its original capabilities. These typically include the most capable CPU in a given socket's line, along with voltage regulators or other hardware to make it compatible with older boards. Sometimes these CPUs are advertised as if they belonged to the next-higher class, as in claims that a 486 upgrade produces Pentium-class performance. These upgrades don't do miracles, but if you're on a tight budget and have an older machine available, they can be helpful in stretching the useful life of the machine.

Speed Recommendations

Surprisingly, a blazing CPU is not a requirement for a Linux server. For a small network, any Pentium-class or better CPU is probably more than adequate for providing most file and printer services. Even a 486 might be acceptable, although 486 motherboards often lacked the peripheral component interconnect (PCI) bus and therefore may not accept the latest in networking or hard disk interface hardware, both of which are important in a server.

One exception to this rule is if the computer is driving high-resolution or color non-PostScript printers as if they were PostScript devices. For instance, if you've connected inexpensive color inkjet printers to a Linux box and made them available on your network as PostScript models, Linux needs to use Ghostscript to interpret the PostScript from the clients. This is a

CPU-intensive task, and if you attempt it with an inadequate CPU, printing performance will suffer. In general, though, a Pentium should still be adequate for handling one color printer in this way. If you've connected several printers to a single Linux print server, you might want to consider using a higher-end Pentium-class system for the task. If you can print on the clients by using native drivers for that model printer, this can reduce the CPU requirements of the server, but at the cost of increased network traffic.

If you intend to use a Linux system for more than file and print services, you might want to look into getting a more powerful CPU. For instance, if you'll have several people logged on to the computer at once, running scientific or engineering simulations or other CPU-intensive programs, you probably need to invest in the fastest CPU possible, or even in a multiple-CPU motherboard. If you expect the system to be used occasionally by one or two people for tasks such as word processing, a midrange to high-end Pentium should be adequate.

Memory Requirements

A computer is useless without memory. In fact, a computer uses more than one *type* of memory for different tasks. This section is concerned with the types of memory that are most directly associated with the motherboard and CPU. Other system components, such as video cards and hard disks, often have their own memory, which I discuss in the sections on those components. Like CPU speed, a server's need for memory is typically not as high as the memory needs of a workstation, although there are exceptions to this rule.

Types of RAM

Memory can be classified in several ways, and there's a great deal of change within each type of memory over as short a period as a year. This can lead to befuddlement because what you learned two years ago about memory types might not apply today.

The general type of memory I discuss here is random access memory (RAM), which can be read from and written to. RAM comes in many varieties that vary in speed and other characteristics.

Memory Classes

A motherboard typically has three or so different classes of memory. Generally, the slower the class of memory, the more plentiful and less expensive it is. A system uses the faster memory types to *cache*, or hold closer to the CPU for processing, data and instructions that are likely to be used again soon. In this way, the CPU can use memory stores that are fast most of the time, and resort to using the slowest types of memory only when necessary. The types of memory you'll find on a typical system are as follows:

- CPU cache—The CPU cache is the fastest and smallest type of memory. It's part of the CPU itself, so you can't replace or upgrade it except by replacing the CPU. CPU caches are sometimes referred to as Level 1, or L1, caches, and they're typically measured in the tens of kilobytes in size.

- L2 cache—Where the CPU cache is an L1 cache, the motherboard typically hosts another type of cache, known as the Level 2, or L2, cache. This cache is slower but more plentiful than the CPU cache, typically being measured in the hundreds of kilobytes to a few megabytes in capacity. The L2 cache is often soldered onto the motherboard, although some boards have upgradable L2 caches. Intel CPUs since the Pentium Pro and the AMD Athlon place the L2 cache on the CPU module, although it's not part of the CPU chip itself. This allows the L2 cache to run faster than it could on the motherboard, improving overall system performance.

- Main memory—The main memory is the type of memory of which you're probably most aware. If you type **free** at a Linux prompt, you'll get a report of how much main memory you have and how much of it is being used. Main memory is typically measured in the tens or hundreds of megabytes, although some very high-end systems may have a gigabyte or more.

As with all things computer related, these figures are bound to change over the next few years. Also, some systems may have another layer of cache in this stack, or may be missing one.

Memory Subclasses

In addition to these broad classes of RAM, each type has several subtypes. For instance, main memory is available in dynamic RAM (DRAM), extended data out DRAM (EDO DRAM), synchronous DRAM (SDRAM), and other formats. These terms refer to the electrical characteristics of the chips. There are also an assortment of physical forms for RAM, such as 30-pin single inline memory modules (SIMMs), 72-pin SIMMs, and dual inline memory modules (DIMMs), as shown in Figure 22.2. When you build a new system yourself or upgrade an existing one, it's important that you know which types of memory your motherboard can accept. For instance, if you have a motherboard that requires SDRAM DIMMs, you need to acquire that type of memory. If you have existing 30-pin DRAM SIMMs, you won't be able to use them in the new motherboard. Similar comments apply to the cache memory on the motherboard (if it's upgradable). Because the CPU cache is part of the CPU, you don't need to be concerned with matching it to other components.

FIGURE 22.2

The 30-pin SIMM (top) was common in 486 motherboards, but is now largely obsolete; the 168-pin DIMM (bottom) is common in recent Pentium, Pentium II, Pentium III, and clone systems.

NOTE

At press time, PC-100 DIMMs are the most common type for new systems. These are ordinary DIMMs that meet specific timing requirements so that they can be used on motherboards with 100MHz busses (hence the name *PC-100*). PC-100 DIMMs are also shorter than the DIMM shown in Figure 22.2. Other memory types are likely to make PC-100 DIMMs obsolete within a year or two, though.

Because these components need to match, I recommend purchasing RAM, the motherboard, and the CPU from the same vendor, if at all possible. Make sure that the vendor understands you intend to use these components together, and that the vendor approves the combination you've selected.

A Linux Server's Memory Needs

If you're using a Linux system solely as a print and file server, it has relatively low memory requirements because its day will be filled with moving data between the network adapter and hard disks or printer ports—tasks that are not very memory intensive. On the other hand, if your system has a great deal of RAM, Linux uses most of that RAM as a cache for disk accesses. This can greatly speed disk access times if your users routinely access the same files, but it doesn't help if your users spend their time accessing a large number of different files. If you have no need to use the computer with X for graphical user interface (GUI) console use, a server might be able to get by with only 16MB of main memory. This value goes up if you're using the computer as a workstation and as a server, if the server load is particularly high, or if your disk access patterns benefit from having a large cache. As with CPU requirements, you might also want more RAM if you intend to serve non-PostScript printers as if they were PostScript models, using Ghostscript. In this situation, the Linux server functions as a PostScript interpreter, and PostScript printers function best with several megabytes of memory, so you need comparable amounts for each printer you serve.

As a general rule, you should probably try to have at least 64MB in any Linux server, just to be safe. If you have less than this amount, you'll get better server performance if you set the system to *not* run X at startup, or at least if you don't log on to it using memory-intensive GUI environments like KDE or GNOME. These tools can easily consume 30MB or more RAM by themselves. Because a server doesn't need these programs running in day-to-day operation, you might as well devote that memory to other tasks.

Disk Requirements

A server's hardware requirements are quite modest in some areas, but hard disk needs are not one of these. Even in a small workgroup of a handful of computers, a server's disks see a lot of action, and you should be prepared to give your Linux server the best hard disks you can afford.

One trick is to use more than one physical hard disk. Suppose you have two users accessing different files on the server. If the files are on the same disk, the disk heads jump back and forth between the two files, degrading performance for both users. If the two files are on different disks, however, there are fewer head movements, and overall performance benefits. Of course, arranging your disk space so that both drives are used equally involves as much guesswork as anything else. If you can split user files into two groups, you might consider using two partitions, one on each physical disk, for this purpose. Alternatively, you can place system files and printer queues (in the /var directory tree) on one physical disk and user files on another.

Linux isn't fussy about brands of hard disk, so choose the model that has the features you want, without worrying about whether it's compatible with Linux. Compatibility is an issue for SCSI host adapters, however (you'll learn more on this shortly, in the following section). EIDE (Enhanced Integrated Device Electronics) controllers seldom pose problems, but to use advanced features such as *direct memory access* (DMA; used to reduce the CPU overhead of disk access), you need kernel support for your specific EIDE controller. Linux includes such EIDE support for the most popular controllers, which are usually included on the motherboard.

The SCSI Versus EIDE Debate

Most x86 PCs sold today include EIDE hard drives. These devices attach directly to modern motherboards, which can support up to two EIDE devices on each of two cables. EIDE drives are inexpensive and come in capacities that are more than adequate for most desktop uses, hence their popularity.

NOTE

The terms *IDE* (Integrated Device Electronics), *EIDE* (Enhanced IDE), *ATA* (AT Attachment), and *ATAPI* (AT Attachment Packet Interface) describe similar hardware and electronics protocols. *IDE* was the term applied to the earliest devices in this family, and is still sometimes used to apply to more recent products. ATAPI generally refers to non-disk devices that plug in to the same IDE controller that handles hard disks, such as CD-ROMs and tape drives. EIDE usually refers to hard disks. You also sometimes encounter terms such as *ATA/33* or *ATA/66*, which refer to the speed of a particular revision of the IDE-derived bus, or *ATA-2* or *ATA-3*, which refer to a revision of the ATA standard.

UNIX servers, on the other hand, typically come with SCSI (small computer system interface) hard drives. These drives are usually more expensive than EIDE drives of similar capacity and are faster. The SCSI interface also offers advantages over EIDE, most notably including up to 7 devices per cable (15 for some SCSI variants) and an improved capacity to handle simultaneous access to more than one device. For instance, if you have two hard disks, and if you simultaneously read large files from both drives, SCSI copes better with this request than does EIDE; the SCSI bus supports simultaneous transmission by more than one device, whereas EIDE does not. These characteristics make SCSI the preferred bus type for servers, which often have multiple hard disks serving an office of several people making simultaneous access demands.

There is a literal cost to SCSI, however, as SCSI host adapters themselves typically cost $100 or more, and SCSI hard disks are usually substantially more expensive than EIDE drives of similar capacity. The SCSI drives are often (but not always) faster than their EIDE counterparts, however, so part of the price gets you better disk speed even in an access to a single device.

Both SCSI and EIDE come in a variety of bus speeds. Most SCSI drives sold today support at least *UltraSCSI* speed (20MBps), with many supporting *UltraWide SCSI* (40MBps) or better. The EIDE line also uses the word *ultra*, in its term *UltraDMA*, which refers to a 33MBps transfer rate. As I write this, 66MBps speeds are being claimed for some EIDE interfaces. Of course, with either bus, you need matching controllers and hard drives; upgrading one without the other won't get you extra speed. Indeed, a single drive is unlikely to be able to take full advantage of the bus's speed.

CAUTION

Many hard drive manufacturers prominently advertise their products' *bus speed*. This speed is almost always substantially higher than the drive's *actual* speed. The physics of hard disk design limits the speed with which the drive can pull data off its platters, and this so-called *media* or *internal* transfer rate is what determines the drive's speed in isolation. In the case of SCSI drives, you can often attain transfer rates that approach those of the SCSI bus itself by combining multiple drives in one system. With EIDE, this is more difficult because you need to place each drive on its own cable to get a speed improvement from multiple drives, and most motherboards support only two EIDE cables. You should pay careful attention to the manufacturers' speed claims and be sure you're working from figures of the *internal* transfer rate when deciding between two drives.

Linux supports a wide variety of SCSI host adapters. Models from Mylex (formerly BusLogic) and boards based on the Symbios 53c8xx series chipsets from a variety of manufacturers are well liked by the Linux community, as are many Adaptec products. As new models come to market, of course, the precise list of what Linux supports changes. If you already have Linux installed, you can check the kernel configuration options to see which boards are supported; or you can check the Web site for a distribution such as Red Hat (`http://www.redhat.com`) to see what they recommend.

NOTE

Because support for SCSI host adapters (and most other hardware components) is a function of the Linux kernel, and because the kernel is the same between all Linux distributions for a given architecture, supported hardware is the same for all distributions. Different distributions may list different hardware, though, because they've tested different hardware, because they use different standards of compatibility, or because they include different drivers in their default kernel compilations.

Disk Space Requirements

A minimal Linux installation can survive on as little as 100MB, but such a system would be woefully inadequate as a server. For a server, Linux itself takes up somewhere between 300MB and 1GB, depending on the options you select at install time and what extra packages you choose to install. Beyond that, your disk space requirements depend on your particular setup. If you're using a Linux server to store the results of complex high-resolution graphics imaging for a motion picture, your disk space requirements may be truly astronomical; but if you're using it for an office of half a dozen people who write memos and other purely textual documents in word processors, you may need only two or three gigabytes total.

Network Interface Card Recommendations

One piece of equipment that's not necessary in every Linux computer but that's vital for a network is the *network interface card* (NIC; see Figure 22.3). If you choose the wrong NIC for your purposes, all the other hardware choices will be for nothing because Linux won't be able to send data over your network quickly enough.

Ethernet address sticker

RJ-45 networking connector

Activity lights

FIGURE 22.3
A typical 10/100 Mbps NIC has an RJ-45 connector and activity lights visible from outside the computer. The card's Ethernet address is often printed on a sticker on the card.

NIC Speed and Type

This book focuses on Ethernet networking. There are other types of network, however, and if you need to use one of these networks, you need to obtain an appropriate networking card and determine how to configure it. Fortunately, Linux includes support for a variety of network types, and much of the information in this book applies even to non-Ethernet networks.

Assuming that you want to use Ethernet, you need to determine what type and speed of network hardware to buy. If you're building a new network, I recommend using 100Mbps hardware, also known as 100BaseT. This hardware connects using cables that resemble an ordinary telephone cord (see Figure 22.4), and is capable of transmitting data at up to 100Mbps (104,857,600bps). 100BaseT hardware is common, reasonably inexpensive, and well supported by Linux. If you're connecting to an existing network, though, you might need to buy a NIC with the appropriate connector. Additional forms of Ethernet are discussed in Chapter 1, "Networking Hardware." You should also consult Chapter 1 for information on the cable used between computers, including the use of *hubs* (p. 20) and *switches* (p. 20).

FIGURE 22.4
The RJ-45 connectors on the ends of 10BaseT and 100BaseT cable are identical, and resemble telephone cord connectors, although the Ethernet cable connectors are wider.

NIC Chipsets

In general, Linux provides drivers for most devices according to the networking *chipset* (p. 18) on the board, not according to the specific brand and model of the board. For instance, you don't find a driver in the Linux kernel for the D-Link DFE-530TX NIC, but you do find a driver for the VIA Rhine chipset used by that board. An exception to this rule is when one company is the exclusive or nearly exclusive user of a chipset, as is the case with many of Intel's NICs. Thus, you should try to find out what chipset a NIC uses to determine its compatibility with Linux. Unfortunately, this is sometimes difficult to do, as board manufacturers frequently prefer to downplay the fact that their boards use the same core circuitry as their competitors' products. Sometimes a board manufacturer even removes the markings identifying a chipset and replaces them with its own.

Linux includes support for almost all the NICs on the market today, so it's difficult to pick a poor board, at least from the point of view of Linux driver support. Among PCI boards, particularly popular and well-supported products include Intel's EtherExpress line, 3COM's EtherLink XL (using the 3c905b chipset), and a variety of products using the Tulip (21x4x) chipset from DEC (now from Intel) or clones of this chipset from PNIC, Macronix, and others. Most of the inexpensive 10/100 Mbps NICs in stores today are based on Tulip clones.

> **NOTE**
>
> The Linux kernel included with Red Hat 6.0 includes a driver for the Tulip chipset, but this driver doesn't work with all the Tulip clones. Therefore, you might need to recompile your kernel with updated Tulip drivers if you buy such a board. These drivers are available from `http://cesdis.gsfc.nasa.gov/linux/drivers/tulip-devel.html`.

Additional Hardware Tips and Recommendations

Although components such as the CPU, hard disk, and NIC are obvious concerns in building a computer, they're not the only components. Others, although perhaps not as critical, deserve mention and are described in the following sections.

Video Cards

It's possible to operate a Linux server without its own monitor, although you need one to install Linux, and the motherboard will probably require that a video card be installed in order to run. If you want to run a Linux system in such a "headless server" configuration, you can buy the video card that's cheapest. Even an antiquated industry standard architecture (ISA) video card will work in such a situation.

If you want to use your Linux system with its own monitor and X, however, you need to get a video card that's supported by Linux—or, more precisely, by XFree86. Because the video card market changes so rapidly, it's difficult to make specific recommendations in a book. In general, though, availability of XFree86 drivers lags a generation or two behind actual video hardware, so if you buy the latest and greatest video board, you might find that it's useless under Linux, except in text mode. Boards by Matrox and ATI generally have good Linux support, as do products with S3 chipsets. You can find more information on current XFree86 driver support at the XFree86 Web site, `http://www.xfree86.org`. In addition, SuSE (http://www.suse.com) develops many of the cutting-edge XFree86 drivers, so you might find an experimental driver there for a relatively new video board. If you find that you're in possession of an extremely new and unsupported board, it's possible that the Xi Graphics (http://www.xig.com) Accelerated X server supports your board; but purchasing this software might be more expensive than buying a replacement video card.

Video boards, like many computer components, have their own memory. This memory is used to hold the contents of the screen, and sometimes to help with 3D rendering or other features. As you increase the resolution and color depth of your display, you increase the amount of memory required on the video board. You can compute the amount required to run the board at any given resolution with the following formula:

$$M = x \times y \times d / 8{,}388{,}608$$

In this equation, M is the memory in megabytes, x and y are the x and y resolutions, and d is the color depth (for instance, 16 for 16-bit color, capable of displaying 65,536 colors). Most video cards on the market today have more than enough RAM to handle a display of 1024×768 or even 1600×1200 at 16-bit, and often at 24-bit or 32-bit. Keep in mind that the speed of the display drops as the screen resolution, and especially the color depth, increases.

Sound Cards

In general, you don't need a sound card for a server. If you want one nonetheless, you should know that there are three major sources of drivers for sound cards in Linux:

- The Linux kernel—The kernel includes a set of drivers for a number of sound cards. Many of these are older ISA designs, but some are newer PCI cards.

- The OSS drivers—4Front Technologies (http://www.4front.com/) offers the commercial Open Sound System (OSS) drivers for Linux. These drivers are related to the drivers in the Linux kernel, but are available only for a fee.

- The ALSA drivers—The Advanced Linux Sound Architecture (ALSA; http://alsa.jcu.cz/) project is working on a new sound model for Linux, and has a set of drivers available.

Linux sound driver development and the sound card marketplace both change rapidly, so it's difficult to make definite recommendations. ISA boards based on assorted Crystal Semiconductor chipsets are well supported, however, under all three driver sets, and PCI boards based on the S3 SonicVibes chipset are also popular.

Additional Printer Ports

If you intend to set up a Linux box as a print server, you might find that you want to serve more than one printer from a single computer. Because most printers come with parallel ports, and because most motherboards have only one parallel port, you might need to add one or more parallel ports to your computer. ISA boards to do this are common, and may contain one or two ports. Linux should have no problem using such ports, assuming that you configure the board properly. Where your first parallel port is `/dev/lp0`, the second is `/dev/lp1` and the third is `/dev/lp2`.

It's difficult to use more than three parallel ports on a standard Intel-architecture machine. Therefore, you might want to look into using a serial port for further printers, either with a printer that accepts serial input or with a parallel-to-serial adapter. Printing via a serial port is typically slower than via a parallel port, however.

The Universal Serial Bus (USB) is another method of attaching a printer. USB support was added to the Linux kernel with version 2.2.8, but was still quite crude at that time. You can find more information on the state of USB support for Linux at `http://peloncho.fis.ucm.es/ ~inaky/uusbd-www/`. USB is becoming a common interface for printers, especially for inkjets, and in theory you can attach several dozen USB printers to a single computer, so when this technology matures it might be quite useful to Linux users.

Finally, if no other options are available, you can purchase dedicated Ethernet print servers or, for some printers, install an Ethernet board in the printer. These devices make one or more printers directly available on your network. In many cases, using such a server obviates the need for using Linux as a print server. If you want to use Ghostscript in Linux to convert PostScript into the printer's native format, however, you still need to configure a printer queue and serve that in the usual way. This sort of configuration increases the traffic on your network because the file goes first to your Linux print server and then to the printer itself.

Backup Hardware

Murphy's Law guarantees that at least one of your network's computers will crash catastrophically, taking its operating system and perhaps user data with it. That's why you should look into using your Linux box as a backup server, using media such as a tape drive for backups. To do this, however, you need appropriate backup hardware, as described in the following sections.

Tape

One of the most popular backup media is tape. Tape drives come in four major types of interface: SCSI, EIDE/ATAPI, floppy, and parallel port. For serious server use, I recommend a SCSI tape unit. These drives tend to be the most reliable, and they're available in some of the largest capacities. An ATAPI unit might be acceptable in a very small network, but remember the limits on the number of EIDE/ATAPI devices—four per system. Floppy- and parallel-interfaced tape backup units tend to be finicky and unreliable, so I recommend avoiding them.

Within each class of tape backup unit there are several different tape formats available. The two most popular are Travan and digital audio tape (DAT). In general, Travan drives are inexpensive but the tapes are pricey, whereas DAT drives are costly but the tapes are inexpensive. Both formats are available in capacities ranging from a gigabyte or so up to tens of gigabytes. If you're backing up many machines or keep a large library of tapes, the costs even out or favor DAT; if you back up only a couple systems and have only a couple tapes per system, Travan is less expensive. In addition to these formats, there are others, typically aimed at large systems, such as digital linear tape (DLT) and advanced intelligent tape (AIT). Some tape systems (even including some Travan units) are available as *changers*, which swap tapes in and out automatically for unattended backups of large quantities of data. If your network has more than three or four computers, you should seriously consider using a high-end DAT system, a DLT drive, or a changer. Expect to pay over $1,000 for such a system.

CD-R, CD-RW, and DVD-RAM

CD-recordable (CD-R) and CD-rewritable (CD-RW) have become popular for a variety of data storage purposes. These media have a capacity of 650MB, and they possess excellent archival qualities (that is, the media last a long time). These characteristics make these media an excellent choice for long-term archival storage of data such as scientific data, financial records, and so on. You can place a CD-R or CD-RW drive on your Linux server and use it to archive data from any or all of your networks' computers. As with other storage media, I favor SCSI units, although Linux CD-R tools also support many EIDE/ATAPI units. Check the Linux CD-R HOWTO (included with most Linux distributions) for details on how to use these devices.

DVD-RAM devices are available, and function much like CD-R or CD-RW drives, but with DVD technology for substantially higher capacities. These drives are currently quite expensive, however, and there are as yet no Linux tools to use them. Both conditions are, of course, subject to change, so you might want to do a search for `linux and dvd-ram` at `http://www.deja.com` to find the very latest information on this technology.

Although they're good for archival storage of important records, the 650MB capacity of CD-R and CD-RW discs limits their usefulness for routine system backups. If your network is highly centralized, with a Linux server dishing out most programs and data, your workstations' contents might each fit on a single CD-R, which could be a useful recovery strategy for them; but you probably want something with higher capacity to back up your server.

Removable Disks

Removable drives, such as the Iomega Zip and JAZ drives or conventional hard disks mounted in removable bays, are sometimes useful as backup media. As with CD-R discs, you can use such media to back up important data files and transport them from site to site.

Removable-media drives typically have capacities that are much lower than those of fixed disks, however, and so they aren't good candidates for backing up an entire network, except perhaps for backing up workstations with limited disk capacities as described for CD-R. If your network is small, you might consider using a small number of removable fixed disks to back up the network or its server. This solution has the advantages of high speed and low cost for a small number of backups, but the disadvantage of rapidly mounting costs as the amount of data to be backed up increases. It becomes quite pricey to maintain a rotating set of, say, a full month's backups by using removable fixed disks.

Where to Save and Spend Money in a Linux Server Design

When you design a Linux server, you should not make the same decisions as you would for building a desktop workstation. A server needs rapid access to all its files, and does not need fancy multimedia capabilities, for instance. If you're on a budget, then, you should consider trimming on these items:

- CPU—A server's needs for raw computing power are limited, so there's no point in investing in the latest Pentium III CPU.

- RAM—A server isn't likely to be running a large number of memory-intensive programs, so you can save on memory. Most computers today come with at least 32MB of RAM, and that should be more than adequate for a small server that need not itself run X or user programs. If you can spend money on a better CPU or more RAM, but not both, though, spend money on the RAM because the server's RAM-based disk cache might help improve system performance.

- Video—A server's video card isn't used much, so don't spend much on this component.

- CD-ROM—Unless you intend to use the machine to serve CDs, you won't use the CD-ROM drive much. Similarly, you probably don't need a DVD-ROM drive in the server, unless you intend to serve DVD-ROMs.

- Sound card—You probably don't need a sound card at all.

You should save by not investing a lot in components from the preceding list and put the savings into the features that do matter:

- SCSI—A SCSI host adapter lets you attach many storage components and use them more efficiently than you could with EIDE/ATAPI.
- Multiple SCSI hard disks—Instead of, say, a single 20GB drive, purchase two 10GB drives. This can improve overall performance, especially if you enable Linux's built-in redundant array of independent disks (RAID) support. Buy the fastest hard disks you can afford. If you need substantial disk space, buying multiple small drives might actually save money compared to buying one large drive.
- Backup hardware—Don't let your network go unprotected! Overall, a SCSI tape unit is probably the best and simplest backup solution, although it's not the only one. You might want to use a combination of strategies, such as a CD-R for workstations and a tape for the server.
- A good NIC—Although not expensive, a good NIC is critical for good network performance. Get the fastest NIC your current network supports, or even faster if you're using 10BaseT.

Summary

Putting together a Linux computer requires more research than does assembling a PC to run Windows, largely because you're not guaranteed to have Linux drivers for many components. New and experienced Linux users also often have questions about Linux's compatibility with specific CPUs or about Linux's requirements in terms of RAM or disk space.

Fortunately, Linux *is* compatible with a wide range of hardware, so even if you randomly select an off-the-shelf computer, you probably won't have to replace much to get it working with Linux. As a general rule, you should probably avoid the very latest devices, particularly in video hardware. Invest your money in fast hard disk storage and adequate network hardware, and you'll be most satisfied.

22

DESIGNING A COMPUTER AS A LINUX SERVER

System Administration

IN THIS CHAPTER

This book is about Linux system administration. It focuses upon a specialized set of administrative tasks—those relating to operating the computer as a server for a small network. There are certain important administrative tasks that don't fall under the heading of any of the specific networking tasks I've covered in the book to this point, however. I cover these tasks in this chapter.

I cover some administrative tasks elsewhere in this book. For instance:

- Chapter 5, "Basic Linux Configuration," covers installation and the handling of user accounts.

- Chapter 6, "Compiling a Kernel for Networking," covers the important topic of kernel compilation.

- Chapter 13, "Using Linux to Back Up Client Machines," includes information on backing up the server itself, as well as client computers.

- Chapter 14, "Preparing to Share a Printer," covers printer configuration.

- Chapter 24, "Maintaining a Secure System," covers system security issues.

You can also consult a book such as Pitts & Ball's *Red Hat Linux 6 Unleashed* from Sams for more information on running a Linux system.

Installing and Removing RPM Packages

In the Linux community, software programs are often referred to as *packages*. A package includes not just the program, but also documentation, configuration files, support programs, and so on. For ease of distribution, packages typically come in a single file. Three distribution formats are common for Linux packages:

- Tarballs—a *tarball* is a group of files bound together in a tar archive and compressed with gzip. Tarballs usually have .tgz or .tar.gz extensions. They can contain either binaries (compiled programs) or source code that you must compile yourself. I describe the process of compiling programs later in this chapter.

- Debian packages—The Debian distribution uses its own package format. These packages' filenames typically end in .deb. Debian package files are more sophisticated than tarballs because Debian's format includes information on the package contents, including *dependency* information that tells the system upon what other packages any given package relies. For instance, the package earth.deb can record that it relies upon sun.deb. That way, if you attempt to install earth.deb without sun.deb, the system can tell you that you must first locate and install sun.deb.

- RPM packages—Red Hat introduced the Red Hat package manager (RPM) format to accomplish much the same task as the Debian package format. RPM, like Debian's format, supports dependencies and other package information. Conceptually, these two formats are quite similar to one another, although they aren't compatible.

Most mainstream Linux distributions use the RPM format for their files. Debian, of course, uses the Debian format. Slackware uses tarballs. A few others, like Stampede, use assorted other formats. You can install the package managers for a foreign distribution on any system. For instance, you can install the RPM utilities on a Slackware system, or the Debian utilities on a Red Hat system. It's best to stick with one package format per computer, though, to avoid conflicts.

> **NOTE**
>
> Because RPM is used so widely, my comments on it apply to non-Red Hat distributions that use RPM, such as Mandrake and SuSE, as well as to Red Hat itself.

Understanding the RPM Database

The RPM utilities maintain a database of packages you've installed in the directory `/var/lib/rpm`. The files in this directory have `.rpm` extensions, but they aren't RPM package files; rather, they're databases that maintain information on installed packages, such as

- Names—The names of the packages that you have installed, such as `glibc` and `samba`.

- Versions—The version number associated with each installed package, such as `2.1.1-6` for `glibc`. The version number includes both the software version (`2.1.1`) and a *build number* (`6`). The build number refers to minor changes to the package implemented at compile time. A revised build might add or delete support files, change the location in which a file is installed, or apply a patch that's not part of the official software release.

- Installed package dependencies—Most packages depend on one or more others for proper functioning. For instance, most programs link against the standard C libraries, which are contained in the `glibc` package. Therefore, most packages depend upon `glibc`. Sometimes a package depends upon a specific version of another package; for instance, a package might depend upon `glibc` 2.1 or later. The RPM system allows searching for dependencies in reverse, too. For instance, if you were to try to remove `glibc`, the system would refuse on the grounds that so many additional packages depend upon `glibc`.

- Descriptions—Each package has assorted descriptive information associated with it, including the system on which the RPM file was created, copyright and distribution terms, and an English description of what the package does.

- Included files—RPM maintains a list of files that are associated with each package. RPM can use this information to delete old files when you update or remove a package. You can also search the database to find out what package owns a specific file.

You don't access the RPM database files directly; instead, you use the `rpm` program, or a GUI front-end such as `gnorpm`, to do the job. I describe these tools shortly.

Source, Binary, and Noarch RPMs

RPM files come in three basic forms: *source*, *binary*, and *noarch*:

- Source—Source RPMs usually contain the string *src* as part of their filenames, as in `icewm-0.9.33-1.src.rpm`. Source RPMs contain source code that you can use to compile the program on your system. Normally you don't need to use source RPMs, but they can be convenient in some cases, as when you want to recompile a program to take better advantage of some new system utility, or when you want to compile the same program for Linux running on computers with different architectures, such as Intel and PowerPC computers.

- Binary—Binary RPMs contain precompiled program code. For Intel-architecture machines, binary RPM filenames generally contain the string *i386*, or possibly a higher *x86* value, such as *i686*, if the program was compiled to take advantage of more sophisticated CPUs' features. Binary RPMs also exist for non-Intel architectures, such as PowerPC, and in such cases they have different CPU codes as part of their filenames, such as *ppc*. You cannot use a binary RPM for an architecture other than the one you're using. You can often recompile a source RPM when all you can find are the source RPM and a binary for an architecture you're not using, though.

- Noarch—*Noarch* stands for *no architecture*. A noarch RPM is one that contains information that doesn't depend upon the architecture. RPMs for Linux documentation are noarch, for instance, as are RPMs that contain only interpreted programs like Perl scripts.

In general, it's easiest to install binary and noarch RPMs. If you can only find a source RPM, though, you can use it to create an appropriate binary RPM and install that. If you can't find an appropriate RPM of any form, it's possible to create an RPM from raw source code, but doing so is beyond the scope of this book. It's generally easier to install a program directly from the source tarball than to create an RPM from the source tarball, but you might want to create an RPM in order to maintain as much information about your system as possible in the RPM database files. This way, you can check the validity of the installed files quite easily, and you can be sure that your program won't overwrite other programs' files, or be overwritten by future installations. You can also more easily uninstall a program in the future if you install it from an RPM.

> **TIP**
>
> If you're running Linux on an unusual architecture, such as PowerPC, you may have difficulty locating appropriate binary RPMs. Most sites that have binary RPMs for Intel also have source RPMs, so you should be able to download the source RPM, create an appropriate binary RPM, install from the new binary RPM, and archive it on a CD-R, Zip disk, floppy, or some other medium.

Locating Worthy Program Files

When you need to install a new program, the first step is to locate it. There are several possible sources for RPM files:

- Your installation CD—Most Linux distributions include lots of programs that aren't installed in a standard installation. The program you want may already be on your CD.

- Another distribution's installation CD—Sometimes a distribution other than the one you're running includes the package you want. If you're using an RPM-based distribution and have another distribution's CD handy, check that CD for the program.

- Distributions' archives—Your distribution maintainer probably has an archive of RPMs that may not be on your CD. Sometimes the RPMs available from the Internet site are newer than what's on the CD, and some sites have additional programs, too. Red Hat, for instance, maintains an archive of RPMs contributed by third parties on their FTP site `ftp://contrib.redhat.com`.

- Program authors' Web sites—Many program authors either provide RPM files themselves or provide links to RPM files maintained by others. It's therefore worth checking a program's official Web site to see if there's an RPM available.

- Independent Internet archives—Many FTP and Web sites host RPMs for a wide variety of programs. One of the best for locating RPM files is located at `http://rufus.w3.org/linux/RPM/`.

In general, I recommend using RPMs that are designed for the distribution you're running. This practice will avoid possible problems with conflicts between libraries or other peculiarities. In most cases, though, you can use RPM files created with one distribution in mind on another distribution. My own Red Hat system has several RPMs installed from SuSE and Mandrake, for instance, and those programs work fine.

23

SYSTEM ADMINISTRATION

Using the rpm Program

The method of RPM management that provides the finest control is the rpm command-line program. I present some basic information on use of this program in this section, but I can't begin to cover the program's full set of features. For more information, check the rpm manpage, or Ed Bailey's *Maximum RPM*, from Sams.

Installing Binary RPMs

If you have a binary RPM file, you can install it by typing

```
rpm -i filename.rpm
```

or

```
rpm -U filename.rpm
```

Using -i results in a standard installation, whereas -U results in an upgrade. If an earlier version doesn't already exist on the system, -U results in a standard install. Therefore, I generally use -U in all cases. If you want to maintain careful written logs of software you've installed, you might want to favor -i because doing so will cause rpm to alert you when a package you're trying to install already exists, and might therefore be an upgrade rather than a fresh installation.

You might also want to add the -vh options, as in

```
rpm -Uvh filename.rpm
```

These parameters result in the display of hash marks across the screen to indicate the progress of an installation. If you want to install multiple RPMs, you can specify them all on one line. For instance, here's what happens when you install two packages:

```
[root@speaker RPMS]# rpm -Uvh zgv-3.0-8.i386.rpm zsh-3.0.5-10.i386.rpm
zgv                  #################################################
zsh                  #################################################
```

If the package you're trying to install requires components you don't have on your system, you'll receive an error message along the lines of failed dependencies, along with a list of the packages or files that are required. You have three choices in a case like this:

- Override the dependency coding—You might have installed the packages you require in a non-RPM form, or in an RPM that's named differently than what the complaining RPM expects. If so, you can tell rpm to ignore dependencies by adding the —nodeps flag, as in

  ```
  rpm -Uvh filename.rpm —nodeps
  ```

  This action causes the system to ignore dependencies and install the package. If you're wrong about support files being present, though, the program won't run correctly.

- Reconfigure required files—RPM allows dependencies to be specified in terms of either individual files or entire RPM packages. If a dependency is given in terms of an individual file, you may be able to reconfigure your system to provide that dependency, if appropriate support exists in another file. For instance, an RPM might look for a library in a location other than the one in which it's installed on your system. In that case, creating a symbolic link from the expected location to the file's true position should allow the RPM to install normally.

- Install the required package—You can install the required RPM package to satisfy the dependency. You can either install the packages in sequence or at the same time (by specifying both on the same rpm line). If the latter, it doesn't matter in what order you list the RPM files.

Another common problem when installing RPM files is in a file conflict. If an RPM you're trying to install contains files that would overwrite files owned by another RPM, the system will refuse to install the RPM. You'll have to determine whether you want to overwrite the existing file on a case-by-case basis. If you decide to install the new RPM, you can do so by specifying the --force parameter, as in

```
rpm -Uvh filename.rpm --force
```

TIP

Before forcing an installation over existing files, you may want to back up the existing files by renaming them or copying them to another directory. That way, if you decide to uninstall the new package, you can easily restore the original files. Similarly, if you prefer to have the original files back while still using the new RPM, you can replace the new RPM's files with the old ones.

On rare occasion, rpm may complain and refuse to allow an upgrade from an older version of a program to a newer one. This happens sometimes when you try to upgrade a program from an RPM created by one person or organization to an RPM created by another person or organization. In a situation like this, you can uninstall the old RPM and install the new one.

CAUTION

It's always wise to back up configuration files related to a program before upgrading. The RPM system contains mechanisms to do this automatically, but only if the maintainer of the RPM specifies the configuration files correctly. I've had configuration files replaced by "updated" files inappropriate for my system when upgrading RPMs.

Creating a Binary RPM from a Source RPM

If you have a source RPM, you can install a working program by a two-step process:

1. Create a binary RPM from the source RPM.

2. Install the binary RPM as described earlier.

To perform the first step, type:

```
rpm --rebuild sourcefile.rpm
```

The rpm program then performs several operations:

1. Extracts the source code from *sourcefile.rpm*, placing a tarball in /usr/src/redhat/SOURCES and the uncompressed source code in a subdirectory of /usr/src/redhat/BUILD.

2. Compiles the source code.

3. Creates a binary RPM file in the /usr/src/redhat/RPMS/*arch* directory (where *arch* is the architecture, such as i386).

4. Deletes the intermediate files, leaving only the original *sourcefile.rpm* and the new binary RPM file.

In most cases, these steps all occur without any direct intervention on your part. When the process finishes, you can install the new binary RPM file directly, copy it to another directory and install the package from there, or even copy the RPM file to another computer and install it there.

> **NOTE**
>
> Depending upon the size of the program and the speed of your computer, creating a binary RPM from a source RPM may take anywhere from a few seconds to quite a few minutes or even hours. During the compile process, you should see a string of compilation commands, but no progress indicator *per se*, so you won't know how long the process will take except by guesstimating from the size of the source package—and that only after you have some experience with compiling packages on *your* computer.

Occasionally the creation of a binary RPM will fail. There are two common causes of such a failure:

- Missing files—If the program relies upon some package, such as Motif or Lesstif libraries, and if this package isn't installed, compilation will fail. The compilation messages may provide some clue about what may be missing, but it won't be as obvious as "install the Lesstif package to compile this program." Try doing a Web search on promising-sounding error messages near the end of the compiler output to find what's missing, or check the documentation for information on libraries and utilities the software requires.

- System incompatibilities—If you're trying to compile an older source RPM for a newer system, or any source RPM for an unusual architecture, you may run into incompatibilities. For instance, the older program might not compile properly with your newer C compiler. Chances are you'll need to modify the source code to get the compilation to succeed. This is a topic well beyond the scope of this book, but if you're familiar with C (or whatever language the package uses), you can take a stab at it by editing the files in the `/usr/src/redhat/BUILD/`*packagename* directory. You'll then need to either build and install the package manually (as described shortly) or create a new source RPM file, which again, is beyond the scope of this book.

Generally speaking, if you can create a binary RPM from a source RPM, you can install it and use it. Occasionally, though, the binary RPM will exhibit odd bugs or not run at all. In such a case, you'll have to debug the program as you would any other.

Uninstalling RPMs

If you decide that you no longer need a program, you can easily uninstall it by using the `-e` parameter to `rpm`, as in

```
rpm -e packagename
```

Note that you don't specify the full filename of the package, just the package's main name. For instance, the package `zsh`, which I used as an example earlier for installation, comes in the file called `zsh-3.0.5-10.i386.rpm`. To install it, you enter the full filename, but to uninstall it, you would type

```
rpm -e zsh
```

If you're not sure of a package's name, you can try using RPM's *query* feature, which you initiate with the `-q` parameter. For instance, you could type

```
rpm -q zsh
```

If the package `zsh` is installed, RPM returns further details—namely, the package name and its full version number. If the package isn't installed, RPM says so. You can therefore try several variant names until you find the one that's correct.

23

SYSTEM
ADMINISTRATION

You can also use -q in conjunction with -f to locate the package that owns a specific file. For instance, suppose you want to uninstall the package that owns the file /usr/sbin/nmbd. Here's what you might type, and see in response:

```
[root@speaker root]# rpm -qf /usr/sbin/nmbd
samba-2.0.5a-1
```

If you're sure you want to delete Samba, you could then do so by typing:

```
rpm -e samba
```

Using the gnorpm Program

Using rpm from the command line is definitely the most flexible way to manage RPM files on your system. You might want to work with a GUI interface, though, either because you're more comfortable with that or because you want to browse through available packages—either those already installed on your system or those on a CD or in some directory on your hard disk. In these circumstances, you can use the gnorpm program.

NOTE

Prior to version 6.0, Red Hat Linux used the glint program rather than gnorpm, and some distributions may still use glint, or some other GUI front-end to rpm. If you type **gnorpm** and don't get the program, try **glint** instead, or check your distribution's documentation. If you use glint, the details of operation differ, but many of the basic principles are the same.

When you start gnorpm, you're greeted by the Gnome RPM window shown in Figure 23.1. This window contains two panes. The left pane shows a hierarchical classification of installed package categories, and the right pane shows the packages that are installed in a selected category.

NOTE

The hierarchical organization of installed packages doesn't correspond to the organization of files in the Linux directory structure. The gnorpm hierarchy exists only to help you locate packages. In fact, because each RPM maintainer must classify his or her own RPM, the classification scheme tends to be confusing and inconsistent, so you may have to look several places to find a specific package.

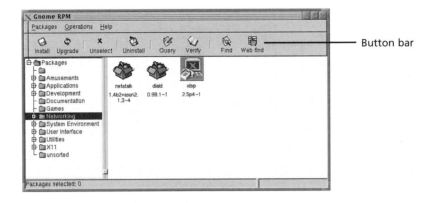

Button bar

FIGURE 23.1

Most RPM files display as generic icons, but some, like xisp in this figure, use custom icons.

You can perform several operations with the gnorpm utility, including

- Uninstalling packages—To remove a package, locate and select it, and then click the Uninstall button in the button bar. The system asks you to confirm the uninstallation with the Continue Removal dialog box shown in Figure 23.2. If you click Yes, the system removes the package. You can also uninstall several packages at once by selecting them all before clicking Uninstall.

FIGURE 23.2

If you select multiple files for removal, you approve removal of all files simultaneously, despite the fact that you can highlight only one in the Continue Removal dialog box.

- Installing packages—To install a package, click the Install button in the button bar. The program displays the Install dialog box, shown in Figure 23.3. You can click the Add button in this dialog box to select RPM files you want to add using a file selector dialog box. When you've selected all the files you want to install, click Close in the file selector and click Install in the Install dialog box. You'll see the Installing progress indicator dialog box, as shown in Figure 23.4, displaying the progress of the installations.

23

SYSTEM
ADMINISTRATION

FIGURE 23.3

You can find information on a package before installing it by clicking Query.

FIGURE 23.4

The installation progress indicator can be useful when you're installing many or large packages; with small packages, it comes and goes almost before you can notice it.

- Query packages—You can find information on a package by selecting it and clicking Query. This action produces the Package Info dialog box, as shown in Figure 23.5. This dialog box includes assorted information on the package, including its size, build and install dates, a description, and a list of files it contains.

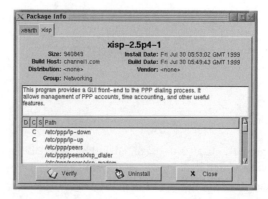

FIGURE 23.5

If you select multiple packages before clicking Query, you can choose between them by clicking their tabs in the Package Info dialog box.

- Verify—You can check that the package's files haven't changed since installation by selecting the file and clicking Verify. This produces the Verifying Packages dialog box shown in Figure 23.6. Some problems, such as a new modification time, likely aren't serious. Others, like file size changes, may indicate corruption or might even be an indication of a cracker's presence on your system, though not always. Changes in file sizes, MD5 checksums, and so on, are quite normal for configuration files, for instance.

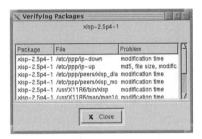

FIGURE 23.6
If you select several packages, you'll get a single Verifying Packages dialog box for all of them.

- Other operations—You can do a great deal more with gnorpm, including locating installed packages that meet certain criteria and finding packages from Red Hat's Web site. Overall, gnorpm doesn't provide all the features of rpm, but it's quite useful for common maintenance tasks.

Compiling Programs from Source

If the program you want to install is available only as a source tarball, or if you have some reason for not using an RPM, you can compile and install the program "manually," using conventional UNIX-style tools like make and whatever installation scripts the program author may have provided. When you install a program in this way, you give up the capabilities provided by RPM, including easy uninstallation, protection against file conflicts, and so on. I therefore favor using RPM (or Debian packages, if you use Debian) rather than source tarballs whenever possible.

Obtaining and Unpacking Source Code

As with RPM files, you have several options for locating source code tarballs, including

- The program's Web site—If the program's author maintains a Web site, the source code should be available on that site, unless it's a commercial program, in which case the source probably won't be available at all.

- Tarball-based distributions—Distributions like Slackware may come with or make available source code in tarball format.

- Linux archive sites—FTP sites like `ftp://sunsite.unc.edu` and `ftp://tsx-11.mit.edu` contain a huge mass of Linux and UNIX source code.

Even if the documentation for a UNIX program you want to use doesn't mention Linux compatibility, there's a good chance the program will work with Linux. You might, however, have to make some changes to its source code or installation routines. Such changes are beyond the scope of this book, and will be very specific to the program you're compiling.

Once you've obtained a tarball, you can uncompress it with the `tar` command, as in

tar xvzf *progfile.tar.gz*

where *progfile.tar.gz* is the name of the tarball. Most tarballs create a subdirectory in which the source files will reside, but a small number dump the files into the current directory. You may therefore want to check the contents of the archive before extracting it by using **tar tvzf** rather than **tar xvzf**. This command will display the contents of the archive without actually extracting it.

TIP

You can extract the tarball as `root` in a system source code directory such as `/usr/src`, as an ordinary user in your normal home directory, or in `/usr/src` or another system directory if you have write permission to that directory. I generally prefer to compile programs as an ordinary user and install them as `root`. This practice reduces the amount of time I must spend as `root`, and therefore the risk that I'll make a disastrous mistake with `root` privileges.

Configuring Programs

One of the files in the source code tarball is probably called README, INSTALL, or something else suggestive of configuration, compilation, and installation instructions. Read this file. It can tell you much better than I precisely what you need to do to compile and install the program. In general, though, there are four methods of precompilation configuration in common use:

None—Particularly simple programs may require no precompilation configuration at all. A few don't even have Makefiles; you must compile these programs by using the compiler directly, or by running them as scripts.

Manual—Older programs and programs from less experienced or less friendly authors often require manual configuration. You may need to dig into a file (probably the `Makefile`) and change compilation defaults by hand. It's helpful to understand something about UNIX programming when you encounter such a program, but if you're lucky you may be able to get by even without extensive programming knowledge.

`configure` script—Many newer programs come with a script, typically called `configure`, that examines your system and builds an appropriate `Makefile` based upon what the script finds. With such programs, you need only type `./configure` and wait a while as the script churns to configure the program for compilation on your system.

`make config`—Some programs incorporate functionality similar to that provided by a `configure` script in the `Makefile`. The `Makefile` is itself a script of sorts run by the `make` program. Normally, the `Makefile` tells the system how to compile your program, but a programmer can include within it instructions on how to configure the compilation process. The Linux kernel uses this method, in fact—when you type `make config`, `make menuconfig`, or `make xconfig`, the system uses this mechanism to prompt you for information on what features you want to include, and examines your system for additional information.

In some cases, you may need to make additional changes to activate particular program features or to customize the program. For instance, you may want to change a program's default color scheme, or fix a bug you've found. Some such changes are simple, and even a non-programmer can probably determine how to make them, given a bit of time to examine the source code. Others require programming skill that I can't pretend to impart in a single chapter. You can consult Warren Gay's *Sams Teach Yourself Linux Programming in 24 Hours* from Sams Publishing for basic Linux programming information, or a book appropriate for whatever language or toolkit your program uses, for more information on modifying a program to suit your specific needs.

Compiling the Source Code

With most programs, you need only type **make** to compile the source code. You'll then see a string of commands execute automatically in order to do the job. This process can take anywhere from a few seconds to several minutes or even hours with a large program or slow computer.

In some cases, you'll need to issue multiple `make` commands, or different commands to compile the program in different ways. For instance, as I discuss in Chapter 6, "Compiling a Kernel for Networking," you can compile the Linux kernel itself in any of several ways (**make zImage**, **make bzimage**, and so on). The kernel also requires that you compile kernel *modules* separately with the **make modules** command. The program's documentation should specify what exact commands you need to type to do the job.

23

SYSTEM ADMINISTRATION

In some cases the compilation won't succeed. You'll need to examine the compiler errors to determine what went wrong. You may be missing some vital library file, or the program might require a different version of the compiler than you've got. It's difficult to offer specific advice for a situation like this, aside from reviewing the documentation that came with the program. If you're not sure if you've got a specific support package, check your system using gnorpm, and check for packages of the specified name on your distribution's install CD. If a package with a name related to the one given by the program's author is on the CD but not on your system, install it. Also, note that many libraries come with both runtime and development packages. You'll probably need the development package in order to compile a program that requires the package.

Sometimes a program fails to compile because of a *version* mismatch between the installed and expected libraries. If you have a more recent library, try to find an updated version of the program. If your library is older than what the program requires, you can either update your library or try to find an older version of the program. Updating your library can sometimes cause problems with other programs that depend upon the library, though, so proceed with caution. Fortunately, you can often install multiple versions of the same library and have them coexist on a system.

Installing the Software

Most source distributions include a make command to install the compiled program. This command is generally called install, so you type **make install** to install the software. In some cases, there will be a separate install script you run instead of a make command. For some particularly small programs, you may need to copy the executable file to an appropriate location manually. For instance, you might type **cp foo /usr/local/bin** to install the program file foo in the /usr/local/bin directory.

Traditionally, you install software that you've compiled yourself into the /usr/local directory tree. Some installation programs place software elsewhere, though. This practice can sometimes cause problems because the new software may overwrite existing software that belongs to RPM packages. Installing locally-compiled software somewhere other than in /usr/local can also make it more difficult to track these files down if and when you want to uninstall the software. You might be able to change the Makefile or install script to alter the installation path, if you're concerned about this.

Once you've installed the software, you should be able to run it by typing the program's name. If you want to create an icon or menu entry for an X desktop environment like GNOME or KDE, consult the documentation for that environment.

Checking Your Log Files

Linux, like most UNIX systems, keeps a set of *log files* describing important system activity. One of the important tasks you face as a system administrator is to monitor these log files. In truth, this can be an extremely dull task because most of the log file entries are routine and uninformative. You normally don't really *care* that ferd logged onto the system at 9:38 AM on Monday, for instance. If, however, you know that ferd is on vacation in Nepal without Internet access, that login should raise a red flag as a potential security violation. Log files can also provide useful diagnostic information when you're installing new programs—and particularly new daemons, which typically log information rather than interact directly with you. You should therefore know something about log files and the tools you can use to help you keep abreast of them without boring you to tears.

The syslogd Facility

Red Hat Linux uses a daemon called syslogd to handle system logging. In principle, it works like this: When a program wants to log a message, it sends that message to the system log daemon, which then writes the message to a file or passes it on to another system. This design allows even user programs to log messages in system files to which the calling user can't normally write because syslogd normally runs with root privileges.

You configure syslogd by editing the /etc/syslog.conf file. The default configuration places most messages in /var/log/messages, but you can change this location. The system logger also handles a number of message types that don't go in /var/log/messages, but in other files. You should read the syslog.conf manpage for more information about the format of this file.

23

SYSTEM
ADMINISTRATION

> **NOTE**
>
> Many commercial UNIXes place messages in /var/log/syslog rather than /var/log/messages, but the files serve much the same function.

Many programs (particularly daemons) have options to turn on or off system logging, or to log more or fewer messages. This characteristic can be quite handy if you're having problems because you can run the daemon with whatever options it requires to log debugging information. You can then examine the last few lines in /var/log/messages to discover what went wrong when a problem occurs. You might find that the daemon choked on a particular option in a configuration file, for instance, or that it received some input that didn't match its expectations.

In addition to or instead of using syslogd, some daemons create their own log files. Samba does this, for instance. Such log files often include information that's not found in the /var/log/messages file, so you may want to check for log files specific to the service you're investigating when you look for information.

The /var/log Directory

Most Linux distributions store their most important log files in the /var/log directory by default. In order to prevent the log files from growing to a size that threatens to overrun your hard disk, distributions include cron jobs that run once a week, early on Sunday mornings, that *rotate* the log files. In Red Hat Linux, five log files are kept for each original: Four previous weeks' files and one current file. (Other distributions may keep the same or different numbers of log files.) For instance, you'll find in /var/log the current file messages along with the preceding weeks' files messages.1, messages.2, messages.3, and messages.4. Each week, the cron job erases messages.4 and promotes each preceding week's log up one number. A new messages file starts empty, but quickly begins to accumulate new messages.

NOTE

Although the log files are rotated once a week, the cron job that accomplishes this task actually runs *daily*. It simply specifies a weekly rotation, and so does nothing six days out of seven. You can alter this behavior by editing the file /etc/logrotate.conf and changing weekly (near the top of the file) to daily, monthly, or size *bytes* to set daily, monthly, or size-based rotation schedules, respectively. See the logrotate manpage for more details.

TIP

Most servers run 24 hours a day, 7 days a week, so this weekly cron job does its thing reliably. If for some reason you normally shut down your server on the weekend, though, you may want to either reconsider that policy or reschedule the cron job. Altering the log rotation to occur daily rather than weekly may be a good option if you leave the computer powered on overnight at least occasionally. Otherwise, you can create a cron job to run logrotate occasionally when the system *is* running, or you can run logrotate manually whenever it's convenient.

Using swatch to Monitor Log Files

Red Hat Linux comes with a utility called swatch that's used to monitor system files. It may not be installed on your system, so check your installation CD. swatch is a Perl script that monitors your system files, either once or continuously. When swatch finds a pattern that you specify in a log file, it can take any of several actions you specify, such as send you email or create a beep sound.

Basic swatch Options and Configuration

You run swatch from a command line or a script by typing **swatch** followed by any of several parameters, including

- -c *config_file*—Specify the name of the configuration file. This file defaults to ~/.swatchrc, which is probably not terribly useful, at least not for a system-wide monitoring utility.

- -r *time*—Restart time, given either as *hh:mm*[*am*¦*pm*] to specify an absolute time or as +*hh:mm*, to indicate a time the specified number of hours and minutes after starting swatch.

> **CAUTION**
>
> When restarted, swatch rereads its configuration file, but does *not* close the file it's monitoring. This means that, if set to monitor a system log file that's rotated, swatch continues to monitor the old (and now static) file. Getting around this limitation requires editing the log rotation configuration file, as I describe shortly.

- -f *filename*—Do a single pass through the specified *filename*.

- -t *filename*—Monitor *filename* continuously. (swatch uses a program called tail to monitor the file, hence the -t switch.)

As an example, here's a line that causes swatch to run a single pass through /var/log/messages using /etc/swatch.conf as the configuration file:

```
swatch -c /etc/swatch.conf -f /var/log/messages
```

The configuration file itself consists of four fields, which must be separated by *tabs* (spaces *will not* work correctly). These fields are

- Pattern—A Perl regular expression pattern or patterns. Each pattern is delimited by slashes (/), and multiple patterns can be separated by commas. Perl patterns are similar to egrep patterns, as described on the egrep manpage.

- Action—The action to be performed when the specified pattern is found. Examples of actions include `bell` (to sound a tone on the console), `exec=command` (to execute the specified command), and `mail=address` (to mail the matched line to the specified address). As with patterns, you can specify multiple actions by separating them with commas. Additional actions are laid out in the `swatch` manpage.

- Time interval—An interval, specified as `[[HH:]MM:]SS`, during which `swatch` will generate only one message should multiple messages that are *identical* except for the time stamp appear. Because many messages include details that won't be identical, such as process ID numbers, this option is of limited use. It is an optional component of the configuration file.

- Timestamp location—The location of the timestamp in the line, specified as a `start:length`. For most entries in `/var/log/messages`, `0:16` will serve as the timestamp location. `swatch` uses the timestamp location merely as a block for information *not* to include when determining if two messages are identical, so you may be able to expand the size of the "timestamp" to include fields with changes that don't concern you, like process ID numbers for login attempts.

As an example, here's a `swatch` configuration file that watches for packet filtering messages, failed login attempts, and any messages related to `root`:

```
/Packet log¦root/        mail=root
/authentication failure/  mail=root  02:00  0:16
```

The authentication failure line includes a time specification so that identical failure messages occurring within two minutes of each other will generate only one email. This configuration file causes `swatch` to mail matching message lines to `root`. For best security, though, you may want to email these notices to an account on another system, if possible. Doing so will make it less likely that a cracker could break in and erase all evidence of having broken in, including `root`'s email, before you get a chance to read about the problem.

Configuring `swatch` for Practical Log Monitoring

Chances are you'll want to configure `swatch` to either check your log files on a regular basis or monitor them continuously. In practice, continuous monitoring is probably the more desirable course of action because it makes it less likely that a cracker will be able to penetrate your system and then erase the evidence. To configure `swatch` in this way (or for a scan at some regular interval), you should do the following:

1. Create a `swatch` configuration file. I use `/etc/swatch.conf` as an example, but you can place yours somewhere else.

2. Start `swatch`. The command

   `/usr/bin/swatch -c /etc/swatch.conf -t /var/log/messages &`

   does this.

3. Create an entry in a system startup file, such as `/etc/rc.d/rc.local`, to start `swatch` on system startup. You should use the same command specified in step #2.

4. To keep `swatch` monitoring the correct log file even after a log rotation, you must edit a syslog configuration file. On Red Hat 6.0 systems, the file is `/etc/logrotate.d/syslog`. At the top of that file is a definition for handling the `/var/log/messages` file. You need to add two lines to this section to restart `swatch`. For instance, you might change this section to read

```
/var/log/messages {
    postrotate
        /usr/bin/killall -HUP syslogd
        /usr/bin/killall tail
        /usr/bin/swatch -c /etc/swatch.conf -t /var/log/messages
    endscript
}
```

> **NOTE**
>
> The documentation for `swatch` suggests that restarting `swatch` should have the desired effect, but with the versions of `swatch` and `tail` included with Red Hat 6.0, restarting `swatch` doesn't reset the file being read by `tail`. Killing `tail` also kills `swatch`, so you can kill `tail` and then restart `swatch` as a workaround. If you use another distribution and if restarting `swatch` in this way causes problems, you can try the command `/usr/bin/killall -HUP swatch` in the preceding example, instead of the `killall tail` and `swatch` commands.

5. Restart the syslog daemon by typing

    `/etc/rc.d/init.d/syslog restart`

    This causes the daemon to reread its configuration files.

If you want to monitor more log files than just `/var/log/messages`, you'll need to perform similar steps for each file you monitor. The syslog configuration file for the log files you monitor may not be the same as for `/var/log/messages`, however: There are other syslog configuration files in `/etc/logrotate.d`.

23

SYSTEM
ADMINISTRATION

TIP

You might want to create a script that starts swatch. You can then call this script in your system startup file, the /etc/logrotate.d/syslog file, and whenever you want to restart swatch manually. If you need to alter your swatch startup procedures, you can then edit one file rather than two (or perhaps more). This practice can be particularly helpful if you want swatch to monitor two or more log files.

CAUTION

If you experiment with swatch, you may find the need to kill swatch and restart it. If you do, you may end up killing swatch but leaving the tail program running. When you start swatch again, it accepts input from two tail instances, thus creating double reports. If you do this again, you'll get *three* reports of each new log file entry, and so on. You should be sure to kill any tail process used by swatch when you kill swatch itself.

Managing swatch's Reports

One problem with swatch is that it generates one report for each line in the monitored file. If you set swatch to send email, and if your system generates ten messages upon which swatch acts, you'll get ten separate email messages. If your system comes under heavy attack from a cracker, you'll spend all your time sifting through swatch's reports, rather than defending against the cracker! One way around this problem is to have swatch *append* its reports to a file tucked out of the way somewhere, and to have a cron job periodically check that file and, if necessary, email it to you. Here's one possible configuration to accomplish this task:

1. Create a swatch configuration file that appends swatch's reports to a file. For instance, here's a variant of the example swatch configuration file I presented earlier:

```
/Packet log|root/        exec="/bin/echo $0 >> /tmp/.swatch"
/authentication failure/ exec="/bin/echo $0 >> /tmp/.swatch"  02:00  0:16
```

This file causes swatch to append its reports to the file /tmp/.swatch, which is a *dot file* (its filename begins with a period) and hence not obvious on a casual scan of the system. For added security, you can place the file in a subdirectory readable only by root, or give it a less obvious and more arbitrary name, like .s1118.

2. Create a cron job to check the contents of the swatch temporary file. If the file exists, email it or perform some other action, and then delete the temporary file. Here's a script that performs this task:

```
#!/bin/sh
if [ -f /tmp/.swatch ]
then
    mail -s "Swatch alert!" < /tmp/.swatch root
    rm /tmp/.swatch
fi
```

If you place this script in /etc/cron.hourly, the system automatically executes it every hour.

3. Start swatch as described earlier, by creating a startup script entry, a log rotation handler for tail, and starting swatch manually.

Your system will now monitor your log files and alert you no more than one hour after the occurrence of any event that swatch has been programmed to recognize. You can mix swatch's actions in various ways. For instance:

- You can run two or more instances of swatch, each of which monitors a different log file, and all of which log to the same temporary file. You'll then receive a single report for actions monitored by all swatch instances.

- In the swatch configuration file, you can specify different actions for different conditions. For instance, you might want to send email *immediately* for any failed attempt to access the root account, while logging other messages for later reporting. You can do so by specifying different actions for each line of the configuration file.

- You can maintain multiple swatch temporary files, in order to obtain reports at differing intervals. For instance, you might maintain one file for hourly reports, another for daily reports, and so on.

One drawback to having swatch maintain a temporary file and then mail reports to you in batches is that it may take a while for you to discover a problem. Of course, the same is true if you're not constantly logged on. Another drawback is that there's always the chance that a cracker could gain access to your system, discover your swatch logs, and delete those logs before they're sent to you. In the end, you'll have to balance these drawbacks against the likelihood that you'll be inundated with many small emails or other messages should your system ever experience repeated swatch-monitored problems.

One other possibility is to have swatch send its output to a printer. If you have access to a disused printer and a spare port to which you can connect it, the printer can make an excellent recording device. In fact, a dot-matrix printer accepting raw ASCII (without processing through Ghostscript) is ideal for such duty. There would then be no need for a temporary holding file and no risk that a remote cracker could erase evidence of an intrusion, provided that swatch detects and logs that evidence.

23

SYSTEM ADMINISTRATION

Finally, if you're running a network with several Linux or UNIX computers, you can configure them to pass log files to a central computer. You do this by editing the computers' /etc/ syslog.conf files and specifying @*machinename* as one of the locations for the log file you want to maintain centrally. You must then configure that target machine to accept remote logs by launching syslogd with the -r option. You'll need to edit the /etc/rc.d/init.d/syslog file to add this option, and then restart the logger by typing:

```
/etc/rc.d/init.d/syslog restart
```

When you restart swatch using the -t parameter, it checks the last few lines of the monitored file and sends you a report on what it finds there. You can therefore expect a few repeat entries, particularly if you configure swatch to send you reports on relatively routine matters, if your system is under attack, or if you restart swatch frequently. If you use swatch to periodically scan the entire log file, of course, you'll get repeat entries whenever you scan without performing a rotation.

Summary

Installing programs and monitoring system logs are two very important system administration topics not covered elsewhere in this book. By far the easiest way to install software on a Red Hat or other RPM-based Linux system is to install binary RPMs, which contain pre-built binary code, often customized for best operation with a Red Hat or similar Linux system. Source RPMs are also usually fairly easy to install, although this approach is more time-consuming and may require more expertise if you encounter problems. Raw source code in a tarball can also be installed on any Linux system. When installing a program from source code, you'll need to read the instructions to learn how the programmer intended the software be installed. If you encounter problems, you'll need to know enough about programming to track the problem down yourself, or ask for help from somebody who has such knowledge. Source code installs do give you something, though, because you can then customize the program in ways that aren't possible with binary files.

Linux generates a large number of system log messages, and it's easy to overlook these log files. Particularly if your system is on the Internet, however, you shouldn't do so because the log files may indicate an attack by a cracker or other important problems with the system. Fortunately, the swatch program can help by sifting through the log files, locating messages that are important, and discarding the rest. swatch can then send important messages to you via email (preferably on another computer), a printer, or some other means. Setting up a log file monitoring system can go a long ways towards keeping your system running smoothly.

Maintaining a Secure System

IN THIS CHAPTER

Throughout this book, I've referred to the security implications of networking services and offered advice on how to provide services without taking undue risks in the process. In addition to care given to specific services, there are steps you can take to safeguard your system as a whole. This chapter discusses some of these more general security issues.

Maintaining a system you can trust is not an easy task. Crackers constantly discover new security problems with specific products, so you must regularly update your software to keep pace. Even if the security world were static, you would have to cope with a large number of potential security breaches, ranging from users with lax passwords to crackers exploiting obscure program bugs. To help you learn more about Linux security issues than I can cover in this chapter, I recommend *Maximum Linux Security* from Sams, which covers common security threats and ways to correct them.

Hackers and Crackers

Newspapers frequently carry headlines such as *Hackers Break Into MegaCorp Mainframe* or *National Security Threatened by Hackers*. Such headlines suggests that these *hackers* are criminals, and indeed, the actions described often *are* criminal in nature.

I've avoided the term *hacker* in this book, however, because its meaning is unclear at best. In particular, although the popular media and most individuals use the term to refer to computer criminals and cyberspace miscreants, the term also refers to individuals who possess programming skill and a love of computer programming. By this second meaning, which actually predates the first, hackers *do not* engage in destructive behavior such as breaking into computers or destroying data. In fact, many of the people who have written Linux and all its support programs consider themselves hackers. Many of these "old-school" hackers rail against the more recent corruption of the term to refer to criminal (or at least antisocial) behavior.

Another word does unambiguously describe individuals who break into computers and (sometimes) destroy data or disrupt operations: *cracker*. It's for this reason that I've used the term *cracker* throughout this book to refer to such activities—its meaning is clear, provided the context doesn't allow for an interpretation of the word as referring to a crunchy edible wafer.

The Importance of Security

How much attention you give to security depends on a number of factors, including

- Your budget—Properly securing a system costs money, either in terms of software and, perhaps, hardware costs, or in terms of wages or consulting fees.

- Your available time—If you're doing the work yourself, on an unpaid basis or as only a part of your job, you must consider the time it takes to secure your network.

- The importance of the data on your computers—If a computer contains non-critical data, you might want to devote fewer resources to protecting it than you do to a machine holding mission-critical information.

- The difficulty of recovery from data loss—If you have copious backups, you can recover from a security breach by restoring an older system and then closing whatever holes the intruder used to get in.

- The consequences of a security breach—Many people overlook the consequences of a breach. Obviously, you might lose time and effort in recovering from the breach, but there are other potential consequences. For instance, if a cracker breaks into your system and then uses it to attack other systems, send spam, or otherwise disrupt the Internet, you may get a lot of attention, and not of a good variety.

- Your perception of the risk—Just how serious *are* the threats? They're real. Individuals operating computers linked to the Internet via DSL and cable modem lines routinely report one or more crack attempts per day against their systems. Highly visible sites are likely to garner more attention. (Most businesses are loathe to discuss such matters in public, but if Joe Public's home system is being attacked on a daily basis, you can be sure that business sites are, as well.)

You should definitely give at least *some* thought to security, even if you're *not* directly connected to the Internet. You may think of security threats as coming from outside, but sometimes they come from within, too.

Internal Security: Protecting Against Local Snoops

If you're reading this book so you can set up a small network at home, and if you live alone, internal security is more-or-less synonymous with the protection of your home against burglary. The physical security of a computer can also be quite important in an organizational setting, particularly if the computer resides in a public location, such as a university computer lab.

The Direct Attack

If a would-be thief has physical access to a computer, your data are not very secure, although you can take steps to slow down a thief, such as:

- Door locks—Placing locks on doors, and ensuring that the room is always locked, is a common-sense precaution against theft. Similarly, window alarms and other physical access controls are worthwhile investments, particularly when you have highly sensitive data or large numbers of valuable computers in one location.

- Computer locks—You can chain a computer to a desk or, better yet, to a wall. Some computer cases are designed with such chaining in mind, but with many, you may need to purchase a special kit that includes an eye you attach to the case and through which you run a chain. You can also purchase special screws with keyed slots that are difficult to unscrew without special tools to prevent a thief from opening the computer and removing the hard disk, including all its data.

- Removable media locks—If you want to prevent the export of information from a computer, you can lock or physically eliminate removable media devices such as floppies and Zip drives. Many computer stores have devices to help in this task. An intruder can also shut down and reboot a Linux computer using a Linux boot floppy, or in some cases a CD or removable-media disk. Once booted with the intruder's boot media, even data owned and readable only by root is open season. Again, media locks can be helpful in protecting against such abuses, as can data encryption of sensitive files.

- BIOS password—Most modern BIOSes support a password which is required to boot the computer. An intruder won't be able to boot the computer, even with his or her own media, without this password. This measure can be overcome by resetting jumpers on most motherboards, however, and of course the BIOS password does no good if the intruder removes the computer's hard disk and uses it in another system. Therefore, physical security to lock the computer case is important if you expect a BIOS password to do any good.

Of course, each of these measures can make a computer more difficult to use, in one way or another. For instance, a BIOS password may result in a need for you to come in and reboot the system after a power failure, whereas the system might boot up automatically if there were no BIOS password present.

Attacks on a Local Network

Typically, you run a server to provide services for computers on your local network. You probably don't want those outside of your network to access the server, and so you may take steps to isolate your server from the outside. For instance, you might install one or more separate firewall computers, as described in Chapter 21, "Configuring a Firewall." If the source of an attack originates from within your organization, though, a firewall won't do much good. You should be aware of two basic classes of internal network attacks:

- Packet sniffing—Normally, network cards ignore packets that aren't addressed to them, so the OS need not examine all of the traffic that passes over an Ethernet network. It is possible, however, to reconfigure a card to pass *all* the packets it receives on up the TCP/IP stack. A person with physical access to your network, therefore, can install a *packet sniffer* program to receive these packets and monitor your internal network's traffic. The usual use of such packet sniffers by crackers is to record other users' passwords sent in cleartext over the network. For this reason, it's best to use protocols that do not send cleartext passwords. Ideally, your protocols won't send *any* data unencrypted, though few protocols meet this ideal (SSH being one that does). I've discussed these issues in the relevant chapters of this book, such as Chapters 11, "Samba: Sharing Files with DOS, Windows, and OS/2," and 18, "Using `ssh` or `telnet` to Log On Remotely."

- Abuse of service—An internal cracker can abuse services provided on your internal network just as an external cracker can abuse services provided on the Internet as a whole. For instance, suppose a new *exploit* (a means of abusing a service to gain special access) is discovered against the Samba package that allows an attacker with a valid password to gain root access. An external cracker might be unable to use this exploit because the cracker lacks a valid password or because the Samba server rests behind a firewall. An internal cracker with an account on the Samba server, on the other hand, *can* use that exploit to compromise your system.

It's not pleasant to contemplate the possibility that one of your coworkers, employees, or students might want to break into your server, but such things do happen. The intent is often not malicious; the individual might simply want to "look around," or might feel that he or she needs freer access to a resource than you've provided. Even in such cases, though, damage can be done, either through ineptitude on the part of the intruder or because of your wasted time in investigating the matter. For this reason, you need to educate your users about the motivations behind the security measures you take. Ideally, your users should be a part of the decision-making process that leads to the security measures. It might be better to loosen the controls on a shared resource to make it easier to access than to lock the system down against outsiders only to find your own users conspiring to break in.

External Security: Protecting Against Crackers

You probably think of external attacks first when you think of computer security in general. In most cases, it's easier to perform an "inside job," but unless you're operating an intranet at a prison for computer criminals, the vast number and skill of potential outside attackers probably outweighs the relative ease of internal access.

In protecting against outside attack, you can take several important steps, including

- Understand networking—If you don't understand how networking functions, you won't know what areas are vulnerable, what services you require, and so on. Without this knowledge, you cannot design an effective security policy.

- Educate your users—Users who understand the reasons for networking policies are more likely to conform to those policies. For instance, a user might not realize that email is far from secure, and so might innocently send sensitive data, such as a guest account password, by email. Once your users understand the risks, they're less likely to compromise your security through ignorance.

- Use secure protocols—Rather than protocols like Telnet, which send passwords and other data in cleartext, use protocols that encrypt data, such as SSH. This step can reduce the chance that an outsider might sniff a password when a legitimate user connects to your computer, or uses an internal computer to connect to one on the outside world.

- Close off unneeded services—If a service isn't needed, shut it down. For instance, Red Hat Linux ships with FTP, Telnet, and a host of additional services enabled by default. You can disable these, often by commenting out their lines in /etc/inetd.conf. I describe methods of providing these services selectively later in this chapter. You might wonder why this step is necessary—after all, if an attacker lacks a password, what harm can the service do? There are two ways the unused service can do harm. The first is that the attacker might obtain or guess a password, say through packet sniffing. The second is that the daemon you run to provide the service may in fact contain a bug that allows an intruder entry even without a password.

- Run a firewall—You can block services you need internally from the outside world by running a firewall computer, as discussed in Chapter 21, "Configuring a Firewall." The firewall itself may be tricky to configure, of course, but it can help protect internal computers from the outside. As I discuss in Chapter 21, though, a firewall is not a *guarantee* of safety; it's only one tool towards that end.

- Run up-to-date software—Because crackers are constantly developing new exploits, you must also regularly check for updates to block those exploits. Red Hat maintains a list of updated packages at http://www.redhat.com/corp/support/errata/. Other distributions maintain similar lists. Many of the errata relate to non-security–related bugs, but others fix security problems. You should make it a point to check for security-related fixes on a regular basis. You should also continue to read and learn about security issues in order to better understand the issues and, hence, better configure your system against attack, even with existing software.

- Test your system—You can run a variety of programs, such as Nessus (http://www.nessus.org) and Crack (http://www.users.dircon.co.uk/~crypto/) to check your system for potential security problems. The details of how to use these programs and interpret the results is beyond the scope of this book, though *Maximum Linux Security* does include some information on these matters. Some Internet Web sites, such as http://www.dslreports.com, offer scanning services that can do some types of security tests, though not others. (Crack tests your password files for vulnerabilities, for instance, and an external service can't do this unless you hand over the password file, which is a very inadvisable practice, and one that a reputable security scanning site won't suggest.)

- Monitor log files—Linux's system log files provide a wealth of information concerning both normal and abnormal system events. You should monitor them regularly. Chapter 23, "System Administration," includes information on how to do so relatively painlessly.

Passwords

One of the most important aspects of system security rests quite literally in the hands of your users: passwords. When using secure transmission protocols like SSH, you can deprive crackers of passwords gleaned from packet sniffing, but if the cracker can obtain a password in some other way, your system is still vulnerable to attack.

Some users may think that their passwords are valueless to crackers because their accounts don't contain any sensitive information. *Not so!* With access to a regular user account, a cracker may be able to overcome security measures on your system to gain access to others' data, or to attack other computers, either on your network or elsewhere. Individuals also often use the same password on multiple computers, in which case a breach on one can translate quite quickly into a breach on additional machines.

Tips for Creating Good Passwords

Linux stores passwords in the /etc/passwd or /etc/shadow file, depending upon whether or not *shadow passwords* are enabled on your system. (More on shadow passwords shortly.) Crackers routinely try to gain access to password files for Linux or UNIX systems because they can attempt to *crack* the passwords—that is, find at least one password for entry to the system.

Normally, Linux stores passwords in an encrypted form. When you log in, Linux encrypts the password you type and compares it to the encrypted password. If the two encrypted passwords match, you're let in; if they don't match, the originals couldn't match either, so you're kicked off the system or asked to try again. The encryption process is non-reversible, so in theory, a password file doesn't do a cracker any good. The trouble is that most people choose passwords that can be guessed relatively easily. To illustrate this fact, let's consider an 8-character password. Assuming a person restricts a password to upper- and lower-case characters and digits, that leaves 62 possible choices for each of the eight characters, or 2×10^{14} possible passwords. Even assuming a computer that could check 1,000,000 passwords per second, locating the correct password by brute force could take up to almost seven years. Suppose, however, that a person uses a common word as a password. If you combine dictionary files from ten languages and add duplicates based on reversals and other small modifications, you get a total of about 5,000,000 words. Our hypothetical 1,000,000-passwords-per-second computer would take only five seconds to locate such a password! (Of course, no computer accessible to the average cracker can approach these speeds, but current computers could still crack such a password in a matter of hours.)

24

Therefore, if a cracker gains access to even the encrypted passwords on a Linux computer, and if even one user on that system has a poor password, the cracker will soon have access to the Linux computer itself, albeit (one hopes) with only normal user privileges—initially. Crackers being what they are, our hypothetical uninvited guest will almost certainly try to gain root privileges, and may well succeed by exploiting buggy software or some other hole in the system's security.

CAUTION

There's no special protection of the root password afforded in any of this. It's therefore extremely important that you pick the best root password you can. If a cracker somehow obtains your password file, runs it through a crack program, and finds the root password, you will have just made the cracker's life *much* easier.

So what makes a good password? Ideally, a password should be a random collection of upper- and lower-case letters, numbers, punctuation, and even control characters (though not quite all characters are legal). In practice, the cognitive strain of remembering such passwords, particularly for users who have multiple accounts on different computers, is too great. A fallback position is to take an easily-remembered base and corrupt it in various ways. Here are some ideas for what to use as a base:

- Two short words placed side-by-side: *bunpen*
- Two short words intermixed: *bpuenn*
- Truncate two longer words; for instance, if you start with *camera* and *door*, you might use a base of *merado*.
- Use an acronym that has meaning just to you. For instance, *yiwttd*, for *yesterday I went to the dentist*.

After you have a base, apply several of the following operations:

- Add random digits, preferably *within* the individual words, if your base is a multi-word mix: *b3unpe9n*
- Add random punctuation, preferably *within* the individual words: *b&unp!en*
- Randomly convert letters to uppercase (or lowercase, if you started with uppercase): *bUnpEN*
- Reverse the order of the letters: *nepnub*

CAUTION

It's important that you apply *several* of these distortions. The reversal distortion alone is particularly ineffective, and should not be used by itself.

Of these practices, adding in numbers or punctuation is perhaps the most important. In fact, many Linux and UNIX `passwd` programs complain or flat-out refuse to accept a password that doesn't contain at least one or two digits or symbols.

NOTE

You may be wondering why I used such short words as bases for passwords. The reason is that many password implementations limit password length to eight characters. If a password is to have two non-alphabetic characters (a good rule of thumb), that leaves only six letters.

There are certain practices you should avoid, even as a base upon which to make further changes:

- Using names—Whether it's your name, your spouse's name, your pet's name, the name of your home town, the name of your favorite TV character, or any other name, you should avoid it. Names in general often appear in cracker databases, and a cracker who targets you specifically may delve deeper into variations of names important to you personally than into random words.

- Using personal numbers—Numbers that should be avoided include birthdays, Social Security numbers, telephone numbers, street addresses, license plate numbers, or any sort of ID number. This comment applies both to numbers that apply directly to you and to numbers that apply to family members or friends.

- Using computer information—Don't even think about using your computer's hostname or your account name. (The latter practice is so common that it has a name of its own: a *Joe.*) Similarly, don't use *another* individual's username or another computer's name, or information that's obvious when looking at the computer, like the manufacturer's name or a regular string of keys from the keyboard, like *qwerty*.

- Using password examples from books—Don't use the examples presented here, or in any other book, magazine article, or online newsgroup posting, as a password. Crackers are likely to add such examples to their databases as soon as possible. An online posting suggesting great passwords might even be *from* a cracker!

- Storing passwords in anything but gray matter—Don't write down your password, give it to another person, send it by email (even to yourself), store it on a disk, or otherwise record it in any way, except in your own brain. In some cases, this may not be practical, or even possible. For instance, as discussed in Chapter 16, "Samba: Sharing Printers with DOS, Windows, and OS/2," when you configure Linux to use a printer shared from a Windows computer, you *must* store a password used to access that printer on your local hard disk. Similarly, you must store an ISP's login password on your system if you use dial-on-demand to initiate PPP connections. When you use such conveniences, you should weigh the security implications carefully, and you should configure your systems such that the password you store on disk isn't used in any other context. For instance, your PPP login password should *not* be the same as the password you use to access any other computer.

One other point bears mentioning here: You shouldn't give your password even to individuals claiming authority, *especially* electronically. As I write this, an outbreak of an old scam has occurred: Email messages, apparently from an individual's ISP, ask the individual to send in his or her password for necessary system maintenance. When a person is duped by this request, the cracker who forged the email gains access to the system. The latest outbreak of this scam uses cracked accounts to send X-rated spam to countless other accounts. If you're an ordinary user, you should be aware that your system's administrators *do not* need your password. Using the root account, an administrator can do anything you can do to your files, and can even use the su command *without* a password to use your account as you would. Therefore, any request by email for a password that appears to come from your system administrator has probably been forged, or may indicate that the system's root account itself has been cracked. If you're an administrator or manager, you should realize there's no reason to keep users' passwords in any form but the system's password file, or possibly on other systems for necessary remote access, as described earlier. Keeping a list of user passwords can actually constitute a security hole, since unauthorized access to that list gives an intruder unfettered access to the system. You should be sure your users realize this, too, so that they don't fall victim to crackers who impersonate you in order to obtain a password.

Changing Your Passwords Regularly

Users should change their passwords occasionally. If a cracker obtains a password—through whatever means—that password won't do the cracker much good if it's changed before the cracker can use it. Even if the password is changed *after* the cracker has used it, changing the password will lock the cracker out unless the cracker has further compromised system security. How often should you change your password? That depends on the security needs of the site. In many cases monthly password changes suffice, but others may need more or less frequent changes. Remember when you set a policy for such changes that people may well find it inconvenient to think up and then remember new passwords on a regular basis. If you enforce too-frequent changes, your users may just think up two or three passwords and rotate through them, which reduces the effectiveness of the password-change policy.

Understanding Shadow Passwords

Originally, UNIX systems, and most Linux systems, stored passwords in an encrypted form along with usernames and assorted other types of account information in the /etc/passwd file. Because some of this non-password information had to be accessible to non-root programs, the /etc/passwd file was world-readable. The reasoning was that the encryption would prevent the file from doing a would-be cracker any good; however, as I've just described, that has proved not to be the case, at least with the increasing speed of computers since the development of UNIX in the 1960s. Therefore, many UNIX and Linux systems today, including Red Hat 6.0, use *shadow passwords*. In this process, the /etc/passwd file is still world-readable, but it doesn't contain any passwords. Instead, the passwords go in another file, typically called /etc/shadow, which is readable only by root. Typically, shadow password packages include a single program for authenticating users, and this program (the *pluggable authentication module*, or *PAM*, in Linux) is given root privileges, and therefore can read the shadow passwords file.

The use of shadow passwords is transparent to most users; logins and other password-related operations occur in the same way as usual. This procedure does mean that no non-root user can read even the encrypted passwords of other users. Therefore, potential crackers among your user population, or crackers who have gained normal user access through one means or another, can't feed the /etc/passwd file's contents through a password-cracking program to gain access to additional accounts, possibly including the root account!

NOTE

The shadow password technique is unrelated to the separate password file maintained by Samba for encrypted password access to Samba shares. This Samba password file (/etc/smbpasswd) does share one characteristic with the shadow password file, though: It's readable only by root. You should protect both the Samba and the regular Linux password files with equal diligence. Ideally, your users should have separate passwords for both systems, so that compromise of one password doesn't automatically translate into compromise of the other.

Enforcing Good Password Practices

By default, Red Hat Linux 6.0 includes some rules to enforce good password practices. Specifically, Red Hat performs a dictionary lookup on the password, and refuses the password if it or some obvious component of it matches any word in the dictionary. For instance, Red Hat's passwd refuses the password *password* (which is, by the way, a notoriously common and poor password choice). This is a good start, but doesn't begin to cover all the ground of good password selection.

> **NOTE**
>
> If you run passwd as root, you can proceed to force use of even the poorest password choices; passwd *warns* root that a password is poor, but will accept it if root types the same poor password a second time.

Enforcing Regular Password Changes

One method of enforcing good password use is to create new accounts with randomly-selected strings as initial passwords. Use a different random string for each user, and configure the system to require a password change on the first login. (I describe enforced password changes shortly.) Similarly, if a user forgets a password and comes to you to set a new one, you can set a random string and require an immediate change. Alternatively, you can have users type a password directly—you run passwd as root, and the user types the password. (You should check to be sure the user doesn't ignore the "bad password" warning, though.) The key here is to avoid providing several users with the same passwords, or with passwords that have ever been written down on a piece of paper that might be found by others. If they aren't required to change them, users have a tendency to leave the password as it was initially, which can cause problems if every user gets the same initial password or if that password is written down anywhere.

You can control when or if your users must change their passwords by setting appropriate options when you create or modify the account. Figure 24.1 shows the linuxconf window in which you set these options (you get to this window by selecting Config, Users accounts, Normal, User accounts and then selecting an existing user or adding a new one and clicking the Params tab). You can adjust one user's settings in this way. You can also set the default settings used when you create new users by selecting Config, Policies, Password & account policies, which provides similar options. (You can also change the minimum required password length and the minimum number of non-alphabetic characters required by the passwd command from this window.) You set the password expiration in terms of the number of days the password is valid. You can also set an expiration date for the account, after which it will be disabled. You can set this either in terms of the number of days after the required password change (the default of -1 disables this feature) or in terms of an absolute date.

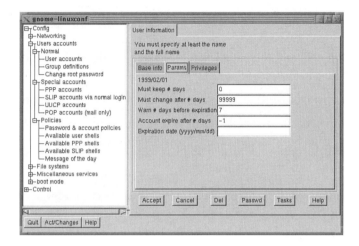

FIGURE 24.1
You can enforce password changes by setting low values in the Must change after # days field; the default value of 99,999 results in a password that must be changed after almost 274 years.

If you prefer to work from the command line, you can set password expirations by using the chage command. The syntax of this command is

```
chage [-m mindays] [-M maxdays] [-d lastday] [-I inactive] [-E expiredate] \
➥    [-W warndays] user
```

The uses for these parameters are

- -m *mindays*—The minimum number of days between password changes. A value of 0 allows multiple changes per day; 1 allows only one change per day; 2 allows only one change per two days, and so on.

- -M *maxdays*—Sets the maximum number of days for which a password is valid.

- -d *lastday*—The number of days since January 1, 1970 since the password was last changed. The system uses this value to determine when a password must be changed. You can also use *MM/DD/YYYY* format if you want to modify this value.

24

**MAINTAINING A
SECURE SYSTEM**

> **TIP**
>
> If you want to enforce a password change soon after a user gets a new account or a new password from you, you can set the -M and -d values appropriately; for instance, -M of 30 and -d of 29 days before the present date. If you don't want to enforce a regular password change, you can make a note to yourself to go back and change the -M value sometime in the next month.

- -I *inactive*—The number of days past password expiration before the system locks the account. Once the account is locked, the user must contact the system administrator to reactivate the account.

- -E *expiredate*—The date on which an account locks automatically, in *MM/DD/YYYY* format, or in days since January 1, 1970. This feature can be useful in setting up temporary accounts, such as accounts given to students requiring an account for a class—you can give an expiration date of the end of the semester.

- -W *warndays*—The number of days before expiration that the user receives warning messages of an impending required password change.

- *user*—The username of the account you want to modify.

The chage command is only usable by root, except with the -l parameter, which provides information on when the password and account are due to expire.

Discovering Poor Passwords

One further password-related task you may wish to undertake is to use a password-cracking program such as Crack (http://www.users.dircon.co.uk/~crypto/). This action should spot many of the weaker passwords on your system, so you can contact the offending users and have them change their passwords.

> **CAUTION**
>
> Be cautious about running Crack, particularly on systems that you don't own. If your superiors find that you're running Crack, they might misinterpret your action as malicious! You should therefore obtain permission from an appropriate individual or organization before running Crack or some other password cracker. You may also want to notify your users of what you're about to do. When you do so, include information on what constitutes a good password and encourage your users to change bad passwords before the date on which you intend to begin your password-cracking exercise. Finally, you should be cautious about the security of the password file

and, especially, reports generated by Crack. In a default Red Hat installation, you must regenerate a standard passwd file from the existing passwd and shadow files (this regenerated file should *not* replace the existing passwd file, though). Place this regenerated file in a directory with restricted permissions (0700, for instance) and ownership (root), and give the file itself similar permissions. Delete it when you're done with the password-cracking activity. Better yet, store all these files on a separate computer that has *no* network connectivity.

Disabling Unneeded Passwords

In a Linux computer that's used only for remote file access, you can disable regular login accounts for users who don't need such access. There are several ways you can do this:

- Disable account logins—In /etc/shadow (or /etc/passwd, if your distribution doesn't use shadow passwords), change the password string to an asterisk (*). The password string is the second field of each file, and on a normal account, it consists of thirteen letters and numbers that closely resemble gibberish. By specifying a single asterisk as the password, you forbid logins of any sort. This approach may be suitable for accounts that are used *only* for remote file access by Samba using encrypted passwords or by NFS, but not for much else. Samba using cleartext passwords and Netatalk both require that the user have a conventional Linux account, including a password.

- Provide limited resources—If you set the user's default account to a read-only directory, and ensure that the user has no write privileges, you can limit the utility of the account for the user. Unfortunately, this action is also likely to limit the utility of the user's access for other purposes, such as file sharing.

- Change the login shell—You can change the login shell from the popup list of shells when you create or edit an account in linuxconf, as shown in Figure 24.2. Alternatively, you can use usermod -s *shell username* to do the task. In either case, the shell must be listed in the file /etc/shells. You can set the shell to a program that gives restricted or even no access to the system. If a user should only be able to use FTP, for instance, you could use /usr/bin/ftp as the shell. This approach also allows the user to use services such as Netatalk, which are not login services but that do require a conventional password.

24

MAINTAINING A
SECURE SYSTEM

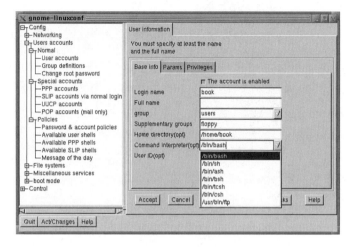

FIGURE 24.2

Set an unusual shell if you want a user to have restricted or no conventional login access.

TIP

You can set /usr/bin/passwd or /usr/bin/smbpasswd as the shell if you want to allow users to change their passwords for access to Netatalk or Samba services. When users log in using telnet or SSH, they'll immediately be prompted to change their passwords, and will be able to do nothing more.

CAUTION

A poor choice in shell can be a major security problem. If the shell program is buggy, a clever cracker might find some way to circumvent the intent and actually gain *increased* privileges on your computer. Scripts can be particularly suspect because they may give a cracker access to the scripting language.

Controlling Network Access

In many cases, one of the biggest security concerns relates to unnecessary network access to a computer. By default, Red Hat Linux ships with many services running that you may not want or need, such as FTP and Telnet. Even if you do have some limited needs for these services, you might not want to make them available to all comers. This is particularly true on a firewall computer or router, on which you might want to make, as an example, Telnet or SSH connections possible from your internal network but not from the outside world. Fortunately, Linux provides many methods of selectively restricting access to services.

Removing Unneeded Services

The first task in controlling network access is to excise from your system those servers that you simply do not need. For instance, if you aren't serving DOS, Windows, or OS/2 computers via SMB/CIFS, and if you don't need to access remote filesystems or printers using these protocols, you can completely uninstall the Samba package. Completely removing the program has the added advantage that an intruder won't be able to use the package against you or against other systems.

> **TIP**
>
> You may want to sift through the installed packages using gnorpm (described in Chapter 23, "System Administration") or a similar tool in order to locate both servers and clients that you're not using. This will help your system security, and it may gain additional disk space you can devote to programs you *do* want available, or to users' files.

In some cases it may not be possible to remove packages entirely. For instance, suppose your users need to use the telnet client program, but you don't want to provide remote access to the system via the telnet protocol. In Red Hat 6.0, both the telnet client and the in.telnetd server come in a single package. In this case, you should track down the method used to start the server and disable it. Three methods of daemon launching are in common use:

- An entry in /etc/inetd.conf—The /etc/inetd.conf file controls several daemons that are launched by inetd. (See Chapter 3, "Networking Services," for more information on inetd. I discuss a replacement for inetd later in this chapter.) You can comment out an /etc/inetd.conf entry by placing a single pound sign (#) at the start of the relevant line.

- A startup file in /etc/rc.d/init.d—Red Hat Linux places scripts that control startup, shutdown, restarting, and otherwise controlling many network services in the /etc/rc.d/init.d directory. It then places links to these scripts in other subdirectories under /etc/rc.d in order to control the precise services offered when Linux is booted to a text-mode login, an X-based login, or in other ways. If you want to disable a service, you can often move the script in /etc/rc.d/init.d to some other location (I use /etc/rc.d/disabled). The startup procedure will then not be able to load the startup script, and the service won't run. You can still start it manually if you like, however, by typing the script's name and, if needed, **start** or some other parameter to signal startup. You may need to disable the service again if you upgrade it, however, because the upgrade process may place a new initialization script in /etc/rc.d/init.d.

- Direct startup—You may need to remove an entry from /etc/rc.d/rc.local or some other startup file for some services. Most servers you install from RPMs don't add lines to startup files in this way, but you may have done so for a few servers, particularly those that you compiled yourself. You can comment out such startup lines by preceding them with pound signs (#).

> **NOTE**
>
> Different distributions sometimes use different service startup protocols. Slackware, for instance, places most of its network startup commands in the /etc/rc.d/rc.inet1 and /etc/rc.d/rc.inet2 files. Consult your distribution's documentation or a good book about your distribution for details.

Sifting through configuration files isn't easy, and you may miss some services in this way. Therefore, you may want to use a *port scanner*, such as Nessus (http://www.nessus.org), to check what ports are open. There are also Internet-based services that will do this job, such as one available at http://www.dslreports.com. Port scanners may also be useful in checking the effectiveness of packet filtering firewalls or other measures.

Using TCP Wrappers

One basic security measure employed by default in Red Hat Linux is known as *TCP Wrappers*. This is a tool that screens incoming connection requests. The TCP Wrappers daemon, tcpd, sits between inetd and the daemon for the requested service, as illustrated by Figure 24.3. When inetd receives a request for service, inetd passes that request, fairly indiscriminately, to the associated server—inetd isn't primarily a security tool, but one to reduce the load on the system. TCP Wrappers, by contrast, serves as a filter, much as a personal secretary can filter phone calls. (My own personal fantasy is to have such a secretary who shields me from telemarketers, while quickly and unobtrusively passing calls from my friends, family, and editors at Sams. TCP Wrappers can do the equivalent for Linux daemons, but sadly not for voice telephone calls.)

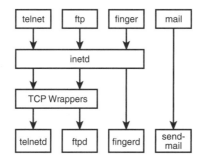

FIGURE 24.3

TCP Wrappers may or may not be used for any given daemon, depending upon the configuration of the daemon and the inetd.conf *configuration. (By default, Red Hat 6.0 actually sends finger requests through TCP Wrappers, but you could reconfigure it as shown here if you wanted to.)*

The TCP Wrappers package is installed by default on Red Hat Linux 6.0, but the default configuration lets anybody connect to the system. You can tell tcpd to do filtering by creating appropriate entries in the /etc/hosts.allow or /etc/hosts.deny files. If you use the former, you block access to all hosts but those specified in the file, whereas if you use the latter file, you create a "black list" of sites to which you want to deny access. Both files' formats are the same, though; it's their meanings that are reversed. If a client appears in both hosts.allow and hosts.deny for a given service, hosts.allow takes precedence, and the client is given access.

The basic form of entries in both files is as follows:

```
daemon-list : client-list
```

These components are composed as follows:

> *daemon-list*—A list of daemons. These names appear in /etc/inetd.conf as the parameter to tcpd. You can also use wildcards for services, such as ALL (for any service).
>
> *client-list*—A list of client computers. Computer names can be specified as names (such as tyler or fillmore.threeroomco.com) or as IP addresses (such as 192.168.43.32). In both cases, you can specify an entire network by using a leading or trailing period, respectively (as in .threeroomco.com or 192.168.43.). TCP Wrappers also accepts a number of wildcards, such as ALL (any host) and LOCAL (hosts whose names don't contain dots). You can exclude one host from a rule by using the EXCEPT keyword, as in 192.168.43. EXCEPT 192.168.43.29.

You should consult the hosts.allow or hosts.deny manpage (they're actually the same) for further details concerning the format of these files, including more advanced options to detect IP spoofing and the usernames of individuals requesting services.

24

MAINTAINING A
SECURE SYSTEM

It's important to recognize that TCP Wrappers only filters connections for services that are specified as being handled by `tcpd` in `inetd.conf`. Not all services so qualify, at least by default. The default Samba configuration, for instance, doesn't go through these services. If you try to configure a service to be run from `tcpd` and `inetd`, don't be surprised if you have problems; not all daemons work well with TCP Wrappers. For instance, the Netatalk `papd` print server doesn't use TCP/IP, and so can't be served by TCP Wrappers. Even servers that do use TCP/IP (and even the TCP protocol) may not work well from `inetd` or `tcpd`, for a variety of reasons.

You should also note that TCP Wrappers will *not* make a service invisible to outside port scanning; it will only deny access to that service (if configured to do so). A determined cracker might be able to deduce to what computers you *are* providing access to a service, perform IP spoofing in a way that circumvents TCP Wrappers, and begin an attack. Of course, these extra steps make your system more difficult to break, which may deter a casual cracker. For tighter control over services, you may want to investigate `xinetd` and packet filtering.

Replacing `inetd` with `xinetd`

Throughout this book, and particularly in Chapter 3, "Networking Services," I've referred to `inetd` as one way to launch network services. This program functions as a "super server," taking over the task of monitoring ports for connection requests and launching the server daemons that handle the monitored ports only when they're needed. The main goal of `inetd` is to reduce the memory load on the system. Using `inetd` in conjunction with TCP Wrappers, however, can provide security benefits, by allowing you to better control access to your computer's services.

The combination of `inetd` and TCP Wrappers does, however, still make the use of the port visible to many port scans, which you may want to block. You can do so, and attain some additional benefits, by replacing the combination of `inetd` and TCP Wrappers with `xinetd` (`http://synack.net/xinetd`).

Obtaining and Installing `xinetd`

The `xinetd` program is not part of a standard Red Hat Linux 6.0 distribution, but it does appear on the CD that accompanies this book in the `sams-extras/security` directory. To use `xinetd`, follow these steps:

1. Install the `xinetd` package.
2. Convert the `inetd.conf` file to one that `xinetd` can use. You do this with the `inetd2xinetd` program. At a minimum, you need to pipe in the original `inetd.conf` file and pipe the output to a convenient location, as in

   ```
   inetd2xinetd < /etc/inetd.conf > /etc/xinetd.conf -daemon_dir /usr/sbin
   ```

The -daemon_dir parameter specifies the location of the directory in which daemon programs reside because xinetd doesn't use a search path (it needs complete pathnames to all the daemons it's to launch).

3. Make any configuration changes you like to xinetd.conf. (I describe the file format shortly.)

4. Uninstall inetd, or at least remove its startup script from /etc/rc.d/init.d.

5. Kill the inetd process.

6. Start xinetd by typing

```
/etc/rc.d/init.d/xinetd start
```

xinetd Configuration

The /etc/xinetd.conf file's format is quite different from that of /etc/inetd.conf. Consider a single /etc/inetd.conf entry as an example:

```
telnet  stream  tcp     nowait  root    /usr/sbin/tcpd  in.telnetd
```

This line handles the telnet service, via tcpd. When a connection comes in on the telnet service port, inetd launches /usr/sbin/tcpd and passes it the parameter in.telnetd. TCP Wrappers (tcpd) is then responsible for launching in.telnetd. Now, let's look at the equivalent entry in /etc/xinetd.conf:

```
service telnet
{
        socket_type     = stream
        protocol        = tcp
        wait            = no
        user            = root
        server          = /usr/sbin/in.telnetd
}
```

For the most part, the xinetd configuration information is the same as that in inetd.conf, but it's labeled more explicitly. If you read the last entry on each line, you see that it corresponds (sometimes with some minor changes) to the equivalent field in inetd.conf. The one exception is that tcpd is no longer in the picture. Instead, xinetd takes over the tasks of *both* inetd *and* tcpd and launches in.telnetd itself.

The xinetd.conf file format supports a *default* configuration, which you can specify like this:

```
defaults
{
        instances       = 50
        log_type        = FILE /var/log/servicelog
        log_on_success  = HOST PID
        log_on_failure  = HOST RECORD
```

```
    bind              = 192.168.1.1
    only_from         = 192.168.1.1 192.168.1.2 192.168.1.3
    disabled          = tftp
}
```

This entry demonstrates several additional parameters you can use in either the default configuration or entries for individual services. These parameters include

instances—The total number of daemons that xinetd will launch for a given service. This can be useful in limiting the number of connections you allow to a popular or less powerful computer. It can also be used to prevent a malicious individual from tying up your resources by launching thousands of connections to your system.

per_source—This parameter is similar to instances, but the limit is applied on a per-source-address basis. For instance, if you specify a per_source of 5, the service will accept up to five connections from the computer tyler.threeroomco.com, five more from fillmore.threeroomco.com, and so on, up to the limit imposed by instances.

disabled—When used in the default entry, this parameter disables a service, even if it's listed later in the file. This parameter makes it easy to temporarily disable a service without commenting out the service's entry.

log_type—Where to log connection information. The preceding example logs information to the file /var/log/servicelog; however, if you use SYSLOG rather than FILE /var/log/services, you log information to the usual system log location (/var/log/messages by default). You can also control logging priority and other factors; see the xinetd.conf manpage for further details.

log_on_success and log_on_failure—determine what information xinetd logs when a server exits and reports a successful session or a failure, respectively. Possibilities include HOST (the remote host's address), USER (the user ID of the user who initiated the request, if available), EXIT (the exit status of the server), and DURATION (the duration of the connection).

bind—This is one of xinetd's most useful features for a multi-homed computer because it allows you to tell the system to respond *only* to requests linked to one particular interface. For instance, if you want to accept telnet connections from your internal network but not from the outside, you could include the line **bind** = ***a.b.c.d*** (where a.b.c.d is your server's address on the internal network). That service will then be *invisible* to any would-be intruder accessing the system from the outside. The interface word is a synonym for bind.

only_from—To restrict access to a service to given hosts, specify them here. You can specify individual hosts (as in the example), networks (as in 192.168.0.0 or 192.168.4.23/16), network names listed in /etc/networks, or computer names. This parameter takes the place of the hosts.allow file's contents.

`no access`—Specify computers and networks as you do with the `only_from` parameter, but these hosts are *denied* access. This parameter provides functionality similar to that in the `hosts.deny` file.

`banner`—Gives the name of a file to be transferred to the would-be client when a connection is denied.

`port`—The port number for a service. Unlike `inetd`, `xinetd` doesn't require that a service name be listed in `/etc/services`. When using an unlisted service, though, you must specify its port number.

`server_args`—Arguments passed to the server.

`access_times`—Specify the times during which a connection will be accepted, as in `08:00-18:00` to allow connections from 8:00 AM to 6:00 PM each day.

`redirect`—Redirects a service request from the host computer to another. When the specified port is accessed, the access request is passed on to the specified remote system and port. The syntax is `redirect = address port`. You can use either an IP address or a hostname for the address, but the hostname is resolved only once, when `xinetd` starts. This feature can be extremely useful if you want to run a server from within an IP masqueraded network. Some clients, though, such as SSH, may detect the redirection and complain or possibly even close the connection.

Many of these parameters support the use of += and -=, in addition, to =, to set values. This feature is useful mainly if you want to override a default. For instance, you can increase the information logged for failure to access a particular service by using **log_on_failure +=**
USER (or some other information not included in the default logging).

If you decide to use `xinetd`, I recommend that you start with a translation of your `inetd.conf` file. You can then add lines to restrict access, change logging operations, and so on. If you need to add a new service, you can copy an existing entry and modify it to suit your needs.

Should you use `xinetd` or the `inetd`/TCP Wrappers combination? Each method has its advantages and disadvantages. Advantages of `xinetd` include

- Support for selective blocking and control of the UDP protocol, in addition to TCP packets.
- Time-based blocking of connections.
- Better hiding of services run on an internal network from the outside.
- Minimal denial-of-service protection in both total and per-client connection limits.
- Easy service forwarding.

Advantages of `inetd`/TCP Wrappers include

- Red Hat Linux's default configuration uses this combination, so it's easier to set up and help is more readily available.

24

MAINTAINING A SECURE SYSTEM

- More likely to work with certain servers. For instance, nmbd (the Samba name browser daemon) doesn't work from xinetd, but it does from inetd.

- Supports blocking by username and by mismatched IP address and claimed hostname.

- Allows exceptions to blocked addresses (xinetd also allows this, but in a much cruder way).

Tip

It's possible to run both xinetd and inetd. You could, for instance, run nmbd through inetd and smbd (the Samba server daemon) through xinetd. Depending upon your needs, you might also want to consider using ipchains to control access to a server that runs continuously, not just when a super server deems it necessary.

Overall, xinetd is probably of most interest on a multi-homed host—one that has two network cards. You can then provide services on one card while denying them on the other. This feature results in some firewall-like characteristics, though xinetd alone does not constitute a true firewall package. Nonetheless, it is a very useful network security tool.

Using ipchains to Control Access

One further method of controlling access is ipchains. This is the utility described in Chapter 21, "Configuring a Firewall," for setting up a packet filter firewall. Because I described ipchains in Chapter 21, I won't go into any detail here. I merely want to point out that this utility can be used to restrict access to specific services in a very fine-grained manner. Some of the advantages of ipchains include the following:

- It performs logging operations that are in some ways superior to those of xinetd. For instance, xinetd does *not* log attempts to access a service from an interface to which that service is not bound. If you use ipchains to block the service from that same interface, though, ipchains can log such an attempt.

- You can use ipchains to block ICMP packets, which is a feat that neither TCP Wrappers nor xinetd can perform. (Even ipchains can't block non-TCP/IP protocols such as AppleTalk's DDP, however.)

- Unlike xinetd, ipchains can block *outgoing* packets, as well as incoming ones.

- Because ipchains is based on controlling packets at the kernel level, it can be used to block data that would normally be handled by *any* server, not just a super server—you need not be concerned with incompatibilities such as that between xinetd and nmbd.

Of course, `ipchains` isn't without its drawbacks compared to `xinetd` or TCP Wrappers. These limitations include

- The `ipchains` rules require more attention to low-level details, and are therefore a bit trickier to set up, particularly if you want to do extensive filtering.

- The kernel must search through `ipchains` rules for all packets. This process can slow down network accesses, particularly if you have many complex rules.

- You can't back-query the originating computer for information such as the user who attempted an access when using `ipchains`—at least, not without involving additional scripts and utilities.

In practice, you may want to use two or even all three of these access control methods. Each alone can contribute to system security, and using each for its unique strengths can provide a great deal of flexibility, as well as added security.

Security Information on the Web

Following the security advice in this chapter, and throughout the rest of this book, can help you to run a system that will be difficult to compromise. Reading another book or two on system security and implementing those books' suggestions can help even more. Books do have certain limitations, though. Prime among these is the fact that they're *static*. These pages won't magically change to inform you of the latest security-related bugs as they are discovered, for instance. For the latest information, you must look elsewhere.

The best sources for up-to-date security information are on the Internet itself. Here are a few suggestions of places to look to learn more, and especially to find advisories of security problems:

- Your distribution's Web site—As I mentioned earlier, Red Hat maintains an errata list at `http://www.redhat.com/corp/support/errata/`, and other distributions maintain similar Web pages. I recommend checking for new errata every week or two, or perhaps more often if your site contains particularly sensitive material.

- The Computer Emergency Response Team Coordination Center (CERT/CC)—This organization is dedicated to public education and responses to Internet security issues. They maintain a Web site at `http://www.cert.org`.

- The United States Department of Energy Computer Incident Advisory Capability (CIAC)—The CIAC database is intended mainly for Department of Energy use, but many of its resources are available to the public. The CIAC Web site is located at `http://ciac.llnl.gov/`.

- Product Web sites—You can check the Web sites for major packages, such as Samba, for security-related updates. It's particularly important that you check such sites routinely if the package in question isn't part of a standard installation of your Linux distribution, such as `xinetd`.

- The `comp.security` newsgroup hierarchy—There are several Usenet newsgroups with names beginning `comp.security`. These groups can be an important source of information on computer security issues.

- Mailing lists—There are numerous security-related mailing lists, mostly concerned with fairly specific topics. If you're interested in locating a mailing list related to a specific topic, try starting at an appropriate Web site and skim for information on mailing lists. You could also try posting a query for information on an appropriate newsgroup. Both CERT and CIAC maintain mailing lists. To subscribe to the former, send a message to `cert-advisory-request@cert.org` with a Subject line of `subscribe`. To subscribe to the CIAC mailing list, send a message to `majordomo@tholia.llnl.gov` with `subscribe ciac-bulletin` as the text of the message.

In addition, there are a plethora of security-related Web sites, including sites concerned with the security of specific products and protocols. Any Web search engine should turn up sites on specific topics in which you're interested.

Summary

Keeping your system from being used or abused by unauthorized individuals is a difficult task, and there's no way to be 100% secure. Even if you had extraordinary knowledge of computer security, you could become the victim of a bug in a program you trust, such as `inetd`, `xinetd`, `sendmail`, or some other server, or even potentially of a client program. For this reason, you should monitor Web sites and other online resources for security update information.

You should close down services that aren't needed on specific interfaces or by sites other than those that do need them. If your FTP server, to name one example, is online *only* so that your colleagues at a specific institution can exchange data with you, you can use TCP Wrappers, `xinetd`, or `ipchains` to block that server to everybody but your colleagues.

You should pay attention to passwords, as well, even when you believe those passwords are only usable on your internal network. Passwords are your first and, sometimes, last line of defense against crackers. Because a Linux server is likely to have many users, it's also likely to have many passwords, and this fact means that your users need to understand the importance of password security, more so than they need to understand the workings of `inetd` or similar administrative details.

Finally, all the network security measures conceivable will do you no good if your computer is stolen, destroyed, or even just physically accessible to a cracker for a time. You should take measures to keep unauthorized personnel away from the computer, and you should also perform regular backups and store some of them off-site.

INDEX

The IT site
you asked for...

It's
Here!

InformIT is a complete online library delivering
information, technology, reference, training, news,
and opinion to IT professionals, students,
and corporate users.

Find IT Solutions Here!

www.informit.com

Get **FREE** books and more...when you register this book online for our Personal Bookshelf Program

http://register.samspublishing.com/

SAMS

Register online and you can sign up for our *FREE Personal Bookshelf Program...*unlimited access to the electronic version of more than 200 complete computer books—immediately! That means you'll have 100,000 pages of valuable information onscreen, at your fingertips!

Plus, you can access product support, including complimentary downloads, technical support files, book-focused links, companion Web sites, author sites, and more!

And you'll be automatically registered to receive a *FREE subscription to a weekly email newsletter* to help you stay current with news, announcements, sample book chapters, and special events, including sweepstakes, contests, and various product giveaways!

We value your comments! Best of all, the entire registration process takes only a few minutes to complete, so go online and get the greatest value going—absolutely FREE!

Don't Miss Out On This Great Opportunity!

Sams is a brand of Macmillan USA.

For more information, please visit *www.mcp.com*

WHAT'S ON THE CD-ROM

INSTALLATION INSTRUCTIONS

Windows 95/98 NT 4

1. Insert the CD-ROM into your CD-ROM drive.
2. From the Windows desktop, double-click the "My Computer" icon.
3. Double-click the icon representing your CD-ROM drive.
4. Double-click the icon titled Readme.txt to learn more.

Macintosh Installation Instructions

1. Insert the CD-ROM disc into your CD-ROM drive.
2. When an icon for the CD appears on your desktop, open the disc by double-clicking its icon.

Linux and Unix

These installation instructions assume that you have a passing familiarity with UNIX commands and the basic setup of your machine. Because UNIX has many flavors, only generic commands are used. If you have any problems with the commands, please consult the appropriate man page or your system administrator.

1. Insert the CD-ROM into the CD drive.
2. If you have a volume manager, mounting of the CD-ROM will be automatic. If you don't have a volume manager, you can mount the CD-ROM by typing

   `Mount  -tiso9660  /dev/cdrom  /mnt/cdrom`

   NOTE: `/mnt/cdrom` is just a mount point, but it must exist when you issue the mount command. You may also use any empty directory for a mount point if you don't want to use `/mnt/cdrom`.
3. After you've mounted the CD-ROM, you can install files from the tcltksoftware/linux or unix folders.

READ THIS BEFORE OPENING THE SOFTWARE